Roland Schrapp

Soul Calendar and Incarnation Cycle

ROLAND SCHRAPP

The Anthroposophical Soul Calendar and the Incarnation Cycle of Man

The Spiritual Archetype underlying the Soul Calendar

Bibliographic information of the Deutsche Nationalbibliothek (German National Library):
The Deutsche Nationalbibliothek lists this publication in the Deutsche Nationalbibliographie
(German National Bibliography);
Detailed bibliographic data are available on the Internet at http://dnb.de.
© 2020 Schrapp, Roland

Production and Publishing: BoD – Books on Demand, Norderstedt (Germany)

ISBN 978-3-7526-9010-1

In reality the human being is not an earth-being. In reality
the human being is a cosmic being,
a being belonging to the whole universe.

Rudolf Steiner, Lecture of 31 October 1920, GA 200

Anthroposophy is a path of knowledge,
to guide the Spiritual in the human being
to the Spiritual in the universe.

Rudolf Steiner, beginning oft he first Leading Thought, GA 26

But now comes the time when the view of the human being as a spiritual being that undergoes a development between death and a new birth, becomes a living feeling, a living sensation, where one must live in the imagination of the supernatural meaning of human souls. For without this imagination the culture of the earth will be killed.

Rudolf Steiner, Lecture of 6 February 1920, GA 196

CONTENTS

Introduction

In today's materialistically oriented time, many people are filled with the sobering idea of living on planet Earth as an insignificant "speck of dust" on the edge of a galaxy, among myriads of other celestial bodies in a cosmos which is infinite but predominantly hostile to life. The modern, enlightened person feels his own body no longer only as the material basis, but rather as the cause of his consciousness and of his inner soul experiences, of which he can be robbed of at any time because of the body's mortality. Only the constant suppression of the certainty of death makes the supposed temporal limit of existence bearable for many. Since the blossoming of materialistically oriented natural science in the 19th century, the human being can not find any support that grants him inner security, neither in the large, wide world nor in his own being. For many people, this transition of their conception from an existence that was spirit-saturated and god-supported, in which man knew he was safe, to a spiritless, godforsaken existence is combined with a feeling of insecurity and dissatisfaction of the soul. Even if it may be not fully aware of it, it still exists. Rudolf Steiner often pointed out the importance of the great change of human consciousness in the course of the 19th century and the resulting consequences for the beginning of the 20th century. Even countless people of the 21st century suffer from this, not less, but rather more.

As long as a person clings with his soul only to his transient body, he submits himself to transience and the idea of imminent destruction. Only when he understands that not only a soul but also an immortal spirit dwells, lives and works in the human body, who is related to the Spiritual working in the cosmos, the All-Spirit, only then can today's human soul again find a proof support that gives security and inner stability. This is the great task of Anthroposophy, the wisdom of the inner being, the spiritual essence of man. Rudolf Steiner summarized this in the meaningful words of his first leading thought:

"Anthroposophy is a path of knowledge that wants to lead the Spiritual in the human being to the Spiritual in the universe. It emerges in people as a need of heart and feeling. It must find its justification in being able to satisfy this need." [1]

However, not only with his spirit, but also with his soul, man is rooted in the nature around him, both terrestrial and extraterrestrial. Therefore, through sympathy of the soul with nature's annual cycle, he can follow a path of self-knowledge by feeling. Rudolf Steiner writes about this in his preface to the first edition of the Soul Calendar in the year 1912:

"In this way, the year becomes the archetype of human soul activity and thus a fruitful source of true self-recognition. In the following Soul-Year-Calendar, the human spirit is thought of in such a position in which he can sense his own soul-weaving on the seasonal moods from week to week in the image on the impressions of the course of the year. It is meant as a self-recognition through feeling. This feeling self-recognition can experience the cycle of the soul-life as a timeless one on the time by the given characteristic weekly sentences. Expressly, it is meant to be a possibility of a path of self-recognition."

"Timeless" is the cycle of human soul-life in so far as it is connected with the immortal, eternal spirit of man, which is not subject to the limitations of the Temporal. Consequently, the Soul Calendar ultimately leads to the knowledge of the spirit and thus overall to a deeper knowledge of the psycho-spiritual being of man in general. An extraordinarily deep meaning lies hidden behind the often mysterious formulations of the weekly verses, which has not yet been revealed in the last hundred years since the publication of the Anthroposophical Soul Calendar by Rudolf Steiner. A thick veil is spread over it, a veil of Isis, the goddess of the soul, of which it is known that no mortal can lift it. Only the immortal, psycho-spiritual human being, who knows himself at home in the extrasensory, higher worlds, is capable of doing this. Only to him the weekly verses unveil themselves as a travel guide through these worlds and lift him up into ever higher spiritual-cosmic realms until he experiences God, from where he gradually descends again into a new life on Earth, enriched in spirit and fertilised in his soul. If the reader embarks on this journey, the spiritual archetype of the Soul Calendar underlying the weekly verses is ultimately revealed to him. In addition, a much broader understanding of the human being opens up to the reader. And since the psycho-spiritual human being as the "Son of Man" is intimately connected with Christ, the "Son of God", a deeper understanding of the human being can only be truly attained if it is accompanied by a deeper understanding of the Christ Being.

Looking behind the veil of Isis, is only possible, if one rises into a meditative mood. Rudolf Steiner wrote in his first preface at the turn of the year 1912: *"It would be easy to say: So, as stated here, the soul should*

---

[1]   GA 26 "Anthroposophische Leitsätze" (Anthroposophical Leading Thoughts)

meditate if it wants to cultivate a bit of self-knowledge. It is not said, because man's own path is to take inspiration from something given, not to submit pedantically to a «path of knowledge»." However, this does not mean that the weekly verses are no meditation formula. It simply means that it should be put into every person's free will how he or she deals with the verses and whether at all. Perhaps a person prefers verses of a completely different kind for meditation on his or her individual path of development. On the other hand, even people who have not yet found access to meditation can certainly find their very own way of dealing with the weekly verses. – But, insights that were granted a human soul, who did not meditate on the weekly verses in the narrower sense, but let them work inwardly in a meditative mood for several years and traced the spiritual depths hidden therein, his insights into the terrestrial nature and the extraterrestrial cosmos, especially into the psycho-spiritual being of man, which far surpasses all limits of the Temporal, and in addition into the relation between man and the Christ Being, is the subject of this book. Moreover, numerous quotations from Rudolf Steiner's lectures and books uncover the enormous depths of his weekly verses.

The greatest gain in knowledge will come to the reader when the individual chapters are read in sequence beginning with the Easter verse as the first, since they build on one another in content and there are many references to previous chapters. This is the only useful manner to follow the gradual development of the flow of reflections and to fully comprehend their content. Since Easter is a movable celebration, the exact date for the Easter verse will vary from year to year, as well as for the weekly verses of the first half of the year preceding and following the Easter verse. However, this should not give rise to pedantic mathematical calculations, since usually several weekly verses are carried by similar moods of soul and nature and there are many content-related connections, which will have to be dealt with in more detail in the course of the reflections.

Rudolf Steiner himself also provided us with information in this regard. According to Johanna Mücke[2], the questions about shifting of the date appeared as early as 1913. She wrote in a letter: *"At that time I asked Doctor about it and he said: the main thing is that the first stanza always begins at Easter. The shift would not mean much, as he always kept three stanzas of the weekly verses in the same mood."* (Johanna Mücke's letter of 12 April 1938 to Marie Steiner) In connection with eurythmic work in later years, he also explained to Marie Steiner: *"The verses are designed internally in such a way that three verses each follow a basic mood, then in turn three comprise the next mood."* (Marie Steiner, in a letter to Hans Arenson, dated July 15, 1948) [3]

Regarding the other question of how to handle the weekly verses by people living in the southern hemisphere of the Earth, the following statement by Rudolf Steiner from one of his lectures may be referred to:

"Now the human soul feels also: When in the north the soul of the Earth moves out to the stars [i.e. at St. John's Day] and to a certain extent appears to the spiritual view like a comet tail which extends out to heaven, on the other side the soul of the Earth withdraws into the Earth, and it is Christmas. And again vice versa, when the soul of the Earth withdraws here, on the other side the comet's tail extends out into the cosmos. That happens at the same time." [4]

From such sympathy of the human soul with the annual rhythm of nature we may conclude that at the same time, when the readers of the northern hemisphere devote themselves to the 12th weekly verse, the "John-Atmosphere", for the people of the southern hemisphere the 38th weekly or Christmas verse, the "Consecration-Night-Atmosphere", is the appropriate one.

Now the reader is cordially invited to enter into the soul- and spirit-depths of the hitherto unexplored fifty-two weekly verses with the help of the following reflections, so that the spiritual archetype of the Soul Calendar may gradually reveal itself to him and he may achieve an expanded view of the human being as well as his connection with the cosmos and the Christ Being. – An overview of the fifty-two weekly verses is added at the end of the book.

---

[2] Johanna Mücke was the director of the Philosophisch-Theosophischer Verlag (Philosophical-Theosophical Publisher) founded by Marie von Sivers (from 1914 Marie Steiner) in 1908, which was renamed the Philosophisch-Anthroposophischer Verlag (Philosophical-Anthroposophical Publisher) after the separation from the Theosophical Society.

[3] "Beiträge zur Rudolf Steiner Gesamtausgabe" (Contributions to the Rudolf Steiner Complete Edition), Nr. 37/38

[4] GA 226 "Menschenwesen, Menschenschicksal und Welt-Entwicklung" (Man's being, his destiny and world-evolution), Kristiania (Oslo), Lecture of 21 May 1923

Finally, the author would like to thank Benjamin Schmidt (Germany), a friend in mind, who accompanied the development of this work from Christmas 2016 to Easter 2018 as a first reader and, through his feedback, occasionally gave the author the opportunity to explain one or the other difficult feature in more detail. It turned out that the translation of the text into English was completed just at Easter-time 2020, with the friendly support of Dr. Gopi Krishna Vijaya (Utah, USA) in proofreading the author's English translation.

Note on the translation of the weekly verses:

Due to the great importance of every single word of the fifty-two weekly verses, the translated stanzas were placed side by side with the original German wording. In this way, readers with knowledge of German may always compare the translations with Rudolf Steiner's original words. Since in many cases he created new combinations of German words in order to express the deeper meaning of the verses in an appropriate way, corresponding new word-combinations had to be created in English as well.

Rudolf Steiner chose his words not only according to their meaning, but also according to their sound based on their consonants and vowels. Of course, this could often not be maintained in English. Basically, wherever possible, translations more literal and similar to the German original sound were preferred to the more common ones. For example, the first line of the first weekly verse or Easter verse "Wenn aus den Weltenweiten" was translated "When from the vastness of the world" in order to retain its sound character. The consonants "W" and "V" are the consonants of the zodiacal sign Aries as Rudolf Steiner told us in his lectures on eurythmy[5], and they resound three times in this line. This could be maintained. For the same reason German terms like "Weltenwort", "Weltenselbst" and "Weltenwärme" were not translated using the more common terms Cosmic Word, Cosmic Self and cosmic warmth or cosmic heat, but "World Word", "World Self" and "world-warmth". Priority was given to fidelity with regard to the meaning or the original sound over a possibly smoother linguistic or poetic sound.

We must accept, that the original German verses often sound strange and unusual even to German readers. Therefore it would have been a wrong strategy for translation to look always for words sounding more familiar to the English ear than the chosen ones.

Kassel, Easter-time 2020

Roland Schrapp[6]

---

[5] GA 279 "Eurythmie als sichtbare Sprache" (Eurythmy as a visible language), Dornach, Lecture of 8 July 1924
[6] spoken: Shrupp

Rudolf Steiner's Prefaces to the Soul Calendar

Preface to the first edition 1912/13

The human being feels connected to the world and its change of times. He feels his own being as a likeness of the world-archetype. But the likeness is not a symbolic-pedantic imitation of the archetype. What the great world reveals in the course of time corresponds to a pendulum beating of the human being, which does not run in the element of time. In fact, man can feel his being, insofar as it is devoted to the senses and their perceptions, as corresponding to the summer nature interwoven with light and warmth. The foundation in himself and the life in his own world of thoughts and will impulses he can sense as a winter existence. Thus, in him, the rhythm of outer and inner life becomes what nature presents in temporal alternation as summer and winter. But great secrets of existence may be revealed to him if he relates his timeless rhythm of perception and thought in a corresponding manner to the time-rhythm of nature. In this way, the year becomes the archetype of human soul activity and thus a fruitful source of true self-recognition. In the following Soul-Year-Calendar, the human spirit is thought of in such a position in which he can *sense* his own soul-weaving on the seasonal moods from week to week in the image on the impressions of the course of the year. It is meant as a self-recognition through *feeling*. This feeling self-recognition can experience the cycle of the soul-life as a timeless one on the time by the given characteristic weekly sentences. Expressly, it is meant to be a possibility of a path of self-recognition. It is not intended to give «prescriptions» in the manner of theosophical pedants, but rather is pointed to the vivid weaving of the soul as it can be. Everything that is destined for souls takes an individual colouring. For this very reason, however, *every* soul will find its way in relation to an individually marked one. It would be easy to say: So, as stated here, the soul *should* meditate if it wants to cultivate a bit of self-knowledge. It is *not* said, because man's own path is to take inspiration from something given, not to submit pedantically to a «path of knowledge».

Preface to the second edition 1918

The course of the year has its own life. The human soul can sense this life. If the soul allows itself to be effected by what speaks variously out of the life of the year from week to week, only then will it really find itself through such participation. It will feel how forces will be growing up by that, which strengthen it from within. It will notice that these forces want to be awakened in it by the share the soul can take in the meaning of the course of the world as it takes place in the sequence of times. Only by that it will become aware of the fine but meaningful threads of connection, which exist between itself and the world into which it was born.

For each week, in this calendar a verse of such kind is inscribed, which inspires the soul to witness what is going on in this week as a part of the entire life of a year. What this life causes to resound in the soul, when the soul unites with it, is intended to be expressed in the verse. It is thought of a healthy «feeling at one» with the course of nature and a powerful «finding oneself» arising from it, in the belief that sympathizing with the world's course in the sense of such verses is something the soul yearns for, if it rightly understands itself.[7]

---

[7] Both prefaces as well as all weekly verses of the Anthroposophical Soul Calendar are taken from volume GA 40 "Wahrspruchworte" (True-Verse-Words / Truth-Wrought-Words)

Weekly Verses
of the Summer Half-Year

SUMMER HALF-YEAR

Experiences of the Soul in Spring – Ascension to the higher worlds

Spring in Life on Earth – 1st Week

1 Easter-Atmosphere (7 – 13 April)	*1 Oster-Stimmung (7. – 13. April)*
When from the vastness of the world	Wenn aus den Weltenweiten
The sun speaks to the human sense	Die Sonne spricht zum Menschensinn
And pleasure from the depths of soul	Und Freude aus den Seelentiefen
Unites with light, in looking,	Dem Licht sich eint im Schauen,
Then soar, out of the selfhood's sheath,	Dann ziehen aus der Selbstheit Hülle
Thoughts to the distant space	Gedanken in die Raumesfernen
And dully bind man's essence	Und binden dumpf
To the existence of the spirit.	Des Menschen Wesen an des Geistes Sein.

In the first weekly verse, entitled "Easter-Atmosphere" by Rudolf Steiner, the special kind of the people's experience during their life on Earth is characterized in carefully selected words full of wisdom. As soon as we "see the light of the world" through physical birth, we come under the direct influence of sensations that touch us every day from the outside. They first speak to our sensory organs and attract the attention of our soul to the outside. Particularly intensively we notice this at the beginning of spring, when the days become longer than the nights, due to the fact that the Sun rises higher and the light prevails over the darkness. Then life in nature also celebrates its resurrection and, through its increasing sprouting, growing and blooming, brings us the astonishing variety of forms and colours of the plant world, which emerges anew each year. But within the animal world as well, the new life, initially born protected by the forest or the stable, is striving more and more out of its hiding places and ventures to the outside world, which is so tempting with its sensory stimuli. It is impressions of this kind that we humans love most about spring. They also lure us out into nature. We feel refreshed and enlivened by the miracle that sprouts every year and which now takes place all around us on the surface of the Earth.

Strangely, in the first weekly verse of his Soul Calendar, Rudolf Steiner mentions nothing of these numerous births of new bodily life in the nature around us, although this verse is nevertheless titled "Easter-Atmosphere" and we associate with Easter time just the annual resurrection of new life on Earth. Completely contrary to our expectations, Rudolf Steiner draws our attention away from the Earth's surface and the earthly nature with his very first words, up into the atmosphere that surrounds the Earth filled with "light", and even further out into the "vastness of the world" and the "distant space", that is, into the area of the extraterrestrial. If one lets the words of the first weekly verse have an impartial effect on oneself, a feeling of astonishment may arise at first and raise the question in one's soul: Why does Rudolf Steiner so completely ignore the extremely impressive and wonderful, even enchanting spring events on Earth? Why, in this time of the births of the bodies, does he direct our gaze so consistently away from the Earth, out into the vastness?

On closer inspection, we notice in addition that only one single thing of the entire terrestrial nature is mentioned at all. It is the bodily sheath of the human being. But even this is briefly and concisely described simply as a "sheath" of something that Rudolf Steiner calls "selfhood". He obviously wants to draw our attention to a process of consciousness that is taking place on this sheath of man, namely on its outside, especially in its sense of sight, the main sense of the human being. As such, sight is particularly emphasized with the term "human sense", although it certainly also stands for all other senses of the human being. The reason for the special emphasis of the sense of sight is certainly that with it we perceive the "light" surrounding the Earth and, following this, are able to penetrate farthest into "the vastness of the world" and the "distant space", much further than the sense of hearing would allow us, not to mention the senses of touch, smell and taste that give information only about the immediate surroundings of the body and the body itself. As a consequence of the effect of the sunlight on the "human sense" something is triggered in the human soul. As a response of our inner world, a compassionate feeling of joy rises "from the depths of soul" towards the sensory impressions approaching us from the outside. In the course of this process of looking at the outside world, man awakens to a first timid consciousness of his "selfhood". He becomes aware of something that is to a certain extent independent in relation to the outside world, his self, which he calls "I". In a lecture from Volume 5 about karmic connections, Rudolf Steiner points out in short, concise words: *"that we stand here on Earth as human beings, enclosed in our skin, so to speak in terms of space. Everything within our skin we call ourselves. Everything that is outside our skin, we call the world. And we look out into the world from what is within our skin."* [8]

Right at the beginning of the weekly verses of the Soul Calendar, man is thus described not as a merely physical, living body-being, but in particular as a consciousness-being that even awakens to the realization of "selfhood", to the consciousness of his "I", on the basis of a trinity consisting of body ("the selfhood's sheath"), soul ("joy from the depths of soul") and spirit ("thoughts"). In this threefold composition man was born in the course of a long evolutionary process out of the whole Divine, which surrounds us as nature. The Rosicrucians of the Middle Ages summarized their knowledge of this process of the development of the human members of being in the words "Ex deo nascimur" – "Out of God we are born, we emerge" – and hid their knowledge in the letter sequence "E D N". With the Easter season, in which the birth of new bodily life reaches its climax in nature, this "Ex deo nascimur" finds its sensory perceptible likeness in the course of the year and its fulfillment. Although the creative activity of building new bodies will continue in the following months of spring, it will then decrease more and more and eventually fade away in the course of the summer months.

However, when God gives birth to something, it is of His nature and essence. The actual human being developing in and on his lower sheaths is indeed of divine nature, as we know through Christ himself. In John 10:34, the Gospel tells us how Christ pointed this fact out to the Jewish scribes, saying, *"Is it not written in your law, «I have said, you are gods?»"* Here Christ referred to Psalm 82, verse 6, which the scribes knew and which reminds men of their divine origin: *"I said: «You are all gods and sons of the Most High.»"* But if we are sons of the Most High, we are sons of the Father. What kind, however, is our father of whose kind we are? Rudolf Steiner commented on notes from a private lesson as follows:

"The first force, the unmanifested Deity, is also called the Father; the second force is the Son, who is both life and creative substance, and the third force is the Spirit. Together they appear as these three primal forces, that is, as Father, Son and [Holy] Spirit, as c o n s c i o u s n e s s, l i f e and f o r m." [9]

On another occasion, when Rudolf Steiner spoke about the three kinds of creation, he elucidated about the threefold deity:

"But wherever we have an emerging out of nowhere, there we have the first Logos. Therefore, the first Logos is often called the one, who hidden in the things themselves, the second Logos the substance that rests in the things, which creates the living from the living, the third Logos the one, who combines all that exists, who puts the world together with the things. These three Logoi always interpenetrate mutually in the world. The first Logos also includes inner wisdom and will. The creative activity of the first Logos includes experience, that is, collecting thoughts out of nothing and then again creating according to the thoughts out of nothing. However, creation out of nothing is not meant as if nothing had been there, but that experiences are made in the course of development and that in the course of becoming there is created something new, so that what is there melts down, so to speak, and something new is created from experience." [10]

These two statements of Rudolf Steiner can be summarized in the words: The Father is highest divine, creative consciousness. He is hidden within himself. He does not need an outside world to be aware of himself. His life-creating activity is the Son born out of the primordial unity, the only begotten Son. The Spirit shows itself as forms or materials of the most diverse levels of density and in the most diverse combinations. The Son has a direct share in the Father's consciousness and is creative himself. The purpose of every revelation of the Father is to develop new consciousness in the manifested form up to the highest creative level of consciousness, where it can reunite with its origin, but then enriched with all the

---

[8]   GA 239 "Esoterische Betrachtungen karmischer Zusammenhänge" (Esoteric reflections on karmic connections – karmic relationships), Volume 5, Paris, Lecture of 25 May 1924

[9]   GA 89 "Bewusstsein – Leben – Form" (Consciousness – Life – Form), an undated private lesson "Über die Logoi" (About the Logoi), probably 1904

[10] GA 93a "Grundelemente der Esoterik" (Foundations of esotericism), Berlin, Lecture of 30 October 1905

new experiences that have been made on the path of development. *"So in the end there is something that was not there at the beginning: all the experiences. What was there at the beginning flowed out in all sorts of things and beings. A new consciousness has been created in the end with a new content, a new content of consciousness."*

To accomplish this great work of Creation, the Son sacrifices himself and descends to the densest states of form, pervades them, enlivens and ensouls them. Thereby on the one hand, He gradually makes the divine sparks inherent in them suitable to develop an ever stronger and more comprehensive creative power as well as, on the other hand, an ever stronger and more comprehensive power of consciousness. That is why He says of Himself: *"I am the way, the truth and the life."* (John 14:6) He is the way to the Father.

In ancient times of evolution of the human consciousness we already passed through three lower levels of consciousness, the dull trance consciousness, the deep sleep consciousness and the dream consciousness. In a further evolutionary step on Earth, we developed up to an outer object consciousness, which enables us to gain the knowledge of ourselves on an outside world, the self- awareness or consciousness of the "I". From there, under Christ's guidance, we can now ascend to the next higher levels of consciousness:

"There are seven stages of human consciousness: trance consciousness, deep sleep consciousness, dream consciousness, waking consciousness, psychic, superpsychic and spiritual consciousness. There are actually twelve stages of consciousness in total; the five others are creative stages of consciousness. They are those of the creators, the creative gods. These are related to the twelve signs of the zodiac. Man has to go through these twelve stages one after the other. ...

One can imagine a high being, who set all twelve stages of consciousness out of himself. He himself is there as the thirteenth and will say to himself: I could not be what I am if I had not exuded these twelve stages of consciousness out of myself. – We have this case given in Christ with the twelve apostles. The twelve apostles represent the stages of consciousness through which Christ passed." [11]

Christ develops the human consciousness of the "I" up to the highest state predetermined to the Son of Man, the consciousness of the Son of God. The thirteenth state of consciousness is that of the Son, who has returned to the Father. *"Become perfect as your Father in heaven is perfect"* (Mt 5:48) and *"I and the Father are one"* (John 10:30). But there is only one being that can lead us to the goal of our development. Therefore Christ also says: *"No one comes to the Father except through me."* (John 14:6).

"Through the Christ impulse this «I» shall be found in an appropriate way. And the fact that within Central Europe this «I» connects itself most purely with the Christ impulse is expressed linguistically by the fact that in our [German] word «Ich» [English: «I»], through an inner spiritual necessity of progressing development, the initials of Christ, I-C-H, Jesus Christ, are expressed. This may seem like a dream to those who want to remain in the field of dreamful science today. To the one who awakens from this dreamy world view, to him this is a great, significant truth. «Ich» expresses man's connection with Jesus Christ." [12]

The twelve steps of evolution from the human being to the being of God, which culminate in a thirteenth, highest state, have their reflection in the course of the year. However, the development of creative power is reflected there separately from the development of consciousness. Just as the earthly man consists of a lower man, the metabolic man, and an upper man, the conscious man, the stages of development for

---

[11] Ibidem, Lecture of 26 September 1905

[12] "Jesus, the Anointed One" in ancient Greek did not begin with the letter "J" but with "I": Ἰησοῦς Χριστός (Iēsous Christos). – See also GA 166 „Notwendigkeit und Freiheit im Weltengeschehen und im menschlichen Handeln" ("Necessity and independence in world affairs and in human action), Berlin, Lecture of 8 February 1916 – In another Lecture Rudolf Steiner spoke on the same topic: *"The effective power is expressed in the fact that through inner vision, through true mysticism, communion with Christ is possible. This was also integrated into the language. Europe's first Christian initiate himself, Ulfilas*, put it into the German language in order that man found the «Ich» [English „I"] in the language. Other languages express this relationship to the I through a special form of the verb, for example in Latin "amo", but the German language adds the I. «Ich» is: J.Ch. = Jesus Christ. This is intentionally put into the German language, it is no coincidence. It is the initiates who have created language. Just as one has AUM for the Trinity in Sanskrit, we have the sign «ICH» for the inner being of man. This created a centre through which the world's passions can be transformed into rhythm. They have to be rhythmized by the I. This center is literally the Christ."* – GA 93a „Grundelemente der Esoterik" (Foundations of Esotericism), Berlin, Lecture of 27 September 1905)

  * Ulfilas or Wulfila (ca. 311 - 383 AD), Bishop of the Gothic tribe of the Terwingen, developed a scripture and created new words for the Gothic language to accomplish the earliest Bible translation into a Germanic language: the so-called Wulfila Bible.

attainment of the substance-producing divine creative power are reflected in the natural moods of the "lower half of the year", the dark winter half, whereas the stages of development associated with the attainment of the divine power of consciousness are reflected in the natural moods of the "upper half of the year", the light summer half.

In the Soul Calendar, Rudolf Steiner describes to us in his wisely chosen formulations of the weekly verses, which are partly appearing mysterious, how we can participate feelingly with our souls in the developments of the divine creative power on the one hand and the divine power of consciousness on the other hand, inspired by the changing natural moods in the course of the year. The first weekly verse of the year therefore begins immediately with the birth of the human "I"-consciousness at its lowest stage of development. This birth happens by means of a physical body equipped with physical sensory organs and a physical outside world. This gives man the already described impression that he would dwell within his body as in his "selfhood's sheath", which clearly separates him from the world around and places him opposite to it. That is why he describes everything in his surroundings as "objects".

The human soul, however, is by no means as clearly separated from the outside world as it appears with regard to the body. Man's sympathy with the play of light around him causes that his soul "unites with light, in looking". Inside and outside world interpenetrate mutually each other, pervade each other. Through this touch of the inner soul by the outer sensory world, the I begins to loosen its close connection with the body, although it still remains closely connected with it. Accordingly, we first feel our I-consciousness as belonging to our body and living in it.

On closer inspection, however, it turns out that we experience our I predominantly outside the body. This is also shown by the fact that we are able to view our body from the outside, from the feet to the chest, even to the shoulders and the arms, and to separate it from the outside world as the "selfhood's sheath". But we cannot see our own head, unless we use a mirror. By experiencing ourselves, however, with our I just at the border of our body to the outside world, it becomes clear that our I is already part of this outside world, and indeed of its underlying Spiritual, which comes to us in the image of a physical outside world. This arouses our intellectual interest. Through the sensory stimuli that approach us from the outside world, we are stimulated anew, just in spring and Easter, to contemplate the new variety of perception in our environment and to expand with our thinking far into this outside world. Finally we are outside with our attention, with our I, out with the things, with the blue sky, with the warming, brightly shining sun. "Then soar, out of the sheath of self, thoughts to the distant space." In this way we gain the possibility to grow beyond our corporeality and to realize that on the one hand we have a body equipped with sensory organs with which we awaken to our I, but on the other hand we also have a soul which is able to connect with the spirit of the outside world, to unite with it. In thought we can move out with our own Psycho-Spiritual and our I-consciousness into the sensory world and the psycho-spiritual world underlying it. In fact we are much more connected to this world through our thought life than we are initially conscious of in life on Earth, as the thoughts that we cherish here are immediately absorbed by the beings of the next higher Hierarchy of spiritual beings during the whole time of our stay on Earth:

"And just as we humans have to take our iron, our wood from the subordinate kingdoms – that is, first from the mineral, from the vegetable kingdom – to put together our machines, so the Angeloi, Archangeloi, Archai also need materials to do, well, say, to build – although this expression is of course very coarse – what they are to build. And what are their materials? For much what the Angeloi, Archangeloi, Archai have to accomplish in the spiritual world, the materials are just the thoughts that people consider their property. And that's the way it is: As we walk through the world and cherish our thoughts, looking at our thought life, as it were, from the inside and viewing it as our property, the Angeloi, Archangeloi and Archai work at our thoughts, without our knowledge. The very least that lives in our thoughts comes to our consciousness, because thoughts mean much more than what comes to our consciousness, much other than what lives in our souls. While we think and remember our thoughts, the named beings of the higher Hierarchy, the next Hierarchy, work, so to speak, from outside in their own way, according to the way they can use our thoughts. So imagine every human being in such a way that what happens to his consciousness is only one side of his thought life. While he is thinking, the beings of the named Hierarchies are constantly hovering around him and working with the help of his thoughts. These are their materials. And what they work in this way is part of what is needed so that Jupiter, Venus, Vulcan can emerge from the Earth. This belongs to what causes progress in the development of the universe. And during our whole life until death the mentioned beings of the higher Hierarchy work from the outside on the thoughts, in so far as these are, as it were, enclosed by our being." [13]

---

[13] GA 174b "Die geistigen Hintergründe des 1. Weltkrieges" (The spiritual backgrounds of World War I), Stuttgart, Lecture of 15 March 1916

Rudolf Steiner's choice of words points out in the first sentence of the Easter weekly verse already that our outside world includes psycho-spiritual beings. He does not say here at all what today's man, predominantly influenced by science, would formulate usually: "When from the vastness of the world the sun *shines* to the human sense." No, Rudolf Steiner says: "When from the vastness of the world the sun *speaks* to the human sense." A large glowing gas ball cannot speak. It can only shine, glow or radiate. "Speaking" means the revelation of something Psycho-Spiritual. When we humans speak, we reveal a part of our own Psycho-Spiritual to those to whom we address our words. If we want to take seriously the statement of the Easter weekly verse saying that the sun "speaks", then we must assume that behind the image of the radiant sun a psycho-spiritual being is hidden, which reveals a part of its own inner life to us and through this lightful revelation causes everything that triggers pleasure in the depths of our souls, leads our human Psycho-Spiritual – "man's essence" –, out of the bodily sheath and raises it above the merely Earthly. The psycho-spiritual essence of the Sun and the psycho-spiritual existence, which in its revelation gives light, life and love to earthly beings, wants to connect with the human being. Who does not feel reminded hereby of the words of the great Sun Spirit Himself, who connected Himself to mankind through the Easter event two thousand years ago. He said: *"I am the light of the world"* (John 8:12) and *"I am the Resurrection and the Life"* (John 11:25). In addition, the first weekly verse even shows us the way how we can get closer to Him: by growing beyond our mortal sheaths, formed from the Maya of the sensory world. For Christ is not only life, but as He says of Himself: *"I am the way, the truth and the life."* (John 14:6)

If we take the sensory outside world as a parable of a more comprehensive worldview, we can regard nature in its entirety as a Creation out of which we were born, accomplished according to the will of the Father and formed by the Spirit. The brightly shining Sun in the sky, which gives us life, light and warmth, then becomes the likeness of the Son, born of the Father's universal oneness. The Son speaks to the human sense in the sheath of sunlight as the World Word and causes in doing so, especially at Easter time, a bodiless, spiritual birth: the birth of the human I. In 1912, the year of the first edition of the Anthroposophical Soul Calendar, Rudolf Steiner himself indicated in one of his lectures about this meaning of the Easter verse:

"What the calendar has as its exterior is only the exoteric side, for in reality we have the year 1879. The temporal relations, which can be observed through occult observation, are to be expressed here actually. This should be started here, because it is, of course, only the first step. With the mystery of Golgotha is given the birth of the I-consciousness within humanity. And this fact will gradually be more and more recognized in the spiritual culture of our Earth as important for all future of mankind. Thus one will gradually understand that it is justified to count the year 1879 today, that is, 1912 less 33, which also means that the time is counted from Easter to Easter, that we do not begin with January, because if one sees something essential for the spiritual development of humanity in the birth of the I-consciousness, it is also justified to be reminded every year by referring this birth of the I-consciousness to the relationships of microcosm and macrocosm. A significant feature in the relationship of microcosm and macrocosm is given when Easter is commemorated in connection with the birth of I-consciousness." [14]

In the same way that two thousand years ago on Golgotha the Christ Being had to leave its mortal human body in order to be born into the environment of the Earth and to higher life, so we too must move out of the earthly body with our I into the vastness of the world. As long as we remain in the earthly body, our consciousness remains dusky and our thoughts "*dimly* bind man's essence [his soul and I] to the existence of the spirit." Only when we develop beyond the mere sensory experience to out-of-body perception can we, starting from the first stage of the bodily-born I-consciousness, tread the path to an ever higher development from the still childlike I of the earthly human being up to a cosmic I. Few people who are ahead of the general development of humanity, since they walk on the path of spiritual discipleship, can already within life on Earth rise to a consciousness outside "the selfhood's sheath" and achieve some of those stages of consciousness which the human I will develop on its evolutionary journey to a cosmic I, as it is determined to it by divine procreation. All people, however, can already experience these future stages of consciousness after the death of their physical bodies, in the period between death and a new birth. During that time, the Christ Being becomes our guide through the spiritual worlds. We experience Him as the Lord in the extra-bodily existence, the living one among the supposed dead. The ancient Egyptians worshiped Him in this capacity as Osiris, the ruler of the afterlife, and knew that every human being dies towards Osiris, into the Osiris. The ancient Rosicrucians also recognized these connections and put them into the words "In Christo morimur" – "Towards Christ or into Christ we die." They hid this knowledge in the letters "I C M" or "I J M" (In Jesu morimur).

---

[14] GA 133, "Der irdische und der kosmische Mensch", (Earthly and Cosmic Man), Berlin, Lecture of 23 April 1912

We recognize the astonishing spiritual depth of the words of the first weekly verse and that a very intimate, spiritual Easter-Atmosphere hides behind their shell. In this mood resonates the fact that the "Ex deo nascimur" finds its fulfillment in the course of the year with the Easter time and the birth of the earthly human I on the physical and bodily sensory experiences of the outside world, as the germinative birth of the Son of God in the human soul. The possibility of any further development of the newborn earthly I is given to man solely through the power and guidance of the Son. Through the new impulse of the "In Christo morimur", He immediately shows us the way from the earthly corporeality and the Earth's surface into the spiritual vastness of the world, which we can experience with the physical senses at first only as "distant space", but behind which are hidden extra-bodily worlds to which we will all belong after death. We contribute to this development from the dull earthly consciousness up to the clearest and highest spiritual-divine consciousness, if we already feel and experience beforehand the individual developmental steps every year in the successive moods of nature in its annual cycle. For the course of the year, like everything material, is only a reflection of a higher, wider process of development, entirely in the sense of Goethe's saying at the end of the second part of his Faust drama: *"All that is transient is but a likeness. The unobtainable – what we cannot yet attain within the world of the transient – here it becomes achieveness"* [15], in the world beyond the veil of the senses.

It may seem strange to some readers to see the mood of Easter and of spring, with the new birth of earthly life that takes place everywhere, associated with man's death and afterlife. However, such disconcertment can arise only in our present, materialistically oriented time, in which all instinctive clairvoyance of the ancient times has completely disappeared. In the past, a sympathizing with the course of the year gave completely different experiences to the people, just contradictory experiences compared to our times:

"But above all, man experienced the course of the year in such a way that when he followed the soul of the Earth out into the cosmos towards the spring time and towards the time of St. John's Day, he learned every year by this following also to follow the spiritual beings of the higher Hierarchies and especially to follow the deceased souls who had already died in the world. In ancient times, people were aware that when they sympathized with the course of the year, they learned to follow the deceased souls, so to speak, to see how their deceased were doing. And people felt: spring not only brings them the first flowers, spring also gives them the opportunity to look at their deceased, to see how they are doing. – Something Spiritual was very concretely connected with the experience of the course of the year." [16]

From these reflections we can already see what great, truly breathtaking depths we can expect in the further weekly verses of the Soul Calendar. Now we also understand better the mysterious reference that Rudolf Steiner gave us in the preface to the first edition of the Soul Calendar on Easter 1912, when he prophesied what the weekly verses are able to reveal to man:

"But great secrets of existence can be revealed to him, if he brings his timeless rhythm of perception and thought to the temporal rhythm of nature in an appropriate manner. Thus the year becomes the archetype of human soul activity and thus a fruitful source of true self-knowledge.".

What Rudolf Steiner meant with "self-knowledge", and thus true "knowledge of the human being", illuminates a different statement of him:

"Knowledge of the human being will only be possible if it can start with the lowest forms of the phenomenal world, with everything that manifests itself to man as the material world. And what thus begins with the contemplation of what manifests as the material world must end with the contemplation of the hierarchical world. From the lowest forms of material existence up to the highest forms of spiritual

---

[15] Here Goethe designed his terms in artistic creativity: the German term "das Unzulängliche", usually used in a completely different way (meaning the inadequate), is etymologically yet related to "das Nicht-Erlangbare", "the unobtainable", which, according to Goethe, only can be achieved and become an event in the heavens. The combination of the terms "the achieved" and "event", which we find in the English language as "achievement" is accomplished by Goethe through the artistic fusion of the German words "das Erreichte" (what has been achieved) and "Ereignis" (event) to the word "Erreichnis", which otherwise does not exist in the German language, but rhymes with "Gleichnis". In the translation above this was reproduced with the words "achieveness" and "likeness".

[16] GA 226 "Menschenwesen, Menschenschicksal und Welt-Entwicklung" (Man's being, his destiny and World-Evolution), Kristiania (Oslo), Lecture of 21 May 1923

existence, up to the world of Hierarchies, must be sought that, which can then lead to real knowledge of the human being." [17]

Rudolf Steiner has left us a very great spiritual treasure with his Soul Calendar. It can turn into a true guide through the extrasensory worlds if we are only able really to penetrate to those depths that are hidden behind the words of the weekly verses, although they are always referring to the sensory world. Through this reference to the sensory experiences of external nature we are repeatedly "grounded" and protected from the drive to be alienated from the Earth too much and too early, in our consideration on the psycho-spiritual depths behind the weekly verses.

We may guess already as well, what a high goal will be at the end of this journey, if we allow ourselves to be guided by Christ. He Himself is the path through the metamorphoses of life. Where this path leads us, he revealed to us with the words: *"No one comes to the Father but through me"* and *"Become perfect as your Father in heaven is perfect."* (Mt 5:48) The Father from whom we were born – ex Deo nascimur – is our origin and also our goal. But before we can find the Father, we must first find the Son. That we are able to walk this path we owe to Christ, the only begotten Son. At Easter about two thousand years ago he opened the way through the mystery of Golgotha to all of us. Since then, the "in Christo morimur" has been possible for all of us. And that is necessary, because otherwise we would lose with death not only our physical body, but also our I-consciousness that we can only acquire in life on Earth.

"For, the physical body disintegrates at death. If we have acquired our I-consciousness through it, then the anxiety arises, which is quite a scientifically founded fearfulness: How do we carry our I-consciousness through death?

This question is only solved by the mystery of Golgotha. Never would humanity be able to carry the I-consciousness through death, unless this I-consciousness, developed in the physical body, unites with the Christ, who holds it, when it would melt away with the physical body from the human soul. The I-consciousness is acquired through the physical body. In death it would melt away with the physical body from the human soul, if this I were not connected to the being of Christ, in the sense of Paul's words «Not I, but the Christ in me»; for the Christ takes it and carries it through death." [18]

Christ preserves our I-consciousness until the great midnight hour of existence in the midst of two incarnations, where we are endowed with new powers to cope with the descent to a new life on Earth and the further development of the human I-consciousness to ever higher levels in ever closer union with Christ.

Ascension to the Moon Sphere – 2nd Week

The first weekly verse describes, how, at Easter time, excited by the sensory stimuli of the increasing sunlight, man's thoughts "soar out of the selfhood's sheath", the physical body, "to the distant space" and thereby "dully bind man's essence to the existence of the spirit". In the second weekly verse, the expansion of the psycho-spiritual essence of man is continued. It is driven to the moment when he finally leaves his earthly body, passes through the portal of death and experiences his "In Christo morimur". First and foremost, the amazing experience of the soul results for him: *"You have gone out of your physical body and are leaving this physical body behind."* [19] But while the deceased person experiences himself as being separated from his physical body, frees himself from his earthly materiality and returns it to Earth, all the contents of his consciousness gained in life on Earth go the exactly opposite way. It is true, that for a few days they appear in front of his soul's eye in a large commemorative tableau, so that he can once again overlook his entire past life on Earth. But soon the newly deceased person notices how his entire world of thoughts, all his memories, detach themselves from him and escape into the cosmos. They are taken away from him by the beings of the so-called third Hierarchy, the Angeloi, Archangeloi and Archai, who work out a large etheric overall-tissue from the thoughts of the individual human beings:

---

[17] GA 230 "Der Mensch als Zusammenklang des schaffenden, bildenden und gestaltenden Weltenwortes", (Man as symphony of the creative, building and shaping Cosmic Word), Dornach, Lecture of 9 November 1923

[18] GA 125 "Die Philosophie, Kosmologie und Religion in der Anthroposophie" (Philosophy, Cosmology and Religion in Anthroposophy), Dornach, Lecture of 13 September 1922

[19] GA 153 "Inneres Wesen des Menschen und Leben zwischen Tod und neuer Geburt" (Inner nature of man and life between death and new birth), Vienna, Lecture of 13 April 1914

"And when we pass through the portal of death, then, as we already pointed out in my previous presence, some time after we have passed through the portal of death, our ether body will be taken from us and woven into the general world ether. Not only that, which we see by looking at one side of our thought-tissue at last, is interwoven here, but also that, which the above-mentioned beings have worked out, is interwoven into the general world ether. While working, so to speak, on our individual thought-tissue during our lives, they then assemble the individual thought-tissues of one, of the other, of the third person, as they may be needed, so that something new may come about in the course of the further development of the world. This must be interwoven into the general world ether, which they can acquire by assembling the individual human ether bodies they have worked on during the time of physical life.

... What we can give to these beings, the Angeloi, Archangeloi, Archai, forms for the whole time, which we then live between death and a new birth, something we have to look at, we have to watch. We know that it is taken from us a few days after we have passed through the portal of death. But while living on between death and a new birth, our soul's gaze is constantly focused on that which we have been able to give for the general world-ether-tissue. And while we ourselves now in turn have to contribute to the production of that which will later on connect with physical matter in order to give us a new incarnation, this work of ours is influenced by the view of what we have given to the great world. In short, concerning the way we will be able to prepare for our new incarnation, much will depend on whether we have something to look at from which we can draw new impulses for a next incarnation in this thought-tissue interwoven with the world ether, or whether we cannot." [20]

The second weekly verse speaks of this process of detachment of the ether body and its interweaving into the general world ether, its interweaving with the ether bodies of all the other deceased persons by the beings of the spiritual world. In short, it speaks of the transition of the separate existence of human thought life to a general existence.

2nd Week (14 - 20 April)	*2. Woche (14. – 20. April)*
Into the outside of the sensory universe	Ins Äußere des Sinnenalls
Thought power loses own existence.	Verliert Gedankenmacht ihr Eigensein;
Thus, spirit-worlds now find	Es finden Geisteswelten
The human shoot again,	Den Menschensprossen wieder,
Which has to find its germ in them,	Der seinen Keim in ihnen,
Its own soul's fruit yet in itself.	Doch seine Seelenfrucht
	In sich muss finden.

How does man himself experience this fundamental change of his thought life, which starts just a few days after death?

"When the moment comes when man steps through the portal of death, then little by little – it takes a few days –, after the physical body is put off, that, which I have called the ether body or the formative force-body in my writings, separates from the I and from the astral body. This separation is such that the person, who has passed through the portal of death, feels that his thoughts, which he has hitherto only regarded as something that is within himself, are realities, which are expanding more and more. Two, three, four days after death, man has the feeling: You actually consist of thoughts, but these thoughts diverge. – Man as a thought being becomes larger and larger and finally man's entire thought being dissolves into the cosmos." [21]

Bearer of the entire thought being of man is his ether body. Before our birth on Earth, we pulled it together from the cosmic perimeter, which the Sun marks on its daily and annual circular path in the sky, from "the outside of the sensory universe". At death, the ether body detaches from us and returns to where it was taken, just as we return in the opposite direction the substances of our physical body to the Earth from which we once took them. During our earthly life, the Earth is polar in its relation to "the outside of the sensory universe", the perimeter, because we experience the Earth as its centre. The material sheath that was temporarily taken from the Earth as well as the thought experiences of man excited through it are thus separated and flee from the psycho-spiritual man, the astral body and the I, each in exactly the opposite

---

[20] GA 174b "Die geistigen Hintergründe des 1. Weltkrieges" (The spiritual backgrounds of World War I), Stuttgart, Lecture of 15 March 1916

[21] GA 226 "Menschenwesen, Menschenschicksal und Welt-Entwicklung" (Man's being, man's destiny and world evolution), Kristiania (Oslo), Lecture of 16 May 1923

direction. Everything material flees towards the centre of the sensory world. All thoughts flee into the vastness of the cosmos. But there they become something completely different than they were to us during our life on Earth.

"But nowhere around the Earth do we discover thoughts as such. They are only present in humans and come out of them. When we step out of the earthly sphere of death into the spatial sphere of thoughts, then at first no beings live there; at first we do not meet beings in the vastness of space – neither gods nor humans –, but we meet world thoughts everywhere. It is that way, when we have gone through death and are entering the vastness of the world, as if here in the physical world we would not first see people, but if, when we approach a person, we would first perceive his thoughts, without seeing him. We would see a cloud of thoughts. And we see a second cloud: We do not encounter beings, we encounter the world thoughts, the general world intelligence. Man lives in this sphere of cosmic intelligence a few days after his death. And in these world thoughts, weaving there, appears like a detail, I would like to say like a special cloud we look at, one's own last life on Earth, which one has experienced. This is inscribed into the world intelligence. One looks at one's own life all at once, in a large tableau all at once for a few days. With each day – there are only a few – that which was inscribed into the world intelligence becomes weaker and weaker. It expands into the cosmic space, it disappears. While at the end of life on Earth there is the aspect of death, at the end of the experience after a few days there is the disappearance into the vastness of the world. So after the first aspect, which we may call the aspect of death, we have the second aspect, which may be called the aspect of the disappearance of the earthly life." [22]

Once we descended to Earth from "spiritual worlds" and brought the "spirit-germ" of our physical body. It was united with the fertilised egg cell in the womb of our earthly mother, so that an earthly human could be born. Now, at the end of our life on Earth, we return to our spiritual home as beings who sprouted out of our earthly body. This after-death process of sprouting from the Earth finds its analogy in the sprouting and shooting of the plant world around us at the beginning of spring. A plant shoot can only grow out of the Earth as a bodily-living creature. The "human shoot", on the other hand, grows out of life on Earth as a psycho-spiritual being, which carries into the higher worlds the totality of its experiences between birth and death as his treasure of memory, his soul's fruit matured within him during life on Earth,.

"What we can call a fruit of the last life, we feel as if it would not remain as it was during the tableau of remembrance, but as if it were going into the distance, as if it were going away, as if it were going into the future of the times and would vanish into the future of the times. So our fruit of life, after we have achieved such a one, is going into the distance, and we know in the soul: this fruit is somehow existent, but we have lagged behind it. You have the consciousness, you have remained at an earlier point in time, the fruit of life moves quickly, so that it arrives earlier at a later point in time, and we must follow it, this fruit of life. What I have now said, this inner experience, that the fruit of life is in the cosmos, is existent, we must imagine quite vividly, because that gives the foundation for our consciousness, for the beginning of our consciousness after death. Our consciousness must always be stimulated by something, so to speak.

When we wake up in the morning, our consciousness is newly kindled – whereas we are unconscious while sleeping – by immersing ourselves into the physical body and by facing the outer things, by something working from the outside. In the situation immediately after death, this consciousness is kindled by the inner feeling and experience of what is the fruit of our last life, what we have achieved, conquered for us. That exists, but it exists outside of us. Through this feeling and experiencing of our innermost earthly being we have the first enkindling of our consciousness after death, and this consciousness is invigorated by this.

... Oh, this treasure of memory during life, it is something completely different than a mere treasure of memory! When we are out of the physical body, then we see this whole treasure of memory as a living presence, then it is there. Every thought lives as an elementary being. We know now: During your physical life you thought. Your thoughts appeared to you. But, while you were in the delusion you would bring forth thoughts, you created many elementary beings. This is the new thing you have added to the entire cosmos. Now there is something that has been born by you into the Spirit. Now what your thoughts were in reality arises before you. One learns first in direct view what elementary beings are, because one learns to recognize those elementary beings first, which one has created oneself. This is the meaningful impression of the first time after death that one has the memory tableau. But it begins to live, really to live, and as it

---

[22] GA 239 "Esoterische Betrachtungen karmischer Zusammenhänge" (Esoteric reflections on karmic connections – Karmic Relationships), Volume 5, Paris, Lecture of 23 May 1924

begins to live, it transforms into many elementary beings. Now it shows its true face, so to speak, and the cause of its disappearance is that it becomes something completely different." [23]

We see how vividly the second weekly verse describes this after-death experience: "Into the outside of the sensory universe, thought power loses own existence. Thus, spirit-worlds now find the human shoot again, which has to find its germ in them, its own soul's fruit yet in itself." But that, which flees out of man's inner being is only that part of his soul's fruit which was connected with his consciousness, especially with his thought life. There is another part, which remained unconscious to him during his life on Earth and was therefore not connected to his thoughts. He now carries this part into the Moon sphere. In it he assimilates consciously in reverse course of time all those experiences which he made in an unconscious state during his sleep on Earth. Here it turns out that the Moon is the ruler of the night also in a completely different sense than we usually think:

"First of all, directly after passing through the portal of death, man experiences the going away of his imaginary world. The imaginations, the forces of thinking, become objective, become like effective forces that spread out into the world, so that man first feels going away from him all that he consciously went through in life on Earth between birth and death. But while – and this is something that happens in a few days – the mentally experienced earthly life moves away from man into the vast cosmos, now a consciousness rises up from within of all that man unconsciously went through in the sleeping states during life on earth. And this happens in such a way that man now experiences his life on Earth in reverse order in a third of the time. During this time, the human being is actually very busy with himself. One could say: During this time man is still intensively connected with his own affairs of the earthly life. He is completely interwoven with what he went through, say, during the various nights, that is, in his sleeping states. ...

By this I have hinted to you how the dead one lives in the time in which he experiences his life backwards in accordance to what he always went through in the sleeping states. In this period, man, who has now left his physical, his ether body, feels in the region of the spiritual Moon forces. We must clearly realize that everything that is a celestial body, Moon, Sun, other stars, insofar as they appear to the physical eyes, are really only the physical formation of the Spiritual. Just as the individual person who is now sitting here on the chair is not just the flesh and blood that we can regard as matter, but soul and spirit, so soul and spirit live everywhere in the whole universe, in the whole cosmos, and not merely a unified psycho-spiritual being, but many, infinitely many spiritual beings. And thus are linked to the Moon, which we see only outwardly with the physical eye as the silver disc, numerous spiritual beings. We are in their realm as long as we live our earthly life backwards in the manner described, until we have returned to its starting point. So we can say that we are in the Moon region all that time." [24]

With regard to the numerous spiritual beings mentioned here, which we encounter in the Moon sphere, the encounter of the deceased ones with their guiding Angelic beings, the Angeloi, is of particular importance:

"But the growing into the spiritual world is also such that it comes closer more and more to beings, which are beyond man. In the Moon region we are still very much among beings who have lived with humans on Earth, in the main part. [25] *But in the Moon region we already behold those beings who lead us from life on Earth to life on Earth. There are the beings I have denoted in my books according to an ancient Christian manner with the name of the Hierarchy of Angeloi."* [26]

Under the care of his respective Angelos, each person completes a whole series of significant steps of development in the course of his after-death passage through the Moon sphere, which have the goal of gradually weaning him from earthly life:

"It has already been said that the human soul, in the first time after it has passed through the portal of death, is essentially dependent, so to speak, on looking back in a certain way on what it could experience on Earth. The Kamaloka period, as it is also called, is a life that still completely deals with the earthly

---

[23] GA 153 "Inneres Wesen des Menschen und Leben zwischen Tod und neuer Geburt" (Inner nature of man and life between death and new birth), Vienna, Lecture of 13 April 1914

[24] GA 226 "Menschenwesen, Menschenschicksal und Welt-Entwicklung" (Man's being, his destiny and World-Evolution), Kristiania (Oslo), Lecture of 17 May 1923

[25] In the Moon sphere, we encounter beside the other deceased people the so-called "primordial teachers of mankind", who in the time of ancient Lemuria were still connected with the Earth and with humanity on Earth. But then they moved to the outer environment of the Earth, together with the Moon, and thus became Moon beings.

[26] GA 239 "Esoterische Betrachtungen karmischer Zusammenhänge" (Esoteric reflections on karmic connections – karmic relationships), Volume 5, Paris, Lecture of 24 May 1924

conditions. *This Kamaloka period is basically a time in which the soul must feel called to gradually get rid of everything that still lives in it of direct connection with the last embodiment on Earth. ...*

But because of the fact that man remains attached to the sensory impressions, that he still retains the desire for the sensory impressions, he first goes through the R e g i o n   o f   D e s i r o u s   A r d o u r *in life after death. He still wants to have sensory impressions for a long time. But he cannot have them since he has shed off the sensory organs. A Life that flows onward in yearning for sensory impressions and with the inability of having sensory impressions, such is life in the Region of Desirous Ardour. Indeed, this life burns within the soul. This life is a part of the actual life in Kamaloka, when the soul is longing to have sensory impressions, to which it got used here on Earth, and – since the sensory organs are shed off – cannot get such sensory impressions.*

A second region of the Kamaloka-life is that of flowing stimuli. This region is experienced by the soul in such a way that, when it lives through this special region, it has already given up its desire for sensory impressions, but still has a desire for thoughts, for such thoughts that are gained in life on Earth by the instrument of the brain. ... This earthly thinking is weaned off in the R e g i o n   o f   F l o w i n g   E x c i t a b i l i t y*. There man gradually experiences that thoughts, as they are conceived on Earth, basically matter only in life between birth and death. ...*

Then, when man has given up cherishing thoughts that depend on the physical instrument of the brain, he still experiences a certain connection with the Earth in the forms of what is contained in his wishes. Just remember that wishes are actually something that is more intimately connected to the soul than, one might say, the world of thought. Every person's wishes have a certain colour. And although one has other thoughts in the youth, others in the middle parts of one's life, others in old age, it is easy to recognize that a certain kind of wishing runs through the whole of human life on Earth. This form, this nuance of wishing is only given up later in the R e g i o n   o f   W i s h e s*.*

And then, last but not least, in the R e g i o n   o f   P l e a s u r e   a n d   D i s p l e a s u r e*, the longing is put off to live together with a physical earthly body at all, with that physical earthly body with which one was together in the last embodiment. While one is going through these regions, of the desirous ardour, of the flowing excitability, of the wishes and that of pleasure and displeasure, there is still a certain longing for the last life on Earth. First, so to speak, in the Region of Desirous Ardour. There the soul still yearns to be able to see with eyes, to hear with ears, although it can no longer have eyes and ears. When it has finally weaned off to be able to have such impressions of eyes, ears and so on, then it still longs to be able to think through a brain as it had on Earth. Once it has finally given up this habit, it still longs to be able to wish with such a heart as one had on Earth. And at last the person no longer longs for sensory impressions, no longer for the thoughts of his head and not for the wishes of his heart, but still for his last embodiment on Earth on the whole. The human being then gradually separates himself from this longing, too. All this which is to be gone through in these regions exactly corresponds to the experiences of the enlarging soul up to that region which we have called the Mercury sphere, that is, the expansion of the soul through the Moon sphere out to the Mercury sphere.*" [27]

Ascension to the Mercury Sphere – 3rd Week

The third weekly verse describes to us the entry of man, coming from the Moon sphere, into the next higher and next larger sphere, the Mercury sphere. The transition between these two takes place in the middle region of the soul world, the Region of Pleasure and Displeasure, i.e. between the actual Moon sphere and the Mercury sphere:

"Up to the Region of Pleasure and Displeasure, thus up to where the soul is, so to speak, between Moon and Mercury, it is still intimately afflicted with a longing for its last life on Earth. However, also in the regions of Mercury, of Venus, of the Sun, the soul is not yet completely free from its last incarnation on Earth, but it has to come to terms with itself regarding what exceeds merely personal experience; has to come to terms in the Mercury region with what has developed within it or has not developed as moral concepts." [28]

---

[27]   GA 141 "Das Leben zwischen Tod und neuer Geburt im Verhältnis zu den kosmischen Tatsachen" (Life between death and new birth in relation to cosmic facts), Berlin, Lecture of 1 April 1913

[28]   Ibidem.

There the person releases himself from his last penchant for corporeality. More and more he understands himself as a being completely independent of the body, which now has a much more real existence than during his life in the earthly body. The psycho-spiritual human being gradually begins to understand its "real essence":

"The Region of Pleasure and Displeasure in the soul world, which has been described above as the fourth, imposes special trials on the soul. As long as the soul lives in the body, it participates in everything that is related to this body. The weaving of pleasure and displeasure is connected to it. It gives the soul a sense of well-being and comfort, displeasure and discomfort. During the physical life, the human being feels his body as his self. What is called sense of self is based on this fact. And the more sensual people are, the more their sense of self takes on this character. – After death, the body as the object of this sense of self is missing. The soul, having maintained this feeling, feels like hollowed out. A feeling, as if it had lost itself, strikes the soul. This lasts until it understands that the physical is not the true human being. The effects of this fourth region therefore destroy the illusion of the bodily self. The soul learns to not continue in feeling this corporeality as something essential. It is healed and purified from the penchant to corporeality. By doing so it has overcome through what it had been previously strongly chained to the physical world, and it can fully unfold the forces of sympathy that go outward. It has, so to speak, departed from itself and is ready to pour out itself sympathetically into the general soul world." [29]

3rd week (21 - 27 April)	*3. Woche (21. – 27. April)*
And to the universe now speaks,	Es spricht zum Weltenall,
Forgetting gradually itself,	Sich selbst vergessend
Recalling yet its origin,	Und seines Urstands eingedenk,
The growing I of man:	Des Menschen wachsend Ich:
In you, I free myself	In dir, befreiend mich
Out of the fetters of my personal traits	Aus meiner Eigenheiten Fessel,
And fathom out my real essence.	Ergründe ich mein echtes Wesen.

More and more the human I, gradually awakening to itself and growing both in self-knowledge and in cosmic expansion, learns to comprehend itself as an immortal being born from the spirit. It gradually forgets its former earthly self and instead increasingly remembers its "origin" in the spiritual world from which it had once descended to Earth. Now it is turning its attention and aspiration more and more to the universe. For this it must free itself from "the fetters of its personal traits". What Rudolf Steiner means by the words "personal traits" becomes clear to us through one of his early lectures from 1904, where he uses the same word as a collective term for a person's mental abilities and talents, i.e. for his very specific, very personal soul being:

"What does it mean that a Psycho-Spiritual only comes from Psycho-Spiritual? Psycho-spiritual is when we encounter the fate of a person as it depends on external facts, on talents and abilities, on the whole character. Only the one who is not able to observe the fine, intimate p e r s o n a l t r a i t s of a human soul in its becoming, only the one who merely has a sense for the rough physical, can deny that we see something growing up in the child, which may just as little be explained as coming from a non-psychological, a non-spiritual as the earthworm from the mud. Schiller's nose, Schiller's red hair and many other things in his physiognomy can certainly be explained by bodily inheritance, just as the carbon parts and the oxygen parts in the earthworm come from other carbon and oxygen parts of the environment. The inanimate parts of the earthworm come from the inanimate parts of the surrounding nature and so do the physical parts of our bodies come from the physical environment. But we cannot explain Schiller's abilities and talents from the surrounding area just as little as we can explain the earthworms from the mud." [30]

Growing beyond the merely personal, man frees himself from the "fetters of his personal traits". Gradually, his super-personal, eternal, true and real essence dawns on him. Before that, the soul power of antipathy prevailed in him and segregated him from his surroundings as a separate being. In the three lower regions of the soul world, which Rudolf Steiner summarizes under the term Moon sphere, it was the predominant power. In the fourth and middle region of the soul world, the power of antipathy gets into a state of equilibrium with its counterforce: sympathy. In the course of man's transition from the Moon sphere

---

[29] GA 9 "Theosophie" (Theosophy), Chapter "Die drei Welten" (The three worlds), Section II "Die Seele in der Seelenwelt nach dem Tode" (The soul in the soul world after death)

[30] GA 54 "Die Welträtsel und die Anthroposophie" (World's mysteries and Anthroposophy), Berlin, 15 February 1906

to the Mercury sphere, taking place in this region, he, as described above, abandons his desire for an earthly sense of personality. When he then enters the Mercury sphere, the fifth region of the soul world, he begins to detach himself from any attachment to a physical-sensory environment at all. From now on he recognizes himself as belonging to the universe, into which he has expanded more and more, and increasingly turns his attention away from the Earth. He begins a psycho-spiritual communication with his new environment. Therefore, it says in the third weekly verse, "And to the universe now speaks ... the growing I of man."

"The fifth stage of the soul world is that of the soul-light. Sympathy with others has already a high validity in it. Souls are related to it, insofar as they have not been absorbed in the satisfaction of lower cravings during physical life, but rather had joy and pleasure on their environment. The rapture of nature, as far as it had a sensual character, is subject to purification here, for example. But one has to distinguish this kind of rapture of nature from that higher life in nature which is of a spiritual kind and which seeks the spirit manifesting in the things and processes of nature. This kind of sense of nature belongs to the things that develop the spirit itself and establish something lasting in this spirit. However, this sense of nature must be distinguished from such a pleasure in nature, which has its basis in the senses. The soul needs to be purified from this just as much as it needs to be purified from other tendencies that are rooted in mere physical existence. Many people see a kind of ideal in institutions that serve sensual welfare, in an educational system that primarily brings about sensual comfort. It cannot be said of them that they only serve their selfish desires. But their soul is directed towards the senses and must be healed by the power of sympathy that prevails in the fifth region of the soul world, which lacks these external means of satisfaction. The soul gradually realizes here that this sympathy must take other ways. And these ways are found in the outpouring of the soul into the soul-space[31] caused by the sympathy with the soul-environment. – Those souls also, who first expect an increase in their sensual welfare from their religious activities are purified here. Be it that their longing is focused to an earthly, be it to a heavenly paradise. They find this paradise in the «soul-land», but only for the purpose to comprehend its worthlessness. All these are, of course, just a few examples of purification taking place in this fifth region. They could be multiplied at will." [32]

As for the beings with which man comes into contact in the fifth region of the "soul land", the Region of Soul Light or Mercury sphere, beings from the Hierarchy of the Archangels or Archangeloi are now joining in to those human beings, which are close to us, and to the Angeloi: *"And these Archangeloi become important for us when we look at the Mercury existence. Within the Mercury existence, we are in the world of the Archangeloi."* [33]

If we look at the first three weekly verses in an overview, it becomes clear that they comprise a three-stage process of detachment of the psycho-spiritual human being from life on Earth. At the beginning, in the first weekly verse, the Sun as the highest phenomenon of the sensory world lures the human psycho-spiritual out of the body into the wider earthly environment through the stimuli of light and warmth at the sensory organs of the earthly human body. Thereupon the second weekly verse leads the being who has sprouted from the body, the "human shoot", completely out into the cosmic environment of the Earth. He returns his body to the Earth. His thought life, on the other hand, flees from him in the opposite direction "into the outside of the sensory universe". Man as a soul-being is thus reduced to the abilities and talents of his soul that he acquired in life on Earth, his "personal traits". The third weekly verse then describes how, on the one hand, the earthly human I gradually forgets his inner drives still adhering to his past life on Earth and the associated earthly sense of personality – "forgetting gradually itself" – but on the other hand now begins to fathom out its "real essence" as a psycho-spiritual being belonging to the universe, endowed with I-consciousness. What begins in the first weekly verse and is in full swing in the second finds its completion

---

[31] The word "soul-space" may lead to ambiguous ideas, since Rudolf Steiner uses the term "space" here only comparatively. In the soul world we are in deed no longer in the spatial, but rather in a retrograde temporal. Rudolf Steiner expressly points this out elsewhere in his book "Theosophy":

"It would exceed the bounds of what this book is intended to observe, if further characteristics of these higher worlds were to be dealt with. For what can be compared with spatial conditions and the course of time, in relation to which everything is completely different here than in the physical world, can only be spoken of in an understandable way if one wants to present it in a very detailed way" (GA 9, Section "The Soul in the Soul World after Death", last paragraph)

[32] GA 9 "Theosophie" (Theosophy), Chapter "Die drei Welten" (The three worlds), Section II "Die Seele in der Seelenwelt nach dem Tode" (The soul in the soul world after death)

[33] GA 239 "Esoterische Betrachtungen karmischer Zusammenhänge" (Esoteric Reflections on Karmic Connections – Karmic Relationships), Volume 5, Paris, Lecture of 24 May 1924

and temporary conclusion in the third weekly verse. In principle, a complete turning inside-out of the human being has taken place here. The words of Rudolf Steiner, which he once said to Johanna Mücke, confirm that *"he has always kept three stanzas of the weekly verses in the same mood".*[34] In the context of his eurythmic work in later years, Rudolf Steiner expressed himself to Marie Steiner in the same sense: *"The verses are designed internally in such a way that each three verses follow a basic mood, then again three comprise the next mood."*[35]

Step by step, the deceased person becomes more and more aware of his inner unity with the world around him. He actually learns increasingly to understand his higher self. However, all the after-death steps of development have their parallels in the successive natural moods of the course of the year. Rudolf Steiner pointed this out right at the beginning of the preface to the second edition of his Soul Calendar:

"The course of the year has its own life. The human soul can sense this life. If the soul allows itself to be effected by what speaks variously out of the life of the year from week to week, only then will it really find itself through such participation. It will feel how forces will be growing up by that, which strengthen it from within. It will notice that these forces want to be awakened in it by the share the soul can take in the meaning of the course of the world as it takes place in the sequence of times. Only by that it will become aware of the fine but meaningful threads of connection, which exist between itself and the world into which it was born."

Ascension to the Venus Sphere – 4th Week

With the fourth weekly verse, a new trinity of interrelated developmental steps begins. Let us first remember that at his death man left behind on Earth his physical body, the selfhood's earthly sheath, and that the ether body, the bearer of thought life, fled from it into the cosmos. Now the human I is still enveloped in the astral body, which derives its name from the stars according to the Latin adjective "astralis", which means belonging to the stars, concerning the stars. It is this body that carries us into the planetary spheres, the spheres of the wandering stars. There we experience ourselves as psycho-spiritual beings predominantly in feeling and will.

"When the soul no longer lives in the physical body, it must develop other abilities, which only slumber during the physical life, it must, with the echo of feeling and will still working in it for years, ripen out of this context what it can use now for the spiritual world also in this relation, forces which I have described by saying that it is something like a feeling desire or a desiring feeling. We know of our feeling and our will, they are located within our souls. But from such a feeling and desire, as they are in our souls, we basically have nothing after death. They must gradually dim and dull; and that is what they do after years. However, during this dimming and dulling, something of feeling and will must develop, which is useful for us after death. ... We must gradually develop – and we are developing – a will that pours out of us, that undulates and waves from us to where our living thoughts are. It pervades these, because on the waves of will the feeling floats, which in physical life is only within us. On the waves of will the feeling floats. Out there, the sea of our will is undulating and waving, and on this floats the feeling. Namely it floats then, when the will hits on a thought elemental being. Then, through this collision of the will with the thought elemental beings a glowing of the feeling occurs, and we perceive as a true reality of the spiritual world that our will is thrown back. Let me put it this way: Suppose there is an elemental being in the spiritual outside world. When we have worked ourselves out of the state we have to go through first, then our will, which is now going out of us, surges towards the elemental being. There, where it hits on the elemental being, it is thrown back. But it does not come back as will, now it comes back as feeling, which floods back to us in this sea of will. As a feeling, which comes back to us in the floods of will, lives our own being poured out into the cosmos."

The first two lines of the fourth weekly verse point to this type of human experience, which had its beginning in the Mercury sphere already, but is now growing to particular strength in the Venus sphere, the Region of Soul Power: "I feel now essence like my essence, so speaks sensation ..." Again we are addressed from the outside, similar to the speaking of the sun in the first weekly verse, when we still experienced ourselves inside the sheath of the body. But now our previous inner being has become our

---

[34] Letter of Johanna Mücke from 12 April 1938 to Marie Steiner. Johanna Mücke was the director of the Philosophical-Theosophical Publisher founded by Marie von Sivers (from 1914 Marie Steiner) in 1908, which was renamed Philosophical-Anthroposophical Publisher after its separation from the Theosophical Society. In this capacity Johanna Mücke was also entrusted with the printing of the Soul Calendar.

[35] Letter of Marie Steiner from 15 July 1948 to Hans Arenson.

outside world. Thus, from our own sensation, the recognition by feeling speaks: "I feel now essence like my essence."

"But yet another soul power must come out of us, which is still slumbering in much deeper layers of the soul than the feeling will or willing feeling: the creative soul power, which is like an inner soul light, which must shine out over the spiritual world, so that we not only see the living weaving objective thought beings swimming on the waves of feelings that come back in the sea of our will, but so that this spiritual world is illuminated with spiritual light. Creative spiritual luminosity must go out from our soul into the spiritual world. It awakens gradually. ...

This creative soul power, which we radiate like a soul light out into the spiritual space – if I may use the expression «space» here, for it is actually not space, but one has to bring these conditions to understanding in a certain way by expressing oneself figuratively –, this soul light slumbers deep down in us, because it is connected with something that we must not and cannot know anything about in life. At the very bottom, there is slumbering within us during our life on the physical plane, something, that is then redeemed as light and then enlightens and illuminates the spiritual world. What radiates from us must be transformed and used during our physical life so that our bodies really live and can hold consciousness. But deep below the threshold of consciousness this spiritual luminosity works in our physical bodies as the power, which organizes life and consciousness. We must not bring it into the earthly consciousness, otherwise we would rob our bodies of the power that has to organize them. Now, as we have no body to supply, it becomes spiritual luminosity and irradiates and shines and illuminates." [36]

No external sun illuminates our outside world anymore. Now that we have to prepare ourselves in the Venus sphere for the next higher Sun sphere, we must learn to become more and more similar to the Sun, to radiate ourselves, to pour out ourselves into the world. We ourselves make our environment a "sunlit world" through our own "floods of light" and, pouring ourselves out, we perceive our own being as belonging to this outside world. For what is it, this psycho-spiritual environment that we illuminate? It is our own former inner world. Its essence is our own essence. We find there our own feeling and will, as Rudolf Steiner explained in the above quotation: "On the waves of will the feeling floats. Out there, the sea of our will is undulating and waving, and on this floats the feeling." Thereby, we do not only feel ourselves one with our feeling and will, but also with the floods of light radiating from us.

4th Week (28 April - 4 May)	*4. Woche (28. April – 4. Mai)*
I feel now essence like my essence:	Ich fühle Wesen meines Wesens:
So speaks sensation,	So spricht Empfindung,
Which in the sunlit world	Die in der sonnerhellten Welt
Unites with floods of light;	Mit Lichtesfluten sich vereint;

But this sensation, which pervades us in the Venus sphere, is not a passive sensation as we know it from life on Earth. It is active, filled with willpower. In the fourth weekly verse, we therefore find the strange formulation that the sensation "wants" something. Feeling and will are one there. They are feeling will and willing feeling at the same time.

"You see, my dear friends, the feeling will and the willing feeling we have, as long as we live in the physical body, at least, I would like to say, differentiated into the sibling-pair of feeling and will in us. We have them as two, while it is a unity then, when we have passed through the portal of death."

In this sense, Rudolf Steiner describes in the fourth weekly verse not only feeling but also a sensation that is wanting:

I f e e l now essence like my essence:	Ich f ü h l e Wesen meines Wesens:
So speaks sensation,	So spricht Empfindung,
...	...
It w a n t s to give to thinking	Sie w i l l dem Denken
Warmth for the clarity	Zur Klarheit Wärme schenken
And firmly bind together	Und Mensch und Welt
Man and the world in unity.	In Einheit fest verbinden.

---

[36] GA 153 "Inneres Wesen des Menschen und Leben zwischen Tod und neuer Geburt" (Inner nature of man and life between death and new birth), Vienna, Lecture of 13 April 1914

The sensation wants two things. On the one hand, "it wants to give to thinking warmth for clarity". This refers to the warmth of the soul, the ability of man to love, which is of particular importance in the Venus sphere.

"Suppose, when we passed through the portal of death we left a person behind, whom we loved very much. Yes, now after death as we get accustomed to the situation, after we have started with our own elemental creations, we gradually become able to see the elemental beings of other humans. Now we can familiarize ourselves in seeing thoughts of other persons as elemental beings. We gradually learn based on our own elemental beings, to see as well what the other people we have left behind think, which thoughts live in their souls; we see it. For it is expressed in the elemental beings, which appear before our souls in mighty Imaginations. So in this respect we can already have much more connection with the inwardness of a person concerned than we had with him or her in the physical world. For while we ourselves were in the physical bodies, we could not look at the thoughts of the other people; now we can. But we need, as it were, the memory based on feeling – please pay attention to the words –, the memory based on feeling, the feeling connection with our own last life on Earth. We must feel, as it were, what we felt in the body, and this feeling must resonate in us. Then the relationship comes to life, which we would otherwise have only as a picture, which expresses of the thoughts of the others. So we get a living connection indirectly through our feelings. And that is basically the case with everything.

You see, it is a working out of a state that can be characterized by saying: It is a time in which we need still have to draw the forces from our last life on Earth to come into living relations with our spiritual environment. We still have to be connected with this life on Earth. We love the souls we have left behind, whose soul-contents appear to us as thoughts, as elemental beings. But we love them because we still live from the love we have developed for them during our life on earth."

Our "sensation" in the Venus sphere does not "want" only to give us clarity about what our fellow human beings think, with whom we are karmically connected, but through our emotional connection, our soul warmth, our loving feeling, which we had for them, it wants to give us access to them and thereby revive our relationship with them and reunite us with them.

As a second thing, however, our "sensation" in the Venus sphere also "wants" to give us the clarity that what appears there as the world around us is we ourselves, in the sense as has been explained above.

Undoubtedly, the fourth weekly verse also refers to the earthly sensory experience of light and warmth, which we can experience during the weeks when the strengthening physical Sun passes through the Venus sign of Taurus. However, the statement that the increasing warmth brings clarity to thinking does not make any sense in the physical world. During life on Earth you need just the opposite for the clarity of thinking: "a cool head", as a German saying quite rightly says. A warming of the head, as it can be experienced in feverish conditions, immediately dampens the clarity of thinking and makes it dreamy to fantasizing. If, on the other hand, we relate Rudolf Steiner's statement that "the sensation wants to give to thinking warmth for the clarity" to our after-death experience in the Venus sphere, as described by Rudolf Steiner in the above quotation, then only it really makes sense and reveals how carefully and wisely he chose his formulations, what delicate ties he formed between the seasonal experience of nature on Earth and the analogue psycho-spiritual experience in the spheres. In this context, a statement by him from 1912 should be recalled:

"Long occult experience and research is squeezed into these fifty-two formulas that can be the formulas of time for an inner soul experience that may thereby be connected to the processes of divine-spiritual experience. They are something timeless, which represents the relationship between the Spiritual and the sense perceptible. Everyone will gradually understand the value of this «Soul Calendar», which will retain its meaning for all years, and will gradually find its way from of the human soul into the spirit, which lives through and weaves through the whole universe. But it is not so easy to make these meditation formulas your own in their very deep meaning. That takes the human soul years and years. Thus, this calendar reveals not a mere idea that has suddenly come, but an action that is organically connected with our whole movement, and little by little it will be understood why this is done this way and that is done the another way in it." [37]

The fourth weekly verse has parallels to the first weekly verse. There, too, was talk of sunlight and of the "binding of man's essence to the existence of the spirit". However, this bond was initially only "dull" in life on Earth. In the Venus sphere, on the other hand, the psycho-spiritual of man and that of the world already interpenetrate mutually so intensively that "man and the world" can now become "firmly" bound

---

[37]   GA 133, "Der irdische und der kosmische Mensch" (Earthly and cosmic man), Berlin, Lecture of 23 April 1912

together "in unity". In this sense, the fourth weekly verse proves to be like the higher octave to the first weekly verse.

In the Moon sphere, adjacent to the Earth sphere, man has put off the egoistic parts of his in the course of his after-death development, and in the Mercury sphere he has grown beyond his desire for a natural environment based on external sensory experiences. Now he still carries impulses of will within himself, which on the one hand are already of a higher kind, such as those that aim at artistic activity or scientific knowledge, but on the other hand still seek their satisfaction in sensory experience.

"Through the sixth region [the Venus sphere], that of the active Soul Power, the purification takes place of that part of the soul, which is thirsty for activity, which does not have a selfish character, but has its motives in the sensual satisfaction which deeds bring. On the outside, natures who develop such a desire for action certainly give the impression of idealists, they appear to be self-sacrificing persons. In a deeper sense, however, it does matter to them to exalt a sensual feeling of pleasure. Many artistic natures and those who devote themselves to scientific activity because they like it so much belong here. What chains them to the physical world is the belief that art and science are there for such a pleasure." [38]

However, not only the artistic and scientific aspirations in his soul that man brings from life on Earth play a role in the Venus sphere or the "Region of active Soul Power", but especially also the religious feeling he cherished during his past life on Earth:

"Then go on and search to read in «Theosophy» what is said about the active soul power, and you will understand that through the inner experiences in the Region of the active Soul Power must occur, which was mentioned here as significant when passing through the Venus sphere. In this context has been elucidated that the soul must have developed religious impulses in a certain way in life on Earth. To be able to pass through this Venus sphere properly, so that the soul does not have to remain lonely there, but can develop a sociable life, it must have those qualities that have been described here, it must be ensouled by certain religious concepts. Compare what has been said about it with the description of the Region of active Soul Power in «Theosophy», and you will find the accordance in the fact that these conditions have been presented from the inside at one time and from the outside at another." [39]

In another lecture Rudolf Steiner also told how important it is for our after-death experiences in the Venus sphere, whether we have only developed cold thinking in our life on Earth, or whether we were also filled with "religious warmth".

"Those who were not religious, who did not assimilate the eternal, the divine, who could not have psycho-spiritual relations to other human souls in the Mercury time, will also become a hermit in the Venus time, whereas we are sociable beings also there, when we were together with like-minded beings in the Mercury time and unfolded religious warmth among ourselves. Atheists will become hermits in the Venus time. Monists[40] will have to live in the prison of their own soul, so that one cannot approach the other. To be a hermit means to have a dull consciousness that does not enclose the other, to be a sociable being, means to have a bright consciousness that finds its way into the other." [41]

In order that we can "have a bright consciousness" in the Venus sphere, our religious feeling brought from life on earth wants and is able "to give to thinking warmth for the clarity". In the Mercury Sphere the Archangeloi turn human thought into wisdom, but still within the framework of human intelligence, whereas the Archai in the Venus sphere add love, the source of all religious warmth, to this thinking.

"From the Mercury region, man then enters the region of Venus existence. That which man is able to bring from himself to the Venus region is transformed by those beings, who inhabit Venus – and who are still much further away from earthly beings than the Mercury beings –, in such a way that it can develop further at all in the spiritual region. But this is only possible because man enters a new element when he enters the Venus region. When we live here on Earth, it is important that we have ideas, have concepts, have imaginations. For what would man be on Earth if he did not have imaginations and ideas. Thoughts, they hold him, they are valuable, and we as human beings are, because we have thoughts that are good

---

[38] GA 9 "Theosophie" (Theosophy), Chapter "Die drei Welten" (The three worlds), Section II "Die Seele in der Seelenwelt nach dem Tode" (The soul in the soul-world after death)

[39] GA 141 "Das Leben zwischen dem Tode und der neuen Geburt im Verhältnis zu den kosmischen Tatsachen" (Life between death and the new birth in relation to the cosmic facts), Berlin, Lecture of 1 April 1913

[40] The German Association of Monists, an organization of the early 20th century which propagated an atheistic-scientific world view.

[41] GA 130 "Das esoterische Christentum und die geistige Führung der Menschheit" (Esoteric Christianity and the spiritual guidance of mankind), St. Gallen (Switzerland), notes from the Lecture of 19 December 1912

for something, we are therefore intelligent. Especially today, it is regarded important when people are intelligent. Today almost all people are intelligent. It wasn't always like that, today it is like that. And the whole life on Earth depends on people having thoughts. From the human thoughts the great technique has sprung up. Finally, everything comes into being with the help of thoughts, what man puts into practice in good or evil on Earth. But the thoughts still have an effect in the Moon region; because the beings in the Moon region judge according to the way in which the good and evil deeds originated from the thoughts. But the beings in the Mercury region, too, judge the diseases they have to remove from the people still according to the thoughts. In a certain sense, however, here is the border up to where thoughts – in general, that which still reminds of human intelligence – have a meaning. Because if one comes out of the Mercury region into the region of Venus, then there prevails that which we experience in life on Earth in its reflection as love. Love replaces wisdom, so to speak. We enter the region of love. Only in that way can man be carried on into the Sun existence that love leads him out of the sphere of wisdom into the Sun existence." [42]

As a part of the same lecture Rudolf Steiner later added to his description of the Archai as Venus beings:

"At the same time one learns to recognize which beings are preferably connected with the Venus existence: the beings from the Hierarchy of the Archai, the Primordial Forces. And now you get to know an important truth, again something that, when you really get to know it, astonishes you tremendously. One looks at the beings connected with the Venus existence, which shine into human life after sexual maturity. And these beings are those who are connected as Primordial Forces with the origin of the world itself. These beings, which as Primordial Forces are connected with the origin of the cosmos itself, are also active in their reflection in the genesis of physical man in the sequence of generations. The great connection between the cosmos and the human life reveals itself in this way."

Exactly in this sense ends the second part of the fourth weekly verse, which refers to the passage of man through the Venus sphere, for after the words: "It wants to give to thinking warmth for the clarity" follows the supplement: "and firmly bind together man and the world in unity".

Ascension to the Sun Sphere – 5th Week

When the physical and the ether body have been discarded, the after-death passage of the human being through the sub-solar spheres – the spheres of Moon, Mercury and Venus – is aimed to purify the astral body, which is still remaining as the last bodily sheath, from all self-centered personal traits under the direction of beings of the so-called third Hierarchy. On his further path through the higher worlds man is only allowed to take with him that part of the astral body, which has been transformed by the I, as a pure extract that remains eternally with him. But the part, which has not yet been transformed by the I, must be dropped as a kind of third corpse:

"After having passed through Kamaloka[43], a kind of third corpse is discarded. First it was the physical corpse, then the etheric one that dissolves in the general world ether, and now it is the astral corpse. It contains all of man's astral body which he has not yet purified and ordered by his I. What once was given to him as the bearer of his impulses and passions, and what he did not spiritualize through the I, shifts away after the Kamaloka state. On his further path man takes along an extract of the astral body: first, the sum of all good will impulses, and, second, everything he has transformed by the I. Everything of his drives that he has refined: the beautiful, the good, the moral, forms the extract of his astral body. Now, at the end of the Kamaloka period, the human being consists of the I, and stored around, as it were, the extract of the astral body and the ether body, the good will impulses." [44]

Only in this sublime, pure state, the psycho-spiritual human being is granted access to the region of the creative and thus divine beings in the Sun sphere:

"Angeloi, Archangeloi and Archai act on man in such a way that they do not yet use the forces of nature for their work, but they only use what affects man psycho-spiritually, i.e. language, contemporary ideas and

---

[42] GA 239 "Esoterische Betrachtungen karmischer Zusammenhänge" (Esoteric Reflections on Karmic Connections – Karmic Relationships), Volume 5, Paris, Lecture of 24 May 1924

[43] With regard to this term, see in particular the reflections on the 2nd weekly verse (Moon Sphere).

[44] GA 109 "Das Prinzip der spirituellen Ökonomie" (Principle of spiritual economy), Budapest (Hungary), Lecture of 6 June 1909

so on. Their activity does not affect the lower members of his organization, neither the ether body nor the physical body. On the other hand, from the Exusiai upwards we have those beings who act on man, but also work in the natural forces outside, who are the leaders and controllers of air and light, of the different kinds of processing of the nutrients in the kingdoms of nature. They are the ones who preside over these kingdoms of nature. What we have in thunder and lightning, in rain and sunshine, the way that in one area this or that kind of nutrients grows, in short the whole distribution and order of earthly conditions, we attribute to spiritual beings whom we seek among the beings of the higher Hierarchies. If we look up to the Exusiai, then we see their results not only in those invisible effects which are, for example, the manifestations of the Time Spirit, but we see in the Exusiai that which has an effect on us as light, and also has an effect on plants as light." [45]

The first part of the fifth weekly verse refers to these creatively working, generating beings, the Exusiai or Spirits of Form, who have their main abode in the Sun sphere. Light is the physically visible revelation of these beings as the weekly verse says. The life-giving powers of the Sun weaving therein bring about the fertility of the earthly plant world:

5th Week (5 – 11 May)	*5. Woche (5. – 11. Mai)*
Within the light that out of spirit-depths	Im Lichte, das aus Geistestiefen
Reveals the gods' creative work	Im Raume fruchtbar webend
By weaving fertilely in space: ...	Der Götter Schaffen offenbart: ...

The subsequent second part of the fifth weekly verse describes in addition the soul life of man in the Sun sphere. There he experiences himself in an almost opposite way to his existence in the Moon sphere. The polarity between the Moon as the weakly shining ruler of the night and the Sun as the ruler of the day that outshines everything with the brightest light also finds its expression in the soul experience of man as he passes through the spheres of after-death life. In the Moon sphere he is mainly occupied with himself. Everything personal and everything self-centered is experienced once more with great intensity and, insofar as it has affected other people, it is also suffered by him. There man is given the task of finding "his own soul's fruit yet in himself", as it is said in the second weekly verse. As long as the soul is bound to a personal body, ultimately to its remaining astral body, it is filled by emotions of selfishness. It makes a difference between its personal experience as an inner world and the outside world surrounding it. This separation continues until the Venus sphere or the region of the Archai. Therefore, the latter are also called Spirits of Personality. Only in the Sun sphere does the soul become free from its restrictive, personal impact. Unhindered by the astral body, it follows its own quest for pure soul-existence. Like the radiant sunlight pouring out into space, it expands to a world-existence. Like a butterfly out of the narrow pupa's shell, it emerges from its subjective existence and rises into an objective world-existence, freed of personality. In this way it gloriously accomplishes in the light its resurrection "from narrow selfhood's inner power":

In it, the essence of the soul appears	In ihm erscheint der Seele Wesen
Expanded to the world-existence	Geweitet zu dem Weltensein
And resurrected	Und auferstanden
From narrow selfhood's inner power.	Aus enger Selbstheit Innenmacht.

The Sun sphere is the seventh and highest region of the soul world. Rudolf Steiner also describes it as the "Region of actual Soul Life". Before man was allowed to enter here, he did not only cast off everything corporal, but also all wishes, emotions and goals that were directed towards a world of corporeality:

"The seventh region, that of the actual soul life, frees man from his last inclinations towards the sensorial-physical world. Each preceding region absorbs from the soul what is related to it. What now still envelopes the spirit is the opinion that its activity should be entirely directed to the sensory world. There are highly gifted personalities, who, on the other hand, do not ponder much about anything else than the processes of the physical world. One can call such a faith a materialistic one. Such faith must be destroyed, and this will happen in the seventh region. The souls see that there are no objects for materialistic conviction in true reality. This faith of the soul melts away here like ice in the sun. The soul's essence is now absorbed by its world. The spirit is rid of all fetters. It rises into the regions where it lives

---

[45] GA 124 "Exkurse in das Gebiet des Markus-Evangeliums" (Excursions into the field of the Gospel of Mark), Berlin, Lecture of 16 January 1911

only in its own environment. – The soul has fulfilled its previous earthly task, and after death, all that has remained of this task as a fetter to the spirit was dissolved. By overcoming the earthly rest, the soul itself is given back to its own element." [46]

When the human being experiences his spiritual resurrection in the Sun sphere, he has matured to enter into a closer relationship with that divine cosmic soul, who had experienced his bodily Resurrection on Earth. For further after-death experiences in the Sun sphere it is of extraordinary importance for man that he brings along from his last life on Earth an understanding for the Resurrection of the God from the earthly body, for the mystery of Golgotha.

"In the Venus sphere, people are as it were secluded in areas like those areas in which the peoples, the races, are living together on Earth. Thus, in the Venus sphere there are areas where those who are related in their religious feelings get together. But this is not sufficient for the Sun sphere. In the Sun sphere one feels lonely if one was only prepared on Earth for a certain kind of religious feeling in the soul. In the Sun sphere one is a sociable being only if one has developed an understanding, in the best sense of the word, for every religious feeling, if one has, so to speak, developed the deeper tolerance for all religious systems of the Earth. From the mystery of Golgotha until our time, the external Christian creed was in a way sufficient, for this Christian creed actually includes in a certain way an understanding that in a completely different way reaches further beyond a limited religious system than it is the case with other religious systems. You can really easily convince yourself of that. Many other religious systems are still limited to certain areas of the Earth, and one can, if one only wants to see, very easily see how the confessor of the Hindu religion, of Buddhism and so on speaks of an equality of all religions and religious wisdom in general. But if one goes deeper into what he means, one finds that he only means his own religion. He basically demands of the other people to recognize his own religion. This is what he calls equality of religions. Try to read theosophical journals that come from the area of India. There, what the Indians say is presented as the general world religion and those who do not acknowledge it are said to be not honest theosophists. Original Christianity was not attuned to this tone right from the start, especially where it has become occidental religion. If it were the same in the Occident as it is in India, we would have a Wotan religion today. That would then be what the Hindu religion is to the Orient, for example. The Occident, however, did not take the religion that had grown out of itself, but from the beginning the religion of a founder who lived outside the Occident, the Christ Jesus. Unegoistically, the Occident has absorbed a religion into its essence. That's a fundamental difference. And basically, true tolerance towards every religious system is inherent in the essence of Christianity, even though this essence has perhaps been poorly understood by occidental Christians.

Actually, for the Christian everyone is a Christian, however he may name himself otherwise. And it is only narrow-mindedness if one wants to spread Christian dogmas everywhere. Openness is something completely different. If you look at the Hindu, the Chinese, the Buddhist, if you go into the deeper elements of their beings, you will find everywhere the beginnings of Christianity, you will point out from what they themselves think, those parts which are the beginnings of Christianity, without having to mention the name of Christ. But this closer Christendom, in the way it is given to the people today between birth and death, is actually only a preparation for the Sun sphere after death. There is something else that is necessary for this Sun sphere: the thing that is necessary is what in the right and true sense we call Theosophy. It gives us that inner understanding for all religious systems of the Earth, for the essence of all religious systems of the Earth. If we acquire this understanding here on Earth, then we prepare ourselves in the right way for the Sun sphere. We must have this understanding for the different religions and for the mystery of Golgotha, for the Christ impulse, if we are not to become hermits towards other human souls and towards the spirits of the higher Hierarchies in the Sun sphere between death and new birth.

When we enter the Sun sphere between death and new birth, we find two things. The first thing we find is something we can only express figuratively: we find an empty throne, an empty world-throne. And what we can look for on this empty world-throne, we can only find in the images of the Akasha Chronicle. On this throne, which we find empty when we live through the time between death and new birth, the Christ once sat within the Sun sphere. He has expanded himself into the Earth sphere through the mystery of Golgotha, and since that time the inhabitants of the Earth must be able to acquire an understanding of the Christ impulse here on Earth and keep this impulse in memory: then they can recognize the image that appears in the Akasha Chronicle when they live into this Sun sphere. He who has not gained this understanding here on Earth does not recognize who once sat on this throne and what is now only present as a picture, and he cannot find his way in life within the Sun sphere between death and new birth. Thus we see how it is the

---

[46] GA 9 "Theosophie" (Theosophy), Chapter "Die drei Welten" (The three worlds), Section II "Die Seele in der Seelenwelt nach dem Tode" (The soul in the soul world after death)

earthly mission of the human souls to seek here the connection with the mystery of Golgotha in the way we seek it within our spiritual movement. By doing so we sustain the memory of the Christ impulse between death and new birth and do not become a hermit within the Sun sphere, but a sociable being through the forces that we have brought along; so that we then, as it were, through our own power we brought along, enliven the image – which is only an image in the Sun sphere – of the Christ. And we must bring along so much power from the time on Earth that this power remains with us also for the following time and cannot be lost.

But we find a second thing in this Sun sphere, a second throne, and this is now occupied by a real being, Lucifer. And so, between death and new birth, when we have reached the Sun sphere, we feel as has just been described, on the one hand facing the Christ, on the other facing Lucifer. If we had not assimilated the Christ impulse, Lucifer alone would have to become our leader. But when we have assimilated the Christ impulse, we are on the long journey through the universe under the guidance of the Christ impulse on one side, and on the other side of Lucifer; for we need him as well in the following times. We also need Lucifer, because he now leads us in the right way through the other world spheres, first to the Mars sphere." [47]

Ascension to the Mars Sphere – 6th Week

The fourth, fifth and sixth weekly verses describe in three big, coherent steps an exceedingly astonishing metamorphosis of the human being soon after his death on Earth. He experiences his transformation from a human soul to a cosmic soul. In the after-death ascension into the Venus sphere, this process finds its expression at first purely sensitively in a gradually increasing feeling of an inner connection of man and world. But, his sensation as a personal being of his own remains: "I feel now essence like my essence, so speaks sensation ... It wants ... firmly bind together man and the world in unity." In the course of the expansion of his consciousness, which man subsequently undergoes in the Sun sphere, his soul-essence radiates, like the light of the physical Sun in the sensory world, across the entire soul world and thus the soul perceives a new sensation. It feels as being "expanded to the world-existence and resurrected from narrow selfhood's inner power". Thereby, further remnants of personal existence are overcome. However, this process only comes to a certain conclusion in the Mars sphere. Only now everything personal, all mental and psychological personal traits, are given away. Man has matured from a soul-being to a spirit-being. His self has "arisen out of separate being". His experience is no longer subjective, but objective. A first insight into the spiritual truth underlying the Maya of the sensory world is achieved here. While in the earlier periods after death he still felt his last earthly body as an expression of himself, he now experiences, in a higher truthfulness, the entire world-body as an expression of himself. Then, however, he no longer lives in time and space, but in the midst of the forces that underlie them, in temporal and spatial forces; because everything is active force in the spiritual world, is in continuous creative activity, especially in the Mars sphere. This is the very realm of action of those high spirit-beings, which are called Dynamis by the Greek word for power.

6th Week (12 – 18 May)	*6. Woche (12. – 18. Mai)*
Arisen out of separate being	Es ist erstanden aus der Eigenheit
Is now my self and finds itself	Mein Selbst und findet sich
As revelation of the world	Als Weltenoffenbarung
In temporal and spatial forces;	In Zeit- und Raumeskräften;
The world presents to me all over,	Die Welt, sie zeigt mir überall
As divine archetype,	Als göttlich Urbild
The truth of my own likeness.	Des eignen Abbilds Wahrheit.

"When the soul has passed through the Sun region, it is finished with all that can be experienced in a certain way with regard to the «personality» of man. What is experienced outside the Sun region, outside the Region of the actual Soul Life, is then spiritual; that goes beyond everything personal. What the soul then experiences as «That are you» – and especially in our time, when it undergoes what can be

---

[47] GA 140 "Okkulte Untersuchungen über das Leben zwischen Tod und neuer Geburt" (Occult investigations on life between death and new birth), Stuttgart, 17 February 1913

experienced on Mars as the Buddha impulse, what looks so strange here on Earth but no longer looks strange on Mars – the impulse, which is denoted by the word «Nirvana», i.e. the getting away from everything that receives its significance on Earth, thus the coming closer to the great cosmic significance of the world space, all that the soul experiences in such a way that it frees itself from what is personality. In the Mars region, the lowest region of the spirit land, where the soul comes to understand the «That are you», or in our time to assimilate the Buddha impulse[48], there it frees itself from all connections with any thing of an earthly nature. After it has freed itself from this with regard to the soul – to which it must be enabled by the Christ impulse –, it then frees itself from this with regard to the spirit by understanding everything that is blood bonds, which can be bound on Earth, in its earthly definiteness, and subsequently it passes to new states."[49]

In the Mars region, the first or Continental Region of the spiritual world, the human soul, who has become a world soul, encounters a higher reality behind the physical world. It gets to know the archetypes as the higher truth underlying the physical images, i.e. the illusions of the sensory images or the Maya:

"Then it enters the cosmic-spiritual life, joins the Mars region. This Mars region now coincides with what you find in my «Theosophy» as the first part of the spirit land. In this description in «Theosophy» you will find characterized from the inside the spiritualisation of the human soul to such a degree that it now sees what is, so to speak, the archetype of physical corporeality, of the physical conditions on Earth in general, as something external. All archetypes of physical life on Earth appear as a kind of Continental region of the spirit land. Into this Continental region is drawn in what are the outer forms of the various incarnations. With this region of the spirit land is characterized from the inside the same that man has to go through when speaking cosmically, in the Mars region."[50]

As early as in the first years of his anthroposophical lecturing activity Rudolf Steiner described the experiences of the human being entering the spiritual world:

"I have explained that the lowest region is the realm of archetypes. But that is to be understood figuratively; it is a condition. Within this world we have to find the archetypes for everything that we encounter in the sensory world. I have said that in the spirit world we live within the Spiritual just as we live within the sensory world through the senses, and we sense the spiritual world as we sense the sensory world with the senses, as we hear and see this sensory world and so on. What is a thought in this earthly world is a living being in the spiritual world. What passes through our mind as a thought is only the shadow of a spiritual being. This spiritual being appears to us as a thought, because it must penetrate through the veil of physical corporeality. Man imprints his thoughts and imaginations on the world, and through them he makes the Earth more perfect. In the spiritual world these thoughts are things between which man walks. And just as we here walk between physical things, as we bump onto them and touch them, so we walk in the spirit land between thoughts. The archetypes of the sensory world can be found in the lowest region of the spirit land. Here we are in the «workshop» where the sensory objects are «produced». We see there the archetypes of the physical forms of plants, animals and humans. We must think about what we have seen. These thoughts remain in the background like a shadowy silhouette, and man does not believe in the reality of thoughts because they have such a shadowy existence. Just as a watch is created in such a way as its inventor first bore it in his head, so every single thing is created according to the thought, and the thought being appears to us in the spirit land.

Thus, in the spirit land, the whole sensory world, which we see here, appears to us in its archetypes. We see everything there, how it is produced. We see how the plant, the animal sprouts out of the animal- and plant-creating power. We learn to see that, which is here, from another side; we see, as it were, the spiritual negative in relation to the physical positive. We enter a world whose description must seem fantastic to those who have no sensation for it, but which is infinitely more real than the physical world to those whose senses are awakened for this world. It is the world of archetypes, the world of causes. There a spiritual transformation starts with us, which intensifies more and more, the more we become at home in this world.

---

[48] It would go beyond the scope of the description of the weekly verses to go into more detail on the meaning of Buddha's work in the Mars sphere. Further details can be found in GA 130 "Das esoterische Christentum und die geistige Führung der Menschheit" (Esoteric Christianity and the spiritual guidance of mankind), Neuchâtel, Lecture of 18 December 1912.

[49] GA 141 "Das Leben zwischen dem Tod und einer neuen Geburt im Verhältnis zu den kosmischen Tatsachen" (Life between death and new birth in relation to cosmic facts), Berlin, Lecture of 1 April 1913

[50] Ibidem

I would like to characterize the walk through this world for you. It is meaningful because it sheds a light into this world, a light of unspeakable significance. Our own corporeality, the body we call our own, appears to us as a thing among things. It appears to us as belonging to the outer reality. We see the way it is coming into being and we see its decay. Thus the archetype of our body appears to us as a member within the outer reality. We feel like we are facing it. We no longer say to the body «That is me», but we know that it belongs to the objective reality. And one learns a sentence of the highest Indian Vedanta wisdom, the sentence: You must realize that you yourself are a member of the whole great one – «That are you».

In this sphere, the human being in the most impressive way has that experience which Rudolf Steiner summed up in the words of the sixth verse: "The world presents to me all over, as divine archetype, the truth of my own likeness."

"What builds our body we see as if we are stepping on a rock. It's something completely foreign. From experience we learn to understand the sentence: «That are you». And when we exercise this sentence, it is nothing more than a reminder of what we experienced previous in the spirit land. We bring this memory into consciousness and experience a faint reflection of the spirit world in the body world. But that carries us away from the sensory world. That raises us to higher spheres. We feel as spiritual beings. We know that we are a member of the primordial spirit, a ray, as it were, emanating from it. We know this from knowledge at first hand.

The second principle of Vedanta wisdom is immediately fulfilled as well in the first region of Devachan: «I am Brahman». The primordial spirit is called «Brahman». When man has come to feel himself as a member of this primordial spirit, then he says: The primordial spirit lives in me. He himself is my essence. – «I am the primordial spirit» is an immediate experience which the soul already has in the lowest region of the spirit land. This is the purpose of life in the first region of Devachan." [51]

If we finally take a look at the second trinity of the weekly verses, the fourth to sixth verses, we again see a three-step development process of the psycho-spiritual man in life after death. In the fourth weekly verse, an impulse arises in the human soul, which wants to "firmly bind together man and the world in unity". Here the goal of the second trinity of the weekly verses is set. In the following fifth weekly verse "the essence of the soul appears expanded to the world-existence". In the sixth weekly verse, the unity between man and world is then accomplished through the realization: "The world presents to me all over, as divine archetype, the truth of my own likeness." Once again, we can say that what begins in the first weekly verse of this trinity and is in full swing in the second, is completed and temporarily concluded in the third weekly verse. Here, a higher truth is found, the truth of the spiritual world, whose first sphere is the Mars sphere. But at this point it is evident already that the following weekly verses will lead to an even higher truth, to the truth of the higher spiritual world or even higher worlds. Again, three consecutive weekly verses are carried out in the same basic mood.

With the entry of the soul into the spirit world, the region of the gods or in Indian the "Devachan", man enters the first of those worlds which esoteric Christianity calls the celestial world. Thus, with his entry into the Mars sphere, he begins his "Ascension" and completes the first stage of it with the conclusion of the sixth week after Easter. It is exactly at this time that we celebrate on Earth the Ascension of Christ. This feast is celebrated 39 days after Easter Sunday, i.e. on the 40th day of the series of the Easter and post-Easter feast season. Until the end of the sixth week after Easter it is 6 x 7 = 42 days. It is true, that the Mars sphere still is connected to earthly corporeality, for we find here the archetypes of all earthly corporealities. Nevertheless it is here, where the Ascension starts. It comes into full swing with the after-death ascension of the human being into the Jupiter sphere and thereby with the transition from the sixth to the seventh week after Easter.

Ascension to the Spheres of Jupiter and Saturn – 7th Week

Only a few days after man has put off his physical body at death on Earth, he realizes, combined with a certain feeling of anxiety, that his world of thoughts, his experiences, imaginations and memories accumulated in life on Earth, escape from him out into the cosmos. In the spiritual world he now has the reversed experience. It is he himself who is extending further and further into the cosmos, becoming a being that gradually expands across the entire planetary system. Here the power of Lucifer comes to his

---

[51] GA 88 "Über die astrale Welt und das Devachan" (About the astral world and the Devachan), Berlin, Lecture of 11 February 1904

help, through which the human soul is more and more turned into a cosmic world-soul and released from the forces of the Earth, which work in the direction of the centre. The same influence, which would have a harmful effect on man during his life on Earth, because it would have prematurely detached him from Earth, without having carefully collected all the experiences only possible on Earth before, this same influence has its full justification when the human spirit-soul reaches the spheres of the outer planets after a fully completed life on Earth. Nevertheless, even then man needs the protection and constant accompaniment of the Christ Being in order to be able to accomplish his ascension into the wider spiritual world in a way that is healthy for him. At this point, because of its great importance, we should recall a statement by Rudolf Steiner, which was already quoted at the end of the contemplation of the fifth weekly verse:

"But we find a second thing in this Sun sphere, a second throne, and this is now occupied by a real being, Lucifer. And so, between death and new birth, when we have reached the Sun sphere, we feel as has just been described, on the one hand facing the Christ, on the other facing Lucifer. If we had not assimilated the Christ impulse, Lucifer alone would have to become our leader. But when we have assimilated the Christ impulse, we are on the long journey through the universe under the guidance of the Christ impulse on one side, and on the other side of Lucifer; for we need him as well in the following times. We also need Lucifer, because he now leads us in the right way through the other world spheres, first to the Mars sphere." [52]

After having passed the Mars sphere, Lucifer leads us, accompanied by Christ, out into the adjoining, even wider spheres, more and more towards the starry sky, the extraplanetary cosmos. The spiritual world light of the universe exerts an increasingly stronger attraction on the human world-soul, and it undergoes this expansion, an even greater one than it was allowed to experience in the Sun sphere already, once more with a certain concern, similar as it was with the escape of the thoughts after death, but this time with the anxiety that its own self could flee away.

7th Week (19 – 25 May)	*7. Woche (19. – 25. Mai)*
My self is threatening to flee away,	Mein Selbst, es drohet zu entfliehen,
By world's light mightily attracted.	Vom Weltenlichte mächtig angezogen.

Of the planetary spheres beyond the Sun, only two, the Mars sphere and the Jupiter sphere, are facing the inner solar system, i.e. the Sun sphere and the lower planetary spheres encompassed therein. In the reflection on the previous weekly verse the effect of the Dynamis as spatial and temporal forces in the Mars sphere was already described. In the following Jupiter sphere the Kyriotetes are active in keeping the life processes within the planetary system going on through their wisdom-filled influence. For, life is only possible if the material invigorated by the Dynamis is pervaded by wisdom-filled processes. Since this wisdom flows out of the Kyriotetes, they are also called Spirits of Wisdom. From the Saturn sphere, the Thrones or Lords of the Flame are active in pervading everything that is alive with soul-warmth. All emotions within our planetary system present themselves here as a great unity. As soon as a living organism is pervaded by a soul and thus raised from the plant level to the animal level, it shows an inner, will-like drive to move. Precisely in this sense, as Spirits of Will, the Thrones have an effect from the Saturn sphere not only on the Earth, but on all planets of our solar system.

"... if we take this outermost planet of our solar system, Saturn, then we have to imagine it ... as the leader of our planetary system in space. It pulls our planetary system in the world space. It is the body for the outermost force that guides us around in the lemniscate in the world space. It drives and pulls at the same time. So it is the power of the outermost periphery. If it only worked alone, we would only move in a lemniscate." [53]

---

[52] GA 140 "Okkulte Untersuchungen über das Leben zwischen Tod und neuer Geburt" (Occult investigations on life between death and new birth), Stuttgart, 17 February 1913

[53] GA 201 "Entsprechungen zwischen Mikrokosmos und Makrokosmos. Der Mensch eine Hieroglyphe des Weltenalls" (Equivalences between Microcosm and Macrocosm. Man as a Hieroglyph of the Universe), Dornach, Lecture of 2 May 1920

Distributed over many lecture cycles, Rudolf Steiner made very diverse, often almost contradictory statements about planetary movement. That a consistent examination of these statements ultimately leads to the realization that, by the interaction of the twelve forces of the zodiac, from the planets' lemniscatory impulse of motion the physically observable spiral paths of the planets come about at the end, is elucidated by the author of this book, step by step, in his essay entitled "The Lemniscatory Path System – An evolution

The fact, that the planets ultimately do not move *"only in a lemniscates"*, but on helical paths, as observed by modern astronomy, is caused by the influence of even higher beings, the Cherubim, which act from the zodiacal sphere on the planetary system enclosed by it.

"We have further seen that if only these higher beings were effective up to the Spirits of Wisdom, the planet would stand still. That it moves outwards, that it has a movement impulse, we had to attribute to the Spirits of Will, and that this movement is regulated in the plan of the entire planetary system, we had to attribute to the Cherubim. But with this we have already assembled the planetary system, because by regulating the individual movements of the planets in such a way that they together form the system, the prerequisite is given that the whole is directed from the fixed stars. And in the Seraphim we then have that which speaks from the planetary system to the outer world space, to the neighbouring planetary systems." [54]

The Saturn sphere, in which primarily the Thrones operate, is as the outermost sphere of the traditional seven-fold series of planets the transition to the extra-planetary world. This strong devotion of the Saturn sphere towards the surrounding zodiac becomes understandable when one considers that it owes its own origin just to these extra-planetary, stellar realms. This oldest sphere of our solar system was formed directly from the cosmic surroundings:

"Thus, we see that ancient Saturn is formed by the Thrones contracting themselves from the surroundings of the universe at one point of the world space and, I would say, doing on a large scale what the silk moth does in a lower sphere when it spins out its own body as the silk thread. They, the Thrones, spin out the heat material, sacrifice it at the altar of ancient Saturn." [55]

In the Jupiter sphere on the one hand and the Saturn sphere on the other hand two forces coming from different sides meet each other. Until Jupiter, it is predominantly the forces of the planetary system that are active. From Saturn onwards, the extra-planetary, stellar, cosmic forces of the first Hierarchy, the Thrones, Cherubim and Seraphim, are at work. The overlap of these two types of force is expressed in the seventh and therefore middle of the thirteen weekly verses of spring. This may be the reason – perhaps only one of several – why Rudolf Steiner summarized the after-death passage of the human soul through the spheres of Jupiter and Saturn in a single weekly verse. Seven lower stages of development meet, so to speak, seven higher ones and overlap in the middle, so that not fourteen but thirteen weekly verses result, which are completely in accordance with the thirteen weeks that all together form a quarter of a year, one of the four seasons.

During its stay in the Mars sphere at the beginning of its Ascension, the human soul still found a certain hold on the spiritual archetypes or thought-beings, which underlie all physical objects. This is no longer the case for the after-death experiences in the spheres of Jupiter and Saturn. There we encounter the spiritual archetypes of life and soul. Our thinking that we develop on earth, however, is primarily based on terms and ideas of things that can be experienced through our physical sense organs and stimulate us to waking consciousness and I-consciousness. Our conceptual world is therefore primarily based on "the sense-appearance", on the world of Maya. Even anthroposophy must use terms from the sensory world in order to make extrasensory experiences understandable to earthly thinking, at least in analogies. In our modern times of materialism, however, these terms essentially refer to the lifeless. The etheric world, the actual sphere of life, remains still closed to most people as an immediate experience at the present stage of development in life on Earth. Consequently, for the vast majority of people today there is no possibility of being able to develop based on the world of the Living their own, more far-reaching world of concepts and a thinking of the Living or a living thinking. Even more closed than the etheric world are the soul-world and the spiritual world to today's earthly humanity. Therefore, as soon as we go beyond the realm of the physical and beyond that part of the spiritual world still facing this physical, we are confronted with the inadequacy of human thinking. "The might of thinking is about to lose itself in the sense-appearance", to say it in the words of the seventh weekly verse. It is the basis of the sensory world, and for this very reason it is also turned downwards, towards the sensory world. Everything that surrounds the coarse sensory

---

of the Copernican worldview based on statements and sketches by Rudolf Steiner on planetary movement". (http://www.rolandschrapp.de/lemniskaten.html). Parts 1 and 2 of the treatise were published in the German edtion of the journal JUPITER by the Mathematical-Astronomical Section of the Goetheanum (JUPITER Sept. 2010, Vol. 5 No. 1, and Sept. 2011, Vol. 6 No. 1).

[54] GA 136 "Die geistigen Wesenheiten in den Himmelskörpern und Naturreichen" (Spiritual beings in the celestial bodies and in the kingdoms of nature), Helsingfors (Helsinki), Lecture of 10 April 1912

[55] GA 110 "Geistige Hierarchien und ihre Widerspiegelung in der Physischen Welt" (Spiritual Hierarchies and their reflection in the physical world), Düsseldorf, 13 April 1909

objects as a fine, supernatural, auric appearance can only be surmised or intuitively assumed by man at first.

Now exercise, intuitive assumption,	Nun trete du mein Ahnen
Your rights with strength,	In deine Rechte kräftig ein,
Replace the might of thinking,	Ersetze mir des Denkens Macht,
Which in the sense-appearance	Das in der Sinne Schein
Is just about to lose itself.	Sich selbst verlieren will.

However, this limit for the might of thinking only arises for humans who have completely devoted themselves to a materialistic way of thinking in life on Earth. Thinking itself is able to extend to the extrasensory worlds, provided it has been trained to do so, because, like feeling and will, it has its origin in one of the three highest worlds of human evolution. Thinking is rooted in Devachan or the spiritual world, which is therefore also called world of thoughts or mental plane. Feeling is a reflection of the Budhi plane in the human soul and will is a reflection of the Atma plane. In this way the three human soul powers are an expression of the divine Trinity of Father, Son and Holy Spirit. In principle, therefore, thinking is suitable as a cognitive power throughout Devachan or the mental plane. Only the transition to the Budhi plane marks an absolute limit. Therefore we find the following statement in a lecture by Rudolf Steiner:

"But there is one thing that remains the same throughout all worlds until Devachan, which does not change: That is the logically trained thinking. Only on the Budhi plane thinking does no longer have the same validity as on the physical plane. There has to be another way of thinking. But for the three worlds below the Budhi plane, for the physical, astral and devachanic plane, the same thinking applies everywhere. So whoever trains himself properly in thinking through study in the physical world will have a good leader in this thinking in the higher worlds and will not stumble as easily as the one who wants to ascend into the spiritual realms with confused thinking. Therefore, Rosicrucian training teaches people to move freely in the higher worlds by encouraging them to discipline their thinking. Whoever reaches up into these worlds in fact gets to know ways of perceptions that do not exist on the physical plane, but he will be able to master them with his thinking." [56]

However, special conditions are predominant in the higher spiritual world, because it is pervaded by the Budhi plane. For into the upper half of each world, the next higher one protrudes and thereby influences the states of existence prevailing there. Rudolf Steiner once explained this using the example of the physical world and the soul world or astral world with the help of his drawing shown in Figure 1.

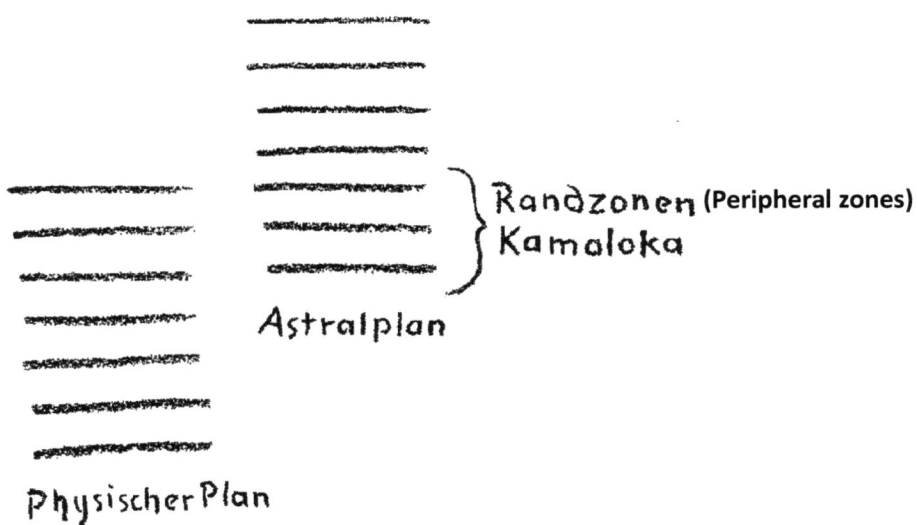

Figure 1: Interpenetration of the Physical Plane and the Astral Plane

---

[56] GA 96 "Ursprungsimpulse der Geisteswissenschaft" (Original impulses of the science of the spirit), Berlin, Lecture of 20 October 1906 with the title "Der rosenkreuzerische Schulungsweg" (The Rosicrucian training path)

"If we start from the physical plane, we have here (it is drawn) seven subdivisions of the physical plane; then seven subdivisions of the astral plane would follow. Of these, the three lowest coincide with the three highest of the physical plane. We must consider the astral plane pushed together with the physical plane so that the three uppermost parts of the physical plane are also the three lowest parts of the astral plane. We can speak of a peripheral zone, which is the one that our souls cannot leave after death when they are still bound to Earth by desires. It is called Kamaloka." [57]

Mostly, Rudolf Steiner uses the Indian term Kamaloka for the lower astral plane – sometimes in the broader sense also for the entire astral plane – only when he describes the human path of development after death. In other lectures he uses a European expression and speaks of the elementary world instead. Above it is the lower spiritual world, pervaded by the upper parts of the astral plane. Above them is the higher spiritual world, pervaded by the lower parts of the Budhi plane, which reaches with its higher parts up to the Atma or Nirvana Plane.

"When we use European expressions, we call the physical plane the small world or the world of mind, the astral plane the world of the Elementary, the lower Devachan the celestial world and the upper Devachan the rational world. And because the European spirit is only gradually working its way up to have the corresponding real expressions in its language, that which is above the devachanic world has received a religiously coloured expression and is thus called the «world of providence», that is the same as the Budhi plane. What is above that, in fact could be seen through the ancient clairvoyance and old traditions could give it to mankind, but no name could be given to it in the European languages, because today only the clairvoyant works up to it again. So that above the world of providence is a world for which the name in European languages must not yet exist in a completely honest and correct manner. It is really there, only thinking is not yet so far as to be able to characterize it; for it cannot be used any name for what is otherwise called in Oriental «Nirvana» and what exists above the «world of Providence»." [58]

Rudolf Steiner's drawing shown as Figure 1 can consequently be extended to Figure 2 by adding the Mental or Devachan Plane, i.e. the spiritual world, upwards according to the given law and the three lowest regions of the Budhi plane pervading its top three regions.

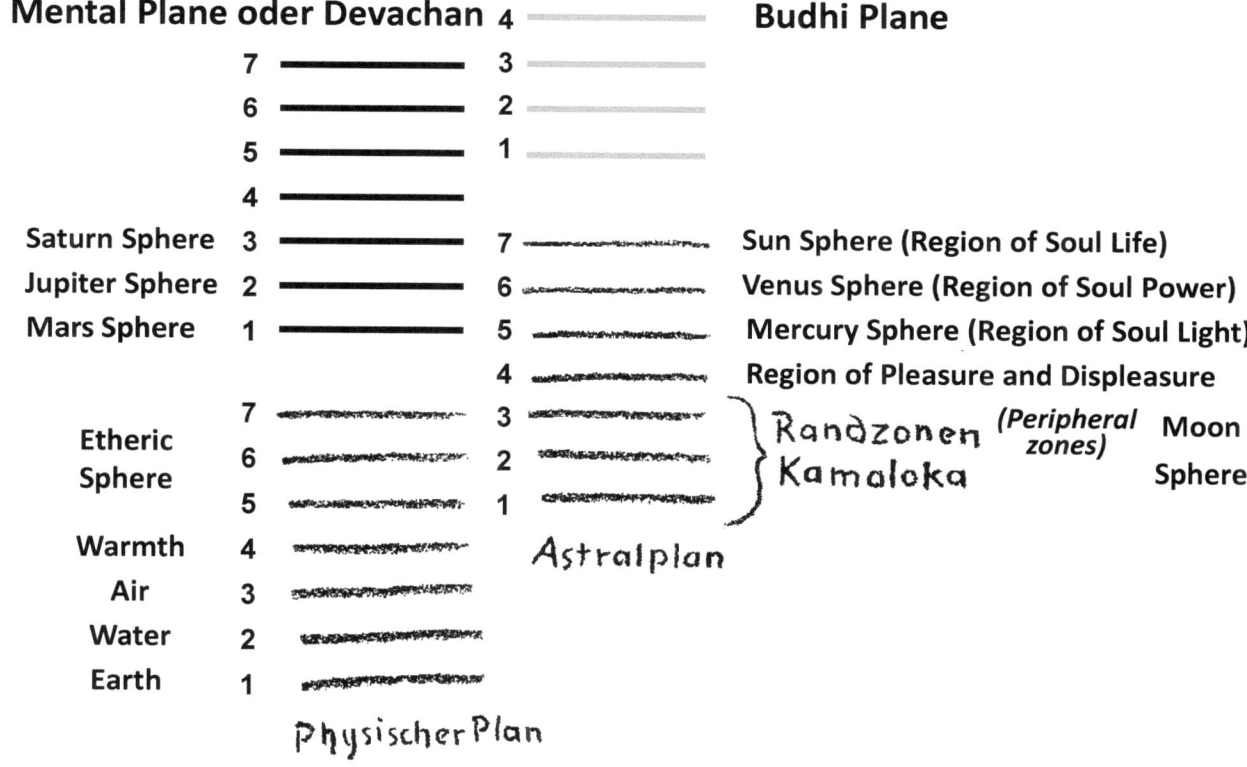

Figure 2: Interpenetration of the worlds

[57] GA 101 "Mythen und Sagen – Okkulte Zeichen und Symbole" (Myths and legends – Occult signs and symbols), Cologne, 27 December 1907

[58] GA 116 "Der Christus-Impuls und die Entwicklung des Ich-Bewusstseins" (The Christ impulse and the development of the I-consciousness), Berlin, Lecture of 25 October 1909

Within the physical world the different regions of the higher worlds are reflected until the Saturn sphere or the third region of the spiritual world. The fourth region already corresponds to the zodiac or the visible starry sky. In the light of the stars, something from even higher regions just shines into the sensory world. The higher regions themselves, on the other hand, correspond to the dark background of the universe, which no longer gives us a concrete sensorial perception that we could grasp conceptually. There thinking loses itself in the sense-appearance, speaking with the words of the seventh weekly verse. But since the nature of the Budhi plane, which is related to human feeling, is already taking effect there, an emotionally pervaded thinking proves to be suitable as a cognitive force for the higher spiritual world, something that we know in earth life as intuitive assumption or the related supposition. Therefore, the seventh weekly verse, with its description of the transition from planetary to stellar existence, states:

Now exercise, intuitive assumption,	Nun trete du mein Ahnen
Your rights with strength.	In deine Rechte kräftig ein,
Replace the might of thinking,	Ersetze mir des Denkens Macht,
Which in the sense-appearance	Das in der Sinne Schein
Is just about to lose itself.	Sich selbst verlieren will.

This intuitive assumption, this sensing, can even be an incentive for us to follow the path of spiritual training and to work towards the development of higher organs of perception in order to reach true perceptions and insights of the higher worlds, too. As long as such organs of perception have not yet been developed, we are just helped by intuitive assumption or assuming that everything anthroposophy teaches us about the after-death life of man in the higher worlds – especially in the spiritual world, which is so completely different, in comparison with the physical world, even almost contrary in part – is based on reality indeed.

"He who thinks trivially – and today's world is all too inclined to think trivially – will easily accuse us of rapture and obscurity. But we theosophists know what the three words mean, which were often mentioned in the first centuries of Christianity, when Christianity was still one of the most profound religions in the world: Perceive, think, assume. – These three words were mentioned side by side. The fact that assumption was mentioned alongside perception and thinking proves that people were not as immodest in terms of knowledge as they are today. Yes, people today are immodest in terms of knowledge, immodest because they are hostile to everything that their senses and minds do not understand. Imagine, if the snail took the liberty of saying that there is nothing else here in the hall but what it perceives. Shouldn't we say of this snail that it has a great immodesty with regard to knowledge? Don't be mistaken. In the worst sense of the word it is the same with man when he says: What my mind cannot perceive and cannot comprehend does not exist in this world. – Two things, perception and thinking, are what give us beauty, size and number in the world. But there is a third that makes us always modest, that makes us aspire, that leads us deeper and deeper into the world: that is the assumption, the assumption that there could be something else than what we know.

The theosophical movement differs in that from all other cognitive movements. What does the ordinary scientist who is proud of his culture and immodest in his ordinary recognition want? He wants to pursue everything he can perceive and recognize, and he wants to apply his findings to countless things. It is as if the snail crawls around in all directions and perceives what it can perceive. It would perceive nothing but what its snail organs can perceive. It's the same with humans. Therefore, the assumption has been added to perception and thinking, the assumption that as we evolve, higher sensory organs will open up to us, unlocking what is usually closed to us in the world. The theosophist's attitude differs from that of the ordinary scientist in the fact that he wants to develop himself, he believes honestly and righteously in the development of his abilities and strives to work on himself. This, ladies and gentlemen, is the theosophical attitude: to work on ourselves so that higher organs will open up for us, so that we will be able to perceive something meaningful, significant in what is around us. This must become more and more western attitude if western mankind does is not to merge completely into the materialistic current. When this theosophical attitude spreads more and more, one will realize that all external physical facts and phenomena are the results, the effects of deeper causes that exist in the astral world or in even higher worlds. Usually western science is satisfied with exploring the body in all its components. But the theosophical attitude asks the question: Is this body put together by itself? Where could be the cause? Can we believe that the forces outside in nature feel the need to put together a human being? No. He who is able to see in the higher world knows that the human beings, before living in the physical organism, before their birth, lived in an astral existence. Just as true as the fact that we had an astral existence before our physical existence, before birth, is it true that we also have an astral existence after our birth, and this reaches further than our physical body. All this is included in what we call the mystery of birth and death." [59]

The human being develops new senses, spiritual senses, under the guidance of divine entities, not only in the astral world, but also in the spiritual world, in order to be able to comprehend this as an even much higher reality. What begins in life on Earth as the intuitive assumption or presumption of an existence of higher worlds, finds its completion with the higher senses in the spiritual world. So there as well the intuitive assumption is obviously the driving force for the development of higher spiritual senses. Materialistically minded people, who in their thinking are completely fixed on the sensory world, who reject the existence of higher worlds and do not allow themselves to at least surmise or sense them, will indeed have little affinity with the regions beyond the planetary spheres. Even the Mars sphere, the so-called Continental Region of the lower spiritual world, still has an affinity to the physical world, because the spiritual archetypes living there produce all physical things. The consciousness in the next higher sphere, the Jupiter sphere or Oceanic Region, however, already requires religious feeling and admiration for the unity of all life, in the Saturn sphere even for the unity of all soul life. Here, too, the element of feeling comes into play. Religious feeling is always developed on the basis of intuitive assumption, since it refers to extrasensory realms. Who has shown little interest in this regard during his life on Earth, will at best bring a powerless intuitive assumption into the spiritual world, which cannot "enforce its rights with strength" to bring the necessary spiritual senses to full formation in the outer planetary spheres and even more so in the transition from the planetary to the stellar regions. Instead of clear knowledge, only a dull intuitive assumption will be able to take its place, which has little potential for development.

"The next region [Jupiter sphere] is the region in which the common life of the earthly world flows as a thought entity, as it were, as the fluid element of the «spirit land». As long as one looks at the world in physical embodiment, life appears bound to individual living creatures. In the «spirit land» it is detached from these and flows through the whole country, as it were, as the life blood. There it is the living unity that is present in everything. During life on Earth only a reflection of this appears to the people. And this is expressed in every form of worship that man shows towards the whole, the unity and harmony of the world. People's religious life is caused by this reflection. Man becomes aware that the comprehensive meaning of existence is not based on the transient, the separated. He regards this transient as a «likeness» and image of an eternal, of a harmonious unity. He looks up to this unity in adoration and worship. He offers to it religious acts of worship. – In the «spirit land», it is not the reflection that appears, but the real shape as a living thought being. Here man can truly unite with the unity he has worshipped on Earth. The fruits of religious life and everything related to it become evident in this region. Man now learns from spiritual experience that his individual destiny should not be separated from the community to which he belongs. The ability to recognize oneself as a member of a whole is developed here. The religious sensations, everything that has already aspired in life to a pure, noble morality, will draw strength from this region during a large part of the spiritual intermediate state. And man will be re-embodied in this regard with an increase in his abilities.

While in the first region one is together with souls to whom one was connected in the previous physical life by the close bonds of the physical world, in the second region one enters into the realm of all those with whom one felt one in a broader sense: through a common worship, a common denomination and so on. It must be emphasized that the spiritual experiences of the previous regions remain during the following ones. Thus a person is not torn from the family ties, friendship and so on when he enters the life of the second and subsequent regions. – Also, the regions of the «spirit land» do not lie apart like «divisions»; they interpenetrate mutually, and man experiences himself in a new region not because he has «entered» it in some form externally, but because he has attained the inner abilities in himself to perceive that within which he was previously unperceptive.

The third region of the «spirit land» [Saturn sphere] contains the archetypes of the soul world. Everything that lives in this world exists here as a living thought being. One finds there the archetypes of desires, wishes, feelings and so on. But here in the spirit world there is nothing of selfishness attached to the soul. Just like all life in the second region, in this third all desire, wishes, all pleasure and displeasure form a unity. The desire and the wish of the other do not differ from my desire and wish. The sensations and feelings of all beings are a common world that includes and surrounds everything else like the physical circle of air surrounding the Earth. This region is, so to speak, the atmosphere of the «spirit land». Everything that man has done in earthly life in the service of commonality, in selfless devotion to his fellow human beings, will bear fruit here. For through this service, through this devotion, he lived in a reflection of

---

[59] GA 88 "Über die astrale Welt und das Devachan" (About the astral world and the Devachan), Berlin, Lecture of 28 October 1903

the third region of the «spirit land». The great benefactors of humankind, the dedicative natures, those who do the great services in the communities, have acquired their ability to do so in this region, after having acquired the prospect to a special relationship with it in previous lives". [60]

The interpenetration of the spheres results in that the Mercury sphere forms a kind of unity with the Mars sphere. Both are facing the physical world. In the course of the after-death passage through the Mercury sphere, man gradually frees himself from his basic need to be surrounded by a sensory outside world, a need that was created by habit during his life on Earth. All kinds of pleasure and lust on the environment as well as rapture of nature are put off there, as explained above. The Mars sphere, on the other hand, contains the spiritual formative forces of all physical corporeality and hence also of the entire physical nature. Both spheres are therefore "thematically" related to each other.

In the Jupiter sphere, the human being processes, as already described, *"the fruits of the religious life"* that he lived on Earth. This task already occupied him during his passage through the Venus sphere, as it was described in the reflection on the fourth weekly verse. The spheres of Venus and Jupiter interpenetrate each other and form a kind of unity also, whereby during the passage through the Venus sphere after death the focus is on subjective soul-experience, but during the later passage through the Jupiter sphere on objective spirit-experience.

Similarly, our after-death experiences in the Sun sphere are intimately linked with those of the Saturn sphere. In the Sun sphere, we undergo a metamorphosis to a world-soul (see 5th weekly verse), whereas in the Saturn sphere we experience the spiritual archetypes underlying all soul life, which appears there as a great unity. Especially the ability for selfless dedication and fellowship finds its further development here, because we no longer distinguish between our own soul experiences and those of other people. A consequence of this interpenetration of the Sun sphere and the Saturn sphere is that today we live with the theory that the Sun would pull the planets through space. It appears to us as the main carrier of the principle of heat, fire or will in our solar system. Only the higher spiritual view reveals that the planet-moving power comes from Saturn as the driving force of the whole system. Rudolf Steiner therefore emphasized with regard to the physically observable helical movement of the planets in space:

"The helical line continues in space. Not that the planets are moving around the sun, but these three: Mercury, Venus, Earth, follow the sun, and these three: Mars, Jupiter, Saturn go ahead." [61]

Ascension to the Sphere of the Zodiac – 8th Week

Beyond those extra-sensory regions, which find their physical image in the seven traditional planets observable with the naked eye, exists the sphere of the fixed stars or the Zodiac as an eighth sphere according to the statements of the ancient astronomers. Outside this sphere, they imagined a ninth, tenth or even eleventh sphere at that time. As a result of the increasing materialization of the entire world view, the planetary system together with the surrounding fixed stars was more and more reduced to a "machina mundi", a world machine and everything was to be explained only according to the laws of mechanics. The spheres were thought of as rotating, crystalline hollow spheres to which the planets and fixed stars were attached. Up to the 16th century, astronomers were convinced of an assumed rotation of the sphere of the fixed stars as the cause for the observed shifts of the vernal equinox in the zodiac. Copernicus first brought the starry sky to a standstill by proving that the retrograde movement of the vernal equinox's position in the zodiac, the so-called precession movement, by no means originated in the starry sky, which he still regarded as a sphere, but in a slow, retrograde rotation of the oblique axis of the Earth. [62]

---

[60] GA 9, "Theosophie" (Theosophy), Section IV "Der Geist im Geisterland nach dem Tode" (The spirit in the spirit land after death)

[61] GA 300a "Konferenzen mit den Lehrern der Waldorfschule" (Conferences with the teachers of the Waldorf School), Vol. 1, Conference of 25 September 1919

[62] As late as 1522, the Nuremberg clergyman and mathematician Johann Werner in his treatise "De motu octavae sphaerae" (About the movement of the eighth sphere) tried to prove the starry sky's rotational movement as generated by a ninth and tenth sphere. Copernicus opposed this opinion in a public report that caused a sensation at the time and pointed out the errors in Werner's calculations (Leopold Prowe, "Nicolaus Coppernicus", Volume II, 10th book, 5th section). More than a decade earlier Copernicus had already announced in his "Commentariolus" his research result that the starry sky was immovable and that both its

As already shown in the reflections on the first weekly verses, all materialistic ideas about the world vanish into thin air in the Mercury sphere at the latest. The spheres themselves do not even prove to be places of residence, but should better regarded as successive states of consciousness, which man experiences sequentially after his death. We have already followed the ascension of the human spirit-soul, which has become a world-soul in its after-death development through the three lower regions of the spiritual world. In its lowest region, the Mars sphere, man looks at the archetypes of all physical forms that make up our environment in the sensory world, including the archetype of his own physical form. In the two next-higher regions he experiences life from a spiritual point of view as something uniformly effective, first in the Jupiter sphere as the bodily life flowing through all forms of plants, animals and humans, which manifests outwardly in the processes of nutrition, growth and reproduction, and subsequently in the Saturn sphere as the soul life which is internally effective in all animals and humans. Thus man has advanced to the limit of the planetary spheres when we take the Earth as the centre from where he started his ascension. He himself has now become a cosmic being and as such has matured to encounter the sublime entities of the Zodiac sphere. Since the earliest primeval times of world creation, since ancient Saturn, he has been connected with them:

"You remember as well that we said: As soon as this Saturn globe has progressed to the Sun globe, in the surrounding of the Sun globe appear clearly those beings which constitute the zodiac. – But I already hinted at that time that this zodiac was already around ancient Saturn, even if it not yet, I would like to say, was so dense, so compact as during the Sun existence. So in the circumference of ancient Saturn we think of Thrones, Cherubim, Seraphim at work, and these actually are to us first in the spiritual sense the zodiac. This line is for the time being the zodiac, in the spiritual sense. You will reply: Is that consistent with the current name of the zodiac? – Oh, it's perfectly consistent as we will be completely convinced in the course of the last lectures. But first you have to imagine it this way: Think you could stand somewhere on this ancient Saturn globe in a certain place. If you now lift up your hand and point out with your finger, then above this place is the region of certain Thrones, Cherubim and Seraphim. If you move a bit further and point out, another of the Thrones, Cherubim and Seraphim is where you point, for these three groups of beings form a circle around ancient Saturn. And now imagine, you wanted to indicate the direction in which certain Thrones, Cherubim, Seraphim are located, so to speak. There is not one like the other. They are not like twelve completely identical soldiers, but each one of them is very different from the other. They are all individualized, so that one points to different beings when one points out from different places. And so that one can point to the right one of the Thrones, Cherubim, Seraphim, so to speak, one marks that for oneself by a certain star constellation. So that's a mark. And thus it is said: In this direction here are the Thrones, Cherubim, Seraphim, which are called Gemini, in another direction those, who are called Leo and so on. So these are like marks to indicate the direction where the beings concerned are. We first interpret the peculiar star constellations as such marks. They are something else as well, but first we have to realize that we are dealing with spiritual beings when we speak of the zodiac." [63]

Just as the Sun sphere is the gateway to the outer planetary spheres or regions of the lower spiritual world, so the Zodiac sphere, as the fourth region of the spiritual world, is the gateway to the starry sky, which amazes us in cloudless nights with its breathtaking splendour.

"And what is described as the fourth region of spirit land already goes beyond our planetary system. There the soul expands, so to speak, into other spaces, into the wider starry sky. And you will find in the description, which was given at another time[64] *from the viewpoints of the inner soul, that the characteristics of the soul experiences regarding the fourth region of the spirit land are given in such a way that you notice about them: they cannot be experienced where we are still in such a spatial cosmic relation to the Earth as the entire planetary system. Something is brought in from the fourth region of the spirit land which is so foreign that it cannot be thought together with all that can be experienced within the last planetary sphere, the Saturn sphere."* [65]

On his path of development after death through the planetary spheres to the Saturn sphere and finally to the Zodiac sphere with the visible part of the starry sky, man undergoes a whole series of metamorphoses of form and consciousness:

---

apparent movement and the progression and regression of the planets were only the result of a movement of the Earth's axis or, respectively, of the Earth itself.

[63] GA 110 "Geistige Hierarchien und ihre Widerspiegelung in der Physischen Welt" (Spiritual Hierarchies and their reflection in the physical world), Düsseldorf, 17 April 1909

[64] In Steiner's book "Theosophie" (Theosophy, GA 9)

[65] GA 141 "Das Leben zwischen dem Tod und einer neuen Geburt im Verhältnis zu den kosmischen Tatsachen" (Life between death and new birth in relation to cosmic facts), Berlin, Lecture of 1 April 1913

"When man has stepped through the portal of death, to the spiritual gaze of the Imagination he actually still looks similar to what he was here on Earth. Because what man bears within himself here on Earth, are the substances which are more or less in granular form, say, in atomistic form; but the figure of man, that is spiritual. ... This figure, however, man still retains, when he has passed through the portal of death. You see it shimmering, iridescent, shining in colours. But the first thing that man loses, is the shape of his head; then the other part gradually melts away. And at the time between death and a new birth when he has entered the region of Seraphim, Cherubim and Thrones, man has been completely metamorphosed, has become a kind of likeness of the cosmos.

So when one follows man between death and a new birth, one sees him first, I would say, continue to weave and gradually lose his figure from top to bottom. But by losing the last of the bottom, so to speak, something has already formed which is a wonderful spirit-figure, which is in itself a kind of likeness of the whole world sphere and which at the same time is the model of the future head which man will bear. Man is involved in an activity in which not only the beings of the lower Hierarchies, but the beings of the highest Hierarchies, the Seraphim, Cherubim and Thrones, participate." [66]

But the head is precisely that part of the human body which bears the main sensory organs through which man gains his I-consciousness, which makes him so unique within the earthly world and distinguishes him quite substantially from the surrounding mineral, plant and animal kingdoms.

"We already face something complicated when we look at the relationship between the planetary sphere and the life process, between the Zodiac sphere and the areas of the senses. But the matter becomes even more complicated when we ascend to the processes of consciousness, when we enter those areas that have a certain connection only with these spheres: the I with the zodiac, the astral body with the planetary sphere of man, the human being's movable sphere of life." [67]

That fact that man can find his way to an I-consciousness is due to the special configuration of his head with the sensory organs, of which according to Rudolf Steiner there are altogether twelve, which are connected to the individual signs of the zodiac, external senses as well as internal, which have their common centre in the main organ of the head, the brain. In addition to the generally known five senses of seeing, hearing, smelling, tasting and touching, we also have a sense of balance and a sense of warmth. But, there are also inner senses in our organs and muscles such as the sense of life and the sense of movement. Furthermore, according to Rudolf Steiner, there are spiritual senses such as the sense of speech, the sense of thinking and the sense of the I. To take a more detailed look on this subject would go beyond the scope of the present considerations. Readers with a deeper interest will find more detailed information in Rudolf Steiner's corresponding lecture cycles.[68] Here, above all, the connection of the I with the zodiac is the subject. In this regard, therefore, in addition to the above quotation, a further statement by Rudolf Steiner is given:

"It is quite true: the more the I aspires the highest point of its development, the more it works into the zodiac. Nothing happens in the innermost of the I, which does not draw its consequences up into the zodiac. That is quite true." [69]

The fourth mystery play "The Soul's Awakening" [70] leads the reader as far as to the after-death experiences of the people in the Saturn region and thus to the border of the planetary spheres. Rudolf Steiner prepended to his drama a seal, which likewise points to the connection of the I with the zodiac. It includes twelve letters, encircled by a snake that bites its tail. Reading clockwise, starting at the eye of the snake, one gets the German words "Ich erkennet sich", in English "I recognizes itself", if one continues to read after the twelfth letter including the first three letters once more, according to the Principle of a snake biting its tail. As the German word "Ich" begins with a "J", it turns into the initials of the name "Jesus Christ" and refers to the work of the Christ in the I or with the words of the Apostle Paul the "Christ in me". Three of

---

[66] GA 230 "Der Mensch als Zusammenklang des schaffenden, bildenden und gestaltenden Weltenwortes" (Man as symphony of the creative, building and shaping Cosmic Word), Dornach, Lecture of 11 November 1923

[67] GA 170 "Das Rätsel des Menschen – die geistigen Hintergründe der menschlichen Geschichte" (The riddle of the human being – the spiritual background of human history), Dornach, Lecture of 13 August 1916

[68] For example GA 169 "Weltwesen und Ichheit" (Cosmic being and I-ness), Berlin, Lecture of 13 June 1916, or GA 208 "Anthroposophie als Kosmosophie – 2. Teil" (Anthroposophy and Cosmosophy – Part 2), Dornach, Lecture of 30 October 1921

[69] GA 102 "Das Hereinwirken geistiger Wesenheiten in den Menschen" (Influence of spiritual beings upon man), Berlin, Lecture of 27 January 1908

[70] GA 14 "Vier Mysteriendramen" (Four Mystery Plays), 4th Drama "The Souls' Awakening"

the twelve letters are highlighted by lightning-like jagged lines. Read backwards, they give the German word "ist", in English "is", which may be taken as an indication that beyond the nine human members of being, most of whom belong to the Creation as a region of appearance, there are three worlds of higher, true being, the "IST" ("IS"), three divine regions that also have their representatives within the twelve zodiacal forces.

Figure 3:
Seal of the 4th Mystery Play

As the basis of the I-consciousness, the twelve senses of man and the combined part of the head's configuration, especially the brain, are creatively produced in the zodiacal sphere by the beings of the first Hierarchy. When we passed through the Sun sphere, we were already allowed to experience the work of the gods, but at first only indirectly, that is, in the manner it revealed itself there: "Within the light that out of spirit-depths *reveals* the gods' creative work by weaving fertilely in space." But now, in the Zodiac sphere, we are allowed to participate directly in the creative might of the gods that brings forth the human senses. The closer we come to this sphere, the more the creatively effective might in the human senses grows, as the 8th weekly verse says:

The senses' might is growing
In league with the creative work of gods.

Es wächst der Sinne Macht
Im Bunde mit der Götter Schaffen,

"One can already notice that the I-consciousness, as it prevails in daytime-waking, is essentially linked to the presence of sensory content. So that we can say: We experience our I together with the sensory content at the same time. With regard to our everyday consciousness we do not experience our «I»s any differently than with the sensory content. As far as the sensory content goes, I-consciousness is present, and as far as I-consciousness is present – at least for ordinary life – so far does the sensory content go. Indeed, it is justified at first, to start from the standpoint of this everyday consciousness, not to separate the I from the sensory content, but to say: While red, while this or that sound, while this or that sensation of warmth, touch, taste or smell is there, the I is also there, and insofar as these sensations are not there, the I, as it is experienced in the ordinary state of wakefulness, is also not there." [71]

In the sphere of the zodiac, the place of creation of the human senses and the human head as a basis for human I-consciousness, all human thinking must be silent. Here we would only disturb the creative activity of the divine beings and harm ourselves. Therefore, we are relieved of conscious participation. Nevertheless, we participate dreamily, but guided by the beings of the first Hierarchy, who pervade our cosmic soul-being with their own powers:

8th Week (26 May – 1 June)

The senses' might is growing
In league with the creative work of gods.
It presses down the force of thinking
To dullness of a dream.
When divine being
Wants closer union with my soul,
Then human thinking must
Be content with a state of dream.

8. Woche (26.5. – 1.6.)

Es wächst der Sinne Macht
Im Bunde mit der Götter Schaffen,
Sie drückt des Denkens Kraft
Zur Traumes Dumpfheit mir herab.
Wenn göttlich Wesen
Sich meiner Seele einen will,
Muss menschlich Denken
Im Traumessein sich still bescheiden.

Sensory perception and thinking are two very different things. Human thinking is an inner process of the soul that follows after the actual experience of the senses. The bearer of the soul-force of thinking, apart from the ether body, is primarily the astral body. This is active when we form imaginations within ourselves according to the sensory perceptions on which we awaken to the I-consciousness:

"But this living in imaginations, it leads us far away from what is the very essence of our I-experience in the sensory perception. We cannot say that we have a strong I-consciousness in the same sense when we only imagine. On the contrary, in mere imagining it always happens that this I-experience wants to darken.

---

[71] GA 206, "Menschenwerden, Weltenseele und Weltengeist" (Man's becoming, world-soul and world-spirit) , Dornach, Lecture of 12 August 1921

This manifests in the transition to a dreamy state or even to a kind of drowsy state during mere imagining. We dive deeper into our inner being when we merely imagine than when we live in the sense-perception in connection with the outside world. Reference must be made to the self-observation of each individual. One will be able to notice how there is a tendency to dampen the I when sensory perception has been damped. When we supplement the sensory experience by the imagination, then get from our «I»s into our astral bodies.

So that we can say: Just as life in sensory perception belongs to the I-experience, so the living in imaginations belongs to the astral body. Above all, this damping of the I shows – and this is actually the most important thing one has to refer to if one wants to understand what I am actually explaining now – that we have something completely individual in living in our sensory perception. The complex of sensory perceptions we face at a moment, no one else can face it in exactly the same way. It is something very individual, and on this very individual we have our I-experience at the same time." [72]

In order for the creative process on the human senses as the basis of the I-consciousness to proceed undisturbed, everything astral that still belongs to the planetary sphere must be left out. Only when our participation in the creative work of the divine beings of the Zodiac sphere is released from everything planetary, can creative powers be planted within us for our next life on Earth. Everything Spiritual that we carry down into the sensory world through our human consciousness with its cognitive ability and inventive spirit, but also everything that we raise from our sensory experience through art into the noble, religious and spiritual, all this has its origin in this central region of the spirit land, as Rudolf Steiner explains in more detail in his book "Theosophy":

"With the fourth region begins the «pure spirit land». But even this region is not yet so in the full sense of the word. It differs from the three lower regions in the fact that in these the archetypes of those physical and soul conditions are present which man finds in the physical world and in the soul world before he himself intervenes in these worlds. The conditions of everyday life are combined with the things and beings that man finds in the world. The perishable things of this world direct his gaze to their eternal origin. And also the fellow creatures to which he dedicates his selfless attitude are not there by man. But through him are in the world the creations of the arts and sciences, of technology, of the state and so on, in short everything that he integrates into the world as original works of his spirit. Of all that, without his contribution, there would be no physical likenesses in the world. The archetypes of these solely human creations can be found in the fourth region of the «spirit land». What man develops as scientific results, as artistic ideas and figures, as thoughts of technology during earthly life, bears its fruits in this fourth region. Artists, scholars and great inventors therefore draw their impulses from this region during their stay in the «spirit land» and increase their genius here in order to be able to contribute in a greater extent to the further development of human culture in a re-embodiment. – One should not think that this fourth region of the «spirit land» is only important for particularly outstanding people. It is important for all people. Everything man is engaged in physical life that reaches beyond the sphere of everyday life, desire and will has its source in this region. If man did not pass through it in the time between death and a new birth, he would, in another life, have no interests which would lead beyond the narrow circle of the personal life-style to the general-human. – It has been said above that even this region cannot be called the «pure spirit land» in the full sense. This is because the condition in which human beings have left the cultural development on earth has an effect on their spiritual existence. In the «spirit land» they can only enjoy the fruits of what they were able to do according to their talent and the degree of development of the folk, state and so on, into which they were born." [73]

In this border region the human being lives directly before his transition to the higher spiritual world. But before he can be granted entry there, this higher spirituality must first get closer to him and pervade the human spirit-soul, which has become a cosmic one, with "holy spirit", for only what has become sanctified is allowed to enter holy regions. This event in man's after-death development process has its reflection in life on Earth in the celebration of Pentecost. On the fiftieth day after Easter Sunday, on Pentekoste Heméra, in ancient Greek πεντηκοστὴ ἡμέρα, the ancient Jews celebrated Shavuot, the feast of the revelation of the Torah, the five books of Moses, and thus the revelation of the holy spiritual teachings to their people by Yahweh. In Christian culture, on this day we celebrate the fulfillment with the Holy Spirit sent by the Son of God, which took place for the first time, as a first Pentecost, about two thousand years ago in Jerusalem. In the weeks preceding the first Pentecost, the disciples got into a kind of dreamlike

---

[72] GA 206, "Menschenwerden, Weltenseele und Weltengeist" (Man's becoming, world-soul and world-spirit), Dornach, Lecture of 12 August 1921

[73] GA 9 "Theosophie" (Theosophy), Chapter "Die drei Welten" (The three worlds), Section IV "Der Geist im Geisterland nach dem Tode" (The spirit in the spirit land after death)

state, as Rudolf Steiner describes it. But just this state made them receptive to the influx of the Holy Spirit. This event also finds its expression in the words of the eighth verse, which coincides with the Pentecost week:

When divine being	Wenn göttlich Wesen
Wants closer union with my soul,	Sich meiner Seele einen will,
Then human thinking must	Muss menschlich Denken
Be content with a state of dream.	Im Traumessein sich still bescheiden.

"All that is transient is but a likeness", Goethe once wrote so aptly. In this sense, the four elements earth, water, air and fire are symbols of four worlds. The element earth represents the physical world, the element water the astral world, the element air the spiritual world and the element fire or warmth the Budhi world or Budhi plane, as will be elaborated below. This fourth world pervades the upper part of the third world. Therefore the state of the higher spiritual world is intimately connected with the elements air and fire (see Figure 4). In ancient Greek πνεύμα (pneuma) means both air and spirit. According to this inner connection, the disciples of Christ Jesus, who were gathered again in the Upper Room of the House of the Last Supper, experienced the outpouring of the Holy Spirit into each of them as roaring air and fiery flames.

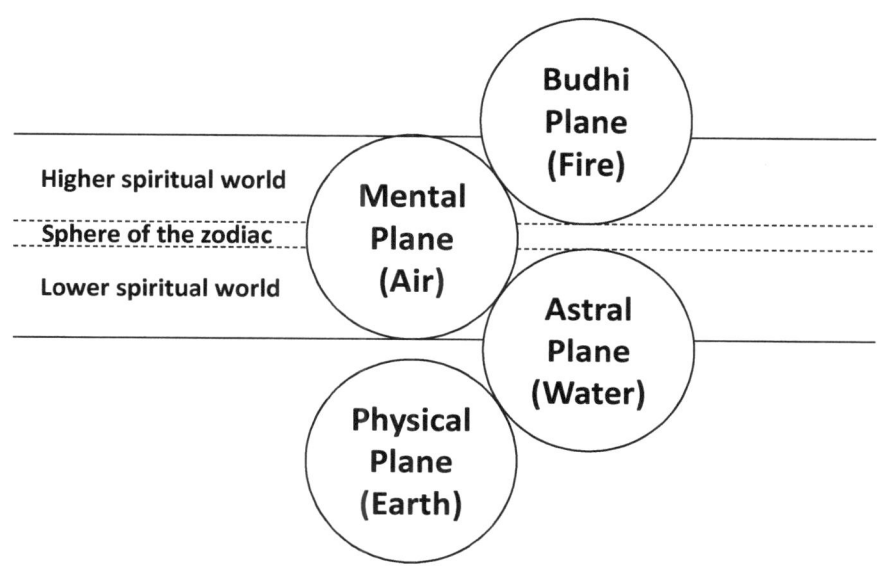

Figure 4: Relationship of the lower 4 worlds to the 4 elements

Since the element air is most closely related to the spiritual world or mental plane, the Holy Spirit is often portrayed as a being of the air, a dove descending from heaven. According to Rudolf Steiner, this does not only correspond to a purely intellectual analogy, but is also an inspired Imagination from the spiritual world.

"And it is quite according to this, when the Holy Spirit was portrayed in the form of a dove by those who drew attention to Inspiration. In which way should we conceive it today when we hear spoken of the Holy Spirit as in the form of a dove? We have to interpret in the way that we say: those who spoke like that were inspired people in the ancient atavistic sense. In that region where the Holy spirit showed himself to them purely spiritually, they saw him as an Inspiration in this form." [74]

But the figure of the dove is just one of the ways in which the Holy Spirit, descending from the higher spiritual world, presents himself. He may as well reveal himself as a rushing mighty wind and tongues of fire, just as it was the case at the first Pentecost. The tongues of fire represent the Budhi, the selfless love which unites itself as the gift of the Son in the higher spiritual world with the gift of the Holy Spirit:

---

[74] GA 214 "Das Geheimnis der Trinität" (Mystery of the Trinity), Dornach, Lecture of 28 July 1922

"Should I make clear what this Budhi means in the spiritual realm, I can only do so through a parable. ... I would like to quote such a parable for Budhi. If you imagine the ordinary productive power in ordinary sensory life, coupled with love, not as a love that receives, but as a love that gives entirely: that is Budhi." [75]

Being filled with the Holy Spirit and with selfless love, which the apostles could receive initially only in a dreamlike state of consciousness, they were ultimately awakened to higher knowledge, not to one which originated from "human thinking", but to sacred, divine knowledge.

"Yet the time came when the apostles felt as if they had spent a long time of many days as in a dream-filled sleep, from which they now awoke with this Pentecostal event. And this awakening, they already felt this in a peculiar way: they actually felt as if something that could only be called the substance of the all-effective love had descended upon them from the universe. As if fertilized from above by the all-effective love and as if awakened from the dreamlike state of life described above, this is how the apostles felt. As if they would have been awakened through all that pervades and warms the universe as the original power of love, as if this original power of love had sunk into the soul of each of them, so they felt themselves. And to the other people who could observe the way they spoke now, they seemed quite strange. These other people knew, that those were people who had lived in an extraordinarily simple way, but some of them had behaved a bit strangely, as if lost in dreams, in the last few days. This was known. But now it seemed to the people as if those were transformed: like people who had indeed attained a whole new attitude, a whole new mood of the soul, like people who had given up all the closeness of life, all the selfishness of life, who had won an infinitely wide heart, a comprehensive inner tolerance, a deep understanding of the heart for everything that is human on Earth, who could express themselves in such a way that they were understood by everybody who was present. One felt, as it were, that they could look into the heart and soul of anybody and guessed secrets of the soul from the deepest inside, so that they could comfort anyone, could tell what he needed at that moment.

Of course, it was highly surprising for these observers that such a transformation could happen with a number of people. But those people themselves who had experienced this transformation, who were raised, so to speak, by the spirit of love of the cosmos, these people now felt a new understanding in themselves, felt an understanding for that which had taken place in intimate communion with their souls in deed, but which they had not understood at the time when it had taken place: Only now, at the moment when they felt fertilized with cosmic love, an understanding for what had actually happened on Golgotha occurred before their souls' eyes." [76]

Although a large number of disciples were present in the Upper Room in Jerusalem at that time, in Christian art we usually find depicted – not without a deeper reason – the twelve apostles with the Mother of Jesus in their midst and tongues of flames above their heads. This refers to the zodiac with its twelve signs, whose earthly representatives are the twelve apostles. The Mother of Jesus, the only one among them who was already filled with holy Spirit from her youth, represents the unity of the twelve as the Thirteenth. Therefore, she is often portrayed with a circle of stars above her head. But all other saints as well bear the sign of the zodiac, the glowing, circular halo above their heads as an expression of their fulfillment with cosmic, holy Spirit.

Why, however, the 8th weekly verse, if it refers to the I, does not say as one might expect, "When divine being wants closer union with my I", but "When divine being wants closer union with my soul"? This could be sensed as a contradiction. But the reason for this is the fact that the I is enveloped by the soul. Whatever "wants closer union" with the I, can only achieve this by closer union with the soul, too. *"The soul [has] its centre in the I. ... The sensory phenomena reveal themselves to the «I» from one side, the spirit from the other."* The former reveal themselves to the I through the sentient soul. *"Just as it does with the body, the sentient soul also interacts with thinking, with the spirit. At first thought serves it. Man forms thoughts about his sensations. That's the way he learns about the outside world. ... The sentient soul does not merely receive the impressions of the outside world as sensations; it has its own life, which is just as fertilised by thinking on the other side as by the sensations on the one side. So it turns into the intellectual soul."* The sentient soul forms a unity with the soul body and thus connects itself with the world of corporeality, the physical world. The intellectual soul is receptive to the influences of the lower spiritual or mental world. But for everything that reveals itself to the I from the higher spiritual world and the lower part of the Budhi plane, the consciousness soul is the receptive part of the human soul and reservoir of experiences.

---

[75] GA 54 "Die Welträtsel und die Anthroposophie" (World's mysteries and Anthroposophy), Berlin, Lecture of 15 February 1906

[76] GA 148 "Aus der Akasha-Forschung – Das fünfte Evangelium" (From Akasha-Research – the Fifth Gospel), Kristiania (Oslo), Lecture of 2 October 1913

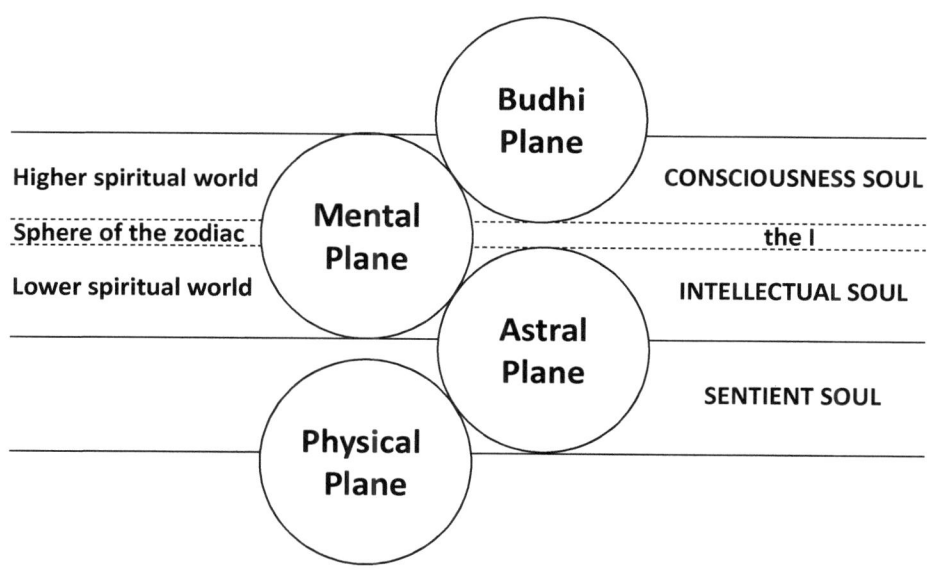

Figure 5: Connections of the soul-members and the I with the world planes

"When man lets revive in his inner being the independent true and good, he rises above the mere sentient soul. The eternal Spirit shines into it. A light brightens in it that is imperishable. If the soul lives in this light, it partakes of something eternal. It connects its own existence with it. What the soul bears as truth and good in itself is immortal in it. – That which brightens in the soul as eternal is here called consciousness soul. ... The kernel of human consciousness, the soul in the soul, is meant here with consciousness soul. The consciousness soul is distinguished here as a special member of the soul from the intellectual soul. The latter is still involved in the sensations, the desires, affects and so on. Everyone knows how he at first considers that to be true, which he prefers in his emotions and so on. But only that t r u t h is the enduring truth which has rid itself of all the tastes of such sympathies and antipathies of the emotions and so on. The truth is true, even if all personal feelings rebel against it. The part of the soul in which this truth lives is called here the consciousness soul. ... Consciousness soul and spirit self form a unity. In this unity the spirit man lives as the life spirit." [77]

Just in this sense the 8th weekly verse says: "If divine being wants closer union with my s o u l."

Ascension to the Sphere of the Spirit Self – 9th Week

After the expansion of the cosmic spirit-soul of man into the region of the zodiac and the visible starry sky, it extends into even more distant regions, which are so sublime that there is no longer any sensory image of them in the physical world. These regions belong entirely to the Invisible already. It is the "pure spirit land" or the higher spiritual world, which is composed of the three highest regions of the spiritual world. There, the forces and beings underlying the zodiac are at home. As we enter this kingdom of the Holy Spirit, we also enter the regions of the Trinity. In complete harmony with this event, Christianity on Earth celebrates "Trinitatis", Trinity Sunday, on the ninth Sunday of the Easter and post-Easter feast season.

In these regions filled with holy spirit, man on his after-death path of development can only be lifted up when he completely frees himself from any attachment to his last incarnation. For this purpose, he must also put off even the most hidden and unconscious personal will impulses that still connect him with his existence as a formerly incarnated separate being. Only when really the very last remnant of this "peculiarity of will" has been "forgotten" by him, when the spirit-soul has completely left behind its former personal existence, can it find itself in his higher, superpersonal, purely spiritual self, its eternal individuality, which exists behind and above all incarnations. Hence, the ninth weekly verse begins with the words:

---

[77] GA 9 "Theosophie" (Theosophy), Chapter "Das Wesen des Menschen" (The essential nature of man), Section IV, "Leib, Seele und Geist" (Body, soul and spirit)

From now on it is no longer the will of man, but the will of God that matters. Here, man lives in a kingdom beyond the archetypes of the three lower regions of the spiritual world and also beyond the formative powers of the fourth and middle region of the spiritual world. Towards the end of the reflection on the 7th weekly verse it was already explained and illustrated by figures that the three lower and the three upper regions of a world interpenetrate mutually with the three regions of the next lower or respectively next higher world. This is also the case with the three upper regions of the spiritual world. They are pervaded by the three lower regions of the next higher world, the Budhi plane, as shown in Figure 6.

The three upper regions of the Budhi plane, in turn, are pervaded by the Atma plane. These two worlds are still beyond the developmental possibilities of a current average person. Therefore their regions are depicted grey. The actual three worlds in which man is still developing are the Physical plane, the Astral plane or the soul world, and the Mental plane or the spiritual world, which is also called Devachan. It could as well be called the Manasic world or Manas plane. The Indian word "manas" is linguistically related to the English word "man" and the German word "Mensch" (man or human being). It denotes man as an intellectual being, which by his thinking carries down the spirit from higher worlds to earthly existence. For this reason the Manas plane is also called thought world or Mental plane, from Latin "mens", i.e. spirit, mind, thinking, thought.

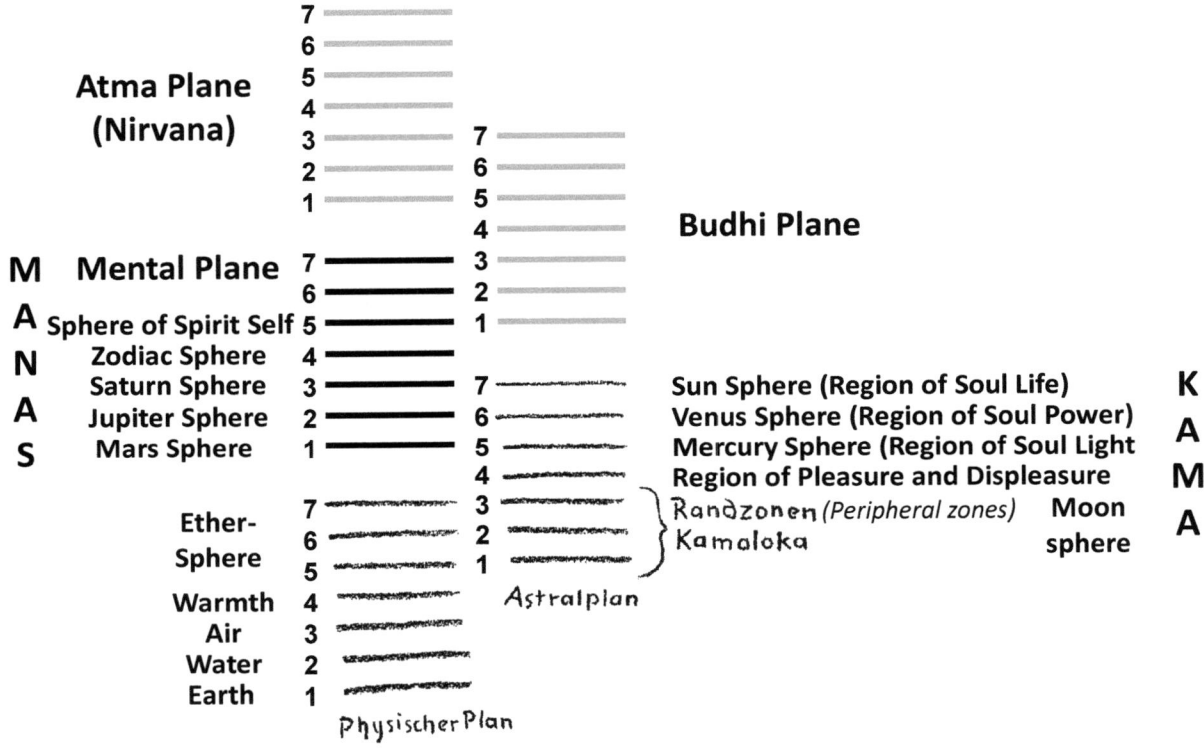

**Figure 6: Mutual interpenetration of the worlds
from the Physical Plane to the Atma Plane**

As a result of the mutual interpenetration of the lower three regions of the Manas plane with the upper three regions of the Astral plane, "Kama-Manas" is generated. "Kama" denotes the general desire-like nature of the Astral plane. Kama-Manas therefore corresponds to the lower or ordinary thinking of man, which, with regard to the soul, Rudolf Steiner also calls the intellectual soul. In the upper three regions of the Mental plane Manas connects with Budhi to "Budhi-Manas", the higher spiritual cognition of man. In one of his early essays, Rudolf Steiner relates this term to the consciousness soul which is imbued with the spirit self (see Figure 5 in the previous chapter). The fact, that both are in addition pervaded by Budhi finds its expression there in the attached Indian term "Buddhi manas", at that time still written in the Theosophists' style of notation with a double d.[78]

The term "manas" is used in three ways. In the broadest sense, it denotes the entire Mental plane, just as Budhi includes the entire Budhi plane and Atma the entire Atma plane. In a somewhat narrower sense manas denotes only that part of the human being which expands through the upper three regions of the spiritual world and is pervaded by Budhi, i.e. actually Budhi-Manas. In an even narrower sense manas or spirit self refers only to that part of man which is located in the fifth region of the spiritual world. In this narrowest sense, the fifth region is the actual sphere of the spirit self, for in the sixth and seventh regions of the Mental plane the life spirit of the Budhi plane and the spirit man of the Atma plane are already clothed in their germ-covers. There is planted what is to blossom to full maturity only in the distant future on the Budhi plane and the Atma plane.

If one wants to borrow an image from the sensory world for the Budhi as an illustration, it may be compared with the life-creating warmth:

"Let's look at the hen that hatches its egg. It is completely absorbed by its breeding business and, by doing so, feels a sense of well-being when it experiences, as in a dream, the hatching of the small winged chick. This sense of well-being in creation can be found at all stages of cosmic development, and everywhere it releases a corresponding warmth. If one imagines the cosmic intelligence as the world of thoughts accessible to the higher I (manas), one immediately notices this power of warmth that pervades the universe, emerging virtually from the creative source of all life (Life spirit: Budhi). And through it one may pre-sense this world of creative power, which was before ours and envelops it. One then rises from Manas to Budhi and from Budhi to Atma." [79]

As man gradually "forgets" his lower I, his individual "peculiarity of will" and thereby completely detaches himself from his last incarnation, grows beyond it to his eternal spirit self, he enters the higher spiritual world, which is pervaded by Budhi, the "warmth that pervades the universe", in short, the "world-warmth". From this point it begins to fulfil more and more man's "spirit and the essence of his soul", i.e. the spirit self and the consciousness-soul, and thus, figuratively speaking, announces an imminent time of "summer-warmth", which man may experience on even more sublime stages of development in his after-death life. In the course of the year, this finds its earthly expression in the mood of nature at the beginning of June. Rudolf Steiner genuinely summarized this important event in the fifth region of the spiritual world in the few words of the first sentence of the 9th weekly verse:

9th Week (2 – 8 June)	9. Woche (2. – 8. Juni)
Forgetting my will's peculiarity,	Vergessend meine Willenseigenheit
World-warmth, announcing summer,	Erfüllet Weltenwärme sommerkündend
Fills up my spirit and the essence of my soul;	Mir Geist und Seelenwesen;

In the higher spiritual world, starting with the fifth region, man lives in a sphere of formlessness. It differs from the lower spiritual world in the fact that nothing there has yet been formed to a concrete shape, as is the case with the archetypes of the lower three regions. Also, the shaping forces of the fourth region are not yet effective there. In the upper three regions everything is still highly ideational, wholly formless.

---

[78] GA 34 "Lucifer-Gnosis 1903 – 1908", Note 2 to Rudolf Steiner's essay "Wie Karma wirkt" (How Karma works), first published in "Lucifer", No. 7, December 1903:

"For those who are accustomed to the usual theosophical expressions, I note the following. (I borrow my expressions for certain reasons from an occult language, which differs somewhat from the terms used in the widespread theosophical writings, but it is, of course, completely identical in substance. That's why I want to put side by side one mode of expression with the other.) Each of the above entities: body, soul, spirit, consists of three members. Thus the human being appears as composed of nine members. The body is composed of: 1. the actual body, 2. the life-body, 3. the sentient body. The soul is composed of 4. the sentient soul, 5. the intellectual soul and 6. the consciousness-soul. The spirit is composed of 7. spirit self, 8. life spirit, 9. spirit man. In the incarnated human being, 3 and 4 as well as 6 and 7 merge (flow into each other). As a result, the nine members appear drawn together to seven members and one receives the usual theosophical subdivision of man. 1. the actual body (Sthula sharira), 2. the life-body (Prana), 3. the sentient body, pervaded by the sentient soul (astral body, Kama rupa), 4. the intellectual soul (Kama manas), 5. the consciousness-soul, pervaded by the spirit self (Buddhi manas), 6. the life spirit (Buddhi), 7. the spirit man (Atma)".

[79] GA 94 "Kosmogonie" (Cosmogony), Paris, Lecture of 9 June 1906

Accordingly, this area of the spiritual world is called the Arupa region, i.e. the region of formlessness. Every human being passes through this high region in his after-death development:

"Man always enters the higher spiritual world, which we also call the «Arupa sphere», between two embodiments. The undeveloped one stays there for a shorter time, the developed one for a longer time. Everyone must pass through this region." [80]

However, the formlessness prevailing there must not be understood as emptiness. Rather, it is a world of higher will impulses, intentions and goals, as Rudolf Steiner makes clear in his "Theosophy":

"Thus, the self is in the realm of intentions and goals when it lives in the fifth region of the «spirit land». Just as the architect learns from the imperfections that have revealed to him, and just as he integrates into his new plans only that which he was able to transform into perfections from these imperfections, so the self in the fifth region wipes off from his results of earlier lives that which is connected with the imperfections of the lower worlds, and fertilizes the intentions of the «spirit land» with which he now lives together, with the results of his earlier lives. It is clear that the power that can be drawn from this region will depend on how much the self has acquired during its embodiment of such results that are capable of being absorbed into the world of intentions. The self, which during its earthly existence sought to realize the intentions of the Spirit through an active thought-life or through wise, active love, will acquire a great expectancy of this region. The one who has been completely absorbed in everyday conditions, who has lived only in the Transient, has not sown any seeds which can play a role in the intentions of the eternal world order. Only the little, which he worked beyond the daily interests, can unfold as a fruit in these upper regions of the «spirit land». But one should not think that above all here comes into consideration what brings «earthly glory» or the like. No, here is called into question precisely that, which in the smallest circle of life leads to the consciousness that everything has its own significance for the eternal development of existence. One must become familiar with the idea that man in this region has to judge differently than he can do in physical life. If, for example, he has acquired little that is related to this fifth region, the urge arises in him to engrave on himself an impulse for the following physical life, which makes this life run in such a way that in his fate (karma) the corresponding effect of the lack becomes apparent. What then appears in the following life on Earth as painful fate, from the point of view of this life – perhaps even as one that is deeply lamented – man finds quite necessary for himself in this region of the «spirit land».

Since man in the fifth region lives in his actual self, he is also lifted out of everything that envelops him from the lower worlds during embodiment. He is what he always was and always will be during the course of his embodiments. He lives in the activity of the intentions which exist for these embodiments and which he integrates into his own self. He looks back on his own past and he feels that everything he has experienced in it will be integrated into the intentions he has to realize in the future. A kind of memory for his earlier biographies and the prophetic foresight for his later ones flashes. It can be seen: that which has been called the «spirit self» in this scripture lives in this region, as far as it is developed, in a reality appropriate to it. It develops and prepares itself in order to make possible an executing of spiritual intentions in reality on Earth during a new embodiment." [81]

In his earlier writings Rudolf Steiner often called the spirit self the "cause-body" or "causal body" with regard to its capacity as bearer of all the fruits of our previous embodiments:

"When man returns to the very self, to his original being himself, when he gets to know the fifth region, then his gaze widens over his own incarnations, then he is able to survey his past and his future. He experiences a flash of memory of his past incarnations and can relate them to what he may accomplish in the future. He overlooks the past and the future with a prophetic view. Everything he accomplishes seems to him to flow out of the eternal self. This is what the self acquires in the fifth region of the spirit land. That is why we call this self, insofar as it runs free in the fifth region and becomes aware of its own being, the bearer of the causes of the human being, which transmits all results of the past life into the future. That which reappears in the various embodiments, is the cause-body, until such time as man passes over to higher states where higher laws than those of reincarnation apply. Since the beginning of planetary life we have been subject to the law of reincarnation. The causal body is that which transmits the result of a

---

[80] GA 88 "Über die astrale Welt und das Devachan" (About the astral world and the Devachan), Berlin, Lecture of 4 November 1903

[81] GA 9 "Theosophie" (Theosophy), Chapter "Die drei Welten" (The three worlds), Section IV "Der Geist im Geisterland nach dem Tode" (The spirit in the spirit land after death)

previous life into the coming lives, it is that which enjoys as fruits that which was worked out in previous lives." [82]

The substantiality of the higher spiritual world is revealed to the spiritual senses of the human being as flowing light. Like its physical counterpart in the sensory world, the sunlight, it appears as a unit, formless and undifferentiated, although it includes a multitude of forces, of which Goethe mentioned, for example, the sounding of the Sun that is accessible to spiritual perception:

> In ancient manner sounds the Sun,
> competing with his brother-spheres in song and talk,
> and he accomplishes his predetermined journey's run
> with rumbling, thundering walk. [83]

In a comparable manner, the region of formlessness reveals itself to the visionary eye and spiritual sense of hearing. But in the higher spiritual world the sound becomes a meaningful word and a spirit-talk:

"As I described a week ago, the Devachanic world may be divided into three lower realms and three higher realms. The three higher realms sound and shine into the three lower realms. We have called the lower Devachanic realms – in theosophical language «rupa-realms» – the mainland, the ocean, the airspace, whereas beyond the fourth realm – (Akasha) – the three highest realms of Devachan spread, which in theosophical language are called «arupa-realms». Of all that which is below Devachan – that is, the astral realm and the physical realm – there are the primal states in the higher Devachan. These arupa-realms are inhabited by beings of the most sublime kind. The masters of the original Christian wisdom have described these realms. They were known in Christian wisdom until the 13th century. Then knowledge of them was lost. No one understands the Christian wisdom of previous centuries unless he realizes that some scriptures speak of the three supreme realms of Devachan. These three realms are, as said, inhabited by sublime beings who control and direct all processes in the lower realms.

Goethe also points to the first stage of the higher Devachan [the fifth region] in a passage of the fairy tale of the green serpent and the beautiful lily. You can read there: What is more glorious than the light? Speech (or talk, in German: Gespräch). – That is one the deepest words that Goethe spoke. From the kingdom of light in Devachan arises the so-called kingdom of speech or talk, that kingdom in which not only light but also a stream of insight flows as light, and it is through this stream that the higher beings enunciate in man the eternal truths, it is through it that the speech or talk of the cosmos resounds. Thus we come up to the higher realm, in which, as it were, the words are begotten for this talk, in which the voice sounds, in which the origin of the world is inherent, which the people call the «Word» out of which the worlds have come into being. In the realm of speech or talk, the realm of the light of knowledge, live a series of most sublime beings, which in Christian wisdom have been named Exusiai. These are beings that are difficult to describe with a term of the occident. These beings become visible in the garment of the light of insight. I have already indicated that such a being appeared to Moses in the burning thorn bush. This indicates a being of the Exusiai. From the substance of this kingdom the garment of these beings is weaved; they become visible and proclaim the truth to those who are mature to hear it." [84]

It is clear from these words that the cosmic spirit-soul of the human being in the state after death is here already about to approach the encounter with Christ or God. The divine will-impulses, intentions and goals are first clothed in the speaking "light of insight" of the fifth region. In looking at this will-imbued light, the human spirit-soul begins to understand how to behave there. After it has forgotten its "will's peculiarity", it no longer follows its own will-impulses, but is stimulated by the divine will-impulses of the higher spiritual world. For this reason, the spiritual view of this light "commands" the human being even "to lose" himself into this very light:

---

[82] GA 88 "Über die astrale Welt und das Devachan" (About the astral world and the Devachan), Berlin, Lecture of 11 February 1904

[83] Goethe, "Faust" Part 1, Prologue in heaven. German original text:
> Die Sonne tönt nach alter Weise
> In Brudersphären Wettgesang,
> Und ihre vorgeschriebne Reise
> Vollendet sie mit Donnergang.

[84] GA 88 "Über die astrale Welt und das Devachan" (About the astral world and the Devachan), Berlin, Lecture of 28 January 1904

To lose myself into the light,	Im Licht mich zu verlieren
I am commanded by the spirit-vision,	Gebietet mir das Geistesschauen,
And strongly tells presentiment:	Und kraftvoll kündet Ahnung mir:
Now lose yourself to find yourself.	Verliere dich, um dich zu finden.

Through inner "presentiment", which is now more feeling than thinking and strengthened by high spiritual beings, the message goes to man here that his losing himself will lead to a finding himself on a higher level, to finding himself in the true self. In this process not only the Exusiai will become visible to him, but even more sublime beings:

"One definitely has to lose one's earthly I to get the real, true self in view. And whoever would not develop this devotion, he just cannot get to this true I. One would like to say: The true I does not want to be sought if it is to appear, if it is to reveal itself; and it hides itself if it is sought. For it is found only in love. And love is the surrender of one's own being to the foreign being. Therefore, the true I must be found like a foreign being.

And in the same moment that one gains this beholding of one's own true I, one simultaneously comes to behold what now lives in another world, in the actual spirit world. One meets the beings of the first Hierarchy: Seraphim, Cherubim, Thrones.

And just as one finds one's I there again, of which one actually only has a reflection here in earthly life, so one finds for the whole world of the earthly environment its true spirit-shape. One must lose this earthly world as well for this insight in order to find its true world of origin together with our true I." [85]

If somebody, who strives for the spirit as a spirit-disciple in his life on Earth already, wants to rise beyond the limits of his present incarnation into the higher regions of the spirit land and thus also to the knowledge of his earlier incarnations, he must abstain from a thing which otherwise becomes an obstacle to him: Alcohol.

"There is a certain level of occult development at which man no longer regards the doctrine of reincarnation as a theory, but recognizes it per se. He sees this clairvoyantly in himself and in other people. No person can ever come to this realization as long it still enjoys a drop of alcohol. Man can acquire other powers through training, but these never." [86]

Nevertheless, alcohol has an important role to play in the evolution of mankind. It helps the people to develop from the soul conditions in the Saturn sphere, in which the animal kingdom also has a share, up to the stage of personal I-consciousness, which is rooted in the zodiacal sphere.

"The wine, the alcohol has occurred only in a certain time in the history of the world and of mankind. And it will disappear from it again. We see here the deep truth of occult research. Alcohol was the bridge that leads from the genus-I, from the group-I to the independent, individual I. Never would man have found the transition from the group-I to the individual I without the material effect of alcohol. This generated the individual, personal consciousness in the human being. When humans will have achieved this goal, they will no longer need alcohol, and it will disappear from the physical world again. You see, everything that happens has its meaning in the wise guidance of human development. Therefore, today no one should be contradicted if he drinks alcohol, whereas on the other hand those people who have hurried ahead of the rest of humanity and promoted their development to such an extent that they no longer need alcohol should avoid it. Christ has appeared to give powers to mankind so that the highest I-consciousness can be attained in the sixth period. Alcohol thus helps the human being to become a personal I as we develop it within an incarnation." [87]

On another occasion a year before, Rudolf Steiner expressed himself in the same sense:

"So that man would think that one incarnation was the only one, it was necessary that something cut off the brain from the knowledge of the higher principles in man, of Atma, Budhi, Manas, and from the knowledge of reincarnation. For this purpose people were given the wine. Previously, only water was used in all temple-worship. Then the use of wine was introduced, and even a divine being. Bacchus, Dionysos, was the representative of wine. The most profoundly initiated disciple, John, reveals in his Gospel what

---

[85] GA 84 "Was wollte das Goetheanum und was soll die Anthroposophie" (Purpose of the Goetheanum and of Anthroposophy), Dornach, Lecture of 22 April 1923

[86] GA 94 "Kosmogonie" (Cosmogony), Appendix, "Ergänzendes zum Vortrag vom 9. Juli 1906" (Supplement to the lecture of 9 July 1906)

[87] GA 100 "Menschheitsentwicklung und Christuserkenntnis" (Human development and understanding of Christ), Basel, Lecture of 25 November 1907

wine means for inner development. At the wedding of Cana in Galilee, the water is turned into wine. Through wine, man was prepared in such a way that he no longer understood reincarnation. At that time, the sacrificial water was turned into wine. Now we are about to turn the wine into water again. He who wants to reach up into the higher realms of existence must abstain from every drop of alcohol." [88]

These words could lead to the opinion that a person, while still occasionally consuming some alcohol, cannot be fully convinced of reincarnation or even know concretely of one or more of his earlier incarnations. However, it would be a misinterpretation of Rudolf Steiner's statement above, for we have another one in which he states that knowledge of earlier incarnations can also be granted at relatively early stages of spiritual discipleship as a demonstration of grace by the spiritual guidance of man. His angel, the guardian of his spirit self, may reveal it to him if he considers his protégé to be mature enough.

"Now you know that what we call the actual eternal kernel of the human being, the individuality, continues from incarnation to incarnation. But you also know that for the vast majority of people there is still no awareness of life in the previous embodiments, that people still do not remember what happened to them in former incarnations. Only those who have developed to some extent to clairvoyance look back into their former incarnations. – What cohesion would there be between the incarnations of a human being on Earth, who does not yet remember his former embodiments, if there were not certain beings who, so to speak, unite the separate incarnations, who watch over the advancement from one incarnation to the next? For every person we must presuppose a being that, as it is one level higher than man, guides the individuality from one incarnation to another. Mind you, these are not the beings that regulate karma and whom we are yet to talk about. They are simply vigilant beings that preserve, so to speak, the memory from one incarnation to another as long as man himself cannot do this. And these beings are the Angeloi or angels. So that we can say: Every human being is a personality in every incarnation. But every person is watched over by a being that has a consciousness which reaches from incarnation to incarnation. That is what makes it also possible that for certain lower degrees of initiation, even if man does not yet know anything of his former embodiments, he is nevertheless given the opportunity to ask his angel. This is quite possible for certain lower degrees of initiation." [89]

For all those who wish to find access to their former incarnations already during their earthly life, let us remember the following words of Rudolf Steiner, which show how important the intensive study of anthroposophy or spiritual science is even in this respect:

"And at a certain point in time between death and a new birth, the thought creatures of the spiritual environment have such a strong effect that without any impulse of will the described forgetting is brought about. And with it emerges the living in the «true I». By empowerment of the soul-life and as a spiritual act of free will, the clairvoyant consciousness brings about that which is, as it were, a natural event for the experience between death and new birth. However, within the physical-sensory experience a memory of former lives on Earth can never occur if the ideas have not been directed to the spiritual world within those lives on Earth. One must always have known of something beforehand, of which a clearly recognizable memory is to emerge later. Thus, in life on Earth one also has to acquire knowledge of oneself as a spiritual being if one rightly wants to expect for the next earthly life to be able to remember the preceding earthly life. But this knowledge need not be acquired through clairvoyance. Whoever acquires an immediate knowledge of the spiritual world through clairvoyance, in his soul a memory of the former life can appear in the lives on Earth that follow the one in which he attains this knowledge in the same way as in the sensory world the memory of something self-experienced emerges. Whoever gains a deeper understanding of spiritual science, even without spiritual vision, will find this memory arising in such a way that it can be compared with one in the sensory existence, which one has preserved from an event of which one has only heard a description." [90]

---

[88] GA 97 "Das christliche Mysterium" (The Christian mystery), Düsseldorf, Lecture of 9 February 1906

[89] GA 110, "Geistige Hierarchien und ihre Wiederspiegelung in der geistigen Welt" (Spiritual Hierarchies and their reflection in the physical world), Düsseldorf, Lecture of 15 April 1909

[90] GA 17 "Die Schwelle der geistigen Welt" (The threshould of the spiritual world), "Von dem wahren Ich des Menschen" (About man's true I)

Ascension to the Sphere of the Germ Sheath of the Life Spirit – 10th Week

In the sixth and seventh regions of the spiritual world the two highest members of the human being have their reflections, the life spirit of Budhi as the sixth member and the spirit man or Atma as the seventh member. Rudolf Steiner describes both together as the "life kernel" of man. Their real home is located in the two next-higher worlds, the Budhic and the Atmic plane. At the present stage of human development, however, they only exist germ-like and these germs or early preliminary stages are enveloped with the substance of the two highest regions of the spiritual world.

"From the element of the thought world only the germ sheath is taken, so to speak. And this encompasses the very life kernel. Thus we have reached the border of the «three worlds», for the kernel comes from even higher worlds. When man, according to his components, was described in a preceding section, this life kernel of him was specified, and the «life spirit» and «spirit man» were given as its components. For other world-beings there are similar life kernels as well. They come from higher worlds and are transferred to the three specified in order to accomplish their tasks in them." [91]

When the spirit-soul of man has arrived in the sixth region of the spiritual world, it has previously given up two of its three soul powers, thinking, feeling and will. Already in the fourth region, the Zodiac sphere, "the force of thinking" was pressed down to "dullness of a dream" and "human thinking" had to be "content with a state of dream" or to be transformed into "assumption". In the next-higher fifth region, the actual region of the spirit self, spiritual beings caused the spirit soul, expanded into the cosmos, to lose its human will, its "will's peculiarity". A veil of oblivion was spread over it. Of the three soul forces, therefore, only human feeling remains. In the sublime state of cosmic feeling the spirit self, pervaded by divine powers, is carried further and further out into the cosmos of the spiritual world and finally towards the Budhic plane, from which the all-pervading "world-warmth" emanates. In this way, figuratively speaking, man reaches "summer's heights". He could never achieve this on his own at his current stage of development. Rather man is taken along as a feeling spirit-soul by beings who are the spiritual essence of the Sun and "rise" into the realms of spiritual light and divine warmth as "the sun's bright being" under the guidance of Christ, the highest of the Sun Spirits.

10th Week (9 – 15 June)	*10. Woche (9. – 15. Juni)*
Up to the summer's heights,	Zu sommerlichen Höhen
The sun's bright being rises;	Erhebt der Sonne leuchtend Wesen sich;
It takes along my human feeling	Es nimmt mein menschlich Fühlen
Into its spatial vastness.	In seine Raumesweiten mit.
Sensation stirs inside,	Erahnend regt im Innern sich
Like a presentiment announcing dimly,	Empfindung, dumpf mir kündend,
Once you will recognize:	Erkennen wirst du einst:
A divine being has felt you now.	Dich fühlte jetzt ein Gotteswesen.

Through the upward movement of the feeling human spirit-soul, it gets into regions in which divine feeling draws near. They both interpenetrate here mutually. Of course, only as much of the human feeling as is related to divine feeling can participate. Only human feeling pervaded by selfless, divine love and warmth can persist here beside the divine feeling. The more a person has developed of this in his life on Earth, the more "human feeling" he will be able to preserve itself here. But since the life spirit is still germ-like, enveloped in the substance of the sixth region of the spiritual world, this is sufficient at best for a "dull" sensation or sensing insight that one is felt or rather felt through by a "divine being". Only later will this sensation be able to mature into clear knowledge.

As the second highest region, the sixth region of the spiritual world is inwardly connected with the second lowest region of this world. There the human being has experienced life as a power already that flows through everything, acting uniformly. For the after-death life in this second region of the spiritual world, the Jupiter sphere, man's capacity for religious feeling is of great importance, as has been stated above. The reason for that is this inner connection of the second region with the sixth region, in which human feeling is completely pervaded by divine feeling. The second region of the spiritual world, the Jupiter sphere, in turn pervades the Venus sphere of the soul world. [92] Rudolf Steiner seems to explicitly make a

---

[91] GA 9 "Theosophie" (Theosophy), Chapter "Die drei Welten" (The three worlds), Section III "Das Geisterland" (The spirit land), last paragraph

[92] See the consideration of the 7th weekly verse and the illustration there

reference to this in both the 4th and 10th weekly verses in which he lets the "sensation" speak or proclaim to man. The 4th weekly verse about the Venus sphere says: "So speaks sensation ..." In the 10th weekly verse about the second highest region of the spiritual world Rudolf Steiner formulates: "Sensation stirs inside, like a presentiment announcing dimly ..." Only in these two weekly verses does he use the word "sensation". We cannot find it in any other weekly verse. As mentioned above, already in the Venus sphere the focus of human experience is in the religious feeling that man has brought from his last earthly life. On Earth it constantly supplied the life body or ether body with new, fresh forces and thus contributed to its refinement and gradual transformation into life spirit.

"A powerful means of purification and refinement of the ether body is religion. The religious impulses thus have their great mission in human evolution. What is called conscience is nothing other than the result of the work of the I on the life body through a series of incarnations. When man realizes that he should not do this or that, and when such insight makes such a strong impression on him that it propagates into his ether body, conscience arises." [93]

Conscience is a kind of noble feeling, which is particularly related to the sixth region of the spiritual world. A well developed conscience anchored in the ether body is an important basis for spiritual discipleship. All the initiates of the various degrees consciously work on the refinement of the life body and its transformation into life spirit already in life on Earth. By doing so, they acquire a special kinship with the sixth region of the spiritual world in their after-death life. Being intensely pervaded by divine feeling they are enabled there as a consequence to carry a deep religious sincerity, a firm conviction and unshakable faith down into their next life on Earth, where they can witness the reality of the spiritual world.

"These are those who can affirm from personal experience that the teachings of Theosophy are truths and facts. But it is also they who have the duty, as often and as well as they can, to proclaim to others what was revealed to them as incontrovertible truths and to arouse in them the high feeling and the power that leads the human being further up the ladder of knowledge. The one who can believe in reincarnation, who knows that it is something possible, has already reached the first stage. Who believes – even if only dully – that reincarnation is possible, can expect that this thought in him turns into the understanding of its reality, because faith, which works as a living power in the human soul, produces miracles in the soul of man. He who does not know how that works which comes out of spiritual depths, calls such people enthusiasts and dreamers because he does not realize that they create out of a much deeper consciousness than he himself. But the course of the world is a continuous embodiment of what dreamers and idealists once thought." [94]

The sixth region of the spiritual world is thus above all the region of the spirit-disciples, the Chelas. Most people today are already working on the purification of their astral body and its gradual transformation into Manas or spirit self by the forces of the I. However, the work of the Chelas extends further and includes the ether or life body. They work on it with the help of the power of religiosity:

"That which is consciously worked into the astral body by the I is called spirit self or Manas. With the I's conscious working in begins something very peculiar. Before this Manas is developed, however, that part in the astral body, which the animal has likewise, remains completely unchanged. Despite an increase in intellect, the astral body may remain essentially unchanged, full of animal desires, for example. But there are influences that indeed transform the sentient body: conscious religiosity and art. From these we draw force for self-conquest and refinement. This is a much stronger might than mere morality. Man has so much of Manas or spirit self as he has worked into his astral body. This is not something external, it is a product of transformation of what formerly was the sentient soul.

As long as I work only on my sentient body, I use my achievements to modify this astral body. All the moral of the world and intellectuality as well cannot accomplish more. But, if true religiosity works in me, this stronger power pushes itself through the astral body and works into the next lower, the ether body. This is of course a much stronger accomplishment, as if the I merely modifies astral material, because the raw material of the ether body is much coarser, much more resistant than the finer astral body. The result of this transformation we call the life spirit or Budhi. So the life spirit is the spiritualized life body. In the Orient, a person who had brought this to the highest level was called a Buddha. This tremendous moral power originates from consciousness when the three souls are governed by a strong I. For humanity in general, these are preparatory steps. In a fully conscious way only the Chela works into his ether body. The Chela

---

[93] GA 34 "Lucifer-Gnosis 1903 – 1908", Aufsatz "Die Erziehung des Kindes vom Gesichtspunkte der Geisteswissenschaft" (Essay "The education of the child from the perspective of the Science of the Spirit")

[94] GA 88 "Über die astrale Welt und das Devachan" (About the astral world and the Devachan), Berlin, Lecture of 11 February 1904

aims at spiritualizing everything into his ether body. The chelaship is complete when he has made Budhi completely flow into his life body, so that the life body that he ennobles from the I has become life spirit.

On the third stage, man achieves the highest principle that we can reach for the time being. He is able to work down into his physical body. He thus exceeds the level of a Chela and becomes a «master». When on the second stage Budhi glows through his ether body, man, apart from moral principles, gains control of his character. He can change his temperament, his memory, his habits. The human being of today masters all this only very imperfectly. To understand the task of a Chela, compare yourself, as you are today, with yourself when you were ten years old. How much knowledge have you achieved since then, and how little your character has changed! The content of the soul has changed thoroughly, but habits and inclinations have changed only very little. Who as a child was irascible, forgetful, envious, inattentive, is often still so as an adult. How much our ideas and thoughts have changed, how very little our habits have changed! This gives you a clue to estimate how much tougher, firmer, heavier the ether body is in relation to the astral body. Conversely, how much more fertile and with more consequences is an improvement achieved on the ether body!

As an example of the different tempo of the possibility of conversion, the statement may apply: What you have learned and experienced has changed like the minute hand of the watch, your habits like the hour hand. Learning is easy, giving up is hard. You can still be recognized by the handwriting of former times, because they also belong to the habits. It is easy to change views and insights, hard to change habits. To change this tough thing, habit, more and more, that's the job of the Chela. This means to become another person by creating another ether body, i.e. to transform the life body into life spirit. This gives you forces of growth in your hands. Habits are obvious forces of growth. If I destroy them, then growth power, vis vitalis, is released at my disposal, for my conscious control. Christ says: «I am the way, the truth and the life.» – Christ is the personification of the power that changes the life body." [95]

In another lecture, which Rudolf Steiner gave only five months later in Berlin, he pointed with even clearer words to the strong effect of religious impulses on the transformation of the ether body into the man's sixth member of being, the Budhi, and to its most intimate connection with Christ:

"But the religious impulses have the strongest effect on the ether body. Under the influence of such impulses, a part of the ether body separates in order to turn into Budhi, the Logos, the Word. In esoteric Christianity this is called the Christos."

With regard to the three divine persons, Rudolf Steiner emphasized in the same lecture summarising:

"Thus we have to distinguish within Christian esotericism: the Holy Spirit: so much does the Christian have in himself of the Holy Spirit as he has refined the astral body; then the Son, Logos, the Word: so much does the Christian have in himself of the Son, of the Logos, of the Word, as he has transformed the ether body; and thirdly the Father: so much does the Christian have in himself of the Father – only an initiate can consciously have the Father in himself – as his physical body has been transformed, made eternal." [96]

Ascension to the Sphere of the Germ Sheath of the Spirit Man – 11th Week

The ascension of the human spirit-soul into the seventh and highest region of the spiritual world leads even nearer to Christ and the Father. In life on Earth this can only be achieved by higher initiates and masters in an extra-corporal state. The prerequisite for this is a consciously performed work on the physical body and its gradual transformation into the spirit man or rather a further development of its preliminary stage, as far as this is already possible in the course of the Earth development.

"The seventh stage can only be achieved by the one, who has been an initiate in this life, who has understood the meaning of the mysteries, who can participate in the construction and plan of the divine world order. After having performed his task in the lower regions, he directly enters the highest region, from

---

[95] GA 94 "Kosmogonie" (Cosmogony), Munich, Lecture of 28 October 1906

[96] GA 96 "Ursprungsimpulse der Geisteswissenschaft" (Original impulses of the science of the spirit), Berlin, Lecture of 25 March 1907

where the source of existence originates, where all life impulses and streams of existence flow. The initiate alone has the absolute prospect of the seventh degree of Devachan or spirit land." [97]

After having accomplished life on Earth we may all participate in this sublime "hour of the sun" in after-death life. However, the vast majority of people pass through it unconsciously, i.e. asleep. Nevertheless, here they absorb forces which will enable them to consciously experience the passage through this high region sometime in the future.

Let us remember that in the higher spiritual world there are also the germs and preliminary stages underlying the archetypes of the lower spiritual world. The still unformed germs are parts of the so-called first elementary kingdom. – How this world of the Unformed, the Arupa world, is experienced by an initiate, the following words of Rudolf Steiner describe:

"Whoever has an eye for this system of all other world germs knows that these germs are of infinite beauty and grandeur. Everything that appears later on is only a faint reflection of what is germ-like in the first elementary kingdom. In this, there are the great intentions of the divine primordial Spirit, the intentions he has with the various worlds. And just as (developments) lag behind intentions, they also lag behind with regard to the world-existence, not as a whole, but in details. In the great variety of infinity, the intentions are wonderfully fulfilled. That is why Theosophy calls this first elementary realm the world of the unformed, which only later gives birth to the form out of itself." [98]

An extraordinarily sublime, highly spiritual "beauteousness of the worlds" is experienced by the disciples and initiates in the higher spiritual world, the Arupa sphere. This increases to the seventh region of the spiritual world, which is the home of the higher initiates and masters. They experience this "beauteousness of the worlds" combined with the inner call to surrender completely to it. In addition, they are called there to awaken to the insight, "to recognize the wise news", that now the "hour of the Sun" has come, in which they are enabled to reach the unio mystica, to unite or become one with the I of the World through intensive, feeling experience of the divine feeling that pervades themselves, as already described in the 10th weekly verse.

11. Week (16 - 23 June)	11. Woche (16. – 23. Juni)
In this hour of the sun,	Es ist in dieser Sonnenstunde
It's up to you, to recognize wise news:	An dir, die weise Kunde zu erkennen:
Surrendered to worlds' beauteousness,	An Weltenschönheit hingegeben,
Pervading feelingly your self in you by living through:	In dir dich fühlend zu durchleben:
The human I can lose itself	Verlieren kann das Menschen-Ich
And in world's I retrieve itself.	Und finden sich im Welten-Ich.

Truly it is an "hour of the sun" when man is allowed to experience that the human I, which has long since become cosmic, is finally allowed to surrender to the "worlds' beauteousness" of the divine intentions forming its environment, to lose himself into them and thereby find himself in the world's I. Rudolf Steiner described this highly sublime experience once again in the year after the publication of the weekly verses of the Soul Calendar in his fourth mystery drama "The Souls' Awakening" as part of Maria's experiences, who as the most advanced disciple of Benedictus is allowed to progress to the experience of the so-called world-midnight or midnight hour of existence between two incarnations. Before this occurs, the human spirit-soul goes through a state of highest spiritual light, a true "hour of the sun". This is why Maria speaks of "bright fields of light". Towards the end of Scene 10 of the fourth mystery drama, she tries to open the way for Johannes – who is intimately connected with her and in his aspiration following her example – to the two highest regions of the spiritual world, where he can see her in her true self. To this end, she radiates to him the power she has gained through a holy vow: [99]

---

[97] GA 88 "Über die astrale Welt und das Devachan" (About the astral world and the Devachan), Berlin, Lecture of 11 February 1904

[98] Ibidem, Lecture of 11 November 1903

[99] GA 14 "Vier Mysteriendramen" (Four Mystery Plays), 4th Drama "Der Seelen Erwachen" (The Souls' Awakening), 10. Bild (Scene 10)

MARIA:	MARIA:
Maria, as you wished to see her,	Maria, so wie du sie schauen wolltest,
She's not in worlds where shines the truth.	Ist sie in Welten nicht, wo Wahrheit leuchtet.
My holy solemn vow radiates power	Mein heilig ernst Gelöbnis strahlet Kraft,
That should preserve for you, what you achieved.	Die dir erhalten soll, was du errungen.
You find me in bright fields of light,	Du findest mich in hellen Lichtgefilden,
Where beauty radiantly creates life's forces;	Wo Schönheit strahlend Lebenskräfte schafft;
Seek me in world foundations, where souls	In Weltengründen suche mich, wo Seelen
Want to obtain the feeling of the gods	Das Götterfühlen sich erkämpfen wollen
Through love that sees the cosmos as the Self.	Durch Liebe, die im All das Selbst erschaut.

The generation of "life's forces" through radiant beauty as Maria describes it, clearly points to the sixth region of the spiritual world, where the preliminary stage of the life spirit wraps itself in its spiritual germ sheath. In the 10th weekly verse, which deals with the experiences in this sphere, reference was already made to the mutual interpenetration of human feeling and divine feeling. In Maria's words we additionally find the content of the 11th weekly verse, the finding of one's own self in the self of the universe or the world. Maria also mentions here the power that makes this possible for her. It is the love which as a unifying power flows from the higher Budhi plane through the upper three regions of the higher spiritual world. This love is a completely selfless one. It can only unite with a "human feeling" that has cast off all its "will's peculiarity", as it already happens with the entry into the fifth region of the spiritual world, as expressed accordingly in the 9th weekly verse. This shows that the contents of the 9th, 10th and 11th weekly verses belong together. They again are a set of three. What begins in the 9th weekly verse with the words "And strongly tells presentiment: Now lose yourself to find yourself" and leads to the interpenetration of human feeling by divine feeling in the 10th weekly verse, finds its fulfillment in the 11th weekly verse with finding the "human I" in "the world's I".

When we speak here of "human I", of course neither the I-consciousness of the terrestrial person is meant, nor the I on which this is based at the level of the Zodiac sphere, the fourth region of the spiritual world, but the I in the higher spiritual world, which is filled by the spirit self, quite in the sense of Rudolf Steiner's words in his book "Theosophy":

"The spirit develops the I from inside to outside. ... The spirit developing an «I» and living as an «I» is called «spirit self», because it appears as the «I» or «self» of man." [100]

In his book "Theosophy" Rudolf Steiner later gives further information about the sublime experiences of man in the seventh region of the spiritual world:

"The seventh region of the «spirit land» leads to the border of the «three worlds».[101] Here man faces the «life kernels» that are transferred from higher worlds to the three described ones in order to accomplish their tasks. When the human being is at the border of the three worlds, he thus recognizes himself in his own life kernel. This implies that the riddles of these three worlds must be solved for him. So he overlooks the whole life of these worlds. In physical life the abilities of the soul, through which it gets the experiences in the spiritual world described here, are not conscious under the ordinary circumstances of life. They work in its unconscious depths on the bodily organs that bring about the consciousness of the physical world. This is precisely the reason why they remain unperceivable for this world. The eye does not see itself either, because the forces that make other things visible are working in it." [102]

Today's average person lives in the materialistic worldview of his earthly I at the lowest border of the "three worlds", completely in the mineral sphere of the physical world, where he strives to satisfy his lower needs with the help of lifeless technology. The high initiates who guide humanity find their true I at the opposite border of the "three worlds", where they are pervaded by divine will, divine feeling and divine knowledge of truth. However, there is a mirror-like, intimate connection between this highest region of the spiritual world and the lowest region of the physical world. The "life kernel" of man – which, as already

---

[100] GA 9 "Theosophie" (Theosophy), Chapter "Das Wesen des Menschen" (The essential nature of man), Section IV, "Leib, Seele und Geist" (Body, soul and spirit)

[101] The "three worlds" are the physical world, the soul world and the spiritual world within which we develop during our present evolutionary phase. But through the germs of the life spirit and the spirit man, the "life kernel", which comes from even higher worlds, already further, future stages of evolution are planted in us in a germinal state.

[102] GA9 "Theosophie" (Theosophy), Chapter "Die drei Welten" (The three worlds), Section IV "Der Geist im Geisterland nach dem Tode" (The spirit in the spirit land after death)

mentioned above, consists of the life spirit or Budhi and the spirit man or Atma, both of which are only present in man as early preliminary stages – is only found as the "germ sheath" of the spirit man in the seventh and highest region of the spiritual world. In order to develop its early preliminary stage, man must work fully consciously on the transformation of his physical body, which is much more difficult than the work of the Chela on the ether body, which bears our habits, or even all our work on the astral body, which bears our emotions:

"There is something even more difficult to get under the control of free will than our habits, than emotions: that is the physical body in its animal and vegetative, mechanical or reflexive dependence. There is a stage of human development in which no nerve is activated, no globule of blood rolls without man's conscious will. This self-transformation intervenes in conditions and states that were fixed long, long before Atlantis and Lemuria, thus being the most habit-hardened, the most difficult to reverse: into primordial cosmic states. By this work man develops Atman, the spirit man. A preliminary stage for this is present in every person today. This whole cycle depends on the attainment of the fully clear I-consciousness.

The strongest, most powerful laws are those of the respiratory process. The whole spirit man depends on the breathing of the lungs, because it is the outer expression of the gradual moving in of the I. In the ancient Atlantean time this preliminary stage then came out by saying I. In Lemuria, man did not breathe through lungs but through gill-like organs. He also did not walk as he does today, but floated or swam in the more liquid element, where water and air were still undivided. To maintain the balance, he had an organ analogous to the swim bladder of a fish. The more the air gradually separated, the more this air bladder changed to our current lung. Parallel to the development of the lungs, the development of the I-consciousness is going on. This is preserved in the words: «And God breathed into him his breath of life, and he became a living soul.» Atman means nothing more than «breath» (in German: Atem). Breath regulation is therefore one of the strongest tools in yoga work, which teaches to master all functions of the body. With this we look into a future in which people will have transformed themselves from within." [103]

The regulation of the breath for the development of the early preliminary stage of the spirit man or Atma involves extraordinary dangers, since it works into the physical body. Moreover, the Eastern yoga methods which teach such breathing exercises are by no means beneficial to Western people, but virtually harmful because of the different constitution of their members of being. Moreover, a proper and health supporting breathing exercise is only be given directly by the teacher to the disciple.

"In the yoga training, the disciple brings a certain rhythm to his breathing by adjusting his inhaling, stopping breathing and exhaling to a certain number of seconds. However, the way of these breathing exercises can only be specified by the teacher to the disciple. Through the exercises for conscious regulation of the breathing process, nothing less is done than the beginning of alchemy." [104]

In this regard, overestimation of oneself is the greatest foolishness and actually only shows the student's immaturity. Anyone who follows the path of spiritual discipleship with real prudence will be fully aware, which great task the Chela's work on his life body is. Only if this is carried out consistently and responsibly, the Chela can expect that one day the master will in addition reveal to him the breathing exercises suitable for him, which he may then apply under the supervision of the master.

Ascension to the First Sphere of the World of the Life Spirit – 12th Week

With the ascension into the world of the Life Spirit or the Budhic plan we enter into the world of the Son, which exists beyond the world of the Holy Spirit. The lower three spheres of the former reach down to the upper three regions of the latter, so that the world of the Holy Spirit and the world of the Son mutually interpenetrate there. An initiate who is raised to the extraordinarily high level of consciousness in the lowest region or sphere of the world of the Son reaches the twelfth and highest human stage of consciousness for the time being. This is the topic of the 12th weekly verse.

Let us remember that the weekly verses of spring describe a development of the human I-consciousness, which starts with the birth of the I in life on Earth. As it says in the first weekly verse, the thought-based earthly I-consciousness only "dully bind(s) man's essence to the existence of the spirit". What begins there in a "dull" initial state is destined to develop through twelve stages up to world or cosmic

[103] GA 94 "Kosmogonie" (Cosmogony), Munich, Lecture of 28 October 1906

[104] Ibidem, Leipzig, Lecture of 10 July 1906

consciousness with the participation of the human being in the consciousness of God. Here once again some words of Rudolf Steiner, which were already quoted in the reflection on the first weekly verse:

"There are seven stages of human consciousness: trance consciousness, deep sleep consciousness, dream consciousness, waking consciousness, psychic, superpsychic and spiritual consciousness. There are actually twelve stages of consciousness in total; the five others are creative stages of consciousness. They are those of the creators, the creative gods. These are related to the twelve signs of the zodiac. Man must go through these twelve stages one after the other." [105]

Humanity will completely have reached the fourth level of consciousness, the I-consciousness or awake consciousness, only at the end of the Earth's development. At present, this consciousness is still on its mineral stage in most people. It therefore has a feature of the dull character of the trance consciousness. Man perceives himself as an I. But what this I actually is, that it is of divine nature and includes an almost breathtaking potential for development, most people today do not even have the slightest idea of it. Only in their deepest unconsciousness are they connected with the spiritual world in which their «I»s are rooted. The fact, that "I" and soul live in higher worlds every night, remains unconscious to them. In future epochs of evolution on Earth, human consciousness will unfold the evolutionary stages of the I-consciousness, which are analogous to trance, deep sleep and dream consciousness up to the goal of full waking and I-consciousness.

A bit later in the same lecture by Rudolf Steiner, from which the above quotation is taken, he opened up to his listeners another yet extremely important context:

"One can imagine a high being who has put all twelve stages of consciousness out of himself. He is there as the thirteenth, saying to himself: I could not be what I am if I had not separated these twelve stages of consciousness from myself. – We have this case in Christ with the twelve apostles. The twelve apostles represent the stages of consciousness through which Christ passed."

The representative of the lowest stage of consciousness, the I-consciousness in the sensory world, is Judas Iscariot. He lives entirely in the sensory world and is therefore most easily seducible, since his essence is only "dully" connected to the world of the spirit. He therefore expected the Kingdom of Christ to be established on Earth as a kingdom in the material world, and his betrayal is rooted, among other things, in his deep disappointment that all this did not happen. Judas thus represents materialism.

"Already in the time of Christ, the Spiritual had to be betrayed by the merely Material. Judas Iscariot had to betray Christ. But one can say: If there had been no Judas, there would be no Christianity either. Judas is the first one, who is attached to money, that is, to material culture. The whole material time incarnates in Judas. This material time has obscured and darkened the Spiritual. Christ becomes the Redeemer of the material time through his death." [106]

At the table of the Lord's Supper Judas sat directly opposite John, the disciple whom Jesus loved, as it says in John's Gospel. He corresponds to the exact opposite, twelfth and highest stage of consciousness. Hence he sat at the right hand of Christ.

"John had to develop up to Budhi in order to become able to comprehend what was revealed as the Christ Jesus. The other three evangelists were not so highly developed. John gives the highest. He was an awakened one. John is the name of all who are awakened. This is a generic name, and the Raising of Lazarus in the Gospel of John is nothing more than the description of this awakening. The writer of the Gospel of John – we will hear his name later – never names himself other than «the disciple whom the Lord loves». This is the term for the most intimate disciples, for those in whom the teacher and master has succeeded in awakening the disciple. The description of such an awakening is given by the author of the Gospel of John in the Raising of Lazarus: «the Lord loved him», he could awaken him. Only if we approach in deepest humility to such religious documents as the Gospel of John, may we hope to reach to the literal understanding and to open at least a small part of its sacred content to our understanding." [107]

That Christ loved John meant that he could pervade John's selfless soul and I with Budhi in an intensity that was not possible with any other of the twelve disciples. This intimate connection was illustrated to the other disciples by John resting on the breast of Jesus Christ, on his "heart, flaming with love", the Budhi organ.

"The whole gospel of John speaks in a strangely imagining language. Let's take an example. What does this mean: The disciple whom the Lord loves? – Just think that the writer of John's Gospel names himself:

---

[105] GA 93a "Grundelemente der Esoterik" (Foundations of esotericism), Berlin, Lecture of 26 September 1905

[106] GA 93a "Grundelemente der Esoterik" (Foundations of esotericism), Berlin, Lecture of 3 October 1905

[107] GA 94 "Kosmogonie" (Cosmogony), Munich, Lecture of 28 October 1906

«whom the Lord loves» and *«who lies on Jesus' breast»*. *This disciple is the external representative of the heart, the Budhi organ. What the heart is in the human body is John in the midst of the twelve disciples."* [108]

And in another lecture of the same cycle Rudolf Steiner explicated:

"The heart is organized for the future. It will be a very important organ. As Manas is now nourished in man by the blood circulation, thus will Manas work in the heart and from the heart then." [109]

Manas and Budhi will work together. All wisdom will then come from the heart, from the warmth of love, the Budhi. This wisdom is the spiritual source of the Gospel of John. Only a person, initiated by Christ Jesus himself, as John the favourite disciple was, could and can consciously be raised to this high stage. Therefore, the 12th weekly verse is rightly entitled with the words "John-Atmosphere" and dated June 24, on which Christianity commemorates the birth of John the Baptist. A further explanation about the "favourite disciple", intended by Rudolf Steiner, which due to his illness he unfortunately could not give as a second part of his so-called "last address", has been preserved as a verbal statement from him by Dr. Noll. He treated Rudolf Steiner together with Ita Wegmann. According to the verbal statement John the Baptist was intimately connected from the spiritual world with Lazarus, who was initiated by Christ himself and awakened to the "disciple whom the Lord loved" and who later wrote the Gospel of John.

"At the awakening of Lazarus the spiritual being of John the Baptist, who had been the spirit overshadowing the crowd of disciples since his death, entered the previous Lazarus from above to the consciousness soul and from below the being of Lazarus, so that the two interpenetrated each other. After the Raising of Lazarus, this is John, the «disciple whom the Lord loved»." [110]

There were two persons taking part in this high level of initiation. Hence their names are associated with it. Rudolf Steiner, however, did not entitle the 12th weekly verse with the words "John the Baptist", "John-Lazarus" or "John the Evangelist", but chose the title "John-Atmosphere" to express that this is a certain rank of initiation or a "generic name", as it says in the above quotation.

An exact assignment of the ten other disciples to the ten stages of consciousness or initiation between Judas and John is not handed down to us. However, it is obvious to associate the apostle Peter with the eleventh level and thus with the highest region of the spiritual world, the sphere of the germ sheath of the spirit man or Atman, the last stage below the Budhi plane. Through the highest human member of being the power of the Father-God works into us. This may be the reason why Peter was able, according to John 6:68, to say the words, *"You have words of eternal life; and we have believed and recognized that you are Christ, the Son of the living God"* or as it says in Matthew 16:16 *"You are Christ the Son of the living God"*, to which Christ replied, *"Blessed are you, Simon, Son of John; for flesh and blood has not revealed this to you, but my Father in heaven."* (Mt 16:17). Peter's connection with the Father-God is also expressed in the fact that he sat at the table of the Lord's Supper on the left of Christ Jesus, as the seer Anna Katharina Emmerich, for example, told us. [111] So Christ sat at the right hand of Peter, as the Son in heaven sits at the right hand of the Father. [112] Moreover, Peter was the one whom Christ himself instructed to follow him. Peter followed him through death. John the Baptist had already gone ahead. In this respect Peter was a son or successor of John. Accordingly, Christ called Simon Peter a "son of John" (Bar-Jonah) when he tested him for his relationship with Budhi three times, asking: *"Simon, son of John, do you love me more than these?"* (John 21:15-17) Christ knew that Peter had yet to go through death to find Budhi, the path that both John the Baptist and Lazarus had already taken. Therefore Christ added the meaningful words to Peter: *"Amen, Amen, I say to you, when you were younger, you girded yourself and went where you wished. But when you have grown old, you will stretch out your hands and someone else will gird you and lead you where you do not wish to go. This He spoke, signifying by what death he would glorify God. After these words He said to him: «Follow Me!»"* (John 21:18-19)

---

[108] Ibidem, Lecture of 6 November 1906

[109] Ibidem, Lecture of 31 October 1906

[110] GA 238 "Esoterische Betrachtungen karmischer Zusammenhänge" (Esoteric reflections on karmic connections – Karmic relationships), Volume 4, "Ergänzende Bemerkungen zum Inhalt der Ansprache vom 28. September 1924 (letzte Ansprache)" (Complementary remarks on the content of the speech of 28 September 1924 [last address])

[111] See, for example, A. K. Emmerich, "The bitter suffering of our Lord Jesus Christ", Chapter "Last Supper", Publisher: Pattloch Verlag; or Judith von Halle, "The Last Supper", Chapter "Annunciation at the Communion Table", Publisher: Verlag am Goetheanum

[112] e.g. letter of the apostle Paul to the Ephesians (1, 20)

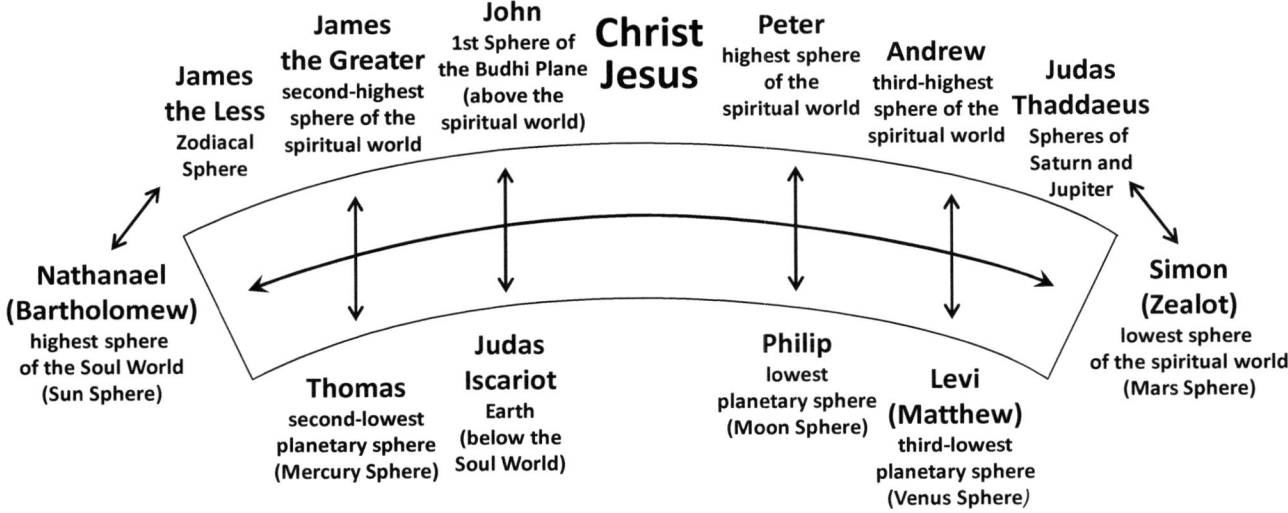

Figure 7: The 12 Apostles as representatives of the 12 stages of consciousness in the 12 spheres

A third one of the twelve disciples whom Christ raised to a higher level of consciousness was James the Greater, the brother of John Zebedee. He was allowed to witness the Transfiguration of Christ on the mountain, which means in the higher spiritual world, and to witness his spiritual conversation with the two deceased persons Elijah, who was reborn in John the Baptist but had already been murdered at this time, and Moses. James the Greater might represent the state of consciousness of the sixth region or second highest sphere of the spiritual world. According to this, at the Transfiguration, Christ would have presented himself clothed in the germ sheath of the life spirit in the higher spiritual world. Perhaps this is the deeper meaning of the words: *"His clothes became shining, exceedingly white, such as no launderer on Earth can whiten them."* (Mark 9:2-9) or *"As he prayed, the appearance of His face was altered, and His robe became bright white."* (Lk 9, 28-36). At the Communion table James the Greater was assigned the place next to John, the favourite disciple. He was therefore the second-nearest to Christ. (See figure 7)

The place at Peter's left hand was likewise the second-nearest to Christ. There, Andrew was placed, Peter's brother. According to Matthew 4:21 and Luke 5:10, Andrew and Peter, together with the two Zebedee sons, were among the first called disciples with whom Christ surrounded himself. All four were called as fishermen on the Galilean Sea. Andreas would thus represent the stage of consciousness of the fifth region or third highest sphere of the spiritual world, which is just pervaded by the lowest region of the Budhi plane. He had in common with Christ that he was crucified as well, on the Andrew Cross that was named after him.

Proceeding our consideration in this way, always looking alternately from left to right and each time one place further away from Christ Jesus, the next one would be James the Less, who sat beside James the Greater. The identical first names of the two might point to the very close connection between the evolutionarily older spirit self, the preliminary stage of which we have already received on the ancient Moon, and the younger I belonging to the evolution of the Earth, as Rudolf Steiner expresses in the words already quoted: *"The spirit developing an «I» and living as an «I» is called «spirit self», because it appears as the «I» or «self» of man."* [113] The I originates in the Zodiac sphere, as was explained in connection with the 8th weekly verse. James the Less would thus be the representative of the first extra-planetary or stellar state of consciousness. Consequently, together with Andrew, James the Greater, Peter and John, he may be assigned to the five creative stages of consciousness mentioned above by Rudolf Steiner, which exist beyond the seven planetary stages of consciousness.

The next disciple would be Judas Thaddaeus, who sat next to Andrew. This seat would certainly fit the stage of consciousness of the Saturn sphere, as this outermost of the seven planetary spheres is already oriented towards the starry sky. This fact would also correspond to the peculiarity of the 7th weekly verse, insofar as it additionally refers to the Jupiter sphere as the foundation of all life in the sensory world.

---

[113] GA 9 "Theosophie" (Theosophy), Chapter "Das Wesen des Menschen" (The essential nature of man), Section IV, "Leib, Seele und Geist" (Body, Soul and Spirit)

According to the law of reflection, the second region of the spiritual world is closely related to the sixth region of this world, from which the germ sheath of the life spirit, Budhi, is formed. With it the series of six apostles sitting on the same side of the table as Christ is concluded.

Simon the Zealot and Nathanael (Bartholomew) sat or lay at the two ends of the table, i.e. at the transverse axis between the rear and front half of the table. If one takes the rear half of the table on which Christ sat as a symbol of the spiritual world and the front half as a symbol of the soul world, the ends of the table between these two halves would represent the transition spheres from the spiritual world to the soul world. That would be the Mars sphere and the Sun sphere. Simon the Zealot would fit quite well to the Mars sphere as a "zealous" person. Nathaniel (Bartholomew) would then correspond to the level of consciousness of the Sun sphere, another quite sublime sphere. Here the side-change in the descending order of the spheres is reversed. Now it runs from right (Mars) to left (Sun), instead of from left to right as is the case with the upper half of the table. Apparently at this point the law of reflection becomes effective, in the sense that the higher is mirrored in the lower, which appears therefore mirror-inverted.

Levi (Matthew), who was sitting at the right-hand end of the table, next to Simon the Zealot, but at the front of the table, would therefore represent the level of consciousness of the Venus sphere, the first of the three sub-solar spheres, which are more facing the Earth. Levi was a customs officer. He already shows the influence of the sensory world, of earth- and matter-relatedness.

Thomas, sitting at the right of Bartholomew, but at the front of the table, may represent the Mercury sphere. That would fit in so far as Mercury rules arms and hands. Thomas needed a physical proof of the Resurrection. Christ took Thomas' fingers and put them into his wounds.

The Moon Sphere as the last one would be represented by Philip, who sat to the right of Judas. As Christ multiplied the bread, he asked Philip, testing him, where he should get the "bread" for the many people. Philip understood this in the material sense and replied that they only had 200 denarii at their disposal (John 6:7). Only Judas thought more materially and financially, who even let himself be paid for his betrayal with earthly currency and thus clearly represented the lowest level of consciousness. Figure 7 shows these seating arrangements of the twelve apostles at the Communion table. The place directly opposite Christ Jesus was kept free for serving up the food and also because none of the disciples reflected Him in His entire being. Rather, He reflected Himself in various ways in the Twelve.

Judas, who represents the state of consciousness just below the Moon sphere and thus below the soul world, sits opposite John, who represents the state of consciousness just above the spiritual world. Philip, the representative of the lowest state of consciousness of the soul world, i.e. the Moon sphere, sits opposite Peter, the representative of the highest state of consciousness of the spiritual world. The same mirror-image opposites exist between James the Greater (second highest state of consciousness of the spiritual world) and Thomas (second lowest planet sphere – Mercury sphere) as well as between Andrew (third highest state of consciousness of the spiritual world) and Levi (third lowest planetary sphere – Venus sphere). James the Less and Nathanael (Bartholomew) actually do not sit opposite each other, since the latter sits at the left longitudinal end of the table and is thus the table neighbour of the former. Perhaps this expresses the close relationship between the zodiac (James the Less) and the Sun (Nathaniel), which manifests in the fact that the sun follows a path in the sky through the signs of the zodiac and that together with this course in the succession of the months the forces of the zodiac are shown to us. Similarly, Judas Thaddeus and Simon the Zealot sit next to each other with Simon the Zealot at the right longitudinal end of the table, so that the two representatives of the upper three planetary spheres (Saturn/Jupiter and Mars) sit together. Upwards these spheres are bordered by the zodiac, downwards by the sun, whose representatives sit opposite them at the other longitudinal end of the table. In all these sets of two, both the Oppositional and the Common is emphasized every time. The seating arrangement of the twelve apostles at the table of the Lord's Supper, prescribed by Christ Himself, therefore certainly supports the attempted assignment of the twelve apostles to the twelve stages of consciousness.

But now back to the reflection of the 12th weekly verse, the "John-Atmosphere". Describing man's entry into the Budhi plane Rudolf Steiner combines it with the name of the favourite disciple John. As we can see in his highly spiritual gospel and his Apocalypse, he is one of the great, leading teachers of mankind, the so-called Bodhisattvas. They are human beings who in their development are so far ahead of the rest of humanity that they can function as teachers and spiritual leaders. They alone are able to rise fully consciously beyond the three worlds to the Budhi plane. All other people develop still within the three worlds below. But it is possible for them, though with more or less clear consciousness, depending on their respective stage of development, also to gain an insight into the Budhi plane from the higher spiritual world and to follow the way of the Bodhisattvas there to a certain extent:

"The human being, I said, goes up between death and a new birth to the upper Devachan or the world of reason. There he looks into higher worlds, in which he is not himself inside, and sees those beings

standing above him working in these higher worlds. While man is living his life in worlds from the physical plane to the Devachan plane, it is normal for a bodhisattva being to go up to the Budhi plane, which we in Europe call the world of Providence. This is a good word, for it is their task to lead the world from age to age with providence." [114]

Right at the beginning of the 12th weekly verse it becomes clear that the impulse to expand the consciousness of the human spirit to the Budhi plane does not originate from man himself. Here the human being is completely seized by the divine will, which now comes from an even more sublime world than that of "worlds' beauteousness" and flows through the human I that has become a world-I. But what is more sublime and noble than the "worlds' beauteousness" already mentioned in the 11th weekly verse? It is the aura surrounding it, its sheen or just "the sheen of the worlds' beauteousness". From this comes the impulse of will, which now elevates the human I to the "world-high flight" into a region beyond the three worlds, to the Budhi plane.

12 *John-Atmosphere (24 June)*	12 *Johannes-Stimmung (24. Juni)*
The sheen of the worlds' beauteousness	Der Welten Schönheitsglanz,
Compels me from the depths of soul	Er zwinget mich aus Seelentiefen
To set my own life's divine powers	Des Eigenlebens Götterkräfte
Free for the world-high flight;	Zum Weltenfluge zu entbinden;
To leave myself	Mich selber zu verlassen,
And confidently seek myself	Vertrauend nur mich suchend
In world-light and world-warmth.	In Weltenlicht und Weltenwärme.

The mutual interpenetration of the three lower regions of the Budhi plane with the three higher regions of the spiritual world has the consequence that in the latter not only the love power of the Budhi, but also its power of radiance and its sheen are perceptible.

"The other three regions of Devachan, which are even higher, are regions that are even more distantly connected to the Earth, regions that shine across, so to speak, from a completely different world. And when man, either as seer or in the time between death and a new birth, raises into this area, then he takes from this area everything that one would like to call the heavenly spark that man brings into this world. It is what appears to him as divine, as higher spiritual, as the real Idealistic that pushes in from the higher world and can only enter the physical world by him as higher morality, higher religiosity and finer spiritual science. All wisdom, all the higher sheen of existence that man, as a messenger of God, brings into this physical world, he takes from these three higher regions of Devachan." [115]

The origin of the "higher sheen of existence", however, is on the Budhi plane. There the "heavenly spark" of the human being is rooted, which endows him with his "own life's divine powers". The expansion of an initiate's consciousness to the Budhi plane is accomplished by means of an extremely intense impulse from his environment. It is so strong that Rudolf Steiner describes it as "compelling". For a descriptive characterization of the Budhi plane the terms are gradually missing. The highest things we find in the outside world of earthly existence are light and warmth. They can be borrowed as concepts from the sensory world in order to describe the shining, flaming divine love of the Budhi plane as "world-warmth" and the divine wisdom of the higher spiritual world arising from it as "world-light". This is where the divine part of the human being spreads. He can only do it because he is inwardly related to them.

Man's rising to the Budhi plane goes hand in hand with the complete removal of all being something special, even as a being of the starry world. Now all selfhood, all rudimentary feelings of separation from others must be left behind. Man must leave himself, his self, his own being, in order to be able to become one with and share in the universal and God-Self. Here, the human spirit-soul approaches its all-oneness in and with God in order to finally reach the knowledge of its unity of being with all beings. They all came out of God and are therefore of the same nature as him. But although every drop of the ocean is of the same nature as the ocean, it is not the ocean itself, just as every ray of light is of the same nature as the universal and world light and yet not this itself. Unity of being, however, is the basic condition for an existence on the Budhi plane. Only the one who has turned to the spiritual worlds in life on Earth already

---

[114] GA 116 "Der Christus-Impuls und die Entwicklung des Ich-Bewusstseins" (The Christ impulse and the development of the I-consciousness), Berlin, Lecture of 25 October 1909

[115] GA 53 "Ursprung und Ziel des Menschen" (Origin and destination of humanity), Berlin, Lecture of 17 November 1904

and moreover was able to feel his inner equality of being with all beings can hope to be allowed to experience this high state in a conscious way.

About one of those high initiates who were given access to the high region of the transition from the spiritual world to the Budhic world in their life on Earth, i.e. about the philosopher Philo of Alexandria[116], a description of his personal experience of this "worldhigh flight" has been handed down to us. Rudolf Steiner quotes the passage as part of his consideration of Philo's path of knowledge:

"This is the description of a path of knowledge that is held in such a way that one sees, whoever goes this way, is aware, that when the Logos comes alive in him, he flows together with the Divine. This is also clearly expressed in the words: «When the Spirit, seized by love, takes his flight into the holiest, with joyful swing, winged by God, he forgets everything else and himself, he is only filled by and clung to whom, whose satellite and servant he is and to whom he offers the holiest and most chaste virtue as a smoke-offering.»" [117]

Significantly, this initiate, who was allowed to experience the "world-flight" caused by Budhi or love, bears the name Philo from ancient Greek φίλο (philo) = to love.

Like Philo, Rudolf Steiner points out in the 12th weekly verse with the words "to leave myself" that for the person, who is experiencing this world-flight, even self-feeling is now lost after "will's peculiarity" has long been "forgotten".[118] Here the I leaves the "three worlds" within which it is to develop, solely by divine will. The whole Creation, and thus also man as part of it, once emerged from the divine Word, the Son of God. In the middle between two lifetimes on Earth he is allowed to return to his origin for some time and reunite with it. For this purpose the human I, which has become a world-I, spreads out or into the infinite Deity with the help of divine powers predisposed in him and fanned by the Deity himself. Now, however, there can no longer be any talk of "finding" the I. In infinity it remains in the state of searching, completely trusting in the divine love by which it feels carried and raised beyond the entire Creation.

Arrival in the Second Sphere of the World of the Life Spirit – 13th Week

In the physical world, the astral world and the spiritual world the human I is working on the transformation of its different sheaths. By doing so it acquires powers and develops itself to ever higher levels. For this development work it needs something outside of itself, an outside world. This is perceivable to the human I by means of the senses, which are parts of its sheaths in the respective world. So there are physical, astral and spiritual senses. At the upper limit of the three worlds, at the transition from the higher spiritual world to the Budhic world, the human spirit-soul, which has become a world-soul, reunites with the deity from which both it and all external worlds, which it has experienced on its path of development, emerged before primeval times. Everything is revelation from the inside of the Deity. Here, therefore, all external experience loses its meaning. Here is the highest limit, beyond which the soul experiences are no longer comparable to any sensory experiences. The "senses' heights" have been reached here. With the end of the sensory experience, however, all outside world is extinguished at the same time. Instead of this, the unity of the human self as well as the unity of the world with the Deity is now dawning on to man in immense and extraordinary experiences from within his world-soul, his "soul's depths". This transition from a cosmic outside world to a cosmic divine inside world does not happen suddenly. It was gradually prepared already in the spheres of the spiritual world. In a similar way as we are first devoted to the outside world illuminated by the Sun in life on Earth in the state of waking, but gradually tire with the waning light of the Sun and finally withdraw into our inner world through dream and sleep in order to accumulate new powers for the next day, so rhythmically two states always alternate with each other also in man's passage through the spheres after death.

"So the soul undergoes changing states. It is not always in the state that it radiates its spiritual luminous power spiritually over its environment, so that human souls and other beings are around it and spiritual processes are experienced by it. Thus, it is not always the case that the soul lives in the outer spiritual world, but this state must alternate with a state that the soul feels this radiating of spiritual luminous power

---

[116] Philo of Alexandria, Jewish philosopher and theologian (ca. 15/10 BC to after 40 AD).

[117] GA 8 "Das Christentum als mystische Tatsache" (Christianity as mystical fact), Chapter "Plato als Mystiker" (Plato as a mystic)

[118] See 9th weekly verse

deadening, so to speak. The soul becomes dull inside, it is no longer able to radiate its light on the environment. It must concentrate in itself its whole existence. And now the moment comes when in the meantime between death and a new birth the soul lives a completely lonely life. This takes a long time. If you want to compare it with ordinary life, you can say: As in ordinary life, man has to alternate between sleep and wakefulness, so after death he has to alternate between a life that pours out into the outside world and a life of inner solitude, when everything that one experienced before in the state of widening has been absorbed, when the soul knows however: You are now quite lonely with yourself. Just as one becomes unconscious in sleep, so one withdraws into oneself here, but does not become unconscious. The soul gains a strengthened consciousness especially in these times of solitude, but it experiences it in such a way that it knows: out there is the spiritual world, but you are alone with yourself. Everything that you experience, you experience in yourself. – The experiences within oneself are the echoes of what one has experienced outside of oneself. Only in this way the inner luminous power can regain its strength and emerge from the soul. And then one wakes up spiritually again and undergoes the other state again.

It is one of the strangest experiences to really learn to understand the statement that for the time between death and a new birth the soul lives in spiritual conviviality and solitude, that this alternation of states of social experience and loneliness in the spiritual world – but for much longer periods than day and night – means regarding this after-the-death experience something like sleeping and waking in the physical experience. I have hinted at these conditions in my penultimate book: «The Threshold of the Spiritual World».[119] But when living on between death and a new birth, the soul experiences a gradually dulling, a fading of its luminous power. One would like to say: The experiences of inner loneliness are getting stronger and stronger. They gradually become such that man experiences a whole world inside, one would like to say a whole cosmos. Truly, it becomes so, that it is justified to say: something like the feeling of fear of himself overcomes man when he discovers what is down there in the undergrounds of the soul, and what comes out now, approximately in the middle of life between death and a new birth." [120]

13th Week (30 June – 6 July)	13. Woche (30. Juni – 6. Juli)
And am I in the senses' heights,	Und bin ich in den Sinneshöhen,
Then flames in my soul's depths	So flammt in meinen Seelentiefen
Out of the spirit's fire-worlds	Aus Geistes Feuerwelten
The Truth Word of the Gods:	Der Götter Wahrheitswort:
In spirit's backgrounds seek, by sensing,	In Geistesgründen suche ahnend
To find yourself akin to spirit now.	Dich geistverwandt zu finden.

Rudolf Steiner dealt with the passage of the soul through the midnight hour of existence also in his fourth mystery drama "The Souls' Awakening" and gave some explanations in his lecture cycle "The Secrets of the Threshold":

"What the souls experience in their Devachanic time is different, depending on whether the souls have undergone this or that preparation on Earth. When the soul passes through what is called the world-midnight with consciousness in the Devachanic time, this must be understood as a significant soul experience. Souls who are not prepared for this, experience this world-midnight in such a way that the souls sleep, so to speak, in that time which can be called the Saturn time of Devachan. For the successive times that the souls undergo between death and a new birth, may be described with reference to the individual planets as Sun time, Mars time, Mercury time, and so on. Some souls oversleep, as it were, this world-midnight." [121]

Rudolf Steiner's subdivision of man's development between death and new birth into periods, which he relates to the planets, must not be confused with the planetary spheres. It only shows that the spiritual experiences in the after-death life may be meaningfully structured in various ways, without the different views to contradict each other. Rather, they complement each other as observations from different perspectives.[122] In his Soul Calendar, Rudolf Steiner has chosen an even more specific approach. He

---

[119] GA 17 "Die Schwelle der geistigen Welt" (The Threshold of the Spiritual World)

[120] GA 153 "Inneres Wesen des Menschen und Leben zwischen Tod und neuer Geburt" (The inner nature of man and life between death and rebirth), Vienna, Public Lecture of 8 April 1914

[121] GA 147 "Die Geheimnisse der Schwelle" (Secrets of the threshold), Munich, Lecture of 24 August 1913

[122] For more information, see the chapter "Reflections of the human incarnation cycle in the annual rhythm of nature" after the 41st weekly verse

subdivides the course of time from life on Earth to the world-midnight in thirteen sections, corresponding to the thirteen weeks of a quarter of a year. Further it says in the lecture above:

"Prepared souls awake in the time of their spiritual life at that world-midnight. But this does not yet mean that such souls, who consciously, i.e. being awake, experience the world-midnight through their corresponding preparation between death and a new birth, also bring an awareness of this experience into life on Earth when they come to physical existence. For Maria, for Johannes Thomasius this happens in such a way that they experienced the world-midnight appropriately prepared in their spiritual time between death and new birth, but that in the beginning of their earth life and through long times of it, a kind of soul-gloom has spread over the experience in the world-midnight, and that it emerges in a later stage of the present earth life. It only appears, however, when a certain inner calmness and cohesion of the soul has occurred."

In the mystery drama "The Souls' Awakening" Rudolf Steiner describes the way in which in Maria and Johannes the memory of their passage through the world-midnight between their last life and the present dawned, experienced by them with waking consciousness. Of course, in life on Earth, the process is somewhat different than being experienced in the state after death. At first, to Maria's introspection is shown an icy cold spiritual light. But then flames ignite in the depths of her soul. In this coldness and the flaming fire her thinking and feeling fight with each other. Mary finally struggles her way through to the experience of the world-midnight. The flames turn out to be the Budhi working down into the regions of the spiritual world. They exhaust her thinking, because the events of the world-midnight can only be experienced with the soul power of feeling:[123]

MARIA:

The ice's cold is burning in my self,
Igniting flames in my soul's depths;
The flames exhaust my thinking.

MARIA:

Des Eises Kälte brennt in meinem Selbst,
Es zündet Flammen mir in Seelentiefen;
Die Flammen zehren mir das Denken auf.

Benedictus tells her that Johannes is experiencing something similar:

BENEDICTUS:

In your soul's depths the fire's flaming,
That in the world-frost flares up to Johannes.

BENEDICTUS:

In deinen Seelentiefen flammt das Feuer
Das sich im Weltenfrost Johannes zündet.

The parallel of Maria's soul experiences with the 13th weekly verse, in which it says "And am in the senses' heights, then flames in my soul's depths out of the spirit's fire-worlds the Truth Word of the Gods" cannot be overlooked. As a student of Benedictus, Maria experiences here her view into the Budhi plane as the flare-up of a spiritual fire world in her soul's depths. According to Rudolf Steiner, the full ascension to the Budhi plane is still reserved for the Bodhisattvas, who encounter the Christ Being there, who comes to meet them from even higher worlds. But they only precede all others, for their disciples will also gradually mature to be able to follow their masters:

"From the other side He [Christ] also works into those worlds into which the Bodhisattvas ascend when they leave the region of mankind[124] to learn for themselves so that they can then become teachers in mankind. From above, from the other side, such a being as the Christ approaches them. Then they are the disciples of the Christ. Twelve Bodhisattvas surround such a being as Christ is, and we cannot speak of more than twelve at all, for when the twelve Bodhisattvas have accomplished their mission, we have finished the time of earthly existence.

The Christ was physically there one time and has gone through that which includes descent, arrival on Earth and ascension. He comes from the other side and is the being in the middle of the twelve Bodhisattvas, who get there what they have to carry down to Earth. So the Bodhisattva beings ascend between two incarnations up to the Budhi plane, and down to the Budhi plane reaches that which comes to meet them fully-consciously as teacher: the Christ being. On the Budhi plane the Bodhisattvas encounter the Christ. And when people progress and develop the qualities that are instilled in them by the

---

[123] GA 14 "Vier Mysteriendramen"(Four mystery plays) – 4th Play "Der Seelen Erwachen" (The Souls' Awakening), at the end of Scene 4

[124] The "region of humanity" encompasses the three worlds below the Budhi plane: the physical, astral and spiritual worlds. Cf. here the consideration to the 12th weekly verse.

Bodhisattvas, then they will also become more and more mature in order to reach up into the same sphere." [125]

At this point the question may arise, how it is possible that the Bodhisattvas and their disciples are able to encounter the Christ at the upper pole of the human incarnation cycle, on the lower levels of the Budhi plane, whereas Christ has connected himself with the Earth since the mystery of Golgotha and is to be sought by humans especially in their lives on Earth. Even in the Sun sphere he no longer can be found, but only his "Akasha image" and his "empty throne", as we have learned from the reflections on the 5th weekly verse. How could it be possible, still farther away from the Earth, even in the most remote region at all, to encounter Christ so directly and vividly? The reason is given in the fact that humans do not only spatially move away from the Earth on the path of their after-death development. Space loses its meaning relatively quickly. In the soul world, time is the predominant characteristic. Already during life on Earth all soul experiences are going on in time, forming a series of memories, completely independent of all spatial conditions. The influence of time reaches up to planetary spheres and thus to the upper limit of the lower spiritual world. In the Sun sphere, for example, the principle of time is still effective. For this reason, there are different experiences before and after the mystery of Golgotha in this sphere. However, with the transition from the planetary spheres into the Zodiac sphere, the gateway to the higher spiritual world, the human spirit-soul leaves all connection with the Temporal and enters the realm of eternity and duration. For this reason, the Bodhisattvas experience the Christ there as he is in eternity, in full glory and sublimity, uninfluenced by all temporal limitations, although they receive teachings from Him with the participation of the Holy Spirit, which they then carry down into time and space to the various cultures and peoples. The experiences on the Budhi plane are therefore in no way in conflict with today's unity of the Christ Being with the Earth. Christ is also always our companion and the keeper of our I throughout our entire incarnation cycles.

Thus, after the 12th weekly verse, which Rudolf Steiner himself associates with John as representative of the highest level of human consciousness, in the 13th weekly verse follows the reference to the Logos by the phrase "the Truth Word of the Gods". In the prologue of his Gospel, it is John, who describes Him as the Word through which everything came into being:

"In the prime beginning was the Word; and the Word was with God, and the Word was a God. This was in the prime beginning with God. Everything has come into being through this, and without this nothing of what was made has come into being. In this was the life, and the life was the light of men. And the light shone into the darkness, but the darkness did not comprehend it.

There became a man, sent from God, with his name John. This one came for a witness, to bear witness of the Light, that through him all should believe. He was not the Light, but a witness of the Light. For the true Light which enlightens all human beings, was to come into the world.

It was in the world, and the world has come into being through it, but the world has not recognized it. It came to the individual human beings (it came as far as the I-humans); but the individual human beings (the I-humans) did not receive it." [126]

Christ is the Creator Word. But He is even more. He says of himself: *"I am the way, the truth and the life. No one comes to the Father but through me."* (John 14:6) He is therefore also the way of all creatures back to the Father. He is also the truth, or "the Truth Word" observed by all creative spirit-beings of the Hierarchies who serve Christ, "the Truth Word of the Gods", and He is the spirit of life, the life spirit or the Budhi. Therefore, we must ascend to the Budhi plane if we want to meet Him directly in His own world. As we die we die towards him, get ever closer to Him through all astral and spiritual spheres until we finally and really die into Him. The "in Christo morimur" becomes an absolute reality here. But it is precisely through this dying into Christ that we may have a share in Him, in eternal life, which is sublime above the three lower worlds. The Creator Spirit, the Truth Spirit, the Life Spirit rises here in us, so that we may also experience the words of Paul: *"But now no longer I live, but Christ lives in me"* (Gal 2:20) in absolute reality during the world-midnight. "Out of the spirit's fire-worlds", from the Budhi plane, "flames in our souls' depths the Truth Word of the Gods", flames in us the Budhi, flames in us the life spirit. [127]

---

[125] GA 116 "Der Christus-Impuls und die Entwicklung des Ich-Bewusstseins" (The Christ impulse and the development of the I-consciousness), Berlin, Lecture of 25 October 1909

[126] John 1:1-11, translated by Rudolf Steiner in GA 97 "Das christliche Mysterium" (The Christian Mystery), Heidelberg, Lecture of 3 February 1907. Rudolf Steiner himself added the words inserted in brackets in handwriting.

[127] See also the 19th lesson of the First Class of the School of Spiritual Science

By opening up the access to the Budhi plane for us, Christ has opened a door to our redemption from the cycle of incarnation. However, we are only allowed to pass through it after we have got all the experiences that can be accumulated during our numerous lives on Earth across the many ages. Only when we have reached the appropriate maturity of development will we become free through and in Christ. He brought us a preliminary stage of the Budhi as a heavenly gift already in ancient Lemuria. As the highest of the Sun spirits, already then he had the most significant influence on human evolution on Earth.

"Many such Fire Spirits had developed on the Sun and were high Spirits on Earth. One of these Fire Spirits was called to pour out his being upon all mankind. For the whole Earth there was a communal spirit that could pour out the element of the Sun Spirits or Fire Spirits, the Budhi or the life spirit, over all mankind into all its members. But in the Lemurian race and in the Atlantean period people were not yet ripe to receive anything from this Sun Spirit. In the Akasha chronicle one can see something very strange about that time, namely that humans consisted of physical body, ether body, astral body and the spirit self. But the spirit self was only in a very weak way in men. The Budhi or the life spirit floated around everyone, but this could only be noticed in the astral space. Everyone had such a Budhi-environment in the astral space; but this Budhi, which floated around man from the outside, was not yet ripe to penetrate into him. It was part of the one great Fire Spirit, who had poured out his drops on the people; they just could not yet penetrate into the people. Through the deed of Christ on Earth, the preliminary states were developed in the human beings, that they could receive into their Manas what we call Budhi.

What Christ did on Earth was prepared by the other great teachers who preceded, Buddha, the last Zarathustra, Pythagoras, who all lived about six hundred years before Christ. These were such spirits who had already integrated much of what the other people had only floating around them. They had absorbed this spark of Christ into the I-man. Moses also belonged to these spirits. But the other people had not yet received this spark in the I-man.

What entered the physical body, ether and astral body of Jesus of Nazareth is this whole Fire Spirit, the common source of all these spiritual sparks for mankind. This is the Christ, the only divine being who in this way is not present on Earth in any other form. He came into the Jesus of Nazareth so that those who felt connected to the Christ Jesus, received the power to absorb the Budhi. With the appearance of the Christ Jesus the possibility begins to receive the Budhi. This is what John called the divine Creator Word. The divine Creator Word is this Fire Spirit who poured out his sparks into men." [128]

But Christ is the "Truth Word" as well, or as it says according the words quoted above from the prologue of the Gospel of John: *"the true light which enlightens all human beings"*. We can take it into our consciousness soul, which is pervaded by the spirit self, so that Budhi-Manas[129] is formed. This connection between the consciousness soul and the truth may be pointed out once again with the words of Rudolf Steiner quoted already at the end of the reflection on the 8th weekly verse:

"When man lets revive in his inner being the independent true and good, he rises above the mere sentient soul. The eternal Spirit shines into it. A light brightens in it that is imperishable. If the soul lives in this light, it shares in an Eternal. It connects its own existence with that. What the soul bears as truth and good in itself is immortal in it. – That which brightens in the soul as eternal is here called consciousness soul. ... The kernel of human consciousness, the soul in the soul, is meant here with consciousness soul. The consciousness soul is distinguished here as a special member of the soul from the intellectual soul. The latter is still involved in the sensations, the desires, affects and so on. Everyone knows how he first considers that to be true, what he prefers in his sensations and so on. But only that t r u t h is the enduring truth which has detached itself from all the tastes of such sympathies and antipathies of the sensations and so on. The truth is true, even if all personal feelings rebel against it. The part of the soul in which this truth lives is called here the consciousness soul.

Thus, as in the body, one would also have to distinguish three members in the soul: the sentient soul, the intellectual soul and the consciousness soul. And as the corporeality has a limiting effect on the soul from below, so the spirituality has an expanding effect on it from above. For, the more the soul fills itself with the true and the good, the wider and more comprehensive the eternal in it develops. – To the person who is able to «see» the soul, the shine that emanates from man, because his eternal expands, appears as a reality just as the light that radiates from a flame is real to the sensual eye." [130]

---

[128] GA 97 "Das christliche Mysterium" (The Christian Mystery), Cologne, Lecture of 2 December 1906

[129] See also the reflection on the 9th weekly verse

[130] GA 9 "Theosophie" (Theosophy), Chapter "Das Wesen des Menschen" (The essential nature of man), Section IV, "Leib, Seele und Geist" (Body, soul and spirit)

In another lecture Rudolf Steiner elucidated in the same context about the meaning of the I, which is so closely connected with the spirit self and the consciousness soul:

"In man, it is the I that first crystallises out the state of equilibrium and shows him the way in life. The I also gives man his concepts, his thoughts, his knowledge. In the animals we only have instincts. Through his knowledge man gains wisdom, t r u t h. So we can say: in childhood, man takes up the enlivening forces of the universe through the work of the I. It gives him his life. Through the I man straightens himself up, he finds his way. Through the I, man gains knowledge that leads him to the truth. In early childhood, it thus works on the formation of the human body, unconsciously for the human being. The same, raised to a higher level, sought in a spiritual way, comes close to man when he pervades himself with Christ. When the Christ has come to life in the soul, when the soul has thereby found the direction of its goal, of its way, when it recognizes the truth of the higher worlds, then this I, which is present in man, speaks: I am the way, the truth and the life. – And man feels: thus is not spoken by his personal earthly I, but so does the Christ speak in man." [131]

The truth is in intimate connection with the divine life forces or the Budhi, as Rudolf Steiner emphasized in lectures in Berlin and Heidenheim:

"When you hear from occultists that lying is murder and suicide, it acts as an impulse with such an ethical force that it cannot be compared to the simple admonition: You shall not lie. – If you know what lies and what truth is, if you know that everything has its imprint in the spiritual, then things will change. The narrative corresponding to the t r u t h produces the life forces for further development. The incorrect assertion hits the truth and hits back at man himself. Each lie of a person, he later will have to feel. Lies are the greatest obstacles to further development. It is not for nothing that the devil is called the Spirit of Lies and Obstacles. The explosive substance of a lie objectively kills and it breaks over the one who sends it out." [132]

"Everything has an effect in life. If man abandons himself to an error or a lie, even if he is not aware of this in his ordinary consciousness, it is still present in the subconscious, where it acts as a destructive force not only for the individual person but for the entire evolution of the world. Likewise, when a person unites with the forces of truth, this continues to work as a life-creating force for the whole development of the world and humanity." [133]

Truth really is a very significant power, connecting us with the Budhi, the eternal life. But by doing so it has yet another effect of great importance: it sets us free. Christ, the Truth Word himself, has proclaimed this to his disciples already during his life on Earth:

"Then Jesus said to the Jews who believed in him, «If ye abide in my speech, ye are my true disciples, and ye shall know the truth, and the truth shall make you free.»" (John 8:31-32)

Some readers may ask at this point perhaps wondering: "But, are not love and compassion much more important than the knowledge of the truth?" Rudolf Steiner replied to this:

"You always hear people say, «The main thing is love and compassion». Certainly love and compassion is the main thing, but only knowledge can make love and compassion fruitful. It gives a comfort, and this is not rare, even among those who believe that they aspire to the spirit. To say «love» is something you can learn in a second. – To acquire knowledge for the redemption and blessing of mankind, needs an eternity. And to take up this in consciousness in us that knowledge is the basis of all real spiritual activity, this must increasingly become the point of the theosophical movement." [134]

In the same sense, Rudolf Steiner spoke at a lecture in Düsseldorf:

"So the great mission of man is that he should bring free will into the world, and only together with free will that which is called love in the true sense of the word. Because, without free will, love is impossible. A being who must necessarily follow an impulse, just follows it; for a being who can also act differently, there is only one power to follow: love. Free will and love are two poles that belong together. Therefore, if love should enter into our cosmos, this could only happen through free will, that is, through Lucifer and his

---

[131] Beiträge zur Rudolf-Steiner-Gesamtausgabe Nr. 54, Ostern 1976 (Contributions to the Rudolf Steiner Complete Edition, No. 54, Easter 1976), Lecture by Rudolf Steiner of 4 March 1911 in Hanover

[132] GA 96 "Ursprungsimpulse der Geisteswissenschaft" (Original impulses of the science of the spirit), Berlin, Lecture of 12 June 1907

[133] GA 127 "Die Mission der neuen Geistesoffenbarung" (Mission of the new revelation of the spirit), Appendix, Heidenheim, Notes from the lecture of 30 November 1911

[134] GA 96 "Ursprungsimpulse der Geisteswissenschaft" (Original impulses of the science of the spirit), Berlin, Lecture of 7 May 1906

conqueror, and at the same time through the Saviour of man, through the Christ. Therefore, the Earth is the cosmos of love and free will.

... And what will be said about man when we classify him among the Hierarchies? After the Archangels and Angels, the Arch-Messengers and Messengers, the Spirit of Free Will or the Spirit of Love will have to be added to the series of Hierarchies, and this is, starting from above, the tenth of the Hierarchies, which however is still developing. But it belongs to the spiritual Hierarchies. There is no repetition in the universe, but every time when a round is completed, something new is added to the evolution of the world. And adding this new is always the mission of the corresponding Hierarchy, which is at the level of its mankind." [135]

When today's man has become a universal world-soul in the higher spiritual world and has subsequently returned to the divine source of his own origin, he cannot yet fully preserve his I-consciousness. Therefore, the last two weekly verses have in common that they emphasize the searching and pre-sensing through which the spirit-soul, which has become the universe, strives to find itself. "And confidently seek myself in cosmic world-light and world-warmth" says the 12th weekly verse. The 13th weekly verse elaborates on this with the words: "In spirit's backgrounds seek, by sensing, to find yourself akin to spirit now." It seems as if at the time of the midnight hour of existence man is threatening to lose himself rather than to find himself. But that will not always be the case. With each incarnation on Earth the human I will be strengthened and it will become more and more possible for the people to maintain their I-consciousness also on the higher planes. The individualized human souls can be compared to water drops that have emerged from a common, divine primordial sea. Every single one of these soul-water-drops is coloured according to his very individual experiences, which he collects in the course of his numerous incarnations on Earth and the passages in between through the spiritual spheres.

"Being absorbed in the universal consciousness is redemption – as they say in the East. It won't be like that. Formerly, prior to the first embodiment, there was no I-consciousness. But it will be there after the last incarnation. Each drop of the one soul fluid colours itself with a very specific colour, each with a different one. In the end, each one brings his own colour, and the formerly bright, clear water becomes iridescent of infinitely beautiful, shining colours. But each one is there on its own. Each person brings along his own particular colour, his individual consciousness, which is unloseable. Harmony of all consciousnesses is the universal consciousness at last. By free will, the many will be one unit, because they want to be so! We should imagine what it's really like. Every single consciousness is completely contained in the universal consciousness." [136]

Developing free will and love is the mission of mankind. The way in which after death, on the one hand, we carry our I-consciousness through the "in Christo morimur" from the Earth up to the source of all truth, the Truth Word, on the Budhi plane, in order to develop free will, this is described in the first thirteen weekly verses of the summer half-year. The way in which in the course of our "in Christo morimur", on the other hand, we reach to the source of all love in the "love-worlds of the heart", and thereby develop the creative power of our I, the acting out of love, we will find described in the weekly verses of the winter half-year. In this way, the two great missions of humanity, the development of free will and the development of love, are distributed over the two halves of the year. We develop free will by learning to see through the outer Maya, the illusion, the error, and expand our consciousness until the knowledge of truth. We develop love by learning to overcome our inner egoism, the desires and instincts, and by advancing towards doing the good out of selfless love. In the development of free will through the realization of truth, the natural moods of the summer half-year help us to direct our attention out into the external world. In the development of love, on the other hand, the natural moods of the winter half-year help us by encouraging us to withdraw into ourselves and direct our attention inwards.

But free will through knowledge of the truth also requires an alert, clear I-consciousness. Free will without I-consciousness is just as impossible as free will without knowledge of the truth. Therefore, the development of the I-consciousness is at the centre of humanity's evolution. We will only be able to bring it to full bloom together with Christ. Without the Christ impulse we would be able to maintain our I-consciousness only on Earth, but not during the after-death ascension to the higher spheres and certainly not at the time of the great midnight hour of existence, which we are to live through more and more I-consciously. After we have given up our personal thinking, willing and feeling and after their replacement with divine thinking, divine willing and divine feeling, our last own, which remains, is only our I-consciousness.

---

[135] GA 110 "Geistige Hierarchien und ihre Widerspiegelung in der physischen Welt" (Spiritual Hierarchies and their reflection in the physical world), Düsseldorf, Lecture of 18 April 1909

[136] GA 97 "Das christliche Mysterium" (The Christian Mystery), Leipzig, Lecture of 17 February 1907

"Until that point in time, we have to preserve the connection with our I. We must, as it were, preserve the one memory: You were this I on Earth. This I must remain as a memory. That we are able do so in our time cycle depends on the fact that the Christ has brought the power into the Earth aura, which otherwise would not be brought along from earthly life, the power that enables us to preserve the memory until the midnight hour. There would be a rupture, a gap, so to speak, that would make our existence inharmonious in the middle between death and a new birth, if the Christ impulse did not flow through the earthly world. Long before the midnight hour, we would forget that we have been an I in the last life. We would feel the connection with the spiritual world, but would forget ourselves. And this is caused by the fact that we really develop our I so strongly on Earth. Since the Mystery of Golgotha, it has become necessary to come more and more to this I-consciousness. However, as we gain more and more our I-consciousness on Earth, we use up the powers we need after death in order to really not forget ourselves until the midnight hour of existence. To preserve this memory, we must die into the Christ. Hence the Christ impulse had to be there: Until the midnight hour of existence, He maintains for us the possibility not to forget our I." [137]

At the current stage of development, if we allow ourselves to be fulfilled with the Christ impulse, we are enabled to carry our I-consciousness up to the lowest regions of the Budhi plane. The aim of the I-development, however, is that we unite it once on the Atmic plane with the primordial power of all consciousness, with the Father.

"Jesus says: «We shall dwell with the Father.» That was the most important thing at the outpouring of the Spirit, which began with the words: «May Your heart remain calm.» For his intimate disciples, Christ goes to prepare the dwelling: «In the house of the Father are many dwellings.»

Let us be clear about these words. Man can never lose the degree of consciousness that he once attained. You should give up any other idea. People so often indulge in «being absorbed in the universal consciousness» and think that this is a redemption. Such kind of universal consciousness does not exist and will never exist. The ability to say «I» is now achieved by man. And the more he says «I» and works from the I on the purification of his three lower bodies, the astral body, ether body and physical body, the more strongly he develops his I and develops into the future. So man can become consciously selfless because he wants to. One day all human beings will have reached the summit of I-development. Nevertheless they can selflessly comprehend the spirit of community. We are sitting here in this room, and the common spirit inside is like a point from which everything radiates in common. But this common spirit can also radiate voluntarily out of every heart and buzz through space. Let us remember how Deity is reflected in the world. He poured all His life into His mirror image through the great sacrifice. Now let us imagine that we could also pour our lives into countless mirror images, so that every single mirror image would say: I and my origin are one. – Thus, once all human beings emerged from the womb of Deity like mirror images of the Deity. They are finally empty «I»s with a transformed astral body, ether body and physical body, and they enter the spiritual world and say the deepest mystery of their being: «I and the Father are one!» The animal men of the Lemurian time could never become spiritual on their own; only by taking in the divine drops. At the end of their development, purified and purged, they can say: «I and the Father are one.» ...

The Father Spirit, the spirit of the common origin, must enter into the individual «I»s. Then the I works on the Father principle; then each I builds its own house, and yet they are all united by the Christ principle. «In my father's house, there are many dwellings», says Christ. This refers to the dwelling that the «I»s are building for themselves. Christ, however, must prepare the place, the dwelling place. But this to happen, the Spirit must come who unites the human beings. That is the Spirit of truth." [138]

The "Spirit of Truth" is the Holy Spirit, who opens to the human beings the understanding of the Son of God, the Truth itself, through universally valid wisdom teachings that unite the human beings of all peoples and languages. In this sense Plato also spoke in his song of praise about the love of truth or, as he calls it, of the "true philosophy". It is handed down to us at the end of its Timaios, from which Rudolf Steiner once quoted the following passage and commented afterwards:

"«And now we would also like to assert that our discussions about the universe have reached their goal, for after this world has been equipped and filled with mortal and immortal living beings in the manner described, it has (by that) become itself a visible being of this kind, which encompasses everything visible, a likeness of the Creator and a sensorily perceptible God and has become the greatest and best, the most beautiful and most perfect (which could exist), this one world, born out of unity.»

---

[137] GA 153 "Inneres Wesen des Menschen und Leben zwischen Tod und neuer Geburt" (The inner nature of man and life between death and rebirth), Vienna, Lecture of 14 April 1914

[138] GA 97 "Das christliche Mysterium" (The Christian Mystery), Cologne, Lecture of 8 March 1907

But this one world, born out of unity, would not be perfect if it did not also have the likeness of the Creator himself among its likenesses. Only from the human soul can this likeness be born. Not the Father Himself, but the Son, the offspring of God, who lives in the soul and resembles the Father: to Him, man can give birth.

Philo, who was said to be the resurrected Plato, called this wisdom born out of man, which lives in the soul and has as its content the reason that exists in the world, the «Son of God». This world-reason, the Logos, appears as the book in which «all the world-store is registered and drawn in». It appears further as the Son of God: «imitating the Father's ways, looking at the archetypes, He forms the figures». The platonizing Philo addresses this Logos as the Christ: «Since God is the first and only king of the universe, the way to him has rightly been called the Royal; but let us regard philosophy as this way ... the way, which the choir of ancient ascetics walked, which was turned away from the bewitching magic of lust, devoted to the worthy and serious care of the beautiful; this Royal Way, which we name true philosophy, is called the law: God's Word and Spirit.».” [139]

Such words can only be spoken by someone who was allowed to raise himself up into the highest regions of spiritual life, into the immediate presence of Christ on the Budhi plane. Persons of that kind are in particular those who undertake very special missions for the evolution of mankind. Probably the most important of them is "the disciple whom Jesus loved", who was initiated and awakened in his consciousness during his life on Earth up to the Budhi plane, by Christ-Jesus. But there are more human beings who have already been "awakened" to the highest truth as well as to the highest life. The East calls these awakened or enlightened beings "Bodhisattvas". They are able to receive "the Truth Word of the Gods" in the immediate presence and through the immediate sight of the Christ Being, in order to bring it as wisdom teachings to their far less developed fellow human beings on Earth.

"There are regions of spiritual life where one can find, so to speak, purified from all earth dust, this high being, the Bodhisattva, in its spiritual peculiarity, and where one can find the Christ, unclothed from all that he has become on Earth and in its proximity. There, the following is found: One finds, so to speak, the basis of humanity, that which all life emanates from: the spiritual primal source. There is found not only one Bodhisattva, but a series of Bodhisattvas. As we have pointed out to the Bodhisattva that underlies our seven successive cultures, likewise there is a Bodhisattva that underlies the Atlantean cultures and so on. In spiritual heights, you find a series of Bodhisattvas who in their times are the great teachers, the instructors not only of men, but also of those beings who do not descend into the region of physical life. We find them all sitting there, when we are allowed to speak comparatively, as the great teachers. They gather what they are to teach, and in their midst we find a being that is not only great by teaching: and this is the Christ. He is not only great by teaching, but He is in the midst of the Bodhisattvas as a being that has an effect on the surrounding Bodhisattvas by the way that they have the sight of Him. He is seen by the Bodhisattvas to whom He reveals His own magnificence. Whereas the others are what they are, by the fact that they are great teachers, the Christ is what He is to the world through what He is in Himself, through His being. You only have to look at Him; and the revelation of His own being is something that only needs to be reflected in his environment; then the teaching arises thereof. He is not just a teacher. He is life, a life that pours itself into the other beings who then become the teachers. So the Bodhisattvas are those who receive their teaching by enjoying the bliss of having the sight of Christ in their spiritual height." [140]

In the second region of the Budhi plane or world of the life spirit is the peak of our incarnation cycles. This is as far as we can ascend in this day and age. The third sphere of the Budhi plane is already turned to even higher spheres and worlds, as it is the case with the third sphere of the spiritual world, the Saturn sphere. The third sphere of a world always forms a functional unity together with the fourth and fifth spheres with the tendency towards even higher spheres. An example from the sensory world may serve for better understanding:

The lowest sphere of the physical world is the region of the earthy or solid. We like to think of it as a horizontal plane. In reality, however, the Earth's surface forms a globular shell surrounding our Earth globe, a sphere. The next higher sphere, the watery or liquid, nestles very close to it. Although some of the water always evaporates, it returns to the Earth as rain and unites with the water masses in the riverbeds and ocean basins. The earthy and the watery together form a unit. The next higher sphere of the physical world, the atmosphere, the airy or gaseous, already has the tendency to escape the Earth. Each gas wants to expand further and further through an inherent force. Physics calls this force vapour pressure. It increases

---

[139] GA 8 "Das Christentum als mystische Tatsache" (Christianity as mystical fact), Chapter "Plato als Mystiker" (Plato as a mystic)

[140] GA 113 "Der Orient im Lichte des Okzidents – Die Kinder des Luzifer und die Brüder Christi" (The East in the light of the West - The Children of Lucifer and the Brothers of Christ), Munich, Lecture of 31 August 1909

even more when a gas is exposed to heat. The gaseous and the warm or fiery tend to unite, just as the earthy and the liquid. However, they strive in opposite directions: The earthy and liquid to the centre of the Earth, gas and heat to the Earth's outer environment. In addition there is another phenomenon. The third sphere of a world is always intimately connected to the fifth sphere. The latter works into the third and is reflected in it, so to speak. In the physical world, this means that the air not only unites with the heat, but in addition the light ether, as the fifth state of matter in the physical world, pervades the air with a sensorily perceptible image of itself. Thus air, heat or warmth and light, i.e. the third, fourth and fifth material states of the physical world, form a unit. This manifests in their common characteristic of wanting to escape from the Earth into outer space.

We find the same regularity in life on Earth in the human members of being, too. Physical body and ether body form a functional unit. They stay in bed at night. On the other hand, the astral body, the I and that part of man, which has already been transformed to Manas, i.e. the third, fourth and fifth member, separate from the first two and strive towards the Earth's environment. Only after a certain time they return to the ether body and physical body. However, this return only happens during life on Earth. After death, they are set free and, following their own impulses, can take off more and more from the Earth and expand out into the cosmos.

We find this law in the spiritual world as well. The Mars and Jupiter spheres, i.e. the Continental Region and the Oceanic Region, thus the first and second spheres of the spiritual world, form a unity. The third sphere, the Saturn sphere or Atmospheric region, already has the tendency towards the Zodiac sphere and the cosmic spheres above it. Therefore, the 7th weekly verse is a kind of threshold-verse, a transition from the planetary to the stellar spheres.

On the Budhi plane, accordingly, from the third sphere, the tendency starts to take off from the lower worlds and to form a unity with the effectiveness of the fourth and fifth spheres. The fifth sphere, however, is already pervaded by the Atmic plane. Man thus gets in touch with forces that want to detach him from the lowest world, the physical world, and lift him up for one world plane. Therefore the entry into the third sphere of the Budhi plane is reserved for those beings who after several lives as Bodhisattvas on Earth mature to Buddhahood and prepare themselves to enter into a lasting connection with the Atmic world. It is also called Nirvana, i.e. region of blowing away or blowing out, because a person's entry into this world is connected with his leaving the cycle of rebirths and his detachment from the physical world. Buddhas shift the centre of their being from the spiritual world, where the "ordinary" man has his I, one world higher to the Budhi plane. They become Budhas, as the word can be written, emphasizing the connection with the Budhi plane. Such beings embody themselves only down to the astral plane, one world higher than all other human beings.

We, who have not yet matured to Buddhahood, must remain connected to the physical world for our own benefit. For us, the second region of the Budhi plane is the culmination and turning point, as we still lack very much the developmental maturity that is necessary in order to loosen ourselves from the physical world and ascend into the superspiritual worlds. At this turning point in the incarnation cycle all those who have become capable of consciously experiencing the world midnight through appropriate preparation in life on Earth will receive a final consciousness-expanding message of the Truth Word, the Christ. They are called to get at least a sense of the realization that they are in truth not "only" spiritual beings, as they were allowed to recognize through the assistance of the Holy Spirit already in the spiritual world, but that they have their roots and their origin in even higher, in superspiritual worlds, in worlds which underlie the spiritual world, i.e. in "spirit's backgrounds". These are the world of the Son and the world of the Father, the Budhic and the Atmic plane, which here are described as "spirit's fire worlds" and "akin to spirit".

And am I in the senses' heights,	Und bin ich in den Sinneshöhen,
Then flames in my soul's depths	So flammt in meinen Seelentiefen
Out of the spirit's fire-worlds	Aus Geistes Feuerwelten
The Truth Word of the Gods:	Der Götter Wahrheitswort:
In spirit's backgrounds seek, by sensing,	In Geistesgründen suche ahnend
To find yourself akin to spirit now.	Dich geistverwandt zu finden.

From the summit, the second region of the world of the life spirit, people gradually descend again to a new life on Earth, either for achieving further necessary experiences and clearing off their karma or, as is the case with the Bodhisattvas, to assist their less developed fellow men without karmic obligation and to advance them in their development. They are the "masters of wisdom and harmony of sensations", as Rudolf Steiner often called them, who work in selfless service under the guidance of the Christ Being.

The Christ Being

Writing about the Christ Being is truly a difficult endeavour. Christ is so high above us human beings that we are still at the very beginning of an understanding of his sublime being. In the traditional Christian denominations today usually no distinction is made anymore between Jesus and Christ. The differentiation between man and God has been lost there. In some denominations Jesus Christ is completely reduced to the simple man Jesus, who is said to have been a very noble man, but not the Son of God. Others, on the other hand, see Christ as divine, but equate him entirely with the Father-God. The distinction between Father, Son and Holy Spirit has often given way to a rigid, one-sided monotheism that no longer shows any understanding of the original teaching about the divine Trinity.

Through his occult research, Rudolf Steiner has made it possible for us to take a more differentiated look at the mystery of the Christ Being. In his lecture cycle "From Jesus to Christ"[141] and many supplementary lectures he clearly emphasized the distinctions between the man Jesus and Christ, the divine being. Thus, at least in anthroposophical circles, the knowledge of this difference is quite widespread nowadays. The man Jesus of Nazareth was the bearer of Christ, who was able to work in him, as his I and his higher spirituality, for three years in an earthly body and finally accomplish the mystery of Golgotha, through which he overcame earthly death, connected himself with the whole of humanity and the Earth, and since then has been leading, from the etheric outer environment of the Earth, all those who want to be led by him of their own free will towards the goal of human development on Earth.

The statement "Jesus was bearer of the Christ" will therefore find approval among many anthroposophists. The statement "Christ is bearer of the Logos", on the other hand, will cause obvious amazement among most of them, because even anthroposophists usually do not distinguish between the Christ Being and the Logos. The terms Christ and Logos are usually equated. This is quite understandable, for we have many passages in the Gospel where Christ is equated with the second person of the Trinity, the Son of God, the Word or Logos. This is what Peter also called him, when Christ himself asked his disciples: *"But who do you say that I am?"* Peter frankly replied: *"You are the Christ, the Son of the living God."* Christ himself expressly confirmed this statement with the words: *"Blessed are you, Simon, son of Jonah; for flesh and blood did not reveal this to you, but my Father who is in heaven."* (Matthew 16:15-17).

This is also confirmed in the Gospel of John. When many disciples retreated from Christ-Jesus because they were offended by his words that he was *"the bread of life"*, that his flesh was a *"true food"* and his blood a *"true drink"*, Jesus asked the Twelve: *"Do you also wish to go away?"* Simon Peter answered him: *"To whom can we go? You have words of eternal life and we have believed and realized that you are the Son of God."* (John 6:67-69). This formulation clearly refers to the second person of God. In the context of the words quoted above, Christ also spoke several times of his intimate connection with the Father in heaven and that He had sent him. Moreover, it is precisely the Gospel of John, which in its great prologue states clearly, that the Word, the Logos, Himself became flesh and *"dwelt among us, and we beheld his glory, a glory as of the only begotten Son of the Father, full of grace and truth. John bears witness of him, cries out and says: «This was the one I said of: After me will come the one, who was before me, because he was earlier than me.»"* (John 1:14-15). At the baptism at the Jordan, John calls him in addition the *"Lamb of God"* (John 1:29) and the *"Son of God"* (John 1:34).

In view of this intense connection between Christ and the Logos, a statement by Rudolf Steiner, handed down to us from Friedrich Rittelmeyer[142], initially causes astonishment. Rittelmeyer noted in his self-written work "Unpublished Conversations with Dr. Steiner": *"Dr. Steiner very clearly confirmed that Christ is the Supreme of the Sun Hierarchy, but that the second person of Deity, the Logos, is to be distinguished from him. He is above him or, as one might say: behind him. Behind each of the three Hierarchy groups stands one person of the Deity. Christ always spoke with extraordinary reverence when he spoke of the Father.*

---

[141] GA 131 "Von Jesus zu Christus" (From Jesus to Christ), cycle of 10 lectures with a preceding public lecture held in Karlsruhe from October 4 to 14, 1911

[142] Friedrich Rittelmeyer (* 5 Oct.1872 in Dillingen an der Donau [on the Danube]; † 23 March 1938 in Hamburg) was a German Protestant pastor, important preacher, theologian and anthroposophist. He was the co-founder and first "Erzoberlenker" (Arch Senior Guide) of "The Christian Community", also called "Movement for Religious Renewal".

But Yahweh was not meant there, even if the Jews might have understood it that way. Christ would have identified himself with Yahweh." [143]

Christ would have identified himself with Yahweh, in so far as his Sun Being was radiated to the Earth in pre-Christian times by the Moon Being Yahweh first with diminished power, as a light softened for mankind. Even today we cannot look directly to the Sun, but we can look at the shining disk of the full Moon. Since, however, we cannot even behold and really understand the physical Sun, how much less may we expect to behold and understand the high Sun Being Christ or even the Logos Himself, the second person of the Trinity? Christ only became visible to the people on Earth in the physical sheath of Jesus' corporeality. That is why Rudolf Steiner describes us the man Jesus as the bearer of Christ. Obviously, one of his main tasks a hundred years ago was to clearly emphasize the distinction between Jesus and Christ. But it was apparently only a first step towards a more comprehensive understanding of Christ. For in a similar way, according to the above words of Rudolf Steiner, which are certainly truthfully quoted by Friedrich Rittelmeyer, we may understand Christ as bearer of the Logos. As a result, a threefold being was acting on Earth at the time of the mystery of Golgotha: Jesus – Christ – Logos. If we take Jesus as an earth-man and Christ as the highest Sun Being, intimately connected with the planetary spheres, we may regard the Logos as the Universal Being, the creative World-Word, who influences the evolutionary processes within the planetary spheres as well as the evolution of mankind on Earth from the extra-planetary starry sky by means of the twelve forces of the zodiac.

When and in which way did Christ become the bearer of the Logos, the bearer of the World-Word? Rudolf Steiner gave an answer to this. First he pointed out that the Sun Being Christ belongs to the Hierarchy of the Archangels, but developed up to their highest initiate already in the ancient Sun, where the Archangels went through their rank of mankind.

"So these beings [the Archangels] could live on the Sun in such a way that they inhaled and exhaled warmth and fire. Therefore, these spirits are called Fire Spirits. In the Sun they were on the rank of mankind, and they worked in the service of mankind. These beings are named Sun or Fire Spirits. At that time, man was on the stage of sleep consciousness. These Sun-Fire Spirits already had I-consciousness. Since then they also have evolved and ascended to higher stages of consciousness. In Christian esotericism they are called Archangels. And the most highly developed spirit, who was in the Sun as Fire Spirit, who is still active on Earth today, with highest developed consciousness, this Sun or Fire Spirit, that is the Christ, just as the most highly developed Saturn Spirit is the Father God. In terms of Christian esotericism, therefore, such a Sun-Fire Spirit was embodied in the carnal body of Christ Jesus, and that was the highest, the regent of the Sun Spirits." [144]

Unfortunately, about the lecture cycle "Theosophy of the Rosicrucian", in which Rudolf Steiner made these statements, we only have "a transcript, but not literally, jointly produced by Camille Wandrey and Walther Vegelahn, which Rudolf Steiner did not check", as it says in the note attached to the GA 99 edition. Many of the early lectures have not yet been shorthanded, as we know.

The above words *"just as the most highly developed Saturn Spirit is the Father God"* appear to be very abridged. In the context of the statement about Christ as an Archangel Being, made immediately beforehand by Rudolf Steiner, these words can only be understood in such a way that the most highly developed Saturn Spirit, one of the Spirits of Personality, who at that time were passing through their rank of mankind, became the "bearer" of the Father God; for neither an Archangel nor a Spirit of Personality can be equated with the Father as part of the divine Trinity. Rather, we may assume that on the ancient Moon, according to the same law, the most highly developed Angel Being has become the bearer of the Holy Spirit in an analogous manner. Consequently, in the course of the first three planetary states three beings would have evolved up to "bearers" of one person of the divine Trinity at a time, namely the most highly developed one of the Spirits of Personality to the bearer of the Father on the ancient Saturn, the most highly developed one of the Archangels to the bearer of the Son on the ancient Sun, and the most highly developed of the Angels to the bearer of the Holy Spirit on the ancient Moon. – Then it continues in the same lecture:

---

[143] "Unveröffentlichte Gespräche mit Dr. Steiner" (Unpublished conversations with Dr. Steiner) written by Friedrich Rittelmeyer, published in 2016 by Verlag Urachhaus, Germany, with the consent of the leadership of The Christian Community.

[144] GA 99 "Die Theosophie des Rosenkreuzers" (Theosophy of the Rosicrucian), Munich, Lecture of 2 June 1907

"In order that He [Christ, the supreme Sun Spirit] could come to Earth, he had to use a physical body. He had to be subject to the same earthly conditions as man in order to be able to operate here. So we are dealing on the Sun with a solar body, so to speak, a body of the Sun-planet, with I-Spirits[145] who are Fire Spirits, and with a regent of this Sun, the most highly developed Sun Spirit, the Christ. While the Earth was Sun, this spirit was the central spirit of the Sun. When the Earth was Moon, He was more highly developed, but it remained with the Moon. When the Earth came into being, he was most highly developed and remained with the Earth after he had united with it after the mystery of Golgotha. He thus is the highest planetary spirit of the Earth. Today, the Earth is his body, just as the Sun was his body at that time. Therefore we must take literally the words from the Gospel of John: «He who eats my bread lifts his heel against me.» For the Earth is the body of Christ, and when the people who eat the bread taken from the body of the Earth walk on the Earth, they tread on the body of Christ with their feet. Take this word quite literally, just as all religious documents must be taken literally indeed. But first you have to know the letter in its true sense and then seek the spirit."

On another occasion Rudolf Steiner described how the Archangel-Sun-Spirit Christ became the supreme initiate of the ancient Sun by connecting himself with the Logos, taking Him into himself that highest Universal Being which sounded towards him from all directions of space as the World-Word, distributed to the twelve beings of the Zodiac. But to be able to work for the mystery of Golgotha in and through a human earthly body, the Logos needed a link, a bearer, a mediator between the twelve forces of the extra-planetary starry sky and the earthly world. The Sun Spirit Christ was prepared for this supreme task on the ancient Sun already. Christ was charged with the task to reunite that which had been distributed to the twelve beings of the Zodiac and by doing so to become a Logos-Bearer, a Thirteenth among the Twelve, both the twelve zodiacal forces in heaven and later also the twelve apostles on Earth as a microcosmic likeness of the macrocosmic event:

"If you transferred yourself to the Sun today, you would, looking about radially, first look at the twelve constellations of the zodiac. At that time they were not outwardly visible as such. But instead there were twelve figures, twelve beings, who made their words sound from the depth of darkness, from the depth of blackness, since the outer space was not filled with light. What kind of words were these? Well, you see, these were words – the word «word» is again only a surrogate to indicate what it is – these were words that spoke of ancient times, already then ancient times. They were twelve world-initiators. Today, in the directions of these twelve world-initiators are the twelve zodiac images, and from them sounds to the soul, which is open to the whole world, the original kind of the unspoken World-Word, which could be formed from the twelve voices. Lucifer solely – I must now begin to speak figuratively, because human words are just not enough – had the urge in himself to irradiate everything with the light present in him and thus to recognize it, whereas the Christ devoted himself to the impression of this World Word in an inexpressible manner and absorbed it completely, completely in himself; so that they were now united in the Christ Soul, that this Christ Soul was the Unification Being of the great world mysteries, sounding in through the inexpressible Word. Thus we face the contrast between Christ receiving the World Word and the proud Lucifer, the Venus Spirit, who rejects the World Word and wants to fathom everything with his light. ...

We have to take this scene in. Then we will find that during the ancient Sun time the ways of Christ and Lucifer separated. The way of Lucifer went downwards. He had to fall behind in his development, and he therefore in his development also fell behind during the Moon time. The Christ Spirit, the Sun Spirit, went forward and became a forward evolving spirit, who could finally appear on Earth in the form described to you more often. Through his devotion to the universe, through the reception of the divine creative Word, through identification with the Divine-Creative, with the inexpressible Word, through the rejection of any pride and the replacement of any pride by devotion to the World Word, Christ developed from a ruler of a planet, which he was in ancient Sun time, to the ruler of the other planets with the governmental area of the Sun." [146]

In this sense, another statement by Rudolf Steiner to Friedrich Rittelmeyer becomes understandable, about which the latter one records in his document "Unpublished conversations with Dr. Steiner": *"It shocked me, however, when Dr. Steiner once said that it is so often extremely difficult to distinguish Christ from Lucifer. So I asked whether there was a certain characteristic by which one could recognize whether a touch of Christ really emanated from Christ. Dr. Steiner replied: Christ is pure selflessness. That's the only way to identify him."*

---

[145] i.e. spirits who pass through their rank of mankind, developing I-consciousness

[146] GA 137 "Der Mensch im Lichte von Okkultismus, Theosophie und Philosophie" (Man in the Light of Occultism, Theosophy and Philosophy), Kristiania (Oslo), Lecture of 12 June 1912

If we want to create an image of the supreme Sun Spirit, the Christ, we may imagine him as a central being between on the one hand a circle of twelve beings floating above him, which together represent the Logos, streaming into the planetary spheres, and on the other hand a circle of twelve people on Earth standing beneath him, the twelve apostles, which Christ turned into earthly likenesses of the heavenly Twelve, by allowing them to eat the "heavenly breads". This mystery was opened to them through an Imagination, caused by Christ, about the feeding of the four thousand and the five thousand with the breads of the heavens and the fishes:

"A multitude of people was called a «thousand» according to the ancient terminology, and if one wanted to specialize, a number was added that was taken from the most important characteristic. For example, the people of the fourth cultural period were called the «fourth thousand», and those who already lived in the manner of the fifth cultural period were called the «fifth thousand». These are simply termini technici. Therefore, the disciples could say: During the daytime state, we perceive what the Christ power sends us from the forces of the Sun, from the seven constellations of the day, so that we then receive the food intended for the people of the fourth cultural period, for the fourth thousand. And in our nocturnal imaginative clairvoyant state we perceive through the five constellations of the night what applies to the nearest future, to the fifth thousand. Thus the people of the fourth epoch – the four thousand – are nourished from heaven by the seven heavenly breads, by the seven constellations of the day; and the people of the fifth epoch – the five thousand – are nourished by the five heavenly breads, by the five constellations of the night. The division is always indicated, where the daytime constellations meet the nighttime constellations: Pisces (the fishes).

A secret is touched here. Here is hinted to an important mystery process: to the magical intercourse of Christ with the disciples. The Christ makes it clear to them that he does not speak of the former leaven of the Pharisees, but that he conveys to them a heavenly food from the solar forces of the cosmos, which he brings down, though nothing is available, the one time as the seven day breads, the seven constellations of the day, and the other time as the five night breads, the five constellations of the night. In between there are always the fishes that are the division; two fishes are even mentioned once, so that it is particularly clear (Matthew 14:13-21, and 15:32-38)." [147]

Just as the Logos, the World-Word, spoke to the Sun Spirit Christ through the twelve beings of the zodiac, so later also Christ on Earth spoke not only through the body of Jesus of Nazareth, the Thirteenth in the middle, but often through one or the other of the twelve apostles, so that it was quite difficult for his opponents to clearly identify him.

"There was in a way an inner and deep interrelation between the soul of Christ and the souls of the Twelve. Everything going on in the soul of Christ was a meaningful process for the time being, processes of a rich kind, manifold processes. But everything going on in the soul of Christ was, as it were, reflected like a kind of mirror image, like a kind of reflection, in the souls of the disciples, but divided into twelve parts; so that each of the twelve experienced a part of what was going on in the soul of Christ Jesus, but each of the twelve something different." [148]

At a lecture in Cologne; Rudolf Steiner revealed further connections:

"Then, the Christ Being joined with the body of Jesus of Nazareth more and more. And it happened later, when the Christ went among his closest students that they were inwardly linked with him in such a way that he did not live apart from them, so to speak. The more he settled into his body, the more he settled into the innermost being of his students. Now he went through the lands in the flock of his students. At times he spoke through this, at other times through that student by intimate communion, since he settled into the others, so that when they walked in the land, it was no longer the Christ Jesus who spoke, but one of the disciples. However, the Christ spoke through him. And with such intensity he settled into the disciples that the facial expression of the disciple through whom the Christ spoke changed in such a way that whoever listened outside from the people had the feeling that he was the Master. But the other one, who was the Christ, withered so much that he looked as usual. So He spoke soon through this, soon through that in the land around. This was the secret of its effectiveness in the last time of the three years.

And when he thus walked along with his disciples and was regarded more and more dangerous by his enemies, they said: How can we persecute him? We cannot arrest the whole bunch? For you never know as to whether you've got the right one or the wrong one. If you capture the wrong one, the right one has escaped. They never knew if they had the right person in the one they faced. This was the big fear! It was

---

[147] See GA 123 "Das Matthäus-Evangelium" (The Gospel of Mathew), Bern, Lecture of 10 September 1910

[148] GA 139 "Das Markus-Evangelium" (The Gospel of Mark), Basel, Lecture of 21 September 1912.

known that at times this one spoke, at other times another, and the right one was not recognizable, because he turned into the usual form of another.

There was something wonderful about this crowd. Therefore, it was necessary that a betrayal happened. For, the way in which things are usually presented, they weren't. What did it mean that Judas had to give a kiss to the one who was the right one? According to the usual description, that would not have been difficult to catch Jesus of Nazareth. The kiss would have no meaning if not someone who knew exactly which one was the right one, had to show it to those who didn't know that. But for the reason given, the enemies didn't know who the right one was." [149]

Christ, who used the human bodily sheaths of Jesus as bearers for his life on Earth, could apparently work through the members of being of the twelve apostles, too. But, what about his own members of being? Which is his lowest, which his highest member? The following explanations by Rudolf Steiner should help us to better understand the sevenfold member structure of the Christ Being:

"When we speak of man in the sense of spiritual science, we say that the complete human being whom we contemplate, whom alone we are able contemplate, is a sevenfold being consisting of physical body, ether body, astral body, I, spirit self, life spirit and spirit man. He is not yet complete today, but he will be when his sevenfold being has come to full formation. But in the large universe there are not only such beings as man is in his development. There are other beings, for example such as those, about whom we may not say that they have a physical body as the lowest member of being, like today's man. There are beings where we have to count differently. We may write down the members of the human being like this:

7. *Spirit Man*
6. *Life Spirit*
5. *Spirit Self*
4. *I*
3. *Astral Body*
2. *Ether Body*
1. *Physical Body.*

Now there are beings whose lowest member of being is the ether body. These are also sevenfold beings who then have an eighth member above the spirit man. They begin with the ether body, astral body and so on, and they end with a member that exists above our Atma, above the spirit man. There are other beings whose lowest member of being is the astral body. But then they have an eighth and a ninth member above the spirit man. There are beings whose lowest member of being is the I, who therefore do not have a physical body, ether body and astral body in our sense, but who manifest themselves in such a way that the I pushes outward, without the three sheaths, thus beings who send «I»s to the outside everywhere. They then have an eighth, ninth and tenth member. They are described in the Apocalypse as «living creatures, full of eyes». Then there are beings who begin with the spirit self, with Manas, as the lowest member. They even have an eleventh member. And finally there are beings, who begin with the life spirit. They then have a twelfth member. So there are beings who – just as man has a physical body as the lowest member – they have the Budhi as the lowest member, and who therefore have a highest member, which we best call the number twelve. These are high, sublime beings, who reach far above anything a human can imagine. …

If we write down the human being into the zodiac, we have him there reaching to Libra. That being, who with his essence belongs entirely to the zodiac, whose forces belong entirely to the zodiac and who manifests Himself in planetary life only in His lowest member, which is signified by Libra – like in humans the lowest member is signified by Pisces – that is the being who, as you can see, spreads life over our whole universe. [see Figure 8]

Man absorbs life, whereas this being radiates life over our whole universe. This is that being who is able to accomplish the great sacrifice and who is inscribed into the zodiac as the being sacrificing himself for our world. Just as man soars into the zodiac, this being sends us his offering from Aries, which belongs to him like Libra to man. And just as man turns up his I to Libra, so this being streams his essence over our sphere as a sacrifice. Therefore, this being is named the sacrificial «mystical Lamb», for the Lamb is the same as Aries; hence the name of the sacrificial Lamb or Aries for Christ. Christ is now characterized to you as belonging to the whole cosmos. His I strives until Aries; and if the I streams until Aries, He Himself

---

[149] GA 148 "Aus der Akasha-Forschung – Das fünfte Evangelium" (From Akasha-Research – the Fifth Gospel), Cologne, Lecture of 18 December 1913

thereby becomes the «great sacrifice» and by doing so He is in a relationship with all mankind, and in a sense those beings and powers which are on Earth are His creations. With His whole being He stands in the Sun and is connected in his creations with the Moon and the Earth and his power lies in the constellation of the Lamb. So the powers to become creator of those beings, lie in the constellation of Aries or the Lamb. The name «sacrificial lamb» or «mystical lamb» is taken right from heaven." [150]

		♈	Aries	12th	Member	
		♉	Taurus	11th	Member	
		♊	Gemini	10th	Member	
		♋	Cancer	9th	Member	„Mystical
		♌	Leo	8th	Member	Lamb"
7th	Spirit Man	♍	Virgo	7th	Member	
6th	Life Spirit	♎	Libra	6th	Member	
5th	Spirit Self	♏	Scorpio			
4th	I	♐	Sagittarius			
3rd	Astral Body	♑	Capricorn			
2nd	Ether Body	♒	Aquarius			
1st	Physical Body	♓	Pisces			

Figure 8: The 7 members of the human being and of the Christ Being (GA 102)

These statements by Rudolf Steiner may certainly be reconciled with his different statement above, according to which Christ is one of the Archangels. For, it's true that on the ancient Sun they had a physical body as their lowest member consisting of fiery air and are therefore called Fire or Sun Spirits. But the initiates of various degrees rush ahead of their fellow-brothers through further development by evolving their three highest members of being as high as possible. They then can sacrifice their lower members, which they have ennobled by the effectiveness of their "I"s, to their fellow beings and, if necessary, always form new lower members for themselves. In this way it becomes possible for the highest initiates to even unite themselves with their three highest members of being so closely that they can use their middle members, the "I"s, as their lowest members. For each sacrificed lower member, however, a new higher member of being is added to them, so that they ultimately become sevenfold beings again. Rudolf Steiner already elucidated this process in 1908 in the context of an esoteric lesson with the example of the Spirits of Form, who in the course of their normal development since ancient Saturn reached a stage which their initiates had achieved a long time before, namely the gradual laying down of their lower members of being and the associated attachment of new, higher members:

"Spiritual Beings encased this [ancient] Saturn like a cloak, among them the Spirits of Form. They also passed through a development. As lowest members they had bodies on Saturn, comparable to man's ether body today. Furthermore they had astral bodies, «I»s, spirit-selves, life spirits, spirit-men, and a member one degree higher than what man can achieve. ... The Spirits of Form mirrored their own likenesses into the fiery material of Saturn, and man has become a likeness of the Deity as early as that time. ... Secondly: in the Sun, the Spirits of Form radiate their vital bodies completely into it. They are not reflected back. The human preliminary stages are pervaded with them. In times before, the Spirits of Form have mirrored their likenesses. Now they pervade these likenesses with their own life forces. They give up their ether bodies. Now they have the astral body as lowest member, and attach another member upwards. ... Third: on the Moon, the Spirits of Form also give off their astral bodies and keep the «I»s as their lowest members. Upwards, they again attach one member, the tenth member. Outwardly, they form nothing but «I»s. These

---

[150] GA 102 "Das Hereinwirken geistiger Wesenheiten in den Menschen" (The influence of spiritual beings upon man), Berlin, Lecture of 27 January 1908

Spirits of Form work from the outside through space into the Moon with their «I»s. They have given off to the human preliminary stages the astral body. Everything that the human beings have, has flowed down from the cosmic environment, is a sacrifice of this cosmic environment. Fourth, now the Earth condition: Man forms his body in the primal Earth out of the elements of the Earth. The high Sun Beings come over. The Spirits of Form again totally sacrifice their lowest member, the «I»s. They retain for themselves as their lowest member Manas, the spirit self, the flooding wisdom of the world. It surrounds us as the lowest member of the Spirits of Form. We live, weave and are in this wisdom-life of the Spirits of Form." [151]

If we now assume, that already on the ancient Sun the Christ as highest initiate of the Archangels was able to develop up to the I and thus to the Zodiac sphere – which first made possible to him the above mentioned absorption of the World Word by the forces of the zodiac – we may assume likewise that in the course of the subsequent planetary development of the ancient Moon he could rise one stage higher, i.e. could ascend to the spirit self as his lowest member of being, just as his Archangel siblings could rise one stage higher than their human stage during the Moon evolution. In the course of the subsequent Earth evolution the Christ Being could apparently develop another stage upwards so that now he has the Budhi, the life spirit, as his lowest member of being. Thus it becomes understandable that Rudolf Steiner characterizes the Christ Being to us both as an Archangel and as a being who has the Budhi as his lowest member.

What does this mean in relation to the different planes or worlds? How far does a sevenfold being like Christ tower above the three worlds in which we develop? Human beings essentially accomplish their incarnation cycles within the physical, astral and spiritual worlds. Only a few humans today are already able to consciously reach to the two lowest spheres of the Budhic world. For the vast majority of people, contact with these sublime regions takes place unconsciously, but nevertheless as a quite important process in their "souls' depths", as it is said in the 13th weekly verse. Beyond the Budhic plane or the world of the life spirit, the Atmic plane or the world of the spirit man exists. It is also called Nirvanic World. Only a person who has long served the evolution of humanity as a Bodhisattva and finally developed up to the stage of Buddhaship is able to enter Nirvana, as it is termed in the Eastern mystery schools. The Sanskrit word nirvana means to blow away or to go out. We could also say: dissolve into nothing. However, Nirvana is by no means Nothing. Rather, it is none of all that we can imagine in any way. Therefore its condition may only be described by a negativum. Today it is not yet possible for us to have any appropriate ideas of the Atmic world, for this exceeds our comprehension.

Beyond Nirvana there are even higher worlds. The next higher one is just called the world above the Nirvanic plane, the Paranirvanic plane, because other words are missing. If one imagines the worlds not as one above the other, but as threedimensional spheres, with the higher spheres always containing the lower ones, then it appears more appropriate to use the word Parinirvanic plane, which means the plane encompassing the Nirvanic plane. Beyond this world is an even more sublime, even larger world. It has therefore been preceded by the prefix maha = big, so that it is called the Mahapara- or Mahaparinirvanic plane. Altogether seven worlds are described to us. [152] Beyond these, there is the region of the threefold Deity or the threefold Logos.

As already mentioned, the lowest member of the Christ Being is Budhi. As a sevenfold being, he consequently extends into the region of the threefold Deity, the threefold Logos, as is shown in Figure 9. The four lowest members of Christ are in the area of the four uppermost worlds and thus outside the region of the Logos. His three highest members, however, are in the region of the threefold Deity. It pervades them and, in a sense, makes up the higher self of Christ. In this way, Christ fully and completely is a bearer of the Logos. In the ancient Sun, when his lowest member was the I, he reached into the Trinity with only one of his members. At the same time, however, this opened up the possibility that the Logos could connect with him. On the ancient Moon, the Christ Being reached up into the Trinity even with his second highest member, and, during the development of the Earth, finally with his third highest member. Therefore he spoke the truth to the apostle Philip when he told him about himself: *"He who sees me sees the Father. How do you speak: Show us the father? Do you not believe that I am in the Father and the Father is in me? The words that I speak to you, I do not speak on my own. But the Father who dwells in me does the works."* (John 14:9-10). The Father-God of the Trinity "dwells" in the highest member of the Christ Being and works through it down into his lower members, down to the Budhi. Thus Christ really became the representative of the threefold Deity within the Creation, the "Deity, who reveals Himself" to the world and its creatures. That is just the Son principle of Deity.

---

[151] GA 266a "Aus den Inhalten der esoterischen Stunden" (From the contents of the esoteric lessons), Volume I, Berlin, 14 March 1908, record C

[152] GA 93a "Grundelemente der Esoterik" (Foundations of esotericism), Berlin, Lecture of 30 September 1905

There is absolutely no contradiction to the statement above that the actual bearer of the Father Principle within the seven worlds is the highest initiate of ancient Saturn, a being from the ranks of the Archai or Spirits of Personality, who evolved in the periods between ancient Saturn and the Earth development up to the Atma or spirit man as the lowest member. His middle member, which in man corresponds to the I, therefore no longer exists within the seven worlds, as is the case with the Christ Being, but already in the Hidden, in the divine primal foundation, the region of the threefold and triune Deity. There, the concept of development loses all meaning and turns into the concept of perfection.

But through his lowest member of being Christ is also "the life". By accomplishing the great sacrifice and offering up the Budhi, he rises further and "goes to the Father". The higher self of Christ, however, which is united with the Trinity, above all development and by whose volition Christ acts, does not have a benefit from this sacrifice. It is an act of supreme selflessness out of the highest free will and God's supreme love for his creatures. The offering of life, the Budhi, is a longer process that did not begin at the times of the mystery of Golgotha, but much earlier in ancient Lemuria, as was already described with Rudolf Steiner's words in the reflection on the 12th weekly verse.

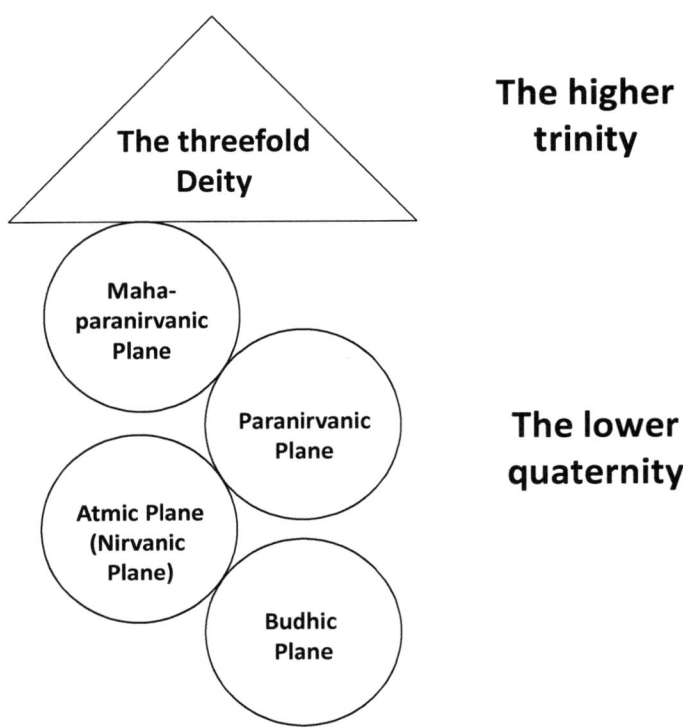

Figure 9: The upper 4 worlds and the Trinity

Figure 9 shows that the Christ Being's structure of members is the macrocosmic model of the human structure of members. The threefold Deity is the higher self or higher trinity of Christ. By analogy, the three Bearers of the Trinity, the highest initiates of ancient Saturn, ancient Sun and ancient Moon, form the higher self of man with their lowest members, Atma, Budhi and Manas, above a lower quaternity consisting of the I, astral body, ether body and physical body. Thus, the Christ Being's structure of members is the archetype of that prayer which he himself gave to humanity, the "Lord's Prayer". Rudolf Steiner pointed out the connection of this prayer with the human members of being in an early lecture in 1907, when he summarized the details in an illustration with the words:

"In the so-called spiritual or occult science, the upper trinity was always mentioned, and for the human being, who was created in the middle of the Lemurian race, the triangle and the quadrangle were chosen as a scheme, especially in the Pythagorean school, so that for the composed human being the following scheme results." [153] (see figure 10)

---

[153] GA 96 "Ursprungsimpulse der Geisteswissenschaft" (Original impulses of the science of the spirit), Berlin, Lecture of 28 January 1907

The three highest members of the human being, Manas, Budhi and Atma, are macrocosmic members. This fact manifests in their connection to the spheres beyond the zodiac. Manas is the lowest macrocosmic member of the human being. It basically spreads over the entire mental plane, the so-called spiritual world, which is also named the Manasic plane. Primarily, the principle of the Holy Spirit works in it. There he causes a reflection of the macrocosmic, stellar members of being into microcosmic, planetary members of being. For this purpose, the Zodiac sphere, the middle region of the spiritual world, serves as a "mirror surface". It encloses the planetary spheres like the womb encloses the embryo. With man's passage through the stage of humanity and his associated development up to the zodiac, the region of the I, the possibility opens up to him, in each subsequent planetary development cycle, to discard one of his lower microcosmic members of being and to receive the seed of a new macrocosmic member of being on top, as is the case with all hierarchical beings developing within the seven worlds and as it has already been explained above using the example of the Spirits of Form.

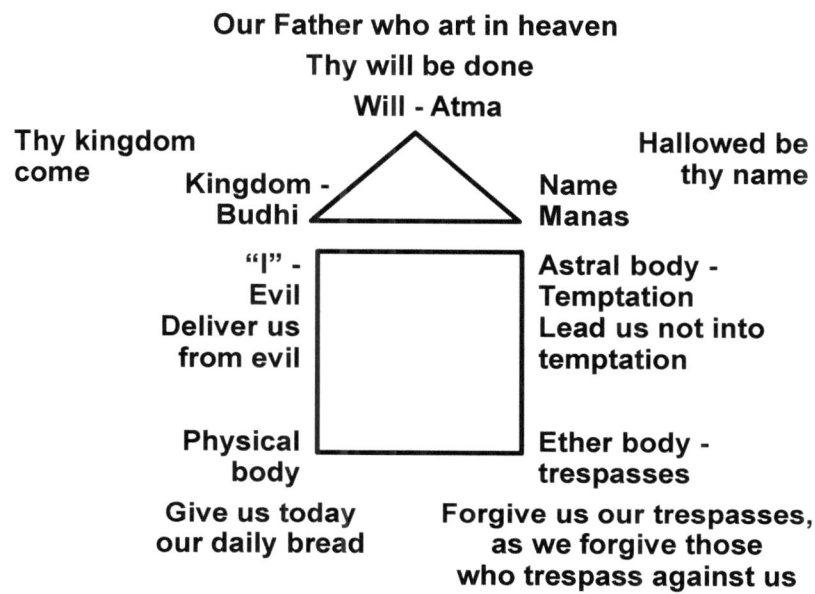

Figure 10: The Lord's Prayer and the members of the human being (GA 96)

In the middle of the seven worlds, the lowest of Christ's members of being is located, the Budhi. For this reason it is related to the middle of man's members of being, the I. Christ does not only have an influence on the Budhi of the people, but also on and through their "I"s. Man is called to move the center of his being to the Budhi plane one future day. Then he will have fully and completely connected his I to Christ. In this connection he will be able to pass through the next pralaya, the superspiritual condition between the Earth development and the future Jupiter development. For this purpose he will rise into the spheres above the Arupa sphere under the guidance of Christ.

But back to the Logos, which completely fills the higher self of the Christ Being. How can we come to an idea of him as a threefold Deity? Rudolf Steiner spoke on this subject in his lectures on "the three Logoi":

"There are three definitions of beings who create a planetary chain, who are underlying a planetary chain. They are called the three Logoi. The third Logos creates by combination. If out of the single substance something else emerges with new life, it is the second Logos who creates. But wherever we have a coming out of nothing, there we have the first Logos. Hence, the first Logos is often called the Hidden in the things themselves, the second Logos the substance resting in the things, which creates the living out of the living, the third Logos the one who combines all that exists, who puts the world together out of things. These three Logoi always interpenetrate mutually in the world." [154]

In addition may be given a statement by Rudolf Steiner from one of his early private lessons in which he spoke from different points of view about the three Logoi:

---

[154] GA 93a "Grundelemente der Esoterik" (Foundations of esotericism), Berlin, Lecture of 30 October 1905

*"The first power, the unmanifested Deity, is also called the **Father**; the second power is the **Son**, who is both life and creative substance, and the third power is the **Spirit**. Together these three primordial powers appear as Father, Son and Spirit, as **consciousness, life** and **form**."* [155]

This statement leads to an understanding of how the three Logoi – Father, Son and Holy Spirit – manifest themselves within the Creation:

Christian esoteric describes the states of consciousness as *Father*.   **A**
             the states of life as *Son* or *Word*.   **B**
             the states of form as *Holy Spirit*.   **C**

Theosophy calls   **A the first**
                      B the second } **Logos.**
                      C the third

The following overview of evolution results, when considering that

> **the 1st Logos reveals himself in man as Atma,**
> **the 2nd Logos reveals himself in man as Budhi,**
> **the 3rd Logos reveals himself in man as Manas."** [156]

In the course of the seven planetary stages of evolution from ancient Saturn to Vulcan, seven successive degrees of consciousness are evolved by the power of the Father. Within each of these planetary periods of Creation, the beings developing pass through seven states of life by the power of the Son. For this purpose, they move in seven circuits or rounds across the seven globes or states of form made by the power of the Holy Spirit. With the exception of the physical globe, always two of them exist on the same world level. The astral and the plastic globe both are located on the lower astral plane, which pervades the higher physical plane, i.e. the ether sphere. The rupa globe and the intellectual globe both exist on the lower mental plane, which is pervaded by the higher astral plane. The arupa globe and the archetypical globe both are on the higher mental plane, which is pervaded by the lower Budhi plane. [157]

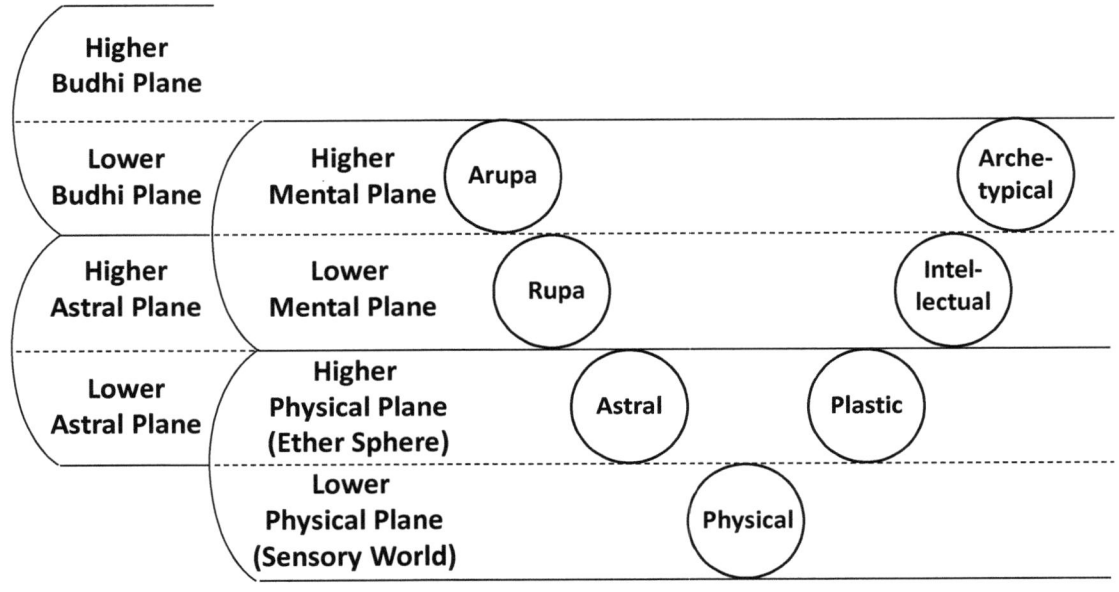

Figure 11: The 7 globes or states of form

---

[155] GA 89 "Bewusstsein – Leben – Form" (Consciousness – Life – Form), private lesson with the title "Über die Logoi" (About the three Logoi), undated, presumably 1904

[156] GA 104 "Die Apokalypse des Johannes" (The Apocalypse of John), "Zeichen und Entwicklung der drei Logoi in der Menschheit" (Signs and development of the three Logoi in humanity), from Rudolf Steiner's script for Edouard Schuré in May 1906

[157] See the explanations and figures in the chapters about the 7th, 8th and 9th weekly verses.

But, if we strive to gain a deeper understanding of the Christ-Logos-Being, we must not focus our attention on the globes or states of form, but turn to the "states of life", i.e. the rounds or circuits of the evolving beings along the seven globes. They take place in the three lower worlds, the physical plane, the astral plane and the mental plane, which, as a result of their mutual interpenetration, manifest in four world levels, as shown in Figure 11, which is based on a sketch by Rudolf Steiner from a lecture in Berlin. [158]

According to the occult law "as in the large, so in the small", the incarnation cycles of man likewise extend across the three lower worlds, or the four world levels formed by them. In periods between our lives on Earth we every time pass through the same spheres, in which the seven globes are located. By doing so, a contact with the Budhic plane is only possible to us because it pervades the Arupa region, the higher spiritual world, as described above. These states of life as well as our incarnation cycles are furthermore reflected on a smaller scale in the course of each year on Earth, as the reflections on the thirteen weekly verses of spring have clearly shown. The whole process ultimately culminates in the encounter with Christ on the Budhi plane. Additionally, our incarnation cycles are reflected on an even smaller scale in the daily cycle. But, since we sleep during a good third of it, we cannot use it practically to consciously re-experience our entire incarnation cycle on it. The situation is different, however, with the course of the year. Here we have the opportunity to consciously re-experience our entire incarnation cycle and thus the work of the Christ Being, who is advancing our development. Thus the Anthroposophical Soul Calendar with its weekly verses is not only a guide through the higher worlds, but also to Christ. And only now we really understand the answer, given by Rudolf Steiner to a question from Friedrich Rittelmeyer:

"To my question what should be done to prepare for Damascus-like Christ-events, he [Rudolf Steiner] replied: This is only possible if one experiences Christ in the course of the year. Also for that purpose, one may see our meditations." [159]

Even if this statement only referred to the monthly meditations of the year given to the priests of the Christian Community in their breviary by Rudolf Steiner, they are closely connected to the meditations of the Soul Calendar as well. Moreover, the fifty-two weekly verses of the Soul Calendar as meditation formulas are much more detailed than the twelve monthly verses of the breviary. Rudolf Steiner himself described the connection as follows:

"Well, with the weekly verses are meant the moods, which are in the Soul Calendar. The one who seeks these things out of the spirit, out of the real extra-sensory experience, always faces the very concrete situation, doesn't he? And in trying to research for your breviary, I faced your minds with my soul. When I formulated the twelve annual moods and the weekly verses, I had before me the different moods of an anthroposophical constellation, within which one could not yet know that an insight would arise anywhere, that a religious renewal was necessary. But, when you compare what we have in mind here as a breviary, with the moods of the annual weekly verses, you will feel, that things will fit in well with each other, that one will bear and enlighten the other." [160]

With the fifty-two weekly verses of the Soul Calendar, we indeed have an extraordinarily precious spiritual treasure, which may bring us a great deal closer to an understanding of the Christ Being. Who really wants to prepare himself to become able to see the etheric Christ in a Damascus experience must first acquire a deeper understanding of the Christ Being, for in all spiritual things the understanding precedes the seeing, even brings forth the latter, as Rudolf Steiner emphasized at the end of the introduction of his early book "Theosophy" already:

"The principle: to acknowledge higher worlds only when one has seen them is an obstacle to this seeing itself. The will first to understand through healthy thinking what may be seen later, promotes this seeing. It magically sets free important powers of the soul that lead to this «seeing of the seer»." [161]

So here too, the understanding of Christ precedes seeing the Christ:

"If a number of people will have evolved a feeling for it through spiritual-scientific understanding, then it will happen that these people will just as well be able to convince themselves of the truth of the Christ-event as Paul was able to convince himself at the event of Damascus. Between 1930 and 1940 there will

---

[158] GA 89 "Bewusstsein – Leben – Form" (Consciousness – Life – Form), Berlin, Lecture of 5 November 1904 and supplement to a letter to Marie von Sivers of 25 November 1905

[159] See notes 142 and 143 (pages 77 and 78).

[160] GA 343 "Vorträge und Kurse über christlich-religiöses Wirken" (Lectures and courses on Christian-religious activity / Courses for the Christian Community), Vol. II, Dornach, Questions to the Lecture of 9 October 1921 in the afternoon

[161] GA 9 "Theosophie" (Theosophy), last sentence of the introduction

be a small number of people who will evolve this ability, and then during 2500 years more and more people will see the Christ in his ether body. When they evolve to etheric vision, people will see Christ in the ether body, which they only achieve through spiritual-scientific understanding and feeling. This is the new descent of Christ to mankind on Earth. In truth, it is rather an ascent, for it will no longer be that the Christ will embody himself in the flesh. But those people who evolve up towards him will be able to perceive him in the ether body. They will know from immediate experience that Christ is alive. For those who want to recognize Christ, he will reappear in his etheric body. They will know of the Christ by seeing." [162]

In other lectures on the forthcoming vision of the etheric Christ, Rudolf Steiner also pointed to the importance of the previous attainment of an understanding of the Christ Being; for example in the lecture of 1911 in Milan:

"The understanding of Christ, as we have discussed it right now, can only be acquired on the physical plane. To make this possible, in the next three millennia people will have to acquire in the physical world the ability to see the extra-sensory Christ, and that is what the spiritual-scientific movement is for. This is its mission: to create the conditions, which bring about on the physical plane the understanding of Christ, so that the Christ can be seen. Whether, at the time when Christ intervenes in humanity as the etheric Christ, we are in a physical body or between death and new birth, this does not matter if we have acquired the ability to see him here. Let us assume, for example, that a person, because he dies earlier, could not achieve to see the Christ in his present etheric embodiment, then he would nevertheless be able to see the Christ between death and new birth, if he has acquired the understanding for it here. He who is far from spiritual life and does not acquire an understanding of Christ will stay away from the knowledge of Christ until the next life and then acquire it in the next life." [163]

Christ as the being who rules over the further development of all life in rhythmic cycles, be it either in the rounds along the seven globes, be it in the incarnation cycles of man or in the course of each year on Earth with its rhythm of monthly and weekly moods, everywhere He proves to be the driving force of development, the power of metamorphosis and transformation of the lower into higher. This is why Rudolf Steiner made metamorphosis the main subject of his architectural work of art when he was constructing the first Goetheanum, and why he named it after Goethe, the new founder of the teaching of metamorphosis. And at the foremost point of the first Goetheanum, he intended to place a wooden sculpture of the power and being, who brings about all metamorphosis and development, the Christ, the representative of man, who at the same time is the representative of God, and thereby connects man and God.

From this point of view, the twenty-six weekly verses of the summer half-year as well as those of the winter half-year, each form a kind of small Goetheanum, constructed according to the archetype of the incarnation cycle with its manifold psycho-spiritual metamorphoses of the human being. And in the middle of each of these two little Goetheana, the Christ Being stands as the central figure, as the developmental goal and future ideal of us all.

---

[162] GA 118 "Das Ereignis der Christuserscheinung in der ätherischen Welt" (The event of the appearance of Christ in the etheric world), Düsseldorf, Lecture of 20 February 1910

[163] GA 130 "Das esoterische Christentum und die geistige Führung der Menschheit" (Esoteric Christianity and the spiritual guidance of mankind), Milan, Lecture of 21 September 1911

Experiences of the Soul in Summer – Return to Life on Earth

Turn Back in the Second Sphere of the World of the Life Spirit – 14th Week

Christ, the representative of the second Logos or the Son within the Creation, who directs the states of life of all planetary beings, leads mankind towards its destiny, the development of free will and love based on I-consciousness. This evolution process takes place in the course of seven cycles along the seven globes in the lower three worlds or the four world levels formed by them. In a comparable way, Christ also leads each individual person in his incarnation cycles through the same worlds. In addition he acts as sustainer of the human I-consciousness in life after death. Hitherto, man has been able to sustain his I-consciousness by his own power only in direct contact with the sensory outside world on Earth. The ability to preserve it until the world-midnight, even after all personal thinking, willing and feeling have been given up in the course of passing through ever higher spheres of the spiritual world, this ability we owe solely to our inner attachment to Christ.

"I have told you, in this whole period of the first half of life between death and a new birth, we alternate between inner life and outer life, between loneliness and spiritual conviviality. The conditions of the spiritual world are first of such kind that every time we return to our loneliness in this spiritual world, in our inner activity we always bring before our soul again that which we have experienced in the outside world. Through this, there is a consciousness which spreads as with wings of infinity across the whole spiritual world. The wings contract again in the loneliness.

But we must sustain one thing that must remain there, no matter whether we spread out into the great spiritual world or withdraw. Before the mystery of Golgotha happened, it was possible, through the forces by which man was related to primeval times, to hold the firm I-cohesion, not to lose this I-cohesion, i.e. to retain completely clearly one thing as a memory of the past life on Earth: you were an I in that life on Earth. This must extend through times of loneliness and conviviality. Before the mystery of Golgotha, this was provided by inherited powers. Now this can only be done because with that, which we detached from us as our earthly goods, which we felt departing as soon as we left the physical body, a soul fulfillment remains connected, the soul fulfillment, which we can have by the fact that the Christ has flown out into the Earth aura. This imbuement with the Christ-substance, this is what in the present gives us the possibility to preserve the memory of our I in the transition from physical life to death until world-midnight, despite all the expansion into the spiritual world, despite all the contraction into loneliness. Until then, the impulse emanating from the Christ power lasts so that we do not lose ourselves." [164]

Thus, until world-midnight our I-consciousness can be sustained through the memory of a past life on Earth in which we have connected ourselves with Christ. When we then live through the middle of the world-midnight, being completely surrendered to these sublime experiences of universal existence in the depths of our souls, the highest and most divine experiences, in which we may participate at all on the present stage of human evolution, then we live with this universal life, this universal existence, and are threatened to more and more forget that we were and are special beings, who have gone through a long after-death developmental process. In order to come to a distinction between us and the universe, we need a new outside world on which we can wake up to ourselves again. Therefore, towards the end of the world-midnight, a longing begins to stir out of our divinely interwoven feelings, which endow us with the power to gradually awaken fully to ourselves again. This process may certainly be compared to man's awakening every morning in life on Earth. Then, too, at nighttime, the human being is fully immersed in his inner life, even though he brings no memory of it into his daytime consciousness. At the end, however, a longing for experiences of an outside world arises as the driving force for awakening. It causes memories of events of the last preceding days to rise within us from a state of unconscious emotional experience and to form dream images. Gradually even our thought life awakens again and our will impulses begin to stir. In an analogous manner, during the "awakening" from the world-midnight experienced in the depths of our souls, the longing for the previously perceived spiritual outside world rises in us, which we once irradiated and illuminated with our own light strengthened by divine powers.

---

[164] GA 153 "Inneres Wesen des Menschen und Leben zwischen Tod und neuer Geburt" (The inner nature of man and life between death and rebirth), Vienna, Lecture of 13 April 1914

"But then, out of the longing, a new spiritual force must kindle our longing to a new light. This power is only present in the spirit, in spiritual life. My dear friends, in the physical world there is nature and the divine, from which we are born into the physical world and which is pervading this nature. There is the Christ impulse that is present in the Earth aura, i.e. in the aura of physical nature. But the power, which comes to us in the world-midnight to make our longing shine over our whole past, only exists in the spiritual world. It exists only where no bodies can live. And when the Christ impulse brought us to the world-midnight, and the world-midnight was experienced by the soul in spiritual solitude – for world-darkness has occurred because the soul-light cannot radiate from ourselves then – when the Christ led us until there, then out of the word-midnight, out of our longing, something spiritual emerges, which creates a new world light and spreads a shine across our own being, through which we grasp ourselves anew in the world existence, through which we awaken anew in the world existence. The spirit of the spiritual world that awakens us, we get to know him by the process that a new light shines out from the world-midnight, irradiating our past humanhood. In Christ we died. Through the Spirit, through the bodiless Spirit, who by a technical word is called the Holy Spirit, that is, the one living without the body, for this is meant by the word «holy», without the weaknesses of a spirit living in a body, through this Spirit we are reawakened in our being out of the world-midnight.

Thus, through the Holy Spirit we are awakened in the world-midnight.

Per spiritum sanctum reviviscimus." [165]

In his lecture of the following day, Rudolf Steiner directly referred to these descriptions:

"In this, my last lecture, I would like to continue from where we ended yesterday. We have ended at what I allowed myself to call «the great world-midnight-hour of spiritual existence between death and a new birth», that midnight hour when the human inner experience becomes most intense, and what we may call spiritual conviviality, the being in contact with the spiritual outside world, has reached its lowest degree, so that in certain respects spiritual darkness is around us during this midnight hour of spiritual existence. But it has been said that the longing for the outside world has again an effect in us and that this longing becomes active through the Spirit, who works in spiritual worlds, and that this longing generates a new soul-light out of ourselves, so that it becomes possible for us to see an outside world of a very special kind now. This outside world that we then see is our own past..." [166]

Until the middle of world-midnight it is primarily the forces of Christ coming from the Budhi world that lift us up into ever higher regions and in addition, if we have already connected ourselves with him on Earth, sustain our I-consciousness in memory of our life on Earth. From the middle of the world-midnight, it is primarily the forces of the Holy Spirit from the spheres of the Arupa region that take their place and enable us to remember ourselves again and thus to reawaken us fully to ourselves.

Gradually the events experienced by us in the regions of the higher spiritual world before the begin of the world-midnight-hour dawn as a memory and spread around us as a new outside world, illuminated by our own shining light, which now regains strength through the force of the Holy Spirit. We start to remember that we were devoted to all those sublime experiences, which revealed themselves to our spiritual senses in the course our ascension to the Arupa region after death. Looking back, we re-experience that, a long time ago, when we entered the fifth region of the spiritual world and thus the higher spiritual world, we lost or forgot "own being's drive", in the words of the 9th weekly verse: "Forgetting my will's peculiarity". Then a memory reaching back even farther awakens in us, that prior to this our thinking had to "be content with a state of dream" as soon as we entered the zodiac region and the starry sky, as it says in the 8th weekly verse. It is this awakening of the remembrance of such experiences, brought about by the Holy Spirit, which led us out of the very last remnants of separate existence into a cosmic and universal existence, that is outlined in the first two sentences of the 14th weekly verse, in which Rudolf Steiner in a quite analogous way put the two verbs exceptionally in the past tense to mark the characterized experience as a retrospective:

14th Week (7 – 13 July)	14. Woche (7.- 13. Juli)
Surrendered to the senses' revelation, I lost own being's drive,	An Sinnesoffenbarung hingegeben Verlor ich Eigenwesens Trieb,

---

[165] GA 153 "Inneres Wesen des Menschen und Leben zwischen Tod und neuer Geburt" (The inner nature of man and life between death and rebirth), Vienna, Lecture of 13 April 1914

[166] Ibidem, Vienna, Lecture of 14 April 1914

| A thought-dream seemed, benumbing, | Gedankentraum, er schien |
| To rob me of my self, | Betäubend mir das Selbst zu rauben, |

The further awakening to ourselves takes place in a similar way as in life on Earth. Every morning the newly appearing sensory stimuli from our outside world help us to full mental awakening. Something similar happens at the opposite point of our incarnation cycle. The perceptions of the bright "sense-appearance" of our new spiritual outside world awaken us again to mental recognition and distinction between the inside and the outside world. Just as in life on Earth with its impressions of the senses, additionally the corresponding thoughts come up to us – even though today we may think that we would generate them by our own within us – so the "world-thinking" pervaded by the Holy Spirit "draws near" in the "sense-appearance" of the higher spiritual and the superspiritual world.

| World-thinking yet draws near | Doch weckend nahet schon |
| In sense-appearance to wake me up. | Im Sinnenschein mir Weltendenken. |

When we arrived at our after-death ascension in the fifth region of the spiritual world or the sphere of the spirit self in the narrower sense, we became aware of our higher self which bears inside the fruits of all our past incarnation cycles. The memory of this great all-round view of everything we have experienced and done in the course of our own evolution as human beings is now coming back to us. It pictorially forms before us as a new spiritual outside world. Rudolf Steiner elaborated this, after his words quoted above:

"This outside world, which we then see, is our own past, as it happened through earlier incarnations and the interim times between the deaths and the new births, and which we now see as an outside world, when we are looking back on what we have got and enjoyed from our cosmic existence and on what we have owed to this cosmic existence."

A little later in the same lecture Rudolf Steiner summarized these statements with the words:

"Then, in the midnight hour of existence, the Spirit approaches us. Now we have preserved the memory of our «I»s. If we carry it in until the midnight hour of existence, until the time when the Holy Spirit draws near to us and gives us the retrospection and the connection with our own inner world like an outer world, if we have preserved this connection, then the Spirit can now lead us to our re-embodiment, which we bring about by generating our archetype in the spiritual world."

All creation starts with awakening at a new world morning and takes place based on the memory of the preceding events. Likewise at the beginning of the Elohim's great work of creation there was a memory of former states of creation, as described by Rudolf Steiner in his lecture cycle on the biblical story of creation:

"Yes, the Elohim again created through their pondering, as if out of their memory, what I have called the complexes of existence. – And in a certain respect, these Elohim fared in the same way as we are doing when we create something out of the memory. But, we develop such activity only in a much lower field." [167]

In life on Earth we can only work in a much lower field, indeed. However, during our centuries-long stay in the spiritual and superspiritual worlds, we work in communion with the gods. There, we are involved in far more sublime activities than we are able to do in earthly life. We are allowed to witness and participate there in the process through which – based on the memory of our past incarnations – a new, future man is formed and equipped with new spiritual cognitive powers and the resulting new powers of selfhood, on the one hand, and with a new earthly corporeality, on the other.

In the following weekly verses of the Summer Quarter we find outlined the process through which, out of the universal and cosmic self, a human individual self is gradually formed, a human spirit-soul-being, which carries its new goals and will impulses, developed together with the gods, down into his next life on Earth, in order to finally awaken there to full I-consciousness. The creation of his sheaths, his new astral body, ether body and physical body, on the other hand, is the subject of the weekly verses of the Winter Quarter, which are more focused on the material processes of creation. In this way the Soul Calendar emphasizes the polarity between Cosmos and Earth. For, at the same time, when in spring and summer everywhere on Earth a physical development, fruiting and ripening takes place, in the cosmos a psycho-spiritual development is going on, a fruitening and ripening of human spirit-souls as an opposite pole. When, on the other hand, in autumn and winter the outer bodily life on Earth comes to rest and the people withdraw more into their psycho-spiritual inner world, thus becoming internally active, then the creative body-forming powers awaken in the cosmos to full effectiveness in order to develop the substantial foundations for a new

---

[167] GA 122 "Die Geheimnisse der biblischen Schöpfungsgeschichte" (The secrets of the biblical story of creation), Munich, Lecture of 22 August 1910

spring and summer as well as for new earthly corporealities. This is why the pregnancy of many animal species occurs particularly in winter, when cosmic forces make new bodies grow in the wombs for the next generation.

This seasonal division of the cosmic activities in the weekly verses and the polarity between earthly and cosmic processes is fully in accord with the Imaginations of the four seasons revealed by Rudolf Steiner. He likewise describes that in summer Uriel's cognitive powers, which comprehend everything and test for truth, are in cosmic culmination, that the human virtues carried up to him in the heights, the psycho-spiritual qualities of the people, appear there as beauty images woven from sun gold, which become part of the "worlds' beauteousness" (11th weekly verse) and the "sheen of the worlds' beauteousness" (12th weekly verse), while Gabriel's materially nourishing, body-forming powers show their effects on and in the living creatures on Earth. In the winter half-year, on the other hand, Gabriel is in cosmic culmination and prepares, working down from the spiritual worlds, the new material bearers of the living creatures on Earth. At the same time Uriel then works on Earth and endows the incarnated people inwardly with stronger powers of knowledge, wisdom and judgment so that at the turn of the year they may come to new decisions, goals and will impulses for the new year. [168]

Return to the First Sphere of the World of the Life Spirit – 15th Week

In the course of our after-death ascension into the spiritual and superspiritual world we were allowed to get to know ever higher entities as individual spirit-beings. We were allowed to experience their work in harmony with world-thinking, world-willing and world-feeling and even participate in their work. When we gradually awaken to ourselves after the world midnight, or are awakened by the world-thinking guided by the Holy Spirit, and our own past turns into a new outside world, our perception of the numerous individual spirit beings, who are involved in the evolution of humanity and the world, changes.

"Then another condition occurs. What was before was of that kind that one really saw the various spirit beings as individualities. One got to know the spirit beings, so to speak, face to face, by working with them. Then, at some point, a condition occurs – I would like to say, it is only figuratively spoken, but you can only apply pictures to these things – that these spirit beings become indistinct and even more indistinct and a general spirit-formation appears. One may express this by saying: A certain period between death and a new birth is experienced in such a way that one lives in direct contact with the spirit beings. Then comes a time when you live only in the manifestation of the spirit beings, when they manifest themselves to you. – I want to use a rather trivial example. If you see such a small grey cloud in the distance, you may think of it as a small grey cloud. When you move closer it turns out to be a swarm of mosquitoes. Now you see every single mosquito. Here it's the other way around. You perceive – first as separate individualities – the divine-spiritual beings with which you work. Then you live on in the way that you perceive the general spirituality like the swarm of mosquitoes as a cloud, where the separate individualities rather disappear, and then you live, I would say more in a pantheistic way in a general spiritual world." [169]

The weaving and working of spiritual beings in the shining light of the spiritual world is becoming more and more obscured. While the world-beings in their individual diversity were previously allowed to be experienced directly, the immediacy and truth are now replaced by a mere appearance, a "world-appearance", into which the spirit beings interweaving the cosmos seem to be "enchanted". The soul power with which we perceive this is not the world-thinking that awakens us, but the world-feeling by which we may participate even in events that are not clearly and distinctly perceivable to our spiritual vision. From now on we feel more the weaving of the spirit than that we can clearly discern it distinctively.

---

[168] GA 229 "Das Miterleben des Jahreslaufes in 4 kosmischen Imaginationen" (The experience of the course of the year in 4 cosmic imaginations), Dornach, Lecture of 13 October 1923

[169] GA 226 "Menschenwesen, Menschenschicksal und Welt-Entwicklung" (Man's being, his destiny and World-Evolution), Kristiania (Oslo), Lecture of 17 May 1923

15th Week (14 - 20 July)	15. Woche (14. – 20. Juli)
I feel the spirit's weaving in the world-appearance	Ich fühle wie verzaubert
As if concealed by an enchantment:	Im Weltenschein des Geistes Weben:
It has enwrapped my very being	Es hat in Sinnesdumpfheit
In senses' dullness	Gehüllt mein Eigenwesen,
To give the force to me,	Zu schenken mir die Kraft:
Which, powerless to give it to itself,	Die, ohnmächtig sich selbst zu geben,
My I cannot give, in its limits.	Mein Ich in seinen Schranken ist.

As the numerous spiritual individualities are withdrawing more and more from our perception and become blurred to the indeterminate, all our individual former experiences with all the fruits of life, which we collected in our previous incarnation cycles, take their place ever more clearly. This increasingly opens up to us new, most important insights about ourselves. On the basis of these findings, we are to develop the goals and capabilities for a new life on Earth. For this purpose the spiritual world endows us inwardly with a power which we at our present stage of development would never be able to develop from ourselves alone:

"Especially when we have this review of our previous experiences, we are confronted with two things with great intensity. We enjoyed this and that – this is shown to us by spiritual view, so to speak – this and that of joy, of pleasure of existence was given to us. We can overlook all what we have ever got as joy, as pleasure of existence. But we overlook it in such a way that it appears to us in its spiritual value, so to speak, that it appears to us in relation to what it has made of us.

Let's take a concrete case. We look back on something that has been given to us as enjoyment, as satisfaction in the time that has passed in any of our lives of existence. Then we feel: This is not something past; it is a thing of the past in so far as you had the enjoyment of it, but it's not something that is absolutely past. It is something that carries on its effect into all times, carries on in such a way that it waits for what we make of it.

When we have had a satisfaction, an enjoyment, we feel within ourselves – we experience it directly in our soul-existence looking back – : This must become a force in you, a force of your soul, and this force of your soul you may allow to work within you in two ways. In this spirit-existence after the world midnight, in which you are now, you have this twofold possibility. The spiritual world simply gives you abilities to make one of these possibilities a reality. You may transform this past enjoyment, this past satisfaction within you into an ability so that you develop a certain force in your soul through the past enjoyment, which enables you to this or that, through which you create something in the world, be it the smallest or the greatest, that has a value for the world. That is one thing. The other thing is that we may say to ourselves: Well, I have had the enjoyment, I want to be satisfied with the enjoyment, I want to take the pleasure into my soul and I want to feast on the fact that I have had this enjoyment in the past. If we bring about such a possibility with much of what we have enjoyed, what has satisfied us, then it happens that we create in our inner being a force on which we gradually degenerate, suffocate spiritually. And this is one of the most important things that we can learn in the spiritual world, that we become debtors of the world-existence even through enjoyment, through all that satisfies us. The prospect appears before our spiritual eye to suffocate in the after-effects of the satisfactions, of the enjoyments, if we do not decide at the right time to create abilities from past satisfactions, from past pleasures that can bring forth something valuable in life. You see again how the Spiritual and that, which happens on the physical plane, interact.

In anyone who, in the sense of yesterday's lecture, more and more familiarizes himself with the findings of the spiritual science, this spiritual science will merge into the instinctive life of his soul, and he will, so to speak, like the stirring of an inner conscience, even towards the enjoyments, towards the satisfactions he has on the physical plane, develop the mood: You must not accept any pleasure, joy, lust only for your own sake. Instead, he will pervade this lust with a kind of sense of gratitude towards the cosmos, towards the spiritual powers of the cosmos. Because he will know that he will become a debtor of the universe through every enjoyment, through every satisfaction. Most easily and safely we cope with the transformation of those pleasures and joys which are of a spiritual nature. Such pleasures and desires, which can only be satisfied by the bodily tools or at all only by the fact that man bears a body on the physical plane, are also faced by us in the indicated time between death and a new birth as something, which must be transformed, if we do not want to suffocate in it little by little. We feel the need for transformation, but we also feel the one thing, that many incarnations will be necessary, so that between these incarnations we will always be in the spiritual world again and may finally bring about the transformation. Then we find something else in the spiritual world. We find that in our present cycle of humanity with such pleasures, with such joys, in which our Psycho-Spiritual completely perishes on the physical plane, as it were, and the enjoyment, the satisfaction takes on a subhuman, I don't want to say, animal character – because joy and pleasure can take on subhuman character – that in fact with such enjoyments we cause infinite pain for certain beings of the spiritual world, who only then approach us when we enter this spiritual world. And the sight of this pain that we cause for certain beings in the spiritual world is so tremendously disturbing, oppressive, pervading our souls with such forces that we by no means get along well with the harmonious formation of the connections for the next incarnation.

With regard to what we experience on Earth of pain, of suffering – to discuss the other –, it becomes apparent on the spiritual plane that pain endured on the physical plane, suffering endured, continues to have an effect and pervade our souls on the spiritual plane with forces in such a way that these forces become will powers, that we become stronger in the soul and have the possibility to transform this strength into moral power, which we are then able to bring to the physical plane in order to have not only such abilities, through which we may create something valuable for the environment, but also to have the moral power to characterfully allow these abilities to run free.

These and many other experiences we have immediately after the spiritual midnight hour of existence. We feel, we experience, what we have become worth by our past existence. We feel, we experience, which abilities we may achieve in the future." [170]

The 12th and 13th weekly verses described that at the border of the higher spiritual world the human spirit-soul was called to a "world-flight" out into the Budhi plane and thereby was elevated for some time to its divine source beyond the spiritual world. In this sense, these two weekly verses form a unit. A similar unit is formed by the 14th and 15th weekly verses. They describe the way in which man's attention is gradually withdrawn from the Budhic world and directed back to the higher spiritual world. In the course of this process of turning back, an endowment with new powers occurs. For this to be possible, however, man's perception through spiritual senses, by means of which he was allowed to experience the sublime beings of the higher spiritual world beforehand, must be dimmed or dulled. Only in this way, they now can work from within, instead of from outside, as power-giving beings in him and endow him with the abilities necessary for a new life on Earth, which he could never develop out of and by himself.

In the lowest region of the Budhi plane, just before returning to the higher spiritual world, man finds himself in an almost contradictory situation as he was, when in the Zodiac sphere or fourth region of the spiritual world he was prepared for his after-death ascension to the higher spiritual world. At that time the "might" of his spiritual senses had to increase – "the senses' might is growing in league with the creative work of gods" – and at the same time his "force of thinking" had to be suppressed to "dullness of a dream", as it says in the 8th weekly or Pentecostal verse. It was only in this way that "divine being" could unite itself with his soul and elevate him to a higher level. But now, in the lowest sphere of the Budhi plane, at the beginning of his prenatal descent into the higher spiritual world, in an almost reverse process man must be awakened from his "thought-dream" by the "world-thinking", and at the same time the power of his spiritual senses must be dampened, dulled so that the divine spiritual beings are able to endow his soul and his I with a new power of selfhood.

I feel the spirit's weaving in the world-appearance As if concealed by an enchantment: It has enwrapped my very being In senses' dullness To give the force to me, Which, powerless to give it to itself, My I cannot give, in its limits.	Ich fühle wie verzaubert Im Weltenschein des Geistes Weben: Es hat in Sinnesdumpfheit Gehüllt mein Eigenwesen, Zu schenken mir die Kraft: Die, ohnmächtig sich selbst zu geben, Mein Ich in seinen Schranken ist.

"The divine-spiritual beings of the higher Hierarchies withdraw from him. And it appears to him only something like a manifestation, like a reflection, as if the gods would have withdrawn and their misty after-images were still before the human soul, and as if a kind of veil is woven as a misty after-image of what had been woven in reality formerly. The intuitive consciousness that one had beforehand is turning to a cosmic inspired consciousness. One no longer lives with the divine-spiritual beings, one lives with their manifestation. But instead of that an inner I is developing more and more within the soul-consciousness. At, I would like to say, the high stage of life between death and a new birth one lives completely with the divine-spiritual beings of the higher Hierarchies; the I has no inner strength, it only becomes internally

---

[170] GA 153 "Inneres Wesen des Menschen und Leben zwischen Tod und neuer Geburt" (The inner nature of man and life between death and rebirth), Vienna, Lecture of 14 April 1914

conscious of itself again when the gods withdraw and only the manifestation of the gods is there. The appearance of the gods, the radiation, turns into a kind of inspired consciousness; but, on the other hand, man feels himself as an individual being. And what first awakens in man then is a kind, I would say, desire, a kind of longing." [171]

As man approaches the higher spiritual world, the realm of intentions and goals, as Rudolf Steiner calls it in his book "Theosophy", something will-like, a "longing", as it is called in the above quotation, awakens in him besides his feeling. Through that he gradually returns to a condition similar to the one he developed soon after his last death on Earth. At that time his willing feeling or feeling will led him away from the Earth and further and further out into the spiritual cosmos. Now his feeling craving strives in the opposite direction, as Rudolf Steiner explains in the same lecture from which the above was already quoted:

"At the moment when man no longer lives in the worlds of the gods, but in the manifestations of the worlds of the gods, the desire to embody himself again on Earth awakens in him. Just by the fact, that the I-consciousness is growing stronger and stronger, this desire to embody oneself again on Earth awakens."

Return to the Sphere of the Germ Sheath of the Spirit Man – 16th Week

With the 16th weekly verse a new group of three starts, which describe the early prenatal experiences of man in the three spheres of the higher spiritual world.

If man were to remain permanently in the state of universal existence, he would completely lose his own self at his current stage of development, for only at the end of the Earth's evolution that part of mankind, which will have preserved its capacity for development hitherto, will have evolved sufficiently strengthened selves then. Today, man is still a long way from being able to unite universal consciousness and I-consciousness, allhood and selfhood, in the long term. Many times man will have to commute to and fro between these two opposite poles of consciousness. In much the same way that a young child on Earth learns to walk independently and freely only through a frequently repeated change of standing up straight and returning to the ground, whereby with each new standing upright the strength and ability as well as the duration of standing upright and walking freely increase, so also the psycho-spiritual man on his incarnation cycles must change in a rhythmic way many times between allhood and selfhood. After having lived in the centuries following his death on Earth as a universal being expanded across the cosmos, he now – using an image of geometry – has to turn from a circle's circumference back to a circle's centre. At his present stage of evolution, with regard to his consciousness the latter is only possible for him in an earthly human body, which through physical sensory perception gives him the experience of being a centre of an external world surrounding him from all sides. But this is also the first stage of I-consciousness. Through the connection of Christ with the Earth and humanity, we have been given the opportunity to maintain this I-consciousness up to the highest state of becoming universal, even if it is completely based then on the memory of the past life on Earth. This memory is the necessary link between earthly human self and world self. Only through this memory, the evolving psycho-spiritual human being retains his inner continuity and permanence.

By his encounter with God in the course of the great midnight hour of existence between two incarnations at the exact opposite pole to life on Earth, the human spirit-soul is endowed with highly sublime powers from the Budhic and Atmic plane as divine bounties from the Father and the Son. This process has an effect like a fertilisation in the depths of the human soul. It has its analogy within earthly life in that period of the vegetation life which immediately follows the summer solstice, when the Sun has already passed its highest point and fertilised germs appear everywhere in the plant world, which are destined to ripen into fruits. During this time (in the northern hemisphere) the Sun moves through the zodiac sign of Cancer, the mother sign ruled by the Moon, or the sign of the soul. Now the (northern) Earth proves to be fertilized by the Sun. We find the corresponding spiritual, even superspiritual analogy to this event on Earth characterized in those four weekly verses, which begin with the 12th weekly verse, the "John-Atmosphere", immediately after the summer solstice, and which end with the 15th weekly verse four weeks later, when the Sun passes the last degrees of the zodiac sign Cancer. (In the southern hemisphere, all this and the following manifests itself delayed by half a year.)

---

[171] GA 218 "Geistige Zusammenhänge in der Gestaltung des menschlichen Organismus" ("Spiritual relations in the configuration of the human organism), The Hague (Netherlands), Lecture of 5 November 1922

In the following month the Sun travels through the zodiac sign Leo, the sign of fruiting and ripening in the summer heat. This period of time is analogous to the spiritual developmental phase of man *after* having gone through the world midnight, the encounter with God on the Budhi plane and the psycho-spiritual fertilization that took place as a result. Similarly, like a mother on Earth only weeks after a fertilisation notices that it has taken place, so the human spirit-soul becomes fully aware of the divine fertilisation that already has happened only afterwards. This requires the intervention of the Holy Spirit. He leads man consciously from the Budhi plane back to the regions of the higher spiritual world. Only there does he realize that in the course of his passing through the midnight hour he truly has been fertilized in his soul depths, that something has been placed into him that is to ripen into a fruit. At first rather like a presentiment, but then ever more intensely and impressively, man becomes aware of the given task to preserve the spirit-gift, which he received during the midnight hour of existence as a fertilising seed in his inner being, so that the divine bounties, granted by the allness in the depths of his soul, may mature in him from now on, in order that allhood will become selfhood again, which is the prerequisite for further fruits that only can mature in the state of selfhood.

16th Week (21 - 27 July)	*16. Woche (21. – 27. Juli)*
To save the spirit-gift within,	Zu bergen Geistgeschenk im Innern,
Is my presentiment's strict order,	Gebietet strenge mir mein Ahnen,
That divine bounties, ripening	Dass reifend Gottesgaben
And fruiting in soul's grounds,	In Seelengründen fruchtend
May bring the selfhood's fruits.	Der Selbstheit Früchte bringen.

When the human being, on his after-death path of development, ascended from the lower spiritual world into the fifth region of the spiritual world and thus for the first time into the higher, purely spiritual world, he got the order, commanded by his presentiment: "And strongly tells presentiment: Now lose yourself to find yourself", as it says at the end of the 9th weekly verse. When, long time later, with regard to his consciousness man descends from the Budhi plane into the higher spiritual world and thus arrives there exactly from the opposite side, now coming from above, then he again receives a clear and unmistakable order through his presentiment: "To save the spirit-gift within, is my presentiment's strict order". With this remarkably similar choice of words at the beginning of the 16th week's verse, Rudolf Steiner makes clear that this is a soul experience which is quite comparable to the entry into the higher spiritual world from below, coming from the Zodiac sphere. The 9th and 16th weekly verses, each are the initial verses of a group of three about the experiences of the human spirit-soul in the higher spiritual world. They are related to each other.

Although the higher spiritual world is primarily the working site of the Holy Spirit, each of its three spheres are intimately related to one of the three divine Persons of the Trinity. In the seventh and highest region of the spiritual world, in which the germ sheath of the spirit man or Atma is located[172], man is particularly close to the power of the Father and thus to the source of his selfhood. The Father, however, is hidden from us. The Son stands before him as a mediator. He who sees Him, sees the father.[173] The Son acts according to the Father's will. By bringing the selfhood, the "I am", to humanity on Earth, Christ brings us a part of the Father power, which at first works fertilisingly in our soul, whereas its fruits are to be brought to maturity by the Son.

"Let us think of a power moved to the Earth that rightly brings to humanity the awareness that this «I am» can live in every single person, a power that makes it clear to man that God has sunk a drop of his substance into every person. This power would say: This «I am» is something that is within each of you. It is a part of the one divine power. That which you feel as your individual «I am» is one with the «I am» of the Father. Whoever of you has developed the awareness of this fact may say, «I and the Father are one.»" [174]

In pre-Christian times, the Father principle was effective on Earth among the ancient Hebrews through their ancestor Abraham. He turned into a kind of group-I of the ancient Israelite people, whose I-consciousness was still bound to the blood relationship and the succession of generations emanating from Abraham. But later on, the mission of the Son, the Christ, was:

---

[172] See reflection on the 10th weekly verse.

[173] John 14:9-10

[174] GA 100 "Menschheitsentwicklung und Christuserkenntnis" (Human development and understanding of Christ), Basel, Lecture of 25 November 1907

"to give man an I-consciousness, which is no longer linked to blood relationship, an I-consciousness that could say: In myself, I find the connection with the spiritual Father, with the Father, who does not let his blood physically roll down through the generations, but who sends his spiritual power into each individual soul. The I that is in me and that has a direct relationship with the spiritual Father, it was before Abraham was. Therefore I am called to pour such a power into the I, which is strengthened by the awareness of the connection with the spiritual Father power of the world. «I and the Father are one», not I and the father Abraham, who is a bodily ancestor, are one." [175]

On the border of the Budhi plane to the higher spiritual world, the human I emerges directly from God's I. At the Christmas Conference in 1923 Rudolf Steiner expressed this supreme truth with the words that "the own I comes into being in God's I". The memory of this event rests in the depths of the human soul and only those who practice "spirit-recalling" may hope to become able to lift this memory into consciousness one day. Therefore it says in the foundation stone meditation: *"Practise spirit-recalling in soul's depths, where in the working world-creator-existence the own I comes to being in God's I; and you will truly live in the world-being of Man."* [176]

However, man will have to go through many incarnation cycles before, through his ever more intimate connection with the Christ within, he may so surely know himself to be united with the "I am" of the Father, that he too will one day be able to say: *"I and the Father are one"* (John 10:30). After passing through the midnight hour of existence, man must first carry down to Earth the reverse knowledge from the highest spiritual regions: The Father and I, my Self, are one. The All- and World-Self lives in me. Out of it my selfhood emerges like a germ, which is to ripen into a fruit.

That divine bounties, ripening	Dass reifend Gottesgaben
And fruiting in soul's grounds,	In Seelengründen fruchtend
May bring the selfhood's fruits.	Der Selbstheit Früchte bringen.

This realization that the God- and World-Self is the origin and foundation of the human self, that the true human self is of the same nature as the God-Self – in a similar way as a drop of water in the ocean is of the same nature as this and yet not the ocean itself – man must preserve in himself until his new birth on Earth. The realization of the highest truth "I and the Father are one" makes man free. For God is above all limitations of Creation and one day we will return to Him as independent beings and by free will. However, the knowledge of the unity of our essence with God also includes the knowledge of the unity of the essence of each individual being with that of every other being, since they all emerged from God and are therefore of his nature. In the state of universal and world existence, man therefore also knows himself united with all beings. Therefore, in the course of the world midnight, when the truth makes man free, compassion with all beings, the ability of selfless love, is simultaneously germinated in his reawakening selfhood. And since man lives through the midnight hour of existence predominantly with the soul power of feeling, the divine basic feeling of oneness with all beings, which he is to carry down to Earth, arises in him. Only in this way his selfhood can develop fruitfully without slipping into cold egoism. Only in this way his selfhood can bear the fruits willed by God.

During his after-death ascension, the power of the Son helped the human being to carry up to the spiritual midnight hour the I-consciousness, which had been kindled on the earthly sensory experiences, and to remember: "You were this I on Earth." In his prenatal descent from the high spirit worlds, the power of the Holy Spirit now helps him to carry the consciousness of the allness of the human self and of the unity of his essence with all beings down to Earth, so that he may be able to remember even there: Once you were one with the whole universe. You came forth as a human self out of the great World Self. In the future this consciousness will be expressed more and more distinctly in man and will increase in clarity and intensity with each descent to a new life on Earth. We will owe this to the Christ impulse as well, for it does not work only until the midnight hour of existence, but even beyond that to strengthen the power of the Holy Spirit.

---

[175] GA 112 "Das Johannes-Evangelium im Verhältnis zu den drei anderen Evangelien", Kassel, (The Gospel of John in relationship to the other three Gospels, Lecture of 2 July 1909)

[176] GA 260 "Die Weihnachtstagung 1923 – 1924" (The Christmas Conference 1923 – 1924), for example Lecture of 25 December 1923 a.m. – Rudolf Steiner's original words: *"Übe Geist-Erinnern in Seelentiefen, wo in waltendem Weltenschöpfer-Sein das eigne Ich im Gottes-Ich erweset; und du wirst wahrhaft leben im Menschen-Welten-Wesen."*

"The Christ impulse does not merely endow us with such power that we just barely find the connection, but it may give us so much that if the Spirit did not approach us, the Christ impulse could propel us over. With the memory, however, we would not be able to find the connection, but the Christ impulse would propel us over. This is of great importance, and the fact that we receive such an impulse from Christ, which exceeds the most necessary degree, will become more and more necessary for man as he develops into the future. Already now it is necessary that man not only gets to know the most necessary things about Christ, so to speak, during his life on Earth, but that the Christ impulse as a powerful impulse sets itself into his soul, so that it still propels him over the midnight hour of existence. For in this way the impulse of the Spirit is strengthened by the impulse of the Christ, and we carry the impulse of the Spirit more strongly through the second half of life between death and a new birth than we would otherwise carry it through if the impulse of Christ were not there. ...

The spirit would otherwise only be for the spirit and it would cease to work at our birth. By pervading ourselves with the Christ impulse, the Christ impulse strengthens the impulse of the Holy Spirit. And thereby also such an impulse of the Spirit can be brought into our soul, which then, when we enter into earthly incarnation, is a force which we do not consume like the other forces, which we bring along through birth, in the earthly incarnation. That's what I emphasized, that we transform the forces, which we bring from the spiritual world, into our inner organization. But what we get in this way as a plus, as an extra, by the fact that the Christ impulse reinforces the spiritual impulse, that is what we carry into existence without any need to be transformed during life on Earth. The more we approach the future, more and more people will be necessary for the Earth's development, who carry something of their pervasion by the Christ impulse and the spiritual impulse into earthly life through their birth at a new incarnation. The spirit, it must work stronger so that it not only works until birth, and everything from spiritual life is transformed into inner organizing forces with the consequence that only a little consciousness remains, which teaches us knowledge about our physical environment and about what the intellect is able to grasp, which is bound to the brain. If we, as human beings evolving towards the future, would not gradually bring along a surplus of spirit, which arises in the characterized way, then humanity on Earth would cease more and more to sense that there is a spirit at all, during earthly life. Then only the unspiritual spirit, Ahriman, would reign during earthly life, and the people would only be able to know of the sensory-physical world, which one perceives through the senses, and of that, which one can grasp with the intellect bound to the brain. In a certain way, in the further development of mankind all such things are in formation right now, when mankind is in danger of losing the Holy Spirit.

But it will not lose it. Spiritual science wants to be the guardian for this, so that humanity does not lose this spirit, this spirit which approaches the soul in the midnight hour of existence in order to revive in it the longing to behold itself in its past, in all its values. No, spiritual science will have to speak of the Christ impulse increasingly, more and more insistently, so that ever more spirit in more and more people comes into physical existence through birth, and that in this physical existence more and more people arise who feel: It's true that I have within me the forces that need to be transformed into organizing forces, but something lights up in my soul that does not need to be transformed. The Spirit who only belongs to the spiritual worlds, I have brought something of him with me into this physical world, although I live in my body. It will be the Spirit who makes people see what is said of Theodora in my mystery drama «The Portal of Initiation»: That people will see the etheric figure of Christ. The power of the Spirit that thus enters the bodies will give the spiritual eye to see and understand the spiritual worlds. First you will have to understand them, then you will start to look at them with understanding. For, the looking will come because the Spirit will seize the souls in such a way that they will bring this Spirit into the bodies, and also in their earthly incarnations the Spirit will light up: first in a few only, then in a number the Spirit will light up. And may we say on the one hand: Through the Spirit, through the Holy Spirit, we are awakened in the great midnight hour of existence, so on the other hand we must say, looking to what the Spirit is doing in the Earth's development for the future: Even in the physical body the best of the soul, that which gives the view into the spiritual worlds, will be awakened more and more by the Holy Spirit. Being awakened by the Holy Spirit in the midnight hour of existence, man will also be awakened when he lives in his physical body, when he lives into the physical existence. He will awaken inwardly by being awakened through the Spirit from his sleep, on which he otherwise would be set by merely looking at the sensory world and by the intellect that is bound to the brain. People would always sleep through the mere view of the senses and through the intellect bound to the brain. But into this human sleep, with which otherwise humanity would be overcome increasingly darkening towards the future, into this sleep the Spirit will also shine in man during his physical existence. Just in the dying spiritual life, just in the spiritual life which is dying through the mere view of the senses, through the intellectual world on the physical plane, the human souls will be awakened by the Holy Spirit also in the physical existence. – Per spiritum sanctum reviviscimus." [177]

Thus, in order to become able to see the etheric Christ in earthly life and to really recognize him, three things are of importance: First, we must unite intimately with Christ on Earth in order to absorb the Christ impulse with sufficient strength so that it works over into the time after the great midnight hour to strengthen there as a second thing the power of the Holy Spirit, which will make us see. We have to bring this power down from the three regions of the higher spiritual world into our next life on Earth. As a third, however, in addition, it is necessary for man to acquire a further understanding of the Christ Being on Earth, especially *"to experience the Christ in the course of the year"*, as Rudolf Steiner once revealed to Friedrich Rittelmeyer in a personal conversation as a further prerequisite for *"Damascus-like Christ events"*.[178] The present book is intended in particular to make a contribution to the latter.

Return to the Sphere of the Germ Sheath of the Life Spirit – 17th Week

After man has "saved" in his "soul's grounds" the father powers of the "I am", "the spirit-gift" of the midnight hour of existence, as far and comprehensively as he is capable to do this at all according to his level of development, and after he has thus finished his task in the seventh and highest region of the spiritual world, then the process of internalization of the divine bounties continues. In the next lower region, the sixth region of the spiritual world, man becomes aware that he has been filled not only with the power of the Father, but also with the power of the Son, the World Word, whose germ sheath exists there. At first, this power first flowed from the outside to the spiritual "senses' doors" of man in order to be absorbed and internalized by him. In this way, he was prepared on the one hand for a better transformation of his next human ether body into life spirit, and on the other hand for the ability to find the Christ more and more clearly and distinctly also within himself in his future life on Earth.

17th Week (28 July – 3 August)	*17. Woche (28. Juli – 3. August)*
The World Word speaks,	Es spricht das Weltenwort,
Which through the senses' doors	Das ich durch Sinnestore
I was allowed to lead into soul's grounds:	In Seelengründe durfte führen:
Imbue your spirit-depths	Erfülle deine Geistestiefen
With my worlds' vastness	Mit meinen Weltenweiten,
To find me within you one time.	Zu finden einstens mich in dir.

Again, the past tense of the verb – "which ... I *was allowed* to lead into soul's grounds" – points to an event that had already taken place before. But now the World Word reveals itself in the soul-grounds of man and thus comes fully to consciousness. It lights up as world thoughts.

"Between death and a new birth we have the perception that the words, which are spread out in the universe and which mean the essence of the universe, enter us when we inhale our being and reveal themselves as the World Word within us. Here on Earth, we speak exhaling. In the spiritual word, we speak inhaling. And by uniting with us what the Logos, what the World Word tells us, the world thoughts light up within our being. Here, we work hard through our nervous system to think the thoughts of the Earth. There we draw into ourselves the world thoughts from the language of the Logos, which appears after we have first spread our being across the universe. ...

Actually, when man streams down to Earth with respect to his spirit germ – we ourselves then still remain for some time in the spiritual world above, as I have explained – he is not prepared by the spiritual world for thinking in the earthly sense or for speaking in the earthly sense, nor for walking in the sense of earthly gravity, but he is prepared for movement and orientation between the beings of the higher Hierarchies. He is not prepared for speaking, he is prepared for making the Logos resound in him. He is not

---

[177] GA 153 "Inneres Wesen des Menschen und Leben zwischen Tod und neuer Geburt" (The inner nature of man and life between death and rebirth), Vienna, Lecture of 14 April 1914

[178] See notes 142 and 143 (pages 77 and 78) as well as the complete quote in the chapter "The Christ Being"

prepared for the dark thoughts of earthly life, he is prepared for the thoughts that become shining in him, within the cosmos." [179]

For the reason that in our innermost being we are created from divine essence and filled with divine essence, we are enabled to retrieve God in ourselves, not only during our prenatal stays in the spiritual world, but also in the following lives on Earth, insofar as we seek for Him in most sincere prayer or in meditation:

"Thus, we see that both in prayer and in meditation we seek what may be termed the union of the soul with the divine currents pervading the world, which at the highest level is the so-called unio mystica, the mystical union with the deity. The beginning of it is in prayer, the beginning of it is in meditation. Man never could unite with his God, never come into contact with the higher spiritual beings if he himself were not an outflow of this divine-spiritual entity." [180]

In the sixth region of the spiritual world, religious feeling and striving is planted into us, which gradually transforms the human ether body or life body into life spirit as that higher member of being through which Christ, the Son works in us, who reveals himself as the World Word. Here, we get planted into us already, whether in our next life on Earth we will be able to recognize the Christ outside of us in his ether body and also find the Christ within us. Many people will probably see the etheric Christ, since etheric vision will develop as a natural gift in humanity. However, only those who have already found him in themselves will see him with understanding and only by that recognize him. Rudolf Steiner once described the relation between Christ and the sixth member of the human being, using the example of a parable given to us by the Son of God himself:

"Another parable that I will mention briefly is that of the five foolish and the five wise virgins. That also gives us a lot to think about. Let us take a closer look at it: «Then the kingdom of heaven will be like ten virgins who took their lamps and went out to meet the bridegroom. But five of them were foolish, and five were wise. The foolish took their lamps, but they did not take oil with them. But the wise took oil in their vessels, with their lamps. As the bridegroom was delayed, they all became drowsy and fell asleep. But at midnight there was a shout, «Look! Here is the bridegroom! Come out to meet him.» Then all those virgins got up and trimmed their lamps. The foolish said to the wise, «Give us some of your oil, for our lamps are going out.» But the wise replied, «No, lest there should not be enough for us and for you; you had better go to the dealers and buy some for yourselves.» And while they went to buy, the bridegroom came, and those who were ready went with him to the wedding; and the door was shut. Later the other virgins came also, saying, «Lord, Lord, open to us.» But he replied, «Truly I tell you, I do not know you.» Keep awake therefore, for you know neither the day nor the hour, in which the Son of man is coming.»

Here it is indicated that this parable relates to the fact that Christ will appear again in the future. Let's make it clear. We can do that if we look at the parts of the human being again. When I work on the astral body, then the Holy Spirit in the Christian sense arises. When the I works on the ether body, then what we call Budhi or Christ or the Logos arises. In my «Theosophy» the Holy Spirit is called spirit self, and Christ, the Logos, is called Budhi or life spirit.

When we look at today's man, we find that of the people as they live today have developed physical body, ether body, astral body and I. If the I is working on the astral body, the Holy Spirit, the spirit self, Manas, develops from the astral body. And because the I has already worked a bit on the astral body, there is also some Manas, some Holy Spirit in the human beings. This Manas works into man through the outpouring of the Holy Spirit. There will come a time when mankind will enter the sixth of the root races. Then Manas will be developed in those people who have really done something for their development. Manas will be developed in them. They will be ready to receive Budhi, the Christ, the sixth basic part. In the sixth race, people will develop Christ, the majority of them. We are approaching this point in time. It is a time when the Christ Jesus will appear. At this point men will be given the strength to move where they may receive the Christ in a new form as fruit, where the Christ has laid the seed, like a mustard seed, so to speak, that will rise in the soul. The Christ will appear in visibility to those who have developed the Christ Eye in themselves. What man develops in himself is described by a parable, by a symbol. Just as the physical man is created by the interaction of the male and the female, it is imagined that the other parts of man are also fertilized, that the different parts are also fertilized in a certain way. In primeval times, only the physical body of man existed. That was in Saturn time. Then the ether body and then the astral body

[179] GA 219 "Das Verhältnis der Sternenwelt zum Menschen und des Menschen zur Sternenwelt" (The relationship of the starry world to man and man to the starry world), Dornach, Lecture of 26 November 1922

[180] GA 96 "Ursprungsimpulse der Geisteswissenschaft" (Original impulses of the science of the spirit), Berlin, Lecture of 28 January 1907

evolved. This emergence of new moments of development may be imagined as a fertilisation. There you can also see, especially in this example, how deeply the words of the Bible are to be grasped. It is not for nothing that the Bible says, «And Adam recognized his wife» for the fact that she has been fertilized. For, the consciousness of a spiritual fertilization is presupposed. To recognize means to be impregnated with something. Self-knowledge means nothing else than being fertilized with the divine self. Know yourself, means: let yourself be impregnated with the divine self that pervades the world.

Something similar underlies the parable of the five foolish and the five wise virgins in Christian esotericism. It presents this fertilisation in the image of the lamp that has received oil. Thus, each of these parts of man is imagined as a virgin, who has still remained unfertilized, and the fertilised members of man as the virgins, who have poured oil on their lamps. The undeveloped part of humanity stagnates, has no oil on the lamp, does not raise its members to Budhi. The developed one made the spirit work on their bodies, poured oil on their lamps, so to speak. The others did not pour oil on their lamps. They did not develop their five members. The former have developed them, they have prepared themselves at the important time when Christ will be coming. Then it is the time, when the Christ comes. Some will have poured oil on their lamps, their souls will become bright and ready to receive the Christ. The others who have remained dark in themselves will see that others have developed this and they will go to receive wisdom from the others. They will have to get the oil from the dealers. But they're too late. And what will the Christ say to the wise virgins? I know you. – And what will he say to the unwise virgins? I do not know you.

So the parable, applied to fertilization, means: He will come to fertilize the sixth basic part and he will move into the sixth basic part." [181]

Although Rudolf Steiner relates this parable to man's encounter with the etheric Christ on Earth, it also refers to man's encounter with the Christ Being in the midnight hour of existence. There too, Christ is the bridegroom of the virginal human spirit-soul. Accordingly the parable says: *"As the bridegroom was delayed, they all became drowsy and fell asleep. But at midnight there was a shout, Look! Here is the bridegroom! Come out to meet him."* – Whoever is not sufficiently prepared for this event, because he does not have enough oil for his lamp of wisdom, cannot acquire it in the spiritual world in a short period. He first has to descend again into a life on Earth in order to *"get the oil from the dealers"*.

Even when the great midnight hour of existence is over, the human spirit soul remains for a long time in a state of supreme receptivity, and he experiences an extremely significant realization of the fertilization that has already taken place through the powers of God. In the sixth region of the spiritual world, this awareness primarily concerns the Budhi, the life spirit, the lowest member of the Christ Being, who has its germ sheath there. The more intensively a person is able to consciously participate and collaborate in these processes, the more he will succeed in earthly life in finding the Christ both in the outside world as an ether figure and the Christ in himself, and the more glorious the marriage of the virgin human spirit soul with Christ as the bridegroom will be.

Return to the Sphere of the Spirit Self – 18th Week

In the seventh and sixth regions of the spiritual world the human being was devoted to the reception and internalizing of the World Word streaming to him from the vastness of the world. In the fifth region, this process of internalizing the spirit-happening continues. It should connect closely with the human soul in the long term. The soul is to become the sheath of the spirit, "the spirit's dress". Of the three soul members of man, the intellectual soul and first of all the consciousness soul are qualified for this. Comparable to a calyx and a bloom, they are able to widen in order to receive the spirit and, above all, to take into themselves the power of the Holy Spirit here. Although he is the sovereign of the entire spiritual world, in its fifth region, the region of the spirit self in the narrower sense, he presents himself with special intensity, since he works, above all, through the human spirit self.

"By making the independent true and good liven up in his inner being, man rises above the mere sentient soul. The eternal Spirit shines into it. A light emerges in it that is imperishable. In so far as the soul lives in this light, it participates in an Eternal. It connects its own existence with it. What the soul carries in itself as truth and good is immortal in it. – That which lights up in the soul as eternal is here called the consciousness soul. – ... Consciousness soul means her the kernel of human consciousness, the soul in

---

[181] GA 96 "Ursprungsimpulse der Geisteswissenschaft" (Original impulses of the science of the spirit), Berlin, Lecture of 27 April 1907

the soul. It is distinguished here from the intellectual soul as a special soul member. The latter is still involved in sensations, drives, affects and so on. Everyone knows that he considers to be true first, what he prefers in his sensations and so on. But only that truth is the enduring one that has detached itself from all tastes of such sympathies and antipathies of the sensations and so on. The truth is true, even if all personal feelings rebel against it. That part of the soul in which this truth lives may be called the consciousness soul.

Thus, as with the body, one would have to distinguish three members in the soul, too: the sentient soul, the intellectual soul and the consciousness soul. And as the corporeality has a limiting effect on the soul from below, so the spirituality has an expanding effect on it from above. Because, the more the soul fills itself with the true and the good, the farther and more comprehensive the eternal becomes in it. – To the one who is able to «see» the soul, the shine that emanates from man, for the reason that his eternal expands, is a reality just as the light that radiates from a flame is real to the sensory eye. To the «seer», the bodily person is only a part of the whole person. The body exists as the coarsest structure in the midst of others, which interpenetrate mutually. The physical body is imbued by the ether body as a life-form. At all sides projecting this the soul body (astral form) is discernible, and projecting over this in turn the sentient soul, then the intellectual soul, which becomes all the larger the more it absorbs of the true and the good. For this true and good causes the expansion of the intellectual soul." [182]

Here again we see a contradiction between the physical and the spiritual world. In the physical world, a sheath, a container, has a fixed size and shape. The content that is poured into it has to adapt completely to the sheath. In the spiritual world, however, conditions are exactly the opposite. There the container must adapt to the content, the soul to the spirit, which wants to pour itself into it and wrap itself with it, connect with it. Quite in this sense it says in the next weekly verse:

18th Week (4 – 10 August)	*18. Woche (4. – 10. August)*
Can I expand the soul	Kann ich die Seele weiten,
That it unites itself	Dass sie sich selbst verbindet
With the received World-Germ-Word?	Empfangnem Welten-Keimesworte?

Rudolf Steiner's carefully chosen words are really intimately in harmony with his statements in the paragraphs quoted above. However, they also raise the question: What does he mean by the "World-Germ-Word"? This term is a completely new creation. If we want to understand the full meaning of what Rudolf Steiner wants to tell us here, we must therefore look for information and explanation in his writings and lectures. In case we find such information there, then what we find should also be in inner connection with the higher spiritual world, from which the soul is finally to receive the "World-Germ-Word" according to the wording of the 18th weekly verse. – In fact, we find what we are looking for in his early book "Theosophy", as has often been the case:

"The fifth, sixth and seventh regions [of the spiritual world] are significantly different from the previous ones. For the beings within them provide the impulses for the activity of the archetypes of the lower regions. In them one finds the creative powers of the archetypes themselves. The one who is able to rise to these regions becomes acquainted with the «intentions» that underlie our world. The archetypes still exist here as living germinal points, ready to take on the most diverse forms of thought beings. If these germinal points are put into the lower regions, then they swell up as it were and show themselves in the most diverse forms. The ideas by which the human spirit appears creatively in the physical world are the reflections, the shadows of these G e r m T h o u g h t B e i n g s of the higher spiritual world. The observer with the «spiritual ear», who rises from the lower regions of the «spirit land» to these upper regions, becomes aware of how the sounding and tones are translated into a «spiritual language». He begins to perceive the «s p i r i t u a l w o r d», through which for him now not only things and beings proclaim their nature through music, but express it in words. They tell him what may be called in the science of the spirit, their «eternal names»." [183]

Now we understand what Rudolf Steiner means using the term "World-Germ-Word". In the fifth region of the spiritual world, our future, new incarnation initially is also "only" a spiritual archetype, a germ thought that sounds as a word, a World-Germ-Word that streams to the consciousness soul from the surrounding

---

[182] GA 9 "Theosophie" (Theosophy), Chapter "Das Wesen des Menschen" (The essential nature of man), Section IV, "Leib, Seele und Geist" (Body, soul and spirit)

[183] GA 9 "Theosophie" (Theosophy), Chapter "Die drei Welten" (The three worlds), Section III "Das Geisterland" (The spirit land)

spiritual world. Obviously the Thought Germ Beings of the higher spiritual world are always composed of two parts: germ and sheath. Accordingly, Rudolf Steiner continues in his description immediately after the above quotation from "Theosophy":

"One must imagine that these Thought Germ Beings are of a composite nature. From the element of the thought world only the germ sheath is taken, so to speak. And this encompasses the very life kernel. Thus we have reached the border of the «three worlds», for the kernel comes from even higher worlds. When man was characterized according to his components in a preceding section, this life kernel of him was specified, and the «life spirit» and «spirit man» were given as its components. For other World Beings there are similar life kernels as well. They come from higher worlds and are transferred to the three specified in order to accomplish their tasks in them."

The spirit man filled with the powers of the Father, which as a life kernel belongs to the Atmic world, and the life spirit filled with the powers of the Son, which is at home in the Budhic world, they both are enveloped in germ sheaths constituted of the material in the higher spiritual world. The creative Truth Word of the great midnight hour of existence, during which the Son reveals himself to us from the Budhic world – and through him the Father, too –, envelopes itself in the higher spiritual world in Manasic spirit sheaths. The spirit self, Manas, thus becomes the outer sheath of the two highest spiritual members of the human being and by that the bearer of the World-Germ-Word. This spirit self, in turn, is now to be enveloped in man's consciousness soul, which for this purpose should be shaped to "the spirit's dress" in the fifth region of the spiritual world. The human being must actively contribute to this. And obviously he becomes aware that, first of all, he has to find the appropriate strength to be able to master the task at hand. Accordingly, the 18th weekly verse continues:

I sense that I must find the strength	Ich ahne, dass ich Kraft muss finden,
To shape the soul worthy of it,	Die Seele würdig zu gestalten,
To mould it to the spirit's dress.	Zum Geistes-Kleide sich zu bilden.

In his lecture cycle on the Gospel of Matthew, Rudolf Steiner explained precisely this task of man and illustrated it with a sketch (see figure 12).

"Man, we have said, develops upwards in such a way that he unfolds in his being the consciousness soul in which the spirit self may appear. But when he has developed the consciousness soul, then spirit self, life spirit and spirit man have to descend towards him so that his opening bloom can receive this upper trinity. We may also graphically depict this upward development of man as an upward development of a kind of plant.

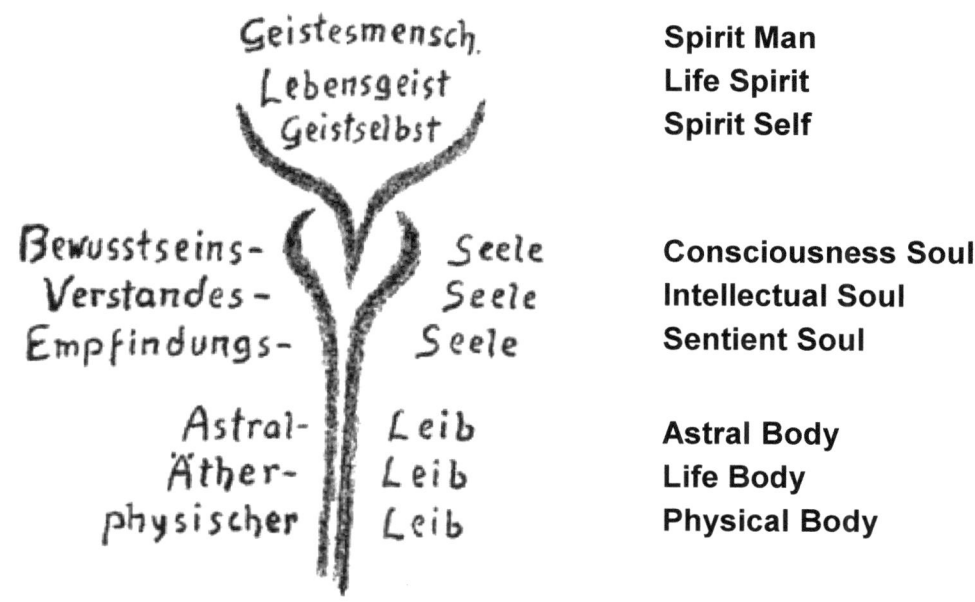

Figure 12: Comparison of the human members of being with a plant (GA 123)

In the consciousness soul man opens up, and the spirit self or Manas, the life spirit or the Budhi and the spirit man or Atma approach towards him. So this is something that, as it were, descends from above towards man as the Spirit-Fertilizing." [184]

But where could man find the strength which, in the course of his prenatal descent to a new earthly life, he needs in order to become able to widen his consciousness soul enough and shape it to a "dress" that is worthy of the spirit in the fifth region of the spiritual world, the actual sphere of the spirit self? He receives it from those spiritual beings, who in ancient Lemuria sacrificed the I as the fourth member of being to him and subsequently took over the care of the development of the spirit self. They are the Exusiai, the Powers or the Spirits of Form, the lowest Hierarchy of creative spirit beings, whose lowest member of being is the spirit self.

"In the beginning of the development of the Earth, man has got his physical body as a preliminary stage, then his ether body and astral body. The Spirits of Form come over from the Moon. Their lowest member is the I. They then sacrifice this I, too, and fertilize man in his preliminary stage with the I so that the I, as it appears on Earth, is a fertilizing power which now streams out from the Spirits of Form; and the Spirits of Form retain the spirit self or Manas as the lowest member of their being. So if we wanted to describe them, we would have to say: the Spirits of Form rule over us in our environment in the Earth's atmosphere. Their lowest member is spirit self or Manas, in which they live and weave, and they have sacrificed that which they once had on the Moon, the I, which works in all directions. It trickled down and fertilized man." [185]

Today man is called to widen his consciousness soul more and more so that it becomes able to take in and wrap up like a dress the Manas which streams to it from the spiritual environment, filled with the germs of Atma and Budhi, as the composite World-Germ-Word of the higher spiritual world.

"Just as in the past the I was around us, then entered into us and works as God in us, so the present lowest member of the Spirits of Form is spread around us: Manas-wisdom. Through the I we are able to develop human wisdom first. But spread around us in the cosmos is divine wisdom. What man should gradually attain is spread out, secretly interwoven into the world that surrounds us. And we ourselves will be filled with this divine wisdom when the Earth will have reached the goal of its evolution, because in us is effective the God in man, the I. Wisdom belongs to the members of the Spirits of Form, wisdom is to them what the physical body is to us. Wisdom-light is the Deity's dress." [186]

The spirit self, Manas, the outer sheath of man's two highest members of being and by that the "Deity's dress", must be wrapped in another "dress", the consciousness soul of man. Thus at the end of his descent through the higher spiritual world – just before he moves into the Zodiac sphere, the fourth region of the spiritual world – he becomes a World Soul Being which is filled with a threefold spirituality pervaded with divine powers as the Trinity's divine bounties. Rudolf Steiner summarized this in a few words in his "Theosophy":

"Consciousness soul and spirit self form a unity. In this unity the spirit man lives as the life spirit." [187]

In this way, man himself becomes a bearer of Trinitarian effectiveness. The 18th weekly verse obviously presents itself to us as an analogue to the 9th weekly verse, which describes the human being coming into direct contact with the powers of the Trinity during his after-death ascension from Earth to the fifth region of the spiritual world, the region of the spirit self, and thus from the opposite direction. In harmony with this, Christianity celebrates the feast of the Holy Trinity on the 9th Sunday of the Easter and post-Easter feast season (the 8th Sunday *after* Easter). When on his prenatal descent to a new life on Earth, man enters the fifth region of the spiritual world again, but coming from higher spheres this time, he again experiences a Trinitarian mood, now as the conclusion of his direct encounter with the threefold and triune Deity. Here, the period of his receptivity to the direct influences of the higher spiritual world ends. In the following process, the consciousness soul will carry down to Earth as much as possible of the received spirit content, according to its respective level of maturity, in order that the divine goals and intentions of the higher spiritual world will have an effect there and may ultimately result in earthly deeds through will impulses that have become human.

---

[184] GA 123 "Das Matthäus-Evangelium" (The Gospel of Mathew), Bern, Lecture of 11 September 1910

[185] GA 102 "Das Hereinwirken geistiger Wesenheiten in den Menschen" (Influence of spiritual beings upon man), Berlin, Lecture of 29 February 1908

[186] GA 266a "Aus den Inhalten der esoterischen Stunden" (From the contents of the esoteric lessons) (From the contents of the esoteric lessons) Volume I, Berlin, esoteric lesson of 14 March 1908

[187] GA 9 "Theosophie" (Theosophy), Chapter "Das Wesen des Menschen" (The essential nature of man), Section IV, "Leib, Seele und Geist" (Body, soul and spirit)

Return to the Sphere of the Zodiac – 19th Week

The time of immediate receptivity to the Trinity's divine gifts comes to an end with the return of the human spirit-soul to the Zodiac region, the fourth region of the spiritual world. But before man may again direct his attention more towards himself, he is first given the task to take up all experiences of the higher spiritual world, everything he received there, into his memory in order to preserve it for his further descent to a new life on Earth. That, however, is only possible because the immediacy of spirit-experience diminishes, just as in life on Earth our memories become a mere shadowy image of the physically experienced and recede into the background of our consciousness. A mysterious process transforms past experiences into memories. By encompassing this precious good as something of his own, man now withdraws more and more from the other beings of the higher spiritual world and begins to densify himself into an individual being. This process of closing off one's own Psycho-Spiritual from the All-Soul and the All-Spirit finds its image in the physical world in the nocturnal starry sky in the constellations of the zodiac, which delimits an inner space of its own from the surrounding universe and encompasses it like a circle. In this way something independent is created, which may now awaken to its own development. In the fifth region of the spiritual world the human spirit-soul still felt to be a member of the higher spiritual world and its beings. In the fourth region, however, man's own psycho-spiritual powers are now awakened so that more and more an independent human self may emerge by this process.

19th Week (11 – 17 August)	19. Woche (11. – 17. August)
To encompass the newly-got	Geheimnisvoll das Neu-Empfang'ne
With memory mysteriously	Mit der Erinn'rung zu umschließen,
Shall be my aspiration's further point:	Sei meines Strebens weiterr Sinn:
This shall awaken, getting stronger,	Er soll erstarkend Eigenkräfte
Own powers in my inner being	In meinem Innern wecken
And, growing, give me to myself.	Und werdend mich mir selber geben.

The ability to remember is inseparably linked to the I-development. It is not our sensory perceptions, whether attained through physical senses or through spiritual senses, that make us an I. The plants already have sensory perceptions. Likewise, it is not the presence of feelings, wishes and impulses of will that makes us a human I, for such are already found in the animal kingdom. Only our very personal memories, which run like a unifying thread through the life of each person, enable us to have a continuity of consciousness and by that to have an I-experience. Each human being collects a limited amount of very personal contents of consciousness in the course of his life and thereby individualizes himself into an I. By "encompassing" the spirit self, which is connected with the consciousness soul by the I, man on his prenatal descent from the higher spiritual world ultimately individualizes everything he has been allowed to receive from the highest divine truth and in this way makes himself an individual spirit-soul-being.

"And in the I the spirit is alive. The spirit radiates into the «I» and lives in it as in its «sheath», just as the «I» lives in body and soul as its «sheaths». The spirit develops the «I» from inside to outside, the mineral world from outside to inside. The spirit, developing an «I» and living as an «I», is called «spirit self» because it appears as the «I» or «self» of man. The difference between the «spirit self» and the «consciousness soul» can be made clear in the following way. The consciousness soul touches the truth which is independent of any antipathy and sympathy and exists through itself; the spirit self carries within itself the same truth, but absorbed and enclosed by the «I», individualized by the latter and taken over into the independent being of man. By making the eternal truth so independent and connected with the «I» to an entity, the «I» itself attains eternity. The spirit self is a revelation of the spiritual world within the «I», just as from the other side the sensory sensations are a revelation of the physical world within the «I»." [188]

When mankind will have completed its evolution along the seven planetary stages from ancient Saturn to Vulcan in the distant future, it will have outgrown all planetary existence and will be able to operate in the Zodiac region with full I-consciousness. Then the I will be our lowest member of being, to which spirit self, life spirit and spirit man, as well as the germs to even higher members, will follow upwards. In this composition we will then ascend into the vastness of the stellar cosmos for a development we cannot grasp yet, in order to contribute as zodiac forces to the formation of a new planetary system and to enable cosmically younger beings to develop their own. But this evolutionary stage is still a long way off for us.

---

[188] GA 9 "Theosophie" (Theosophy), Chapter "Das Wesen des Menschen" (The essential nature of man), Section IV, "Leib, Seele und Geist" (Body, soul and spirit)

First of all, we must become self-aware "I"s, capable of acting independently. For this, we must be able to detach and distinguish ourselves from the general spiritual world and its beings.

"But on the other hand, if we could only experience between death and a new birth, what makes us one with the beings of the higher world, if we never came to ourselves in the spiritual world, then it would be impossible for us here on Earth to ever come to free will, to the consciousness of free will, to the consciousness of our personality, which is basically identical with the consciousness of free will. So by developing morality and free will here on Earth, morality and free will are memories of that rhythm which we experience in the spiritual world above, between death and a new birth, in the manner described. But by directing our gaze to the soul, we may determine even more precisely what remains in the soul as echo on the one hand of that becoming one with the spiritual beings, and on the other hand of that spiritual self-awareness which we experience alternately with it. That which remains us as an echo here in life on Earth within our soul of the union with the beings of the spiritual world is the ability to love. This ability to love is connected with moral life more intimately than you think. For without the ability to love, there would be no moral life here on Earth. Every moral life emerges from the sympathy we have for the other human soul, emerges from the longing to accomplish what we do in sympathy for the other human soul. The way we behave selflessly towards other people, the way we can become moral in love, is essentially an echo of living together with the spiritual beings in the world between death and a new birth."

As already mentioned, mankind is given the high goal of maturing into a tenth Hierarchy of spirit beings, who will be allowed to bear the sublime name "Spirits of Free Will and Love". The development of love and moral forces in man is the basic subject of the weekly verses of the winter half-year, whereas the development of free will is that of the weekly verses of the summer half-year. Therefore, the words of the 13th weekly verse, the last in the series of those weekly verses sketching our after-death ascension, point out to us that at the great midnight hour of existence "flames in our souls' depths out of the spirit's fire-worlds the Truth Word of the Gods". We are thus reminded of the words of Christ, which he spoke on Earth after having emphasized his unity with the Father: *"You will know the truth and the truth will set you free."* (John 8:32) Shortly afterwards, he described his task as the Son of God with the words: *"If the Son makes you free, you shall be free indeed."* (John 8:36). In order to become free, in the sense of independent, soon after the great midnight hour of existence the human being must become an individual again out of his universal existence in which he knew himself one with all other spiritual beings. For this to happen, the higher spirit beings withdraw from him, hide themselves from him and only reveal their weaving activity in the world existence, which man is able then to perceive intuitively. Accordingly it says in the 15th weekly verse: "I feel the spirit's weaving in the world-appearance as if concealed by an enchantment." Besides periods of communal experience with other spirit beings, man must also alternately go through periods of lonely experience during which he is given the power of self-becoming. Only in this way he can turn into an independent self again. Quite in this sense, Rudolf Steiner continues after his lecture excerpt quoted above:

"And what remains for us of this, I would like to say, lonely experience – for that is how it is – of the lonely experience of our self in the spiritual world? For, we feel lonely when we exhale, so to speak. Inhaling is like experiencing spiritual beings, exhaling like experiencing our self. But the feeling of loneliness, you see, the echo of this feeling of loneliness, is here on Earth the ability of memory, of remembrance. We would have no memory as human beings if this were not an echo of the feeling of loneliness just described. We are real men in the spiritual world because we are able, I cannot say to withdraw into ourselves, but to free ourselves from that which is in us of higher spirits. Thereby we are human beings, independent people in the spiritual world. And here on Earth we are independent people, because we can remember our experiences. Just think what your independence would look like if you could only ever live in the present with your thoughts. Your remembered thoughts are what makes you have an inwardness at all. Memory makes us a personality here on Earth. This memory is the echo of that experience of loneliness in the spiritual world that I have described." [189]

The formation of a sense of self through separation and shutting ourselves from other spiritual beings has already been compared above with the image of the zodiac, which surrounds a limited space in the cosmos. Similarly, the skin surrounds our body and separates it from its environment. It is the epithelial cells of the skin that form our sensory organs, which provide the basis for our I-consciousness on Earth. Furthermore, only through the body surface of the skin, which encompasses the human organism, and through its external sensory organs the typical human form comes about. In its twelve sections, from crown

---

[189] GA 218 "Geistige Zusammenhänge in der Gestaltung des menschlichen Organismus" (Spiritual relations in the configuration of the human organism), Stuttgart, Lecture of 4 December 1922

to sole, it is an imaginative image of the twelve forces of the zodiac and the human I, projected into the physical world.

The region of the zodiac is the border between the higher and the lower spiritual world. From here man descends into the planetary spheres not only to individualize as a spirit among spirits through the I, but also as a soul among souls.

Relationships between the Weekly Verses

The detailed reflections on the deeper contents of the thirteen ascending weekly verses of the spring quarter and the immediately following first six descending weekly verses of the summer quarter, offer sufficient material to take an interim look at the quite important subject of the relationships between the weekly verses.

The best known are certainly the relationships between the so-called "mirror verses". They owe their name to the fact that they are always at the same vertical distance from the horizontal mirror axis Easter – Michaelmas. For example, the first saying of the summer half-year, the 1st weekly or Easter verse, just above the mirror axis, is in a mirrored relationship to the immediately preceding last saying of the winter half-year, the 52nd weekly verse, which is just below the horizontal mirror axis. The second last one, the 51st weekly verse of the winter half-year is the mirror saying to the 2nd weekly verse of the summer half-year and so on. The mirror verses reveal their relationships right on the face of it by strikingly similar design and choice of words. The beginning of the 1st weekly verse "When from the vastness of the world ..." is reflected in the same words at the beginning of the 52nd weekly verse "When from the depths of soul ...", whereby the reflection is additionally accompanied by a polarity of content between the "vastness of the world" pointing to the outside world and the "depths of soul" pointing to the inner world. A similar mirror-image relationship and polarity exists between the initial words of the 2nd weekly verse "Into the sensory universe's outer region ..." and those of the 51st weekly verse "Into the inside of the human being ..." Here, too, the "sensory universe" refers to the outside world or the "vastness of the world". On the other hand, the words "into the inside of the human being" are aimed at the inner world, the "depths of soul" of man. Thus, a few words immediately reveal the whole polarity between the weekly verses of the summer half-year and those of the winter half-year.

Nearly all weekly verses show such a striking pairing oriented on the mirror axis. The only exceptions to the rule are the Michaelmas verse and its subsequent saying, which, as 26th and 27th weekly verses, do not outwardly express their mirror relationship in a similar design and choice of words, although it exists in terms of content. A consistently executed regularity would probably be too rigid and ahrimanic. In everything that is regular there must always be at least one irregular element, at least one exception to the rule. But, the obvious relationship between two mirror verses is by no means based on a merely abstract rule. There is a deeper meaning in the fact that both verses describe experiences of the human soul within the same planetary or cosmic sphere. Their nonetheless existing diversity results besides the reason already mentioned additionally from the fact that these spheres are passed by humans once ascending and once descending.

Apart from such vertical mirror relationships between the spring and winter verses on the one hand and the summer and autumn verses on the other, there are additional relationships of content between the weekly verses of spring and the diagonally opposite weekly verses of autumn. In both cases the after-death ascension of man through the different spheres is characterized, albeit with different subjects, once leading into the vastness of the world and once into the soul's depths. The same relationship exists between the weekly verses of the summer quarter and those of the winter quarter. Both groups of verses deal with the descending prenatal development of man, once with the focus on the psycho-spiritual formation of man out of the world self, in the summer verses, and once with the focus on the bodily origin of man out of the universe in the winter verses. In this way, for each verse there is an associated one, but diagonally opposite to it in the course of the year. For this reason, such pairings may be termed "diagonal verses" or "opposite verses".

But even within a half-year there are pairings. Verses, which are on the same height above the mirror axis Easter - Michaelmas, describe experiences of man within the same sphere, however, once at his after-death ascension and once at his prenatal descent. Such pairings may therefore be called "horizontal verses" or "parallel verses".

Consequently, over the entire course of the year, always four weekly verses describe human experiences within the same planetary or cosmic sphere. In Figure 13, this is illustrated graphically using the example of the verses relating to the Zodiac sphere or the fourth region of the spiritual world, i.e. the 8th, 19th, 34th and 45th weekly verses.

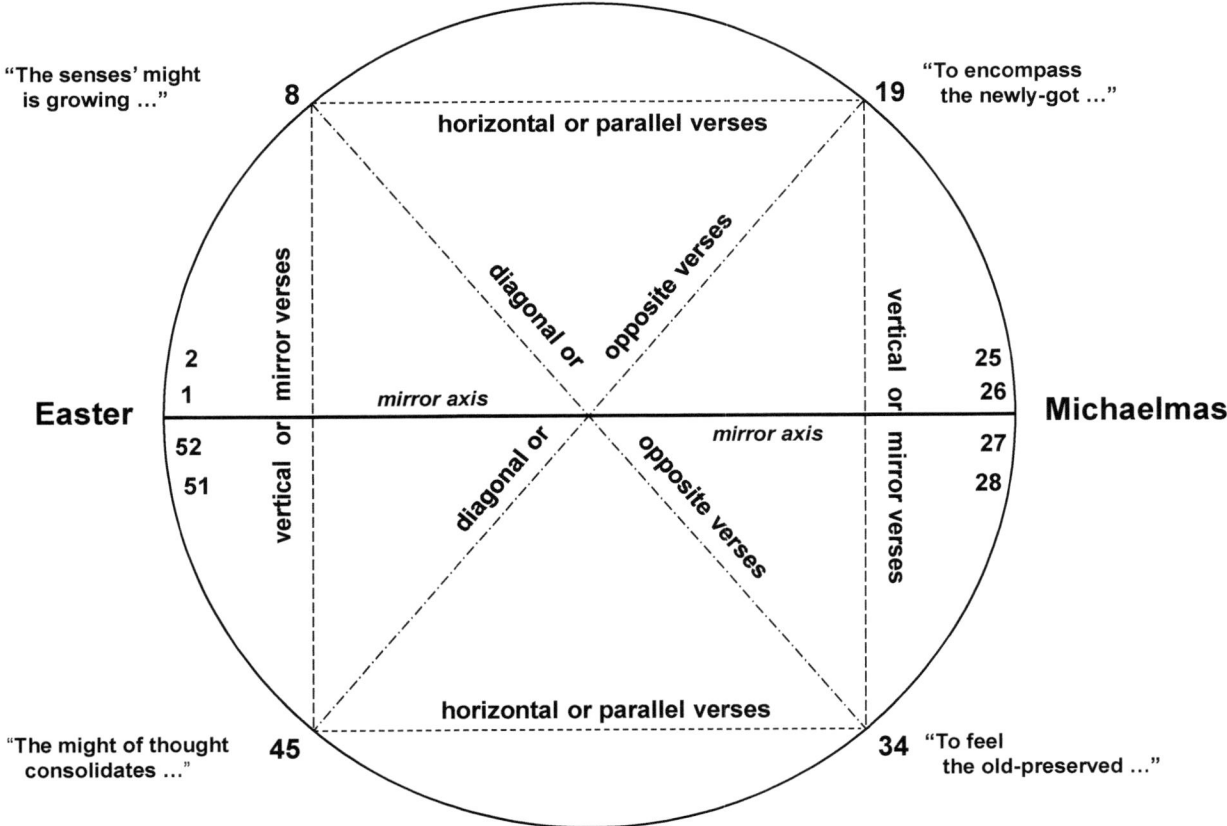

Figure 13: The three main relationships between the verses

The special phase of development that begins with the 8th weekly verse in the Zodiac sphere – the damping down of man's own powers and pushing back of the "human thinking" by the increasing might of the spiritual senses ("the senses' might is growing"), so that man's capacity for devotion and receptivity can be sufficiently increased and a fertilization with the powers of the divine Trinity becomes possible – is concluded in the 19th weekly verse. Then what was to receive has become the "newly-got" and the human being, who has returned to the zodiac region, is allowed to grow in his own powers. These appear first as powers of memory, through which, on the one hand, man is to preserve "the newly-got" and, on the other, to be completely awakened from the "dullness of a dream" in order become aware of himself as an independent I. Thereby the parallelism is uncovered between the 8th and 19th weekly verses. A similar relationship exists between their two mirror verses, the 34th and 45th weekly verse. But this will be discussed in more detail only in the context of the weekly verses of the winter half-year.

However, the relationships between the weekly verses with regard to their content are by no means exhausted. There are a whole series of other relationships. The mere fact that the spring verses describe the after-death ascension of the human soul and the subsequent summer verses the prenatal descent, inevitably results in an analogy, but in the opposite direction. The 1st weekly verse of spring, the Easter saying, describes the awakening of the earthly man to the first stage of I-consciousness through his sensory experience. The first two verses of the summer quarter, the 14th and 15th weekly verses, on the other hand, deal with man's awakening from the All-Self to the first stage of an independent self, to a "separate being". The 1st weekly verse is based on the experience of a midpoint, the I-experience of man on Earth. The 14th and 15th weekly verses, on the other hand, which together form a unity, are based on a circumcircle experience, the All-Experience of man in the cosmos. So although these verses are analogous to each other, they nonetheless describe exactly opposite processes. Such pairs of weekly verses within the same half of the year are therefore referred to as "reversal verses" below. Rudolf Steiner himself expresses the principle of reversal effective here through his carefully selected words in the verses. For example, the 1st weekly verse says: "Then soar, out of the selfhood's sheath, thoughts to the distant space". In the 14th weekly verse, on the other hand, it says: "World-thinking yet draws near in sense-appearance to wake me up." So in the 1st weekly verse man's thinking is going away, whereas in the 14th weekly verse world-thinking is approaching. The exact opposite procedure is described. In a similar reversal, in the 1st weekly verse the physical sensory experience is depicted as light and clear – "When from the vastness of the world the Sun speaks to the human sense" – and the I-consciousness as dull – "and dully bind man's essence to the existence of the spirit". In the 15th weekly verse, on the other hand, the experience of the spiritual senses is dull – "it has enwrapped my very being in senses' dullness" – and the human I is intensely enforced to an individual self – "to give the force to me, which, powerless to give it to itself, my I cannot give in its limits."

In an equally reversal relationship, the spring triad, which follows the 1st weekly verse from the 2nd to the 4th weekly verse, describes that in the lowest three planetary spheres man sheds off his bodily sheaths and thereby detaches himself from his previous life on Earth as far as possible. The analogous summer triad of the 16th to 18th weekly verse, on the other hand, describes the exactly opposite task of man in the highest three spheres of the spiritual world. There he should preserve, internalize and connect with himself as much as possible of his experiences during the midnight hour of existence. The task at the beginning of the prenatal descent is thus exactly the opposite of that at the beginning of the after-death ascension. According to the 16th weekly verse, man has the task to "save" something "within" and thus preserve it. In the 2nd weekly verse, which deals with the experience in the Moon sphere, he "loses" something to the outside, "into the sensory universe's outer region". In addition, both verses speak of the "soul-fruit" of the human being. In the 2nd weekly verse it is the experiences from man's past life on Earth, which he must now find as his "own soul's fruit (yet) in himself". In the 16th weekly verse, on the other hand, the divine bounties granted to him during the midnight hour of existence are to "fruit in soul's grounds" and to "bring the selfhoods fruits". In this way Rudolf Steiner establishes a clear relationship between these two verses and it becomes clear how ingeniously and aptly he chose every single word, for his intention was that each verse, in addition to its relationship to its analogous reversal one, expresses also its relations already described above to its vertical mirror saying, to its diagonal opposite saying and to its horizontal parallel saying.

So what does the reversal relation look like between the saying of the second lowest planetary sphere, the Mercury sphere, i.e. the 3rd weekly verse, and that of the second highest spiritual sphere, the 17th weekly verse? The 3rd weekly verse begins with the words "And to the universe now speaks ... the growing I of man". In the 17th weekly verse, we again have the opposite situation. It begins with the words: "The World Word speaks ..." In the first case the I speaks to the world, in the reverse case the world speaks to the I. And while the human I in the 3rd weekly verse is to forget his midpoint-like earthly self – "forgetting gradually itself" – and to expand to the universe – as "growing I" – in order to reach to the higher I – "In you... I fathom out my real essence" –, in the 17th weekly verse the World Word gives man the order to internalize everything experienced and received as far as possible, to pervade himself with cosmic experiences and powers – "Imbue your spirit-depths with my world's vastness" – to ultimately find the World-I in himself – "to find me within you one time". In the first case the I pours out into the universe and has a fertilizing effect on the universe, in the second case the universe pours into the I and has a fertilizing effect within the I.

Also between the experiences of the third lowest planetary sphere and those of the third highest sphere of the spiritual world such a reversal relationship exists. The 4th weekly verse tells us that, in the Venus sphere, through the feeling of his soul, which expands into the world with the spiritual floods of light, man connects himself with the world through this widening: "and firmly bind(s) together man and the world in unity". This connection of man and world is again our task when we return to the lowest region of the higher spiritual world, the third highest spirit sphere. There, too, the soul has the task to expand and to connect with the world: "Can I expand the soul that it unites itself ..." However, here the human soul is the receiving one. It is to "unite" with the "received World-Germ-Word", whereas in the first case the universe receives the expanding human being.

What about the 5th weekly verse, the Spring saying of the Sun sphere, and the 19th weekly verse, the Summer saying of the Zodiac sphere? Here, too, we find an analogous reversal: The human being, widening to the Sun sphere after death, has finally "resurrected from narrow selfhood's inner power". When, on the other hand, he contracts to a zodiac, descending from the wide universe, then he feels that this "shall awaken, getting stronger, own powers in my inner being and, growing, give me to myself". Man is to become an independent self again, although not yet "selfish", as it can only take place during the passage through the sub-solar planetary spheres. But, here, the Sun sphere and the Zodiac also form an analogous pair.

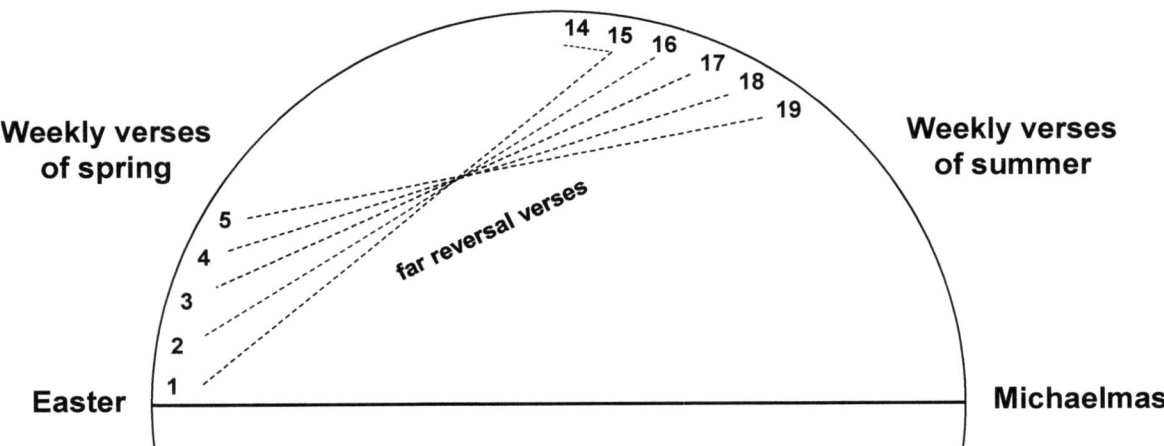

Figure 14: Far reversal verses in the summer half-year

The relationships between the reversal verses are shown in Figure 14. There they are called "far reversal verses", since their relationships exist between verses of the lower and the upper half of a half-year. In fact, there are also "close reversals", as will become apparent in a moment.

As if relations were still not enough, there are additional relationships between those verses of a half-year, all of which belong to its upper half, but also between those, all of which belong to its lower half. This is exemplified in the following for the upper spring and upper summer verses.

After his after-death ascension to the Sun sphere, man is "resurrected from narrow selfhood's inner power" there, as it says in the 5th weekly verse. The one of the 12th week, at St. John's Day, however, speaks of a much more far-reaching resurrection, through which man even leaves himself with the help of the divine powers inherent in him in order to seek his innermost, divine kernel of being in the super-spiritual spheres: "To set my own life's divine powers free for the world-high flight; to leave myself and confidently seek myself ..." This saying is in a reversal relationship to the zodiac saying of the 19th week, because there man, who is unselfed and undressed of his sheaths, is brought back to himself and it is not the "powers of God" but his "own powers" that are awakened in him. Thus, instead of "leaving myself", man experiences a "giving me to myself". See Figure 15.

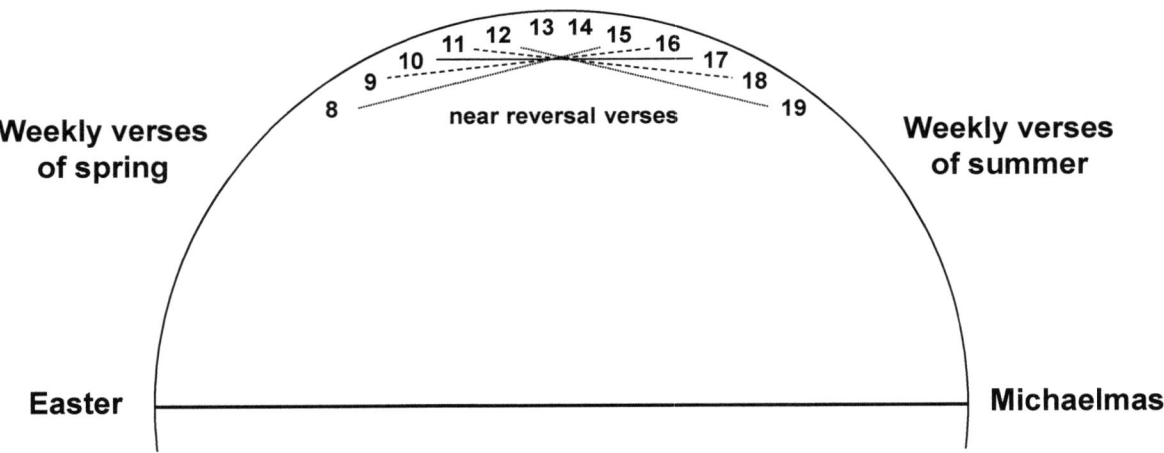

Figure 15: Near reversal verses in the summer half-year

The 8th and 15th weekly verses are in the same reversal relationship. The former says, "the senses' might is growing" and man's I-consciousness based on thinking is pressed down "to dullness of a dream". In the latter, on the other hand, man's separate being has been "enwrapped ... in senses' dullness" so that it receives "the force" for individual existence.

There is a similar relationship between the 11th weekly verse, which describes the after-death experiences of the human soul in the seventh region of the spiritual world, and the 18th weekly verse, which deals with the prenatal experiences of the human soul in the fifth region of the spiritual world. In the 11th weekly verse, "wise news" from the environment are revealed to man: "The human I can lose itself and in world's I retrieve itself". There, the world is to receive the human. In the 18th weekly verse, on the other hand, man's task is to receive the world, for there it says: "Can I expand the soul that it unites itself with the received World-Germ-Word?" In the first case the human I is finally expanded to the world-I, in the latter, on the other hand, the world-self is lastly drawn together to a human self, to the spirit self of man, which then in a further step in the sphere of the zodiac completely closes itself off from the outer cosmos or world-self.

The 10th and 17th weekly verses are intimately related because they both portray experiences of the same sphere, the 6th region of the spiritual world. They are therefore horizontal or parallel verses. According to the statements of both verses, the deity protrudes into the human being, one time feeling through his inside, in the other case putting itself into it.

The reversal relationship between the 9th and the 16th weekly verse is given in the fact that in the former, man is made aware that he should lose himself – "and strongly tells presentiment: Now lose yourself". In the latter, the order goes out to man by presentiment that he should save something in him and thus preserve, i.e. the exact opposite of losing: "To save the spirit-gift within, is my presentiment's strict order."

Couples of weekly verses, which are all in the upper half of a half-year, as well as those which are all in the lower half of a half-year and have reversal relationships of the type just described, are therefore called "near reversal verses".

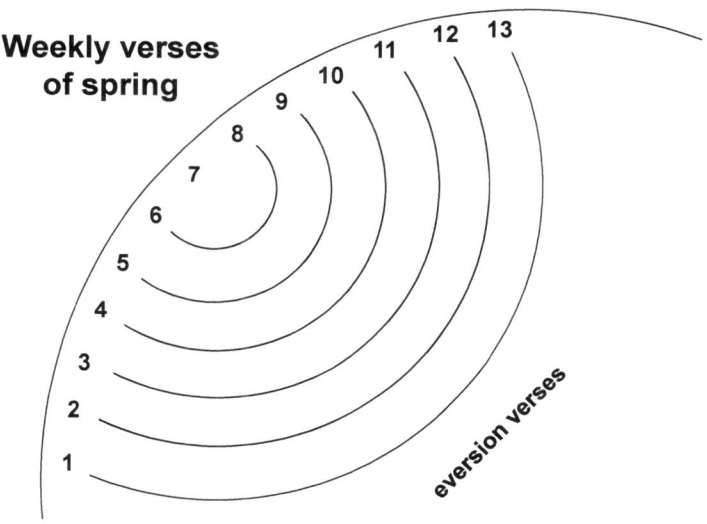

Figure 16: Eversion verses of spring

However, there are not only relations between the weekly verses of the two great halves of the year or between those of the four seasons. In fact, there are in addition relationships between weekly verses that belong to the same season. These have the peculiarity that they express an eversion rather than a reversal. In the weekly verses 1 to 6 we find a description of a human being still marked by his past life on Earth, whereas the weekly verses 8 to 13 characterize the Divine, the spiritual source on which the Universe is based, working into man. In the 1st weekly verse the human being is completely devoted to the Sun and the vastness of the world. In the 13th weekly verse, on the other hand, he is completely devoted to the divine flaming of the highest Sun Spirit, Christ, in his soul depths. In the 2nd weekly verse his thoughts developed on the earthly outside world soar for a world flight, whereas in the 12th weekly verse, this is done by the divine kernel of his being, which is hidden deep inside him. In the 3rd weekly verse man speaks to the universe, but in the 11th the wise news of the universe is given to him. In the 4th weekly verse the human being feels his own being and in the 10th weekly verse he feels a divine being. In the 5th weekly verse the human soul expands with the light and resurrects to higher selfhood. In the 9th weekly verse this expanding merges into loss. Man loses his sense of self in order to find his higher self. And when, on the one hand, man recognizes the world as his divine archetype in the 6th weekly verse, in the 8th, on the other, he may come in closer connection with "the creative work of gods", which underlies this archetype. The middle of the first thirteen weekly verses is the 7th one. It tells us about the transition from a still earthly marked human being into a divine-spiritual universal being, whereby man has the feeling that his self escapes from him. All these relationships are shown graphically in Figure 16.

Even with this, not all relationships between such weekly verses that belong to the same season are given. There are even those that are based on the fact that processes, which begin in the first region of a world, find their conclusion in its third region. The same applies to processes that begin in the fifth region of a world and end in the seventh region of the same world. But, what has been described so far may suffice to show the extremely diverse network of relationships between the weekly verses as a true reflection of the equally manifold relationships between the quite diverse experiences of the human spirit-soul on its after-death and prenatal journey through the different spheres.

In the following, we return the attention of our considerations to the further development of the human spirit-soul, which now gets ready to move into the lower spiritual world and thus into the planetary spheres.

Return to the Spheres of Saturn and Jupiter – 20th Week

With the entry of the human being into the Saturn sphere, the so-called "Atmospheric Region" of the lower spiritual world, in which the entire emotional life of all earthly beings lives out in a great unity, both that of the animal kingdom and that of humans, the emotional experience as such comes again to the fore, understandably. After the human spirit-soul has been separated from the wider universe through the zodiac, it is able to intensively feel its own existence now. By this its sense of self is strengthened. But the sublime experiences, in which the human spirit-soul was allowed to participate in the higher spiritual world and to a certain degree even in the super-spiritual world, continue to have an effect on it. The spirit-soul remembers the birth of its self out of the wider spirit cosmos and feels with great intensity that its own existence could never arise out of itself, could not even sustain itself. Man's own existence is completely born out of the world. Without the world he would have to die as a special being. A selfhood that wanted to live entirely separated from the world as its origin would inevitably deprive itself of its own source of life and ultimately have to deaden itself. It is this most important prenatal insight of man that we find expressed in the words of the 20th weekly verse:

20th Week (18 – 24 August)	*20. Woche (18. – 24. August)*
In this way only, I feel my existence,	So fühl ich erst mein Sein,
Which far from world-existence	Das fern vom Welten-Dasein
Would in itself obliterate itself	In sich, sich selbst erlöschen
And, building merely on its own foundation	Und bauend nur auf eignem Grunde
Inside, would deaden finally itself.	In sich, sich selbst ertöten müsste.

In the course of his after-death ascension through the spheres, man increasingly turned into the world, penetrated deeper and deeper into the secrets of world-existence and grew in his knowledge of the world in order to finally arrive at the full truth and find his origin in the world. Rudolf Steiner advised several of his students to meditate on this intimate connection between world and man. Some of his meditation formulas were preserved; for example, the dedication saying that Rudolf Steiner added to the second edition of his Soul Calendar for his close colleague Elisabeth Vreede on Christmas Eve 1918:

When man does recognize himself:	Erkennt der Mensch sich selbst:
The self becomes the world to him;	Wird ihm das Selbst zur Welt;
When man does recognize the world:	Erkennt der Mensch die Welt:
The world becomes the self to him.	Wird ihm die Welt zum Selbst.[190]

---

[190] GA 40 "Wahrspruchworte" (True-Verse-Words / Truth-Wrought-Words), Section "Widmungssprüche" (Dedication Verses)

In the volume "Wahrspruchworte" (True-Verse-Words or Truth-Wrought-Words) of the Rudolf Steiner Complete Edition a series of similar verses is given to us, of which at least one is reproduced here:

If you want to know your Self,
Look out into world's vastness.
If you want to see through world's vastness,
Look into your Self inside.

Willst Du Dein Selbst erkennen,
Schaue hinaus in die Weltenweiten.
Willst Du die Weltenweiten durchschauen,
Blicke hinein in das eigene Selbst.

V. *Breslau, 8 June 1924*

In the lower spiritual world the soul power of thinking reawakens in man, besides his feeling. With this, man primarily turns to the world. Therefore, it is less suitable for strengthening his individual existence. For the latter, his feeling serves him first of all.

"Thinking and feeling correspond to the dual nature of our being, which we have already thought of. Thinking is the element through which we participate in the general events of the cosmos; feeling is that through which we can retreat into the narrowness of our own being. Our thinking connects us to the world; our feeling leads us back into ourselves, makes us an individual. If we were merely beings, who think and perceive, our whole life would have to flow in indiscriminate indifference. If we could only recognize ourselves as a self, we would be completely indifferent to ourselves. Only through the fact that we feel the sense of self together with the self-awareness, desire and pain with the perception of things, do we live as individual beings whose existence is not exhausted by the conceptual relationship in which they are to the rest of the world, but which even are of a particular value to themselves.

One might be tempted to see in the emotional life an element that is richer saturated with reality than the contemplation of the world by thought. To this is to be replied that the emotional life has this richer meaning only to my individual. To the world as a whole, my emotional life can only receive any value if my feeling, as a perception on my Self, connects with a concept and, in this way, integrates itself into the cosmos.

Our life is a continuous oscillation between the experience of general world events and our individual existence. The further we ascend into the general nature of thinking, where we are interested in the individual only as an example ultimately, as a specimen of the concept, the more we lose the character of a special being, a very specific individual personality. The further we descend into the depths of our own life and make our feelings resonate with the experiences of the outside world, the more we separate ourselves from the universal existence. A true individuality will be the one who reaches farthest with his feelings up into the region of the ideal.

... A completely thoughtless emotional life should gradually lose all connection with the world." [191]

If we rise from subjective, error-prone personal thinking to objective, true world-thinking and from personal feeling to world-feeling, we connect ourselves with the spiritual and super-spiritual worlds, where we are rooted and have our source of life. On the other hand, if we become more and more detached from the world through too much self-esteem because we hold the opinion that we do not need it, we deprive ourselves of our own source of life and wither and waste away. If we ended this path consistently, we would "deaden" ourselves.

In the Jupiter region, the "Oceanic Region" of the spiritual world, we experience that all life in the world is a unity. This world life keeps us, too, alive. It is a gift of the world to us and has its origin in the Budhi plane, the world of the life spirit, in which we were allowed to encounter the Christ Being. Thus, on our prenatal descent into the Jupiter sphere, all religious feeling revives powerfully, depending on the intensity of our memories of the sublime experiences in the higher spiritual world and the encounter with God at the great midnight hour of existence. On the reminiscences in the Jupiter sphere it will therefore depend how far our religious feeling will extend beyond the boundaries of denominational differences of churches and communities of faith in the forthcoming life on Earth, for here, all religious feelings are one undivided unity as is all life. Anyone who is able to carry his religious disposition down into life on Earth from here will seek and find the Divine in all religions. He will feel in the sense of a cosmic world religion and think in the sense of cosmic wisdom.

But with his entry into the outermost planetary spheres man also comes under the influence of the soul world already, for the lower spiritual world is pervaded by it. Even from the lowest planetary sphere, the

---

[191] GA 4 "Die Philosophie der Freiheit" (The philosophy of spiritual activity), Chapter VI "Die menschliche Individualität" (The human individuality)

Moon sphere, forces take effect up to the Saturn sphere. The seven planetary spheres constitute a coherent psycho-spiritual organism. In the same way that the nervous system has its headquarters in the head of the earthman, but works into the far-off tips of the fingers and toes, and just as the blood system has its centre in the heart, but is effective as far as the periphery, the outer body surface, so the influence of the Moon sphere also reaches up to the Saturn sphere. But, although the Moon is one of the seven planets, as a satellite of the Earth it is very much turned towards the Earth and therefore has a special position. Through it the forces of the Earth work up into the planetary plane as shown in Figure 17, actually up to its upper limit in the Saturn sphere. There, the Moon dampens the still objective world-experience and brings about the beginning of a subjective self-experience. Before that, man felt still one with the entire universe. Now he merely feels one with the planetary world of our solar system. The separation of subject and object, of "my" and "your", comes about in this way. Rudolf Steiner expresses this clearly in the 20th weekly verse through the use of the possessive pronoun "my": "In this way only, I feel *my* existence." Henceforward, the universal, stellar existence of man lives only in his memory. Planetary existence is now his environment, even though he still feels himself as a member of the whole world-existence, but already as a delimitable member with a certain degree of individual existence.

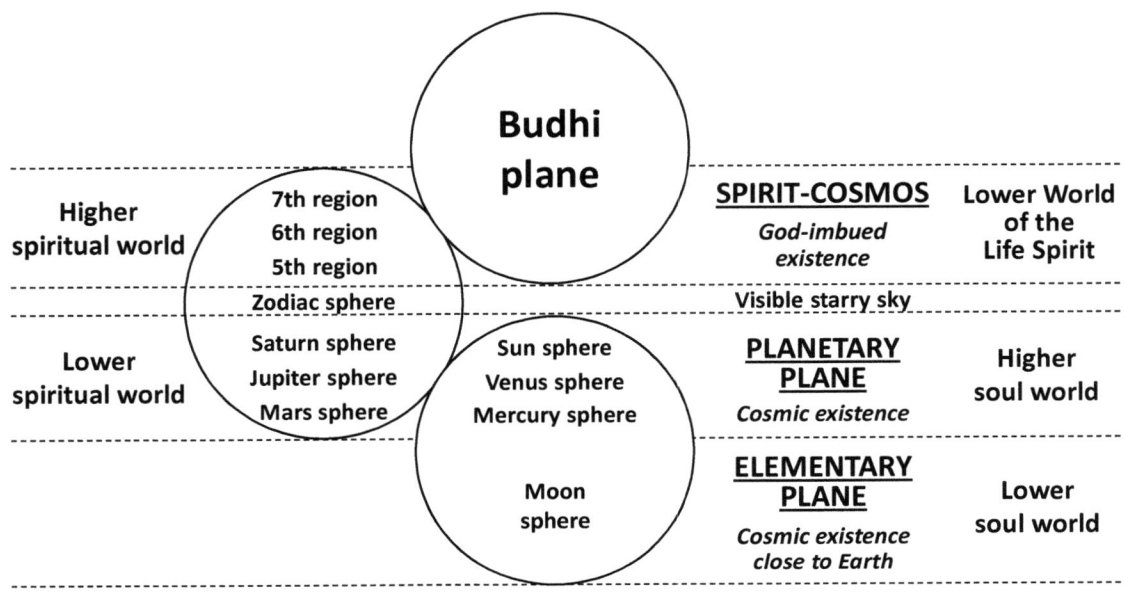

Figure 17: Spirit-cosmos, planetary and elementary plane [192]

"What man experiences in the first stage of his pre-earthly existence, characterized today, in a clear, bright consciousness, is that which is then post-experienced in the earthly existence as a likeness, as an emotional likeness in his religious disposition, in the feeling of a connection of man with the divine foundation of the world. For, if man as a soul in pre-earthly existence wants to give an account to himself of how this peculiarity of his soul appears here in the earthly existence, one could say: At the moment when man passes from experiencing a living spiritual cosmos to experiencing its mere manifestation under the influence of the Moon forces, man would have to say to himself in this moment of his pre-earthly existence: I pass from a god-imbued existence to a cosmic existence. Under the influence of the Moon forces, I am now beginning to contract that bright cosmic consciousness that I have developed universally in previous times, into a more inner consciousness. – I said that the bright cosmic consciousness is dimmed, but the more it is dimmed, the more a subjective consciousness emerges within the human soul, which is confronted with the manifestation of the cosmos as something objective. And so we can say: Man proceeds to an Inspiration in which he knows himself to be a member of the cosmos. He experiences cosmology in this second stage of pre-earthly existence.

What in his life on Earth man has as an aspiration for cosmological wisdom is just as much an after-effect of these just characterized experiences of his pre-earthly existence as religious consciousness is an

---

[192] See also Figures 1 and 2 with the corresponding explanations in the reflection on the 7th weekly verse, which, as a parallel saying to the 20th weekly verse, deals with the after-death ascension of man through the Jupiter and Saturn sphere.

after-effect of the stage described first, of the god-imbued consciousness. These things are experienced in pre-earthly existence. They have their after-effects in the earthly existence, in which they present themselves as a religious or cosmological disposition of the human soul..."[193]

Return to the Mars Sphere – 21st Week

In the three regions of the higher spiritual world the human spirit-soul lives in a God-imbued universal consciousness. After having experienced the great midnight hour of existence, the spirit-soul is increasingly endowed with a power that enables it to turn from a state of allness, into which it has completely expanded and to which it has completely surrendered itself, into selfhood again, to close up to a preliminary stage of an I. This process finds its analogy in earthly nature in the way a fruit of a tree develops from the forces of the entire tree. Gradually, it becomes a separate, delimitable member on the tree, yet remains, until having fully matured, a part of the tree, by which it is nourished and advanced in development. The forces of the sky working and weaving around the tree, sunlight, solar heat, air and rain contribute to this. In a quite comparable manner the various Hierarchies, through which the World Word works and weaves in the universe shaping and evolving Creation, contribute to the development of the human self out of the All-Self. In this process the human self contracts more and more from an initially universal-wide germinal state until, in the course of its passage through the Zodiac sphere, it finally delimits itself from the wider cosmos and proceeds to denser states of planetary existence. Then only, it becomes receptive to a new influence. A force of a completely different kind begins to intervene in the next stages of the process of its fruit formation and fruit ripening. It is the Moon Forces already mentioned in connection with the preceding weekly verse. Their influence does not stream from the wide perimeter of the universe to the human self, but from exactly the opposite direction, from the region near the Earth, i.e. from the centre of the planetary spheres. First therefore man senses this as a "strange power" that intervenes in his process of fruit formation. However, he also feels that the gradual increasing of this very power also strengthens his self, and he becomes more and more aware of himself by this. With a very precise description of this experience, the 21st weekly verse starts:

21st Week (25 – 31 August)	*21. Woche (25. – 31. August)*
I feel strange power fruiting,	Ich fühle fruchtend fremde Macht
Increasing, giving now myself to me.	Sich stärkend mir mich selbst verleihn.

When a tree fruit increases in size and shape, it soon comes under the influence of the Earth's gravity. This pulls ever more strongly at it, in order to detach it from the tree at the end of its ripening process and bring it down to the Earth. The Moon forces likewise have the effect of bringing man back to Earth, after his ripening in the planetary spheres as a fruit of the world self. For this purpose, the Moon forces intervene quite early in this process of fruiting and ripening. Already in the Mars sphere they become clearly noticeable to the human being. He feels, it is precisely through them that a more and more independent, subjective life begins to develop within him and that his selfhood is strengthened. It is interspersed with own powers and will impulses. This whole process, however, still takes place in the realm of the Psycho-Spiritual. Man does not have a separate corporeality yet. With such, he will only envelop himself on further steps down to a new life on Earth. In the Mars sphere, only in the psycho-spiritual sense he is a separate being, a fruit of the universe. He still senses the entire planetary system as his body during this time and himself as a member of the cosmos.

This implanting of own power and own will into the human self also finds its analogy in nature. As soon as a fruit has reached a certain state of maturity by the forces of the tree on which it grows and under the influence of the celestial forces taking effect on it, its own germination begins in its interior. A fruit kernel begins to develop, which during a period of immersion in the Earth's forces will be endowed with the ability to make a new tree growing out of it, which in turn will grow towards heaven. This reproductive power is given to the germ inside a fruit primarily by the influence of the Moon, which increasingly intervenes both spatially from the centre of the planetary spheres and psycho-spiritually from a kind of midpoint in the

---

[193] GA 215 "Die Philosophie, Kosmologie und Religion in der Anthroposophie" (Philosophy, Cosmology and Religion in Anthroposophy), Dornach, Lecture of 11 September 1922

psycho-spiritual man. More and more clearly he notices that a germ begins to mature in his own interior due to the "strange power" that intervenes in his fruit-forming process making this germ stronger and stronger. And in preparation for his future deeds on Earth, man himself participates in the Mars sphere on the formation of this will-germ. From the abundance of divine goals and intentions which he was allowed to experience "by sensing" in the higher spiritual world, the Arupa region, an extract of individual goals and intentions develops in him, which will underlie his soon new life on Earth. It is not so much the will impulses we are aware of in earthly life that condense and fix themselves here in the human spirit-soul, but rather those impulses that mysteriously push us forward in life, the impulses of our higher self that manages our way in life on Earth from the spiritual world. Through the soul light, which clearly increases in the Mars sphere already, we sense more and more intensively that our selfhood gains strength and power as a result.

I sense the seed maturing, and	Den Keim empfind ich reifend
Presentiment weaving with its light	Und Ahnung lichtvoll weben
Within me on the selfhood's power.	Im Innern an der Selbstheit Macht.

The establishment of a reproductive organ both in a plant fruit and in the purely psycho-spiritual fruit of the human self takes place in a completely virginal way. Here are by no means those passionate forces at work which are connected with the process of reproduction of humans and animals in life on Earth. The Moon forces still show their completely pure, virginal side here. In the course of the year this process finds its parallel in the transition of the Sun from the zodiac sign of Leo to the sign of Virgo. Insofar as the Moon, close to Earth, is a cosmic image of the soul and the female principle with its ability to bring human spirit-beings down to Earth as seeds of the universe, to condense them and give birth to them, is illustrated to us in the zodiac in the image of a Virgin as expression of the purest powers of the soul and the female principle. Therefore, in the various religions, the reference to the purest soul powers of man we always find connected with the worship of the Virgin, as for instance the Virgin Mary in Christianity or the ancient Egyptian goddess Isis, who both bear a divine child from the world of the spirit, or the ancient Greek Demeter as mistress of fertility and grain. In this sense, the Virgin holds an ear with wheat-germs in her hand in that zodiacal image into which the Sun is entering now. They represent the virginally brought about germs of the world spirit, capable of growing and prospering.

In such a virginal way, however, the Moon forces only work in the planetary spheres extending beyond the Moon sphere, i.e. only in the realms of the lower spiritual world and the higher soul world pervading it. But, although the Moon forces take an effect in the spheres of Saturn and Jupiter, they become clearly perceptible to man only after his entry into the Mars sphere, where they increase in strength. The virginal influence of these forces reaches down to the Mercury sphere, but not into the Moon sphere, where man after his death left behind all that karma he did not get through yet. That is why we often find in Christian art the Virgin Mary depicted with the moon under her feet or enthroned above a crescent moon. And it is, of course, not by chance that in our Soul Calendar precisely those four weekly verses that describe the pre-natal descent of man through the spheres of Mars, Sun, Venus and Mercury, which still are above the realm of the Moon, are connected with that time in which the sun travels through the zodiac image of Virgo.

With the entry of the Sun into the next sign Libra, on the day of the autumn equinox, the Sun already leaves the bright half of the zodiac. From then on, the nights are longer than the days. The dark forces of the Earth's depths are becoming active, which is indicated in the Plutonian autumn sign Scorpio following Libra. From an astrological point of view, the Moon is "in fall" there, which means that it expresses its passionate powers above all, which in life on Earth are connected with sexuality and reproduction. These forces come from the actual Moon sphere, the lower soul world or the Kamaloka, in which the impulsive parts of human psychic life are rooted.

The ambivalence of the Moon forces finds its expression in Greek mythology in the story of Demeter, the goddess of fertility, and Pluto, the god of the underworld, as well as in the marriage of Demeter's daughter Persephone with him. Persephone spends the bright half of the year together with her mother, the dark half of the year with her husband, who once robbed her, in the underworld. In this context, Persephone, who also was named the Grain Girl, is the personification of the grain of wheat that is exposed to the powers of the Earth's depths during the dark winter months, but develops by that the force to break through the Earth's crust in spring and grow towards the bright realm of its above-earth mother-power again.

In the sky, this ambivalence of the Moon forces appears to us in the rhythmic alternation between the bright full moon and the dark new moon. In the female organism it finds its bodily expression in the fertile and infertile days of the monthly cycle, in the soul in lightful joy and gloomy sadness. Accordingly, Demeter mourns deeply during the winter months, when she misses her daughter, and rejoices even more in spring and summer when she gains reunion with her. Persephone oscillates between these two extremes. On the one hand, the grain girl as a germinating, blossoming seed represents the growth in spring and the time of increasing light, of which we are reminded of every month by the shape of the waxing crescent in the night sky. On the other hand, as the condensing seed of the late summer which develops a solid form, the grain girl also represents the time of the waning light, which we find illustrated in the form of the waning crescent in the sky. With regard to the spirit, however, Persephone represents the old soulful, pre-sensing, dream-like clairvoyance, which was the transition between the clear, bright spiritual vision of Demeter on the one side and the plutonic darkness of the sleep, the younger brother of death, on the other. So it is precisely the rhythmic change of all Temporal that finds its pictorial expression in the myth of Demeter-Persephone-Pluto with respect to the physical, the psychological as well as for the spiritual parts of the human being and the world.

The relationship of the soul and the female with the principle of the rhythm of time and the changing phases of the Moon is definitely also connected with the world planes. In the higher spiritual world man lives in the kingdom of eternity. There he overlooks the entire series of his former incarnations. He exists out of time, looking from the outside, so to speak, at the Temporal. When he enters the planetary spheres, he increasingly comes in touch with the forces of the soul world and thus with the principle of time. Along with it there is an ever-increasing awakening of an inner soul life in man. Accordingly, the ancient calendars of mankind always were based on the representative of the soul in the sky, the Moon. The exact length of the lunar year was much easier to determine from the easily observable phases of the Moon than the length of the solar year, the exact duration of which remained controversial until the sixteenth century.[194]

However, every Temporal is inescapably linked with transience and from this reason the necessity of reproduction arises immediately. We see this in the development of the prenatal human spirit-soul in the higher worlds. There, it finds its expression in the formation of a condensing will-germ or will-seed within the soul. This germ has the task to carry God's will as an individualized human will or the power of selfhood of the human I down to Earth and to make it turn into the energy of action there, the earthly expression of Mars-power. Persephone, the dreamlike and pre-sensing force of old clairvoyance, continues to contribute to this seed-forming in the human soul even today by consolidating the I, the selfhood, into an inner power, precisely in the sense of the words of the second sentence of the 21st weekly verse:

I sense the seed maturing, and	Den Keim empfind ich reifend
Presentiment weaving with its light	Und Ahnung lichtvoll weben
Within me on the selfhood's power.	Im Innern an der Selbstheit Macht.

Rudolf Steiner spoke about this contribution of Persephone in the consolidation and condensation of the human I within the soul in a lecture of the year 1911:

"Yes, we can say that this robbery of Persephone has been going on since the earliest times until our times; the old clairvoyant culture disappeared. But in truth nothing disappears in the world, in truth things just change.

Where did Persephone go? What is she doing as the ruler of the ancient clairvoyant forces in human nature today? You will be able to deduce from the first statements of a book, which will be available here in a few days and which essentially reflects my last Copenhagen lectures[195], that the whole extent of the human soul is far greater than that which the human soul knows through its intellect, through its mind. There is something that one could call wider, a more extensive soul life, a subconscious soul life that works in us, but does not appear in the consciousness of the majority of today's people. It is better to call it subconscious than unconscious soul life. In this subconscious life of the soul, in that, which works in man today without him giving a reasonable, intellectual account to himself through his consciousness, there is Persephone, there the ancient clairvoyant forces have gone down. While in primeval times they worked in the human soul in such a way that this soul could clairvoyantly look into spiritual worlds, today these forces work in the underground of the human soul, in the depths of the soul, participate in the development and

---

[194] The calendar reform, which became more and more urgent in the course of the Middle Ages, could not only take place before 1582 with the replacement of the ancient Julian calendar by the Gregorian calendar, since only the astronomers of the 16th century succeeded in calculating a more precise value for the duration of the solar year.

[195] GA 15 "Die geistige Führung des Menschen und der Menschheit" (The spiritual guidance of man and humanity)

formation of our «I»s, making these «I»s ever firmer and firmer. Thus, in ancient times they were devoted to the activity of giving man clairvoyant forces. Today they are engaged in the strengthening, the consolidation of our «I»s. So they are really drawn down into a human soul-underworld, these Persephone forces, they are embraced by what rests in the depths of the human soul; they are robbed in a certain sense by the depths of the human soul. And so, in the course of humanity's historical development, this robbery of Persephone has been carried out by those forces of the human soul that sit deep in its depths and are externally represented in nature by Pluto. This Pluto dominates the underground of the Earth in the sense of the Greek doctrine of the gods. But the Greeks were aware that the same forces that work in the depths of the Earth also work in the depths of the human soul." [196]

For man to become able to develop a clear I-consciousness in the forthcoming life on Earth, already during his prenatal descent through the Mars sphere a kind of soul-centre must be concentrated, condensed, consolidated in him, like a kernel or seed in a fruit. This seed, which condenses to "the selfhood's power", is completely volitional at first. It is a will-germ in the human soul, which is intended, among other things, to form in the Subconscious the resting, firm basis of the I-consciousness in order to be developed later on, in the next life on Earth, as Rudolf Steiner further explained on the above topic in the lecture of the following day.

"For without man having a will, he would never come to an I-consciousness. Now we may ask the question – this time, from a different point of view than yesterday – what did the Greek feel when he asked himself the question: What is out there spread in the macrocosm as the same forces that evoke in us the will impulses, the whole will-world? What's out there? Then he answered with the name Pluto. Pluto as that central power outside in macrocosmic space, closely bound to the clenched planet, was for the Greek the macrocosmic counter-image of the will impulses that pushed down the Persephone-life into the undergrounds of the soul life, too."

Pluto was to the Greeks not only the ruler of the underworld, but also of everything inanimate in the physical outside world. Accordingly, the spiritual forces which underlie all physical formations originate from the Mars sphere, which is related to Pluto, as the lowest region of the spiritual world. This is clearly expressed in Rudolf Steiner's choice of words for the 21st weekly verse, where he twice uses the Martian word "power" in addition to the word "increasing".

I feel strange power fruiting,	Ich fühle fruchtend fremde Macht
Increasing, giving now myself to me.	Sich stärkend mir mich selbst verleihn.
I sense the seed maturing, and	Den Keim empfind ich reifend
Presentiment weaving with its light	Und Ahnung lichtvoll weben
Within me on the selfhood's power.	Im Innern an der Selbstheit Macht.

Return to the Sun Sphere – 22nd Week

When, in the course of its after-death development, the human spirit-soul had matured to that high superpersonal state which enabled it to expand into the regions of the higher spiritual world beyond the Zodiac sphere, it began to identify with the spiritual light of the world's vastness and to find itself in this light, as it says in the 9th weekly verse: "To lose myself into the light, I am commanded by the spirit-vision, and strongly tells presentiment: Now lose yourself to find yourself". The human spirit-soul has spent centuries in those noble regions in the kingdom of eternity in order to be impregnated and gifted there with the highest divine purposes and powers. Its task is then to bring these divine bounties, received in the light of the cosmic vastness, more and more to consciousness in retrospect, so that when it returns to the Zodiac sphere and concomitant with it takes leave from the higher spiritual world, they are finally completely encompassed with its memory, as the 19th weekly verse gives it. In this way man delimits himself from the outer depths of the universe into a planetary self-existence. Now he is no longer the universe, but a delimitable member of it, a planetary system that has condensed out of the tree of the whole universe, like a fruit on the world tree. And just as during the fruit formation on a tree on Earth all forces of the whole tree pour something of themselves into the fruit in order to live on in the fruit in a germinal state from then on and continue to work forcefully in it, so also the spiritual light from the vastness

---

[196] GA 129 "Weltenwunder, Seelenprüfungen und Geistesoffenbarungen" (Wonders of the world, probations of the soul and revelations of the spirit), Munich, Lecture of 19 August 1911

of the higher spiritual world lives on and works on forcefully in the human spirit-soul, after it has internalized this light and condensed itself to planetary existence beforehand. The full internalization, however, can only take place with the entry of man into the soul world. Only there, all outer spirit light can be transformed into inner soul light and as such liven up strongly. This process is described in the first words of the 22nd weekly verse:

The light out of the vastness of the world,	Das Licht aus Weltenweiten,
It lives on forcefully inside:	Im Innern lebt es kräftig fort:
It turns into a soul-light ...	Es wird zum Seelenlichte ...

Rudolf Steiner called the Sun sphere, the highest region of the soul world, that of "the actual soul life".[197] Just as man in earthly life feels his heart as the centre of his emotional life and points by hand to the centre of his chest when he wants to point to himself, so the Sun sphere, among the planetary spheres, is that region which man senses as the actual home of his soul being and his selfhood. However, the soul is there still a world-soul. It feels belonging to the entire planetary system. And since the three higher regions of the soul world are pervaded by the three lower regions of the spiritual world, the spiritual light of the world's vastness can draw into the human world-soul, can internalize in it. Inevitably, it is subjected to a transformation through this process. It can no longer continue to be one with the entire universe, for it has contracted to form a partial world light within the planetary spheres. From the Sun sphere, the human world-soul illuminates the depths of the spiritual world from its own point of view now. By that the spiritual light loses its all-embracing objectivity. It picks up a subjective nature. Spirit light thus becomes soul light. But this process makes it possible for man to take in as much as possible of the manifold aims and powers of the spiritual world, to pick as many spirit fruits as possible for himself from the tree of the spiritual world, to detach them out, to release them so that a seed as rich as possible from the totality of the sublime powers of the entire universe may be planted into his soul's inside.

The fruits which man releases from the spiritual world, especially in the Sun sphere, are in particular the higher, noble impulses, the virtues. They are transformed there to forces of the heart and qualities of the heart, for in the Sun sphere primarily the finer design of the heart for the new earthly human body is worked on. Rudolf Steiner once listed the virtues in reference to their affiliation to the twelve forces of the zodiac, as communicated by H. P. Blavatsky beforehand, beginning with the sacrificial power as the virtue of Aries, progress as the virtue of Taurus, then continuing with fidelity, catharsis, free will, kind-heartedness, equanimity, insight, sense of truth, redeeming power, power of meditation and love.[198] In the Sun sphere, each human being absorbs just as much of this as he is capable of doing so in accordance with his level of development. Only after a series of further incarnations, the virtues of the spiritual world will be able to reach full development in human earthly life. Until then, they will be ever growing. This evolutionary process is made possible by the soul light, which in the Sun sphere is now evolving strongly within the human being, and which originally was a world-wide spiritual light.

22nd Week (1 – 7 September)	*22. Woche (1. – 7. September)*
The light out of the vastness of the world,	Das Licht aus Weltenweiten,
It lives on forcefully inside:	Im Innern lebt es kräftig fort:
It turns into a soul-light	Es wird zum Seelenlichte
And shines into the spirit-depths,	Und leuchtet in die Geistestiefen,
To loosen fruits	Um Früchte zu entbinden,
That make mature the human self	Die Menschenselbst aus Weltenselbst
Out of the World Self in the course of times.	Im Zeitenlaufe reifen lassen.

The soul light that man is now able to radiate into the surrounding spiritual world with full illuminating power and magnitude is a quality of him not merely in the Sun sphere, but in all three regions of the higher soul world. Only with the help of this light can he make his spiritual outside world experiencable to himself.

---

[197] GA 9 "Theosophie", Chapter "Die drei Welten" (The three worlds), Section II "Die Seele in der Seelenwelt nach dem Tode" (The soul in the soul world after death)

[198] GA 245 "Anweisungen für eine esoterische Schulung" (Instructions for an esoteric training), Chapter I, Section "Die zwölf zu meditierenden und im Leben zu berücksichtigenden Tugenden" (The twelve virtues to meditate and to consider in life)

Already during his after-death ascension into the Mercury sphere, which is pervaded by the Mars sphere as the lowest region of the spiritual world [199], the necessity arose to him that he becomes able to make this soul light radiate from him. There, its luminosity was only at the beginning and by no means of the power and abundance that it reaches in the Sun sphere as the highest region of the soul world. Nevertheless, already in the Mercury sphere it becomes the basis of the experience of the spirit, as Rudolf Steiner revealed to his listeners in one of his Viennese lectures on human after-death life:

"But yet another soul power must come out of us, which is still slumbering in much deeper layers of the soul than the feeling will or willing feeling: the creative soul power, which is like an inner soul light, which must shine out over the spiritual world, so that we not only see the living weaving objective thought beings swimming on the waves of feelings that come back in the sea of our will, but so that we have also illuminated this spiritual world with spiritual light. Creative spiritual luminosity must go out from our soul into the spiritual world. It's awakening gradually.

You see, my dear friends, while we live in the physical body, we have at least, I would like to say, differentiated the sibling pair of feeling and willing within us. We have them as two, whereas it is a unit when we have passed through the portal of death. This creative soul power, which we radiate like a soul light out into spiritual space – if I may use the expression «space» here, for it is actually not space, but one has to bring these conditions to understanding in a certain way by expressing oneself figuratively –, this soul light slumbers deep down in us, because it is connected with what we must not and cannot know anything about in life. At the very bottom, there is slumbering within us during our life in the physical plane, something, that is then redeemed as light and then enlightens and illuminates the spiritual world. What radiates from us must be transformed and used during our physical life so that our bodies really live and can hold consciousness. But deep below the threshold of consciousness this spiritual luminosity works in our physical bodies as the power, which organizes life and consciousness. We must not bring it into the earthly consciousness, otherwise we would rob our bodies of the power that has to organize them. Now, when we do not have to supply a body, it turns into spiritual luminosity and radiates and shines and illuminates everything. – These words mean true realities." [200]

Endowed with this ability to irradiate the outer spirit-vastness and spirit-depths, to the prenatal human being, who is a fruit on the world tree, the opportunity is given to extract additional fruits for himself from the spiritual world and to unite them with him in the form of all the abilities, gifts and will impulses which he is to carry down from higher worlds into the next life on Earth. How well he succeeds will depend on his level of development. The higher the quality of the spiritual fruits loosened from the universe, the more the human self as a microcosm can become a true image of the macrocosm.

When man descended into the zodiac region, coming from the higher spiritual world, he had the task to condense the totality of all forces of the universe to a twelveness of forces. In the Sun sphere he now makes his soul light shine in the twelve cardinal directions in order to fulfil the task "to loosen fruits that make mature the human self out of the World Self in the course of times", out of the World Self, which manifests itself as the World Word from the depths of the cosmos and consolidates itself in the twelve forces of the zodiac. Therefore, man once again absorbs divine gifts when he now, from the Sun sphere, turns his attention to the surrounding spiritual world and the zodiac. His situation here, albeit at a lower level, is comparable to that in which Christ was when he, as the highest initiate of the ancient Sun, absorbed the World Word, the Logos, into his soul. Because of the great importance for a deeper understanding of the Christ Being and because they make clear the way in which Christ became the ruler of Sun sphere, the supreme Spirit of the Sun, which is of utmost importance for the further evolution of mankind, Rudolf Steiner's words in this regard are given here once again:

"If you transferred yourself to the Sun today, you would, looking about radially, first look at the twelve constellations of the zodiac. At that time they were not outwardly visible as such. But instead there were twelve figures, twelve beings, who made their words sound from the depth of darkness, from the depth of blackness, since the outer space was not filled with light. What kind of words were these? Well, you see, these were words – the word «word» is again only a surrogate to indicate what it is – these were words that spoke of ancient times, already then ancient times. They were twelve world-initiators. Today, in the directions of these twelve world-initiators are the twelve zodiac images, and from them sounds to the soul, which is open to the whole world, the original kind of the unspoken World-Word, which could be formed from the twelve voices. Lucifer solely – I must now begin to speak figuratively, because human words are just not enough – had the urge in himself to irradiate everything with the light present in him and thus to

---

[199] See Figure 2 at the end of the reflection on the 7th weekly verse

[200] GA 153 "Inneres Wesen des Menschen und Leben zwischen Tod und neuer Geburt" (Inner nature of man and life between death and new birth), Vienna, Lecture of 13 April 1914

recognize it, whereas the Christ devoted himself to the impression of this World Word in an inexpressible manner and absorbed it completely, completely in himself; so that they were now united in the Christ Soul, that this Christ Soul was the Unification Being of the great world mysteries, sounding in through the inexpressible Word. Thus we face the contrast between Christ receiving the World Word and the proud Lucifer, the Venus Spirit, who rejects the World Word and wants to fathom everything with his light. ...

We have to take this scene in. Then we will find that during the ancient Sun time the ways of Christ and Lucifer separated. The way of Lucifer went downwards. He had to fall behind in his development, and he therefore in his development also fell behind during the Moon time. The Christ Spirit, the Sun Spirit, went forward and became a forward evolving spirit, who could finally appear on Earth in the form described to you more often. Through his devotion to the universe, through the reception of the divine creative Word, through identification with the Divine-Creative, with the inexpressible Word, through the rejection of any pride and the replacement of any pride by devotion to the World Word, Christ developed from a ruler of a planet, which he was in ancient Sun time, to the ruler of the other planets with the governmental area of the Sun." [201]

When we connect our soul and our I with the Christ Being in earthly life, forces flow to us which enable us between two incarnations to loosen a rich harvest of spiritual fruits from the spirit-depths in the Sun sphere and thereby, as human selves, to truly become children of the World Self.

"Thus, we see that it is the earthly mission of human souls to seek here [on Earth] the connection with the mystery of Golgotha, as we seek it in our spiritual movement. In this way we keep the memory of the Christ impulse between death and new birth and do not become a hermit in the Sun sphere, but a sociable being through the forces that we have taken with us; so that we then, so to speak, enliven the image of the Christ – which in the Sun sphere is only as an image – through our own, brought-in power." [202]

The Christ light, the "light out of the vastness of the world", then lives up all the more forcefully in our inner being, and the human self is all the more faithfully modelled according to the World Self in the Sun sphere. But if man as a microcosm is indeed a fruit of the world, of the macrocosm, then, just as a new tree emerges from the fruit of a tree, someday in the future a new world must also emerge from man. Rudolf Steiner, looking into the distant future with his spiritual vision, predicted that this will really happen:

"Today man works on his soul; in this way he makes his body more and more similar to the soul. When the Earth will have reached the end of its path, its mission, man will have shaped his body in such a way that it will be an outer image of his soul that has absorbed the Christ. This human being will live over and will plant his so formed powers into the next embodiment of our Earth. Jupiter will look as the human beings can make it by assembling it from their own bodies. This Jupiter will first get his shape from what man has made of himself. Think that all the bodies that were formed will merge into a single globe: that will be Jupiter. You have as a seed in your soul that which will be the figure of Jupiter, that which it will contain as forces. And out of Jupiter shall be born the beings of Jupiter. Thus man today works in advance for the birth of the Jupiter bodies." [203]

In the Sun sphere, today's human being experiences himself with subjectivity in the soul already. However, this is still very strongly pervaded by a humanity-wide feeling. In the interaction of "the light out of the vastness of the world", coming from the circumference, with the powers of the Moon sphere, emanating from the centre of the planetary system, the primal I of humanity once was formed. Its consciousness in the Sun sphere first was on a dreamlike level. The ancient Greeks still knew about this. Although they did not have an overview of the entire incarnation cycle of the human being any more, they still knew of its prenatal, psycho-spiritual pre-existence and the origin of the human self in higher worlds. The ancient Greek initiate regarded the human astral body, the bearer of soul light and forces of consciousness, as a microcosmic counter-image of the heavenly world-astrality, which is filled with spiritual light. For him, this was an expression of a divine being, which he called Zeus, the Lord of the light phenomena in the sky. In addition, the ancient Greek also knew a power that was independent of this one, a power which promoted the independent I-hood of man and was more closely related to the forces of the Moon and the Earth. This power he called Persephone. It was her, who gifted people with the original dreamlike clairvoyance, too. According to the ancient Greek view, the primal I of mankind arose by the interaction of these two powers.

---

[201] GA 137 "Der Mensch im Lichte von Okkultismus, Theosophie und Philosophie" (Man in the Light of Occultism, Theosophy and Philosophy), Kristiania (Oslo), Lecture of 12 June 1912

[202] GA 140 "Okkulte Untersuchungen über das Leben zwischen Tod und neuer Geburt" (Occult investigations on life between death and new birth), Stuttgart, 17 February 1913

[203] GA 104 "Die Apokalypse des Johannes" (The Apocalypse of John), Nuremberg, Lecture of 26 June 1908

"In the way we speak of our «I»s today, a person of ancient times could not yet speak of an intellectual I, but he could speak of something that arose from the interaction of the Zeus forces anchored in the astral body and the Persephone forces. What came into being in him through the union of these two, Zeus and Persephone, was he himself. It was something given to him only from one side, from Zeus, to which the other had to be added, on which Zeus as such had no direct influence. What Persephone was as the daughter of Demeter, was connected with the forces of the Earth itself." [204]

In a similar way as the Moon emerged from the Earth, so Persephone, the daughter, emerged from her mother Demeter, the mistress of the life forces on the Earth's surface. From the union of Persephone with Zeus arose their son Dionysus Zagreus, the human primal I, which bears the qualities of both parents in itself, both the forces of Zeus striving for the bright celestial heights and the vastness of the macrocosm and those forces of Persephone striving towards the centre, towards the Moon and Earth sphere. In this sense, Rudolf Steiner summed up his further remarks in the same lecture with the words:

"In the Greek myth, for all the reasons I have given, Dionysus the Elder, Dionysus Zagreus, is a son of Persephone and Zeus, with good explanation. All the forces in earthly life, which prepared the human I-consciousness in ancient times, if we look at them microcosmically in the inside of man, they were the ancient clairvoyant consciousness. If we look at them macrocosmically, as they surge through the elements of the Earth, they are the elder Dionysus. Thus, at those times, when the human being had an I, which was not yet today's I with its intellectual power, but the forerunner of today's I, the ancient clairvoyant consciousness that has become subconscious nowadays, in those times this human being – it was also still the case with the Greeks – looked out to the macrocosmic forces, which make these I-powers flow into us, and he called them Dionysus Zagreus, the old Dionysus."

The Hebrew secret doctrine likewise tells of the creation of the first human I through the interaction of the Sun-Elohim, who work in the world light, and the Moon-Eloha Yahweh, which damps and reflects the sunlight. The consciousness of Dionysos Zagreus of the Greeks and that of the original Adam of the Hebrews encompassed the whole humanity, since it was not yet dismembered into individual beings, into individual "I"s, but general-human, even if only dreamlike clairvoyant. However, due to the influence of the forces of the Moon and the Earth, the unified human self was divided into an ever greater multiplicity. The ancient Greek myth therefore tells of the dismemberment of Dionysos Zagreus by the Titans, the primeval powers of the Earth. The ancient Hebrews report in accordance of the release of Eve from the earthly body of the primordial Adam and of the descendants resulting from both in ever-growing numbers.

Through this process of fragmentation and division of the human primeval I from a unity into a multiplicity that took place at the beginning of the Lemurian epoch, all today's individual human "I"s emerged. This process has its counter image in an exactly reverse process, which today's man experiences every time he comes into the Sun sphere after his death, into the border region between the soul world and the spiritual world. There he takes his heart qualities, his virtues, which he developed further in his life on Earth, and gives them in an improved condition back to the world's vastness, to the spiritual starry sky from which he once received them seed-like. In the course of this process, the Dionysian-divided individual I also finds its way back to its higher, spiritual unity:

"Then comes the moment when man no longer appears as a unit, but when, to a certain extent, man appears as a multiplicity, where man experiences himself in such a way that one virtue, one feature, moves towards a certain star, the other towards another star, when man perceives his being distributed throughout the world, and when he simultaneously perceives that the parts of his being quarrel, harmonize or disharmonize with one another. Man feels, that what he experienced on Earth during daytime or at night, is distributed over the whole cosmos. And just as during the three days after death, when the thoughts flew away, that is to say, everything that was our daytime life flew away, and we concentrated on what our nocturnal experiences were and lived back to the starting point of our life on Earth, in the same way as we held on to our nocturnal experiences, we hold then, when our entire human experience flies out into the cosmos, on to what we actually are as human beings of an extrasensory world order.

Now our true self emerges from our split, I would like to say from our Dionysically split human being. Little by little, the consciousness emerges: You are spirit. You have only lived in a physical body, you have only gone through what the physical body has brought about you, even in the nocturnal experiences. You're a spirit among spirits.

Now, one enters into a spiritual existence among spiritual beings, whereas one sees split and divided into the whole cosmos what one was as an Earth-person. What we are going through here on Earth is

---

[204] GA 129 "Weltenwunder, Seelenprüfungen und Geistesoffenbarungen" (Wonders of the world, probations of the soul and revelations of the spirit), Munich, Lecture of 20 August 1911

divided out into the cosmos so that it can turn into food for the cosmos, that the cosmos can continue to exist, that the cosmos can receive new impulses for its star movements and star populations. Just as we have to feed our lives with earthly food so that we can live as physical people between birth and death, so the cosmos has to live from human experiences, has to absorb them. And in this way we get to feel more and more like a cosmic human, we find our whole human being transmitted into the cosmos, but transmitted into the spiritual cosmos." [205]

In this way, man contributes to the work on the seed for a new cosmos, and by doing so he becomes aware of his very individual part in the great work "to make mature the human self out of the World Self in the course of times". In the Sun sphere, before his descent into a new life on Earth, the divine insight brightens up in his soul once again, that the human self shall mature to an ever more worthy fruit of the World Self until the end of the Earth's evolution and that this can only succeed if man, in the course of his incarnations on Earth still to come, connects his I and his soul ever more intimately with the Christ Being, the highest spirit of the Sun and the bearer of the Logos[206] as the "new Adam", who brings together the multitude of human beings that emerged from the ancient Adam to a higher unity, while retaining their I-consciousness acquired in earth life.

Return to the Venus Sphere – 23rd Week

In its existence as a cosmic being, the human spirit-soul lives spread across the universe for centuries after its death on Earth, or at least across the entire planetary system in the later phases of its prenatal development. It is nourished by the cosmos and matures to a holistic human self on the cosmos or on the spiritual beings, which it perceives only in their light-filled revelation ultimately. When the period of its existence in the Sun has come to an end, an intense feeling of fulfillment has arisen in the human spirit soul. Man has been completely spirit-saturated. His desire for further spiritual perceptions, which his spiritual senses made possible to him, is totally satisfied and decreases considerably as a result therefore. Man really gets tired and weary of cosmic existence. He yearns for attenuation of the sun-like light-revelation of the spiritual world. Just as in life on Earth in the late evening, the autumn time of the day, we are tired of all the sensorial stimuli, get weary of them, long for the senses' rest, go to bed with our bodies and finally switch off the light, so the prenatal man's desire for cosmic sensory stimuli diminishes at his entrance into the Venus sphere and he yearns for a dimming of the spiritual light around him. It won't completely go out yet. But it is already beginning to fade mistily, to wrap itself in veils. In this sense, the first half of the 23rd weekly verse tells us about the human soul's experiences at its prenatal descent from the Sun sphere into the next lower Venus sphere. Hence we see that the incipient fog formation observable in Earth's nature in September and the autumnal dimming of sunlight are sensory likenesses of a supernatural process that speaks to the depths of our souls by means of a picture of mood in terrestrial nature, but normally does not reach up to our usual waking consciousness.

23rd Week (8 – 14 September)	*23. Woche (8. – 14. September)*
Autumnally is dimming now	Es dämpfet herbstlich sich
The senses' quest for stimuli;	Der Sinne Reizesstreben;
Into light-revelation	In Lichtesoffenbarung mischen
The mists' dull veils are blending.	Der Nebel dumpfe Schleier sich.

The 23rd weekly verse explicitly does not speak of physical light, but of "light-revelation", i.e. of the Spiritual that reveals itself as light. Also in the physical world light is only the outer expression of spiritual beings.

---

[205] GA 226 "Menschenwesen, Menschenschicksal und Welt-Entwicklung" (Man's being, his destiny and World-Evolution), Kristiania (Oslo), Lecture of 16 May 1923

[206] See the chapter "The Christ Being"

"In which element of nature ... do the Spirits of Form express themselves? ... To our observation they are concentrated in what we call the radiating rays of the Sun. Thus, light is the element in which the Spirits of Form first of all weave and live." [207]

In the Sun sphere this light-revelation of the Spirits of Form presents itself in a very special splendour. In the Venus sphere it is opposed in a dimming way by a group of Spirits of Personality or Archai, who have their main place of action there:

"And just as the advanced Spirits of Personality ... are put in their place by the Elohim, so they use in order to bring about all order, all the lawfulness of our Earth's becoming, those Archai, those Spirits of Personality, who have fallen behind, who do not reveal themselves through the light but through the darkness. They are put in the right place so that they can make their contribution to the regular becoming of our existence." [208]

Having arrived in the Venus sphere, man feels the dimming and darkening influence of the retarded Archai as extraordinarily beneficial. There, he not only becomes weary and tired of light-filled spiritual perceptions, but begins even to develop a real fear of cosmic existence, as Rudolf Steiner once explained quite drastically in one of his Dornach lectures from 1922:

"Thus, what is thought-like in the human being in the terrestrial, but actually Spiritual in the extraterrestrial, that is what we find as content of the soul before man descends into the physical world. The other, which is content of the soul, cannot be described otherwise, if we want to take the terms from earthly life, than by saying: It is fear. At the time that precedes the physical life on Earth in the soul lives something that pervades it completely as fear. But, of course, when something like that is said, you must be aware that fear as an experience outside the physical body is something completely different from what it is in the physical human body. So, before man descends to Earth, he is a Psycho-Spiritual, pervaded by an element of feeling, which is only comparable to something that man experiences as fear in life on Earth. This fear has its proper justification during the time of human life I'm talking about. In the life between death and a new birth, man has made all kinds of experiences that can be made at all in this cosmic unity with the universe. To a certain extent man has become tired of this cosmic life at the end of his existence between death and a new birth, just as man is tired of his life on Earth through the drying up, through the increasing paralysing of his bodily organization at the end of his earthly life. Man has in a way become tired of extraterrestrial life. And this becoming tired is not expressed as tiredness, but rather as fear of the universe. Man flees the universe, in a sense. What is the basic characteristic of the universe, he now perceives as something alienated from him which no longer gives him anything. He feels a kind of shyness which can be compared to fear, of the element in which man is therein. He wants to pull himself out of this universal feeling and he wants to contract himself into what is human corporeality." [209]

In the Mars sphere, above the Sun sphere, the cosmic forces were still familiar to man, whereas the forces of the Moon and Earth spheres coming up from the opposite direction were first strange to him, so that, according to the words of the 21st weekly verse, he "felt strange power fruiting". In the Venus sphere, below the Sun sphere, his experiences are exactly opposite now. Here, he feels more connected to the forces of the sub-solar planets already and it is the cosmic forces of the spheres beyond the Sun sphere which he senses as something that has become strange to him, which he is increasingly fleeing. His soul's gaze turns now in the direction of the earthly spatial world. It still is in the distance. But, looking from the Venus sphere, we can already perceive, quite symbolically speaking, the soul-autumn "in the distant space", which is connected with a dimming of the spiritual light and which will ultimately, by complete dimming, turn into the soul's winter sleep in life on Earth. Everything that we could absorb from the bright spiritual realms for our further development towards a new earthly incarnation, we have internalized then. The soul-summer has really surrendered itself to us. Accordingly, the 23rd weekly verse continues:

I see, out in the distant space,	Ich selber schau in Raumesweiten
The autumn's winter sleep.	Des Herbstes Winterschlaf.
The summer has given utterly	Der Sommer hat an mich
Itself to me.	Sich selber hingegeben.

---

[207] GA 121 "Die Mission einzelner Volksseelen" (The mission of folk-souls), Kristiania (Oslo), Lecture of 11 June 1910

[208] GA 122 "Die Geheimnisse der biblischen Schöpfungsgeschichte" (The secrets of the biblical creation story), Munich, Lecture of 21 August 1910

[209] GA 210 "Alte und neue Einweihungsmethoden" (Old and new methods of initiation), Dornach, Lecture of 17 February 1922

In which way does this manifest as a psycho-spiritual experience of the human being in the Venus sphere? What does he see "out in the distant space", which is of course not yet meant in the physical sense here, but as a pictorial transcription for the more distant areas of the supernatural experience? In a certain sense, the prenatal experience is here quite similar to the after-death experience. It must be taken into account, however, that in addition to the mutual interpenetration of the three regions of the higher soul world with the three regions of the lower spiritual world, as schematically shown in Figure 2 towards the end of the reflection on the 7th weekly verse, in reality an additional mutual interpenetration takes place. Every single sphere always pervades with its upper half the lower half of the next higher sphere. This may seem strange and confusing to our ahrimanic marked earthly consciousness, which we develop on the firmly circumscribed sensory forms of the earthly outside world. We would like to have everything neatly separated from each other and imagine the individual planetary spheres as superimposed layers. But that would be far from reality. Precisely because of the fact that the upper half of the Sun sphere pervades the lower half of the next higher sphere of Mars, the Sun sphere becomes the gateway to the spiritual world and makes possible the transformation of "light out of the vastness of the world", in the words of the previous weekly verse, into "soul light". Hence the psycho-spiritual experience in the upper half of the Sun sphere is not only turned towards its neighbouring Mars sphere, but basically already towards all three planets above the Sun sphere, even towards the zodiac, as already explained above. It is exactly the reverse with regard to the soul's experiences in the lower half of the Sun sphere. Into it, the upper half of the Venus sphere rises from below, and for this reason the forces of all three sub-solar planets flow up too, even the forces of the Earth.

It is not the human soul's prenatal experiences in the Sun sphere but instead its quite comparable after-death experiences that Rudolf Steiner described vividly, by making them the theme of the 5th scene of his mystery drama "The Souls' Awakening".[210] This scene is clearly divided into two halves. In the second half, the character of Capesius is used as an example to portray the experiences of those human souls in the Sun sphere, who have already ascended to its upper part and therefore feel attracted to the planets above the Sun. In the first half of the 5th scene, on the other hand, the examples of the two characters of Felix Balde and Strader illustrate the experiences of human souls who find themselves exposed to the after-effects of their past earthly existence for a long time after death, which extend up to the earth-facing lower part of the Sun sphere and thus, according to the above explanations, also to the upper part of the Venus sphere. Even the elemental spirits of the solid earthly substance, the gnomes, work up to that region. They are perceived there as mist, right in the sense of the words of the 23rd weekly verse: "Into light-revelation the mists' dull veils are blending." In his mystery drama Rudolf Steiner lets Felix Balde's soul look towards the gnomes and experience how the "shining existence" disappears in the distance, i.e. figuratively speaking "in the distant space", and misty pictures appear that are connected to the forces of the Earth.

FELIX BALDE'S SOUL:
(looking at the group of gnomes):

There in the distance, shining existence disappears.
It floats as misty pictures to the depths;
It wishes to give weight itself in floating.

FELIX BALDES SEELE:
(mit dem Blick nach der Gnomengruppe):

In Fernen dort entschwindet leuchtend Sein;
In Nebelbildern schwebt es nach den Tiefen;
Es wünscht im Schweben sich Gewicht zu geben.

The more advanced soul of Hilarius Gottgetreu (his surname means: faithful to God), who in the Middle Ages lived on Earth as a Grand Master of a mystery covenant, explains to Felix Balde what this is all about:

HILARIUS' SOUL:

The mist of wishes is the Earth Star's
Mere reflection, projected into spirit's realm;
That star for which you're working in *this* world
Out of soul-substances an own thinking existence.
For you it's just a fleeting misty weaving;
But they are beings, feeling soul-dense in themselves.
On earth, they work creative with world's reason
In the old fiery bottom that thirsts for forms.

HILARIUS' SEELE:

Der Wünsche-Nebel ist des Erdensterns
Ins Geistgebiet geworfner Widerschein;
Des Sterns, für den du dir in *dieser* Welt
Ein denkend Sein aus Seelenstoffen wirkst.
Für dich ist's nur ein flüchtig Nebelweben;
Für sich sind's Wesen, seelendicht sich fühlend.
Auf Erden schaffen sie mit Weltverstand
Im alten formendurst'gen Feuergrunde.

---

[210]   GA 14 "Vier Mysteriendramen" (Four mystery plays)

FELIX BALDE'S SOUL:	FELIX BALDES SEELE:
I don't want to be burdened by their weight.	Ich will, dass ihr Gewicht mich nicht belaste.
It gives resistance to the urge to float.	Es schafft dem Schwebetrieb den Widerstand.

AHRIMAN:	AHRIMAN:
Your word is good. I'll grasp it quickly,	Dein Wort ist gut. Ich will es schnell erfassen,
To keep it unspoilt for myself;	Dass ich es unverdorben mir erhalte;
You cannot cherish, furthermore, it for yourself.	Du selber kannst es dir nicht weiter pflegen.
But you would hate it down on Earth.	Auf Erden aber würdest du es hassen.

On Earth we need the earthly heaviness connected with the work of the gnomes in order to be able to develop as an earth person in an earthly body. In the Venus sphere, however, the upper half of which is pervaded by the Sun sphere, these forces hinder us from further after-death ascension and their obstacle is all the stronger the more we have connected ourselves to these forces in the past life on Earth.

But it is not only the light-revelation that is dimmed by the mistily active Earth forces in the Venus sphere. Spiritual hearing undergoes a change there as well. While in the spiritual world the "spirit word" is directly audible, in the Venus sphere only its sound and echo can first be experienced in after-death life. Just as the mist, as an expression of the darkness, counteracts the light, so now an echo caused by the Earth forces becomes noticeable as a contrast to the spirit word.

STRADER'S SOUL:	STRADERS SEELE:
A word in sound and in its echo audible.	Ein Wort im Hall und Widerhall vernehmlich.
It shows a meaning, the sound yet disappears;	Es gibt sich sinnvoll, doch der Hall entschwindet;
The echo feels the lust for own existence.	Den Widerhall ergreift die Daseinslust.
In which direction will it want to go?	Wohin wird er die Richtung nehmen wollen?

Strader's soul forces, which appear in his Imagination as four female figures before him, give him the answer to his question. First, those two speak to him who are most closely related with the element of love in the Venus sphere, which is not by chance named after the goddess Venus. In the mystery drama these two soul powers bear the name "Philia", according to the Greek word "φιλία" for the psycho-spiritual, amicable love as an expression of the psycho-spiritual Venus principle. In the preliminary remarks to the fourth mystery drama, Rudolf Steiner refers to the character of "the other Philia" as *the bearer of the element of love in the world to which the spiritual personality belongs*". The three other characters Philia, Astrid and Luna represent the sentient soul, intellectual soul and consciousness soul of man, here in particular the corresponding soul parts of Strader. Their names show their relation to the sphere of Venus (Philia), to the sphere of Mercury (Astrid, like the Latin word aster for star, here especially for Mercury, the brightly shining morning star) and to the Moon sphere (Luna, the Latin word for Moon). In this way, they are in a special connection to the three sub-solar planetary spheres and above this through "the other Philia" to the Earth, on which man is to develop from physical love to spiritual love.[211] For this purpose, also the "echo" of the spirit word moves towards the Earth, which is surrounded by floating misty pictures, as is revealed to Strader in the following.

THE OTHER PHILIA:	DIE ANDRE PHILIA:
It's moving off, in the desire for own weight,	Er ziehet sich, Gewicht begehrend, fort
To that place where the bright existence disappears	Zum Orte hin, wo leuchtend Sein entschwindet
And penetrates the depths with misty pictures.	Und nebelbilderhaft in Tiefen dringt.
If you can keep its meaning in your realm,	Bewahrst du seinen Sinn in deinem Reich,
I'll carry to the mist the force for you.	So trag' ich dir die Kraft zum Nebel hin;
Then you will find it down on Earth again.	Du wirst sie dann auf Erden wiederfinden.

---

[211] *"The other Philia is also in certain respects the other self – but the other self which still rests in the depths of the soul and has not completely detached itself, which is related to something most similar to the spiritual world here in the physical world, which is related to all-powerful love, and which can lead you up to the higher worlds because it is related to this love."* (GA 147 "Die Geheimnisse der Schwelle" (Secrets of the threshold), Munich, Lecture of 30 August 1913)

PHILIA:

The misty creatures I will care for you,
So that they guide your will, without your knowing,
I will entrust it to the cosmic light,
Where they create the warmth for your own being.

ASTRID:

I radiate blissful shining starry life
To creatures, densing forms therefrom.
They will enforce your earthly body,
From knowledge far, but close to heart's desire.

LUNA:

The weighty essence, which they heavily create,
I'll hide in your sense-body then,
That in your thinking you may not turn it to evil
And thus stir up a storm in earthly life.

PHILIA:

Die Nebelwesen pflege ich für dich,
Dass sie den Willen dir nicht wissend lenken;
Vertrauen will ich ihn dem Weltenlicht,
In dem sie deinem Wesen Wärme schaffen.

ASTRID:

Ich strahle wonnig helles Sternenleben
Den Wesen hin, dass sie's zu Formen dichten;
Sie werden deinen Erdenleib erkraften,
Dem Wissen fern, doch nah' dem Herzenstriebe.

LUNA:

Gewichtig' Wesen, das sie lastend schaffen,
Verberg' ich dir im Sinnenleibe künftig;
Dass du es denkend nicht zum Bösen bildest
Und so im Erdensein den Sturm erwühlest.

It becomes clear from these words of the soul forces that the gnomes appearing in the Venus sphere as misty creatures, who carry the forces of the Earth up to the Sun sphere, participate in the formation of the will germ of man and his future earthly body already in his after-death life. Philia, Astrid and Luna, all three, speak of the fact that they form in advance the forces for the next life on Earth, which however will be hidden below the threshold of consciousness of the earth man, because he will not be able to fully lift the will forces into awake-conscious thinking in life on Earth. Philia chooses the words "without your knowing", Astrid says "from knowledge far, but close to heart's desire" and Luna formulates "in your thinking ... not". The will forces of man work directly in the material. Therefore the elementary spirits of the earthly substance also work on them as well as on the earthly body of man. – At the end, Strader reviews his experience and sums it up for himself:

STRADER'S SOUL:

The three were speaking sunlike words; –
These work here in my field of vision.
They are creating many shapes;
The impulse germinates in me to redesign them
Meaningful to unity by strength of soul.
Wake up to me, you royal power of the Sun,
That I can dampen you at the resistance,
Which my desire carries from the Moon's own range. –
Already stirs a glow of gold, it feels so warm,
And silvery sheen, thought-spraying, cold;
Now smoulder, Mercury's desirous drive,
And wed with me the separated world-existence.
So do I feel, again a part has been created
Of that picture, which I must work out here
From cosmic spirit-forces.

STRADERS SEELE:

Die drei, sie sprachen Worte sonnenhaft; –
Die wirken mir in meinem Blickekreis.
Gestalten viel an Zahl erschaffen sie;
Es keimt in mir der Trieb, zur Einheit sie
Mir seelenkräftig sinnvoll umzubilden.
Erwache mir, du Sonnenkönigskraft,
Dass ich dich dämpfen kann am Widerstand;
Ihn trägt mein Wunsch vom Mondeskreise her. –
Schon regt sich Goldesleuchten, fühlend warm,
Und Silberglanz, gedanken-sprühend, kalt;
Erglimme noch, Merkurs Begierdetrieb,
Vermähle mir getrenntes Weltensein.
So fühl' ich wohl, dass wieder mir ein Teil
Des Bildes sich erschaffen, das ich hier
Aus Welten-Geistes-Kräften wirken muss.

With these words Strader makes a clear reference to the three sub-solar planetary spheres, the silvery sheen of the Moon sphere, the golden glow of the Sun sphere and the feeling warm effect of the Venus sphere[212] as well as the influence of Mercury on the will germ forming in man. With the phrase "that I can dampen you at the resistance" another word is given besides "mist", which Rudolf Steiner uses with regard to the dimming of the Sun's luminosity in the Venus sphere in the 23rd weekly verse, which begins with the words "Autumnally is dimming now ..." and then points to the "mists' dull veils".

---

[212] See also the parallel saying to the Venus sphere: the 4th week verse.

Perhaps some readers feel reminded here of the mist-saturated atmosphere of the ancient Atlantis, which dimmed and veiled the physical sunlight. In fact, there is an inner relation between the 23rd weekly verse and the experiences of the human beings during their earthly incarnations in times of the Atlantean epoch. The physical masses of mist and fog of the ancient Atlantis not only darkened the outer, physical sunlight. Also into the soul life of the Atlanteans, who knew themselves in intimate communion with divine beings through an only instinctive, but nevertheless light-full psycho-spiritual clairvoyance, the initially still foggy sensory perceptions of a physical, spatial earth environment intermingled. On the one hand, people sensed, on the other hand, they also learned from their Atlantean oracles that the time of a soul life illuminated by spiritual sunlight will come to an end and a dull soul-autumn will follow the bright soul-summer. Therefore, the words of the 23rd weekly verse also apply to the ancient Atlantean era: "Into light-revelation the mists' dull veils are blending. I see, out in the distant space, the autumn's winter sleep. The (soul-)summer has given utterly itself to me."

The seven great epochs of human development on Earth are not only repetitions of the evolutionary processes of ancient Saturn, ancient Sun and ancient Moon at a higher level of evolution, but they are also physical reflections or repetitions of events that already happened on the higher globes and in the different planetary spheres before the actual process of forming the Earth. We relive them again and again as regularly recurring parts of our incarnation cycles. In the preceding chapter, the connection between events in the Sun sphere and those of the Lemurian epoch on Earth has already been pointed out. Both in the Sun sphere and on Earth at the time of ancient Lemuria, humanity was under the direct guidance of the Spirits of Form or Elohim. They were the ones who, in collaboration with Yahweh, the Moon-Eloha, endowed the human beings with an I by separating the primordial I out of themselves, which in the course of time was destined to divide into billions of single individuals. Not only the extrasensory beings of the Earth and the Moon but also those of Venus and Mercury were and still are involved in this process of division. The Archai or Spirits of Personality, the actual Venus Spirits, who are one rank below the Elohim, worked primarily on the human corporealities during the course of the Atlantean epoch, so that the separate bodily forms could have an effect on the people's consciousness by bringing out separate personalities as the basis of individual I-consciousness.

"It is indeed the case that the physical form which we receive by birth and which we give off with death, emerges out of the realm of the Archai, the Primordial Sources, the Primordial Forces, so that we actually have our physical form by being enveloped by a spirit from the realm of the Archai. ...

If you now imagine that only in the Lemurian time – as I explained in these days – man emerges as such a being as the earth-man is and that he only gradually takes on this form, then you get through what can be provided as a description of the transformation of the human form, in the way I gave it in «Occult Science - An Outline», – just remember how I specified it in the description of the Atlantean world – then you get what the Archai really do; then you get a description of how the Archai work from their realm down into the Earth's realm, how they metamorphose the human form.

This metamorphosis of the human form from the Lemurian period to the time when the human form will disappear from the Earth is quite something that is constituted, shaped down from the realm of the Archai. And in working on man in such a way, the Archai produce at the same time that which in the true sense of the word is the Time Spirit. For this Time Spirit is closely connected with the shaping of the people, by bringing their skin into a certain form, so to speak. The Time Spirit is essentially seated in people's utmost sphere of sensation. And if one understands the work of these Archai, then one also understands that not only the human forms change, but also how the Time Spirits change in the course of the earthly existence". [213]

The dismembering of the individual human "I"s out of the general human primordial I of the Sun sphere starts in the Venus sphere with the division of humanity into religious communities, which appear in earthly life as the great world religions with their many subgroups.[214] This process found its reflection on Earth when humans were differentiated into diverse physical races in the mist-saturated atmosphere of the ancient Atlantis. Additionally, however, there was a division in religious aspects by connecting each group of humanity to one of the seven Atlantean oracle sites.

---

[213] GA 205 "Menschenwerden, Weltenseele und Weltengeist" (Man's becoming, world-soul and world-spirit) Part 1, Dornach, Lecture of 17 July 1921

[214] See the 4th weekly verse, the parallel saying on the Venus sphere

Return to the Mercury Sphere – 24th Week

At the time when man had transferred his entire thought life to the cosmos by his ether body in the course of his after-death life, when he had lived through the Moon sphere and expanded to the Mercury sphere, he was given the further task to detach himself from his past existence as an individual human being on Earth even with regard to the unconscious parts of his will, in particular his selfish volitional impulses. Man gradually had to learn to recognize himself as a cosmic being. "Forgetting gradually itself", the human I was called to "fathom out its real essence" in the vastness of the psycho-spiritual universe.

In the opposite way, when the human soul descending from higher spheres to a new life on Earth arrives at the Mercury sphere, it is faced with the task to condense its soul-existence, to become self-like – not selfish – in order to become able to feel more and more as a self of its own, to become aware of itself. Such awareness is not yet I-consciousness, but rather a feeling or sense of self and the experience of an individual will, which in the next life on Earth, though resting deeply in the subconscious, will give the necessary basis for the I-consciousness, which will be developed then. The task of the human soul in the Mercury sphere is no longer a widening cosmic creativity, but a self-creation and self-perception through contraction and densification.

24th Week (15 – 21 September)	24. Woche (15. – 21. September)
By constant self-creation The soul-existence perceives itself;	Sich selbst erschaffend stets, Wird Seelensein sich selbst gewahr;

Only through densification of its soul-existence into self-will the sense of self can develop, which is necessary for a life as an earthly person. Without this self-will man in life on Earth would never be able to call himself I, as Rudolf Steiner expressly declared:

"So while you must preferably combine man's activity of memory with the physical body, man's activity of thinking with the ether body, man's activity of feeling with the astral body, you will therefore have to combine man's activity of will with the I preferably. Man only says "I" to himself, because he is a will-being." [215]

So the coming out of oneself and losing oneself to the world in the after-death ascension into the Mercury sphere must be contrasted by a finding oneself, even a willing oneself and enjoying oneself in the prenatal descent into the Mercury sphere. Man must develop a certain degree of self-love or self-centeredness there, that power, which may become such a great obstacle for the meditating person, since it is unfortunately intensified by the exercises that strengthen the soul life:

"Two things occur when a person seeks, through proper meditation, by concentrating his whole soul life on individual imaginations called into consciousness by his arbitrariness, to bring out these forces resting in the depths of the soul. First, a quality, which is otherwise always present in the soul, but can be defeated in ordinary life by relatively easy measures, is reinforced together with the other qualities that are otherwise dormant in the depths of the soul. Because, spiritual development does not occur otherwise than that in a certain respect one makes the whole soul life more active, energetic inwardly. That quality which is thus reinforced together with what one is trying to strengthen is what one may call self-centeredness, self-love of man. Yes, one may say, this self-centeredness, this self-love of man, one only really gets to know when one goes through a spiritual-scientific training. Only then do we know how deep this self-love is present in man's soul, slumbering there." [216]

After man had been a spirit being spread across the cosmos for centuries and was revitalized by the Holy Spirit in his self-cognition as a cosmic spirit towards the end of the great midnight hour of existence, quite in the sense of "per spiritum sanctum reviviscimus", he is now, in the Mercury sphere already near the earth, given the task to condense the knowledge and goal orientations newly gained in the vastness of the spiritual cosmos into very personal will impulses in order to become by that a will-fruit on the world-tree. In this sense, it continues in the 24th weekly verse:

---

[215] GA 157 "Menschenschicksale und Völkerschicksale" (Destinies of individuals and nations), Berlin, Lecture of 20 April 1915

[216] GA 62 "Ergebnisse der Geistesforschung" (Results of spiritual research), Berlin, Lecture of 6 March 1913

The cosmic spirit keeps on striving,	Der Weltengeist, er strebet fort
Revitalized in self-cognition,	In Selbsterkenntnis neu belebt
And forms out of the darkness of the soul	Und schafft aus Seelenfinsternis
The will-fruit of the sense of self.	Des Selbstsinns Willensfrucht.

All our will impulses are rooted in the depths of our being, in the "darkness of the soul", into which the weak light of our earthly consciousness cannot shine:

"But when we have an impulse of will – we only need to check ourselves – it comes out of the depths of our being: I want this, I want that. – But how often do we feel instinctively pushed to one or the other! Our mind often tell us: This should not happen at all; our mind often tell us: We are actually dissatisfied with what is going on. – Then, however, on the other hand, when we look back at our own soul life and ask about our feelings, we must say: Stimulated by a certain feeling has happened, with which we even may be dissatisfied and which is rooted in the dark depths of the soul in such a way that its quality even remains unconscious to us according to its origin. And what we feel, I would like to say, plunges in a similar way down into this unconsciousness, into this darkness of will." [217]

This striking turn of the last summer verses towards will, in contrast to the emphasis on thinking in the first weekly verses of spring, shows that man's life after death is essentially divided into two parts. At first, in the course of his after-death ascension, man utilizes all that he can bring to the spiritual world as fruits from the Earth as newly acquired knowledge of his thought life, and his thoughts become pictorial. Then man already contributes to the creative work on his future earthly corporeality, but at first only as an image. Therefore, in the 5th scene of the mystery drama "The Soul's Awakening" Rudolf Steiner lets Strader, who after his death ascended to the upper Venus sphere and thus also to the lower Sun sphere, as it is explained in the previous chapter, say the words: "So do I feel, again a part has been created of that picture, which I must work out here from cosmic spirit-forces." Rudolf Steiner elucidates this division of our life after death as follows:

"In the moment we die, the thought becomes what it should not become in ordinary consciousness: then thought turns into Imagination. This Imagination, which is strived for with great effort in occult development, appears when man passes through death. All his thoughts turn into pictures. Man then lives completely among pictures. One can therefore understand the deceased only if one has gotten to know this pictorial language. Immediately after death, thoughts turn into pictures. With these pictures, man lives for some time between death and a new birth. Then the pictures gradually turn into Inspiration. In this way the soul actually continues to grow. The pictures turn into Inspiration. This is the time when man begins to perceive the music of the spheres. To him, the music of the spheres becomes something real. He lives in the world of world sounds. And finally, he merges with the objective-spiritual universe. His soul turns becomes all Intuition. He becomes one with the universe, so to speak." [218]

But from world-midnight onward, a force flows to man from the fatherly God-will, which gradually fills these images with creative will in order to ultimately transform them into material realities; for all matter is nothing but condensed will. Rudolf Steiner accordingly continues his above explanations with the words:

"But when man has arrived at the world-midnight, that is, after he has gone through the state of Imagination, through the state of Inspiration, through the state of Intuition and, so to speak, has reached the height of life between death and new birth, then Intuition fills itself again with will. The thought becomes volitional again, and this will saturates more and more the soul, which now in turn strives to Inspiration, then to Imagination. When it has arrived at the Imagination and has experienced it for a while, then it is ripe again to be embodied here. In the way I described it, from the pictures is formed what then appears as a transformed limb-metabolic man of his previous incarnation. ...

Throughout this time the human being absorbs will. And when man reaches physical existence again, we see that what is working in, out of the cosmos, which he absorbed into himself from his previous incarnation, is in the picture, and the will is still in the picture. So we have a will-saturated Imagination then. Thus, when man arrives at a new physical life before conception, he has an Imagination, but an Imagination saturated with will.

---

[217] GA 212 "Menschliches Seelenleben und Geistesstreben im Zusammenhang mit der Weltentwicklung" (Human soul life and spiritual aspiration in connection with world development), Dornach, Lecture of 29 April 1922

[218] GA 205 "Menschenwerden, Weltenseele und Weltengeist" (Man's becoming, world-soul and world-spirit), Part 1, Dornach, Lecture of 3 July 1921

From the Imagination, which is essentially what was already there as a picture, the head arises and what belongs to it, and the will takes hold of the new limbs and the metabolism, so that it distributes across the head and the rest of the human being. The head is essentially, I would say, crystallized, frozen thought; what lives in the rest of the human being is organized will. Actually, man can really wake up only in his head. You know your thoughts, don't you? Your imaginations are in your ordinary consciousness. That can be said of all today's people. What is going on in the will, is just as unknown to the people as what is going on in sleep, as I mentioned several times. For, do you know in your ordinary consciousness what is going on, when you lift your arm? You perceive that the arm is lifted, you have the imagination, but the act of will as such remains in sleep, relatively like the sleep between falling asleep and waking up. So one can say, with regard to the limb-metabolic man people sleep even in daytime."

In the post-Atlantean epoch, the development of the "will-fruit" of the human sense of self or self-love in the "soul-darkness" of the unconscious soul depths steadily increased. During the Atlantean epoch, under the rule of the Archai, each person still felt one with his race, one with his physical ancestors, and his memory extended over a long physical line of ancestors far into the past. In our fifth great epoch, the so called post-Atlantean epoch, on the other hand, the work of the Archangeloi or Archangels, who have their spiritual home in the Mercury sphere, comes more into effect. Under their rule, the large religious communities and races formed by the Archai or Venus spirits have been more and more divided into individual peoples. Along with this, people's sense of self has become more and more national. The identification of the individual with the people he belonged to was enormous. The Greek was first and foremost Greek, the Persian clearly felt himself to be a Persian, the Egyptian quite naturally Egyptian. Even today many people still feel folkish. But in the future, the nations will be further divided and man will reach complete individualization. All this is already preparing today for the next great epoch. Just as the division of mankind into races under the direction of the Archai or Spirits of Personality took its very earliest beginnings in the middle of the third or Lemurian epoch and the further division of the races into peoples under the direction of the Archangels as their Folk-Spirits already in the middle of the fourth or Atlantean epoch, so the individualization of man has already taken its beginning in the middle of the fifth or post-Atlantean epoch. It was during the fourth culture of this epoch, the Greek-Latin period, when the next step towards I-development of man could start. Marriages, which crossed the borders of nations, weakened the influence of the Folk-Spirits in an increasing number of human beings, making them all the more subordinate to the direction of their Individual Spirits, the Angels. Today we are in the midst of the struggle between nationalism, which is already in the late stages of its development, and individualism oriented towards the coming sixth epoch, which will make it possible to recognize all human beings as human siblings of equal value, regardless of any racial, ethnic or religious affiliation.

However, the consolidation of the "will-fruit" in man as the basis of an individual sense of self must not happen unrestrained. It would go beyond individualism and lead into the worst egoism, which ultimately would disintegrate the individualized I and cause people to fall into a beastlike libidinousness through loss of the I. Therefore, at the same time when individualization began, in the Greek-Latin period, the middle of the fifth great epoch, the Christ Being had to intervene instantly, to remind the people of their general-human spiritual origin in the Sun sphere. As a counterforce to the incipient individualization of human beings into individual "I"s, the highest Sun Being, who in full truth could say of Himself "I am the light of the world", had to incarnate on Earth as the superior cosmic I and the I of mankind in the Dionysian general-human, provisional primal I of the soul of the Nathan Jesus-boy.[219] Only those "I"s, who along with their ever-increasing sense of self as the firm centre of their psycho-spiritual being will in addition pervade themselves and connect more and more with the general-human Christ impulse, can escape the fall into egoism. For this purpose, Christ not only accomplished the great selfless sacrificial act on Golgotha for all human beings and the future of the Earth, but he also taught his immediate contemporaries social, moral action based on compassion and general human love, by making concrete and vivid the second commandment "You shall love your neighbour as yourself" (Lk 10:27) through the parable of the Good Samaritan (Lk 10:30-36), at the request of a Jewish teacher of law. In this parable, the one who acts according to God's commandment is not a devout Jew, but a Samaritan who was looked down and even despised by the Jews because his tribe had mixed with members of other peoples and cultivated its own kind of worship. The Samaritan, however, did not ask about the ethnic or religious affiliation of the one who needed help. As a human being, he helped a needy other human being based on pure compassion.

A person that acts socially, morally, compassionately and lovingly, along with his increasing individualization, will come under a new, rightful influence of the Archangels, through which they bring forth the formation of communities of individual "I"s. Therefore, the experiences of man soon after his death in

---

[219] GA 114 "Das Lukas-Evangelium" (The Gospel of Luke), Basel, Lecture of 18 September 1909

the realm of the Archangels, the Mercury sphere, depend on how far he already matured in his social and moral actions, i.e. how much of the relevant impulses of will live effectively in his soul depths.

"One can say that the person who has developed the qualities of compassion, of love, those qualities that are usually called moral-good, lives into the next sphere in such a way that he is able to get in contact with the beings who are in this sphere too, that he is able live with them, whereas the person who brings poor morality into this sphere lives like a hermit. This is the best description that the Moral prepares us to live together with the spiritual world. The Immoral of our heart as well as that of our thinking and behaviour in the physical world condemns us to tormenting loneliness in which we always have the yearning to know the other, yet cannot. And either as a hermit or as a sociable spirit, who is a blessing in the spiritual world, we live into the second sphere, which has always been called the Mercury sphere in occultism. Today it is called Venus in external astronomy; as we know, an inversion of names has happened, as I have often said." [220]

During man's descent through the planetary spheres is prepared what he carries down from the spiritual world into his next life on Earth as morality, compassion and love. In the Sun sphere his virtues of the heart are planted into him already, in the Venus sphere his ability to love and in the Mercury sphere his social sympathy with his fellow human beings. Only if all this was included in his will-fruit, in addition to a healthy degree of self-love and sense of self, which he also must develop during his descent, will this will-fruit be a good one, beneficial not only for others, but for himself, too. Ideally, self-love should not become stronger than love for the other, as the second great divine commandment teaches. Very few of us are so far developed already today that they can truly live up to this commandment, and especially in the present age of the consciousness soul, which has the task to advance the individualization of the human beings, a strong selfish and antisocial trait goes through our souls. This makes it all the more important, especially for today's man, to remember not only the first commandment but also the second commandment in particular.

Return to the Moon Sphere – 25th Week

With the prenatal entry into the Moon sphere the last stage of the psycho-spiritual life of man begins before his next incarnation on Earth. Here, he completes his new ether body, which will later seize the substances of his physical body, pervade them with its formative forces during his entire following life on Earth and thereby keep it alive. In the preparation of this ether body, the Moon forces respectively the Moon beings are involved in a very special way.

"When man has gone through the time between death and a new birth, when he has completed everything that must be completed between death and a new birth with regard to the psycho-spiritual, then man gets ready to descend to Earth, to connect himself with what is handed over to him by father and mother as his physical-bodily part. But before he can find the possibility of connecting with the physical body from his I and his astral body, he must clothe himself with an etheric body which he draws from the surroundings of the cosmos. ... Since the Moon has split off [from Earth], man receives these forces, which he needs to form his ether body, from outside the Earth, just from the Moon split off from Earth, so that immediately before his entry into earthly life man must appeal to that which is inherent in the Moon forces, that is, to something cosmic, in order to form his ether body. ...

Everything that happens on the Moon, whatever happens to ensure that man gets the right forces he needs to form his ether body, all that depends on the observation results, at which the beings in the Moon arrive, who, so to speak, live in the Moon and observe the wandering stars of our planetary system, Mercury, Sun, Moon and so on.

It was a knowledge that existed in certain mysteries. There was ancient mystery knowledge of certain mystery sites that the constellations, the movement conditions of the planetary system, which belongs to our Earth, were observed from the Moon and the deeds of the Moon beings were determined based on that." [221]

---

[220] GA 140 "Okkulte Untersuchungen über das Leben zwischen Tod und neuer Geburt" (Occult investigations on life between death and new birth), Vienna, Lecture of 3 November 1912

[221] GA 233a "Mysterienstätten des Mittelalters" (Mystery sites of the middle ages), Dornach, Lecture of 21 April 1924

While staying in the Moon sphere on our descent to a new incarnation on Earth we observe together with the Moon beings the constellations and movement conditions in the planetary system. Thus, we focus our attention on a temporal happening. We integrate this into the formation of our new ether body, which is first and foremost a temporal organization, in contrast to the physical body as a spatial organization. But in the Moon sphere we are still out of space and live in temporal activity.

"If one then looks back on man then, one finds also in man his ether body in accordance with what is etheric outside. But this ether body does not appear in such a way that you can say: here is the physical person, there is his ether body. Of course, you can draw it that way, but that's just a fixed section of it. You never see merely the present ether body, but when you observe a person with respect to his ether body, you see this section that can be drawn adjacent to that which precedes it. You always see the whole ether body until birth. The temporal is something uniform. You cannot simply see the twenty-year-old ether body if you are facing a twenty-year-old person, but you can see everything that happened in his ether body up to birth and a bit beyond. Here, time really becomes space. Just as you look into an avenue and the trees are pushed closer and closer to each other through perspective, just as you look into the whole avenue according to the space, in a similar way you look at the ether body as it is at the present time, but you look back at the whole structure, which is a temporal structure. The ether body is a temporal organism. The physical body is a spatial organism." [222]

The observation of the effect of time in the constellations and movement conditions of our planetary system is only one part of our activity in the Moon sphere, however. The other part consists of a last look back at our experiences in the higher spiritual world, which we summarized and encompassed with memory in the Zodiac sphere, and later on received again from the zodiac and interiorized them in the Sun sphere. In this way we preserved the knowledge of the divine origin of our "I"s, which has grown out of the God- and World-Self as a human self. In a similar way as we looked back to the zodiac from the Sun sphere, we look back to the Sun sphere from the Moon sphere in the last time before a new birth, and thus gain an additional, strong influx of forces for our "I"s. We do not look into the physical space world and not into the ethereal temporal work of the other planetary world, but into a direction beyond space and time, where both do not have any meaning, into "the dark of space and time", into the transition region from time to eternity, because the Sun sphere is the gateway to the spiritual world and connected through the zodiac with the higher spiritual world, which is pervaded by the lower regions of the Budhi plane. There Christ, as an extracosmic Being, has his lowest member of being, whom we were allowed to meet during the great midnight hour of existence. Making the inner soul light shining in this direction during his last prenatal stage in a final retrospect, man's sense of self is once again intensely strengthened and firmly founded in him. Man now knows that he is an I and allowed to live on in the near future without having to live together with the cosmic life from which he escaped more and more since the Venus sphere. He realizes: I may belong now to myself! This experience is the content of the first sentence of the 25th weekly verse, which does not by chance begin with the word "I":

25th Week (22 – 28 September)	*25. Woche (22. – 28. September)*
I may belong now to myself	Ich darf nun mir gehören
And brightly spread the inner light	Und leuchtend breiten Innenlicht
Into the dark of space and time.	In Raumes- und in Zeitenfinsternis.

Rudolf Steiner described the prenatal, observing view of man from the Moon sphere to the Sun, in community with the Moon beings, in the same lecture quoted above as follows:

"And what was observed? Well, there one mainly observed – the other [see above] was also observed, but mainly there was observed this – that forces from the Sun come from beings, who must not interfere in the formation of the ether body of man. One looked towards the Sun as to something that had a dissolving, destructive effect on the ether body. They knew through this: Forces emanating from the Sun beings must not be absorbed by the ether body, but they must be absorbed by the higher members of human nature, by the I and the astral body. Only on those the Sun forces are allowed to act. So they knew that one does not turn to the Sun for the benefit of ether body of man; for the ether body one turns to the planets. One turns to the Sun for the benefit of the astral body and especially for the I of man. This was known: For the whole inner power of the I, one has to turn to the Sun. This was the second thing that was there at this initiation referring to the mystery of the Moon. It was the second that was known: with regard to the ether body one

---

[222] GA 234 "Anthroposophie – Eine Zusammenfassung nach einundzwanzig Jahren" (Anthroposophy – A summary after twenty-one years), Dornach, Lecture of 2 February 1924

belongs to the planetary system; but one looks towards the Sun for the invigoration especially of the I and of the astral body, too."

It was still possible to get to know of these significant prenatal events by initiation in the ancient Mystery Schools. Hence, the lecture above continues:

"So this initiation included actually that one became one with the moonlight, but through the moonlight-existence of one's own being one looked into the Sun. Then one said to oneself: The Sun sends its light to the Moon, because it must not hand it over directly to man. Then one has the moonlight together with the planetary forces. From these one forms one's ether body. – This secret was known to the person who was initiated in this way. And so he knew to what extent he bore the power of the spiritual Sun within himself. He had observed this. He had become aware of the extent to which he bore the spiritual power of the Sun within himself. And that was precisely the degree of initiation by which man became a Christ-bearer, that is, a bearer of the Sun Being, not a receiver of Sun Being, but a bearer of the Sun Being. Just as the Moon is a sunlight-bearer when it is a full moon, so man became a Christ-bearer, a Christophorus. For this reason the initiation to the Christophor was a very real experience.

Now imagine this quite real experience, through which man, as it were, hurried away from Earth and soared as an initiated earth person up to the Light Being, this ancient, inner human Easter experience, think of it transformed into a cosmic festivity. In later times, people did not know that such a thing could happen: that man can really step out of the conditions of the Earth, unite with the Moon-like and look at the Sun from the Moon. But a reminder of this should be preserved, and this reminder has been preserved in Easter."

In ancient times, Easter was by no means a spring festivity as we know it today. It was an autumn festivity pervaded by Michaelic power. When all physical-etheric natural life withered and strived for sleep, just then man was particularly called to become aware of his Psycho-Spiritual, even of his divine origin, his own immortality as a cosmic being, who through the divine power in his soul depths is able to carry the world-warmth and the life spirit of the Budhi plane as sunny glowing down to Earth and thus to warm up the cold winter time in its nature-dying, to live through and survive it. Quite in this sense, the 25th weekly verse continues with the words:

While nature's being strives for sleep	Zum Schlafe drängt natürlich Wesen,
The depths of soul must be awake	Der Seele Tiefen sollen wachen
And waking carry sunny glowing	Und wachend tragen Sonnengluten
Into the winter's chilly floods.	In kalte Winterfluten.

The idea of immortality and the resurrection of the psycho-spiritual man out of the dying nature as well as from the transient mortal human body is indeed a Michaelic autumnal thought. Only because humanity in the course of its development increasingly turned to the material and lost access to psycho-spiritual experience, today it likewise needs a material image for the process of the resurrection of the psycho-spiritual from the physical-bodily that has died. For this reason, the Festivity of Resurrection had to be transferred from an original Autumn Feast to a Spring Feast, though it is not at all that in its inner nature.

"But this brings us to the point where we have to emphasize that Christian Easter is not at all a festivity that in any way coincides in its inner meaning and nature with the pagan celebrations of the spring equinox, but Easter, conceived as a Christian feast, actually coincides, if we want to go back to the ancient pagan times, with ancient feasts that have grown out of the mysteries and were celebrated in autumn. The most remarkable thing concerning the fixing of Easter, which by its very content is obviously connected with certain ancient mysteries, the most remarkable thing is: especially this Easter reminds us of what radical, what deep misunderstandings occurred in the world view of most important things in the course of human development. For nothing less has happened than that Easter was confused in the course of the first Christian centuries with a completely different feast, so that it was shifted from an autumn feast to a spring feast.

... Now we become aware of a strange development of mankind in the following centuries. The people's engagement in spirituality decreases more and more. The spiritual content of the mystery of Golgotha cannot take hold in the people's minds. The development tends to the formation of a material inclination. One loses the inner understanding of the heart for the following, one loses the understanding that when outer nature presents itself as transience, as a dying desolate existence, the very liveliness of the spirit can be seen. One also loses the understanding of the external festivity: that when autumn comes with its dying, it can best be perceived that the dying of the Earthly-Natural stands opposite to the resurrection of the Spiritual. With this, autumn loses the possibility of being the time for the Resurrection feast. Autumn loses

the possibility of directing the mind from the transience of nature to the Spirit-Eternity. ... One takes the material as a symbol of the Spiritual because one can no longer be inspired by the material to feel the Spiritual in its reality. ... One needs the reference to external nature, to the outer resurrection. One wants to see how the plants sprout out of the Earth, how the Sun gains power, how light and heat gain power again. One needs the resurrection in nature to celebrate the idea of Resurrection." [223]

The greatest helper we may find when we want to direct our gaze away from the world of space and time, i.e. from everything that is connected with the hereditary processes in earthly nature, and instead to the world of the Psycho-Spiritual, is the great Sun-Archangel Michael, who once appeared in front of the Moon-Eloha Yahweh and since the time when Christ was born has been working as the immediate servant of the highest Sun Spirit, the Christ Being. Since 1879, he has also been active as a Time Spirit to promote the evolution of humanity in the Christian sense.

"Michael, approaching man, comes up to man with a clear rejection of much in which man still lives on Earth today. So, for example, everything that develops as findings in human or animal life or in plant life focusing on the inherited qualities, focusing on what is inherited in physical nature, is such that it seems: Michael rejects it dismissively. By doing so he wants to show that such findings cannot be of any use to man for the spiritual world. Only what man finds in humanity, in animals, in plants, independent of what is purely hereditary, can be carried up before Michael. And then you don't get that meaningful, repellent movement of the hand, but you get the approving look in his eyes that tells you: This is thought justly before the dispensation of the cosmos. – For, this is what one learns more and more to strive for: to cogitate, so to speak, to penetrate to the astral light, to look at the secrets of existence and then to step before Michael and get the approving look that tells one: This is right, this is just before the dispensation of the cosmos." [224]

Michael pushes the door to the spiritual world wide open for mankind. But people have to direct their own gaze through this door. In this, they are – strange as it may seem at first – supported and driven on their way by the gradual dying of the earthly nature. The Earth had already reached the climax of its material existence in the middle of the Atlantean epoch. Since then, degradation processes, desertification and the extinction of species have predominated in the plant and animal kingdom. Humanity contributes its share. The transience of everything physical-bodily will become increasingly apparent to the people in future times. When the present post-Atlantean or fifth great epoch with its seven cultures will have come to an end and humanity will live over into the sixth great epoch, mankind will clearly find around it a desolate, autumnally dying earthly nature. All the more intense, however, will be that Michaelic call in their inner being that sounds to us out of the 25th weekly verse:

While nature's being strives for sleep	Zum Schlafe drängt natürlich Wesen,
The depths of soul must be awake	Der Seele Tiefen sollen wachen
And waking carry sunny glowing	Und wachend tragen Sonnengluten
Into the winter's chilly floods.	In kalte Winterfluten.

Preparatory work in the Michaelic sense for this great period of the decline of outer earthly nature is done by all those people who are already turning to the spirit today. Therefore, all sincerely spiritually oriented people are under Michael's care. But among these, those who already today actively seek to expand their consciousness beyond the material world into the spiritual world by practicing the psycho-spiritual inner vision through concentration and meditation, are particularly arousing his interest. To do so, the meditating person has to withdraw completely to himself through an effort of will. By deducting his attention from the sensory world and directing it inward, the spatial world around him sinks into darkness. But even the memories of the experiences from the sensory world stored in his ether body as a temporal organism must remain silent, so that at the end all temporal experience, which still has any connection with the spatial world, sinks into darkness. In this way, the meditating person experiences in full vigilance and intensity the revival of his own timeless, eternal, psycho-spiritual inner being, which only a human can carry down as his inner light into the physical sensory world, where the physical eye searches in vain for the soul- and spirit-light, where in fact in space and time soul-cold darkness would reign completely, far from spirit, if man would not exist on Earth. He alone among all other creatures of the Earth is able to carry divine warmth and

---

[223] GA 233a "Mysterienstätten des Mittelalters" (Mystery sites of the middle ages), Dornach, Lecture of 19 April 1924

[224] GA 233a "Mysterienstätten des Mittelalters" (Mystery sites of the middle ages), Dornach, Lecture of 13 January 1924

spiritual light into this outer darkness by incarnating again and again on Earth. Thus the words of the 25th weekly verse have yet another meaning:

I may belong now to myself	Ich darf nun mir gehören
And brightly spread the inner light	Und leuchtend breiten Innenlicht
Into the dark of space and time.	In Raumes- und in Zeitenfinsternis.
While nature's being strives for sleep	Zum Schlafe drängt natürlich Wesen,
The depths of soul must be awake	Der Seele Tiefen sollen wachen
And waking carry sunny glowing	Und wachend tragen Sonnengluten
Into the winter's chilly floods.	In kalte Winterfluten.

Under the guidance of the Sun Spirit Christ and his servant, the Sun-Archangel Michael, people will gradually learn to see through the Maya of the sensory world and behold the work of spiritual beings behind the veil of the senses. During their life on Earth people will be in such close contact with both the deceased and the still unborn, in addition with their Individual Spirits, the Angelic Beings, as well as with the primal teachers of mankind, that they will feel like living together with them. *"On a higher level the human souls who will then embody themselves will experience that community with a higher world which the Atlanteans have experienced on a lower level"*, as Rudolf Steiner predicts. [225] Already today, in its tender beginnings, the preparation is going on for what will flourish to a first period of glory in the sixth culture following our current culture. Death will lose its threat to those people capable of spiritual development and they will experience their resurrection in the Psycho-Spiritual. However, this will first be only a pre-bloom, which will come to full and true bloom with much greater intensity not before a later epoch, which will also consist of seven periods, the sixth great epoch of the evolution of Earth and humanity.

Autumn in Life on Earth – 26th Week

The transition of man into a new life on Earth takes place, when the etheric forces of formation and becoming, which were prepared in higher worlds by his prenatal psycho-spiritual being and are now effective in the Temporal-Spatial, pervade and seize physical substances on Earth, which are offered for this in an earthly mother's womb as a result of the fertilisation of a human egg cell. Only in this way do all the subsequent complicated processes of embryonic life come about and a new physically visible, living human form emerges. It is not the material that rises to life, as contemporary science takes for granted, but life as an independent, original power actively seizes the lifeless, passive material in order to manifest itself through it in the physical earth-world as an all-encompassing phenomenon and effective principle of the cosmos.

"The physical matter coming from the mother's body fills only that which comes in from the spiritual world." [226]

Just as man is repeatedly born out of the spiritual worlds into the physical world for his successive earthly lives, so the physical world itself and all substances contained therein were born out of higher worlds in primeval times. In the sense of this knowledge, handed down from ancient mysteries, people have ever called their earthly environment "the Born, the Emergent", in Latin "natura" as past participle of the Latin verb "nasci", i.e. to be born, to come into being. The very first beginnings of the physical world took place on ancient Saturn. At that time, it was born as substance or matter, Latin "material" after the word "mater", i.e. mother. The material-mother herself emerged out of the spiritual, thus out of the Unborn and Immortal. In the primal beginning, however, nature and man were one, for in the physical world of that time there was neither an animal kingdom or plant kingdom nor even mineral kingdom, but only a physical human corporeality consisting of pure heat material. In the course of the evolution of ancient Saturn it was emanated and given as a sacrifice by high spiritual entities, the Thrones, whose lowest member of being was similar to human will:

[225] GA 13 "Die Geheimwissenschaft im Umriss" (An outline of occult science), Chapter "Gegenwart und Zukunft der Welt- und Menschheits-Entwicklung" (The present and future of cosmic and human evolution)

[226] GA 234 "Anthroposophie – Eine Zusammenfassung nach einundzwanzig Jahren" (Anthroposophy – A summary after twenty-one years), Dornach, Lecture of 8 February 1924

"In occult science, they are called «radiant lives» or «radiant flames» because of their sublime-delicate radiant body. And because the material of which this body was made has some distant resemblance to the will of man, they are also called the «Spirits of Will». – These spirits are the creators of the Saturn-man." [227]

What externally surrounds man today as a physical world, as the material-mother Natura or Materia, is from a spiritual point of view only the outside of this will.

"If we look at the will with the power of clairvoyance, it becomes thicker and thicker, this will, and it becomes matter. ... because that is the outside of the will, the matter. Inwardly, the matter is will... And outwardly, the will is matter." [228]

Nature arose from what still exists in man today as his innermost will-nature, his will-being. There, nature has the origin of its existence.

"The Exuded solidifies. This is how the other nature kingdoms are created, which are now around us. Man himself keeps the finest for himself. Thus the whole environment was once united with man; he set it out of his essence." [229]

Based on this spiritual insight the human being may speak with full justification the first words of the 26th weekly verse:

Nature, your motherly existence,	Natur, dein mütterliches Sein,
I bear it in the will part of my being;	Ich trage es in meinem Willenswesen;

Even today, man still carries Saturn's heat as his blood heat within him. This is the "finest", which he has retained for himself, as mentioned by Rudolf Steiner.

"These differentiated states of warmth are the only thing that already existed of the present features of our Earth, and in such warmth at that time the initial preliminary stage of the physical human body was expressed. What was there, you still have in yourself today, only it has withdrawn from the outer spatial existence into your inner being. It's your blood heat." [230]

In this blood heat the human I lives and weaves in close connection with the human will, primarily in the warmth organism of the metabolic and limb part of the physical human body. [231]

"The I is first and foremost that in man which puts will into action, gives impulses of will. ... This happens by the fact that the will first of all works in the warmth organism of man." [232]

But, from his divine source man has been endowed with the ability to absorb again everything he once set out of himself and to return it into a will- and warmth-like germinal state. This process is quite analogous to its sensory counter-image in nature, which can be observed in the autumn of the year when even large trees of sometimes enormous dimensions, which once sprouted from a small seed, in turn make all material foundations of their existence flow into a small seed, so that a new, large tree may later emerge from it. A similar process, but at a higher level, takes place when man sees through nature in its underlying spirituality and internalizes the insights he has gained. By doing so he transforms the spiritual foundations of nature into a germinal state of saturnine, will-like blood heat that is closely connected to the human I. Every human being takes up a small piece of nature's spirituality, so that the evolving part of mankind will

---

[227] GA 11, "Aus der Akasha-Chronik" (From the Akasha-chronicle), Chapter "Das Leben des Saturn" (The life of Saturn)

[228] GA 291 "Das Wesen der Farben" (The essence of the colours), Dornach, Lecture of 5 December 1920

[229] GA 53 "Ursprung und Ziel des Menschen" (Origin and destination of man), Berlin, Lecture of 9 February 1905

[230] GA 104 "Die Apokalypse des Johannes" (The Apocalypse of John), Nuremberg, Lecture of 22 June 1908

[231] Rudolf Steiner has always expressly opposed the scientific assumption established today that there are sensitive and motor nerves. According to his research, the so-called motor nerves are sensitive nerves as well. *"The so-called motor nerve does not serve movement in the way as it is supposed by the doctrine of this division, but as a bearer of nerve activity it serves the inner perception of that metabolic process which underlies the will."* (GA 21 "Von Seelenrätseln" [About mysteries of the soul], Chapter 6 "Die physischen und geistigen Abhängigkeiten der Menschenwesenheit" [The physical and spiritual dependencies of the human being]). – *"The will is actually a process of combustion, a process of consumption."* (GA 225 "Drei Perspektiven der Anthroposophie – Kulturphänomene" [Three perspectives on Anthroposophy - Cultural Phenomena], Dornach, Lecture of 22 September 1923)

[232] GA 202 "Die Brücke zwischen der Weltgeistigkeit und dem Physischen des Menschen" (The bridge between universal spirituality and the physical constitution of man), Dornach, 17 December 1920

once have internalized all spiritual foundations of physical nature and thus be enabled, in the distant future, to cause a new nature, a new planetary existence, emerge out of a future primordial man.

The highest power effective in this process and directing all developmental processes is that divine being which we worship as the second person of the divine Trinity, the Son. He created the material world according to the will of the Father, as described in the prologue of the Gospel of John. However, the creative activity of the Son described there is only half of his work. It is supplemented and completed by a second half, which consists in the return of all Creation to the Father, enriched by the experiences which all beings evolving in Creation have gained in the course of its cycle of evolution; for this is the purpose of Creation. The annual harvest time on Earth in autumn, when the people gather the fruits of the trees and fields, is only a small sensory image of that great world-autumn and that great world-harvest, which takes place during the second half of a cycle of creation.

However, man can fully participate in the return to the Father only if he unites himself with the Son as that God-Being, who makes the return possible and controls it, respectively with his Bearer-Being appearing within Creation, the Christ, as he himself proclaimed to us with clear words: *"I am the way and the truth and the life. No one comes to the Father but through me."* (John 14:6)

In this great work of returning nature to the Spiritual through the inner will-being of man, which is connected with the I, in the course of the second half of the Earth's evolution, the Sun-Archangel Michael is active in a very special way as the helper of Christ. With his advancement to the rank of a Time Spirit in 1879, he initialized a new Michael epoch of about three and a half centuries. Since then we humans have been enabled to enter the spiritual world consciously. The ancient Rosicrucians, who, hundreds of years ago, had already strived to transform the knowledge of nature into a higher spiritual understanding, and who yearned for the necessary help of Michael, could not yet accomplish this with full retention of their self-consciousness, but at first only half-consciously, as in dreams.

"But this is the peculiarity since the beginning of the Michael epoch, since the end of the seventies in the last third of the 19th century, that what was achieved during the ancient Rosicrucian period in the described way can now be achieved in a conscious way. So that today one can say: It no longer needs that other state, which is semi-conscious; however it needs a higher conscious state. And then, with the knowledge of nature that is acquired, one can dive into the higher world, and what one has acquired as knowledge of nature, that emerges towards one from the higher world; by reading again what was inscribed into the astral light, it emerges towards one in spiritual reality. And through what you do, through your carrying out into a spiritual world the knowledge of nature gained here or also the creations of naturalistic art or also the sensations of religion, which work naturalistically within the soul, – for even religion has become naturalistic after all – by carrying up all that, one encounters Michael indeed, if one develops the abilities for it. And so we can say: Rosicrucianism is characterized by the fact that its most enlightened spirits had a strong longing to meet Michael. They could only do it as if in a dream. Since the end of the last third of the 19th century, people have been able to consciously encounter the spirit-being Michael. ...

But Michael is a strange being in deed. Michael is a being that actually reveals nothing if you do not bring to him from the Earth what you have achieved here in eager spiritual work. Michael is a silent spirit. Michael is a reserved spirit. While others of the ruling Archangels are much-talking spirits – in the spiritual sense of course – Michael is a quite taciturn spirit, a little talking spirit that gives at most sparse directives. Because, what one gets from Michael is actually not the word, but – if I may say so – the look, the power of the look. And this is based on the fact that Michael actually is most concerned with that what humans create from the Spiritual. He lives in the consequences of what humans created. The other spirits live more with the causes, Michael lives more with the consequences. The other spirits impulse in man what man should do. Michael will be the actual spiritual hero of free will. He lets people do, but then takes up what becomes from human deeds in order to carry it on in the cosmos, in order to continue in the cosmos what a human being can not yet do with it." [233]

In the same sense Rudolf Steiner spoke in another lecture:

"With regard to external nature, man will find his way into the Extrasensory in the right way through Michael. Without being falsified in itself, view of nature will be able to stand next to a spiritual conception of the world and of man, insofar as he is a world being." [234]

---

[233] GA 233a "Mysterienstätten des Mittelalters" (Mystery sites of the middle ages), Dornach, Lecture of 13 January 1924

[234] GA 26 "Anthroposophische Leitsätze" (Anthroposophical Leading Thoughts), Chapter "Das Michael-Christus-Erlebnis des Menschen" (The Michael-Christus-experience of man)

Nature observation of modern man, however, is subject to a strong Ahrimanic influence, which intends to make people believe that there is only a material world, that spirit can only exist always based on matter, if at all, and consequently the spirit would have to perish when the material perishes. If man gives himself over to this influence in a passive-dreamy, weak-willed and sluggish thinking, without developing higher, will-controlled striving for knowledge, he will easily get into fearfulness and a depressive mood in view of the earthly nature, when it begins to wilt and to die in autumn, because he feels thereby reminded of his own transience or, respectively, of that of his body with which he primarily identifies himself. The will to penetrate the physical veil of the senses must grow stronger in man in order to find the way to the spiritual foundations of nature and cosmos as well as to the spiritual human self, which is most intimately connected with them.

"The feast of strong will, that is how we should understand the Michael Feast. If this is the case, if such knowledge of nature joins up with true consciousness of the spiritual human self, then the Michael Feast will attain its right colour, its right colouration." [235]

Being reminded of the transience of physical nature in autumn each year, including the physical corporeality of man, completely loses its threat as soon as a person gains knowledge of the spirit behind the veil of the senses. But, this path must be taken willingly. The human will-being working in the warmth of the blood must become a fiery power, a "fiery might", that strengthens and consolidates the striving for the spirit. If man advances to the insight that everything perishable has emerged from the imperishable, and if he does not connect his sense of self with his mortal bodily sheath, but with his bodiless, spiritual and immortal I and with his will-warmth related to the original state of Saturn, then a new sense of self is born in him. He will become aware of the fact that he is called to develop the ability to hold himself within himself, so that there is no longer need for being dependent on any external perishable nature as a bearer. In this sense, the 26th weekly verse, entirely filled with Michaelic mood, becomes a great consolation with regard to all transience:

26 Michaelmas-Atmosphere	26 Michaeli-Stimmung
Nature, your motherly existence,	Natur, dein mütterliches Sein,
I bear it in the will part of my being;	Ich trage es in meinem Willenswesen;
And my will's fiery might,	Und meines Willens Feuermacht,
It steels my spirit's drives,	Sie stählet meines Geistes Triebe,
That they give birth to sense of self,	Dass sie gebären Selbstgefühl,
To hold me in myself.	Zu tragen mich in mir.

"As long as you live personally with the world, things reveal only what links them to our personality. But this is their transient aspect. If we withdraw ourselves from our transient aspects and live with our sense of self, with our «I» in our permanence, then the transient parts become mediators in us; and what is revealed through them is an Imperishable, an Eternal in the things." [236]

Goethe likewise lets the natural and spiritual researcher Faust, in the scene "In Front of the City-Gate", speak about the will-drive towards the spirit to the student Wagner, who only knows the other spirit-drive that is solely devoted to intellectual science and to the historically handed-down knowledge of the books. Faust himself knows this drive all too well. To him, however, it has a drawing down effect. Besides, he is aware of another, higher impulse of the spirit that pushes him in the opposite direction, so that he painfully feels his soul divided into a lower and a higher part:

Faust I, Verse 1110 – 1117: [237]

You're conscious only of the one impulse at best;
Oh, never get to know the other!
Two souls, alas, dwell in my breast,
One wants to separate from the other;

---

[235] GA 229 "Das Miterleben des Jahreslaufes in 4 kosmischen Imaginationen" (The experience of the course of the year in 4 cosmic imaginations), Dornach, Lecture of 5 October 1923

[236] GA 9 "Theosophie" (Theosophy), Chapter "Der Pfad der Erkenntnis" (The path of knowledge)

[237] German original wording: *"Du bist dir nur des einen Triebs bewusst; o lerne nie den anderen kennen! Zwei Seelen wohnen, ach! in meiner Brust, die eine will sich von der andern trennen; die eine hält, in derber Liebeslust, sich an die Welt mit klammernden Organen; die andere hebt gewaltsam sich vom Dust zu den Gefilden hoher Ahnen."*

One holds, in bawdy love and lust,
On to the world with all his organs as with hands;
The other rises strongly from the dust
To high ancestors' lands.

At the time of Faust, at the end of the Middle Ages, Michael had not yet begun his reign as a Time Spirit. The gate to the spiritual world was not yet open. Thus, Faust's desire for conscious entry into the spiritual world had to remain just as unfulfilled as that of the medieval Rosicrucians.

But to whom do we owe this second impulse of man, turned towards the spirit? Rudolf Steiner answered this question in one of his Viennese lectures. We owe it to both Christ and the Holy Spirit. The power of the latter is strengthened by the Christ impulse, which works beyond the midnight hour of existence, provided that we intimately united ourselves to Christ in the previous life on Earth.

"That, which remains for us of the Christ impulse, increases the impulse of the Spirit. The spirit would otherwise only be for the spirit and it would cease to work at our birth. By pervading ourselves with the Christ impulse, the Christ impulse increases the impulse of the Holy Spirit. And thereby such an impulse of the Spirit can also be brought into our soul, which then, when we enter into an earthly incarnation, is a force which we do not consume as the other forces which we bring along through birth, in the earthly incarnation. ...

Through the Spirit, through the Holy Spirit, we are awakened in the great midnight hour of existence. And we must say on the other hand, looking at what the Spirit is doing in Earth's development for the future: Also in the physical body, the best of the soul, that which gives the view into the spiritual worlds, is being awakened more and more by the Holy Spirit. Being raised by the Holy Spirit at the midnight hour of existence, man will also be raised when he lives in his physical body, when he lives himself into the physical existence. He will wake up inwardly, being awakened by the Spirit from a sleep, in which he would otherwise be biased with the mere looking at the sensory world and with the intellect that is bound to the brain. People would always sleep through the mere sensory view and through the intellect bound to the brain. But into this sleep of man, which would otherwise creep over humanity increasingly darkening towards the future, into this sleep the Spirit in man will also shine during the physical existence. Amid the dying spiritual life, dying on the physical plane through the mere sensory view and intellectual conception, the human souls will also be awakened in the physical existence through the Holy Spirit. – Per spiritum sanctum reviviscimus." [238]

In the future mankind will need more and more the impulse of the Holy Spirit, increased by the Christ impulse. The Earth as a planet has long since passed the middle of its lifetime and is approaching its old age, which will ultimately end with the Earth's death. Until then, people will have to be strengthened in their "I"s so much, that they will be able to hold them in themselves, as the 26th weekly verse puts it.

"We are in a sense already on the descent of the Earth development, and we as human beings have to swing ourselves up, so that we get beyond the Earth development through our connection with the spiritual world. But in doing so, what we cognitively strive for must be recognized as a force that makes it possible for us to pass over as entire humanity into the next stages of development, when the Earth dies below us, as we pass over into other stages of development on a small scale, when the body dies off, when we pass through the portal of death. We walk as a single person through the portal of death, that is, into the spiritual world. The body dies below us. This is how it will once be in the whole of humanity. This humanity as a whole will evolve toward a Jupiter existence – I call it Jupiter existence. The Earth becomes a corpse. This process of dying is going on already. The individual gets wrinkles, gets gray hair. The Earth today has clear signs of its aging for the geologist who can really observe it – I just talked about it recently. The Earth is dying below us. That, which we are looking for spiritually today, is in fact a counteraction against the ageing process of the Earth. It is this consciousness that we are to pervade ourselves with." [239]

Man's I-development started in the course of the third or Lemurian epoch of the Earth, when the Spirits of Form sacrificed their lowest member of being as the human I, and the Moon-Eloha Yahweh breathed it, enveloped by the human soul, into the human bodies. During the subsequent fourth or Atlantean epoch, the higher spiritual Hierarchies worked on the humans primarily through the Archai in order to develop them

---

[238] GA 153 "Inneres Wesen des Menschen und Leben zwischen Tod und neuer Geburt" (The inner nature of man and life between death and rebirth), Vienna, Lecture of 14 April 1914

[239] GA 194 "Die Sendung Michaels – Die Offenbarung der eigentlichen Geheimnisse des Menschenwesens" (The Mission of Michael – The revelation of the intrinsic secrets of the human being), Dornach, Lecture of 6 December 1919

into personalities. Mankind, originally unified, was divided into races. In the fifth great epoch of Earth development, which is still ongoing today, the races were divided into numerous peoples under the influence of the Archangels. In the future sixth epoch, under the guidance of the Angels, the peoples will also be divided into billions of individual human beings. The positively developing human being will no longer feel folkish, but will regard himself as an individual alongside other individuals with equal rights. This is how the great brotherhood of mankind will come into being. When the sixth great epoch will reach its end and the seventh and final epoch of Earth development will begin, then the humans will ultimately be completely released from the leadership of the beings of the third Hierarchy, including the Angels. At the end of the Earth's development, the human I will be so strong that it can hold itself within itself and has become master of the astral body, on whose resistances it has ripened since ancient Lemuria.

"All development of human cultures is nothing more than working the I into the astral body, a development of the astral body. Filled with desires, drives and passions, man enters life. By overcoming these drives, desires and passions, he works his I into his astral body. When the sixth root race, the sixth major age, will be completed, the I will be completely worked into the astral body. Until then, the astral body is constantly dependent on support from the forces of the Devas. As long as the I has not permeated the whole astral body, Deva forces must support the work." [240]

Those ones, who will have reached the goal of development, which is predetermined for mankind until the Earth's death, will then be completely Christ-imbued in their individual "I"s. They will have brought the first and second commandments to reality in their entirety and in the highest humanly possible measure: *"You shall love the Lord your God with all your heart and all your soul and all your thinking and all your strength. That's the first commandment. The second is this: Thou shalt love thy neighbour as thyself. Greater than this is no other."* (Mark 12, 29-31). Whole humanity, being Christ-imbued, will then experience a general-human *"in Christo morimur"*, release its connection with the Earth's dying body and rise under the guidance of Christ and his servant Michael to the astral or plastic globe of the next higher world in order to continue its development to higher goals there.

"Just as in the Lemurian period the Yahweh Spirit poured out himself into the individualities from the element of the spirit, so the Christ Spirit, who has his body in the warmth of the blood, slowly and gradually has been pouring out himself during the ages that preceded the Christ Jesus and those who follow him. And when the whole Christ Spirit will be poured out into the human individualities, then Christianity, the great brotherhood of men, will have conquered the Earth. Then, there will be no longer any consciousness of cliques and small collectives at all, but only the consciousness that humanity is a brotherhood. With the greatest individualization, everyone will nevertheless feel attracted to the other. The small tribal and popular communities will have given way to the community of the Life Spirit, the Budhi, the community of Christ." [241]

In this sense, the 26th weekly verse, filled with "Michaelmas-Atmosphere", describes the conclusion and completion of the development of the human I on Earth as the opposite pole to the birth of the I characterized in the 1st weekly verse with its "Easter-Atmosphere". As a further contradiction of these two horizontal or parallel verses, the focus of reflection in the Michaelmas verse is on the completion of will-pervaded sense of self or I rooting in the depths of the soul, whereas in the Easter verse it is on the birth and beginning of the thought-borne I-consciousness on the surface of the soul, caused by external sensory stimuli. On the one hand, this closes a complete development circle. On the other hand, the autumnal Michael-experience and the Easter Christ-experience stand side by side as two complementary pillars of human evolution. Rudolf Steiner once again referred to this peculiarity in his guiding principles, which he wrote during the last days of his life in the sickbed as a final legacy to us:

"Thus, in the future, the Michael experience and the Christ experience can stand side by side; through this man will find his rightful path of free will between the Luciferic deviation into illusions of thought and life, and the Ahrimanic allurements of future forms which satisfy man's pride but which cannot be his present forms yet." [242]

Apart from the great importance of the Easter and the Michaelmas verses for the development of humanity as a whole, they also have a clear relation to the individual's life on Earth. As a small developmental period, it is modelled on the large and comprehensive general-human process of

---

[240] GA 93a "Grundelemente der Esoterik" (Foundations of esotericism), Berlin, Lecture of 7 October 1905

[241] GA 96 "Ursprungsimpulse der Geisteswissenschaft" (Original impulses of the science of the spirit), Berlin, Lecture of 1 April 1907

[242] GA 26 "Anthroposophische Leitsätze" (Anthroposophical Leading Thoughts), Chapter "Das Michael-Christus-Erlebnis des Menschen" (The Michael-Christ-experience of man)

development. In this sense, the 1st weekly verse describes how man sees the light of the world at birth and how his thought life is awakened in him through the external sensory perception. The 26th weekly verse, on the other hand, renders how man at the end of his life on Earth has internalized in the hidden will-germ of his soul depths everything he was able to extract from earthly nature in the course of his earthly life. This shows an analogy of the weekly verses of the summer half-year to the earthly human life cycle.

Rudolf Steiner gives as average duration of a human life on Earth 70 to 72 years.[243] If we take 71 years as the arithmetic mean and divide this by the number of weekly verses of the summer half-year, i.e. 71 by 26, you get 2.73 years of life for each weekly verse. The 1st weekly verse, entitled "Easter-Atmosphere" begins with the earthly birth of man at the age of 0 years. The 2nd weekly verse starts with 2.73 years of age. Continuing the series and adding 2.73 years for each following weekly verse, the age of 30 years (exactly 30.03) results for the 12th weekly verse, which describes the entry of man into the lowest region of the Budhi plane or Christ sphere after death. It is that age which the man Jesus of Nazareth had reached when John the Baptist performed the baptism at the Jordan, during which the Christ Being, the Being, whose lowest member is Budhi, connected himself with the corporeality of Jesus of Nazareth. In this respect, the title "John-Atmosphere", with which Rudolf Steiner entitled the 12th weekly verse, proves to be an excellent characteristic of the historical encounter of the human being John with the divine Christ, too. It marks the beginning of a development that will enable all humans of good will to gain a conscious and intimate connection between the human "I"s and the divine I in the future.

The terrestrial encounter between John the Baptist and Christ, on the Jordan River, was a historically unique, microcosmic likeness, experienced at the lower pole of the human incarnation cycle, of the repeatedly happening macrocosmic encounter with Christ at the upper pole of the cycle in the great midnight hour between two incarnations. All those people are allowed to have this experience, who feel so intensively connected with Christ inwardly that He can sustain their I-consciousness until the midnight hour of existence between two incarnations, guide them through their encounter with God and strengthen the power of the Holy Spirit within them for their next life on Earth in such a way that it will become possible for them to penetrate the earthly veil of the senses and to reach an ever more comprehensive knowledge of the intimate relationship of nature and the human being as well as of their common origin in the divine primal source.

---

[243] *"This is approximately the average age of man, 70 to 72 years"* (GA 192 "Geisteswissenschaftliche Behandlung sozialer und pädagogischer Fragen" (Spiritual-scientific consideration of social and pedagogic questions), Stuttgart, Lecture of 1 May 1919 – see also GA 175 "Bausteine zu einer Erkenntnis des Mysteriums von Golgotha" (Building stones for an understanding of the mystery of Golgotha), Berlin, Lecture of 13 February 1917)

Weekly Verses
of the Winter Half-Year

WINTER HALF-YEAR

Experiences of the Soul in Autumn – Ascension to the higher worlds

Autumn in Life on Earth – 27th Week

During the summer half-year the earth-man has the natural tendency to turn to the outside world. The natural spectacle of spring draws his attention out into the world and invites him to intensively experience the ever more lively and colourful natural phenomena. As the reflections on the first half of the Soul Calendar showed, on this path the human being may arrive at the knowledge of his own divine-spiritual origin and thus of his own true essence, provided that he walks on this path in a psycho-spiritual way.

In autumn and winter, on the other hand, it is healthier for man not to indulge in the withering and decay that is observable all around in his outer world, but instead to intentionally focus on himself and his inner world, in order to be able to "bear him in himself", as the last words of the preceding weekly verse suggest. If man walks this inner path in a spiritual way, to his great surprise he will be able to find the origin of the large, vast outside world within himself and thus only attain true knowledge of the world.

To several of his students Rudolf Steiner gave meaningful verses for meditative contemplation, which were dedicated to this amazing context. One of them is mentioned here as an example:

Do you want to know your own essence,	Willst du das eigne Wesen erkennen,
Look all around the world in all directions.	Sieh dich in der Welt nach allen Seiten um.
Do you want to truly understand the world,	Willst du die Welt wahrhaft durchschauen,
Look into the depths of your own soul.	Blick in die Tiefen der eignen Seele.
30 March 1924	*30. März 1924* [244]

Man's returning to himself and focussing his gaze on the inner soul-experiences are supported in the autumn time of the year by the fact that the outside world appears increasingly uncomfortable to him. People withdraw into their houses and apartments, and they prefer to make themselves comfortable there. The external warmth is replaced by the warmth inside of their homes. The soul gets into a mood of retrospective contemplation of all the activities of the summer half-year that has just ended. Everybody is pleased about what he was able to put into practice in the past six months, but becomes aware as well of what wishes are still waiting to be fulfilled, which for the present only can be carried over into next year as seeds for new activities.

A very similar mood arises when man reaches the autumn of his earthly existence in advanced age. When his professional life ends and he retires, the summer half-year of his life on Earth comes to an end, so to speak. Now he no longer has to leave his home every day to fulfil his professional and worldly obligations, but may reflect more on himself and on all that he has achieved in life, as well as on that which still lives inside him in unfulfilled wishes and impulses of will. Due to their rich content, the past decades of life offer plenty of opportunity for such a retrospective self-examination. In addition to the external sensory perception, which has been at the forefront until now, an inner living in memories is gradually beginning to develop and to become more and more vivid. Along with this, a desire awakens for evaluation of one's own life's work through joyful appreciation of what has been successful and, in an effort to achieve an at least halfway objective judgment, for thoughtful questioning of what has been less successful, too. From the insights gained hereby, new wishes and impulses of will arise concerning the way in which one or the other thing could perhaps have been done better. Through this, man already penetrates into the hidden depths of

---

[244] GA 40 "Wahrspruchworte" (True-Verse-Words / Truth-Wrought-Words), Section "Sinnsprüche" (Meaningful verses)

his being, even though the fullness of his wealth of experience accumulated deeply in the unconscious only becomes accessible to him in a very initial and presumptuous manner. All in all, however, self-contemplation becomes a new drive for activity, which supplements world-contemplation that was in the foreground in the past decades of life, and the former even surpasses the latter in significance in the last years of life on Earth, if it is an advanced age. The words of the 27th weekly verse put us exactly in this mood of the soul:

27th Week (6 – 12 October)	*27. Woche (6. – 12. Oktober)*
Ingress into my being's depths:	In meines Wesens Tiefen dringen:
This is encouraged by a prescient longing,	Erregt ein ahnungsvolles Sehnen,
So that I find myself in self-reflection,	Dass ich mich selbstbetrachtend finde,
The summer's sunny gift, which warming lives	Als Sommersonnengabe, die als Keim
As germ in autumn-mood,	In Herbstesstimmung wärmend lebt
As drive of forces in my soul.	Als meiner Seele Kräftetrieb.

The drive for self-reflection originates in one's own soul. Throughout lifetime on Earth, it was developed as a silent germ whose hidden existence in the soul-depths of the human being has always been covered up by the intense sensory impressions of the outside world. Only with increasing age, when the longing for ever new sensory stimuli of the outside world gradually decreases, does man begin to sense, in quiet hours of contemplation, that a completely different longing lives in him, too, which directs his attention in the opposite direction, not out into the physical world of space, but into the temporal stream of his past experiences and thus already into the extrasensory region of the Etheric. In this way man gets a new drive for his soul life. New forces for introspection develop and warm the soul from within henceforth. Both the autumn time of his life and the annually recurring autumn time of the earthly nature may be experienced joyfully by man if he is able to direct his attention and inner striving in the right way. Therefore, all the weekly verses of the Soul Calendar, which refer to autumn and winter time, are filled with an extremely joyful, soul-warming and powerful mood. Deepening oneself in these verses can become true refreshment to the soul, especially if one suffers from the increasing darkness and coldness of the outside world.

But what is the nature of this germ, which was formed in the depths of the human being in an advanced age and becomes noticeable only as a "prescient longing" later in life on Earth? The 27th weekly verse basically provides information about this. It speaks of a "drive of forces in the soul".

"Those who have thought about immortality of the soul have always thought of it as something existing in ordinary life and passing through the portal of death; whereas one first has to seek what passes through the portal of death, for it is so deeply hidden in the soul that it is not noticed, that the attention in ordinary life is not directed towards it; but it is there after all. And when he, who really, chemically so to speak, separates the psycho-spiritual from the physical, then experiences how this psycho-spiritual is saved by spiritual beings in a superior extrasensory world, then he also knows that in this, which is hiding in the soul in ordinary life ..., that he has in this something that works completely in secret, between the lines of life, as it were; which absorbs the finest forces of the soul, of the experience, of the moral abilities of man, like the small plant germ absorbs the forces from the whole plant to concentrate them. And as after wilting, after the leaves have withered and the blossoms have died, the plant transfers what lived in the previous plant as a small germ to the following plant, what the plant saved over as a germ – so it is in the human soul. When one distils it out in this way, one notices: the human soul is constantly working out in every moment of life, waking and sleeping, in the undergrounds of everyday life, working out everything that we acquire in abilities. The soul is pervaded, deeply pervaded by what it has done in injustice and justice, beautiful and ugly; it carries that in itself, as the plant germ carries in itself the germ of the whole new plant." [245]

This, which is powerfully active in man in the background, is predominantly of a volitional nature. In several lectures Rudolf Steiner pointed out the enormous importance of this germ of forces and will, which is deeply hidden in the human being. By way of example, the following statements by him are quoted:

"And the will being in man is something embryonic, something germ-like that only fully develops post mortem, after death." [246]

---

[245] GA 64 "Aus schicksaltragender Zeit" (From fateful time), Nuremberg, Lecture of 12 March 1915

[246] GA 194 "Die Sendung Michaels – Die Offenbarung der eigentlichen Geheimnisse des Menschenwesens" (The Mission of Michael – The revelation of the intrinsic secrets of the human being), Dornach, Lecture of 14 December 1919

"For, a germ is something super-real ... a germ becomes something real only later, thus the later real carries within itself a very first developmental state, so that the will is indeed of a very spiritual nature. Schopenhauer suspected this; but of course he could not advance to the realization that the will is the germ of the psycho-spiritual, because this psycho-spiritual unfolds in the spiritual world after death." [247]

"And with respect to the will, we will never gain a correct view unless we realize that what asserts itself as will, is only a germ that only comes to full development when the outer body, in which it develops as in a soil, has been laid down. Certainly, we must develop the moral ideas in a human being, but we must be clear that these moral ideas, by the fact that they are embedded in the will, do not mean merely what they express between birth and death, but that their full life does not appear until this body is abandoned." [248]

"Cherish my statement that a kernel is formed in man, which enters the spiritual kingdom through the portal of death: this kernel is the bearer of our karma." [249]

"And when we die, is still present for a few days – I have often explained this and you will also find it in my books – the last remnant of memory in the etheric body. When we pass the portal of death, we look back at our past life on Earth. Then this memory fades away. And that which the power of love on Earth has given us as a power for life after death winds its way out of this memory. As the power of our memory is the inheritance we have from our pre-earthly life, so the power of love is the germ-power for what we own after our death. This is how the earthly life refers to the spiritual world." [250]

The ability of love is not only of great importance for our life on Earth. It is also important, if not actually more important for our after-death life and even for its preparation, on which we work every night together with higher spiritual beings, when we are – similar to the state after death – outside our physical and ether bodies with our "I"s and astral bodies, and relive the experiences of the past day in reverse order and with karmic judgment from a different, more objective perspective. Rudolf Steiner describes this context in the same lecture just quoted as follows:

"Think for a moment, we must outwardly relive our deeds with our «I»s and our astral bodies. The ability to do this is acquired the more we are able to unfold love. That's the secret of life with respect to love. If a person can really go out of himself in love, love his neighbour as himself, as it were, then he learns what he needs in sleep in order to be able to experience then in reverse fully without torture what he just has to experience in reverse. Because then he must be completely outside of himself. If someone is a loveless being, then this gives a tension when, outside of himself, he is to re-experience his deeds, which he accomplished in lovelessness. That makes him narrow. Loveless people sleep, if I may express myself figuratively, tight-breasted. And so, while we sleep, that which we transplant into our lives through love really becomes quite fruitful for us humans. And in what develops between falling asleep and waking up – it is clear from my presentation just given – we have what goes out through the portal of death and then lives on out there in the spiritual world. In the conditions between death and a new birth, it loses itself into the coexistence with the spiritual beings of the higher worlds; we regain it germ-like through love during our life on Earth. For love reveals its meaning when a person is with his I and his astral body outside his physical and ether body in sleep. The essence of man becomes wide between falling asleep and waking up when he is a loving person and prepares himself well for what should happen to him after death. The essence of man becomes narrow when he is loveless and prepares himself badly for what should happen to him after death. By unfolding love preferably occurs what is germ for that happening, which takes place after death."

Love lives warming as a germ in autumn-mood, as drive of forces in the soul. The more we are able to bring along from earthly life as "summer's sunny gift", the better prepared we are for our after-death life, especially if we were able to develop love, starting from the stage of physical love up to emotional and finally pure spiritual love, which we may feel for all people, not only for those to whom we are close through sensual desire, through family or kinship relationships or through friendship. Love should become general-human in us. Then we carry it as a fully Christ-imbued drive of forces into the higher worlds and our life after death.

---

[247] GA 293 "Allgemeine Menschenkunde als Grundlage der Pädagogik" (General study of man as the basis of pedagogy), Stuttgart, Lecture of 22 August 1919

[248] GA 297 "Idee und Praxis der Waldorfschule" (Idea and practice of the Waldorf School), Stuttgart, Lecture of 24 August 1919

[249] GA 157 "Menschenschicksale und Völkerschicksale" (Destinies of individuals and nations), Berlin, Lecture of 20 April 1915

[250] GA 218 "Geistige Zusammenhänge in der Gestaltung des menschlichen Organismus" (Spiritual relationships in the configuration of the human organism), Stuttgart, Lecture of 4 December 1922

"One can really say that everything that remains hidden inside man at first reveals itself when man has passed through the portal of death. And then even sleep gains cosmic significance, and the existence during winter also gains cosmic significance. We sleep every night in order to prepare the light in which we must live after death. We go through the winter experiences in order to prepare the warmth conditions of psycho-spiritual kind, which we enter after death. And into what we prepare for ourselves as the atmosphere of the spiritual world, so to speak, into that we carry the effects of our deeds." [251]

The effects of our deeds form the germ of forces from which the immortal, higher self of man, together with and under the guidance of higher spiritual beings, creates the basis for a new life on Earth in the course of several centuries of existence in the extrasensory worlds. Enlightenment of humanity about this great cycle of human life, about the reality of reincarnation and, with Michael's support, directing the people's gaze in a scientific manner beyond the boundaries of the sensory world into the higher worlds, is the extremely important task of Anthroposophy or the science of the spirit for the near future of humanity on Earth.

"This fact, that the human soul experiences repeated lives on Earth as a universal being, that each following earthly life is the effect of former earthly lives, this is what spiritual science will gradually incorporate into the spiritual culture of humanity, just as the Copernican worldview was incorporated into the external culture. Of course, it is still true today that people often say: But, what you are telling me, contradicts what the five senses hold as true! Well, people even had to witness something very different, which contradicts their five senses. For thousands of years people believed, according to their five senses, the Sun and the starry sky would move around the Earth. That it is the opposite, and the Earth moves around the Sun, this is what they had to learn despite the contradiction against their five senses. Thus, what contradicts the five senses, that man goes through repeated lives on Earth, must enter into the thinking habits of the people as well. But then man will speak of the immortal part in the human being, based on real science. He will seek this immortal in a sense between the lines of ordinary experiences, will know in himself an inwardly working being, which is sheltered in a spiritual world, in a similar way as the sensorial outside world is saved in our imaginations and thoughts and sensations. Then man will know himself connected with his eternal, his immortal aspect, connected with the spiritual world. That's what in human evolution is about to happen." [252]

Not only Rudolf Steiner's many lecture cycles, but also the fifty-two weekly verses of the Anthroposophical Soul Calendar, which he formulated so wisely, serve this great goal, by attuning us emotionally and perceptively, following the successive natural moods in the course of the year, to the sublime truth of reincarnation and of the immortal and imperishable human being, and in this way confirming Goethe's knowledge of nature, which he lets sound, at the end of the second part of his Faust drama, through the Chorus mysticus as a summarising knowledge of world and man from the spiritual world: "All that is transient is but a likeness."

Ascension to the Moon Sphere – 28th Week

By passing through the portal of death, the psycho-spiritual man returns his physical bodily sheath to the Earth and a short time later it already begins to dissolve into the countless physical-material components of which it was composed. Until right before death, these manifold substances were still under the supremacy of the ether body. Through it, they were integrated into a dynamic equilibrium of composing and decomposing vital processes and thereby kept together. As long as the ether body had to fulfill this task, it remained continuously united with the physical body, even in sleep times, during which the psycho-spiritual part of man, the astral body and the I, separated from the living material body resting in bed, every day or rather every night for about a third of a day. At the moment of death, however, the ether body is completely freed from its task of enlivening the physical body. Now it unites more closely with the astral body, and when this comes out of the physical body it can therefore take the ether body with it. The power of enlivenment remains with the ether body as its basic property. While previously it was used for the outward-adjacent member of the human being, the physical bodily sheath, it now benefits the inward-adjacent member, the astral body. Instead of the exterior, the psycho-spiritual interior of man is now

---

[251] GA 219 "Das Verhältnis der Sternenwelt zum Menschen und des Menschen zur Sternenwelt" (The relationship of the starry world to man and man to the starry world), Dornach, Lecture of 1 December 1922

[252] GA 64 "Aus schicksaltragender Zeit" (From fateful time), Nuremberg, Lecture of 12 March 1915

enlivened. Rudolf Steiner once described the after-death revival of the astral body by the ether body as follows:

"But it [the astral body] takes the ether body along through the portal of death: And now, drawn out of the physical body, the astral body together with the I can develop a full consciousness; it is now flashed through by the life force of the ether body, and consciousness emerges." [253]

This inner revival of the astral body is accompanied by an enormous expansion of consciousness for the recently deceased person. The temporal vastness of his own being opens up to him. All experiences of his past life on Earth present themselves as a tremendous panorama of life before his psycho-spiritual eye. He no longer feels limited to the present-day experiences, but truly expanded into a temporal being. In accordance with this experience, the 28th weekly verse begins briefly and concisely with the words:

I can, revitalized inside,	Ich kann im Innern neu belebt
Feel now own being's vastness ...	Erfühlen eignen Wesens Weiten ...

However, this expansion is only the very first beginning of an ever-increasing expanse into cosmic spheres. As soon as the inner revival of the astral body by the ether body was accomplished and the life panorama as well as the thought-elemental beings[254] made up the main content of the first after-death stage of consciousness of the deceased for a few days, the ether body separates from the astral body and the I, it expands more and more and escapes into the vastness of the cosmos. Only an extract of it remains attached to the astral body and the I furthermore.

"So, first of all, this image of memory stands before the soul of man. Then comes the time when the ether body separates again from the astral body and the I. But a rest of the ether body remains associated with the human being, something one could call the extract of the last life, something like a short extract. Think of this short excerpt, this essence of life, as if you could artfully summarize the contents of a thick book on one page, but in a way that a person could rebuild the contents of the book from this extract. Something like such an essence of life is incorporated into the human being for all future, after he has discarded what he cannot use for his further evolution. We want to keep this in mind in particular. That which is incorporated into man for the future development is the fruit of his last life. Each life forms something like a sheet in the great book of life and all our earthly lives are inscribed into such a sheet. They are incorporated into our being. We take such a fruit out of one life along into all the future ones. This fruit is of great importance for the further development of the human being." [255]

The remaining extract of the ether body offers the astral body and the I an abutment against which they can hit and thereby ignite another kind of consciousness for the deceased in his further life after death, which feels initially strange.

"But then, when it [the astral body] is so enlivened, when the extract is drawn from the ether body so to speak, then what only sustains the vital functions is expelled into the wider ether world, because the ether body is actually the life-provider of the physical body and cannot be used for anything else further on. Man must first struggle through the spiritual consciousness, which arises by the impact of the astral body and the I against the extract of the ether body, until he comes to the use of his new consciousness in which he spends the time between death and a new birth." [256]

With this new consciousness, man experiences his increasing expansion out into the cosmic spheres. The initial words of the 28th weekly verse apply in this second phase of the widening of the human being in the life after death as well: "I can, revitalized inside, feel now own being's vastness."

"If we first look at the astral body, we see that man lives himself out after death – really literally lives himself out by growing larger and larger, so to speak, into all the planetary spheres. Through the expansion of his psycho-spiritual being, man first becomes such a large being during the Kamaloka period – different beings interpenetrate in this process – that he reaches the boundary which is indicated by the circle drawn by the Moon around the Earth." [257]

---

[253] GA 64 "Aus schicksaltragender Zeit" (From fateful time), Berlin, Lecture of 16 April 1915

[254] See the reflection on the 2nd weekly verse.

[255] GA 56 "Die Erkenntnis der Seele und des Geistes" (Knowledge of soul and spirit), Berlin, Lecture of 16 April 1908

[256] GA 64 "Aus schicksaltragender Zeit" (From fateful time), Berlin, Lecture of 16 April 1915

[257] GA 141 "Das Leben zwischen Tod und neuer Geburt im Verhältnis zu den kosmischen Tatsachen" (Life between death and new birth in relation to cosmic facts), Berlin, Lecture of 20 November 1912

With man's after-death metamorphosis from a spatial body-being to a temporal soul-being, the soul forces of thinking, feeling and willing also undergo an enormous transformation. The 28th weekly verse gives us information right at the beginning about the metamorphosis of feeling, insofar as it concerns man's sense of self. Instead of a small earthly human body, the deceased or rather "revitalized" now feels one with a huge bodiless area of space, with the vastness of the near-earth cosmos bordered by the Moon's orbit. Man can now "f e e l own being's vastness."

But what about the soul force of thinking after death? That new kind of thinking with the help of thought-elemental beings, which man got to know immediately after his death, escapes after a few days together with the ether body into the vastness of the cosmos. "Into the outside of the sensory universe, thought power loses own existence", as it says in the 2nd weekly verse. What previously had a defined "own existence" in man becomes the common good of the cosmos or, spiritually speaking, the common good of the Hierarchies. But this transition of thoughts from man to the cosmos, from own existence to universal existence, does not only take place after death. It already happens in preparation during life on Earth every single night, when the astral body and the I expand into the closer earth environment. This again shows how right the ancient Greeks were when they called sleep (hypnos) the little brother of death (thanatos).

"Thus, with regard to our thoughts we are not independent at all, and we are so little independent that our thoughts are carried out into the cosmos just with the Sun's daily cycle. Even with our feelings we are not independent; they are carried out through the cycle of the year. So already in the earthly existence that, which is in our head through thoughts and in our chest through our feelings, lives not only in us, but lives a cosmic existence as well. Only what lives in our will we keep with us until our death. Then, when we have laid down the body, when we have nothing more to deal with the earthly forces, we carry it out through the portal of death.

And then man passes through the portal of death, loaded with what has become of his acts of will. Just as he has around him here, what lives in minerals, plants, animals, in physical human beings, what lives in clouds, rivers, mountains, stars, as far as they are visible externally through the light, as he has this around him during his existence between birth and death, so he has a world around him when he has given away his physical and ether body and passed through the door of death. He has around him precisely that world into which his thoughts entered every night, into which his feelings entered in every cycle of the year: That's what you thought; that's what you felt. – And now it is as if the beings of the higher Hierarchies carry his thoughts and feelings towards him. They looked at them in the way I characterized it. Now his intellect, his emotions are radiating brightly towards him. Just as the sun illuminates here from morning to evening the earthly existence, as it sets and night falls, so our wisdoms radiate brightly towards us as day when we have walked through the portal of death, so the spiritual lights around us darken and dim, and night falls through our accumulated follies. What is day and night here on this Earth is all around us as the result of our wisdoms and follies after we have passed through the portal of death." [258]

Thus, thinking turns into rays of thoughts that approach us from the outside as a spirit-light, which may be compared in its luminosity with the sunlight in the physical world. With the help of the astral body, which no longer has to spend a part of its power to the tasks on the physical human body, such as moving the limbs, but is freed from this task and thus gets an increase in force, man after death can "forcefully" use the thoughts which radiate back to him from the Hierarchies, in order to look at his past life on Earth from a higher perspective and already find first solutions regarding many mysteries of the course of his life. In this sense, the 28th weekly verse not only portrays our feeling after death in the Moon sphere, but immediately afterwards very vividly our new way of thinking, too:

I can, revitalized inside,	Ich kann im Innern neu belebt
Feel now own being's vastness	Erfühlen eignen Wesens Weiten
And forcefully give rays of thought	Und krafterfüllt Gedankenstrahlen
Out of the sun-might of the soul	Aus Seelensonnenmacht
To solve the mysteries of life,	Den Lebensrätseln lösend spenden,

Rudolf Steiner coined the new term "sun-might of the soul" (German: Seelensonnenmacht) to characterize the luminosity of the thought rays that outshines everything. Apparently, the intensity of this light is extraordinarily powerful. The following extract of a lecture gives more detailed information about this

---

[258] GA 219 "Das Verhältnis der Sternenwelt zum Menschen und des Menschen zur Sternenwelt" (The relationship of the starry world to man and man to the starry world), Dornach, Lecture of 1 December 1922

as well as about the great importance of the retrospective reflection on one's own being during this phase of life after death:

"You see, the materialistic thinker usually sticks to the question: Does consciousness remain beyond death at all? – It is a result of spiritual research that when the soul has passed through the portal of death, it really does not suffer from a lack of consciousness, but that it has just too much consciousness. That a kind of awakening occurs only later on is not due to the fact that one has to acquire a new consciousness after death, but from the fact that one has a very dazzling consciousness, that one has too much consciousness, which must be dampened bit by bit. You can find out more about this in the Viennese cycle [259]*, which is also printed. Man after death has too much consciousness, overwhelming consciousness, and he must first orientate himself in this world of overwhelming consciousness. And as he gradually gets this far, he becomes less conscious than before. He first has to dim the consciousness, as one has to dampen the too bright sunlight. So a dimming of consciousness bit by bit is what one has to do. Thus one cannot speak of an awakening like in the physical world, but of recovering from the superabundance of consciousness to the degree that one can endure, depending on what one experienced here in the physical world. For this, something is necessary: In order to find our way in this outshining light-consciousness after death, the knowledge of one's own being is needed as a starting point; this includes the fact that you can look back on your own being, so to speak, in order to find the guidelines, to orient yourself in the spiritual world. The lack of self-knowledge is precisely the obstacle to consciousness after death. We must find ourselves in the flooding light."* [260]

Now that we have learned what kind of feeling and thinking are in the Moon sphere, the question arises what about the third soul force there, the will. In the Moon sphere, feeling and willing do not appear as separate from each other as we know them from life on Earth, but join more closely with each other to a kind of feeling will or willing feeling.

"After the tableau of memories has dimmed, this feeling will, this willing feeling unfolds, becomes stronger in the soul; but it only expresses things that are still connected with the last life on Earth; so that we may characterize these things that we witness there approximately in the following way: Life on Earth never gives man everything in his experience that it could give him. A lot of things remain that we can say: We did not enjoy everything that could have been enjoyed, that could have made impressions between birth and death. Something always remained between the lines of life, so to speak, of desires, of love for other people and so on. The unfinished – to need the trivial expression – in the last life, that is it we spiritually look back on with desires, and indeed spiritually look back on with desires for years. In these years it is, so to speak, that our world consists mainly of what we have been ourselves. We look into our last existence on Earth, we see in it what has remained unfinished." [261]

Besides the manifold desires and passions that have become a firm inner habit in life on Earth, unfulfilled wishes and longings live in the deeper layers of our soul that could not find their fulfillment in the last earthly life. They are clearly in front of our soul consciousness now. Goethe knew that there is much more planted in man than he can bring to development in earthly life. He took this as an indication that the life on Earth must inevitably have a continuation after death.

"The thought arises in Goethe that the human soul, when it tries to comprehend itself, becomes aware that it has potentialities and abilities which it cannot bring to full development and unfolding in a human life; and then from the depth of his being and also from what I called yesterday «the bearing force of the German spirit» the words come up to Goethe: If nature has given me such potentialities which cannot be satisfied in this life, it is obliged to allot me after death another life, where these different potentialities can really unfold." [262]

In fact, in life after death man has the opportunity to unfold his so far undeveloped potentialities according to his inner, deeply hidden desires – be it in the spiritual worlds between two earthly lives or be it in a next life on Earth – in order to attain fulfillment for wishes, of whose possible realization he hardly dared to dream in view of the manifold restrictions in earthly life, so that in the end they have only become a pipe dream for him and a vague hope, to be able to bring them into fulfillment perhaps at some time in

---

[259] GA 153 "Inneres Wesen des Menschen und Leben zwischen Tod und neuer Geburt" (Inner nature of man and life between death and new birth), Vienna

[260] GA 157 "Menschenschicksale und Völkerschicksale" (Destinies of individuals and nations), Berlin, Lecture of 22 February 1915

[261] GA 153 "Inneres Wesen des Menschen und Leben zwischen Tod und neuer Geburt" (Inner nature of man and life between death and new birth), Vienna, Lecture of 8 April 1914

[262] GA 64 "Aus schicksaltragender Zeit" (From fateful time), Berlin, Lecture of 26 February 1915

the future; alas, who knows when and if at all, perhaps never or at best in a next life on Earth. The last two lines of the 28th weekly verse point to this arising awareness of the unfulfilled wishes and the beginning of the work on their future fulfillment.

28th Week (13 – 19 October)	*28. Woche (13. – 19. Oktober)*
I can, revitalized inside,	Ich kann im Innern neu belebt
F e e l now own being's vastness	E r f ü h l e n eignen Wesens Weiten
And forcefully give r a y s o f t h o u g h t	Und krafterfüllt G e d a n k e n s t r a h l e n
Out of the sun-might of the soul	Aus Seelensonnenmacht
To solve the mysteries of life,	Den Lebensrätseln lösend spenden,
And grant fulfillment many a w i s h ,	Erfüllung manchem W u n s c h e leihen,
Though hope already paralyzed its wings.	Dem Hoffnung schon die Schwingen lähmte.

Very aptly indeed, the 28th weekly verse describes man's after-death experiences with regard to that new way of feeling, thinking and willing in the Moon sphere. There, they are already proving to be germs of a next life on Earth. However, in addition to the wishes that are based on our undeveloped potentialities, there are other unfulfilled wishes. They also begin to develop every night during deep sleep in our soul depths when, in an out-of-body state, we look from our astral body and I morally judging at our earthly deeds. The wishes resulting from this judgment also enter our consciousness in the Moon sphere in the clearest way.

"This life is the first germ to what will be realized as karma in the following earthly lives. In this life, which is lived through in a third of an earthly life time, one really gets to know inwardly through one's own feelings and perceptions, gets to know the effects of one's own deeds on other people. And then, my dear friends, a mighty wish existing inside in the spirit-man [263] comes up, that what one experiences then in the spiritual sphere, in the Moon sphere, because one caused it on Earth in other people, is loaded upon oneself in turn, so that a compensation may be done. The decision to put one's destiny into effect according to one's deeds on Earth and one's thoughts on Earth, this wish stands at the end of this Moon time. And when this wish from that experience, which reaches back to birth, has become fearless then the human being has become ripened to be taken in by the next sphere, by the Mercury sphere. Then man enters the Mercury sphere." [264]

Ascension to the Mercury Sphere – 29th Week

During his stay in the Moon sphere, man was with regard to his cognitive capacity completely dependent on that new kind of thinking which, after surrendering his ether body and thus his earthly thoughts to the cosmos, flows back to him as sunlit thought-rays by the Hierarchies in a way from the outside. In the Mercury sphere another metamorphosis of thought is taking place then. Man begins to develop the ability to illuminate his surroundings on his own by his soul. Therefore, in occultism, the Mercury sphere is called the "Region of Soul Light." [265]

"But more and more a force, a soul force, develops in man, which in turn only the spirit researcher knows when he experiences himself psycho-spiritually out of his body. For this, we have really no expression. Of the other force one can at least say: «willing feeling» or «feeling willing», because it has something similar to will and feeling. Even though will and feeling are objectified, the things that surge around out there as «willings» and feelings, are similar to the impulses of feeling and will that we otherwise have in life. But what the soul witnesses then, what awakens as a force in it the more it distances itself in the described way from its last life on Earth, I can only describe with an expression which may sound clumsy in relation to the ordinary language, but which is nevertheless significant. I can only name it:

---

[263] What is meant here is not the Spirit Man, the seventh member of the human being, but the person who lives on spiritually after death.

[264] GA 239 "Esoterische Betrachtungen karmischer Zusammenhänge" (Esoteric reflections on karmic connections – karmic relationships), Volume 5, Paris, Lecture of 23 May 1924

[265] GA 141 "Das Leben zwischen Tod und neuer Geburt im Verhältnis zu den kosmischen Tatsachen" (Life between death and new birth in relation to cosmic facts), Berlin, Lecture of 1 April 1913

creative soul power, creative power of the soul. It is something that the soul now experiences directly. The soul experiences fully that one changes into an activity, but at the same time that this creative power is really developing, really radiating from the soul into the environment and – again it's clumsy, but this expression must be used just so that one can make oneself understood – this power is something that is radiating into the environment like a spiritual light, which illuminates the spiritual processes and beings all around, so that we see them. Just as when the sun rises and we see the outer objects through the sun, so we see the spiritual processes and beings through our own inner luminosity that pours out. Then comes the time when the soul is in the spiritual environment to the extent that this creative power awakens in it in order to illuminate this world." [266]

This new ability that flares up in the human being during his stay in the Mercury sphere is the subject of the 29th weekly verse:

29th Week (20 - 26 October)	*29. Woche (20. – 26. Oktober)*
To kindle thinking's luminousness	Sich selbst des Denkens Leuchten
Vigorously inside oneself,	Im Innern kraftvoll zu entfachen,
Construing the experiences' deeper meaning	Erlebtes sinnvoll deutend
From cosmic spirit's source of forces,	Aus Weltengeistes Kräftequell,
Is now the summer's heritage to me,	Ist mir nun Sommererbe,
Is autumn's rest and winter's hope as well.	Ist Herbstesruhe und auch Winterhoffnung.

The development and application of this new, creative soul power, which at the same time illuminates man's spiritual environment is experienced by him as bliss. After completing the Kamaloka state, he feels for the first time in a state, which the various world religions have assigned to a heaven in the other world.

"And here the religions have used no insignificant expression when they say to designate life after death: This feeling of oneself in the creative power, this settling into a spiritual environment, which becomes visible by sending one's own creative power into it, this experience of oneself in the outpouring of light is a feeling of bliss. Even pains are experienced as blisses in this world. There the soul lives its further life then.

The point now is that the soul can only in alternating states go through this experience, which has just been described. ... It is not always in the state that it radiates its spiritual luminosity from the soul over its surroundings, so that human souls and other beings are now around it and spiritual processes are witnessed by it. It is not always the case, that the soul lives in the outer spiritual world, but this state must alternate with the state that the soul feels in a way diminishing this radiation of the spiritual luminous power. The soul becomes inwardly dull, it can no longer radiate its light on the environment. It must concentrate its whole being in itself." [267]

In a similar manner as in life on Earth where we alternate rhythmically between turning to the world by day and returning to ourselves in the evening and at night, our life in the higher worlds is also marked by a rhythm of turning to the outside world and returning to ourselves. Beginning with the Mercury sphere, however, the essential difference is that we ourselves then must illuminate our surroundings. No sun shines towards us from the outside, as it happened through the physical Sun to the Earth and the "sun-might of the soul" in the Moon sphere.

In yet another respect, the existence in the Mercury sphere differs substantially from the existence in the Moon sphere. There we were mainly occupied with experiencing our past life on Earth in reverse order, including our most hidden longings and wishes as well as moral assessment of our entire thinking, feeling and willing.

"While we are in this experience in reverse, however, something mixes up in our whole life, which then reaches a certain conclusion when we come out of the Moon area after death. Immediately after we have cast off the ether body a few days after death in the manner described above, the moral assessment of our value as human beings asserts itself from these nocturnal experiences. Then we cannot help but judge morally what we experience there in reverse. And it's very peculiar how things develop then. Here on Earth man has a body of bones, muscles, blood vessels and so on. Then, after death, a spiritual body is formed which is constructed from our moral values. A good person gets a beautifully shining moral body, a bad

---

[266] GA 153 "Inneres Wesen des Menschen und Leben zwischen Tod und neuer Geburt" (Inner nature of man and life between death and new birth), Vienna, Public Lecture of 8 April 1914

[267] Ibidem

person a badly shining moral body. This is formed during this reversal. And that is actually only one part of what is attached to us, what now becomes our – if I may express myself in this way – spirit body, because a part of what we now receive in the spiritual world as a spirit body is formed from our moral values. With another part we get simply dressed from the substances of the spiritual world, if I may say so." [268]

From his cast-off earthly body man does not take anything material, but he carries interrelationships of forces into his life after death. That part of these forces, however, which is connected with the human head, is lost in the Moon region already. Only the forces of man's chest region and the region of the metabolic-limb system are carried by man into the Mercury sphere.

"For, with all that, which arrives there as a headless human being, so to speak – forgive the expression – with all that is connected then, after the moral blemishes have been laid down in the Moon region, that, which man has experienced as health or illness during an earthly life. It is important, because it is very significant, surprising and striking that man casts off his moral blemishes already in the Moon region, but that what infested him in illness does not fall off in the Moon region, but can be taken away from man in its spiritual effects only in the Mercury region by those beings, which have not ever been human beings. It is precisely the observation of this fact that is extremely important: Diseases are taken away from man in the Mercury region in their spiritual results. And observing this we experience first then, how in the world of stars that is the actual world of the gods, Physical and Moral interact with each other. The Morally Flawed cannot enter the spiritual world, remains so to speak in the Moon region, which has so much share in the human beings, for among its inhabitants are beings who once lived among mankind. On Mercury, there are inhabitants who never were earthlings. These beings then take the diseases away from the people. These diseases are seen flowing out into the vastness of the world, into the spiritual cosmos, and the spiritual results of human diseases are absorbed, as it were, by the spiritual cosmos, flow out, are received even with a certain pleasure. But the person who experiences this in life between death and a new birth has the first impression then, which is a purely spiritual one actually, and yet as real to him as the Earth was. Just as here on Earth we experience the wind, the lightning, the flowing of the water, so we experience, when we have passed the portal of death and entered the Mercury region, the going away of the spiritual effects of the diseases, see how they are received by spiritual beings, these spiritual effects of diseases, and the impression is that one: Now you are reconciled, O gods!

This is a very important fact in our life between death and a new birth. Once such facts were known, when just those beings were present, who as the great primeval teachers of mankind, who later became inhabitants of the Moon, taught men. Then it was also known that one can only learn about the nature of diseases what is true, when the truth comes from the Mercury beings. Therefore, all healing, all medical knowledge, was the secret of certain mysteries, the Mercury mysteries." [269]

In the Moon sphere already, the human being has received information about some of his riddles of life, as the reflection on the 28th weekly verse showed. All questions that arise from experiences of disease states in the earthly existence, however, can find their answer in the Mercury sphere at the earliest. Only there man learns to understand the meaning of such experiences: why he had to suffer these or those diseases, why some people had to fall ill frequently or severely, but others only rarely and were allowed to enjoy a fairly stable health. The spiritual beings that help man to come to terms with such experiences in the Mercury sphere are the Archangeloi.

"And when man has given away the physical body in death, he first has in his soul the effects also of those experiences which he had to go through by processes of illness. But they are completely put off in the Mercury sphere under the influence of those beings that we call the Archangeloi. So little by little, through the Moon and Mercury spheres, man becomes a being that no longer has any moral or physical weaknesses in himself." [270]

From the great number of Hierarchies which together make up the cosmic spirituality, the Archangeloi reveal themselves to man in the Mercury sphere. They give him the forces to understand the deeper meaning of illness and health. Here man learns about the psychological-moral causes of his illnesses and can therefore construe all the related questions still open, concerning his experiences in life on Earth, with regard to their deeper meaning, just as it says in the 29th weekly verse:

---

[268] GA 226 "Menschenwesen, Menschenschicksal und Welt-Entwicklung" (Man's being, his destiny and world-evolution), Kristiania (Oslo), Lecture of 17 May 1923

[269] GA 239 "Esoterische Betrachtungen karmischer Zusammenhänge" (Esoteric reflections on karmic connections – karmic relationships) – Volume 5", Paris, Lecture of 24 May 1924

[270] GA 239 "Esoterische Betrachtungen karmischer Zusammenhänge" (Esoteric reflections on karmic connections – karmic relationships) – Volume 5, Breslau, Lecture of 8 June 1924

Construing the experiences' deeper meaning	Erlebtes sinnvoll deutend
From cosmic spirit's source of forces,	Aus Weltengeistes Kräftequell

So this settles man's last questions relating to his life in an earthly human body in the physical sensory world. Into the next higher spheres he can only take with him what he developed within himself of such thoughts, feelings and impulses of will, which aimed at supernatural worlds. His religious disposition will play a greater role there. To a certain extent his connection with the earthly world is finalized in the Mercury Sphere. What has been experienced here is, so to speak, the remaining heritage from the "earth-summer". But after man has found a clarification of his riddles of life and understood the meaning of his suffering, a deep peace enters his soul and "autumn's rest" spreads in him. In this calm, serene mood of his soul, he can now confidently look forward to his further development in the spheres as his "winter's hope", as the last lines of the 29th weekly verse express so beautifully in reference to the autumnal mood on Earth:

To kindle thinking's luminousness	Sich selbst des Denkens Leuchten
Vigorously inside oneself,	Im Innern kraftvoll zu entfachen,
Construing the experiences' deeper meaning	Erlebtes sinnvoll deutend
From cosmic spirit's source of forces,	Aus Weltengeistes Kräftequell,
Is now the summer's heritage to me,	Ist mir nun Sommererbe,
Is autumn's rest and winter's hope as well.	Ist Herbstesruhe und auch Winterhoffnung.

Ascension to the Venus Sphere – 30th Week

From one metamorphosis to the other, man proceeds on his after-death path of development through the planetary spheres. In this process, the world spirituality of the cosmic vastness, the spiritual reality behind the physical sensory images, is disclosed to him in an ever more sublime way. With his transition from the Mercury sphere to the Venus sphere, the Archai begin to reveal themselves as the next higher spiritual beings. Under their care and influence he continues to develop from now on.

"From the Mercury region, man then enters the region of the Venus-existence. By those beings, who inhabit Venus and who are much more unlike earthly beings than the Mercury beings, that, which man is able to bring along of himself to the region of Venus, is transformed in such a way that it can be advanced in the spiritual region at all. But this is only possible because man enters a new element when he enters the Venus region. Living here on Earth, it is important that we have ideas, have concepts, have imaginations. For what would man be on Earth if he did not have imaginations and ideas. Thoughts hold him, they are valuable, and we as human beings are, because we have thoughts that are good for something, we are therefore clever. Especially today, it is regarded important when people are clever. Today almost all people are clever. It wasn't always like that. Today it is like that. And the whole life on Earth depends on people having thoughts. From the human thoughts the great technology has sprung up. Everything that man puts into practice in good or evil on Earth, comes into being with the help of thoughts finally. But the thoughts still have an effect in the Moon region, because the beings in the Moon region judge according to the way in which the good and evil deeds originated from the thoughts. But also the beings in the Mercury region judge the diseases, which they have to remove from the people, still according to the thoughts. But in a certain sense there is the border up to where thoughts – everything that still reminds of human intelligence at all – have a meaning. Because, if one comes out of the Mercury region into the region of Venus, then there prevails that which we know in Earth life in its reflection as love. Love replaces wisdom, so to speak. We enter the region of love. Man can be carried on into the Sun-existence only by the way that love leads him out of the sphere of wisdom into the Sun-existence." [271]

These words of Rudolf Steiner could be interpreted that the effects of our thoughts would reach up only to the Mercury sphere and not have any meaning in the Venus sphere, that only what man developed as love during his past life on Earth would matter there. However, such an interpretation of the above lines would be a misunderstanding, because Rudolf Steiner does not speak of an absolute limit for the effectiveness of thoughts in this context. He rather says: "But *in a certain sense* there is the border up to where thoughts – everything that still reminds of human intelligence at all – have a meaning." In fact, the

---

[271] GA 239 "Esoterische Betrachtungen karmischer Zusammenhänge" (Esoteric reflections on karmic connections – karmic relationships) – Volume 5, Paris, Lecture of 24 May 1924

Mercury sphere is an absolute border only for all thoughts referring to the physical sensory world and for insights that are a result of man's mere intellect. Their effects actually do not reach up to the Venus sphere. But the after-effects of those thoughts which aim at the Extrasensory, already in earthly life, which are not based on the mere intellect, but arise from the innermost feelings of the heart and create a religious mood in us, such thoughts are of even extraordinary importance in the Venus sphere. Especially our most sublime spiritual insights really liven up as more ripened fruits of thought in the Venus sphere and achieve their full development there. They are illuminated by the soul light that we are able to radiate outwards from within us since we entered the Mercury sphere. This light increases more and more in luminosity the closer we get to the Sun sphere. Already in the Venus sphere it increases to a true "soul-sunlight" and illuminates the soul world surrounding us. Its full radiance, however, will not be attained before the Sun sphere, the highest region of the soul world.

The first words of the 30th weekly verse speak to us of these new experiences of the psycho-spiritual human being:

In soul-sunlight sprout for me	Es sprießen mir im Seelensonnenlicht
The thinking's ripened fruits ...	Des Denkens reife Früchte ...

Whoever does not think about religious or supernatural subjects in life on Earth and who, for lack of insight that there is also a moral world order besides the natural world order, has not behaved morally towards his fellow human beings, will hardly be able to find any ripened fruits of thinking sprouting in the Venus sphere. Atheistic or purely materialistic thinking on Earth casts its darkening shadows into the soul-sunlight of the Venus sphere.

"Whoever was not religious, who did not assimilate anything eternal or divine, who was not able to have psycho-spiritual relations with other human souls in the Mercury period, will become a hermit in the Venus period, too, whereas we are sociable beings also there, when we were together with like-minded beings in the Mercury period and unfolded religious warmth with one other. Atheists will become hermits in the Venus period, Monists [272] will have to live in the prison of their own soul, so that the one cannot approach the other. Being a hermit means to have a dull consciousness that does not encompass the other. Being a sociable being means to have a bright consciousness that penetrates into the other. Of course, man always rises into the worlds of the stars nonetheless, but the more dimly he perceives a region, the faster he races through the periods and thus comes faster to reincarnation." [273]

An atheist or materialist can little assimilate from the spiritual environment of the Venus sphere, since he has slight affinity in his soul-being with this environment, which is strange to him. Only religious feeling in connection with supernatural ideas opens the soul to the Divine and makes it receptive to the most important principle of the Venus sphere: divine love. Man must absorb this love as much as possible in order to become able to prepare himself in the necessary way for the next metamorphosis, his transition into the Sun sphere.

"Then, in the Venus sphere, purest love prevails in the most spiritual sense. Venus is the element of purest love, and what has remained there of the human being in this way, is carried from the Venus sphere into the Sun existence by the cosmic love." [274]

If a person brings along enough religious feeling, not the soul-cold religiosity of a scribe, which sticks to the letter and looks down condemningly on other men, but "religious warmth", as Rudolf Steiner terms it in the above quotation, then he can bathe in the "soul-sunlight" of the Venus sphere, in divine love, and strengthen himself for his imminent transition to the Sun sphere. The then secure knowledge of being an immortal spirit being, which can live completely without bodily sheaths, even live a much freer and more sublime life, and in addition, the feeling of being completely sheltered in divine love, enveloped, pervaded and carried by divine love, which can be experienced so intensely in the Venus sphere, both together give the human spirit-soul an inexpressible feeling of safeness. This sublime mood is expressed in the lines of the first half of the 30th weekly verse:

---

[272] See note 40 (page 29)

[273] GA 130 "Das esoterische Christentum und die geistige Führung der Menschheit" (Esoteric Christianity and the spiritual guidance of mankind), St. Gallen, notes from the Lecture of 19 December 1912

[274] GA 239 "Esoterische Betrachtungen karmischer Zusammenhänge" (Esoteric reflections on karmic connections – karmic relationships), Volume 5, Breslau, Lecture of 8 June 1924

30th Week (27 October – 2 November)	30. Woche (27. Oktober – 2. November)
In soul-sunlight sprout for me The thinking's ripened fruits, Into safeness of self-confidence All feeling is transforming.	Es sprießen mir im Seelensonnenlicht Des Denkens reife Früchte, In Selbstbewusstseins Sicherheit Verwandelt alles Fühlen sich.

Now the human being can look forward with pleasure to his further soul metamorphoses, which he already begins to surmise. Clearly and distinctly the insight rises in him that the autumnal withering of his soul-connections to the physical-sensory life on Earth into a complete winter rest is accompanied by a constantly increasing awakening of higher cognitive powers, and that the soul-sunlight emanating from him will soon achieve its full radiance and bring about a real summer of the soul.

With pleasure I can sense Autumn's awakening of the spirit: The winter will arouse in me The summer of the soul.	Empfinden kann ich freudevoll Des Herbstes Geisterwachen: Der Winter wird in mir Den Seelensommer wecken.

How splendidly the 30th weekly verse reflects this soul mood of the human spirit-soul, who first has had to become pure light and divine warmth himself and to attain a higher, psycho-spiritual self-confidence before, then having become sun-like, it is able to ascend into the next higher sphere, the Sun sphere.

Ascension to the Sun Sphere – 31sth Week

With the transition from the Venus sphere to the Sun sphere, the soul-light radiating from man into his spiritual environment and illuminating it, increases in intensity once more. The reason for this is that the origin of its power is no longer only in the soul, but rather in its innermost centre, the I, which is spirit-filled.

"Just as the physical body has its centre in the brain, the soul has its centre in the «I». ... The I lives in the soul. Even though the highest expression of the «I» belongs to the consciousness soul, it must be said that this «I», radiating from there, fills the whole soul and has its effects on the body through the soul. And in the I the spirit is alive. The spirit radiates into the I and lives in it as in its «sheath», just as the I lives in body and soul as its «sheaths». The spirit forms the I from inside out." [275]

Through the connection of the spirit with body and soul by the I, the human spirit is individualized. That makes him very different from the animal. The animal is a soul-being. But since it is not I-endowed, the spiritual part belonging to it does not live within the animal, but as a superior group spirit outside of it. The human being, on the other hand, has become an individualized spirit-being through the I, which consequently has a share in the creativeness and creative power of the spirit. This power is will-like. When, in the Sun sphere, man's soul light shines outwards not only from the soul as such, but from the I, from its spirit-filled centre, that is from man's inner spirit-depths, the soul light not only increases in luminosity and becomes completely like a sun, but also reveals itself as a will-like creative power. This special characteristic of the soul light was prepared and awakened in the Mercury sphere already. Since then, it developed ever more strongly. For a better understanding, we would like to quote some enlightening words by Rudolf Steiner, which were already given in the context of the reflection on the 29th weekly verse:

I can only name it: creative soul power, creative power of the soul. It is something that the soul now experiences directly. The soul experiences fully that one changes into an activity, but at the same time that this creative power is really developing, really radiating from the soul into the environment and – again it's clumsy, but this expression must be used just so that one can make oneself understand – this power is something that is radiating into the environment like a spiritual light, which illuminates the spiritual processes and beings all around, so that we see them. Just as when the sun rises and we see the outer objects through the sun, so we see the spiritual processes and beings through our own inner luminosity

---

[275] GA 9 "Theosophie" (Theosophy), Chapter "Das Wesen des Menschen" (The essential nature of man), Section IV, "Leib, Seele und Geist" (Body, soul and spirit)

that pours out. Then comes the time when the soul is in the spiritual environment to the extent that this creative power awakens in it in order to illuminate this world." [276]

What begins in the Mercury sphere, the first region of the higher soul world, finds its culmination in its highest region, the Sun sphere. Consequently, the soul life also reaches its highest degree here, as Rudolf Steiner says:

"What was described as the highest, pure soul region of the soul world, the Region of the actual Soul Life, is experienced by the soul when it passes through the region of Sun life. So we can say: The actual Kamaloka sphere extends a little beyond the Moon sphere[277] as already mentioned; then the brighter regions of the soul world begin, extending to the Sun. What the soul experiences in the sun is precisely the Region of Soul Life." [278]

The soul light, streaming outward like a sun, which is an active, will-like creative power, too, having its origin in the centre of the soul, in the inner spirit-depths of the I, shines in the Sun sphere with particular intensity. The volitional character of this power is transformed into a "life-will-power" because of the fact that the Sun sphere is the region of the actual soul life. It is precisely this significant metamorphosis, summarized in a few words, that is characterized by the first half of the 31st weekly verse:

The light from spirit-depths	Das Licht aus Geistestiefen,
Strives to the outside like a sun:	Nach außen strebt es sonnenhaft:
It turns into a life-will-power ...	Es wird zur Lebenswillenskraft ...

Endowed with this power man is called in the Sun sphere to work under the guidance and together with beings of the second Hierarchy on his spiritual environment, which is illuminated by himself. This outside world, however, which he illuminates like a sun, is first and foremost a moral environment. The way it is experienced by each individual human being is completely dependent on his moral behaviour in the past life on Earth, for in the spiritual world we do not live in a natural, but in a moral world order.

"In this Sun existence, there is only moral correlation. Everything moral there has the power to become reality and indeed to become reality in an appropriate way. ...

In the Sun region, any good intention that man had, even as a most inconspicuous thought, begins to become reality, which is then looked at by Exusiai, Dynamis, Kyriotetes. According to the good that a person has had in himself, according to the way he was able to think and feel and experience the good in himself, he is regarded by the beings of the Sun sphere. Therefore I cannot describe the Sun region to you in a theoretical way, but only vividly. One cannot give a good definition of how this or that good works in the sun region. One must speak in such a way that it becomes clear to the listener: If you have had a good thought as a human being in the Earth region, then you associate with Exusiai, Dynamis and Kyriotetes in the Sun region in the life between death and a new birth. You may live a spiritually sociable life with these beings. But if you have thought evil that you have left behind with your own being, so to speak, in the Moon region, you are a lonely one, abandoned by Exusiai, Dynamis and Kyriotetes. Thus the good becomes reality in the Sun world through our community with these beings. We do not understand the language of these beings if we have not had good thoughts. We cannot step up to them if we have not accomplished good deeds. In the Sun region, everything is reality as the real effectiveness of our good." [279]

The so peculiar occurrence that our moral being, which we perceive in earthly life as our intimate inner life, appears as our outer world in the Sun sphere, is based on the fact that with death a complete eversion of the human being takes place. Already the outer life panorama in the first days after death arises from our memories. In life on Earth they are part of our inner world. Then, however, they were moved outward and formed our new outside world. For this reason, we will seek there in vain what we experienced in life on Earth as the outer nature and the cosmos. Instead, we experience them within ourselves then. Everything has been reversed.

---

[276] GA 153 "Inneres Wesen des Menschen und Leben zwischen Tod und neuer Geburt" (Inner nature of man and life between death and new birth), Vienna, Public Lecture of 8 April 1914

[277] i.e. at most to the 4th region of the soul world, which is also called the "Region of pleasure and displeasure". See Figures 1 and 2 towards the end of the consideration of the 7th weekly verse.

[278] GA 141 "Das Leben zwischen Tod und neuer Geburt im Verhältnis zu den kosmischen Tatsachen" (Life between death and new birth in relation to cosmic facts), Berlin, Lecture of 1 April 1913

[279] GA 239 "Esoterische Betrachtungen karmischer Zusammenhänge" (Esoteric reflections on karmic connections – karmic relationships), Volume 5, Paris, Lecture of 24 May 1924

"Exactly the reverse is the case in life in the Sun sphere. There is the Moon in us, not out of us, Mercury is in us, even the Sun sphere itself with its whole region is in us, not outside us." [280]

The active life-will-power that emerges from the centre of our souls does not illuminate anything in the Sun sphere that could be experienced even approximately with earthly, physical senses. It shines into a realm outside the sensory cosmos, where nothing could be found by the senses. Even the senses of our soul could not see anything, if we were not able to radiate our own creative soul light out there. Thus, it shines "into the senses' dullness" [281], in order to work out of our inner soul-drives, our inner Moral, active and creatively on our next earth-man, there, in this world of morality. We not only acquire forces for our future earthly deeds in the next life on earth, but from then on we actually contribute to a great cosmic "work of Man".

31st Week (3 – 9 November)	31. Woche (3. – 9. November)
The light from spirit-depths	Das Licht aus Geistestiefen,
Strives to the outside like a sun:	Nach außen strebt es sonnenhaft:
It turns into a life-will-power	Es wird zur Lebenswillenskraft
And shines into the senses' dullness	Und leuchtet in der Sinne Dumpfheit,
In order to set forces free	Um Kräfte zu entbinden,
That make creative powers out of soul-drives	Die Schaffensmächte aus Seelentrieben
Ripen in the work of man.	Im Menschenwerke reifen lassen.

Of course, we cannot accomplish this cosmic work alone, because it is far superior to all earthly activity. For this purpose we need the help of the divine Hierarchies, as Rudolf Steiner further states in his lecture of 25 May 1924 in Paris, from which some was cited already above:

"Actually, all human beings on Earth taken together are the bearers of all Hierarchies; these unfold their essence in man. That, which is in man and is much greater than all the stellar world, all movements and phenomena of the stars, that is our outside world in the Sun existence. And with the beings I called Exusiai, Dynamis, Kyriotetes, with the other beings who live in the Moon, with the beings of the Hierarchy of the Angeloi, with the beings who live on Venus, with the beings of the Hierarchy of the Archai, with all the other human souls with whom we are karmically connected, we work out our next earthly existence based on the view of the human body. And this work in the Sun existence for the genesis of the next earth-man, the next human life on Earth, this work, it is much grander than anything man can produce for culture and civilization on Earth. What civilization on Earth finally shows is human work. Man himself is not only human work. In the Sun, he is allowed to contribute to the future life on Earth. Something miserable would come out if man in connection with other human souls would work alone on this miracle that he represents in life on Earth. He has to work together with all higher Hierarchies. Because that, which is born by the mother of a human being, did not originate on Earth, only the site, so to speak, is originated on Earth. In what is given by physical inheritance, a wonderful world-structure embodies that was formed in supernatural worlds in the Sun existence."

What we work out together with the beings of the second Hierarchy in the spiritual-moral outside world is directly dependent on everything we were interested in and by which we were driven to action during our life on Earth. With the words of the above weekly verse we can say: The basis of our creative forming activity is our "soul-drives" brought along from life on Earth. Out of them our "creative powers" ripen through the transformation of soul-drives into talents and abilities.

"Then we live on and notice how the beings of the second Hierarchy, Exusiai, Dynamis, Kyriotetes, are connected with what we acquired here on Earth through diligence, activity, through interest we have had in the things and processes of the Earth. For, these beings transform our diligence, our interest in the last life, into giant images at first: Exusiai, Dynamis, Kyriotetes, they design the images of our talents, of our abilities in our next life on Earth. We recognize which talents and abilities we will have in the next life on Earth, by the images, which the beings of the second Hierarchy unroll." [282]

---

[280] Ibidem, Lecture of 25 May 1924

[281] See also Rudolf Steiner's use of the wording "senses' dullness" in the 15th weekly verse or the words "the dark of space and time" in the 25th weekly verse.

[282] GA 239 "Esoterische Betrachtungen karmischer Zusammenhänge" (Esoteric reflections on karmic connections – karmic relationships), Volume 5, Prague, Lecture of 31 March 1924

For the human being in the Sun sphere, however, it is not so easy to recognize his spiritual-moral environment, which presents itself in giant images as the basis of his future earth-man to which he should contribute. In order to be able to comprehend and understand all this in its cosmic grandeur and dimension, he needs the help of the Christ Being. Rudolf Steiner expressly pointed out this important context, once more in his lecture of 25 May 1924 in Paris:

"But just as radically as the Christ impulse intervenes in Earth life, so also in Sun life. Just as here on Earth it costs us a struggle to deepen the spiritual life in ourselves so that we can experience Christ, that we get inwardly filled by Christ, that we become Christ-imbued, so it is difficult during the Sun life to survey, to have a clear view of the entire man with regard to his being, as I said before. ... Since the mystery of Golgotha we as human beings on Earth have to go through that inner deepening which we can achieve by contemplating the mystery of Golgotha, by living into the mystery of Golgotha, by empathy for the life of Christ. In this way we can gather in ourselves with independent consciousness during our earthly existence those forces, which we can take with us through death and which can give us the strength to see Man in the Sun. Before the mystery of Golgotha, Christ gave the human being the strength to see Man in the Sun during the life between death and a new birth, whereas after the mystery of Golgotha he prepares the human being during life on Earth in order that he may see the entire, whole Human Being in the Sun."

Only with the help of the force that we bring with us from life on Earth through our inner attachment to Christ can we properly accomplish the grand creative "work of Man" in the Sun sphere together with the Hierarchies, especially the second Hierarchy. For all subsequent steps of development in the regions beyond the Sun sphere, however, yet another strange and for most people certainly quite unexpected help is needed.

"So we live our way into the Sun sphere Christ-imbued. Then we live on and get into a region where we have the Sun below us as we had the Earth below us before. We begin to look back at the Sun. And then something very strange begins. At this moment we become aware that we are beginning to get to know yet another spirit in his peculiar manner, the Lucifer Spirit.

If not previously through occult science or initiation, we do not comprehend, what Lucifer is, by mere life after death. Only when we have reached beyond the Sun do we get to know what he was like before he became Lucifer, when he was still a brother of Christ. For his change did not happen before the time when Lucifer remained behind and detached himself from progress in the cosmos.[283] And what he can do badly, extends only to the Sun. Above, there is another sphere where Lucifer can develop his activity as it was before his detachment. There is nothing of harm that he develops there, and when we have properly associated ourselves with the mystery of Golgotha, we, led by Christ, received by Lucifer, move out into the even more remote spheres of the universe in the right way. The name Lucifer is well chosen, just as the ancients choose wise names in general. When we have the Sun below us, the sunlight is also below us. Thus, we need a new light bearer that shines for us out into the universe. Then, we enter the Mars sphere."[284]

The human soul light, which for the first time in the Mercury sphere began to shine from within us and brightened our surroundings, which then increased in the Venus sphere and reached its greatest luminosity in the Sun sphere as the highest region of the soul world, because it could radiate outwards there from our innermost spirit-depths with full power, this light is not sufficient to brighten the spiritual outside worlds beyond the Sun sphere, too. It is a soul-light and therefore serves to primarily illuminate our surroundings in the soul world. Beyond it, in the spiritual world, beginning with the Mars sphere, we need another light, a spirit-light that we cannot produce from ourselves. There, another being must illuminate the new outside world for us. We need a bringer and bearer of spiritual light, a "Luci-ferus"[285] that illuminates the spheres beyond the Sun. Together with him and with Christ, provided we have intimately united ourselves to the latter in life on Earth, we pursue our way out into the vastness of the spiritual cosmos.

---

[283] More on this in the chapter "The Christ Being"

[284] GA 140 "Okkulte Untersuchungen über das Leben zwischen Tod und neuer Geburt" (Occult investigations on life between death and new birth), Vienna, Lecture of 3 November 1912

[285] According to the Latin words "lux" (light) and "ferre" (to bear).

Ascension to the Mars Sphere – 32nd Week

After leaving his physical earthly body and surrendering his ether body to the cosmos, man gives off his astral body, too, layer by layer when he passes through the sub-solar planetary spheres. In the Moon sphere, still close to the Earth, he left the lowest and most libidinous parts of it. Everything in his astral body, which was connected with illness, antisocial tendencies, but also with the fundamental desire for a physical-sensory outside world, he cast off in the Mercury sphere. Religious ideas and aspirations, insofar as they were limited to only one of the world religions or more over narrowly confined in the sense of special denominations, were abandoned by the human being in the Venus sphere. Only with his supreme religious-moral feelings, with his holy of holies, which is connected to the Divine in all religions and all human beings, regardless of their origin and religious affiliation, which is therefore general-human in the sense of the Christ words *"What you have done to one of my least brothers, you have done to me"* (Matthew 25.40), only with this supreme inner feeling, provided it was developed in earthly life, man entered the Sun sphere. Thereby he attained the greatest possible impartiality and was restored to a state of almost childlike purity, indeed returned to the beginning of his past life on Earth in his retrogressive re-experience of it.

"And only then, when man has lived through his whole life, does he enter the celestial world. Religious documents are always truths that should be taken in the literal sense. If you keep in mind what I have just said, you will easily realize that man can really enter the spiritual world – and by the spiritual world is meant what the Bible calls «heavenly kingdom» or «the kingdom of heavens» – only when he has re-experienced his whole life retrogressively until childhood beforehand. And this in truth is underlying the words of Christ: «Unless you become like children, you will never enter the kingdom of heaven.» Then, when man regressively has reached again the stage of his childhood, he slips off his astral body and enters the spiritual world.

Now I have to talk to you about this spiritual world in a narrative way. This kingdom of heavens is even more different from the physical world than the astral world. But since, of course, everything can only be described with expressions taken from this physical world, it is even more true than for the above description of the astral world that all these descriptions may only apply comparatively.

In this kingdom of heaven there is also a triplicity, as here on Earth. Just as we have here the three physical states solid, liquid and airy, and accordingly the Earth is divided into the Continental, the oceans and the air region, we can in the spirit land distinguish three such regions as well, though only comparatively as I said. But, the region of the continents is composed of something else than our rocks and stones. For what is the solid ground of the spirit land there, are the archetypes of everything physical. Everything physical has its archetypes, including man. For the clairvoyant, these archetypes look like a kind of negative, that is, one sees the space as a kind of shadow figure, and there is radiant light all around it. This shadow, however, is not uniform, according to the blood and the nerves for example, whereas a stone or a mineral shows a uniformly empty space in the archetype, around which a light radiation is visible. Just as you walk on solid rocks on Earth, you walk around there on the archetypes of the physical things. From these the ground of this spiritual world is composed. When a person enters this land for the first time, he always gets a very particular view. This is the moment when he sees the archetype of his own physical body. At first he sees clearly his own body there. Because he himself is spirit. After a normal life time on Earth this happens about thirty years after death; and one has the basic sensation in this moment: That is you. – From this knowledge Vedanta philosophy has coined the «Tat tvam asi – that is you» as a fundamental theorem of knowledge. All such expressions are brought out of a deep spiritual cognition." [286]

In this first one of the regions above the Sun, into which the human spirit-soul expands in the course of its after-death path of development, man is not only an observer of the archetypes, but he is actively working there as a spirit being.

"The human being is spirit among spirits. But what he now sees as his world is the wonder of human organization as a cosmos, as a whole world. Just as mountains, rivers, stars, clouds are our environment here, so, when we live as spirits among spirits, the human being in his wonderful organization is our environment, our world. We look out, we look in the spiritual world – if I may express myself figuratively – to the left and we look to the right. Just as here are rocks, rivers, mountains everywhere, there is Man everywhere. Man is the world. And we are working on this world, which is actually the human being. Just as we build machines, create accountancies, make skirts, make shoes, just as we write something here on

---

[286] GA 100 "Menschheitsentwicklung und Christuserkenntnis" (Human development and understanding of Christ), Kassel, Lecture of 19 June 1907

Earth, just as we weave together what is called content of civilization, culture, so we weave there on mankind, but together with the spirits of the higher Hierarchies and the disembodied humans. We weave mankind out of the cosmos. Here on Earth we are finished human beings. There we lay the spirit-germ of the earth-man. This is the great mystery that man's heavenly occupation consists in weaving the large spirit-germ for the later earth-man together with the spirits of the higher Hierarchies. And each of us weaves – but in huge spirit-size within the spirit-cosmos – the web of our own earth-man, who we are when we again descend to life on Earth. Our work is a work done on the earth-man together with the gods." [287]

In order to be able to do this work, the creative power of the human spirit-soul must first become stronger. The intensity in which this process of growing stronger can take place, however, depends on the past life on Earth, primarily on the will impulses carried through the portal of death, even the most hidden ones in our soul- and spirit-depths. The self-will of man, which makes him an individual being, then matures into a fruit, similar to "the thinking's ripened fruits", which already sprouted in the Venus sphere. In the Mars sphere, man senses with ever greater distinctness and intensity, that his self-will, which together with his I constitutes his "own being", is gaining the force which enables him to contribute actively to the transformation of his spiritual outside world, to weave himself into it and thus to participate in the forming process of the cosmic, spiritual archetype of his next earthly body. This intense experience is illustrated in the 32nd weekly verse.

32nd Week (10 - 16 November)	32. Woche (10. – 16. November)
I feel my own force fruiting,	Ich fühle fruchtend eigne Kraft
Increasing, giving myself to the world;	Sich stärkend mich der Welt verleihn;
And my own being I feel forceful	Mein Eigenwesen fühl ich kraftend
Turning to clearness	Zur Klarheit sich zu wenden
In weaving of life's destiny.	Im Lebensschicksalsweben.

Three times here Rudolf Steiner used words that expressly emphasize the Mars character of the saying: "force", "increasing" and "forceful". In a similar way we already found this in the 21st weekly verse, the corresponding mirror saying, which tells about the prenatal descent through the Mars sphere in the direction of a new life on Earth. There it was the double use of the Martian noun "power" in addition to the word "increasing".

In the Mars sphere, the fruiting of the innermost will-germ, which was brought along from the last life on Earth, has the consequence that man imprints the karmic consequences resulting from it on the archetype of his next earthly body. Here, he already begins to weave the destiny of his next incarnation. Now he also gains complete clarity regarding karmic necessity on the one hand and divine wisdom and love on the other, which also underlie the law of karma as basic principles of the moral world order. From this insight and complete inner approval he turns with the innermost of his will to the initial, at first merely picture-like weaving of his future karma or, as it is said in the above weekly verse, to the "weaving of life's destiny". However, this activity in the Mars sphere is at first limited entirely to the archetype of his future physical body, for we live there in the so-called "Continental Region" of the spiritual world, where the creative archetypes of all physical corporealities on Earth are located.

"This Mars region is the same realm, which you find described in my «Theosophy» as the first part of the spirit land. In this description in «Theosophy» you find characterized from inside how the soul of man has become so much spiritualized that it then sees as something external what is the archetype of physical corporeality, so to speak, the physical conditions on Earth in general. Everything that is an archetype of physical life on Earth appears as a kind of Continental Region of the spirit land. Into this Continental Region is inscribed what the outer forms of the various incarnations are. With this region of the spirit land is presented inwardly the same as what man has to go through, when one cosmically says, in the Mars region." [288]

At our next embodiment on Earth we will not have the same body sheath again but at every time a different one, always according to our karmic necessities. We change the image of our cast-off physical

---

[287] GA 226 "Menschenwesen, Menschenschicksal und Welt-Entwicklung" (Man's being, his destiny and word-evolution), Kristiania (Oslo), Lecture of 17 May 1923

[288] GA 141 "Das Leben zwischen Tod und neuer Geburt im Verhältnis zu den kosmischen Tatsachen" (Life between death and new birth in relation to cosmic facts), Berlin, Lecture of 1 April 1913

body in full adaptation to our individual level of maturity, in order to progress along the path of human development.

"On the first stage in Devachan, man corrects his previous image of life: He himself prepares the image of his body for the next incarnation from the fruits of his previous life." [289]

Man experiences this activity completely free of all heaviness and effort as we know it from Earth. He feels his active contribution to the archetype of his future earthly body as really heavenly bliss. However, in his intense devotion to this bliss, he could easily lose himself. Therefore, in addition to this feeling, he needs a second, which holds his I together.

"When the soul passes the border to the Devachanic world, a feeling of blessedness, bliss appears above all. Even if one entered Devachan unworthily, that is, if one could enter through any spell or black magic before death, one would very soon be swimming in a sea of blisses of lesser or higher degrees. Of course, you could say it is strange that even an unworthy entry into Devachan gives blessedness. It is so, is the answer, but in a way, which has its drawbacks, too. On the Devachanic plane, this feeling of bliss, flowing out and flowing along, is inseparably linked to something else, namely the loss of self, of the power of self-consciousness, of inner I-power. We would dissolve unless another nuance of feeling were added. This is what occult science calls the feeling of sacrificial devotion, the ability to sacrifice.

... And it is strange but true that if man on the Devachanic plan did not have the feeling, you should surrender to what is around you, but with his I only wanted to enjoy bliss, he would dissolve in the sea of the Devachanic beings. However, if he is permeated with the feeling: I will sacrifice myself, I will make flow out what I have acquired, then he will save himself in Devachan from dissolving, from decay. The highest feeling of love, creative love, must be there as a second nuance of feeling in Devachan. And that is something that also makes you understand how the work in Devachan is going on between death and a new birth. After the Kamaloka, where man first lived in deprivation and shortened the duration of his stay there by learning to renounce, when man arrives at Devachan he must immediately begin to work on his next incarnation. Slowly he builds up the archetypes of his next life on Earth. He will build it all the better when he has learned to add to the feeling of bliss, which appears inevitably, the sacrificial devotion of his being to what surrounds him. To the extent that he sacrifices himself with his soul, to this extent the archetype of his future personality is forming. If he could not do that, he would either vanish completely or would need a huge amount of time until he could return to an earthly existence. Thus we see, that the soul finds its limits externally in the forms, so to speak, with the transition from the silent, shining astral world to the sounding Devachanic world. But much more important is the manner it lives itself into the other world inwardly." [290]

In the above weekly verse we find this experience of sacrificing oneself and giving oneself to the world, too, for it tells us that, on the one hand, man feels his active spirit-force growing, which brings him bliss, but on the other hand, he is giving himself to the world through this force, sacrifices himself to the world:

I feel my own force fruiting,	Ich fühle fruchtend eigne Kraft
Increasing, giving myself to the world;	Sich stärkend mich der Welt verleihn;

Once again, it is an ability that man can already acquire on Earth precisely through his efforts to understand the great sacrificial deed of Christ Jesus. No other being on Earth has ever shown so vividly this highest level of sacrificial devotion to humanity and the world. The memory of the mystery of Golgotha on Earth will increase our own sacrificial and devotional capacity in the Mars sphere and thereby enable us to build up a better spiritual archetype of our future earthly body than would be possible without it, and in addition it will maintain our I-consciousness. This shows that the fruit of our intimate union with Christ already in life on Earth is of extraordinary importance far beyond into the cosmic spheres.

---

[289] GA 95 "Vor dem Tore der Theosophie" (At the gate of theosophy), Stuttgart, Lecture of 24 August 1906

[290] GA 108 "Die Beantwortung von Welt- und Lebensfragen durch Anthroposophie" (Answering world and life questions through anthroposophy), Vienna, Lecture of 21 November 1908

Ascension to the Spheres of Jupiter and Saturn – 33rd Week

When in preparation for a new incarnation on Earth, after mostly centuries of being expanded into the depths of the universe, man sets off again to a planetary existence, when within the zodiac enclosing him he contracts into the two outermost planetary spheres, the Saturn and Jupiter spheres, then he begins to feel his special existence as a being of his own. Hence, the 20th weekly verse began with the words: "In this way only, I feel my existence." – Exactly the opposite is the case when man ascends into the same spheres after his death. Throughout his life on Earth, he felt as a special being of his own within the skin of his physical body, separated from the world around him. In the course of his expansion into the spheres of Mercury, Venus and Sun, he ever more clearly recognized his relationship and closer connection with the cosmos. But in these regions of the higher soul world all experience was still pervaded by remnants of personal, subjective sensations from the last life on Earth. It was not until his entry into the Mars sphere, and even there with a certain inner distance, that man took a first objective look at the world, combined with the deep insight of "That are you" or "Tat tvam asi", as the occult teachings of the East describe it. He felt his I still separated from the world, the You, at least with regard to his soul. Only with his entry into the spheres of Jupiter and Saturn he begins to also feel himself as the world and to experience sympathetically its life processes. From now on, the human being and the world are going to grow into a unity. Therefore, the 33rd weekly verse, which summarizes the after-death experiences of man in the Jupiter and Saturn spheres, begins with the words:

In this way only, do I f e e l the world ...   So f ü h l ich erst die Welt ...

The duration of our stay in the two outermost planetary spheres as well as the clarity and intensity of the consciousness of the experiences possible there, again depend on our level of maturity already attained in life on Earth, in particular on the intensity of our devotion towards the Divine, which is effective throughout the world.

"In the second region of Devachan [the Jupiter sphere or Oceanic Region], those are staying who already have some preparation. This is achieved by a higher education within life on Earth. Man learns to recognize that the things of earthly life are transient and only expressions of eternal causes. He learns to recognize unity in all life and to look up to unity in adoration. When the simple savage sees divine qualities in the objects and regards them as a symbol of the Divine, this already goes beyond everyday relationships. In this region man learns to recognize the creative work and action of the Deity. There we see the confessors of the different religions developing devotional feelings by approaching their gods humbly, adoringly. After having passed through this second region man arrives at his reincarnation with a higher degree of piety. We see people, who have a sense for the underlying unity, staying for a long time in this second region. We see them living themselves into the oneness of all existence, and we see how these spirits, when they return to Earth, become leading religious personalities. These people see that the interests of the individual can no longer be separated from the interests of the community. This sense of community-life is developed in the second region of Devachan.

Let's move up to the third region. Here we no longer find the archetypes for what lives in the earthly existence, but we find the archetypes of the soul-existence itself. Here are the archetypes of all desires and instincts, all sentiments and feelings and all passions, from the lowest passion up to the highest pathos. For all these there are purely spiritual archetypes, and they exist in the third region of Devachan. Just as in the second region all life, in the third region all sensation, feeling, suffering and so on exists as one great unity. There, the instincts of one being are not separated from the instincts of another being. There, «That are you» is already accomplished. We can no longer distinguish between my feeling and your feeling, as we do in the limited relationships of the sensory existence. The strange woe is the same as ours. We hear the «groan of the creature». We perceive every pleasure and displeasure, whether it is ours or whether it is foreign. We say to everything: That's you. - We sympathize with everything. I have characterized this region as the atmosphere, as the air circle of the spirit land. Just as our Earth is surrounded by the physical air circle, the spirit continent is surrounded by this air circle, by the spheres of woe and misfortune, by the archetypes of human passions as by storms and breaking, rumbling thunderstorms. Living in the third region of Devachan, we learn to understand the phrase of an inspired one and realize what it means to unite with the «groans of the creatures waiting for adoption as children».[291] Thereby another side of sentiment is developing in us, we get to know the earthly sentiment from another side, not as a selfish individual sentiment, but in such a way that we have developed the sense, the compassion for all beings in this third region. What in our embodiment we develop of selflessness, of benevolence towards our fellow human beings, is the memory of this third region of Devachan; that is what we bring with us from this third region. Philanthropists, the geniuses of human charity, train their skills there; they live a long life in the third region of Devachan.

How do these three regions of Devachan relate to our earthly world? In the first region we find the archetypes of corporeal things, in the second the archetypes of life, in the third the archetypes of the soul world, of the drives, instincts and passions. What we need for our work in earthly life, we find in the spirit land." [292]

Drives, instincts and passions are effective in life on Earth not only in humans but also in animals. However, even in the case of plants we find them pictorially expressed, such as love in the form of the red rose. From such preliminary states the highest compassion and purest love should develop in man. This development of love on Earth is still at an early stage yet, whereas another divine quality has already become reality to the highest degree in the earthly outside world: wisdom. It was already developed on the ancient Moon by the Angeloi. What lived within them then, we encounter today as spread out in our earthly outside world. Wherever we look – provided we look with open eyes – we find such a wealth of wisdom everywhere, even in the simplest natural processes and the most primitive creatures, so that the cognitive capacity of humanity is still far from sufficient to grasp this wisdom in its entirety. The mission of the Earth is to supplement this existing abundance of supreme wisdom with an additional abundance of selfless love. So far, this has only been achieved in the first stages.

"The development of wisdom preceded the development of love. Love is not yet perfect. But it can be found in all nature, in the plant, in the animal, in man, from the lowest sexual love to the highest, most spiritualized love. Enormous multitudes of beings, which were produced by the love instinct, perish in the fight for existence. Fight works wherever there's love. The appearance of love implies fight, necessary fight. But it will also overcome it, transform war into harmony. Wisdom is the characteristic of physical nature. Where this wisdom has been permeated with love, there is only the beginning of the Earth's development. ...

Just as animals and humans on the plant, the gods are dependent on humans. The Greek myth put it so beautifully: the gods receive nectar and ambrosia from the mortals. Both mean love. Love is created within the human race. And the race of gods inhales love. It is the gods' food. The love produced by human beings becomes food for the gods. This is much more real than electricity, strange as it may seem at first. Love first appears as sexual love and develops up to the highest spiritual love. But all love, low and high, is breath of the gods." [293]

From the depths of his soul, Goethe sensed that the loving compassion and sympathy of man with nature, the amazed admiration for the grandeur of the divine Creation, has a deeper meaning in life on Earth and that Creation finds its own fulfillment by looking at itself admiringly through the human being.

"When the healthy nature of man works as a whole, when he feels himself in the world as part of a large, beautiful, worthy and valuable whole, when harmonious comfort grants him pure, independent delight, then the universe, if it could feel itself as having reached its goal, would cheer and admire the summit of its own becoming and being. For, what purpose does all the complexity of suns and planets and moons serve, of stars and galaxies, of comets and nebulae, of worlds that have become and will become, if not at the end a happy human being unconsciously enjoys his existence?" [294]

The knowledge of the spiritual foundations of nature and the resulting joy of knowledge and admiration as well as the feeling of deepest veneration for the creative work of God cause the human being to associate compassionately with nature, to feel one with it. It is therefore the human being who carries love and warmth into the wisdomfilled but otherwise cold world. Without the emotional experience of the human

---

[291] St. Paul's Epistle to the Romans, 8:22-23: *"We know that all creatures have been groaning in labor pains until now; and not only the creatures, but we ourselves, who have the first fruits of the Spirit, groan inwardly while we wait for adoption, the redemption of our bodies."*

[292] GA 88 "Über die astrale Welt und das Devachan" (About the astral world and the Devachan), Berlin, 11 February 1904

[293] GA 55 "Die Erkenntnis des Übersinnlichen in unserer Zeit" (Knowledge of the supersensible of today), Berlin, Lecture of 22 November 1906

[294] Winckelmann: "Antikes" (Antique)

soul it "would merely be a frosty, empty life", as the weekly verse relating to the Jupiter and Saturn spheres says:

33rd Week (17 - 23 November)	*33. Woche (17. – 23. November)*
In this way only, do I feel the world,	So fühl ich erst die Welt,
Which, without my soul's experience,	Die außer meiner Seele Miterleben
Would merely be a frosty, empty life	An sich nur frostig leeres Leben
That, manifesting without might	Und ohne Macht sich offenbarend,
To recreate itself in souls,	In Seelen sich von neuem schaffend,
Would in itself find only death.	In sich den Tod nur finden könnte.

The lovingly felt compassion of the human soul with the Creation is for it not only food or "breath of the gods", but more-over it is the precondition for the world as macrocosm to be able to create in the human being as microcosm a germinal system from which, after having matured properly, a new world will emerge some day in the distant future.

"Occult science contrasts man himself as the «small world» with this «large world». In initial developmental states, he already has within him, as a soul, what the «great world» is to become physically. Thus, he is on the way to expand his inner «small world» to a «large world». In him is the creative womb of the latter. In this sense, occult science sees in the soul a creative germinal system for the future, an «interior» that strives to realize itself in an exterior." [295]

If the world-body is the cosmic body of God, then the human being is the germ cell of this world-body. Through man, the world reproduces itself. Therefore, the spirit-germ of the human body is at first a gigantically large world-germ. This macrocosmic process of reproduction has its image in the plant world on Earth. From a certain state of maturity the plant turns all its forces inwards (involution) to collect them in a small seed, which, although completely different in form, is endowed by it with the ability to develop into a new, complete plant out of itself (evolution). Similarly, the world, the macrocosm, develops the human soul into a microcosmic seed that will be able to create a new world, a new macrocosm out of itself after a required process of maturation. And in the same way that the plant seed must first be sunk into the Earth, the human soul must also be sunk into life on Earth, but many times in order to make a little more progress in its maturation each time. The teaching about this extremely important process of involution and evolution immanent to Creation was already part of the students' education in the old Atlantean mystery schools, as Rudolf Steiner reports:

"From the teachers, the student then received formulas and certain drawings. He then immediately perceived the secrets of the world. This sign [Fig. 18] for example told him, how a seed becomes a new plant. Today's man, without interpretation cannot think anything about it, cannot feel anything about it. The people of that time were immediately affected by this sign when they saw it or when it was tapped along its line. The formulas that were used at that time were then taught to the later peoples by the founders of the religions." [296]

In another lecture Rudolf Steiner shared about this sign of occult scripture:

"A common sign of this scripture is the so-called vortex. You can imagine it by thinking of two sixes intertwined. This sign is used to depict certain phenomena that exist in the whole natural and spiritual world, and in order to characterize their inner nature. If we observe a plant, we will find that it develops until the state of a seed. If we put this seed in the soil, a similar plant develops, which looks like the old one. That there would be transferred any kind of matter from the old plant to the new plant is a material prejudice that is not justified by anything and will be refuted in the future. Only the formative power is transferred into the new plant. The old plant dies completely in terms of material, and the new plant is something completely new in terms of material. Not the least amount of matter passes from the old plant to the new plant. This new understanding of the formation and decay of a plant is described by drawing two intertwining spirals, i.e. a vortex, without a

**Fig. 18: Vortex
(from GA 55)**

---

[295] GA 89 "Bewusstsein – Leben – Form" (Consciousness – Life – Form), fragment from the year 1903/1904

[296] GA 97 "Das christliche Mysterium", Leipzig, Lecture of 17 February 1907

connection between the two lines." [297]

Just as in the plant nothing material, but only forces are transferred from the old to the new plant, in the human being as well nothing material passes from one Earth incarnation into the next incarnation, but only forces, which are substantially strengthened in the course of the after-death life. Likewise, nothing material will pass from the evolution of the Earth to the future evolution of Jupiter, but only effects of forces and processes. The inner world of the soul of today's earth-man will be the basis of the outer world of the future Jupiter. World creates itself anew in human souls. Without being able to pass through the stage of humanity, the world would perish and "would in itself find only death" as the weekly verse says.

"Man will later put out into the environment what he feels. This will become part of the fluid element. All fluid of the next planet [Jupiter] will become an expression of what people feel. Today man sends out words; they were written into Akasha. There they remain, even if the air waves melt away. From this, Jupiter is later formed. Thus, if man gives awful speeches today, awful scaffolding will be produced on Jupiter! That is why so much attention must be paid to what we say; that is why so much importance must be attached to the fact that man masters his speech. Later, man will also send out his feelings. The state of Jupiter's fluid will be a result of the feelings on Earth. What man says today will give form to Jupiter; what he feels will give it inner warmth. What man puts into his will today will be the individual beings which will inhabit Jupiter. Jupiter will be built by the basic forces of the human soul.

Just as we can deduce today the rock structure of the Earth from earlier conditions, the rock structure of Jupiter will be the result of our words. The sea of Jupiter, the warmth of Jupiter will arise from the feelings of today's people. The beings of Jupiter will arise from human will. In this way, the inhabitant of the previous planet really creates the basis for the next planet." [298]

The supreme fruit of human soul life, the spiritualized love, will then be just as natural part of the outside world of Jupiter as the wisdom to be found everywhere on Earth.

"And just as we today, standing on Earth, admire the wisdom integrated into it, the beings of Jupiter will once face beings from which love will smell out. They will taste and smell the love out of the beings around them, so to speak. Just as wisdom shines towards us on Earth, towards the Jupiter beings on Jupiter will smell what develops as love from mere sexual love to the Spinozistic divine love here on Earth. It will smell out like today the plants smell in the different flavours. So the degrees of love will flow out as the fragrance that will ascend from the cosmos, which we have called Jupiter as the successor of our Earth. In this way conditions change in the course of evolution, and whenever there is any progress in evolution, the beings participate. Then the beings associated with the respective planetary stage of development rise up to ever higher stages of development. Today, the people who live on Earth are, so to speak, the tools of the development of love." [299]

Ascension to the Sphere of the Zodiac – 34th Week

The mystery of the essential unity of man and world was revealed to the human spirit-soul already in the course of its after-death process of development in the spheres of Jupiter and Saturn. These two spheres and the Mars sphere as the three regions of the lower spiritual world are still pervaded by the soul world. Therefore, the experiences possible there still have a touch of subjective feeling. With the ascension to the Zodiac sphere, man grows out of any influence of the soul world. He then undergoes completely the transition from a human being to a world being. In a sense, he is born out of the womb of the planetary system and hence only then completely out of his last incarnation. After harvesting all fruits of it and learning to understand all karmic consequences resulting from it, he finishes it. But he keeps all that as a precious treasure in his memory henceforward. He preserves the old, the subjectively experienced, in order to open up to a new, an objective cosmic world-life in the higher spiritual world.

Besides this analogy to a process of "being born-out" of man, there is another. Viewed from a different angle, the period of man's stay in the planetary spheres, where he is exposed to the interaction of the planetary forces on the one hand and the forces of the zodiac or starry sky on the other, is closely related

---

[297] GA 55 "Die Erkenntnis des Übersinnlichen in unserer Zeit" (Knowledge of the supersensible today), Berlin, Lecture of 14 March 1907

[298] GA 93a "Grundelemente der Esoterik" (Foundations of esotericism), Berlin, Lecture of 4 October 1905

[299] GA 102 "Das Hereinwirken geistiger Wesenheiten in den Menschen" (Influence of spiritual beings upon man), Berlin, Lecture of 24 March 1908

to the childhood and youth of a human being on Earth, the period during which he still needs education in order to gradually mature into a full age adult human being.

Only with the onset of adulthood, man becomes free from the guardianship of his parents and educators. He begins a completely independent activity and participation in the transformation of the earthly outside world. As an independent member, equal before the law, he is accepted into the circle of adults. His further life on Earth is now subject to the interaction of the forces of the zodiac or visible starry sky on the one hand and higher forces on the other, which belong to the depths of the universe and are not visible to physical eyes. Rudolf Steiner once explained these relations with the words:

"This is the next stage [in life on earth], the next stage we want to consider. It is thought of as if encompassing everything from the moment when man begins to consciously say «I» to himself [300], to the moment when we may dismiss him from his actual upbringing, where he steps out into life independently, the moment when he, as a well-bred or naughty person, has to surrender to the maelstrom of life. ... Thus, the whole planetary system cooperates here with the entire starry sky, and what is going on there between the starry sky and the entire planetary system, these are forces that are active in us during the period when we are brought up. ... If we face a child who already says «I» to himself, which we therefore address in a certain sense as a human being, we must be clear about the following: in him dwells something that is a reflection of something that is active not only outside our earth but outside our planetary system. ... About the correlate of what we experience until the end of our upbringing, we could say, we can still see it. The outermost stars that are barely visible still have a relationship to it. But what we experience afterwards, which can additionally be developed in us [as adults], belongs entirely to the invisible world. We are dismissed from all visible world when we have truly finished our upbringing." [301]

With the ascension to the Zodiac sphere, another important metamorphosis takes place in man's self-experience. In a similar way as he felt revitalized at his birth into the Moon sphere and thereby into planetary existence – "I can, revitalized inside, feel now own being's vastness" [302] – so he feels his entry into the Zodiac sphere and the resulting transition from planetary to stellar existence combined with a strong feeling of inner revitalization, albeit of a somewhat different kind. Everything brought from his last life on Earth and the old-preserved worked up in terms of content in the course of the passage through the planetary spheres will now come to life within him in a mysterious new way. Through this process the cosmic world forces that were not yet awakened in him and remained dormant in the depths of the human I are awakened to a life of their own. Man thus experiences himself with a completely new kind of self-existence and recognizes as his new task to henceforth work on his moral outside world in the higher spiritual world, the world of divine goals and intentions, by use of his own creative powers, in order to imprint the future spiritual archetype of himself into the outside spiritual cosmos as his "exterior work". The experience of this new soul metamorphosis speaks to us from the words of the 34th weekly verse.

34th Week (24 – 30 November)	*34. Woche (24. – 30. November)*
To feel the old-preserved	Geheimnisvoll das Alt-Bewahrte
With newly risen self-existence	Mit neu erstandnem Eigensein
Coming to life inside mysteriously:	Im Innern sich belebend fühlen:
This shall pour forth, awakening,	Es soll erweckend Weltenkräfte
World forces into my life's exterior work	In meines Lebens Außenwerk ergießen
And, growing, imprint me into the existence.	Und werdend mich ins Dasein prägen.

The essential difference to the previous after-death stages of development lies in the fact that the further work on the archetype of a new human body takes place henceforward with the forces of the extra-planetary cosmos, i.e. the starry world as well as the invisible depths of the cosmos on which it is based. In fact, "world forces" come into effect here and they flow into the "exterior work", i.e. into the extra-planetary work of Man. In this way he makes himself part of the outer cosmos and imprints himself into its higher spiritual existence. This activity starts in the Zodiac sphere as a transitional sphere to the higher spiritual world or even as the first sphere that may be assigned to it.

---

[300] from about the third year of his earthly life

[301] GA 161 "Wege der geistigen Erkenntnis und der Erneuerung künstlerischer Weltanschauung" (Ways of spiritual knowledge and the renewal of artistic worldview), Dornach, Lecture of 2 February 1915

[302] See 28th weekly verse.

"But in the life between death and new birth, man watches how the forces from the starry world work on him, on his being, how they gradually rebuild him. From this you can see how different the view is between death and the new birth than here on earth. Here, man stands at a point on the earth, directs his senses out, and then his looking or hearing goes out into the vastness. Thus, he looks out into the vastness from the midpoint where he is. It is just the other way around in life after death. Man feels as if spread out with his whole being, and what he is looking at is actually the midpoint. He looks to a point. There comes a time for man between death and the new birth, when he carries out a circle that passes through the whole zodiac. He looks at his own being from every point of the zodiac, i.e. from different points of view, and then he feels as if he would draw the forces he pours out upon his being from the different parts of the zodiac, so that it gets what it needs for the next incarnation. Thus, we look from the circumference to a midpoint. It is as if you could double yourself here on earth, step out of yourself, and you would let yourself stand in the middle, would walk around yourself and constantly absorb the forces of the universe, the invigorating Soma, which, however, because it takes on a different character from different sides, pours itself in different ways into the being you have left in the middle. That's the way it actually is, translated into the Spiritual, in life between death and the new birth." [303]

In its totality, however, the human being extends far beyond the Zodiac sphere and the visible starry sky into the more distant spiritual cosmos. In this respect, the zodiac is the boundary or transition, respectively, from forces effective also in the animal world to forces effective solely in humans.

"Only that which is under the zodiac with the Earth, the Moon, has a meaning with regard to the animal. But, regarding man that which is outside the zodiac has a meaning. ... Therefore we have to go into the zodiac itself with regard to the animal. ... Regarding the human being we have to go beyond the zodiac if we want to make clear to ourselves what is going on for example in his senses. In this way, man extends beyond the zodiac in his relationship with the cosmos." [304]

In order to understand the earthly animal world, we must look at the zodiac in its components or, as Rudolf Steiner says, "go into the zodiac itself", because its twelve forces are the spiritual foundations of the twelve stages of development of the animal kingdom. In a conference with teachers of a Waldorf School Rudolf Steiner explained that the animal world can be divided into three groups of four, i.e. three quaternities, just as the zodiac [305], which therefore a name was given pointing to the animal kingdom (Greek: zodiakos von zodion = zodiacal image, but also little animal or living creature as diminutive of zoon = living creature. German: Tierkreis = animal-circle). The first group of four consists of the lowest levels of animal development, ranging from protozoa/protists (1), sponges/corals/anemones (2) and echinoderms/urchins (3) to tunicates (4). Rudolf Steiner summarizes them under the term "head animals", because the forces that act in them are also involved in the head-formation of the human form. Following the zodiac row in reverse direction, starting with Cancer, they are expressions of the zodiacal forces Cancer, Gemini, Taurus and Aries. The second and middle group of four is composed of those developmental stages of the animal kingdom which are related to forces which are effective in the rhythmic system of man as well. These are molluscs (5), worms (6), arthropods (7) and fishes (8). They emerge in the same succession from the zodiac forces Pisces (5), Aquarius (6), Capricorn (7) and Sagittarius (8). The formation of the last mentioned fishes does not, as one might expect, origin from the zodiac image of Pisces, but from that of Sagittarius.[306] The highest group of four consists of those animal species that show complete limbs and are therefore connected to the human metabolic-limb system. These are amphibians (9), reptiles (10), birds (11) and ultimately the mammals as the most highly developed animals (12). The zodiacal forces Scorpio, Libra, Virgo and Leo are expressed in them. Thus, the entire developmental series of animals runs backwards through the zodiac – like the precessional movement of the Earth's axis –

---

[303] GA 141 "Das Leben zwischen Tod und neuer Geburt im Verhältnis zu den kosmischen Tatsachen" (Life between death and new birth in relation to cosmic facts), Berlin, Lecture of 10 December 1912

[304] GA 208 "Anthroposophie als Kosmosophie" – 2. Teil

[305] GA 300 c "Konferenzen mit den Lehrern der Waldorfschule" (Conferences with teachers of the Waldorf School), Volume 3, Conference from 12 July 1923, 8 p.m.

[306] Rudolf Steiner comments: *"You must remember that the zodiac came about at a time when there were completely different terms and summaries. In the Hebrew language the word 'fish' does not exist. Therefore it is well founded that you do not find fishes mentioned in the genesis work because the Hebrew language has no expression for fish. They thought of them as birds that live in the water."* – On the other hand, this does not exclude the fact that within another frame of reference the zodiacal image Pisces is related to the fish, for instance when the zodiacal images are assigned to the various professional activities of people, such as the shipping and fishing (see e.g. GA 208 "Anthroposophie als Kosmosophie" [Anthroposophy as Cosmosophy], Dornach, Lecture of 28 October 1921)

starting with Cancer up to Leo as representative of the mammals and the topmost conclusion of the animal series.

In the sense of Darwinism, natural science adds man to this series of twelve as the thirteenth member and thus as a further, albeit higher animal level. By this man is degraded to a higher animal, which from an anthroposophical point of view, he is not, in any way. The twelve-memberedness of the human form and the twelveness of the human senses are rather based on the harmonious interaction of all twelve zodiacal forces in their totality. This is caused by forces coming from the invisible depths of the universe far outside the Zodiac sphere. The human form, the human senses, as well as the human I, which awakens on the human senses to I- or self-consciousness, all three originate in the Zodiac sphere, develop however under the influence of forces that are rooted not only in the three highest regions of the spiritual world, but flow in from the regions of the Budhi plane, the Christ sphere, and with the help of them even from the Atma plane above, the Father sphere. In a similar way as the earthly body of man is only bordered by its outer form, but essentially consists also of that which is within the sheath of his skin, so the actual self of man consists by no means only of the I belonging to the Zodiac sphere, but furthermore encompasses the spiritual content of this I, which originates from higher regions and for which the human I is only the spiritual sheath.

"Through self-consciousness, man describes himself as an independent being closed off from everything else, as «I». In his «I» man summarizes everything he experiences as a being of body and soul. Body and soul are the bearers of the «I». It works in them. Just as the physical body has its centre in the brain, the soul has its centre in the «I». ... And this «I» is man himself. This justifies him in regarding this «I» as his true being. He may therefore regard his body and soul as the «sheaths» within which he lives; and he may call them the bodily conditions through which he works. ... Only from within, only through itself, the soul can call itself «I». By saying «I» to himself, there begins something to speak in man, which has nothing to do with any of the worlds from which the «sheaths» mentioned so far have been taken. ... But the I absorbs into itself the rays of the light that shines as eternal light in man. Just as he summarizes the experiences of the body and the soul in the «I», he also lets the thoughts of truth and goodness flow into the «I». The sensory phenomena reveal themselves to the «I» from one side, the spirit from the other. Body and soul surrender themselves to the «I» to serve it; but the «I» surrenders itself to the Spirit in order to become filled by it. The «I» lives in body and soul; but the Spirit lives in the «I». And what of the Spirit is in the I, is eternal. For, the I receives essence and meaning from what it is connected to. In so far as it lives in the physical body, it is subject to the mineral laws, through the ether body it is subject to the laws of reproduction and growth, through the sentient soul and the intellectual soul to the laws of the spiritual world; in so far as it takes in the Spiritual, it is subject to the laws of the Spirit." [307]

Thus the human being in its totality extends with its essence far into the invisible cosmic depths beyond the visible starry sky. But from the sphere of the zodiac man already begins on his after-death course of development to imprint himself into a higher spiritual existence by the forces which he can develop out of what he has brought along from the Earth, from the "old-preserved". In this way he makes himself a part of a higher reality, of a more real existence, in which his future life on Earth is prepared as a great cosmic exterior work, completely in the sense of the words of the weekly verse:

To feel the old-preserved	Geheimnisvoll das Alt-Bewahrte
With newly risen self-existence	Mit neu erstandnem Eigensein
Coming to life inside mysteriously:	Im Innern sich belebend fühlen:
This shall pour forth, awakening,	Es soll erweckend Weltenkräfte
World forces into my life's exterior work	In meines Lebens Außenwerk ergießen
And, growing, imprint me into the existence.	Und werdend mich ins Dasein prägen.

Ascension to the Sphere of the Spirit Self – 35th Week

When man ascends from the Zodiac sphere or fourth region of the spiritual world to the fifth region, he reaches a state outside all temporal existence. He gets into a realm of eternity, which can only find an imperfect expression in the lower regions through transient and incomplete images and resonances. Here only, he is in a world of true existence. It consists of the three highest regions of the spiritual world.

---

[307] GA 9 "Theosophie", Chapter "Das Wesen des Menschen" (The essential nature of man), Section IV "Leib, Seele und Geist" (Body, soul and spirit)

Together they are the kingdom of the Holy Spirit. Beginning with the fifth region of the spiritual world, the divine goals and intentions on which all creation is based are revealed. How much of these a person is able to absorb as new inner impulses of will and activity pleasing to God for his next incarnation, depends on how intensively he can participate with awake consciousness in the sublime spiritual activity there. This, however, in turn depends on the level of maturity that he has reached in the course of his incarnation series. Of this, he gets a complete overview there. Besides the "old-preserved", which he brought with him as his individual treasure from his last life on Earth, a whole series of additional old-preserved aspects from incarnations more distant in time are emerging then. Everything was preserved in the depths of his spiritual self for eternity, since his very first incarnation. Thereby the single individual I turns into a spirit self, which is aware that it encompasses a multitude of earthly personalities, courses of life and destiny. And as man rises above their respective limitations, he attains an extremely high degree of independence.

"When we ascend to the fifth region of the spirit land, we are completely free from the fetters of earthly existence. Then we are free and capable of development in all directions. Then our environment consists of the element in which our actual, true, real home is. In this higher region we experience the actual intentions, which the world spirit has with regard to earthly development. We participate in the intentions of the world spirit. All things become speaking then. We get to know the goal that the divine world spirit has for the plants, for the animals and for the humans; we get to know the perfect form of which the created is only an imperfect image. What we experience are the purposes, the intentions, the goals – the goals that flow out of the eternal. This is what we get to know here. And when, strengthened and invigorated by this, we return to the physical world, we are messengers of the divine intentions. Then we carry out what is to be inserted into this world as a true Spiritual, as an independent Spiritual.

Now you can easily imagine that what can be drawn from this region will depend on how much the Self has already developed during its embodiment in physical life. If man does not have an inclination to rise to the higher intentions, if he sticks to the ordinary and cannot comprehend what is eternal, then he will only have a brief flashing in the fifth region of Devachan. And the one who is little connected with the Earthly during earthly life, who reflects freely on earthly existence, who does deeds of compassion and charity without egoistic interest, he has in this existence acquired the expectation to stay a longer time in the higher regions of Devachan. This enables him to develop in a higher sense what is independent mental activity. What pours out of the eternal, the divine, flows to him. Here the self takes in the world of thought, unlimited by earthly imperfection.

Every incarnation is only an imperfect image of what man actually is. The spiritual self is in the spirit land, and by moving into the human body, into the human soul, it can only realize a faint image of what it actually is. When man returns home to the real self, to his original selfhood, when he gets to know the fifth region, then his gaze widens over his own incarnations, then he is able to get an overview of his past and his future. He experiences a flash of memory about his past incarnations and can relate them to what he can accomplish in the future. He overlooks the past and the future with a prophetic view. Everything he accomplishes seems to him to flow out of the eternal self. This is what the Self acquires in the fifth region of the spirit land. That is why we call this self, insofar as it runs free in the fifth region and becomes aware of its own being, the bearer of the causes of the human being, which transfers all results of the past life into the future. What reappears in the various embodiments, is the causal body, until man passes over to higher states where higher laws apply than those of reincarnation. Since the beginning of planetary life we have been subject to the law of reincarnation. The causal body is that which transmits the result of a previous life into the coming lives, that which enjoys as fruits, which was worked out in the previous lives." [308]

In the region of the bearer of the causes, the causal body or the spirit self, man experiences not only his true self, but also true existence, which underlies all creation and to which existence in the earthly world almost appears as non-existence. The more he is able to recognize of the true existence in the higher spiritual world, the more he is also able to absorb the divine intentions and goals prevailing there and to assimilate them in such a way that they become a real urge for creation in him to contribute to the shaping of his next incarnation as well as to the further development of all humanity on Earth. But it will depend on the level of the individual's maturity how well he will be able to accomplish this significant task. Therefore, we find the sublime experience in this sphere formulated by Rudolf Steiner as a question in the opening words of the 35th weekly verse:

---

[308] GA 88 "Über die astrale Welt und das Devachan" (About the astral world and the Devachan), Berlin, Lecture of 11 February 1904

35th Week (1 – 7 December)	35. Woche (1. – 7. Dezember)
Can I distinguish the existence So that it reappears In soul's urge for creation? ...	Kann ich das Sein erkennen, Dass es sich wiederfindet Im Seelenschaffensdrange? ...

How much of this urge for creation man's soul can develop in the fifth region of the higher spiritual world depends on the fruits which he brings there from his earthly life. And, which of man's members of being is it that actually carries these fruits to the spirit self? – A link is required between the earthly human body, which makes the I-conscious sensory experience on Earth possible, and the spirit. This link is the threefold soul. What the sentient soul takes up as earthly experiences from the astral body, to which it is closely connected, is processed further in thought and feeling by the intellectual and emotional soul. This one then passes it on to the consciousness soul, which can deepen the mental and emotional insights spiritually and thereby lead them to the spirit self. For this purpose, the consciousness soul joins closely the spirit self to form a unity. Especially the maturity level of the consciousness soul is therefore of enormous importance for man's stay in the higher spiritual world because this soul member transfers the fruits of the past incarnation as nourishment to the spirit self, enriches it, and thus contributes to the further development of the higher human being.

"And the spirit self will become richer and more powerful the more the consciousness soul feeds it. It has been shown that during life, through the assimilated experiences and the fruits of these experiences, this food is supplied to the spirit self. For, the described interaction between soul and spirit can of course only take place when soul and spirit are intermingled, pervaded by each other, that is, within the connection of «spirit self with consciousness soul»." [309]

The consciousness soul makes the spirit self "more powerful", as Rudolf Steiner himself says. However, this power is not an end in itself, but it enables man to live into the World Self with his higher self. For this purpose even more power flows to him from the divine Hierarchies. Accordingly, the 35th weekly verse continues with the words:

I feel, I've been endowed with power To humbly live into the World Self My own self as a member.	Ich fühle, dass mir Macht verlieh'n, Das eigne Selbst dem Weltenselbst Als Glied bescheiden einzuleben.

Rudolf Steiner expounded this special activity of the human being in the fifth region of the spiritual world in his early book "Theosophy", with the express reference that the spiritually matured human being can feel himself there as a member of the divine world order. As the lowest spirit being, still developing towards a future tenth Hierarchy among the other Hierarchies, man can only in full modesty live himself into the divine world order as a member.

"If this «spirit self» has developed so far during a series of stays in the «spirit land» that it can move freely in this country, it will increasingly seek its true home here. Life in spirit becomes as familiar to it as life in the physical reality to the earth-man. Henceforth the points of view of the spirit world work as the relevant ones, which the self accepts as his own ones, more or less conscious or unconscious, for his following life on Earth. The self can feel as a member of the divine world order. The limits and laws of earthly life do not touch it in its innermost being. The power for everything, which it performs, comes to it from the spiritual world. But the spiritual world is a unity. Whoever lives in it knows how the eternal worked on the past, and from the eternal he can determine the direction for the future. The view over the past widens to a perfect one. A person who has reached this level gives himself aims to achieve, which he should carry out in a next embodiment. From the «spirit land» he influences his future so that it runs in the sense of the True and Spiritual. During the intermediate state between two embodiments, man is in the presence of all those sublime beings before whose gazes the divine wisdom is spread out unveiled. For he has reached the stage that he can understand it." [310]

---

[309] GA 9 "Theosophie" (Theosophy), Chapter "Wiederverkörperung des Geistes und Schicksal" (Re-embodiment of the Spirit and Destiny)

[310] GA 9 "Theosophie" (Theosophy), "Die drei Welten" (The three worlds), Section IV "Der Geist im Geisterland nach dem Tode" (The spirit in spirit land after death)

Ascension to the Sphere of the Germ Sheath of the Life Spirit – 36th Week

The human being's entry into the Zodiac sphere as the middle sphere of the seven regions of the spiritual world was accompanied already by his encounter with beings which bring the archetypes in the three lower regions of the spiritual world into a harmonious order. On Earth this is sensorially perceivable in the outer form of the human being, which in the course of evolution has become an expression of the human I and the twelve forces of the zodiac by harmoniously combining all developmental stages of the animal world to a higher unity. The beings of the Zodiac sphere arrange and group all these archetypes in the lower regions of the spiritual world. But they are by no means their creators. The latter ones can only be found in the three regions of the higher spiritual world, i.e. beyond the Zodiac sphere. There, man meets truly creative beings after his death. They are the actual causers of the generation of the archetypes in the lower spiritual world.

"The archetypes of the fourth region do not directly refer to the other worlds. In a certain sense, they are beings that dominate the archetypes of the three lower regions and bring forth their coming together. They are therefore busy arranging and grouping these subordinate archetypes. Accordingly, in this region originates a more extensive activity than in the lower ones. The fifth, sixth and seventh regions differ significantly from the previous ones. For, the beings within them provide the archetypes of the lower regions with the impetus for their activities. In them one finds the creative powers of the archetypes themselves. Those who are able to ascend to these regions will become acquainted with the «intentions» (there is no thought of warming up the old «doctrine of expediency») that underlie our world. Like living germinal points, the archetypes still are here ready to take on the most diverse forms of thought beings. When these germinal points are led into the lower regions, then they swell up as it were and appear in the most varied forms. The ideas by which the human spirit appears creative in the physical world are the reflections, the shadows of these germ-thought-beings of the higher spiritual world." [311]

In these regions not only the preliminary stages of the archetypes exist in a state of germination capacity, but also those of the three highest members of the human being, Manas, Budhi and Atma. The latter two are at home in even higher worlds, the Budhic and Atmic world. According to Rudolf Steiner, they are the real "life kernels" of the spiritual human being. But since the higher members of being always work on the lower ones and by doing so manifest themselves on a subordinate level, we also find them active in the two highest regions of the spiritual or thought world. They dress there in the material of these regions like in a kind of "germ sheath" and thus become perceptible as "germ-thought-beings" or "thought-germ-beings", too.

"We must imagine that these thought-germ-beings are of composite nature. From the elements of the thought world only the germ sheath is taken, so to speak. And this envelops the actual life kernel. Thus we have reached the border of the «three worlds», for the kernel comes from even higher worlds. When the human being was described in a preceding section according to his components, this life kernel was of him was specified and the «Life Spirit» and «Spirit Man» were named as its components. There are similar life kernels for other world beings. They come from higher worlds and are transferred to the three specified in order to perform their tasks in them."

As it is the case in the lower spiritual world, the activity of the thought-germ-beings in the higher spiritual world also reveals itself not only through images, but additionally through sounds. However, the sounding in the upper regions differs substantially from that in the lower ones.

"The observer with the «spiritual ear», who ascends from the lower regions of the «spirit land» to these upper regions, becomes aware of how the ringing and sounding are translated into a «spiritual language». He begins to perceive the «spiritual word», through which for him then not only things and beings show their nature through music, but express it in words. They tell him what may be called in occult science, their «eternal names»."

Through all these beings the "World Word" expresses itself here as the revelation of the Logos or the Son as the second divine person of the Trinity. This connection becomes especially apparent in the sixth region of the spiritual world, since in each of the three worlds within which man develops, always the sixth region is in a closer connection to Budhi, the sixth of man's members of being. We find this connection both in the sound ether as an expression of the World Word in the sixth region of the physical world and in the love-warmth of the Venus sphere as an expression of Budhi in the sixth region of the soul world. In its spiritual germ sheath, however, the Budhi can only be experienced in the sixth region of the spiritual world. And even there Christ himself, whose lowest member is the Budhi, still remains mysteriously hidden from man. His work is at first solely revealed by the sounding of the World Word. But since in the world of aims

---

[311] GA 9 "Theosophie" (Theosophy), Section III "Das Geisterland" (The spirit land), last paragraph

and intentions everything is will-like and purposeful, man experiences this revelation as "urging". So the content of the World Word, i.e. what it intends as aims, does not remain hidden from man. This meaning is revealed to him in his innermost spirit-depths as an assignment of the Christ Being to man for his future activity and his further path of development both in the spheres and in the next life on Earth. This experience is described with impressive words in the 36th weekly verse.

36th Week (8 - 14 December)	*36. Woche (8. – 14. Dezember)*
Within my being's depths now speaks,	In meines Wesens Tiefen spricht
Urging for revelation,	Zur Offenbarung drängend
The World Word so mysteriously:	Geheimnisvoll das Weltenwort:
Imbue your labour's aims	Erfülle deiner Arbeit Ziele
With my spiritual light,	Mit meinem Geisteslichte,
To sacrifice yourself through me.	Zu opfern dich durch mich.

The aims and intentions in the sixth region of the spiritual world are identical to those which Christ himself, as the Creator of the world, has set for the further development of mankind and the world as a whole according to the will of the Father. Man is called there to contribute to this.

"In the sixth region of the «spirit land», man will accomplish in all his actions that which is most appropriate to the true nature of the world. For he cannot seek what he likes, but only that which is to happen according to the right course of the world order." [312]

For this purpose, however, man must renounce all his selfish aims and intentions, which he put off in the Moon sphere some time after his last death before his ascension to the higher spheres, and additionally, in each of his after-death passages through the sixth sphere of the spiritual world, he must take up more and more altruistic aims and intentions into his innermost spirit-depths, even connect his self so intimately with them that one day the Christ will work in him and through him in life on Earth. Man must sacrifice the selfishness of his self, the self-centeredness, and make the world aims of Christ his own aims. In this way he strengthens his higher self and connects it permanently with Christ. Through his power he is enabled to accomplish this great task.

The last words of the 36th weekly verse show moreover how important it is that in the sixth region of the spiritual world the human being is not only assisted by Lucifer as a light bearer, who illuminates the higher spiritual world to him, but the Christ Being contributes in addition his own light from the Budhi plane, which reaches down into the three higher regions of the spiritual world, pervades and warms this. Man should connect the Christ light with his aims in order to have sufficient sacrificial power at his disposal in his next life on Earth, when he will again be exposed to the temptations that are waiting for him in the lower parts of his being, deposited in the Moon sphere, so that he can develop his own higher, selfless powers precisely through overcoming and sacrificing those. In this sense, we may understand the second half of the 36th weekly verse:

Imbue your labour's aims	Erfülle deiner Arbeit Ziele
With my spiritual light,	Mit meinem Geisteslichte,
To sacrifice yourself through me.	Zu opfern dich durch mich.

With every incarnation on Earth man will learn more and more to transform his astral body into spirit self or Manas and thus gradually mature into a true citizen of the higher spiritual world, first of its fifth region, but then more and more of its sixth region.

"When through a series of such pilgrimages on earth the actual spiritual self or the bearer of the causes embodied itself in a physical body and then lives in the spirit land in such a way that it is able to move as freely in the spiritual land as the sensory man moves between the sensory objects – for, this is an experience that we make there: to learn to move in a way that seems to have much more initiative and is higher than within the sensory reality – then we move up to the sixth region of Devachan, then we acquire the expectation to spend some time in the sixth region between two lives. In the sixth region the human self already runs free with the deeper essence of its own inner being; there it lives what we call life in Spirit, in the eternal self. There it lives to the full what it draws directly from the spring of the divine self. There the

---

[312] GA 9 "Theosophie" (Theosophy), Section IV "Der Geist im Geisterland nach dem Tode" (The spirit in spirit land after death)

human being learns to become at home in the spirit land as the physical person is at home in the physical world. The laws of the spiritual world become so familiar to him that he considers himself to belong to them. In this sixth region man learns that he comes into this physical world as a messenger of the purely Divine; no longer does he take the intentions for what he needs in order to work in the physical world from the physical world itself; he carries out the plans of the divine world order itself: he works out of the Spiritual, he acts out of the Spiritual. But he is still no stranger on earth, and he also does not act like a stranger. He has acquired independent impartiality in this sixth region. If he appears in the physical world as a messenger of the spiritual world, his work is all the more fruitful because he does not cling to the things of this world; and since he judges them completely objectively, he will do the proper thing. His action will be the action of the divine world order itself, an expression, a revelation of the divine world order itself.

In this sixth region of the spirit land, man now also enjoys the contact with those sublime beings, of whom I have spoken the last time, who work on the plan of the divine world order. Their gazes overlook the divine wisdom, open and unveiled. The person who has developed to the sixth region is able to understand what they say to him about the divine world plan. When he returns to the earthly plane, he can determine the direction and the aims of his life himself. Then he acts out of himself. He can consciously work on the future. Then he is able to become an initiate here on this earth. The one who is able to become an initiate has attained the expectation to live between two embodiments in the presence of the spirits and to become familiar with the powers and treasures of the spirit land only through deeds which were not connected with the Earthly through egoism, but which he did in selfless sacrifice. When he then returns to the embodiment, his memory is open to his former embodiments. Then he sees that he already lived here and there, and he determines the future of his next embodiment; even if not in all details, for that cannot be determined. Those, who have experienced this in the intermediate state between their embodiments in the spirit land, are the aspirants for initiation into the mysteries; they are the ones who are admitted to the occult schools and will learn there the wisdoms which they have to proclaim to the world so that it may go the way of progress." [313]

Ascension to the Sphere of the Germ Sheath of the Spirit Man – 37th Week

In the seventh and highest region of the spiritual world the human being reaches the border of the three worlds. There he gets to know his own life kernel and finally to understand who or what lives in it and where it originates.

"The seventh region of the «spirit land» extends to the border of the «three worlds». Here man faces the «life kernels», which are transferred from higher worlds to the three described ones in order to accomplish their tasks. If man is at the border of the three worlds, he therefore recognizes himself in his own life kernel." [314]

The real and true life kernel of man consists of the life spirit and the spirit man. To this day, however, they are only like germs in the human soul. As man's two highest members of being, they are at home in the Budhic and the Atmic world. From the Budhic world, Christ pours the power of the Son of God into the higher spiritual world. Man experiences it there as a spiritual light filled with the most intense warmth of life and love, which is clearly different from the pure but nevertheless cold light of knowledge by which Lucifer illuminates the higher spiritual world. Beyond the border of the three worlds, however, even Lucifer's light loses its effect. In this respect, "world-winter-night" reigns there. Only a Christ-imbued spirit-light can have an illuminating effect there. If, in the sixth region of the spiritual world, the human being has fulfilled his innermost will impulses and aims with the spirit-light brought to him by Christ, as we are ordered to do there according to the words of the 36th weekly verse – "Imbue your labour's aims with my [the World Word's] spiritual light to sacrifice yourself through me" – then in the seventh region the deepest desire arises in us, the "heart's drive", to carry this light even to where it originates, out into the "world-winter-night". When the human spirit-soul becomes aware of this sublime longing inside it is filled with a feeling of bliss, as it says in the opening words of the 37th weekly verse:

[313] GA 88 "Über die astrale Welt und das Devachan" (About the astral world and the Devachan), Berlin, Lecture of 11 February 1904

[314] GA 9 "Theosophie" (Theosophy), Chapter "Die drei Welten" (The three worlds), Section IV "Der Geist im Geisterland nach dem Tode" (The spirit in spirit land after death)

| To carry spirit-light into world-winter-night, | Zu tragen Geisteslicht in Weltenwinternacht |
| Is what my heart's drive longs for blissfully ... | Erstrebet selig meines Herzens Trieb ... |

Just at the time when the outer darkness on Earth is approaching its maximum, in the week immediately before the winter solstice, those human soul moods of after-death life, which are experienced in the highest spiritual regions, are reflected in the outer nature mood. The longest winter nights in life on Earth thus become a symbol for the spiritual "world-winter-night" in the transitional region from the higher spiritual world to the Budhi plane or the Christ sphere. It is the period of time that the Christian part of earthly humanity spends in pre-Christmas mood and looks forward to the upcoming holy time of the year, to the imminent beginning of the twelve holy nights. Here a particularly sublime mood rises in the human soul and in the human heart. This is why Rudolf Steiner speaks of the "heart's drive" in the corresponding weekly verse, because the heart as the "Budhi organ" [315] in the earth-man is the centre of both physical warmth and warmth of life as well as warmth of the soul and the purest, most spiritual feeling of love.

The regions into which the human being now strives to carry out the spiritual light of the World Word, following the blissful drive of his heart, are most sublime fields. They are located where the three worlds have their origin, in superspiritual "cosmic grounds". There the germs of the life spirit and the spirit man, which exist only in their first preliminary states in the human soul and are filled with Christ light radiating in from the Budhi world, are to take their roots, out of their germ sheaths, in order to connect themselves with these worlds. Where all Creation has its origin, man also has his origin. Just as a plant finds firm support and food in the ground of the Earth, the spirit-germs planted in the human soul should become rooted in the cosmic grounds as well, by means of the Christ-light within them, because from there man receives his life, from the home of his two highest members of being, which together form his "life kernel". Therefore, the first four lines of the 37th weekly verse read:

To carry spirit-light into world-winter-night,	Zu tragen Geisteslicht in Weltenwinternacht
Is what my heart's drive longs for blissfully,	Erstrebet selig meines Herzens Trieb,
That soul-germs put down roots	Dass leuchtend Seelenkeime
In cosmic grounds luminously ...	In Weltengründen wurzeln ...

At the border to the "cosmic grounds", the World Word itself undergoes a change, too. There it becomes completely evident that it is God who expresses himself through the World Word, that the World Word is only the outer appearance of the "Word of God", the second Logos, the Son, who is capable to lift all existence to ever higher levels and thereby "transfigure" it. This transfiguring sound, however, is accompanied by a brightening and illuminating of a stage of existence, where the previous spiritual senses are no longer able to perceive anything, where it has become dark even to them. In this sense, the 37th weekly verse reads in its entirety:

37th Week (15 - 21 December)	*37. Woche (15. – 21. Dezember)*
To carry spirit-light into world-winter-night,	Zu tragen Geisteslicht in Weltenwinternacht
Is what my heart's drive longs for blissfully,	Erstrebet selig meines Herzens Trieb,
That soul-germs take their roots	Dass leuchtend Seelenkeime
In cosmic grounds luminously	In Weltengründen wurzeln,
And in the senses' darkness sounds, transfiguring,	Und Gotteswort im Sinnesdunkel
The Word of God through all existence.	Verklärend alles Sein durchtönt.

Ascension to the First Sphere of the World of the Life Spirit – 38th Week

Beyond the three worlds there is the Budhic world, the World of the Life Spirit, which is eminently pervaded by the power of Christ, since there he has his lowest member of being, the all-encompassing Budhi glowing in a fire of warmth and selfless love. Even exoteric Christianity illustrates this by pictorial representations of Christ Jesus with the flaming heart. The possibility of coming into contact with this superspiritual region is only given to man because the two regions bordering the spiritual world, the Budhic and the Atmic world,

---

[315] GA 94 "Kosmogonie" (Cosmogony), Munich, Lecture of 6 November 1906

protrude into the highest regions of the spiritual world or, as far as the Atmic world is concerned, at least influence it through their germ-forming activity there. In this way they work to develop the higher spiritual man, who is present as a germ in each human being, to his completeness. In the distant future the I will no longer be the middle one of the human members of being, but the lowest one, followed upwards by Manas, Budhi and Atma, to which the threefold corporeality of man will then be transformed entirely. This higher spiritual human being still exists at an early childlike stage. It rests hidden in the depths of the human soul or – as one could say as well – in the vastness of the cosmos.

But when man has reached the border of the three worlds after death and has been able to maintain his consciousness until then because he has already dealt with these high levels of existence in imaginary and emotional terms during his past life on Earth and thereby acquired an inner relationship with them, then the spirit-child hidden in his soul's womb, which to a certain extent is still enchanted into the lower members of his being and clothed with the germ layers of the higher spiritual world, is revealed to him. At first, however, man cannot perceive it in full clarity of cognition. He rather feels than fully understands already what develops in him as a Divine-Spiritual on a still germinal-childlike level, especially because the feeling has its origin on the Budhi plane. In this experience man towers above the three worlds, even beyond the world of the spiritual light. In relation to this light, there is the deepest night. For that reason, this most exalted experience is related to the longest night of the course of the year on Earth. This is indicated by the first words of the 38th weekly verse, which Rudolf Steiner titled "Weihe-Nacht-Stimmung", meaning "Consecration-Night Atmosphere" and emphasizing the deeper meaning of the German word for Christmas: "Weihnacht".

38 Consecration-Night Atmosphere	*38 Weihe-Nacht-Stimmung*
I f e e l the spirit-child in my soul's womb	Ich f ü h l e wie entzaubert
As if released of an enchantment; ...	Das Geisteskind im Seelenschoß; ...

Not illuminated by the cold cognitive light of the spiritual world, but by the light of Budhi shining in the human heart as the warmth of love or the flaming Christ light, in intimate "brightness of the heart" in other words man is allowed to witness this mysterious process in the first and lowest region of the Budhic world. Here, beyond the borders of the three worlds, from man's true life kernel on the Budhi plane grows in his soul's womb, his consciousness soul, the capability of becoming a bearer of Christ or Budhi of his own. Through God's Son, through the holy World Word, the spirit germ of Budhi is fertilized and the spirit-child is begotten in the innermost sanctuary of the human soul. In a similar way as the consciousness soul grows out of man's lower members of being as the Son of Man, so by the fertilising procreative power of Budhi in the soul-womb of the consciousness soul, which is in close union with Manas or the Spirit Self, the spirit-child emerges, who by its Budhic nature is already superspiritual, since it grows out of the human being's "divine ground" in "cosmic distances".

38 Consecration-Night Atmosphere	*38 Weihe-Nacht-Stimmung*
I feel the spirit-child in my soul's womb	Ich fühle wie entzaubert
As if released of an enchantment;	Das Geisteskind im Seelenschoß;
In brightness of the heart,	Es hat in Herzenshelligkeit
The holy World Word has begotten	Gezeugt das heilige Weltenwort
Hope's fruit from heaven,	Der Hoffnung Himmelsfrucht,
Which jubilantly grows in cosmic distances	Die jubelnd wächst in Weltenfernen
Out of my being's divine ground.	Aus meines Wesens Gottesgrund.

In supreme bliss, in holy jubilation, the person matured enough is allowed to participate in this mysterious process feelingly and empathetically. This is what the seven lines of the 38th weekly verse tell us. However, this experience is still reserved primarily for students of the spirit who are already consciously working on the transformation of their ether- or life-body into Budhi or Life Spirit. It depends on their level of development, how intensively they can participate in the holy event. To the fullest extent it is experiencable to the masters, of course, who are already consciously working on the transformation of their physical body to Atma or the Spirit Man.

How man experiences the development towards Chelaship or Mastership, Rudolf Steiner once summed up briefly and concisely in the words:

"Thus, conscious work on the ether body is Chelaship.
Conscious work on the physical body: Mastership.

Man experiences growing up to these two stages as an opening up of new worlds, new environments, comparable only with the sensations of a child when it emerges from the dark, warm mother's womb into the cold, bright world at birth. In all mysteries, the moment of procreation of Budhi is called second birth, rebirth, awakening." [316]

Even with the birth of a human child from the dark, warm womb of his earthly mother out into the cold, bright light of the terrestrial outside world, this process is comparable, which has been described above in a more spiritual way.

The love streams of the Budhi plane have their own origin in the love of the Father and thus in the Atmic world, because out of love for the world the Father has given the Son to the world. Through the Son the love of the Father is revealed within Creation and only because of the fact that man's "divine ground" lies in the Budhic and Atmic worlds there is a possibility given to him at all for carrying, in the course of the Earth's evolution, love into Creation, which "without his soul's experience, would merely be a frosty, empty life", as the 33rd weekly verse goes. Wisdom that was developed on the ancient Moon is already an integral part of the kingdoms of the earthly nature, the mineral, plant, animal and human kingdoms. Love, the heart-warming sympathy for the Creation and all its beings, can only be carried into the world by man. We all are children of our divine Father, and in our innermost essence therefore of the same kind as He. But just as a drop of water is of the same kind as the ocean and yet by no means the ocean itself, man is of course not identical with God.

In order to incorporate love into the world, mankind was created as one homogeneous human soul from the forces of the Budhi plane. Therefore, its innermost being is the divine love and willingness for sacrifice of the Son. This was lost by that part of the primeval being of man, which was given the task of descending into the physical world, dissecting into a multiplicity on his way there, and finally developing individual I-consciousness and free will as new human abilities. For this purpose the descending and dividing part of the human primeval soul had to undergo the so-called Fall of Man and to become so intensively entangled with the physical world that ultimately he was no longer able to liberate himself by his own efforts. The salvation of the Earth's evolutionary goal became possible only through the intervention of the original pure, childlike primeval soul of mankind under the guidance of Christ. It was only through it that the hope was maintained that the Earth would ultimately culminate as a cosmos of love. With the birth of the childlike soul in the Nathan Jesus-boy on Earth[317] and its ability to bear the Christ or Budhi, but especially through the ensuing mystery of Golgotha, the way was opened for all humans to overcome their selfish parts of being and to become representatives of divine love on Earth.

"Since the mystery of Golgotha, something has been living in our human evolution that entered into our earth's aura and to which we need only appeal in our joy of celebration as hope for the indestructibility of our human being. To remember that is just as necessary for us as it was for the people who enjoyed the simple plays.[318] *Yes, we may even say in addition: We enjoy the simple plays no less. We feel connected with those people who had their joy on these plays because we appreciate in our way what was given to humans, by the fact that the Child of Humanity joined the Earth's becoming, that they were given the strongest hope, the strongest impulse, which man needs so much, so that in winter on Earth, since the time after the Mystery of Golgotha, he can maintain himself by the view that, as in the physical cosmos the Sun prevails over earth-egoism, so in the depths of the human soul more and more the impulse will live, which flowed out through the mystery of Golgotha as the spiritual Sun-impulse of humanity's development on Earth.*

Once the event was there as a historical one, through which this impulse entered life on earth. But it should wake up again and again in the memory, as it can happen through such festivities. For on the one hand it is true that the Christ Being once entered the earth-aura through the mystery of Golgotha; on the other hand it is true what Angelus Silesius said with his beautiful words:

> *Had Christ in Bethlehem a thousand times been born*
> *And not in you, you were eternally forlorn!*

---

[316] GA 94 "Kosmogonie" (Cosmogony), Munich, Lecture of 28 October 1906

[317] GA 114 „Das Lukas-Evangelium" (Gospel of Luke), Basel, Lecture from 18 September 1909.

[318] For example, the "Oberuferer Weihnachtsspiele" (Christmas Plays from Oberufer), performed every year in the anthroposophic branches and at the Waldorf schools. Oberufer was the name of a village at the border between Austria and Slovakia.

What was born in Bethlehem should be born deep and ever deeper in our own souls, so that we may see in our own souls what the medieval feeling wished to see fulfilled when it saw represented the fate of souls pervaded by the Christ impulse in those childlike figures, which are carried up by the angels to the realms of the blessed ones and not captivated by the claws of Ahriman, to whom only those souls remain who have connected themselves with life on earth to such an extent that they appear old, whereas the fate of the soul is to grow not old on earth, but to remain young. And it's only the fate of the body to grow old on earth. Man's higher destiny is to preserve in this aging body the spiritual youth in connection with the mystery of Golgotha, in order to feel more and more in himself the hope that, however intensely the winter storms may rage in the soul and the temptations may live in the soul, never the vivid confidence can die that what flowed into the earth-aura through the mystery of Golgotha and what we want to invigorate in our souls through remembrance by such celebrations, can emerge from the depths of the soul.

So I tried to summarize what we can feel as a Christmas mood precisely from a contemplation that seeks to combine by these few words what we, based on our anthroposophical worldview, feel concerning Christmas, with what people in earlier times experienced in the message of the divine child at such a play, as we have demonstrated it. This is what the words are intended to express:

In human soul-grounds lives	*In des Menschen Seelengründen*
The Spirit-Sun, with confidence in victory;	*Lebt die Geistes-Sonne siegessicher;*
Righteous forces of the mind	*Des Gemütes rechte Kräfte,*
Are able to surmise Him	*Sie vermögen sie zu ahnen*
In my inner being's winter-life,	*In des Innern Winterleben,*
And my heart's impulse for hope:	*Und des Herzens Hoffnungstrieb:*
It beholds the Sun's spiritual victory	*Er erschaut den Sonnen-Geistes-Sieg*
In the blessing light of Christmas	*In dem Weihnacht-Segenslichte,*
As the symbol of the highest life	*Als dem Sinnbild höchsten Lebens*
In the winter's darkest night.	*In des Winters tiefer Nacht."* [319]

The "heart's impulse for hope" finds its firm support in the divine child who, through his ability to bear Christ, has made possible the "Sun's spiritual victory". The Chelas or students of the spirit can become more and more like this divine child if, in the middle of the time between two incarnations, they are able to absorb the power that flows to them from the Budhic world in order to fertilise their soul depths again and again with divine love, so that from incarnation to incarnation it may flame stronger and stronger in them and they in this way become ever more true representatives of the power of Christ on Earth.

Arrival in the Second Sphere of the World of the Life Spirit – 39th Week

After having given off his threefold bodily sheath, the physical body, the ether or life body and the astral body as well as the bodily bearing part of the I already on Earth and in the spheres of the sub-solar planets, the psycho-spiritual human being consists only of soul and spirit. But even in this composition, he appears as a four-membered being, for his soul is also threefold and furthermore has three forces that can be distinguished from one another: will, feeling and thinking. So together with the spiritual part of the I there are again four members of the human being. However, in the higher worlds the three soul forces do not prove to be separated in the same way as they appear in the earthly person. They appear there rather as willing feeling, feeling willing and sensing recognition. Nevertheless, they are quite distinct aspects of the soul life.

The contemplation of the 34th weekly verse showed that in the fourth region of the spiritual world, the Zodiac sphere in the narrower sense, the I rises to a higher level of existence, to "newly risen self-existence", and that the desire stirs in it to imprint itself into the spiritual outside world. But, this outwardly directed process is soon followed by a supplementary, inwardly directed process because even though the spiritual world is to assimilate the I into itself, the I as well in mutual interplay is to assimilate the spiritual world in itself, to become filled with it in order to thereby gain access to the state of eternal spiritual existence in the regions of the higher spiritual world. Rudolf Steiner summarized this in the words:

---

[319] GA 150 "Die Welt des Geistes und ihr Hereinragen in das physische Dasein" (The world of the spirit and its projecting into physical existence), Berlin, Lecture of 23 December 1913

"But the «I» surrenders itself to the Spirit in order to become filled by it. The «I» lives in body and soul; but the Spirit lives in the «I». And what of the Spirit is in the I is eternal. For, the I receives essence and meaning from what it is connected to." [320]

It is the destiny of the I to assimilate the spirit. Each of the three spiritual members of the human being, which are to fulfill the I – Manas or Spirit Self, Budhi or Life Spirit and Atma or Spirit Man –, is closely related to one of the three soul powers.

Manas is at home in the spiritual world. It expresses itself in man as cognitive power both for his outside world as well as for himself, as his thinking, which however in the higher spiritual world rather appears as sensing cognition, especially in the fifth region, the Region of the Spirit Self in the narrower sense. There man, with the help of Manas, as far as he has already developed it, should recognize himself as part of the World Self in order to integrate himself into it in full knowledge. Accordingly, the 35th weekly verse begins with the words: "Can I *distinguish* the existence ...", and states as goal and purpose of this cognition "to humbly live into the World Self my own self as a member".

The sixth member of the human being, Budhi, is in a special relationship to the feeling or willing feeling of man, i.e. his powers of heart, love and sacrifice, as already explained in the previous chapters. Therefore, on his after-death ascension to the sixth region of the spiritual world, where the life spirit works through its germ sheath, man is given the task of fulfilling himself with the love-light of the Christ Being, who reveals himself through the World Word, in order to develop in himself the spiritual foundations for a higher readiness for sacrifice. "Imbue your labour's aims with *my* spiritual light, *to sacrifice* yourself through me", says the 36th weekly verse.

Atma, man's seventh member of being, is closely related to the human will and drive for action. Consequently, the 37th weekly verse, referring to man's passage through the seventh region of the spiritual world, begins with words that emphasize volition striving for activity: "To *carry* spirit-light into world-winter-night, is what my *heart's drive longs for* blissfully."

In this way, in the four upper regions of the spiritual world, the I and the three soul forces of man each pass through separate stages of development, always emphasizing just one of these three soul forces or the I itself.

In the future, man is to pervade himself more intimately with Budhi, i.e. to assimilate the Christ. As Budhi is closest related to the willing feeling of man, this soul power plays a special role in his ascension to the first region of the Budhi plane. Accordingly, the 38th weekly or Christmas verse preceding this chapter, which deals with the conscious turn of the human spirit-soul towards the first region of the Budhi plane, says in the first sentence "I *feel*" and speaks of "brightness of the *heart*". However, in order to pervade with the Budhi, the lowest of Christ's members of being, not only the feeling, but the whole human spirit-soul, there must also take place an imbuement of its thinking, will and I with Budhi.

First, in a further step, the soul power of thinking is Christ-imbued. Through this, man gains a share in the all-encompassing knowledge of the Christ Being. He is allowed to see the world for a time with the eyes of the divine Love Being underlying the world, with the eyes of God. He gains the "World Being's light". In this all-encompassing consciousness, however, he is initially no longer able to find himself by his own efforts. This additionally requires the power of the Holy Spirit from the higher spiritual world, which extends into the Budhi plane by pervading its lower regions. Already during man's passage through the fifth region of the spiritual world, the first one directly connected with the Budhi plane, he was "endowed with power to humbly live into the World Self my own self as a member", as it says in the 35th weekly verse. Now that he has ascended to the Budhi plane, the sensing thought power of Manas is increased by the Holy Spirit into a true "might of thinking". From the interaction of this with the "World Being's light", the seeing of the world through the eyes of God, man recognizes the great importance of the creation of man for the totality of Creation. This stimulates his sense of self and enhances it to such an extent that it becomes a power of its own that reawakens his selfhood.

39th Week (29 December - 4 January)	*39. Woche (29. Dezember – 4. Januar)*
Surrendering to spirit-revelation,	An Geistesoffenbarung hingegeben
I gain World Being's light.	Gewinne ich des Weltenwesens Licht.
Thought power grows and clears	Gedankenkraft, sie wächst
To give myself to me,	Sich klärend mir mich selbst zu geben,
And from the thinking's might emerges	Und weckend löst sich mir
The sense of self to wake me up.	Aus Denkermacht[321] das Selbstgefühl.

---

[320] GA 9 "Theosophie" (Theosophy), Chapter "Das Wesen des Menschen" (The essential nature of man), Section IV "Leib, Seele und Geist" (Body, Soul and Spirit)

Thus, in the highest sphere of all, with which the human being is able come into direct contact in the course of its after-death development, the newly burgeoning sense of self helps the spirit-soul not to completely lose itself in its divine ground, and to feel itself as a spiritual-superspiritual being, rooted in God, but nevertheless determined to a life of its own. Furthermore, man may recognize here, how important he is to the gods, even that the ideal of the Human Being, the ideal of Man, is their supreme goal, indeed the religion of the gods.

"To the gods, the goal of their Creation was the ideal of Man. However, really not that ideal of Man which runs free as the physical man does today, but in such a way as the highest human soul-spirit-life could live up in the fully developed capacities of this physical man. Thus, as a goal, as the highest ideal, as the religion of the gods, an image of Mankind is contemplated by the gods. And as if on the distant shore of divine existence there floats for the gods the temple, which presents the likeness of divine existence in the image of Man as the highest artistic achievement of the gods. And that is the peculiarity that man, while he is forming himself in the spirit land between death and a new birth, gradually makes himself more and more mature there to behold this temple of mankind, this high ideal of Mankind." [322]

Overall, Rudolf Steiner describes a total of four stations on the Budhi plane. The two already described, which deal with feeling and thinking, will be followed by two more. Thus, it can already be guessed at this point that the human spirit-soul, after the great midnight hour of existence, on its subsequent descent through the two lower regions of the Budhi plane towards the spiritual world, will go through two further developmental steps, which will serve to fulfil the will and the I with the power of Budhi. Only then, the psycho-spiritual quaternity of man, consisting of thinking, feeling, willing and I, will be maximally Christ-imbued, as far as it is possible depending on the maturity level of each individual person.

But before we turn to the deeper contents of the next two weekly verses, we want to linger for a while on the summit of the after-death ascension of the human spirit-soul between two incarnations, the great midnight hour of existence, and take a closer look at the intimate connection between Christ and Man.

---

[321] The German term "Denkermacht" not only means "the thinker's might" (des Denkers Macht) but also the power that the thinker owns, the power or even might of thinking. Here, the emphasis is not on the person but on the ability, which has increased to a might, just as in the 44th weekly verse the German word "Schöpferwille" not only means "Creator's will" (des Schöpfers Wille) but also the will to create or the "creative will".

[322] GA 153 "Inneres Wesen des Menschen und Leben zwischen Tod und neuer Geburt" (Inner nature of man and life between death and new birth), Vienna, Lecture of 10 April 1914

Christ and the Human Being

Writing about "the Christ Being" is "truly a difficult endeavour" as was said at the beginning of the chapter of the same name between the weekly verses of spring and summer. This could easily lead to the assumption that, in comparison, it should be quite easy to write about the human being. But, man was created in the image of God, and as a child of God he is of divine nature as well. This inevitably has the consequence that the endeavour to understand and describe the human being as a whole is by no means as simple as it may seem at first glance. In order to approach an understanding of the essence of man, one really has to broaden one's perspective enormously. Alone, in order to understand the origin and evolution of the human physical body, we must go back far into the most distant past, basically to the beginning of all temporal becoming, to that planetary state, which Rudolf Steiner called the ancient Saturn, which was the first incarnation of our solar system. It was followed by the developmental states of the ancient Sun, the ancient Moon and only in fourth place by the development of the Earth. During each of these planetary states, human beings have each been given separate bodily sheaths, in total four: a physical body, an ether body, an astral body and an I-bearer or I-body, as Rudolf Steiner occasionally called it. The I-body differs from the more narrowly three-membered corporeality of man in that it already represents the transition from the sheath nature to the divine part of man's being:

"A being who can say «I» to himself is a world of its own. Those religions that are built on occult science always felt this. They therefore said: With the «I», the «God», who in lower beings reveals himself only from the outside in the appearances of the surroundings, begins to speak within. The bearer of the ability described here is the «I-body», the fourth member of the human being. This «I-body» is the bearer of the higher human soul. Through it, man is the crown of the earthly Creation." [323]

The I-body or bearer of the Divine in man thus occupies a separate place above the three body-members in the narrower sense. But all four members of the human being are by no means the whole man. As created in the image of the threefold God, man also appears as a threeness, consisting of body, soul and spirit. But, God is not only threefold, but triune, too. Therefore we speak of the Trinity (tri-unity). The Trinity of God shows itself in man in the very special function of the I, which unites the threeness of body, soul and spirit into a unity.

In the course of the planetary development, man also received the members of his soul and his spirit as components of his entire being. These are threefold as well. Hence he consists of three times three members of being, which in the I as the tenth member have both their common midpoint and their all-encompassing circumcircle, according to the macrocosmic models of the I on the one hand in the Sun as midpoint, but in the circle of the zodiac encompassing the entire planetary system, too. Therefore, in occultism the number 10 is considered the number of man, and mankind is destined to be included in the series of spiritual beings as a tenth Hierarchy when it reaches its developmental goal. [324]

The spiritual members of the human being only exist in a germ-like state to this day. They originate in much higher worlds than the members of his body and his soul. But the I, which makes man human at all, also belongs to a world which extends beyond the planetary development described above, which begins with ancient Saturn. For this very reason it can serve as a bearer of the higher human being and as an outer sheath for the spiritual members still to be developed. If we want to understand the human being in the truly Christian sense, we must actually go beyond the entire planetary development that has taken place so far.

"The Christ really demands: When you meet a person, you should regard him in such a way that what he shows to you in the outer world is not the whole, full person. You should regard him in such a way that his real nature does not come only from Archai, Archangeloi, Angeloi, but from higher Spirits, who do not belong to the earth development, not even to planetary development, for this begins with the Archai, as you

---

[323]   GA 34 "Lucifer-Gnosis", Essay "Die Erziehung des Kindes vom Gesichtspunkte der Geisteswissenschaft" (The education of the child in the light of anthroposophy), May 1907

[324]   GA 110 "Geistige Wesenheiten und ihre Widerspiegelung in der physischen Welt" (Spiritual Hierarchies and their reflection in the physical world), Düsseldorf, Lecture of 18 April 1909 in the evening

know from «Occult Science - an Outline», but with the higher heavenly Spirits; so that man enters the Maya as something that is supernatural." [325]

Planetary development has its spiritual foundations in the lower spiritual world, where the archetypes of everything physical, living and emotional can be found. The human I, however, comes from a region that is extraplanetary and thus stellar. The visible starry sky, which we summarize in the twelve constellations of the zodiac, is the region of origin of the human I, as has already been discussed in detail in the chapters on the corresponding weekly verses. But the I is destined to be filled with spirit from even higher regions.

"And what is of the Spirit in the I is eternal. Because the I receives essence and meaning from what it is connected to. In so far as it lives in the physical body, it is subject to the mineral laws, through the ether body it is subject to the laws of reproduction and growth, through the sentient soul and the intellectual soul to the laws of the spiritual world; in so far as it takes in the Spiritual [by virtue of the consciousness soul] [326]*, it is subject to the laws of the Spirit."* [327]

Manas has its home in the spiritual world, like the I, whereas Budhi and Atma originate in even higher worlds, which are named after them Budhic plane and Atmic plane. The human being thus extends far beyond the lower three worlds, in which the entire planetary development takes place in seven rounds or circuits around seven globes or states of form. In fact, however, there are not only seven, but a total of twelve settings of development, whereby five exist in the darkness of the Pralayas, i.e. outside the planetary developments, thus before or after them. Rudolf Steiner summarizes the seven rounds with the following five states of Pralaya into the "twelve stages of the World Year".

"Between the last round of a planetary state and the first round of the next one there are five other states beyond consciousness. The seven rounds and the five states of Pralaya are called together the twelve stages of the World Year." [328]

On another occasion, Rudolf Steiner called the planetary rounds "World Days" and the Pralayas that follow them "World Nights". Both are subdivided into "World Hours", according to the development sections on the seven globes and the five states of Pralaya.

"Each cosmic body, Saturn, Sun and Moon, is assigned a succession of World Hours, which are grouped to World Days, and finally in such a way that seven of these twelve periods are outwardly perceptible and five are more or less outwardly imperceptible. One distinguishes therefore seven Saturn circuits or seven great Saturn days and five great Saturn nights. You can also say five days and seven nights, because the first and last days are twilight days. One is used to call such seven circuits, the seven World Days, «Manvantara», and the five World Nights «Pralaya»." [329]

If we convert Rudolf Steiner's information into a graphic by replenishing the simpler Figure 11 (towards the end of the chapter "The Christ Being"), taking into account the mutual interpenetration not only of the worlds, but also of the globes, then the total overview of Figure 19 results. On the one hand, it illustrates that the human development on the seven globes extends up to the Budhic and Atmic plane. On the other hand, it also becomes apparent that the entire cosmic development starts from the highest of the seven worlds, the Mahaparanirvana Plane, where the Christ Being has the fourth and middle of his seven members of being. So everything originates from Christ.

A sketch has been preserved from a Berlin lecture of 1907 in which Rudolf Steiner depicted only three states of Pralaya. However, this does not contradict his different statement above, where he speaks of five states of Pralaya. At that time, he extended his explanations only to the two states of Pralaya, which in Figure 19 are marked with the numbers 9 and 11 and reach down to the higher Atma plane, i.e. to where the highest member of the human being reaches up. Since they are on the same level and, in terms of time, globe 11 originates from globe 9 as its later redesign, he could combine them into one globe in a simplified way. Rudolf Steiner used the old Indian terms calling the Atma plane the Nirvana plane. His statement in this regard is:

"When the earth will have reached its goal, we will be active on the higher Mental plane. Then the transition begins, which leads us over to the next planet. For that we must have Atma on the outside. So

---

[325] GA 172 "Das Karma des Berufes des Menschen in Anknüpfung an Goethes Leben" (The Karma of human vocation as related to Goethe's life), Dornach, Lecture of 27 November 1916

[326] The consciousness soul unites with spirit self or Manas into a unity.

[327] GA 9 "Theosophie" (Theosophy), Chapter "Das Wesen des Menschen" (The essential nature of man), Section IV "Leib, Seele und Geist" (Body, Soul and Spirit)

[328] GA 93a "Grundelemente der Esoterik" (Foundations of esotericism), Berlin, Lecture of 26 October 1905

[329] GA 104 "Die Apokalypse des Johannes" (The Apocalypse of John), Nuremberg, Lecture of 19 June 1908

Karana Sharira [Manas] and Budhi have to disappear outside [as outer sheaths], too. The consequence of this is that we should not imagine nothing would happen at the transition to the new planet – Pralaya is not inaction and sleep –, but that during Pralaya even Karana Sharira and Budhi are slipped off. On the Budhi plane we have to slip off Karana Sharira, and on the Nirvana plane Budhi." [330]

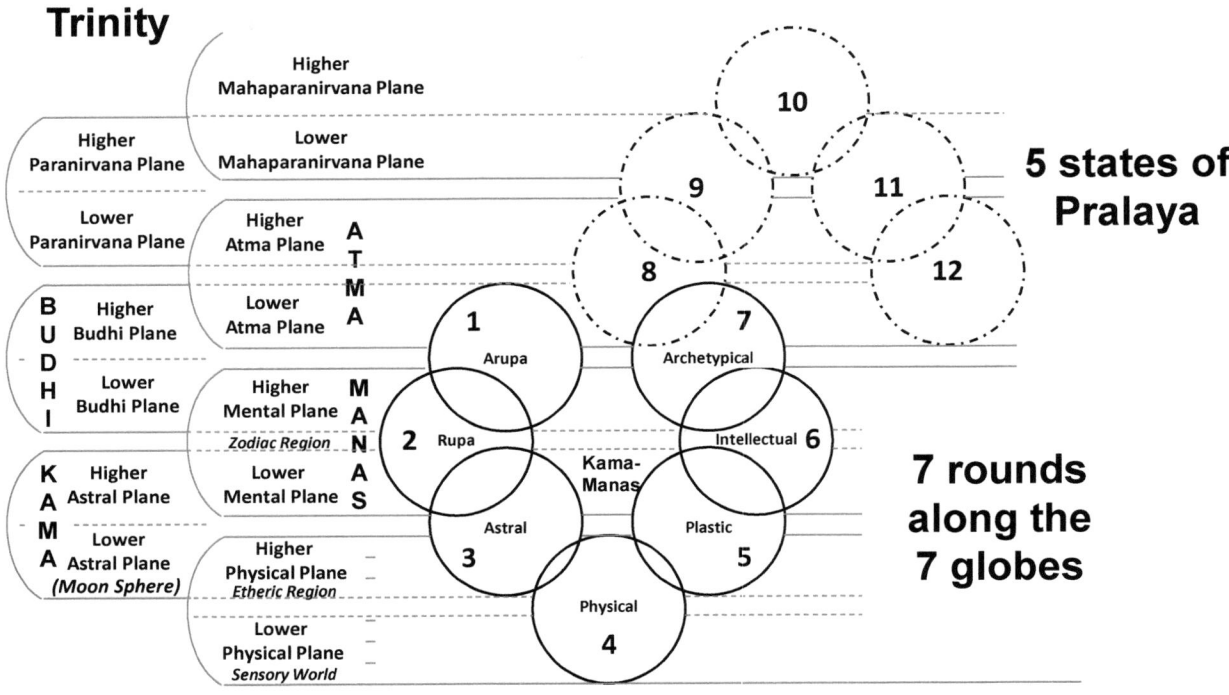

Figure 19: The 7 rounds along the 7 globes and the 5 states of Pralaya as parts of the 12 stages of a World Year

Translated into anthroposophical terminology, the last sentence says: On the Budhi plane we have to slip off Manas, and on the Atma plane Budhi. Globe 7 is on the Budhi plane, but reaches into the higher Mental plane. By slipping off Manas, which belongs to the Mental plane, we rise to globe 8. This is on the Atma plane, but reaches into the higher Budhi plane. By slipping off Budhi, we rise to globe 9. It lies on the Paranirvana plane but reaches into the higher Atma plane. Since Rudolf Steiner's talk was about the members of the human being, and Atma is the highest, he did not extend his considerations beyond, but closed through uniting globes 9 and 11, which both reach into the Atma plane, by the term Nirvana. Of globe 10, man receives a share only when the Christ lives up in him, when he can say with Paul: *"It is no longer I who live, but it is Christ who lives in me."* (Gal 2:20). However, this was not a content of the pre-Christian wisdom teachings of the East on which Rudolf Steiner's lecture above was based. But, of course, it was known that man's Creator exists above him, that He had in a way put man out of Himself. Therefore it says in the lecture: *"But the Creator has Atma as nothing but points in his circumcircle."* What the Creator puts out of himself, he can take in again and put out again, in a similar way as we humans inhale and exhale. In this respect, the human respiratory rhythm is a microcosmic image of the macrocosmic developmental process that is directed outwards on the seven globes and inwards during the five states of Pralaya. Globes 1 and 7 are transitional states, however, insofar as half of globe 1 belongs to the previous Pralaya and half of globe 7 already belongs to the following Pralaya. Therefore we can also speak of 6 outward and 6 inward directed phases of development.

The Zodiac sphere as the fourth region of the Mental plane, from which the human I originates, is the centre and mirror plane between the three lower and the three higher world levels, through which the human being extends in its entirety, reaching from the physical body to Atma. The active participation of man in the development of his spiritual members of being, however, is still in its earliest beginnings. For this purpose, by the Mystery of Golgotha the door to the Budhi plane had to be opened up much further than ever before. In ancient times, only a few chosen ones could penetrate to these high regions during

---

[330] GA 89 "Bewusstsein – Leben – Form" (Consciousness – Life – Form), Berlin, Lecture of 10 November 1904

their initiation experiences and their lives between death and a new birth, with the consequence that the path was completely closed for the majority of mankind.[331] Since the mystery of Golgotha, the path to the Budhi plane, on which Christ's lowest member of being exists, has been open to all mankind, for Christ died for all human beings, rose and ascended one world level higher, into the Ether sphere of the Earth, in order to prepare it for the subsequent ascension of the earth-people in the course of the second half of the Earth's development. For, humanity is to gradually develop from the physical globe 4 to the astral-etheric, plastic globe 5. In this sense too, Christ said: *In my Father's house there are many dwelling places. If it were not so, would I have told you that I go to prepare a place for you? And if I will have gone and prepared a place for you, I will come again and will take you to myself, so that where I am, there you may be also."* (John 14:1-3)

However, each person must make his own contribution to the upward development. Moreover, he or she will only be able to fulfill this task in intimate union with Christ. Without Him as Spirit Guide, no one will succeed in ascension in a blessed way for humanity.

In the course of the human evolution since ancient Saturn, ancient Sun and ancient Moon as well as during the first half of the Earth development, primarily the lower two thirds of the whole human being were developed: the threefold corporeality and the threefold soul. Man has thus been advanced in his development to such an extent that today he can consciously open his soul to his higher spiritual members of being and let himself be filled with them.

In the ancient mysteries, the highest soul member, the consciousness soul, was called the "Son of Man", since it emerged from the human members growing from the bottom upwards. The three spiritual members, on the other hand, coming from divine worlds and streaming from above downwards in order to fulfill the Son of Man, were called the "Son of God" or the "Son of the living God". Rudolf Steiner explained this relation in a lecture of his cycle on the Gospel of Matthew. His words were in part:

"What is the «Son of the Living God» in contrast to the «Son of Man»? In order to understand this concept, we need to supplement the facts we have just said. Man, we have said, develops upwards in such a way that he unfolds in his being the consciousness soul in which the spirit self can appear. But when he has developed the consciousness soul, then spirit self, life spirit and spirit man have to descend towards him so that his opening blossom can receive this upper trinity. We can also graphically depict this upward development of man as an upward development of a kind of plant: [see figure 12 in the chapter on the 18th weekly verse]

In the consciousness soul the human being opens up and the spirit self or Manas, the life spirit or Budhi, and the spirit-man or Atma draw near to him. So this is something that, as it were, approaches man as the spirit-fertilizing from above. Man grows upwards with the other members from below and opens himself to the bloom of the Son of Man, whereas, when man progresses and wants to receive the full I-consciousness, that, which brings him spirit self, life spirit and spirit man, must draw near to him from above."– For, as Rudolf Steiner writes in his Theosophy, *"the I receives essence and meaning from what it is connected to."* [332] The lecture on the Gospel of Matthew continues:

"And the representative of what is brought down to him from above, what points to the farthest future of mankind, who is he? The first gift we receive as the spirit self. Whose representative is he who will bring the gift of the descending Spirit Self? This is the Son of God who lives, the Life Spirit, the «Son of the living God»! Thus, at this moment Christ Jesus asks the question: What must draw near to man by my impulse? That, which is the stimulating spirit-principle from above, must come to man! Thus the «Son of Man», who grows from the bottom up, and the Son of God, the «Son of the living God», who grows from the top down, stand opposite each other. We have to distinguish them.

But we must understand that this question was a very difficult one for the disciples. This question will come to you in all its difficulty for the disciples, especially when you consider that the disciples first received all that which the simplest people after the time of Christ Jesus had already got implanted through the Gospels. The disciples had to take it all in through the vivid teaching power of the Christ Jesus. In the forces they had already developed, there was no ability to understand what could give an answer to the question: Whose representative am I myself? Then, it is pointed out that one of the disciples called Peter gave the answer: «You are the Christ, the Son of the living God» (Matthew 16:16). That was an answer at that moment which, if we may say so, was not from Peter's normal powers of mind. And the Christ Jesus –

---

[331] GA 148 "Aus der Akasha-Forschung – Das fünfte Evangelium" (From Akasha-Research – the Fifth Gospel), Berlin, Lecture of 4 November 1913

[332] GA 9 "Theosophie", Chapter "Das Wesen des Menschen" (The essential nature of man), Section IV "Leib, Seele und Geist" (Body, Soul and Spirit)

let us try to present the matter vividly by appealing in a certain sense to vividness – had to say to himself, looking at Peter: It is much, that out of this mouth has come this answer, which, so to speak, points to a farthest future time. – And when he then looked at what was in Peter's consciousness, what was in him in such a way already, that he could give such an answer with his intellect or with the powers, which he had received by initiation, then the Christ had to say to himself: This is not from what Peter knows consciously; there speak those deeper powers which are in man and which man only gradually turns into conscious powers. ...

The mysterious higher aspect in Peter, what the Christ calls the «Father in heaven», the powers out of which Peter was born, but of which he is not yet aware, they spoke out of him at that moment. Hence the word: «What you are at this stage as a man of flesh and blood has not given you this, but the Father in the heavens» (Matthew 16:17)." [333]

From the highest world just connected to the planetary development on the seven globes, from the Father powers on the Atmic plane, the impulse had to come so that Peter, despite his initiations by Christ himself that had already taken place so far, could call him the Bringer of the spiritual members of the human being, especially Budhi, the Life Spirit, as the lowest member of the Christ Being, could call him the "Son of the living God".

In the sheath of a complete human being, reaching from the physical body up to Atma, the supreme member of the human being pervaded by the Father Power, Christ stood as God in human form, as the Christ Jesus, before his disciples. Only in the transfiguration of Christ, which took place soon after this talk, the meaning of the words spoken by Peter should be revealed to at least three of the disciples in a more comprehensive way, through a higher initiation, which was given to the very limit of what was possible for them. Besides Peter and his brother Andrew, the so-called disciple John, who in the Gospel of John is always named *"the disciple whom Jesus loved"*, also participated. He was the only one who was suitable to receive some time later an even higher initiation beyond the transfiguration experience. The Gospel of John describes it as the Raising of Lazarus. In this event Christ himself united the psycho-spiritual members of John the Baptist, who had already been killed at that time, with the earth-bound members of his disciple Lazarus to form a double being. John the Baptist himself, who in his previous incarnation was the prophet Elijah, as Christ revealed to his disciples[334], pointed in his later incarnation as the Renaissance painter Raphael[335] in his painting of the Transfiguration of Christ to this significant inner connection between himself as the individuality of Elijah and the disciple Lazarus, by raising the third disciple, usually called John, higher than Peter and Andrew on the Mount of Transfiguration, so that he touches with his left hand almost the left foot of the prophet Elijah floating above him as he was in the spiritual world. Obviously the initiation connected with the Transfiguration of Christ was in addition to him the preparation for the later creation of the double being John Lazarus.

Here the question might arise whether Elijah/Johannes the Baptist in his later incarnation as Raphael did confuse Lazarus with John Zebedee. Two statements by Rudolf Steiner, which have been preserved from a personal conversation between him and the two Christian Community pastors W. Klein and Emil Bock in February 1924, point in the direction of an answer to this question:

"To the question: Is the disciple John mentioned in the first three Gospels the same as Lazarus? Rudolf Steiner answered: The author of the Gospel of John is Lazarus. He is called John only as many people of his time. What did John mean, then!

Question: Is Lazarus the same, who was called the Son of Zebedee?

Counterquestion [by Rudolf Steiner]: Did the sons of Zebedee even belong to the inner circle of the twelve? To the star circle in which the Christ saw his being mirrored? There must be some confusion if it's in the Gospels. Confusions should not surprise us in such a case, for the apostles could even exchange their bodies under the completely different spiritual laws prevailing at that time. The three disciples in Gethsemane belonged in any case to the closest circle of twelve and Lazarus also belonged to it." [336]

---

[333] GA 123 "Das Matthäus-Evangelium" (The Gospel of Matthew), Bern, Lecture of 11 September 1910

[334] Christ said to his disciples, *"For all the prophets and the law prophesied until John. And if you are willing to receive it, he is Elijah who is to come."* (Matthew 11: 13-14). Also in connection with his own message of suffering, Christ referred to the decapitation of the Baptist already made by saying, *"Elijah has come already, and they did not know him but did to him whatever they wished."* (Matthew 17, 12, and Mark 9, 13)

[335] GA 126 "Okkulte Geschichte" (Occult history), Stuttgart, Lecture of 1 January 1911

[336] GA 264 "Zu den Zur Geschichte und aus den Inhaltender ersten Abteilung der Esoterischen Schule 1904 – 1914" (On the history and from contents of the first section of the Esoteric School 1904 – 1914), Section

In memoir notes of Elisabeth Vreede, we find an explanation, which she herself put in brackets as an insert, providing further information:

"(Among the twelve apostles, Lazarus-John himself is represented by another so to speak. John, brother of James and son of Zebedee, is not an apostle in the true sense. James and John are one in a sense, they represent among the more intimate disciples of the Christ Jesus the power of the intellectual or emotional soul, which has a double function in man, but is nevertheless a unity. Therefore, they are called "sons of thunder", because thunder is macrocosmically the same thing that is the thought in the human microcosm. But when Lazarus turns into John, he takes the place of the one Zebedee Son, and as such he is the one who lay at the last supper at Jesus' breast.)" [337]

The above statement by Rudolf Steiner *"The author of the Gospel of John is Lazarus"* could easily be misunderstood as if he meant only the Lazarus, insofar as he lived on Earth. From a purely physical point of view, certainly he is the writer of the Gospel, for it was naturally him who wrote with his physical hands. However, Rudolf Steiner refers to Lazarus, who had already gone through his Raising by Christ, i.e. to John Lazarus, who was able to write his Gospel only after this profound transformation of his being. At the end of the 10th chapter, therefore, when he concludes the first half of his Gospel, the writer faithfully calls John the Baptist as witness of the truthfulness of what was said in the preceding chapters about Christ: *"But all that John said about him was true."* (John 10:41). The descriptions of experiences, in which Lazarus participated, do not begin before the 11th chapter, in which his name is mentioned for the first time. Lazarus was always in intimate connection with John the Baptist, who was spiritually present in him. The Gospel writer, therefore, after his transformation, speaks of himself only as "the disciple whom the Lord loves". Therefore, in another context, Rudolf Steiner logically also spoke of John as the "Evangelist", which in German language means the writer of the Gospel, since the German and Latin words for Gospel are "Evangelium".

"John had to develop up to Budhi to comprehend what was revealed as the Christ Jesus. The other three evangelists were not so highly developed. John gives the highest, he was an awakened, a raised one. John is the name of all who are raised. This is a generic name, and the Raising of Lazarus in the Gospel of John is nothing more than the description of this Awakening. The writer of the Gospel of John, we will hear his name later, never calls himself other than «the disciple, whom the Lord loves». This is the term for the most intimate disciples, for those in whom the teacher and master has succeeded in awakening the disciple. The description of such an awakening is given by the author of the Gospel of John in the Raising of Lazarus: «the Lord loved him», he could awaken him." [338]

In all disciples, as in all other people at the time of Christ Jesus, the consciousness soul, the "Son of Man", was not yet fully developed, and even in the initiated ones a connection with the three spiritual members of being, the "Son of God", could only take place for the duration of a three-day initiation sleep. The possibility of a lasting connection while maintaining consciousness was first created by Christ himself.

"All the different peoples before the appearance of Christ on earth had mysteries. In the mysteries was taught what should happen in the future. The students were prepared through long exercises so that they could go through the Entombment. The hierophant could bring the student to a higher state of consciousness, in which he was in a kind of deep sleep. In ancient times, consciousness always had to be depressed when the Divine in man was to emerge. Then the soul was led through the regions of the spiritual world, and after three days man was revived by the Hierophants. Then he felt like a new person. He got a new name. He was then called a Son of God.

In the case of the mystery of Golgotha, this whole process took place outside on the physical plane. In times before, the disciples were revived by a spirit-spark of the Christ, and they were told: One day someone will come who will make it possible for all people to become Christ-imbued. This one will truly be the Word in the flesh. You can experience this for three days only, when you walk through the kingdoms of the heavens. But One will come who always walks through the kingdoms of the heavens, who will carry the kingdoms of the heavens into the physical world." [339]

The Christ Jesus, as the archetype of a "Christ-imbued" human being in its entirety, in which the "Son of Man" was exalted by his connection with the "Son of God", created a second complete human being

---

"Überliefertes aus persönlichen Gesprächen mit Rudolf Steiner" (Handed down personal conversations with Rudolf Steiner)

[337] Ibidem, Section "Über Meisterpersönlichkeiten im Zusammenhang mit den Auferweckungen in den Evangelien" (About the personalities of masters in connection with the Raisings in the Gospels)

[338] GA 94 "Kosmogonie" (Cosmogony), Munich, 28 October 1906

[339] GA 97 "Das christliche Mysterium" (The Christian Mystery), Cologne, Lecture of 2 December 1906

according to his own example in the Raising of Lazarus, and for the first time in such a way that the connection between the "Son of Man" and "Son of God" lasted not only for three days, but for the rest of the earth life of this person. Therefore this disciple received the name: "The disciple whom Jesus loved".

"At the Raising of Lazarus the spirit-being of John the Baptist, who since the time of his death had been the spirit overshadowing the disciples, would have entered into the previous Lazarus from above until the consciousness soul, and from below was the being of Lazarus, so that the two interpenetrated. This was, after the Raising of Lazarus, John, the «disciple whom the Lord loved»."

This statement has been preserved by Dr. Ludwig Noll, who, in addition to Ita Wegmann, treated the already seriously ill Rudolf Steiner in the last months of his life on Earth. Rudolf Steiner intended to reveal even more on this subject – as we know from Marie Steiner – but was not able to finish his last lecture in September 1924 due to his weakened forces. After a notification by Dr. Kirchner-Bockholt, he gave Ita Wegman the further explanation:

"According to the earth powers of this time, Lazarus could only fully develop up to the emotional and intellectual soul; the mystery of Golgotha takes place in the fourth post-Atlantean period, and in this time the intellectual or emotional soul was in development. Therefore he had to be given Manas, Budhi and Atma by another cosmic being from the consciousness soul upwards. Thus, before the Christ stood a man, who reached from the depths of the earth to the highest heights of heaven, who bore in perfection the physical body along with all members until the spirit-members Manas, Budhi, Atma, which can be developed by all people only in the distant future." [340]

In a similar way as in Christ Jesus, two beings were united in the raised Lazarus as well. One of the two was the individuality of John the Baptist, or Elijah, working from the spiritual world since his decapitation. According to Rudolf Steiner, he is none other than Adam, the first man on Earth ever, who descended into an earthly incarnation, and therefore, in contrast to the soul of the Nathan Jesus-boy, he was a soul that was *"ripe, overripe"* [341]. While in the Nathan Jesus the primeval soul of mankind begins its earthly mission as an Adam-being with his first complete incarnation, the mission of the first earthly Adam, who began with his incarnations in ancient Lemuria already, is approaching its end. The new Adam came to replace the old Adam. John the Baptist knew about it and told his own disciples: *"He must increase, but I must decrease."* (John 3:30) By the fact, that the evangelist Matthew ends the first half of his gospel with the Baptist's decapitation (Matthew 14:1-13), he also points to a significant change in the events of that time.

The individuality of Lazarus living on Earth, originated from Cain, the eldest son of Adam, who, unlike his brother Abel, began to understand the Earth as a field of activity for mankind. Lazarus was incarnated in pre-Christian times as Hiram Abiff, the master builder of the temple of Solomon. [342] Unlike Solomon, he had sufficient earthly wisdom as a "Son of Cain" to master the architectural and earthly practical challenges of the enormous temple construction. Since the time of the events around the mystery of Golgotha, he went through a whole series of initiations with the emphasis on the mysteries of the Physical and its spiritualization, in order to continue the development of his earthly wisdom. His gaze was always directed from the Earth up to heaven. Since the Middle Ages, he has been known as Christian Rosenkreutz, the head of the Rosicrucians, who always worked as physicians also.

John the Baptist, on the other hand, the prophetic Elijah individuality, was mainly initiated into the secrets of the Spiritual and the way to combine it with the Physical. His line of vision was from heaven down to Earth. Therefore he was able to contribute to the Christ Being's entry into the body of Jesus of Nazareth at the baptism on the Jordan and also recognize the Christ Being in his spirituality and divinity as the Logos, the creative World Word.

Zarathustra, the third highly developed individuality involved in the events of that time, was primarily initiated into the secrets of the soul as mediator between spirit and body, especially into the secrets of the astral body as the soul-bearer and its purification to the spirit self. [343] Therefore, it was his task to prepare

---

[340] GA 238 "Esoterische Betrachtungen karmischer Zusammenhänge" (Esoteric reflections on karmic connections – karmic relationships) – Volume 4, "Ergänzende Bemerkungen zum Inhalt der Ansprache vom 28. September 1924 (letzte Ansprache)" (Additional remarks on the content of the speech of 28 September 1924 [last address])

[341] Ibidem

[342] GA 265 "Zur Geschichte und aus den Inhalten der erkenntniskultischen Abteilung der Esoterischen Schule 1904 – 1914" (On the history and from contents of the first section of the Esoteric School 1904 – 1914), Berlin, Instruction lesson of 15 April 1908

[343] Zarathustra's great mission began in the primal Persian culture, which was primarily dedicated to the higher development of the astral body. This radiated into the following cultures, which serve the development of the

the soul of the Nathan Jesus-boy as a link between the holy spiritual members of being, brought by Christ, which descended from heaven in the form of a dove as a holy spirit, and the bodily members of Jesus of Nazareth. Rudolf Steiner respectfully calls Zarathustra *"one of the greatest, who has worked in the course of human development".*[344]

Thus, in the world-historical events in Palestine in the times of Christ Jesus, a total of three individuals were involved, highly developed in various ways and initiated for different purposes. Since then, as the three Christian Masters, they have been helpful to all people who sincerely strive to understand the mystery of Golgotha and the events connected with it, as well as to understand the Christ Being in general and its connection with the human being.

In the completed human being John Lazarus, the Adam-Abel-current of evolution, which in the past had remained turned towards the celestial worlds, was united with the Cain-current, which had always remained turned towards the Earth. The former were called "Sons of God" and the latter "Sons of Man".[345] By this completion Christ Jesus produced in John Lazarus a union of two polarities similar to Him, where on a higher level however a true Son of God, the Son of the living God, was united with a true Son of Man, the primeval soul of all human beings. He created John Lazarus as a second completed human being consisting of all members after His image. In front of the true Son of God stood a son modelled on Him. This one was to become his successor and representative on Earth for the time after the mystery of Golgotha. In His last hour in an earthly body, just before his death, looking down from the cross, Christ Jesus appointed John Lazarus in his place as Son, and He did it to such an extent that he even handed him over to his mother as her Son in his place:

"But when Jesus saw his mother, and the disciple whom he loved standing near, he said to his mother, «Woman, behold, your son!» Then he said to the disciple, «Behold, your mother!» And from that hour the disciple took her to his own home." (John 19:26-27)

Now, how would the disciple, whom Jesus loved, have experienced himself as a human being reaching up to the highest spiritual regions, far beyond the planetary spheres of the lower spiritual world, far beyond the visible starry sky and the zodiacal sphere, up to those regions where the highest spiritual members of man's being are at home? Was there a possibility for him to behold himself as psycho-spiritual human being? – It actually was possible to him, but only because he had been prepared by Christ Himself through a whole series of initiation steps. When man is falling asleep, the psycho-spiritual part of his being separates together with the astral body from the physical body and the ether body. If the soul and the I have gone through a series of initiation stages, those higher worlds can be perceived to which the psycho-spiritual parts of the human being belong. What the vast majority of people are only allowed to experience during their after-death ascension between two incarnations is given to the initiated students of the spirit and much more to the masters, of course, already in earthly life. Rudolf Steiner told us how someone who was initiated in such a special way as the favourite disciple of Christ Jesus then perceives his own Psycho-Spiritual.

"What about that, which came out during sleep in an ordinary person, what about the astral body and the I? They too are not conscious at night. In an ordinary person, nothing is experienced within the astral body during night's sleep. But now imagine, you would practice the seven stages of the Initiation of John, these meaningful moments of the Christian initiation by feeling. Then you would not only see what has been described so far. Quite apart from the fact that you can develop clairvoyant power by the contact of the astral body with the ether body, something else would occur. Man becomes aware of the peculiarities of the soul, the psychological human characteristics of the astral world and the Devachanic world out of which he was actually born with regard to his soul. And in addition to this image [the second seal of the Apocalypse][346] *an even higher symbol appears which seems to fill the whole world. To this symbol of the ancient initiation, for the one who passes through the stages of the John-Initiation, something is added that is best represented by the first seal. As a clairvoyant appearance he sees the priest-king with a golden belt, with feet that seem to be made of cast metal, his head covered with hair as if of white wool, a fiery sword*

---

three soul members of man, the sentient, intellectual and consciousness soul. As the latter develops primarily in the Physical, Zarathustra works here together with Christian Rosenkreutz. Since the mystery of Golgotha, Zarathustra has been leading under the name of Master Jesus the more soul-oriented Christian-mystical initiation path. Christian Rosenkreutz leads the Rosicrucian way of initiation, which is more suitable for modern mankind, which is focused on the body.

[344] See note 342.

[345] GA 93 "Die Tempellegende und die Goldene Legende" (The Temple Legend and the Golden Legend), Berlin, Lecture of 29 May 1905

[346] Revelation, Chapters 4 und 5.

flaming from his mouth and the seven stars of the world in his hand: Saturn, Sun, Moon, Mars, Mercury, Jupiter, Venus." [347]

A human being, who underwent such an initiation as the favourite disciple of Christ Jesus made it accessible to his disciples through his Gospel, witnesses in a tremendous macrocosmic Imagination, of which Rudolf Steiner says it "seems to fill the whole world", his own essence as a macrocosmic, psycho-spiritual human being who has become a bearer of Christ, so that the Christ Being himself can speak through him. Rudolf Steiner calls this figure the "priest-king", for a human being who has ascended to the borders of the three worlds and beyond possesses all the wisdom of the world. *"When the human being is at the border of the three worlds, he thus recognizes himself in his own life kernel. This implies that the riddles of these three worlds must be solved for him. So he overlooks the whole life of these worlds."* [348] Man attains a truly royal stage here.

But the higher spiritual world is pervaded by the Budhi plane, in which the life kernel of man is at home. Budhi is the purest love to all beings and to God. This love lived in John Lazarus, too, for he bore Budhi and even Atma in himself. When between two incarnations a human comes into contact with the lower regions of the Budhi plane, where he is allowed to witness the great midnight hour of existence, he has reached his origin, and in the highest royal worldly wisdom and sublime priestly mood he becomes one with God. Thus, at the time when he is furthest away from life on Earth, he turns into a macrocosmic royal-priestly being. He becomes a priest-king like Christ Jesus himself, who united in Himself the Nathan-priestly and the Solomon-royal lineage. Hence, at the place of his origin, the human being experiences himself also in the state of his perfection, the goal of his development. He experiences himself as his Alpha and Omega, as a likeness of the Christ Jesus. However, even then the Christ Being is still far, far superior to him. Therefore, John, the favourite disciple, speaks of Christ, who was revealed to him in the Spirit on a Sunday, as of *"the ruler of kings on earth. To him who loves us and has freed us from our sins by his blood and made us a kingdom, priests to his God and Father, to him be glory and dominion for ever and ever."* (Rev 1:5-6) And in his vision John hears Christ say of Himself: *"I am the Alpha (the beginning) and the Omega (the end), says the Lord and God, who is and who was and who is to come, the All-Ruler."* (Rev 1:8)

In just the reverse manner than a plant on Earth, rooted in the ground below the visible world and growing, blooming and bearing fruit from there up into the world, the human being is with his life kernel rooted in the cosmic grounds above the three worlds, which underlie all visible Creation. And just as the rootstock of a plant is its head from which countless root-hairs protrude into the ground, in a similar way countless hairs grow out of the human head. Today they are horny and hang down from the head due to their weight. Originally they once were spiritual influxes that penetrated the human head from all sides.

"The hairs are the result of the ancient influxes. What is hair on the human body today used to be spiritual influxes from outside into the human body. Dried astral-etheric currents are our hairs today. And such things are actually only preserved where the old truths have remained purely outwardly, in writing, by tradition. In Hebrew, therefore, the word «hair» and the word «light» are roughly written with the same characters, because one had an awareness of the relationship between the astrally inflowing light and the hair; as in ancient Hebrew literature in general documentarily the greatest truths are contained, alone in the words themselves." [349]

Like these spiritual currents around the human head the hair also appears in John's vision of the macrocosmic human being. His head, which corresponds to the rootstock of the plant, appears as a pictorial expression of the Budhi plane beyond the three worlds. Therefore, the love-fire of Budhi shines and flames out of his eyes. But his hair extends above the head to the Atma plane, the highest and purest of all worlds directly connected with the human being, from where the powers of the Father flow to man. These appear in John's vision in the image of pure, snow-white, woolly fine hair.

"I saw one like a Son of Man, clothed with a long robe ... But his head and his hair were white as white wool, like snow." (Rev 1:13-14)

From the eyes of the macrocosmic, psycho-spiritual human being modelled on the Christ Jesus, the Budhi's love-fire flames and his face shines like the Sun, through which the Budhi is expressed in the visible sky.

---

[347] GA 104, "Die Apokalypse des Johannes" (The Apocalypse of John), Nuremberg, Lecture of 19 June 1908

[348] GA 9 "Theosophie" (Theosophy), Chapter "Die drei Welten" (The three worlds), Section IV "Der Geist im Geisterland nach dem Tode" (The spirit in the spirit land after death)

[349] GA 117 "Die tieferen Geheimnisse des Menschheitswerdens im Lichte der Evangelien" (Deeper secrets of the becoming of mankind in the light of the Gospels), Munich, Lecture of 7 December 1909

"...and his eyes (were) like a flame of fire" (Rev 1:13-14) and *"his face was as when the sun shines in its power."* (Rev 1:16)

From the head's mouth sounds the Cosmic or World Word, the Divine Fiat, by which the Father speaks through the Son, by means of the Word. Here, above the three worlds and beyond all time, the World Word has its origin. John therefore writes in the prologue of his Gospel: *"In the prime beginning was the Word; and the Word was with God, and the Word was a God. This was in the prime beginning with God. Everything has come into being through this, and without this nothing of what was made has come into being."* (John 1:1-3)

In order to bring forth Creation, the World Word resounds through the spiritual world, where it creates the foundations of the world. Its power to transform the original unity on the Budhi plane into a multiplicity on the higher Mental plane is perceived by John's spiritual ear like the division of the unified voice into "the voice of many waters".

"...and his voice was like the voice of many waters." (Rev 1:15)

But the mouth itself, from which the World Word emerges, is part of the head on the Budhi plane.

"Here, where the divine thought becomes sound and voice, in the Budhi sphere, is what the Middle Ages called the divine kingdom. Enveloped with Budhi, the Logos now flows into the Mental region, which divides into the Arupa and Rupa levels. Here now the divine thought world flows in. The exemplary ideas surge and mix up. What later becomes separate being and rests enclosed in the Logos in the Budhi sphere, is brought into being here as an exemplary idea." [350]

In order to transform an undifferentiated unity into a multiplicity, the principle of polarity, of oppositeness is required. Therefore, the World Word appears in the image of a sharp, two-edged sword emerging from the mouth of the macrocosmic human being.

"... and from his mouth came a sharp, two-edged sword." (Rev 1:16)

Although John does not report that the sword was flaming in his vision, as it says in Rudolf Steiner's statement quoted farther above, it seems to suggest itself that it may have appeared thus to John Lazarus as Clara Rettich drew it after Rudolf Steiner's instructions on the occasion of the Munich Congress in May 1907, since the sword comes from the Budhi which always reveals itself flamingly (see Figure 20).

As a symbol of the principle of separation, the sword reaches one level lower than the Budhi plane. It therefore protrudes in front of the chest of the priest king down to his hip. The chest and abdomen of the human body represent the higher and lower Mental plane. In their midst, the sharp, double-edged sword or the World Word creates a spiritual image of itself in the form of the fourth region of the Mental plane, the Zodiac sphere in the narrower sense, which separates everything higher from everything lower. There is also the home of the I, which is a prerequisite for the ability to distinguish. The I lives in the fire as well, in the warmth of the human blood and thus in intimate relationship with both the heart as Budhi organ and the creative World Word. Correspondingly, on the occasion of a lecture on the gift of the I to man in ancient Lemuria, Rudolf Steiner said:

"Then he got the double-edged sword, that is the I, which can work from outside to inside and from inside to outside. It has power over the elements of the earth, of water, of fire, which were subject to it. When Kama had been bound to fire, water to life force, matter to spirit, then man formed his armour, then he received the double-edged sword." [351]

The I, which is at home in the Zodiac sphere, is the link of man to Christ. This is why the Zodiac sphere has a special significance in John's vision. It appears there as a girdle in the colour of gold, the metal of the Sun. But, in this vision, the girdle does not run around the waist, as one would expect, but in an unusual way around the chest. Many Bible editions adhere at least in their texts to John's clear statements in this regard. In pictorial representations, however, the golden girdle is often depicted somewhat deeper, shifted towards the middle of the trunk as a sign that it separates the upper half of the trunk from its lower half. But in some illustrations and translations, which have lost the understanding of the deeper meaning, the golden girdle even slips down to the waist, as is customary for earthly people. In John's vision, however, it runs explicitly at the level of the nipples. Just as the zodiac encircles the Sun, so the golden belt the heart. John is very precise in his choice of words here. He describes the macrocosmic Son of Man:

---

[350] GA 89 "Bewusstsein – Leben – Form" (Consciousness – Life – Form), Section "Der erste, zweite und dritte Logos" (The first, second and third Logos), private lesson, Berlin-Schlachtensee, Summer 1903

[351] GA 89 "Bewusstsein – Leben – Form" (Consciousness – Life – Form), Section "Der erste, zweite und dritte Logos" (The first, second and third Logos), private lesson, Berlin, Lecture of 27 March 1905

"clothed with a long robe reaching to the feet (Greek: ενδεδυμενον ποδηρη) and surrounded at the level of the nipples with a golden girdle." (Rev 1:13)

The Latin text reads "praecinctum ad mamillas zonam auream" in close reference to the ancient Greek word "μαστός" (mastós) used by John himself for breast, nipple or hill. This corresponds approximately to the height of the diaphragm separating the chest cavity from the abdominal cavity. The diaphragm is our main respiratory muscle. Heart activity and respiratory activity are the vital functions of humans. This is the centre of their viability. Here Budhi reveals itself as the life spirit within the human organism.

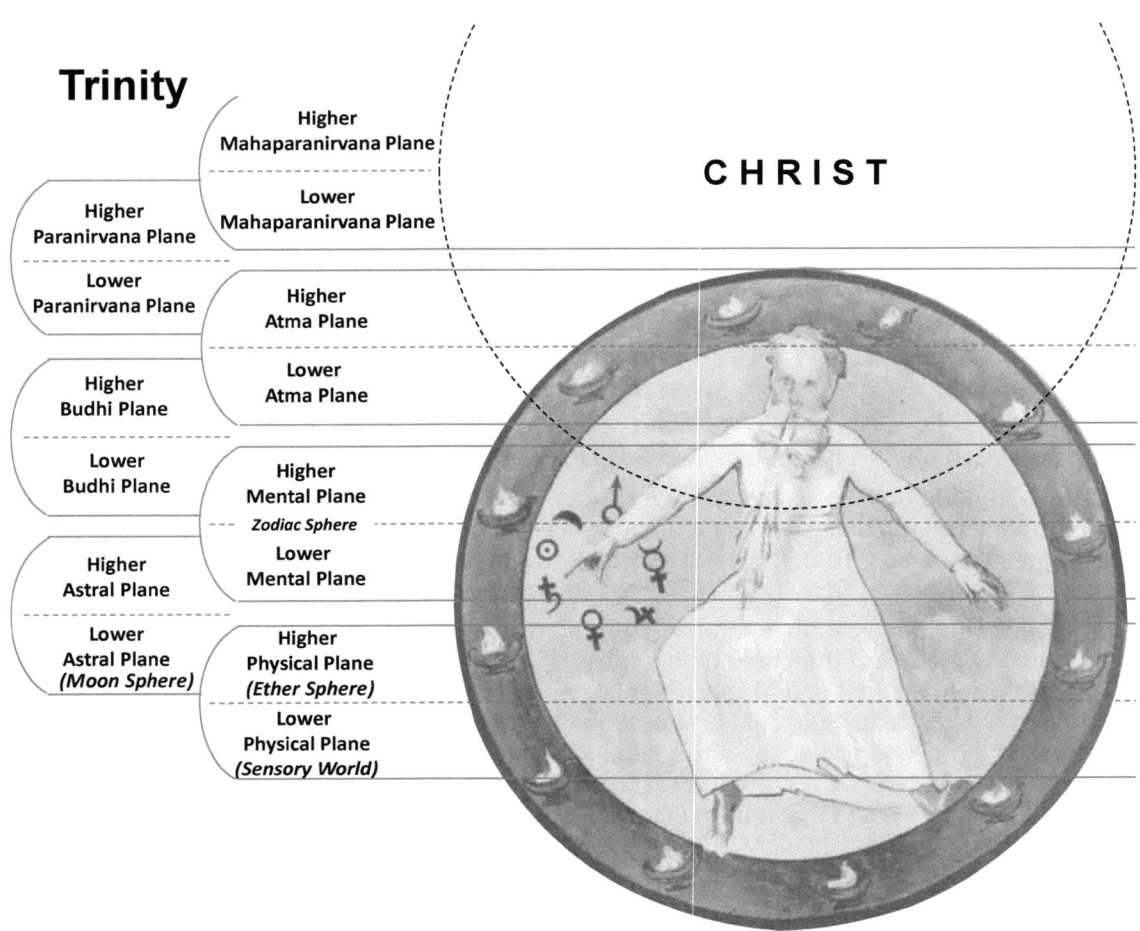

Figure 20: Imagination of the macrocosmic psycho-spiritual Human Being, painted by Clara Rettich according to Rudolf Steiner's instructions (GA 104)

The macrocosmic imagination of the Son of Man, pervaded by the Son of God, that is, the Psycho-Spiritual of John-Lazarus, is obviously structured in such a way that it becomes a likeness of the world planes. The snow-white hair reaches up to the higher Atma plane. The face shining like the sun with its fiery, flaming eyes is an expression of the higher Budhi plane. The double-edged sword reaches down to the hip and thus to the lower end of the spiritual world, that is as far as the World Word sounds through the spiritual world or Mental plane. Strictly speaking, it reaches as far as the genital region, in which the creative forces of the world are effective also. On the other hand, the golden girdle at the level of the nipples, at the transition between the thoracic cavity and the abdominal cavity, marks the Zodiac sphere as a dividing line between the higher and the lower Mental plane.

When a person lets his arms hang down, his hands reach to the middle of his thighs. If he bends his arms at his elbows or raises them to his sides, his hands come up to the level of his belly, which in John's vision corresponds to the lower spiritual world. There is the planetary plane below the Zodiac sphere. The macrocosmic Son of Man rules over this region, too. He works and acts there through the planetary forces.

"... and in his right hand he held seven stars." (Rev 1:16)

This refers to the seven wandering stars or planets, as the first seal of John's Apocalypse, painted according Rudolf Steiner's suggestion, shows. In Figure 20 it is inserted into the series of superimposed yet interpenetrating world planes. The fact that here the planets surround the hand somewhat spaciously may be due to the creativity of artificial representation. It cannot be derived from John's text. Closer would be the idea that the planets hover above his hand, since it is said that he held them in his hand. Nevertheless, also in the drawing of the seal the planets are clearly concentrated on the lower spiritual world as the planetary level, and World Word painted as the sword resounds through this region as the so-called harmony of the spheres.

The Christ Being himself is to be thought as floating behind and above the visionary figure. His highest three members are pervaded by the Trinity, whose bearer within the seven worlds he thereby is. With Budhi, his lowest member of being, the Christ protrudes to the lower limit of the higher spiritual world in order to create places of action in which the Budhi and the World Word can be expressed in a special way in the next lower regions, the Zodiac sphere as far as the spiritual world is concerned, and the Sun sphere as far as the soul world is concerned.

Regarding the two lowest world planes, the Ether sphere and the physical sensory world we do not find any particular details in the macrocosmic Imagination of John. This is not surprising since, according to Rudolf Steiner's words quoted above, the vision refers to the astral body and the I, that is, the psycho-spiritual part of man, which leaves the ether body and the physical body at night. The two lower levels in the seal, in which we find the thighs and lower legs of the Son of Man covered by the long garment, are precisely the home of the two last-mentioned bodies of man. Although in earthly life we tend to first of all identify with them, in the narrower sense they do not belong to the human being at all.

"When man walks around on earth, he actually calls his physical body and his etheric body – of which he does not know much, but at least feels it, insofar as he lives in the forces of growth and so on – he calls this his body. But man has no right to call this his body. For his is only what exists in the I and in the astral body, whereas what exists in the physical body and in the etheric body is the property of the divine-spiritual beings, even when man lives on Earth. The divine-spiritual beings live and weave in it, while man lives on Earth. They continue to work in it, these divine-spiritual beings, even when the human being is not present during sleep. Man would even suffer quite badly if he had to care for his etheric and physical bodies himself in a constant state of wakefulness between birth and death. The human being is forced, again and again ... to hand over his physical and etheric bodies to the gods. This is what ancient times of human development acknowledged by calling the human body, the human corporeality, a temple of the gods." [352]

The weaving and working of the beings who rightly call their own this temple of the gods is the subject of the second seal of the Apocalypse of John. This will be discussed in a separate chapter.

Below the lowest of the depicted world planes, below the visible earth-ground and thus in the interior of the Earth, we nonetheless find a surprising detail of the macrocosmic man, his feet. This expresses the close connection between the Psycho-Spiritual of man and the Psycho-Spiritual of the interior of the Earth. The upward development of man in the course of evolution causes an accompanying transformation of the psycho-spiritual parts of the interior of the Earth as well. To the physical senses it appears glowing-liquid, pervaded by glowing ores and metals. These, however, are only physical images of the psycho-spiritual powers of the planets, which the exalted Son of Man holds in his right hand: Saturn (lead), Jupiter (tin), Mars (iron), Sun (gold), Venus (copper), Mercury (mercury) and Moon (silver). [353] In John's vision, this is reflected in the interior of the Earth as a lower counter-image connected with the Earth's forces, the feet of the macrocosmic man, consisting of the molten ores of the planetary metals.

One of these metals plays a special role here. That is copper, the metal of Venus. For, the mission of mankind is to incorporate the divine love of the Budhi plane into the Earth. Since Budhi is the sixth member of the human being, it is in close relationship to the sixth region of the soul world, the Venus sphere. There man takes up the power of spiritual love in his astral body and his I. On Earth it is reflected in the Venus metal copper. Hence, John writes that the feet of the macrocosmic Son of Man, which reach into the interior of the Earth, look like "chalcolibano" (Greek χαλκολιβανω), a type of copper of whitish luster that was hardened by the addition of earth. In his times, such earth-hardened copper was produced in the Greek populated areas on the southern edge of the Black Sea. [354] John also sees it *"as if burned in a*

---

[352] GA 227 "Initiationserkenntnis" (Initiation knowledge), Penmaenmawr, Lecture of 28 August 1923

[353] See, for example, GA 312 "Geisteswissenschaft und Medizin" (Spiritual science and medicine), Dornach, Lecture of 26 March 1920

[354] In his Etymological Dictionary of the Greek language, the Italian linguist Bonavilla Aquilino gives the following explanation: *"Calcolibano, Chalcolibanus, Chalcolibane. (Stor. Nat.) From χαλκός, chalcos, copper, and from*

furnace", making it shine even whiter. In this way his vision reflects the white-shining face of the cosmic Son of Man with his fiery flaming eyes as an expression of the Budhi in the white-shining, fiery glowing feet made of the earth-hardened metal of Venus. Cosmic love is thus transformed into earthly love and connected to the Earth. Χαλκολιβανω is usually simply translated as bronze, brass, ore, polished ore or even gold ore. But the correct thing would be the translation:

"... and his feet were like white-shining, earth-hardened copper, as if burned in a furnace." (Rev 1:15)

In the course of this consideration, some readers may have got the impression that Johannes Lazarus simply projected the physical form of man from the Earth into the cosmos and thereby created an anthropomorphic image of a God-Man. But that is by no means the case. Precisely the reverse is the case. The human form is an Imagination which can be found in the spiritual world, and which together with the I of man descends into its lives on Earth.

"This [human form] is something thoroughly spiritual. It should cause a solemn mood to perceive a Spiritual with physical senses as a human form in the physical world. For the one who can see spiritually, this is such that he sees in the human form a real Imagination that has descended into the physical world." [355]

In the same sense Rudolf Steiner spoke on another occasion:

"And with the human being we already see the I. What we see there is not the physical body, exactly this is invisible; likewise the etheric body; likewise the astral body. What we see as the human being – outwardly formed, physically formed – is the I. Therefore, for example, to the perception of the eyes, to the visibility, the human being appears outwardly in his 'incarnate', in a colour that is not there otherwise, just as the I is not there otherwise in the other beings. So, if we want to express ourselves correctly, we would have to say: We can only fully grasp the human being if we think of him as consisting of physical body, ether body, astral body and I. What we see before us, is the I, and invisible within is the astral body, the ether body and the physical body." [356]

So, it is not an easy endeavour indeed to describe the human being in its entirety. We experience ourselves only in small aspects and in constant dependence on the sphere in which we live at the present. Only in the period of our greatest distance from the Earth, in the great midnight hour of existence between two incarnations, our gaze opens up to our entire being, which extends across numerous world levels and whose goal of development is to pervade itself with the Christ Being so that it may ascend to ever higher worlds in future planetary stages of development. In doing so, we should become more and more like Christ as our great macrocosmic example, and ultimately become as perfect as our heavenly Father, whose lowest member of being on the Atma plane corresponds to the level of perfection of humanity. We need His power too, which is transmitted to us through Christ, the Son.

It is of great importance that in the future man will increasingly learn to understand himself as truly a cosmic being, to whom life on Earth is a very special and extremely significant period of his life, but nevertheless only one among many others, which only all together make up an entire human life cycle. Now we understand a little better which incredible depth is hidden behind the simple words "Γνῶθι σεαυτόν" (Gnothi seauton) – "Know yourself", which were written at the Apollo Temple of Delphi, and how much the supposed self-knowledge of man is still in its beginnings today, since he tends to understand himself predominantly as a purely physical being.

How important instead a truthful recognition of the human being is for the near future already, was pointed out by Rudolf Steiner many times, for example also with his following clear words:

"It may seem complicated to many people what has to be said when we keep talking about the human being and its connection with the universe. Some people might say, there's so much about the human being! The mere fact that man is formed in a complicated way from the universe is just there and we have to come to terms with it. We must come to terms with this fact especially in the present time, because otherwise – this must be said – it could be too late. People are currently living in incarnations in which it is

---

Hebrew Laban, which means white. It is the name of a type of copper that the Mossineci, peoples of the Black Sea, made, which was very beautiful and white, similar to silver, without adding tin, only hardened with earth, as found in their country." Atti dell' Accad. Ital. Tom. I, f. 212 (Dizionario etimologico di tutti i vocaboli usati nelle scienze, arti e mestieri che traggono origine dal Greco, Milano, 1820)

[355] GA 26 "Anthroposophische Leitsätze" (Anthroposophical Leading Thoughts), Chapter "Erster Teil der Betrachtung: Was offenbart sich, wenn man in die vorigen Leben zwischen Tod und neuer Geburt zurückschaut" (First part of contemplation: What is revealed when one looks back into the previous lives between death and new birth), Goetheanum, at the turn of the year 1925

[356] GA 214 "Das Geheimnis der Trinität" (Mystery of the Trinity), Dornach, Lecture of 28 July 1922

just barely acceptable not to know much about the complicated human nature. But times will come – the human souls will be incarnated again in these times – when this will not be acceptable any longer. The souls will have to begin to know finally how man is connected to the universe." [357]

In this sense let us now pursue the further path of the cosmic, psycho-spiritual human being from the Budhi plane back to a new life on Earth.

---

[357] GA 170 "Das Rätsel des Menschen – die geistigen Hintergründe der menschlichen Geschichte" (The riddle of the human being – the spiritual background of human history), Dornach, Lecture of 7 August 1916

Experiences of the Soul in Winter – Return to Life on Earth

Turn Back in the Second Sphere of the World of the Life Spirit – 40th Week

When Christ was present in the earthly body of Jesus of Nazareth, he said about himself: *"I am the way, the truth and the life."* (John 14:6) In this self-description he states a total of four aspects of his being: The *"I am"* at the beginning of his statement as an indication of his intimate unity with the Father, the *"way"* to the Father through the Son, the *"truth"* as the revelation of the Son through the creative World Word, and *"life"* as an expression of the life spirit. All these may be experienced by the human being during his turning to the Budhi plane, provided that he prepared himself sufficiently for this in his preceding earthly life. At the midnight hour of existence, when the psycho-spiritual human being is in the highest regions of the world accessible to him, in the invisible depths of the universe, yet not in the physical depths of the world, but in the spiritual depths of the world, on the summit of his incarnation cycle, then he is intimately completely one with Christ, with Budhi, with the "I am". Here it is no longer something that could be distinguished from something else, but he simply is. Everything is one in love here. Then he can no longer say of himself "I am this or that", but he can only say of himself: I am, since I am one with the divine "I am". Rudolf Steiner told in this sense about Christ:

> *"We shouldn't think of any other Deity than of Christ in the one, who speaks to Moses about Himself: «I am the I-am.»"* [358]

The "I am" is the same one who reveals himself to the world as Budhi or as the creative World Word. For this reason, as Rudolf Steiner explains in another lecture, *"Budhi is called the «word», which means nothing else than: I am."* [359]

In the depths of the spirit-universe, when the human being, speaking figuratively, rests on the flaming heart of Christ, he is filled with the divine love-power of the Budhi or the fire-power of the World Word in his soul's grounds, that is in the innermost centre of his soul, in his I, for *"the soul has its centre in the «I»."* [360] It flows to him from the Budhi plane, the world of the Son, but its own origin is on the Atma plane, the world of the Father, according to the words of Christ: *"I and the Father are one."* (John 10:30). In this sense Christ as the World Word also said to one of his disciples: *"Do you not believe that I am in the Father and the Father is in me? The words that I say to you I do not speak on my own; but the Father who dwells in me does his works."* (John 14:9-10). Thus, the divine World Word and the divine love do not flow from a single world, but from two worlds: "out of the love-worlds of the heart" as Rudolf Steiner formulated using a plural in the 40th weekly verse, which he meaningfully starts with the words "I am" or "am I".

40th Week (5 - 11 January)	*40. Woche (5. – 11. Januar)*
And am I in the spirit-depths,	Und bin ich in den Geistestiefen,
Then, in my soul's deep grounds,	Erfüllt in meinen Seelengründen
Out of the love-worlds of the heart	Aus Herzens Liebewelten
All separate being's void delusion	Der Eigenheiten leerer Wahn
Fills with the World Word's firepower.	Sich mit des Weltenwortes Feuerkraft.

Even the I as the centre of the soul is Christ-imbued during the great midnight hour of existence, not only the three human soul powers of feeling, thinking and willing. We have already learned about the Christ-imbuement of the feeling from the words of the 38th weekly verse or Christmas verse, which starts with the words "I feel". We found the Christ-imbuement of the thinking characterized in the 39th weekly verse, which reveals to us that the human being is allowed to participate in the "World Being's light", whereby his thought power enhances into a true might of thinking or "thinking's might" in order to "wake up" at least his sense of self on the Budhi plane. But the Christ-imbuement of the human I is the subject of the present 40th weekly verse.

---

[358] GA 109 "Das Prinzip der spirituellen Ökonomie" (The principle of spiritual economy), Cologne, Lecture of 10 April 1909

[359] GA 94 „Kosmogonie" (Cosmogony), Munich, Lecture of 28 October 1906

[360] GA 9 "Theosophie", Chapter "Das Wesen des Menschen" (The essential nature of man), Section IV "Leib, Seele und Geist" (Body, Soul and Spirit)

As long as the human I has not been filled with Budhi, with the flaming divine love, which is also the firepower of the World Word, it has no share in the "I am", the eternal life of the Son and the divine primeval ground of the Father. Until then all selfhood, all separateness is just a void delusion. Again, Rudolf Steiner's words from his Theosophy, already quoted in another context, are confirmed here: *"For, the I receives essence and meaning from that with which it is connected."* [361] Only through the connection with the "I am" does the human I receive a share in divine life.

"Let us think of a power transferred to Earth that really brings to humanity the awareness that this «I am» can live in every single person, a power that makes it clear to man that God has sunk a drop of his substance into every person. This power would say: This «I am» is something that is within each of you, it is a part of the unique divine power. What you sense as your individual «I am» is one with the «I am» of the Father. Whoever of you has developed the awareness of this fact can say, «I and the Father are one.»" [362]

In the midnight hour of existence between two incarnations we can witness how our highest and most spiritual inner being, our true self, the "I am", is born out of the Father God through the Son. Here is the beginning of our "Ex deo nascimur", through which, in the course of the now beginning descent to a new life on Earth, the spirit-germs of our two densest bodies, a new physical body in the higher spiritual world and a new ether body in the lower spiritual world, are first built up for us, filled with the powers of the Father and the Son. [363]

In order to open for all humanity the possibility of ascension to the divine heights on the border between the higher spiritual world and the Budhi plane in the great midnight hour of existence and to be filled there with the flaming love-power of Budhi, Christ himself first had to prepare the way for us. He in fact is, as he says of Himself, also "the way" for the humans to their origin, to the Son and ultimately to the Father. Out of love for mankind, Christ descended to Earth in order to create a new type of man on the physical plane, a new Adam, capable of receiving the two highest members of the human being, Budhi and Atma, not only for three and a half days, as was the case with the pre-Christian initiations, but permanently. At the baptism on the Jordan River, Christ united himself as the "Son of God" with the body- and soul-members of Jesus of Nazareth as the Christ Jesus. By doing so, in a way unique throughout world's history, a Son of God resident on Earth for a longer period was begotten. The divine power of Budhi poured into the Nathanic soul-sheath of the primeval soul of mankind, which before its birth as the Nathan Jesus-boy, which was portrayed in the gospel of Luke, had never fully incarnated and therefore was not subject to the Fall of man. Only for preparation of his later incarnation, this being had undergone a connection with an earthly person as bearer of his soul powers as Krishna.

"Those powers are therein, which are the innermost powers of mankind. We can also call them the Krishna Powers, because we know their origin. What I characterized in the previous lecture as if without a root, this Krishna root reaches up to Lemurian times, to human primeval times. It was connected to mankind at a time before the physical development of mankind started. This root, these Krishna powers, which come together and unify in the Indeterminate, then caused the human inner being to unfold and develop from within. Concretely within a single being, this root is within the Luke Jesus-boy, grows up and remains effective under the surface of the existence after the Zarathusthra-soul entered this special human body. Then, in the moment described in the Bible as the baptism through John, that is, in the thirtieth year of this special human body, that which belongs but to all mankind draws near to this body. In the moment, which is marked by the voice: «This is my beloved Son, today I have begotten him», the Christ draws near to the physical from the other side." [364]

Not only the Son of God but also the Father and the Holy Spirit contributed to the procreation of the new Adam as a prototype of a man who bears within him Budhi and Atma, too. The three synoptic Gospels confirm to us the presence of the Father when Christ entered the body and soul of Jesus of Nazareth by telling us that at the baptism in the Jordan the words sounded down from heaven "This is" (Matt. 17:5) or respectively *"You are"* (Mark 1:11 and Luke 3:22) *"my beloved Son, in whom I am well pleased."* However, they merely state the Father as a witness to the creation of the new human prototype, the new Adam. Rudolf Steiner, on the other hand, in the above quotation gave us the Father's words sounding down from

---

[361] GA 9 "Theosophie", Chapter "Das Wesen des Menschen" (The essential nature of man), Section IV "Leib, Seele und Geist" (Body, Soul and Spirit)

[362] GA 100 "Menschheitsentwicklung und Christuserkenntnis" (Human development and understanding of Christ), Basel, Lecture of 25 November 1907

[363] For more information see from the 42nd weekly verse onwards.

[364] GA 146 "Die okkulten Grundlagen der Bhagavadgita" (The occult foundations of the Bhagavadgita), Helsingfors, Lecture of 3 June 1913

heaven as they were preserved in older Gospel manuscripts. Four years earlier he had already declared to his listeners in a lecture on the Gospel of Luke:

"«This is my beloved Son, today I have begotten him», this is the way it says in the older Gospel manuscripts, and so it should in truth be written in the Gospels (Luke 3:22)." [365]

The text variant of Luke 3:22 mentioned here and omitted in today's popular Gospel translations is confirmed in its existence by Gospel research. In a text-critical treatise on the Gospel of Luke, for example, Wieland Willker not only cites the corresponding Greek wording "εγώ σήμερον γεγεννηκα σε" together with the Latin translation "ego hodie genuit te", in English "today I have begotten you", but also lists a whole series of ancient authors as sources. [366]

In addition to the presence of the Father, in all four Gospels the presence of the Holy Spirit at the baptism in the Jordan is mentioned as a dove floating down from heaven. The Trinity was present and effective in its totality when Christ with his own being as the "I am" attached from above the "Son of God" [367], consisting of the three spiritual members Manas, Budhi and Atma as an expression of the divine Trinity, to the "Son of Man", the three bodily members and the soul sheath of the Nathan Jesus, in order to create a new Adam.

But besides the divine Trinity, a human being as an earthly intermediary also contributed to the mystery of God's becoming a human being. It was John the Baptist who performed the act of the baptism. He was the only one who recognized the influx of the Christ Being into the members of the Nathan Jesus as the "I am", as the bearer of the Logos and the Son of God. In John the Baptist lived the individuality of the ancient Adam, who was the first man to pass through the Fall, and so the ancient Adam contributed to the creation of the new Adam, the Christ Jesus. John was aware that he would be replaced by him, for later he told his disciples: *"He must increase, but I must decrease."* (John 30:3).

Presumably, however, at the baptism of Christ at the Jordan John did not yet suspect that after his decapitation that followed soon after, through a special initiation process in the course of the Raising of another disciple of Christ, Lazarus, he was intended to supplement that one into a complete human being by his own spiritual members of being in order to work from then on as a "Son of God" in Lazarus, the "Son of Man". With this double-being John Lazarus, the God-Man Christ Jesus created a first purely human likeness of the new Adam, that is, of Himself. After the Raising of Lazarus, John Lazarus also reached up from the physical body on Earth to Atma in the highest heavenly heights. Christ Jesus, who said of himself *"I am the way"*, apparently paved the way between God and man in two directions: on the one hand, the way from "the love-worlds of the heart" down to Earth through his own descent into Jesus of Nazareth, who was destined to go through the mystery of Golgotha, and on the other hand the way from earthly humanhood up to himself and the Father through John Lazarus, whom he appointed as his representative on earth (John 19:26-27). [368]

When from the cross, Christ Jesus gave John Lazarus to His mother as her new son, He acted like a father. At this time he already was about to go to the Father through death in order to transform the physical body by the Father Power in such a way that it could become the first precursor of Atma, the supreme member of the human being, which, however, will attain its perfect formation only in the far future, in the last planetary state, the Vulcan. Christ did not always function on Earth only as the Son of God, but often as a representative of the Father too, as he himself revealed to his disciples with the words already quoted: *"The one, who sees me, sees the Father."* (John 14:9) and *"But the Father who dwells in me, he does the works."* (John 14:10)

All the power to transform a physical body comes from the Father. Christ therefore called on the Father for the Raising of the dead Lazarus, who "had lain in the tomb four days already", as the evangelist

---

[365] GA 114 "Das Lukas-Evangelium" (The Gospel of Luke), Basel, Lecture of 21 September 1909

[366] Wieland Willker, "A Textual Commentary on the Greek Gospels – Vol. 3, Luke", Bremen, online published, 12th edition 2015. Willker states as sources inter alia Clement [of Alexandria] (Paed. I, 25, 2), the Gospel of the Ebionites (Epiphanius Panarion 30:13) and Justin (Dialogue with Trypho, 103.8). In addition he says: *"The words are also found in Didaskalia [apostolorum], Origen quotes them (Commentary on the Gospel of John, Book I, 32) as well as several other fathers: Methodius (Symp. 9), Lactantius (Div. Inst. IV, 15), [Aurelius] Augustine (Enchiridion 49), Faustus, Tyconius, Hilarius and Juvencus".* For the latter sources of the fathers, however, Willker makes the restriction: *"Not in all cases it is clear that they really quote from the Gospel of Luke."*

[367] GA 123 "Das Matthäus-Evangelium", (The Gospel of Matthew) Bern, Lecture of 11 September 1910 – see also the reflection on the 18th weekly verse.

[368] See also the preceding chapter "Christ and the Human Being".

expressly emphasized at the beginning of the Raising scene (John 11:17). Christ could revive or re-create an ether body through the power of Budhi or the Life Spirit by his own might. Hence he spoke to Martha: *"I am the resurrection and the life; he who believes in me, will live, though he has died. And whoever lives and believes in me shall not die in eternity."* (John 11:25-26) Everyone who believes in Christ and dies experiences the "In Christo morimur", he dies into Christ, into eternal life. Thus, he will *"not die in eternity"*. But in order to protect a physical body on Earth from decay after death, it additionally requires the willpower of the Father that works in the dead, lifeless material – for *"inwardly, the matter is will"* [369] – and is alone capable of stimulating the spiritual counter-image of the physical body, the Atma sufficiently. Christ therefore called on the Father for help in the Raising of Lazarus to preserve his physical body.

The writer of the Gospel expressly draws attention to this particular situation. Immediately before the Raising of Lazarus he points out for the second time that Lazarus was already four days in the tomb and thus even the time of the death-like initiation sleep of the ancient mysteries had passed: *"Then Martha, the sister of the deceased said to him [Christ]: «Lord, already there is a stench because he has been dead four days.»"* (John 11:39). Additionally, Lazarus John himself, as the Gospel's author, describes that immediately before his Raising Christ was *"deeply moved in the spirit"* or, according to another translation, *"groaned in the spirit"* (lat. fremuit spiritu). Furthermore, he was "grieved", "worried" or "full of inner excitement" (lat. turbavit se ipsum) until he even wept (John 11:33-35). This is also a clear indication that what happened there was by no means just one of the last initiations of the old kind, during which the one to be initiated was put into a deathlike sleep by loosening his ether body. What was going on here was that, which had shuddered the initiates of the last pre-Christian centuries more and more. For a long time they had foreseen that the ether body and the physical body would soon connect so closely with each other in the course of human development that the degree of loosening of the ether body necessary for the initiation process would inevitably result in the death of the person to be initiated and the ancient method of initiation would have to find its final end. This time had come. The ancient initiation resulted in death. The evangelist himself describes us the transition from a death-like initiation sleep to an actual death when he tells us that Christ Jesus first said: *"Our friend Lazarus sleeps, but I go to awake him out of sleep."* At first the disciples were reassured, for they replied: *"Lord, if he sleeps, he will recover."* But he had not spoken of sleep: *"However, Jesus spoke of his death, but they thought that He was speaking about taking rest in sleep."* And finally the real fact was revealed to them: *"Then Jesus said to them plainly, «Lazarus has died.»"* (John 11:11-14) So the evangelist John Lazarus obviously attached the greatest importance on not letting even the slightest doubt arise that at his extraordinary initiation he really had to be led to death, even if only for a short time. One could therefore say that Lazarus "tasted" death.

Only through the interaction of the powers of the Son with the powers of the Father could the person who had just died be recalled to life on Earth again. If Christ had only carried out an ancient initiation process here, he would certainly not have been "worried" and finally even wept. Something quite extraordinary took place here. Christ called on the Father inwardly for help. Only through the body-preserving Atmic power of the Father could the physical body of Lazarus, which was led to the point where the decomposition forces become effective, be renewed: *"So they took away the stone. And Jesus looked upward and said, «Father, I thank you for having heard me. I knew that you always hear me, but I have [also] said this [out loud] for the sake of the crowd standing here, so that they may believe that you sent me.» When he had said this, he shouted in a loud voice, «Lazarus, come out!»"* (John 11:41-43) Christ Jesus acted here not only of his own as the Son of God, but as the earthly representative of the Father, too.

Actually, the words "Lazarus died" and "Lazarus, come out" mentioned in the Gospel of John had already been spoken by the leaders of the ancient mystery schools at the former initiation processes. But in pre-Christian times they still carefully protected the one who was initiated from the real event of death. At the initiation and Raising of Lazarus through Christ Jesus, however, the words, which in pre-Christian times were spoken more symbolically or one could also say prophetically, became historical reality then. A human being was led near to death. But, the powers for revival and raising still had to come from outside. When Christ Jesus raised Lazarus, he acted from the outside like in pre-Christian times the leader of the mysteries did. Only at the mystery of Golgotha this power came from within the one, who himself went through death and overcame it. Thus, for the whole of humanity, instead of the former initiation by a second person from outside, the way for a possible self-initiation and self-raising from within was created for the first time, through the power of the Christ within and his intimate connection with the Father.

By means of the joint work of the Son and the Father at both the initiatory and corporeal Raising of Lazarus, the spirit-soul of John the Baptist, descending from the spiritual world to Lazarus, could bring not

---

[369] GA 291 "Das Wesen der Farben" (The essence of the colours), Dornach, Vortrag vom 05.12.1920

only the Budhi but also the highest member of being, Atma. John could never have done this on his own, for he was initiated only to Budhi, as Rudolf Steiner emphasizes: *"John had to develop up to Budhi in order to become able to comprehend what was revealed as the Christ Jesus."*[370] To this end, the initiation had to be extended as far as the border area between the powers of Budhi and the powers of Atma. Only in that way could this initiation encompass Budhi fully. And since Budhi is the flaming love, John Lazarus became the *"disciple whom the Lord loves"* and who rested at the breast of the Son, at his heart, the Budhi organ. In this way, this very special disciple was prepared so that, from the cross, in the last moments before Christ's own passage through the corporeal death and His return to the Father[371], He could give him to his mother (John 19:26), authorized by Himself as His representative on Earth, as "Son". This scene is very reminiscent of how, according to the tradition of that time, a father handed over his accepted newborn son to his mother.

Thus, by the cross stood John Lazarus as the Son's representative remaining on Earth and beside him the mother of Jesus (John 19:25). She also was a completely unique person. Like Christ Jesus and John Lazarus, she was a composite being. Her transformation to this special state had already taken place long before the Raising of Lazarus. At the same time when the Holy Spirit descended from heaven in communion with the Christ Being at the baptism in the Jordan, a different individuality descended upon the "Mother of Jesus", too. It was the highest female representative of the love-current in human history, the only one prepared to give birth to the future Budhi- and Christ-bearer, whose roots the evangelist Luke expressly leaded back to Adam and his origin directly from God (Luke 3:38). The mother of the Nathan Jesus-boy [372], long since deceased at the time of Christ's baptism at the Jordan, connected herself as a spirit-soul with the mother of the Solomon Jesus-boy [373], who still lived in her earthly body and who represents the wisdom-current in human evolution. In esoteric Christianity, the latter was therefore always called "Sophia" (Greek: wisdom). She was considered a representative of the purified astral body transformed into the spirit self or Manas. Thereby she was predestined to become, in connection with the "blessed", pure, Nathan Mary, the earthly representative of the power of the Holy Spirit, which works through Manas. Rudolf Steiner gave us a statement about the Mother of Jesus and the two other women standing next to her, which is quite in harmony with this.

"In Chapter 19:25 [of the Gospel of John] it says: *«But standing by the cross of Jesus were his mother, and his mother's sister, Mary the wife of Clopas, and Mary Magdalene.»* For understanding the Gospel, it is necessary to know who these three women are."[374]

Immediately after these words Rudolf Steiner wrote a list of the members of the human being on a blackboard, whereby he assigned each of the three women by the cross to one of the three soul-members of man in the following way.

Father	7. Spirit Man	
Son	6. Life Spirit, transformed Ether body	far future
Holy Spirit	5. Spirit Self, Consciousness Soul	Virgin Sophia, purified Consciousness Soul
	4. Intellectual Soul, Astral Soul	Mary, Clopas' wife
	3. Sentient Soul, Sentient Body	Mary Magdalene
	2. Ether Body	
	1. Physical Body	

---

[370] GA 94 "Kosmogonie" (Cosmogony), Munich, 28 October 1906

[371] *"Vater, in deine Hände übergebe ich meinen Geist:"* (Luke 23:46) – griech. παρατίθεμαι = übergebe ich, reiche ich dar, lege ich nieder

[372] The Mary of the Gospel of Luke (Luke 1:27), belonging to the Nathan line originating from David (Luke 3:23-31)

[373] The Mary of the Gospel of Matthew (Matthew 1:16), belonging to the Solomon linie originating from David (Matthew 1:6-16)

[374] GA 100 "Menschheitsentwicklung und Christuserkenntnis" (Human development and understanding of Christ), Basel, Lecture of 20 November 1907

Rudolf Steiner clearly emphasized here the intimate connection of the sentient body with the sentient soul as well as of the consciousness soul with the spirit self, which he so often mentioned. In addition, he marked the latter two as expressions of the Holy Spirit. Thus it becomes understandable why the Mother of Jesus was present among the disciples at the important events after the Resurrection, especially at the outpouring of the Holy Spirit on the first Pentecost.

But there is another connection to be taken into account. According to Rudolf Steiner, the mystery of Golgotha was a divine act of balancing the Fall of Adam and Eve in Paradise to which all subsequent humanity was subjected:

"So, what has happened through the mystery of Golgotha is a matter of the gods, through which a balance has been created to a Lucifer-matter. It is the only matter of the gods that has taken place before the eyes of humans." [375]

But if in paradise Adam and Eve were standing under the tree with the serpent, should we not suppose that under the cross with the Redeemer on Golgotha there also stood Adam and Eve, so that those two primal individualities, which led humanity through the Fall, were also present, filled with the deepest compassion and heartache, as witnesses when Christ accomplished the great balancing act to open the way out of that fall of sin for the whole humanity? – The situation at the Mystery of Golgotha, however, was exactly the opposite of the Fall in Paradise. In ancient Lemuria, the original soul of humanity, the soul of the Nathan Jesus, had been held back in the spirit world to save it from the Fall. Adam and Eve, on the other hand, stood bodily under the tree of Paradise. At the Crucifixion on Golgotha, in exactly the opposite way, the Nathan soul was present in the body at the cross, as the bearer of Christ. Adam (John the Baptist) instead was only spiritually present as the higher part of Lazarus. We hear the same about the Nathan Mary. Like Adam, she too was only spiritually present as the higher part of the Solomon Mary. Does this not suggest to us to assume a connection between her and the individuality of Eve, the primeval mother of humanity? – In any case, the Christians of earlier centuries felt so very clearly.

"In Eve one saw that state where the spiritual mankind became physical, and therefore also sinful. If mankind is to be brought up again to the Spiritual, and if the opposition is to be expressed to the woman who brought the Mortal into the world, then that which is to bring the Immortal back into mankind must be expressed in reverse; the name must be reversed. Therefore, the angel of God addresses Mary with the words «Ave (Hail), Mary!» – Eva (this is the way Eve is named in the German-speaking countries) becomes Ave. This reversal has a symbolic character. ... With this design of the word one sought by pronouncing the words to make man become aware of the occult fact that the physical and the spiritual world have reversed directions in their currents. That has a very deep meaning. Don't see anything arbitrary in it." [376]

Furthermore, Rudolf Steiner gave us the following two statements about the aforementioned connection between the two mothers of the two Jesus-boys:

"At the same moment when this baptism took place in the Jordan, the mother [of the Solomon Jesus-boy] also felt something like the end of her transformation. She felt – she was in her forty-fifth, forty-sixth year then – she felt all of a sudden as if pervaded by the soul of the mother already deceased, who was the mother of the [Nathan or Luke] Jesus-boy, who in his twelfth year had received the I of Zarathustra. Just as the Christ-Spirit had descended upon Jesus of Nazareth, so had the spirit of the other mother, who was now in the spiritual world, descended upon the foster mother with whom Jesus had that conversation. Since then, she felt like that young mother who once gave birth to the Luke Jesus-boy." [377]

"Then the immortal aspect of the original mother of the Nathan Jesus descended again, and transformed the mother who was received into the house of the Nathan Joseph, and made her virgin again, so that the soul of that mother who Jesus had lost is given back to him at the baptism by John. This mother, who has remained with him, thus contains in herself the soul of his original mother, who in the Bible is called the Blessed Mary (Luke 1:28)." [378]

[375] GA 143 "Erfahrungen des Übersinnlichen – Die drei Wege der Seele zu Christus" (Experiences of the extrasensory – The three paths of the soul to Christ), Munich, Lecture of 16 May 1912

[376] GA 101 "Mythen und Sagen – Okkulte Zeichen und Symbole" (Myths and legends – Occult signs and symbols), Cologne, Lecture of 27 December 1907

[377] GA 148 "Aus der Akasha-Forschung – Das fünfte Evangelium" (From Akasha-Research – the Fifth Gospel), Kristiania (Oslo), Lecture of 6 October 1913

[378] GA 114 "Das Lukas-Evangelium" (Gospel of Luke), Basel, Lecture of 19 September 1909

In communion both women are the "mother of Jesus". So, by the cross stood John Lazarus as the future representative of the Son and next to him the "Mother of Jesus" or Mary Sophia, as the future representative of the Holy Spirit. The Father himself, however, could not be represented by a human being, but only by the divine Christ, his Son, for *"No one knows the Father except the Son."* (Matthew 11:27) and *"He who sees me sees the Father."* (John 14:9) The three double beings Mary Sophia, John Lazarus, and Christ Jesus, in each of which a "Son of God" part was united with a "Son of Man" part – in Christ Jesus even directly a God with a human – were particularly closely connected to one of the three main events of Christ's life and underwent their greatest transformations then. The conjunction of the two Jesus mothers into the double being of Mary Sophia was accomplished according to Rudolf Steiner's words quoted above *"at the same moment when this baptism took place in the Jordan"* and immediately afterwards we find them mentioned with the profound name "Mother of Jesus" in the context of the wedding at Cana which took place a few days later – at least according the Gospel of John. The creation of John Lazarus took place through the so-called "Raising of Lazarus", which is described right in the middle of the Gospel of John. After his transformation he bears the new name "the disciple whom Jesus loved". And Christ Jesus himself is intimately connected with the events given at the end of the Gospel, with the mystery of Golgotha, of course, from which he emerges completely transformed in his Resurrection body as "the one risen from the dead".

Christianity on Earth commemorates the first of these events, the baptism on the Jordan, in which Christ entered the bodily and spiritual members of Jesus of Nazareth as the divine "I am", at Epiphany, on January 6, or at least in temporal proximity to it and thus certainly not coincidentally just at that time of the year, when the heavenly fulfillment of the human I in the depths of the soul with the World Word's firepower, the "I am", the Budhi or eternal life, at the time of the midnight hour of existence between two incarnations, has its reflection in the nature mood because it is the time, in which the Earth is also being filled with fresh life forces for a new vegetation year. Possibly the baptism in the Jordan took place on January 6 of the year 30 A.D., which was a Friday. In this case, the event would be clearly related to Good Friday not only in terms of content, but also with regard to the day of the week. The Gospel of John points to this connection by mentioning another significant event that took place "on the third day". If one counts the day of baptism as the first day (just as Good Friday is counted as the first of three days), the third day after the baptism was a Sunday. *"And on the third day there was a wedding in Cana of Galilee, and the mother of Jesus was there."* (John 2:1). In the same chapter John tells us a profound statement of the Christ Jesus during a conversation with the Jews: *"Destroy this temple and in three days I will raise it up."* (John 2:19) The baptism on the Jordan and the wedding at Cana are therefore clearly linked by the evangelist himself to the events of the historic Good Friday and Easter Sunday, at which the Mother of Jesus was present again.

At the baptism on the Jordan River, the double being Christ Jesus experienced its procreation with the entry of the Christ-Spirit into the body and soul of Jesus of Nazareth. Through the death on the cross on the historic Good Friday, His birth into the Earth took place. At the same time, the souls of all human beings experienced their "baptism" by Christ entering into them. As the "bridegroom" he married at this great humanity-wedding the threefold soul and the I of every human being on Earth, which have their external representatives in the "three Mary's" and in John Lazarus. They stood together by the cross as the direct witnesses of the mystery of Golgotha. These two Friday-events, the baptism on the Jordan by John the Baptist and the event on Golgotha are therefore closely connected. In both cases, a birth of the divine I took place in the human being, at the baptism on the Jordan first in preparation in a single human only, in the Jesus of Nazareth, and finally on Golgotha in all humans.

"On Friday, April 3 of the year 33, at three o'clock in the afternoon, the mystery of Golgotha took place. And there also took place the b i r t h o f t h e I in the sense that we have often characterized it. And it does not matter on which point on earth a person lives or which religion he belongs to. What came into the world through the mystery of Golgotha applies to all people." [379]

Return to the First Sphere of the World of the Life Spirit – 41st Week

In the preceding chapters it has already been pointed out that the four weekly verses, which allow us to participate in experiences that are achievable for a human spirit-soul on the summit between two incarnations in the lower area of the Budhi plane, are dedicated to the fulfillment of the three soul powers of

---

[379] GA 143 "Erfahrungen des Übersinnlichen – Die drei Wege der Seele zu Christus" (Experiences of the extrasensory – The three paths of the soul to Christ), Cologne, Lecture of 7 May 1912

feeling, thinking and willing as well as of the I with the power of Budhi, that is their Christ-imbuement, which takes place there. The feeling's Christ-imbuement feeling is the subject of the 38th or Christmas verse. The thinking's Christ-imbuement is described in the 39th weekly verse and that of the I in the 40th weekly verse. The Christ-imbuement of the will is still missing. This is of special importance for the further development of man after the great midnight hour of existence, since he must be inflamed with the impulse to make the human ideal of the religion of the gods, which he was allowed to behold, now become more and more reality through corresponding deeds in the course of the Earth's evolution.

"Thus, as a goal, as the highest ideal, as the religion of the gods, an image of Mankind is contemplated by the gods. And as if on the distant shore of divine existence there floats before the gods the temple, which presents the likeness of divine existence in the image of Man as the highest artistic achievement of the gods. ...

Yonder it is so, that when one has passed the time of the middle between death and a new birth, which still has to be characterized more, when one has passed what I called the midnight hour in my last mystery drama «The Souls' Awakening», that then first there is a certain dullness with regard also to the willing and feeling in view of what stands like a wonderful temple in the far away times. Then divine powers heat and warm our inner soul faculties. It is a teaching that speaks directly to our inner being and that expresses itself in such a way that we gain more and more the ability to really want to go the way towards what we see as an ideal. In physical life we may face a teacher or an educator, and he may face us, and yet we basically feel that he speaks from the outside into our hearts. Here, instead, we feel that our spiritual educators of the higher Hierarchies, by educating us as I have just described, make their own forces flow directly into our inner being. Earthly educators speak to us. Spiritual educators in life between death and a new birth give us their life into our souls by educating us religiously in a spiritual way. And so we feel them more and more within us, these educators of the higher Hierarchies. So we feel ourselves more and more intimately connected with them. But thereby our inner life becomes stronger, gains strength. You are more and more accepted by the gods, more and more the gods live within you, and they help you to become stronger and stronger inwardly! This is what occurs as a basic feeling throughout this life between death and a new birth, especially in its second half." [380]

Here it becomes clear that with the influx of Budhi also forces of the Atma plane are already flowing into the human spirit-soul, for the will is an expression of the Father's power in Creation. Therefore, in Gethsemane, Christ prayed to his Father: *"Not my will but yours be done."* (Luke 22:42) and he also taught his disciples to pray: *"Our Father in heaven... Thy will be done on earth as it is in heaven."* (Matthew 6:9-10). But the Father works through the Son, as Christ himself showed us. The Son accomplishes the Father's will. Above all, Christ carries the divine love into Creation, the flaming love-power of Budhi. From these two together, the aspiration to transform the divine powers of will and love into deeds and works arises in man. For this end, the human spirit-soul, before it leaves the Budhi plane, is gifted with a great creative power, and an extraordinarily intense zest for action awakens in it. It yearns for self-activity, for the implementation of all with which it has been fulfilled in the innermost ground of its heart during its rest at the heart of Christ and its oneness with God on the Budhi plane. To become an instrument of the divine will and the divine love is the aspiration that lives up in the human soul before it leaves the Budhi plane. For this purpose, it is endowed with the necessary powers by beings of the higher Hierarchies. With what wonderful words Rudolf Steiner expresses this experience in his 41st weekly verse:

41st Week (12 - 18 January)	*41. Woche (12. – 18. Januar)*
The soul's creative power	Der Seele Schaffensmacht,
Strives from the heart's deep ground	Sie strebet aus dem Herzensgrunde,
In order to inflame the forces of the Gods	Im Menschenleben Götterkräfte
To right activity in human life,	Zu rechtem Wirken zu entflammen,
To shape itself	Sich selber zu gestalten
In human love and human work.	In Menschenliebe und im Menschenwerke.

By acting according to the divine will and in divine love, man transforms himself, through the karmic retroactive effects of his deeds, more and more into that likeness of the Son of God which he was destined to become from the first day of his creation. In a similar way as Christ once spoke of himself, *"I and the Father are one"* (John 10:30) and *"But the Father who dwells in me does his works."* (John 14:10), we as

---

[380] GA 153 "Inneres Wesen des Menschen und Leben zwischen Tod und neuer Geburt" (Inner nature of man and life between death and new birth), Vienna, Lecture of 10 April 1914

well, in all that we do, should once be able to speak like Paul: "But now no longer I live, but Christ lives in me" (Galatians 2:20) and no longer I act, but the Christ in me. – Nowhere else does man see his final state, the Omega of his own development, so clearly before him as here, at the place of his origin, at his Alpha, from where he once started and where he returns again and again after each of his numerous incarnations in order to become invigorated for his next upcoming developmental tasks and to align himself in his innermost goals with God's will and with divine love.

Rudolf Steiner again points to the heart as the Budhi organ. It is the central organ of the human blood circulation and capable of distributing not only willpower but also the forces of life and love throughout the whole organism. They are cosmic forces that originate on the Budhi plane and in even higher worlds. Christ Himself brought them down to Earth at his baptism in the Jordan and made them flow into a human body. In an immeasurable sacrificial act he finally made them accessible to the whole Earth and to all humanity, so that it may reach its predetermined goal of transforming the Earth into a cosmos of love.

"This cosmic, universal love-power, where did it live on earth first? In the blood that pulsed through the body of Jesus of Nazareth. This blood was really the Christ's physical field of action. The three bodies, the physical, etheric and astral bodies, were taken over by him from Jesus of Nazareth. The blood was completely his own, completely pulsed by his spirit, by the fire of his cosmic, universal power of love. This blood sacrificed itself to the Earth and to all human beings on earth. This blood lives further ethereally in the Earth's atmosphere. This blood-fire has an effect on all people who are willing to take it in, who strive for it, who seek it. Body and soul and spirit of man should gradually take it in. Man's children, his insights, his knowledge, shall be inflamed by this fire and turn him into the one who gives birth to the deeds which realize the Earth's progress. The lower, desire-saturated blood fire will die. The Higher, the Christ in man, will rise in this fire of light. There was no light yet on [ancient] Saturn, it was black; light shone in on the Sun, becoming glowing, yellow. There wasn't red blood on the Moon yet. Red blood could not exist yet. The Moon's light of wisdom was illuminated by wisdom, was white-silvery, as today's moonlight shimmering on a surface of water. On Earth, the I that radiates into the red blood with love-fire is the bearer of man's wisdomful findings by which he is to be led to his earthly deeds. He will recognize the effects of the Sun and the Moon, the proper relationship of the Earth and the people of the Earth to them. The fire of his I will pervade everything. He will oversee discerningly the path of his becoming. In a wisdomful look back at the past he will behold how he is the work of gods. In a love-saturated foresight of the future he will recognize himself as an instrument of the gods in all his members of being that are glowing in the Christ-fire, the I, the astral, ether and physical body." [381]

The earth development's actual mission of bringing love and morality into Creation started with the baptism on the Jordan, when Christ first connected Budhi as the power of divine love and Atma as the Father-God's will for good, for moral action[382], with a human bearer, with the psycho-physical members of Jesus of Nazareth. All former development on Earth was a repetition of previous planetary developments and preparation for the great turning point in the history of the Earth and humanity. For this, red blood had to be developed first as a bearer of the human I and the will forces closely connected with it.

"We could not yet speak of morality during the development of the Moon, for with respect to what man did he was still involved in a necessity there, almost in a necessity of nature. Morality begins on Earth. And it will reach its perfection in the development of Vulcan, when everything that pulsates in the blood's fiery processes will be the purified I, the I purified by morality, the I completely seized by morality: when man's forces of his I and his moral forces will be one and the same, and when his blood, that is his blood heat – because the material is only the outer sign – when his blood heat will be the sacred fire of Vulcan." [383]

Man is created in the image of God and, as a child of God, is destined to develop the divinity planted in him. But since God is so far superior to man, a very long way has to be walked to this end. Not only the three human soul powers and the I are to be inflamed with the Christ fire and the Father will, as it happens on the Budhi plane at the time of the great midnight hour of existence. Also the bodily members of the human being, his physical body, his ether body, his astral body, and his I-bearer or I-body are to be imbued

---

[381] GA 266a "Aus den Inhalten der esoterischen Stunden" (From the contents of the esoteric lessons), Volume I, Berlin, esoteric lesson of 14 March 1908

[382] When Christ was addressed with "good master", he rebuked it and expressed his concern: *"Why do you call me good? No one is good but God alone."* (Luke 18:19 and Mark 10:18) In the Greek text the word for God is "Theos", the same word that John used in the prologue of his gospel for the Father, different from the "Logos", the Word or the Son.

[383] GA 170 "Das Rätsel des Menschen – die geistigen Hintergründe der menschlichen Geschichte" (The riddle of the human being – the spiritual background of human history), Dornach, Lecture of 5 August 1916, last paragraph

with Christ. In the further course, the required reorganisation and higher development of these members of being is the further task of the human spirit-soul, which is increasingly yearning for a new embodiment.

But before the individual steps towards the formation of new human corporealities, the further course of the "Ex deo nascimur", will be considered more closely, it seems appropriate, at the threshold from the Budhi plane to the higher spiritual world, to take a closer look at the way in which the great midnight hour of existence as a part and the supreme turning point of a human incarnation cycle finds its earthly reflection in the annual rhythm of nature.

Reflections of the Human Incarnation Cycle in the Annual Rhythm of Nature

As can be seen from previous considerations, the entire human incarnation cycle is reflected in nature's course of the year exactly in the sense of Goethe's insight: "*All that is transient is but a likeness.*" From this view, some readers may be surprised why Rudolf Steiner in his Soul Calendar does not let the four main axes of the human incarnation cycle coincide with the solstices and equinoxes of the year, but shifted them by two weeks. Would it not have been expected that in the winter half-year the great midnight hour of existence coincides with the winter solstice on December 21/22 of a year or at least on the following Christmas and in the summer half-year with the summer solstice around June 21 or at least on St. John's Eve on June 24 as a mirror image to Christmas Eve on December 24? And would it not have been more appropriate that the Easter saying as the first weekly verse would begin on the spring equinox around March 20, at the time when the Sun enters Aries, the sign of the Lamb? Such questions are quite justified. Some may like to add the further question: If the Sun represents the I of the human being or his Psycho-Spiritual in general, because the Sun sphere is the highest region of the soul world and at the same time the gateway to the spiritual world, would not have been expected that Rudolf Steiner would have made the annual ascent and descent of the Sun with the associated changes in the light conditions and the resulting natural moods on Earth the basis for his descriptions of the human life cycle in the Soul Calendar? After all, all our sensory perceptions of the physical outside world are ultimately experiences of the soul. This would result in a division of the Soul Calendar in two parts by the equinoxes, too, since we are more emotionally turned towards the outside world in the summer half of the year and retreat more into our inner being in the winter half of the year.

Surely no one would take offence if Rudolf Steiner had made such a decision. The weekly verses would then follow the scheme shown in Figure 21. In this case, the darkest or longest night of the year at the winter solstice would have been perfect for the great midnight hour of existence. But, Rudolf Steiner must obviously have had an important reason for not directly following the changes of the physically perceptible sunlight in the course of the year. The reason may be that although we remember two important historical events according to this scheme, both relate mainly to the physical world. Shortly after the winter solstice, on Christmas Eve, we commemorate the physical-bodily birth of the baby Jesus and commemorate all the events on Earth at that time: the count in Palestine, the journey of Mary and Joseph to Bethlehem, the search for a hostel in the cold night, the birth in the warm rock grotto, the shepherds in the field, the angels who spoke to them. The grateful gaze of our soul is directed primarily to the physical-earthly events. The same applies to St. John's Eve. On June 24 we commemorate the physical birth of John the Baptist, who is closely related to the Jesus-child, is so intimately connected to his fate and, as the Gospel of Luke tells us, was conceived and born six months before the baby Jesus (Luke 1:26 and 1:36). In short, above all, we are commemorating the physical-sensory-bodily preparations for the following events changing humanity and the world, from the baptism at the Jordan to the Mystery of Golgotha.

Nevertheless, it would be wrong to claim that Rudolf Steiner's Soul Calendar was not based on the sense-perceptible, physical changes of nature in the course of the year; for in his preface to the first edition in 1912 he wrote:

"The human being feels connected to the world and its change of times. He feels his own being as a likeness of the world-archetype. But the likeness is not a symbolic-pedantic imitation of the archetype. What the great world reveals in the course of time corresponds to a pendulum beating of the human being, which does not run in the element of time. In fact, man can feel his being, insofar as it is devoted to the senses and their perceptions, as corresponding to the summer nature interwoven with light and warmth. The foundation in himself and the life in his own world of thoughts and will impulses he can sense as a winter existence. Thus, in him, the rhythm of outer and inner life becomes what nature presents in temporal alternation as summer and winter. But great secrets of existence may be revealed to him if he relates his timeless rhythm of perception and thought in a corresponding manner to the time-rhythm of nature. In this

way, the year becomes the archetype of human soul activity and thus a fruitful source of true self-recognition. In the following Soul-Year-Calendar, the human spirit is thought of in such a position in which he can s e n s e his own soul-weaving on the seasonal moods from week to week in the image on the impressions of the course of the year. It is meant a f e e l i n g self-recognition. This feeling self-recognition can experience the cycle of the soul-life as timeless on the time by the given characteristic weekly sentences."

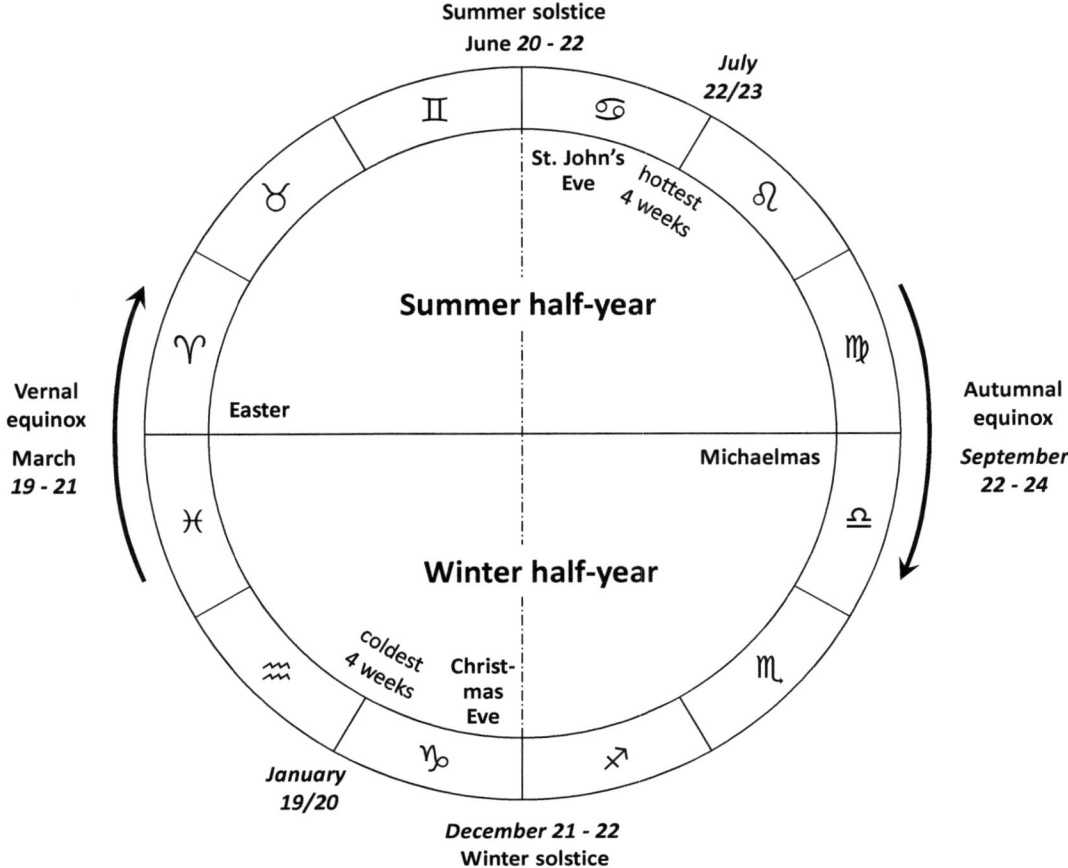

Figure 21: Annual rhythm of light and heat conditions due to the course of the Sun

Right in the first three sentences Rudolf Steiner unmistakably points out that the human being was created as a *"likeness of the world-archetype"* and can also feel himself in this way, but not in a *"sensory-pedantical"* sense, rather that something extrasensory or even extratemporal of the human being is expressed in the temporal rhythm of nature, i.e. something that extends from the realm of the soul, which is still marked by temporal experience, up to the realm of the spiritual-divine, which belongs to the region of timelessness or duration: *"But the likeness is not a sensory-pedantic imitation of the archetype. What the great world reveals in the course of time corresponds to a pendulum beating of the human being, which does not run in the element of time."* This pendulum stroke of the human being, which towers beyond everything temporal, is the life or incarnation cycle of man. The weekly verses are therefore not aimed to help us recognize nature's Psycho-Spiritual immediately, but first the Psycho-Spiritual of the human being itself, which was created according to the world archetype and can therefore reflect itself in nature, can experience and sense itself on it. Therefore, in the spring quarter, there is no sprouting and shooting in the weekly verses as one might expect, but completely unexpectedly in the winter quarter, when the "ex deo nascimur" of the human being is reflected in the external natural mood. In the first instance, the weekly verses of the Soul Calendar are not about recognition of nature, but about self-recognition. Rudolf Steiner attaches great importance to this: *"It is meant as a self-recognition through f e e l i n g . This feeling self-recognition can experience the cycle of the soul-life as a timeless one on the time by the given characteristic weekly sentences."*

And what is it in nature that the human being should sense as the "world-archetype" according to which his own being was created as a likeness? In the weekly verses we will look in vain for references to the

206

variety of solid forms in nature. Nor will we find any relation to the flowing water. Even the word air does not appear anywhere. Instead, our attention is drawn to light and heat repeatedly, to the imponderable, weightless, which is not subject to the earthly heaviness. Even if one of the weekly verses speaks of "the mists' dull veils" [384], that is of moist air, the focus there is clearly on its dimming effect on the light.

In his preface Rudolf Steiner speaks clearly and distinctly of the soul being of man devoted to the physical sensory perceptions of light and warmth. All other phenomena of earthly nature are ignored. And even the light and warmth of the outside world are taken into consideration only with regard to the human soul experiences in the summer half-year: *In fact, man can feel his being, insofar as it is devoted to the senses and their perceptions, as corresponding to the summer nature interwoven with light and warmth."* With regard to the human soul experiences in the winter months, however, Rudolf Steiner points to the inner life of man: *The foundation in himself and the life in his own world of thoughts and will impulses he can sense as a winter existence. Thus, in him, the rhythm of outer and inner life becomes what nature presents in temporal alternation as summer and winter."* This is consistently implemented in the weekly verses insofar as the external light and warmth perceptible to the sensory organs is only mentioned in the summer half-year, whereas regarding the winter half-year is talk of the inner light as an expression of one's *"own world of thoughts"* and the internal warmth as an expression of one's *"own world of will impulses"*.

Presumably, the early anthroposophists around Rudolf Steiner soon also asked the question posed at the outset: If the Soul Calendar with its weekly verses follows nature's *"temporal alternation as summer and winter"*, why does it not coincide with the great turning points in the Sun's path? These or similar questions might have been the reason why Rudolf Steiner undertook the effort to write and prefix a second preface to the weekly verses in connection with the Soul Calendar's new edition in 1918. There he leads the reader's attention in a slightly different direction. He no longer speaks of physical sensory perceptions such as light and warmth at all, but the central subject of the second preface is something extrasensory: l i f e .

"The course of the year has its own life. The human soul can sense this life. If the soul allows to be effected by what speaks variously out of the life of the year from week to week, then only it will really find itself through such participation. It will feel how forces will be growing up by that, which strengthen it from within. It will notice that these forces want to be awakened in it by the share the soul can take in the meaning of the course of the world as it takes place in the sequence of times. Only by that it will become aware of the fine but meaningful threads of connection, which exist between itself and the world into which it was born. For each week, in this calendar a verse of such kind is inscribed, which inspires the soul to witness what is going on in this week as a part of the entire life of a year. What this life causes to resound in the soul, when the soul unites with it, is intended to be expressed in the verse. It is thought of a healthy «feeling at one» with the course of nature and a powerful «finding oneself» arising from it, in the belief that sympathizing with the world's course in the sense of such verses is something the soul yearns for, if it rightly understands itself."

Three times in a row Rudolf Steiner refers to life in the first three sentences, to something etheric, something extrasensory. During the summer half-year, the stimulation of the human soul should certainly also take place through sensory perceptions such as light and warmth – at least according to the content of the first preface, which surely still applies –, but it is much more the seasonal changes of life in nature which the human soul is called upon to sympathize with through the weekly verses. At the same time, however, this also means a turning of the human soul life to that might which exists behind all life and says of itself: *"I am the resurrection and the life."* (John 11:25). The immersion in the weekly verses of the Soul Calendar is obviously to bring about a turn of the soul towards the activity of Christ in the ether or life sphere of the Earth during the course of the year. Thus the anthroposophical Soul Calendar becomes a very valuable tool for preparation of the human being for the encounter with the etheric Christ exactly in the sense of the answer that Rudolf Steiner once gave to Friedrich Rittelmeyer's question:

"To my [Rittelmeyer's] question, what could be done to prepare for Damascus-like Christ-events, he replied: This is only possible when one experiences Christ in the course of the year." [385]

The sun radiates light, warmth and l i f e to the Earth. In the course of the year, however, we do not find the peak of warmth at the same time as the peak of light at the summer solstice. The warmest or hottest weeks in the temperate latitudes of the northern hemisphere usually are in the months of July and August, despite the annual fluctuations. In the middle of this period the transition of the Sun from Cancer to Leo is going on, four weeks after the summer solstice. Correspondingly, the coldest weeks of the year in the same

---

[384] See 23rd weekly verse.

[385] See notes 142 and 143 (pages 77 and 78) – For more details, see the "Introduction" at the beginning of this book.

geographical latitudes are in the months of January and February, approximately divided in two halves by the Sun's sign-transition from Capricorn to Aquarius four weeks after the winter solstice (see Figure 21). So if we do not choose the annual rhythm of sunlight as a likeness of the life or incarnation cycle of man, but the annual rhythm of heat instead, we would according to nature feel the great midnight hour of existence not to be connected with December 21/22, but with January 19/20. Interestingly, both dates are of particular importance in the Soul Calendar, since they mark the beginning and the end of the experiences on the Budhi plane (see the 38th weekly or Christmas verse from December 22 and the 41st weekly verse which lasts until January 18).

But when, on the one hand, the rhythm of light in the course of the year reaches its highest and lowest points at the summer and winter solstice, that is with the transition of the Sun from Gemini to Cancer or, respectively, from Sagittarius to Capricorn, and, on the other hand, the rhythm of heat in the course of the year reaches its highest and lowest points four weeks later, when the sun leaves Cancer or Capricorn and moves to the next signs, wouldn't it be possible that Life as an independent phenomenon has its own highs and lows in the course of the year, which could well be exactly in between, namely when the Sun passes through the middle of the sign of Cancer or, respectively, the middle of the sign of Capricorn? The first sentence of the second preface to the Soul Calendar "The course of the year has its own life" would thus have yet another meaning. The greatest influx of life would then happen in winter together with the great midnight hour of existence on January 5/6, on Epiphany, when we commemorate Christ's baptism on the Jordan and his descent as the Spirit of all life, as Budhi or Life Spirit, to the Earth.

From this point of view it becomes understandable why the main axes of the Soul Calendar are shifted by exactly two weeks in relation to the Sun's annual path and yet the weekly verses are based on the feeling experience of nature, but precisely on the processes in the sphere of life or ether. The annual cycle of life in nature thus becomes a likeness of the human incarnation cycle, which encompasses the successive states of life not only of the earthly person but also of the actual, macrocosmic human being in the higher worlds. Hence Rudolf Steiner's statement in his second preface: "*The human soul can sense this life. If the soul allows to be effected by what speaks variously out of the life of the year from week to week, then only it will really find itself through such participation.*" And since the feeling experience in the course of the year turns in two directions, outwards in summer and inwards in winter, the human soul can feel its entire life cycle twice within one year, at one time following more the Spiritual behind the outer sensory world and at the other time following more the Spiritual behind its own inner being, once moving outwards together with the Earth's soul into the distance and once withdrawing with the Earth's soul into its inner being. But this life cycle of man goes far beyond everything temporal on both occasions: "*What the great world reveals in the course of time corresponds to a pendulum stroke of the human being that does not take place in the elements of time. ... This feeling self-recognition can experience the cycle of the soul-life as a timeless one on the time by the given characteristic weekly sentences.*"

The ideas set out here lead to another question: When the entire life cycle of the human being is reflected on the one hand in the rhythm of light and warmth of nature, as it results from the sensory perceptions in the physical world, but on the other hand is also expressed in the rhythm of life on Earth, in those natural moods which are revealed from the Earth's already extrasensory processes of the life or ether sphere, could it then be possible, that there is a third likeness of the human incarnation cycle, which is based on forces beyond the ether sphere of the Earth, on those from even higher worlds, such as the psycho-spiritual forces of the macrocosm, which are at home in the planetary spheres or even in the starry sky or in other words: in the soul world and the lower spiritual world?

In fact, in his lectures in Penmaenmawr, Great Britain, in August 1923, Rudolf Steiner looked at the human incarnation cycle also from this perspective. Then he made statements which at a first glance seem incompatible with many of his already quoted words, for example:

"*In the epoch in which we live at present, through the action of the world forces it is only possible for the human being to circle through the Mars region completely, so that after death he completes the Mars circle and cannot yet completely enter the Jupiter region, but can only touch it. Only in the course of the further experiences between death and a new birth he will become able to fully enter the Jupiter region and even later the Saturn region. But for the purpose that man, since he cannot yet enter the Jupiter region, nevertheless has a share in the forces of Jupiter and Saturn during the time between his death and a new birth, there are interspersed between Mars and Jupiter the many asteroids, which are discovered again and again in their outer existence by the astronomers, but which are that region which man also passes after death with regard to the Spiritual, because he cannot yet reach Jupiter. And these asteroids have the peculiarity of being colonies of Jupiter and Saturn in their spiritual beings. Beings of Jupiter and Saturn returned to the asteroids. And man, before he is matured for an earthly existence, therefore meets, as it were, in the asteroid region which is interspersed in our cosmos, that which can be a kind of substitute for him provisionally before he can enter the Jupiter and Saturn regions".* [386]

According to this, in the time between death and new birth, man would never get beyond the asteroid belt of our solar system or its spiritual correlation. Through it he receives at least a kind of substitute for the forces to be gained in the Jupiter and Saturn regions. Rudolf Steiner called the highest states that man goes through between two incarnations: Mars, Jupiter and Saturn cycles. The following day he continued on the subject:

"When man has gone through the three cycles and begins the decline, his interest in earthly affairs begins again; and then he looks down, many years before he is born, on the generations that arise in the earth development and at the end of which his father, his mother stand. Already at the moment when man makes this great turning back in the cosmos, he begins to direct his attention down to the earth." [387]

Accordingly, the great midnight hour of existence, which Rudolf Steiner here calls the *"great turning back in the cosmos"*, would occur in the middle between the three ascending cycles of Mars, Jupiter and Saturn and the subsequent three descending cycles of Saturn, Jupiter and Mars, or more precisely in the transition from the ascending to the descending cycle of Saturn. Nowhere is there any talk of the starry sky or the invisible depths of the universe into which the human spirit-soul expands according to other statements by Rudolf Steiner, which have already been quoted many times. A completely different point of view than usual is chosen here, in a sense seen only from the Planetary, from the lower spiritual world, which is the next higher world level above the ether sphere and the lower soul world pervading it.

How can these unusual and, at first glance, confusing statements by Rudolf Steiner become reconciled with his otherwise essentially different statements? In order to arrive at an understanding here, we must first take note of the fact that Rudolf Steiner introduces a whole series of new terms on this occasion. When he speaks of spheres, then he does so mainly with reference to the sub-solar planets Moon, Venus and Mercury. As soon as he refers to the planets above the Sun, to Mars, Jupiter and Saturn, he speaks primarily of region or cycle, i.e. of the Mars region, Jupiter region and Saturn region or the Mars cycle, Jupiter cycle and Saturn cycle. That these terms are by no means identical with the terms Mars sphere, Jupiter sphere and Saturn sphere can be seen from the fact that Rudolf Steiner summarizes the approximately thirty-year passage of man through the sub-solar planets, i.e. from the Moon sphere up to the Sun sphere, the experiences in the entire soul world, under the term Moon cycle. He then also calls this Moon existence and separates it from Sun existence, which includes the entire remaining time of man's life between two incarnations, the duration of which he states as 2160 years. This number is composed of three ascending cycles and three descending cycles, each of which lasts twelve times as long as the Moon cycle, that is 6 x 12 x 30 years or 6 x 360 years = 2160 years, whereby the 30 years of the Moon cycle are not taken into account because of their insignificance, since all numbers are only approximate values anyway. In principle, therefore, man was destined to incarnate only once in each age in order to assimilate everything that the respective Period could give him. In the lecture of the next day, however, Rudolf Steiner relativized this statement:

"I said these 2160 years should actually pass between two incarnations. But man by no means takes in everything that he could pull out of life on earth during his life on earth. Therefore, the periods between death and a new birth are, of course, still very different for many people, for no man 2160 years, but much shorter." [388]

Moreover, the Sun "Sphere" in the narrower sense only is taken into consideration here as the transitional sphere or gate from the soul world to the spiritual world, like the actual Moon "Sphere" as the gate to the soul world.

Since we now know from Rudolf Steiner's other lectures that the people, as long as they are not completely averse to the Spiritual and the Christian in life on Earth, certainly ascend to the Zodiac sphere and find there the limit of their fully conscious experience of spiritual events, but pass through everything that follows rather dreamily, the Zodiac sphere in Rudolf Steiner's differently chosen frame of reference correlates with the asteroid belt. Obviously, everything related to experiences beyond the zodiac or the visible starry sky, i.e. beyond the fourth and middle region of the spiritual world, is brought to men by spirit beings of the higher spiritual world, so that they receive *"a kind of substitute"* for it. The asteroid belt between Mars and Jupiter would then correspond within the given frame of reference to the border between the lower and the higher world, which Rudolf Steiner otherwise associates with the zodiac as an

---

[386] GA 227 "Initiations-Erkenntnis" (Initiation-knowledge), Penmaenmawr, Lecture of 28 August 1923

[387] Ibidem, Lecture of 29 August 1923

[388] GA 227 "Initiations-Erkenntnis" (Initiation-knowledge), Penmaenmawr, Lecture of 30 August 1923

expression of the visible starry sky. A fully conscious experience of the higher spiritual world or even the lower spheres of the Budhi plane after death is reserved for disciples of the spirit anyway, who have not only already worked hard on the transformation of their astral body to Manas – which is going on in its beginnings in almost all people nowadays – but who also work on the transformation of their ether body to Budhi already. From this point of view, Rudolf Steiner's unusual statements can certainly be reconciled with his other lectures on the human incarnation cycle. The result is shown in Figure 22. It is based on the planetary dominations in the zodiac.

The coincidence of the Saturn cycle with the Budhi plane seems quite appropriate, since it presents itself as fiery and flaming and the main characteristic of Saturn is heat as well. Also, the higher spiritual world as an expression of the Holy Spirit is close relationship to Jupiter's sphere of wisdom. Thus, it is by no means an arbitrary classification, but again it shows how manifold the overlaps and reflections of the world levels are among themselves are and from which different points of view they can be watched and described. Within this frame of reference the great midnight hour of existence is on the same days of the calendar as in the warmth rhythm of the year, on January 19 and 20. At this time, the Sun performs its transition from the Saturn-sign Capricorn to the Saturn-sign Aquarius, as shown in Figure 22.

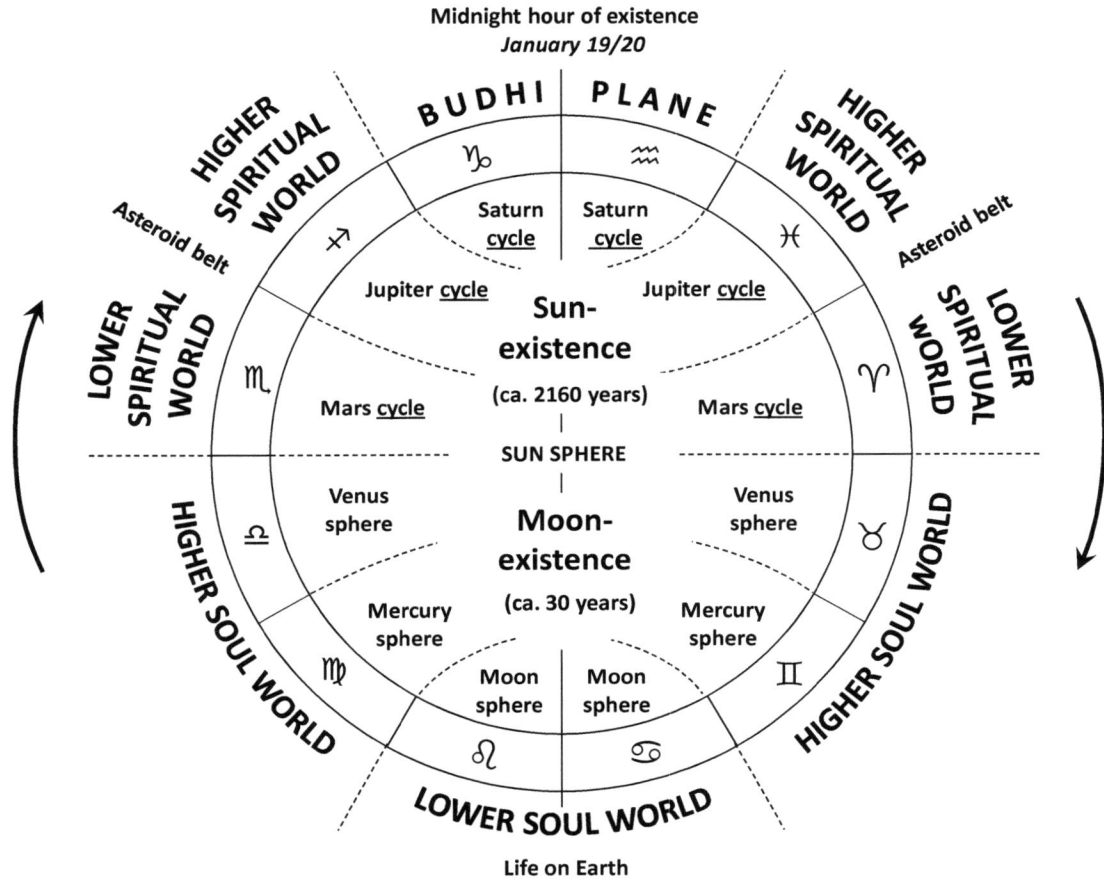

Figure 22: Annual rhythm of planetary force activity in the zodiac

In Figure 21 already the zodiac is shown in a clockwise direction in order to simulate the ascending and descending course of the Sun and to correspond to the usual reading direction from left to right, starting with the vernal equinox. Although the zodiac in the sky is actually left-turning when viewed from the Earth, the clockwise direction has been maintained in Figure 22, because a reversal of the direction of the zodiac would only be more confusing. But this difference is of no importance for the relationships expressed in the figure. The midnight hour of existence is right in the middle between the two Saturn-signs Capricorn and Aquarius. Accordingly, life on Earth is located exactly in the polar opposite middle between the signs Cancer and Leo, and thus below the circle depicted.

We see that there are several ways in which the human incarnation cycle reflects in nature, depending on whether we choose the physical perspective, which can refer in different ways to the annual rhythm of light or heat, or whether we choose the etheric perspective, which is devoted to the extrasensory life processes in the ether sphere of the Earth. Rudolf Steiner obviously chose the latter for his weekly verses for it is precisely by feeling the changes in the states of life during the course of the year that we can most closely approach the spirit being who controls them, Christ as the Life Spirit. A further likeness finally results from the psycho-spiritual point of view of the lower spiritual world, looking at the planetary forces and their interaction with the zodiac.

If there were any other likenesses of the human incarnation cycle in nature, these could only refer to the three lower world levels – the physical-sensory, the etheric and the lower spiritual world levels – because the higher spiritual world does not have any physically-sense-perceptible reflection in nature, at best the uniformly dark background of the universe behind the visible star carpet.

In general, it is significant that in all the reflections of the human incarnation cycle described here, the great midnight hour of existence is always related to the Budhi plane or at least coincides with the time of entry into the Budhi plane as is the case with the annual rhythm of light, or with the time of departure from the Budhi plane as it results based on the annual rhythm of warmth or that of the planetary forces. Only in the annual rhythm of the life forces the great midnight hour of existence is right in the middle between these two, when the Sun passes 15° Capricorn in winter, at the time we celebrate Epiphany, and also when it passes 15° Cancer in summer, two weeks after St. John's day. Perhaps, we may see in this fact the outer expression that the ether sphere is located precisely between the planes of the physical sensory world and the lower spiritual world.

Return to the Sphere of the Germ Sheath of the Spirit Man – 42nd Week

Coming from the Budhi plane, where man originates in the Divine, he gradually begins in the higher spiritual world to turn again to world existence. While doing so, memories of sensory experiences from his former existence appear before his spirit- and soul-eye for the first time again. He begins to "feel, like a presentiment" his approaching descent into the sensory world. Although we cannot even begin to speak of sensory light here, since in relation to the sensory world tenebrous "winter-dark", deepest darkness reigns, inwardly a deep yearning, even a strong drive awakens in man, to work towards the "high" goal of further incarnation in a new human body on Earth. Already before the great midnight hour of existence, he acquired a part of the necessary forces for this by a gathering of forces in the course of his after-death ascension through the higher worlds. In addition, these newly acquired forces were pervaded by the willpower of the Father and inflamed by the love of the Son, so that the will was completely Christ-imbued, as described in the preceding weekly verse.

But now, in man the urge arises to put his new power into action in the higher spiritual world. And since the germ layer of the Atma or spirit man belongs to its seventh and highest region, i.e. that spiritual member of the being which he will form in the future through the fully conscious work of his I on the physical body, his urge for activity here is primarily directed towards first creating a still quite ideal, purely spiritual archetype of a new physical human body which is intended to ultimately manifest itself in the earthly sensory world in order to become his "selfhood's sheath" there, as the first weekly verse calls it.

In all this new creative activity, the Christ-love of the Budhi plane is intensively involved in man. This will always be the case in the two following regions of the higher spiritual world, since the three highest regions are pervaded by the three lowest regions of the Budhi plane. Therefore, all action here is accompanied by the feeling heart-warmth of the Budhi. Whatever man works for his own future on earth, he accomplishes in harmony with divine love. Everything is to develop in such a way that in the next sensory life on earth the possibility for the compensation of karmic guilt from past earthly lives is contained. Far away from all earthly sensory light, man already feels ahead from the point of view of loving warmth of heart. That's the deeper meaning of the 42nd week's verse.

42nd Week (19 - 25 January)	*42. Woche (19. – 25. Januar)*
In this winter-dark,	Es ist in diesem Winterdunkel
To manifest own power	Die Offenbarung eigner Kraft
Is now the soul's strong drive,	Der Seele starker Trieb,
To guide it into darknesses	In Finsternisse sie zu lenken
And feel, like a presentiment,	Und ahnend vorzufühlen
Through warmth of heart the senses' revelation.	Durch Herzenswärme Sinnesoffenbarung.

In more detail, Rudolf Steiner explained to us this creative activity, which begins to stir shortly after the human spirit-soul has gone through the great midnight hour of existence and returned to the spiritual world, in his Vienna cycle:

"After having lived on in the spiritual world for a while, from the gloomy dark of the spiritual environment a clear view emerges then not only of our own passed lives, but especially of everything Human that was connected with these lives, especially everything of that Human, which was more closely connected with these lives. People enter into spiritual relationships with us with whom we had this or that relationship in earlier stages of existence. Not as if the communion with these people had not existed before – in the far greatest time between death and a new birth we always experience a living together with the persons who were close to us in life – but then, by meeting these persons again after the midnight hour of spiritual existence, it appears clearly and distinctly on these persons what we have got to owe them, or what they have got to owe us. Now we do not merely get a view of what was our relation with these human beings between this and that time – we knew that before – but these persons become to us the expression of what is the compensation for the past experiences. Through the manner in which they appear to us, we see by which new experiences on the physical plane we can make up for our previous deeds, for what we owe them or the like. By facing the souls of these human beings, we look, so to speak, at the effects which in the future will be the consequences of relationships we had with them in the past. Of course, the best way to understand this is to take as concrete as possible an individual case.

So let us assume once again that we lied to a person. Now is the time when the possibility is offered in the spiritual world that we are tormented by the truth opposite to our lie. But we are tormented by the fact that our relationship to the person whom we have lied changes in such a way in the time just described so often as we see that person – and we will see him or she often enough with the spiritual eye – in that this person becomes the cause that the truth opposite to the committed lie rises in us and torments us. Thereby the tendency emerges from our depths: You must meet this person again down on earth and you must do something to make up for the injustice you have done through the lie you have committed. For here in the spiritual world that, which was created by your lie, cannot be compensated, here in the cosmos you can only gain complete clarity about the effect of a lie. What has been created on earth of this kind must also be compensated on earth. You know, you need forces in yourself for the compensation, which can only develop when you again move into a body on earth. Thus the tendency develops in our soul: You have to move into an earthly body which offers the possibility to accomplish such an act, whereby the imperfections which you caused on earth will be compensated. Otherwise when you have gone through the next death this person will appear to you again and cause the torture of truth. You understand the whole spiritual technique of how in the spiritual world the impulse is planted in us to create a karmic compensation for this or that." [389]

Especially that part of our new physical human body through which we can come into direct contact with the physical Earth, stand on it, walk on it, move to the places where we want to accomplish our new earthly deeds, that is, our limbs and our metabolic system underlying our movements, all this is built up in the highest region of the spiritual world as a gigantic, macrocosmic, ideal archetype, so that a new earthly tool for our will emerges from it. Filled with divine power and divine love, man works actively and purposefully to ensure that the parts of his next physical body which will serve his volitional life, but also the physical earth-conditions surrounding him then, will best correspond to his goal of karmic compensation of his previous deeds. Of course, this creative activity is only possible for man because he is assisted by high spiritual beings, especially those of the first Hierarchy, whose focus is primarily on karmic compensation.

"Here are the forces that take a person to a certain place. If you have done evil to someone, this is an external fact that goes up into the highest parts of Devachan. In the new integration into a physical body, it acts as forces, which man has left behind, and shifts him, though under the guidance of higher beings, to the place where he then can experience the effects of his deeds in the physical world." [390]

But in the words of the 42nd weekly verse, there is yet another significant content hidden. In the lower spheres of the Budhi plane and the upper regions of the spiritual world pervading them, the human spirit-soul relives the entire evolutionary process of the world's and the human being's creation. Both emerge from a common primeval state. Originally they are one. On the border between the Budhi plane and the higher spiritual world, man overlooks the secrets of himself and the three worlds below the Budhi plane, the

[389] GA 153 "Inneres Wesen des Menschen und Leben zwischen Tod und neuer Geburt" (Inner nature of man and life between death and new birth), Vienna, Lecture of 14 April 1914

[390] GA 99 "Die Theosophie des Rosenkreuzers" (Theosophy of the Rosicrucian), Munich, Lecture of 30 May 1907

spiritual world, the soul world and the physical world, only within which a separation of the concepts of man and world makes sense at all.

"When the human being is at the border of the three worlds, he thus recognizes himself in his own life kernel. This implies that the riddles of these three worlds must be solved to him. So he overlooks the whole life of these worlds." [391]

The densest state of matter that was fully developed on ancient Saturn was the physical warmth. In the course of the second half of the ancient Saturn development, the subsequent Sun development was already preparing. However, there were merely initial steps that only came to their full expression on the ancient Sun. The densest states of matter always appear on the fourth globe of the fourth cycle of a creation period. Consequently, it is only from the middle of the development of ancient Saturn that one can speak of external, material warmth in it. During the first half, the warmth is still present inwardly. Only in the second half it is outwardly perceptible, too.

"This is the peculiarity in the development of Saturn, that the warmth gradually changes from the beginning of Saturn, where it was a merely inner one, to the end, where it becomes more external, more perceptible. ... This is the development Saturn went through: from an inner soul-warmth to an externally perceptible warmth, to what we call external warmth or fire." [392]

Together with the change from inwardness to outwardness the possibility of sensory perception starts, regardless of whether this takes place with the help of physical senses or senses of the soul or the spirit. The five states of life of a Pralaya, the rest between the developments on the seven globes, are not perceptible to all these senses, as Rudolf Steiner emphasizes:

"However, the states of life during the rest periods cannot be perceived with the senses that develop during the «open cycles», just as a person does not perceive during sleep what is going on around him." [393]

All external perception has its beginning in the Arupa region. This is also the home of the first globe. Actually, it is located on the Budhi plane, as can be seen in Figure 19 in the chapter "Christ and the Human Being". But the lower and thus densest part of the Arupa globe protrudes into the upper part of the higher spiritual world. There, too, everything that manifests itself to the outside world is still in the highest degree of spiritual kind, purely ideal and without any form, just "a-rupa". But what begins to manifest itself to the outside world is Budhi, the love of God or the empathic inner warmth of heart. Gradually it changes into outer warmth that can be perceived externally by the higher senses. This externally perceptible warmth condenses step by step from globe to globe, beginning with the Budhic warmth on the Arupa globe of the higher spiritual world, through the spiritual warmth on the Rupa globe in the lower spiritual world and the soul-warmth on the astral globe to ultimately the physical warmth on the fourth globe. However, even on the fourth globe, we can speak of external physical warmth not before the middle of the fourth cycle of Saturn's development. And as the warmth that manifests to the outside becomes the first external sensory experience at all, it is also the beginning of all sensory revelation. By this process, the whole ancient Saturn basically becomes a first great sensory organ in the darkness that develops out of the tenebrous warmth-substances. Into these dark masses of matter, into the darknesses of the ancient Saturn, the human being then directs his power in order to contribute to the construction of his future physical body. We can read the 42nd weekly verse also in this sense.

In this winter-dark,	Es ist in diesem Winterdunkel
To manifest own power	Die Offenbarung eigner Kraft
Is now the soul's strong drive,	Der Seele starker Trieb,
To guide it into darknesses	In Finsternisse sie zu lenken
And feel, like a presentiment,	Und ahnend vorzufühlen
Through warmth of heart the senses' revelation.	Durch Herzenswärme Sinnesoffenbarung.

The matter of ancient Saturn is the manifestation of the Father's willpower. *"Inwardly, the matter is will... And outwardly, the will is matter."* [394] This matter is modified in its conditions by the Son and initially it

---

[391] GA 9 "Theosophie" (Theosophy), Chapter "Die drei Welten" (The three worlds), Section IV "Der Geist im Geisterland nach dem Tode" (The spirit in spirit land after death)

[392] GA 110 "Geistige Hierarchien und ihre Widerspiegelung in der Physischen Welt" (Spiritual Hierarchies and their reflection in the physical world), Düsseldorf, Lecture of 13 April 1909

[393] GA 11 "Aus der Akasha-Chronik" (From the Akasha chronicle), Chapter "Von der Herkunft der Erde" (About the Earth's origin)

thereby appears as the Budhi revealing itself outwardly, as an inner warmth of heart filled with loving will, which turns into the outer warmth of the senses. Warmth of the heart and sensory revelation belong together, because the former was destined from the very beginning to become the bearer of the human I and the latter was and is destined to be the basis of the human I-consciousness. For this purpose, until the later development of the Earth, the ancient Saturn-warmth had to retreat into the interior of the physical human body as its blood heat.

"These differentiated conditions of warmth are the only things that already existed of the present features of our earth, and at that time such warmth was the expression of the first preliminary stage of the physical human body. What existed then, you still have in you today, only it has withdrawn from the outer spatial existence into your interior. It's your blood heat." [395]

The warm human blood is the only thing capable of becoming a bearer of Budhi and Christ, according to whose image the human being is created. This should remind us of Rudolf Steiner's admonishing words that the real origin of the human being is before and above all planetary development:

"The Christ really demands: When you meet a person, you should regard him in such a way that what he shows to you in the outer world is not the whole, full person. You should regard him in such a way that his real essence does not come only from Archai, Archangeloi, Angeloi, but from higher Spirits, who do not belong to the earth development, not even to planetary development, for this begins with the Archai, as you know from «Occult Science - an Outline», but with the higher heavenly Spirits; so that man enters the Maya as something that is supernatural." [396]

In the warmth of the blood, however, not only the human I, but also the will is working as an expression of the Father's power. Therefore, in the seventh and highest region of the spiritual world the human spirit-soul works primarily on the formation of that part of the warmth-organism of its future physical body which will serve the exercise of the will, which is primarily the metabolic-limb system. In this the will works through warmth, also in life on Earth. However, we should not imagine the shape of this spirit-germ as if just the lower man, i.e. his abdomen and his legs connected to it, were formed there, and perhaps the arms as upper limbs in addition. That would give a completely false picture. We come closer to the experience when we first become aware that the metabolic-limb system is only the prevailing factor in the lower man, but works up into the chest-man and even the head-man. Ultimately, it is everywhere where we find blood vessels in the physical human body, which on the one hand promote the metabolism in the whole organism, but through which on the other hand also the will impulses flow and seize the muscles. Instead of the metabolic-limb-man, we could also speak of the blood-man. Even more precisely we should speak only of the blood-warmth-man, because in the Arupa region no blood cells or liquid blood serum are yet developed, but only cosmic currents of warmth, through which Budhi manifests to the outside for the first time.

When we imagine a huge cosmic circle, far larger than our entire solar system, a gigantic, spherical space extending into the tenebrous depths of the cosmos, the "darknesses", as the weekly verse goes, in which the human being, working from the outside under the guidance of Hierarchies, contributes to form dark currents of warmth as the basis of future blood vessels, which will later reach from the innermost centre of the body, from the innermost warmth of the heart, to the outer sensory organs, which thus only "through warmth of heart" will make possible "the senses' revelation", since the sensory organs must also be supplied with blood and warmth, then we achieve a more suitable picture of the first stage of the spirit germ for the new physical body. At the end, however, even this imagination is of course still far too much borrowed from the earthly sensory world to reflect the grandeur and magnificence of the real, spiritual processes.

The prenatal experiences of the spiritual world have an aftereffect in the earthly existence, on the one hand below the threshold of consciousness, but on the other hand they are also reflected in the earthly outside world. Especially at the time, when the wintry sun enters the sign of Aquarius, a feeling-remembrance at least of one's own prenatal invigoration and the associated first, early, own creative activity in the higher spiritual world can be awakened when the soul sympathizes with the changed moods of life and forces in nature. The Aquarius or Streaming Man thus becomes a symbol of the pure spirit-germ which man works out of the dark depths of the universe for his next physical body and his future earthly human form, which is destined to contract more and more in order ultimately to pour itself as a stream of

---

[394] GA 291 "Das Wesen der Farben" (The essence of the colours), Dornach, Lecture of 5 December 1920

[395] GA 104 "Die Apokalypse des Johannes" (The Apocalypse of John), Nuremberg, Lecture of 22 June 1908

[396] GA 172 "Das Karma des Berufes des Menschen in Anknüpfung an Goethes Leben" (The Karma of human vocation as related to Goethe's life), Dornach, Lecture of 27 November 1916

forces into a tiny physical human germ and to appear within the sensory world in this way. It is right in the highest regions of the spiritual world, where the lowest, the Sensory-Physical, has its true origin.

Not for nothing Rudolf Steiner uses the words "manifest" and "revelation" in the 42nd weekly verse, because here, at the border of the Budhi plane to the three worlds, between Creator and Creation, everything that streams out of its divine foundation on the Budhi and Atma planes begins to manifest and reveal itself gradually in ever new ways and in ever lower spheres until it finally becomes apparent in the sensory world of the Earth.

Return to the Sphere of the Germ Sheath of the Life Spirit – 43rd Week

In the sixth region of the spiritual world the "ex deo nascimur" of man progresses. The human spirit-soul is there still in the Arupa region. In its seventh region the manifestation of Budhi as warmth was still subject to the primeval principle of the Father and thus to unity, in which all differentiation has its starting point and origin. But thereafter, in the sixth region of the higher spiritual world the principle of duality comes more to the fore. Here, ancient Saturn's various degrees of warmth differentiate into the opposite poles of heat and cold. The powers of the spiritual world now stand out more clearly from those of the Budhi plane. But the latter pervade the higher, pure or true spiritual world still intensively with warmth. And just as the I gets its meaning only through the spiritual members of being, which fill it, so also the spirit only has its full share in the divine existence when it is pervaded by Budhi and Atma, that is, by the powers "from love-worlds of the heart", as the Budhi and the Atma plane are called in the 40th weekly verse. The three worlds below the Budhi plane are only an appearance as long as they are not connected to the higher Budhic and Atmic reality. Only where the Trinity as a whole is expressed, only where the true, the Holy Spirit cooperates with the powers of the Father and the Son, is true existence. This is the 43rd weekly verse saying:

43rd Week (26 January – 1 February)	*43. Woche (26. Januar – 1. Februar)*
In wintry depths	In winterlichen Tiefen
The spirit's true existence warms.	Erwarmt des Geistes wahres Sein;
It gives to world-appearance,	Es gibt dem Weltenscheine
By powers of the heart, mights of existence.	Durch Herzenskräfte Daseinsmächte;

In order that the warming of the spirit's true existence can take place in the right sense, also in the human spirit soul, which is part of this process, the internally felt Budhic heart-warmth has to grow once more strongly. As a result, the inner soul fire can stand up vigorously against the coldness of the world. Correspondingly, the 43rd weekly verse continues:

The inner fire of the human soul defies,	Der Weltenkälte trotzt erstarkend
With growing strength, the coldness of the world.	Das Seelenfeuer im Menscheninnern.

In the sixth region of the spiritual world, the human spirit-soul additionally witnesses once again everything that was developed in the spirit-germ of the physical body on the Arupa globe in the course of the seven rounds of the ancient Sun. Here the focus was less on the power of the Father, which flows through the metabolic-limb-blood-heat-system of the physical body as willpower, but rather on the power of the Son, the Life Spirit, which rules the vital functions in the chest part of the future new human body and also enables the physical body in general to become a bearer of a life body or ether body. For this purpose, a part of the warmth of the ancient Saturn had to undergo a transformation. On the one hand, this part was compressed to a gaseous state. But this was only possible because at the same time something diluted remained, so that, together with the denser gas, light emerged as a kind of finer, volatilized heat, as a fugitive light ether. To the physical experience of the senses on Earth, sunlight seems to be warm. But in fact, it's cold. The physical heat of the Sun is mainly based on the invisible heat radiation of the Sun, which belongs to the dark infrared range. It projects only marginally into the red range of the visible light spectrum. On the ancient Sun, the dark heat on one side and the cold gas and light on the other side faced each other as a distinct duality. This is still present today in the thoracic organism of the human body as the division into the dark blood circulation, which is permeated by internal heat, with the heart as the Budhi organ on the one hand, and the lung, through which cool, light-filled outside air streams, on the other. It connects us with the outer sensory world, behind which the spiritual outer world hides. The ancient Greeks expressed this relation in their language by using the word pneuma to name both the air and the spirit.

The human spirit-soul very intensely feels the difference between the depths of the spiritual world filled with wintery cold spirit-light and the inner heart-warmth of the Budhi plane, which it left only recently. But at the same time it once again comes into closer contact with the powers of the Son by means of the germ sheath of the life spirit, which is located in the second highest region of the spiritual world. The tendency to want to warm up the world with love, which without the experience of the human soul "would merely be a frosty, empty life", as it says in the 33rd weekly verse, grows here into a strong might, which based on powers of the heart contributes in shaping the existence. Here, man builds for himself the spiritual archetype of his own future "heart-man", the physical support of his life-preserving vital functions, the blood circulation and breathing, but also of his emotional life and his empathetic interest for all beings outside himself. To what extent man, on the basis of love, here is capable of creative work on the spirit-germ of his future physical body, depends however on how much of such love he developed in his previous lives on Earth already.

"With all the details one can observe how that, which was present in one life as inclinations, works on the physical body in the next life. A life that has the tendency to love everything around and to respond lovingly to every being, a life that pours out love, will in the next embodiment have a physical body that will look young and blooming for a long time. Love for all beings, development of sympathy causes a physical body that keeps itself youthful. A hateful life that is full of antipathy to other beings, a life that criticizes and niggles at everything and wants to withdraw from everything, that causes from these tendencies a physical body that ages early and gets wrinkles. Thus the inclinations and passions of one life are transferred to the physical body's life of the next embodiment." [397]

Karmic forces from man's last life interact into everything that he works out here as a spiritual archetype of his future physical body. What was his character at that time, what lived as his inclinations and habits in his ether body, moves one step deeper then and is woven into the archetype of his future physical body in the Arupa region by man himself, together with the spiritual Hierarchies.

"That of which the ether body is the bearer in this life, the permanent character, the dispositions and so on, that occurs in the next life in the physical body, for example in such a way that a person who developed bad inclinations and passions in his life is born in the next life with an unhealthy physical body. A person, on the other hand, who has good health, who is able to endure a lot, developed good qualities in his previous life. One who is constantly prone to illness has worked bad drives into himself. So it is in our hands to create health or illness for us, insofar as they are in the predisposition of the physical body. You only need to eradicate all bad inclinations, because then you prepare a good, strong body for the next life." [398]

So it is we ourselves who, together with the Hierarchies, create the foundations of health, but of disease in the next life on Earth, too, in order to be able to karmically compensate and overcome bad inclinations and passions, which we carried as qualities of character in the ether body of our previous life, by suffering the diseases in the physical body.

At the end of his stay in the two highest regions of the spiritual world, man has worked on the spirit-germ of his new physical body by adding an air-man as the basis of his chest-man to the warmth-man, and through this work he has created the preconditions that later the physical body can be pervaded by an ether body as a bearer of life. However, in order to enable it to also be pervaded by an astral body as a bearer of soul life, a further transformation must take place in the next deeper region of the spiritual world.

Return to the Sphere of the Spirit Self – 44th Week

The further reconfiguration of the spirit-germ of the physical body took place on the ancient moon, again primarily on the Arupa globe that reaches from the Budhi plane into the Arupa region and on which everything physical has its spiritual origin. As soon as the human spirit-soul, together with the Hierarchies that guide it, begins to develop its prenatal activity in the fifth region of the spiritual world, it forms in addition to the twofold spirit-germ of a physical warmth- and gas-organism as a third part the spirit-germ of

[397] GA 99 "Die Theosophie des Rosenkreuzers" (Theosophy of the Rosicrucian), Munich, Lecture of 30 May 1907

[398] GA 99 "Die Theosophie des Rosenkreuzers" (Theosophy of the Rosicrucian), Munich, Lecture of 30 May 1907

a physical water-organism as basis for the nervous system and its spongy-plastic-soft brain and spinal cord floating in the cerebrospinal fluid, the brain- or nerve-"water". The human brain is destined first of all to become the physical bearer of the soul force of thinking and an expression of the spirit, up to the Holy Spirit. Here, therefore, the preliminary stage of a head-man is added to the spirit-germ of the chest-man and metabolic-man. For this purpose, the spirit-germ of the physical body must be enabled to be pervaded by an astral body. Today, through the conscious work of the I on the astral body in the course of life on Earth, the astral body can at least partly be transformed into spirit self or Manas, which here, in the fifth region of the spiritual world, has its home in the narrower sense. The human spirit-soul participates in this activity much more awaken than in the formation of the other two parts of the physical body.

Moreover, in the fifth region of the spiritual world the overview of all incarnations that have taken place so far comes more to the fore than in the two regions before. Here, not only our previous deeds, our inclinations and habits flow into the construction of the spirit-germ of our physical body, but the future head of the new earthly human body is built especially with the help of those physical forces which originate from the physical body laid down on Earth at our last death, yet just without the forces of the former head.

"When we look at a person's head as it is today, it is essentially the result of what has become of the body of the previous incarnation. And when we will have passed through the period between death and new birth, our present body, with exclusion of the head, will have become our head of the next incarnation." [399]

The head is the physical support for all those experiences of the soul in the earthly body that enter our consciousness, especially those of thinking, for with regard to our feeling, which is especially at home in the chest-man that has its centre in the heart, we dream, as Rudolf Steiner says, and with regard to our will, which flows through the interior of our metabolic-limb-part, we even sleep. We are not aware which will-impulse we send to which muscle fibre, so that in the interplay of many muscle fibres just the movement comes about that we intend. Only the external result of all these internal processes ultimately comes to our consciousness. Only in our thinking we are fully awake. And awake in the spiritual sense, we are also in the fifth region of the spiritual world, the region of the spirit self, whereas the higher regions can be experienced completely awake only by spirit disciples and their masters. Most people tend to dream or even sleep there. This circumstance is based on the fact that humanity today has only just progressed to the work on the spirit self by curbing, purifying and transforming the astral body with the help of the I.

From the fifth region of the spiritual world onwards, descending to a new life on Earth, we then become really conscious again of our existence as humans and of our past as earthly persons, besides our world existence. Through this increasing consciousness we attain soul-clarity. This goes hand in hand with an increasing interest in the terrestrial world and mankind on Earth. Man experiences himself as a spirit-soul who has interests and intentions that he wants to put into action on Earth through a suitable physical body. We turn our gaze to the Earth and look there for earthly people to whom we feel spiritually and emotionally related. New impressions, new sensory stimuli are coming to us from Earth:

"You see, as strange as it sounds, when we have passed through the middle of our life between death and a new birth – a number of centuries usually pass between death and a new birth and there is of course a middle, isn't it – then the inner experience of the soul in the spiritual world is directed above all down to Earth. And when you live after this middle, you get more and more impressions from the Earth upwards of what is being done down there, of what people down there think and feel; and each soul gets very specific impressions. So for example a soul can live into the second half of the spiritual life towards its new birth, and more and more it sees those people down there, who, let us say, prepare the next age down there: spiritually active people. Some of these spiritually active people become particularly valuable to the soul. Yes, it happens that one looks down from the spiritual world with particular interest for one or two figures that are active on Earth. Let us assume for example that a human being born in the second half of the nineteenth century was in the spiritual world at the beginning of the nineteenth and in the second half of the eighteenth century; but he looked down upon the significant persons who influenced culture at that time. Some of them he finds particularly valuable, they are particularly dear to him. That is one thing you experience there: that you look down on the people who are developing down there. But by looking down you also influence these people, but not in such a way that free will would be impaired; you influence them so that certain things that live in their soul emerge more easily in their soul by the fact that from the spiritual world some soul looks down on them. In this way earthly people are encouraged to create, to work, by

---

[399] GA 170 "Das Rätsel des Menschen – die geistigen Hintergründe der menschlichen Geschichte" (The riddle of the human being – the spiritual background of human history), Dornach, Lecture of 7 August 1916

souls who are born only later than these earthly people and look down upon them. That may be the case also in further and more intimate matters." [400]

When Rudolf Steiner speaks here of "more intimate matters", this may include our participation in the compilation of our entire ancestral series, because even several centuries before our own reincarnation we are already working intensively on bringing together a large number of people in such a way that ultimately that parent couple may emerge which will be able to offer us the most suitable seed ground for the spirit-germ of our new physical body.

"You start to get an interest in certain people who are down there on Earth, and again in their children and their children again. While one used to have only a heavenly interest, then one gets a strange interest in certain generation series, when the spiritual world becomes a manifestation. These are the generation series at the end of which your own parents are, who will give birth to you when you descend to the Earth again. But you get interested in your ancestors long before. You follow the line of generations down to your parents not only in the course of time, but when this state of manifestation occurs first, you can prophetically overlook the entire line of generations already. You can see through the generations, through the series of human beings your great-great-great-grandfather, great-great-grandfather, great-grandfather, grandfather and so on. You can see in front of you the path that you will make down to Earth in human generations. After we have first grown into the cosmos, we later grow into the real, concrete human history". [401]

This experience is reflected in some people's life on Earth as an interest in genealogy and the compilation of their personal family tree, even if in our materialistic time most people may well reject explicitly the prenatal, spiritual origin of their interest. Rudolf Steiner once described the relevant spiritual experiences in concrete terms using the example of Goethe's prenatal soul:

"Take the soul of Goethe. Long, long before it is born, it already affects its ancestors from the extrasensory worlds, is already related to its ancestors through its powers. It even works in such a way that those men and women come together who, after a long time, can give the right qualities that the soul needs. This is no easy work, because there are many souls involved. If you imagine that people in the eighteenth century stem from the souls of the sixteenth century and that they all have worked together before, you must understand that such communication is an important thing. Souls born in the eighteenth, nineteenth century must communicate as early as the sixteenth century so that all the networks of kinships can be established. There is much to do between death and a new birth. Not only do we have to work in an objective context, that we spend part of our time with services to the spirits of resistance, we also have to work on the forces that make our reincarnation possible at all. Here the thing is that we have to work out the form already as an archetype. This makes an opposite impression of what the seer sees when looking at the sleeping physical and ether body. The physical and ether body present themselves in sleep as something dying; but what builds itself up there as an archetype and becomes part of physical nature, that offers the impression of something sprouting, becoming." [402]

This experience is described in the 44th weekly verse:

44th Week (2 – 8 February)	44. Woche (2. – 8. Februar)
In grasping of new sensory stimuli,	Ergreifend neue Sinnesreize
Soul-clarity, in retrospect of spirit-birth,	Erfüllet Seelenklarheit,
Fills the confusing, sprouting	Eingedenk vollzogener Geistgeburt
Becoming of the world	Verwirrend sprossend Weltenwerden
With the creative will of my own thinking.	Mit meines Denkens Schöpferwillen.

Confusing is the multitude of our ancestors and the innumerable interpersonal encounters on which we work blazing the trail, so that ultimately those qualities may come about on the physical path of inheritance which can best be united with the spirit-germ of the physical body prepared by our own activity. Just consider that although each person has only 2 parents, he or she has but $2^2 = 4$ grandparents and $2^3 = 8$

---

[400] GA 140 "Okkulte Untersuchungen über das Leben zwischen Tod und neuer Geburt" (Occult investigations on life between death and new birth), Bergen, Lecture of 11 October 1913

[401] GA 226 "Menschenwesen, Menschenschicksal und Welt-Entwicklung" (Man's being, his destiny and world-evolution), Kristiania (Oslo), Lecture of 17 May 1923

[402] GA 140 "Okkulte Untersuchungen über das Leben zwischen Tod und neuer Geburt" (Occult investigations on life between death and new birth), Tübingen, Lecture of 16 February 1913

great-grandparents. Extrapolated over several centuries, there easily result 2^8 to 2^{10}, which are 256, 512 or even 1024 ancestors.

However, not only the elaboration of our earthly hereditary current from the entire perimeter of mankind, but also the formation of the spirit-germ for our future physical brain as the centre of the nervous system and physical basis of thinking, out of the wide perimeter of the cosmos and in the image of the entire starry sky, proves to be a truly "confusing, sprouting Becoming of the world". Plastic-aqueous forms sprout up in our spiritual-cosmic surroundings and weave themselves into the warmth- and air-currents of our spirit-germ. More and more complicated and confusing is the gigantic, enormous structure encompassing our entire spiritual horizon, to which we ourselves contribute by our creative activity and into which we fully consciously incorporate our new goals and will impulses, which are still creative forces in the higher world of thought. While our spiritual field of vision is more and more filled with the spirit-germ of our physical body, becoming more and more concrete, surrounding us as a gigantic macrocosm and constituting our external world, the spiritual Hierarchies gradually disappear from our spiritual view. They reveal themselves only through their activity, which we can still perceive as the "confusing, sprouting Becoming of the world".

Man's gaze now focuses even more on himself. In the fifth region of the spiritual world he intensely becomes conscious of himself again. Looking back, he additionally now clearly remembers the spirit-birth of his I or human self out of the divine ground of the Budhi plane and into the higher spiritual world, a process, which he experienced rather dreamlike. But now clarity enters his soul and he participates in the creative power of thinking in the higher spiritual world. This thinking and this will, however, are still world thinking and world will, even if man may identify with it and feel it as his thinking and his will. The human spirit-soul is still embedded in superior spiritual beings. In reality, they are the ones who reveal themselves in world thinking and creative will. But they allow man to participate in it, as far as he is able to do so.

Return to the Sphere of the Zodiac – 45th Week

If the psycho-spiritual human being has matured so far in his prenatal development that he can contract again from the cosmic expanses to the zodiac sphere in the narrower sense, then he settles into the fourth region of the spiritual world. Here his task is to complete the work on the archetype of his new physical body. He adds to the warmth-, air- and water-man, whose spiritual archetype he experiences as his cosmic outside world, the basis for his external form and clear structuring. In the course of human evolution, this work started in the first round of the Earth's development already, namely during the transition from the Arupa globe to the Rupa globe. For the purpose that the new terrestrial man will be able to appear in human form for the future, it must be possible to weave solid materials into him as a prerequisite for a firmly delimitable, external form. In addition, he must also be able to be pervaded by an I. For when we see a human form before us in life on Earth, we do not really see the physical body, nor the ether body or the astral body, but we see an Imagination of the human I.

"And with the human being we already see the I. What we see there is not the physical body, exactly this is invisible; likewise the etheric body; likewise the astral body. What we see with the human being – outwardly formed, physically formed – is the I. Hence, for example, with respect to the perception of the eyes, to the visibility, the human being appears to the outside in his "Incarnate", in a colour that is not there otherwise, just as the I is not there otherwise in the other beings. So, if we want to express ourselves correctly, we would have to say: We can only fully grasp the human being if we think of him as consisting of physical body, ether body, astral body and I. That which we see before us is the I, and invisible within is the astral body, the ether body and the physical body." [403]

"This [human form] is a something thoroughly spiritual. It should stir a solemn mood to perceive a Spiritual with physical senses as a human form in the physical world. For the one who can see spiritually, the thing is such that he sees the human form as a real Imagination, which has descended into the physical world." [404]

---

[403] GA 214 "Das Geheimnis der Trinität" (Mystery of the Trinity), Dornach, Lecture of 28 July 1922

[404] GA 26 "Anthroposophische Leitsätze" (Anthroposophical Leading Thoughts), Chapter "Erster Teil der Betrachtung: Was offenbart sich, wenn man in die vorigen Leben zwischen Tod und neuer Geburt zurückschaut" (First part of contemplation: What is revealed when one looks back into the previous lives between death and new birth), Goetheanum, at the turn of the year 1925

We owe both, the clearly delimited and structured outer form as well as the human I, to the Spirits of Form who control the Earth's development. For this purpose, the spiritual force structure of an earthy physical body and of a symbolic form of the human I were woven into the warmth-, air- and water-man, too. Only in this way it will ultimately be able to connect itself with the earthly substances in a mother's womb, which are given to it from the earthly current of inheritance.

The symbolic form of the human I is a spiritual force-web or network of forces within which the ether body will later integrate the physical substances embedded therein into life processes. Rudolf Steiner occasionally calls this force-web belonging to the physical body the "phantom" of the physical body.

"The phantom belongs to the physical body. It is the remaining part of the physical body and more important than the outer materials. Because, the outer materials are basically nothing else than something that is integrated into the web of the human form." [405]

As Rudolf Steiner further explains, we owe today's form of the human body to the Spirits of Form, thus the same spirits who also gifted us with an I as a fourth member of being. They were able to do so because they had risen to the rank of creative beings who can work by means of the zodiac. Also the Thrones on ancient Saturn created the very first preliminary stage of the physical body with its associated phantom according to the forces of the zodiac region.

"We know that the foundation stone, so to speak the germ to this phantom of the physical body, was laid by the Thrones during the Saturn time, that then the Spirits of Wisdom continued to work on it during the Sun time, the Spirits of Movement during the Moon time and the Spirits of Form during the Earth time. And only thereby what the physical body is has become a phantom. Hence we call them Spirits of Form, because they actually live in what we call the phantom of the physical body."

But the phantom is just the one part of the physical body. Physical substances also belong to it. For this purpose, the human spirit-germ must already prenatally be endowed with the ability to become not only a warmth-, gas- and water-body on Earth, but also an earth-body. In astrology we find this connection illustrated in the fact that the zodiac, along which the cosmic human form extends as a celestial round, is equally interspersed by three fire, air, water and earth signs. We should imagine the form itself as resting, comparable to the earthly embryo in the womb, which cannot yet walk, speak or think or even will, but is completely devoted to other processes. Similarly, in the sphere of the zodiac, the human spirit-soul is still fully devoted to the cosmic processes of becoming in order to bring about his twelve-membered physical form as a pictorial expression of his I.

As a final activity completing the human form, the integration of the twelve sensory organs into the spirit-germ now takes place as tools for igniting the earthly I-consciousness. For although the initial preliminary stages of the sensory organs were already developed on ancient Saturn, by no means all twelve senses of man were created there. In the course of evolution, their number increased only gradually. On the ancient Moon, for example, the human being had only seven senses, which were even more enlivened than the senses of today's earthly man. Their seven-number was an expression of the movement forces of the planets, since the senses were even more pervaded by an ether or life body than is the case with today's senses. Only in the course of the development of the Earth that the human senses have become more and more calm, unmoved and inanimate, so that today they are subdivided according to the twelve zodiacal forces, which are resting in the cosmos and underlie the physical body.

"Seven remain only for the Moon, where the senses are still in motion, where they are still alive. So the life on the Moon, into which the senses are still immersed, is divided into seven members. This is only a small elementary part of what one has to say in order to show that it is not based on arbitrariness, but on living observation of the extrasensory world of facts, which is initially not accessible to the senses of the human being during the earth existence. The further one advances and the further one really gets into the contemplation of the world's secrets, the more one sees that such a thing as this ratio of twelve to seven is not a gimmick, but that it really is effective in all existence, and that the fact that it must be expressed out there through the relation of the resting stellar constellations to the moving planets is also a result of one part of the great mystery of number in the world existence. And the ratio of the twelve-number to the seven-number expresses a deep mystery of existence, expresses the mystery man is subjected to as of a sensory being to a living being, as of himself to a living being. The twelve-number contains the mystery that man can receive an I. By the fact that his senses have become twelve, twelve resting areas, they are the basis of the I-consciousness on Earth. Since during the Moon time these senses were still organs of life, the

---

[405] GA 131 "Von Jesus zu Christus" (From Jesus to Christ), Karlsruhe, 10 October 1911

human being could only have an astral body. At that time, these seven sensory organs, which still existed as organs of life, were the basis of the astral body." [406]

When man, in his prenatal descent from the cosmic expanses, arrives at the middle region of the spiritual world or world of thoughts, the power of the world-thoughts becomes more and more concrete. It noticeably consolidates during the transition from the Arupa region of the higher spiritual world to the Rupa region of the lower spiritual world. This process runs parallel to the "Ex deo nascimur", the spirit-birth of man or his birth from his divine origin on the Budhi plane into the increasingly denser spheres of the spiritual world. Without this increasing power of thought, the sensory stimuli would remain only dreamlike stimuli of the soul. But when the related thoughts join them, the full and clear waking and I-consciousness, based on sensory stimuli, emerges. That's what the first half of the 45th weekly verse refers to:

45th Week (9 - 15 February)	*45. Woche (9. – 15. Februar)*
The might of thought consolidates	Es festigt sich Gedankenmacht
In league with spirit-birth.	Im Bunde mit der Geistgeburt,
It brightens up the senses' gloomy stimuli	Sie hellt der Sinne dumpfe Reize
To total clarity.	Zur vollen Klarheit auf.

However, in order that a recognizing and understanding, clear and fully awake thinking can join the sensory perception, a second spiritual archetype must be created in addition to the spiritual archetype of the physical body, namely that of a new ether body. Its construction essentially takes place in the lower spiritual world and the higher soul world pervading it, that is within the cosmic circle of the surrounding zodiac region and thus in the seven planetary spheres. Therefore the ether body is subject to the seven-number.

And the human soul needs the ether body for another reason too, for a soul is able to connect to a soul body or astral body, but not to a physical body. For this it needs an ether body as a connecting element and link. In addition, an ether body can serve as a material bearer of human thinking and enable a connection of thoughts to the physically experienced sensory impressions.

"The ether body is the bearer of the thoughts" [407], Rudolf Steiner states and continues in another lecture: *"The ether body is actually the bearer of our whole intellect. When we fall asleep in the evening, all our imaginations and memories remain in the ether body actually. Man leaves his thoughts in his ether body and only meets them again in the morning."* [408]

Only through the link of an ether body as bearer and tool of thinking the spirit-filled human soul is able to participate cognitively and intelligently in the outer world events. Only in this way the spiritual light of thought can illuminate the meaning of external sensory impressions. This is pointed out in the second half of the 45th weekly verse:

If soul-abundance	Wenn Seelenfülle
Wants to unite with world-becoming,	Sich mit dem Weltenwerden einen will,
Then senses' revelation must	Muss Sinnesoffenbarung
Receive the light of thinking.	Des Denkens Licht empfangen.

For this purpose, however, thinking must draw nearer to the Sensorial. The still formless (a-rupa) ideas of the higher spiritual world must become formative (rupa), concrete thoughts of the lower spiritual world. The "might of thought" has to "consolidate". Only in this way, later in our life on Earth, thoughts can serve as the spiritual basis of our concepts and words and connect to concrete sensory impressions in the human soul. Therefore, the experiences in the zodiac sphere ultimately result in a necessity for the human spirit-soul to descend into the lower regions of the thought world, into that kingdom in which mainly the planetary forces prevail in order to take up the work on the archetype of a new ether body there and also to draw together a matching astral body.

---

[406] GA 170 "Das Rätsel des Menschen – die geistigen Hintergründe der menschlichen Geschichte" (The riddle of the human being – the spiritual background of human history), Dornach, Lecture of 12 August 1916

[407] GA 93a "Grundelemente der Esoterik" (Foundations of esotericism), Berlin, Lecture of 7 October 1905

[408] GA 130 "Das esoterische Christentum und die geistige Führung der Menschheit" (Esoteric Christianity and the spiritual guidance of mankind), Lugano, Lecture of 17 September 1911

But before this new work can be started, the work on the spirit-germ of the physical body, which mainly takes place in the higher spiritual world, must first be completed. The human I has witnessed his spirit-birth and, through bringing forth the spirit-germ of a physical body, it also has created the prerequisite for the development of an I-consciousness by physical sensory organs. The Hierarchies now gradually take the completed spirit-germ into their care and carry it down to the Earth. As a result, the human soul slowly loses sight of this spirit-germ of his future physical body.

"But I have also indicated that we get lost of this spirit-germ in a way, at a certain point of time. We feel from a certain time on: We have worked out the spirit-germ of our physical organism in connection with other beings of the universe, with beings of higher Hierarchies; we have developed it to a certain point. Then we get lost of it and it immerses into the physical earth forces with which it is related and which come from a father and a mother. It connects with the Human of the hereditary current." [409]

The whole process of losing the spirit-germ of a new physical organism extends from the fourth region of the spiritual world or Zodiac sphere to the third region of the spiritual world, which as Saturn sphere belongs to the planetary spheres already. The reason for the great difference between the higher and the lower spiritual world is that the former is still pervaded by the inner divine warmth of the Budhi plane, but the latter is not. This circumstance is also the reason why all developmental processes on the Arupa globe, which projects from the Budhi plane into the higher spiritual world, are related to the dark warmth states of ancient Saturn, whereas the developmental processes on the Rupa globe, which projects into the lower spiritual world, are related to light and to the ancient Sun's cold currents of light which differentiate from the dark heat. However, the clarity that the light receives as a result makes it suitable to become "the light of thinking". Therefore the spiritual world bears the name "world of thoughts".

Warmth and cold are clearly differentiated from each other in the lower spiritual world, as has been the case since the ancient Sun, on which Christ as representative of the intimate heart warmth and Lucifer as representative of the bright but cold light of knowledge still stood fraternally side by side. Christ chose the ascending path. He remained connected with the Budhi plane and became the bearer of love. Lucifer chose the downward path, turned to the spiritual world with exclusion of the Budhi plane and thus became the bearer of wisdom. He is still the master of the planetary spheres beyond the Sun and the adjacent starry sky. That is why we need his help when we are to extend beyond the Sun sphere after death, from where Christ can lead us to even higher regions and connect us with the Budhi plane, as was already stated towards the end of the reflection on the 5th weekly verse. But on our return from the higher spiritual world, which is flamed through by Budhi, to the much colder but on the other hand brighter lower spiritual world we need Lucifer's help again. Then again he is our "Luci-ferus", our light bearer, who illuminates for us the otherwise dark spiritual world. Only from the Sun sphere downwards does he become an adversary for us, as he disdains the Earth and its mission to develop love in the cosmos under the guidance of Christ. In the planetary spheres beyond the Sun, however, he contributes, in the manner of the ancient Sun state, to the construction of our ether body, which is woven from the emitted and sacrificed substance of the lowest member of being of the Spirits of Wisdom. In this way the ether body becomes the bearer of our thinking and, in life on Earth, we can add a spiritual, mental content to the external sensory impressions with the help of the soul power of thinking in order to be able to enter into a soulful and cognitive relationship with them.

This too is hidden behind the words of the 45th weekly verse:

The might of thought consolidates	Es festigt sich Gedankenmacht
In league with spirit-birth.	Im Bunde mit der Geistgeburt,
It brightens up the senses' gloomy stimuli	Sie hellt der Sinne dumpfe Reize
To total clarity.	Zur vollen Klarheit auf.
If soul-abundance	Wenn Seelenfülle
Wants to unite with world-becoming,	Sich mit dem Weltenwerden einen will,
Then senses' revelation must	Muss Sinnesoffenbarung
Receive the light of thinking.	Des Denkens Licht empfangen.

---

[409] GA 219 "Das Verhältnis der Sternenwelt zum Menschen und des Menschen zur Sternenwelt" (The relationship of the starry world to man and man to the starry world), Dornach, Lecture of 26 November 1922

Return to the Spheres of Saturn and Jupiter– 46th Week

With the entry into the planetary spheres the human soul, coming from the cosmic depths of the star world, enters the realm of the lower spiritual world. Here significantly different conditions prevail than in the higher spiritual world or in the Zodiac sphere, which is the junction between the two. The forces that are particularly effective henceforward, are no longer structured according to the twelve-number, but according to the seven-number. However, they are not as strictly separated from each other as is the case with the clearly defined forms on Earth. The forces of the planets interpenetrate. Although man first enters the Saturn sphere as the highest planetary sphere and then the neighbouring Jupiter sphere, the forces of all seven planetary spheres are effective everywhere within the planetary existence. The Moon sphere as the lowest of these works up into Saturn sphere. However, it has its weakest effect there. Likewise the Saturn sphere works down into the Moon sphere, but only with little intensity. Furthermore, Saturn does not only have an effect inwards, into our planetary system. It also radiates its forces outwards into the surrounding starry sky.

"It is the greatest benefit for us that the forces of Saturn not only shine into the planetary world of the Earth, but also into the vastness of the outer space. – There, however, they are something completely different from the small, insignificant bluish rays of Saturn visible here on Earth. There, the spiritual rays that radiate out into the cosmos and even stop being spatial, shining into a Non-Spatial, appear to us in such a way that between death and a new birth we say to ourselves: We look back here in gratitude to the outermost planet of our Earth's planetary system, to Saturn – for Uranus and Neptune are not actual planets of the Earth development, they joined later – we are aware, Saturn does not only shine down upon the Earth, it also shines out into the vastness of the outer space. We owe to what it radiates out there in spiritual rays that we are undressed of earthly heaviness, undressed of what the physical powers of speech are, of what the physical powers of thought are. Saturn is indeed our greatest benefactor between death and a new birth through its radiating out into the vastness of the world; in this respect, from a spiritual point of view, it is the opposite of the Moon forces.

The spiritual Moon forces bind us to the Earth, the spiritual Saturn forces enable us to live in the vastness of the universe. Here on Earth the Moon forces are of particular importance to us as human beings; I have explained how they even play their part in our daily waking up. What the Moon forces are on Earth to us here, [there] are to us the forces that radiate from the outermost sphere of our planetary system as Saturn forces into the outer space. Because indeed, this radiating out is not that you should imagine: Well, Saturn just has a front side, shines down to the Earth, has a back side, shines out into the universe. It is not this way, but Saturn, if it were this [a sphere has been drawn], moves in this path [a circular path]. Now it radiates out spiritually from everywhere, so that its radiating out happens like this [all around the perimeter]. – On the contrary: physical Saturn appears, I would say, like a hole in this sphere of the World-Saturn, which shines out spiritually into the outer space. It is quite true that what radiates out there covers everything Earthly from a certain time after death, but covers it with light.

Well, cosmically seen it is like this: here on Earth man is under the influence of the spiritual Moon forces, between death and a new birth he is under the influence of the Saturn forces. And as he descends to Earth again, he withdraws from Saturn forces and gradually enters the sphere of the Moon forces. What happens there? As long as the human being is related to the sphere of Saturn's forces – and Saturn, if I may say so, is helped by Jupiter and Mars, who have a special task of which I will speak in the near future here – as long as the human being is under the influence of Saturn, Jupiter and Mars, he actually wants to become a being who does not walk and speak and think in the earthly sense, but who wants to orient himself among spiritual beings, who wants to experience the Logos resounding in himself, who wants the world thoughts to light up in himself. And with these inner intentions, the spirit-germ of the physical organism is indeed now released down to Earth.

The human being, who descends from the spiritual worlds to the Earth, does not have the slightest inclination to submit to earthly heaviness, he has no inclination to walk, to make the speech organs vibrate so that his physical speech sounds, or to think about physical things with a physical brain. He has none of this. He obtains this when he is released, as a physical spirit-germ, from the sphere of the Saturn forces down to the Earth, passes through the Sun and then enters the other planetary spheres, the Mercury, Venus and the Moon spheres. These spheres of Mercury, Venus and Moon transform the cosmic dispositions for spiritual orientation, for experiencing the Logos, for lighting up of the world thoughts within, into the dispositions for speaking, for thinking, for walking. And this inversion is caused by the Sun, that is, the spiritual Sun. When the human being enters the Moon sphere – and the Moon forces are helped by the forces of Venus and Mercury – the celestial dispositions, if I may use this expression, for orientation, for the Logos and for the thoughts, are transformed into the earthly ones." [410]

As long as man stays in the planetary spheres beyond the Sun, i.e. in the three regions of the lower spiritual world, he remains connected to the spirit cosmos and does not yet want to walk, speak or think on his own. He lives with the world thoughts and listens to the harmony of the spheres. But in contrast to the higher spiritual world, where he was able to experience this directly the meaningful World Word and lived in intimate contact with the Hierarchies, both are gradually lost to him in the lower spiritual world. This new world of the harmony of the spheres has an increasingly dazing effect on his former ability to directly perceive the spiritual Word and the spiritual beings. And his life in the region of eternity or duration ends then. With his arrival in the planetary spheres, the human being enters the kingdom of time. There, everything is no longer immediately present, but the experiences disappear in the past. In order to preserve everything experienced, man now needs the ability of memory. His experiences made in the higher spiritual world nonetheless initially live on inside him, and since they are saturated with the divine intentions and will impulses of the Arupa region, they have a reinforcing effect on his changed spiritual vision, which from now on is no longer given as a matter of course, as an "inborn power of the soul", but requires an increasingly greater volitional effort to be exercised. The 46th weekly verse deals with this enormous transformation of the psycho-spiritual experience of man during his transition from the universe of the stars to the planetary world:

46th Week (16 - 22 February)	46. Woche (16. – 22. Februar)
The world is threatening to daze	Die Welt, sie drohet zu betäuben
The inborn power of the soul.	Der Seele eingeborene Kraft;
Come forth, you, memory,	Nun trete du, Erinnerung,
Refulgent from the spirit-depths	Aus Geistestiefen leuchtend auf
And reinforce my looking,	Und stärke mir das Schauen,
Which only by volitions	Das nur durch Willenskräfte
Is able to sustain itself.	Sich selbst erhalten kann.

If the human being would lose the reminiscence of his experiences in the higher spiritual world, he would lose the consciousness of himself, too. Not only in life on Earth but in the lower spiritual world as well, memory is an extraordinarily important human ability, although it appears quite differently on the different levels of existence. Immediately after the spirit-germ of the physical body has been transferred to the hereditary current on Earth, man begins to build up a bearer of memory and thinking for his life on Earth. In the lower world of thought he first creates the spirit-germ of a new ether body. All prenatal experiences are imprinted in this archetype as memories. However, during the earthly life they are only accessible to someone who is a spirit disciple on a certain initiation level provided he can descend consciously with his Psycho-Spiritual into his ether body, transfer himself into courses of time before his birth and walk back through the centuries before his birth.

"It becomes clear to him that the ether body he is now bearing has indeed a long history and that he prepared it over a long time. Long, long before he could enter into existence through this birth, he himself had worked in the spiritual world on the ether or life body which he now bears. And he began to work on this ether body at the moment when the first ancestor, from whom he has just inherited characteristics, entered the physical Earth. This is a true experience of a piece of our ether body. Mere enumerating, that the human being consists of physical body, ether or life body, astral body and I, gives only certain indications, certain core teachings. The only way to get to know what exists as our own inner part in form of a sheath is to become acquainted with the messages of those who really descended into this human work of sheath.

In this way, passing through his own birth, man learns to enter those realms which he traversed before he entered existence through birth; thus, as a mystic, he gets to know a piece of his life before birth, a great piece which encompasses hundreds of years. For he passes through centuries until he arrives at the time when he began to form the archetype of his ether body in the life between his last death and his present birth. At the moment he began, the first germs of those special characteristics shot into a physical person's blood and became more and more pronounced until his ether body was so far developed that it could take on, at birth, the characteristics caused by his own work. This is one side of the experience. What one

---

[410] GA 219 "Das Verhältnis der Sternenwelt zum Menschen und des Menschen zur Sternenwelt" (The relationship of the starry world to man and man to the starry world), Dornach, Lecture of 26 November 1922

experiences there is, so to speak, a reconstructing of everything that one had to do in the spiritual world long before entering existence in this incarnation through birth. What one built there and then pushed together as it were, compressed it into one's present ether body, what condensed into the ether body through centuries, was called «the Upper», the heavenly or the spiritual man. So that the technical expression existed: The human being gets to know his Upper by entering into his ether or life body. This was called the heavenly or spiritual man because man had to sense that aspect of him, which had descended, as being formed out of the spiritual land."[411]

When man will have completed the spirit-germ of his new ether body towards the end of his descent through the seven planetary spheres, he will draw together the ether substances and ether forces fitting to the spiritual archetype, shortly before his entry into the new life on Earth. Thereby, immediately before its connection with the physical human germ in the womb of the future mother, the ether body will appear to the extrasensory perception like a small likeness of the planetary system, surrounded by the zodiac, bounded downwards by the sphere of the Earth. In this way the ether body reveals both its extraterrestrial origin and its developmental history.

"Before he [man] gets the inclination to connect to the physical world through the embryo, he draws to himself the powers of the etheric world. And he forms his ether body by drawing to himself the forces from the etheric world. In order to be able to take this idea more accurately, let us sketch this schematically on the board. Let's assume I wanted to characterize the Psycho-Spiritual, which comes from the spiritual world, by this shape [in figure 23 the darkest circular area in the middle and the slightly brighter hatched circular area surrounding it, which together can be compared to the yolk in an egg].

Of course, this is only done very schematically. Only that which man first draws to himself becomes his etheric body. Thus, descending from the spiritual world, he dresses himself, so to speak, in his etheric body [hatched in orange, the entire star-framed oval]. But the saying that «man dresses himself in his etheric body» does not tell us much; we certainly must touch upon the constitution of this etheric body. This etheric body, which develops in the human being, is to a certain extent a world of its own. However, one might say, a world of its own as an image. It is such, that this etheric body shows something like stars in its surroundings [yellow stars], for example, and that it shows in its lower parts something that more or less looks like an image of the Earth itself. And there even is a kind of image of the Sun and Moon in it.

Fig. 23: Likeness of the cosmos in the prenatal human ether body

This is extraordinarily important that by drawing to ourselves ether forces from the general ether world, when we descend into the earthly world, we bring along a kind of image of the cosmos in our ether body. If we could take the ether body out of man, at the moment when man connects himself to the physical body, we would get a sphere with the stars, with the zodiac, with the Sun and the Moon, much more beautiful than ever mechanically formed."

The forming process of the spiritual archetype of a new ether body thus begins with the entry of the human spirit-soul into the lower spiritual world or Rupa region, where the creative power of the thought archetypes already produces concrete forms. Accordingly, we retrace there the entire past evolution of the spiritual archetypes of the ether bodies from the ancient Sun and the ancient Moon to the Earth. These evolutionary steps always took place on the Rupa globe. During the passage through the Saturn sphere the very first occurrence of the spiritual archetype of a human ether body on the Rupa globe of the ancient Sun is repeated. Since this presented itself to the outside world as shining and gassy, the Saturn region is also referred to as the "Atmospheric Region" based on imaginations and concepts from the sensory world. Just as the clouds in the earthly sky condense out of the light-filled air into visible forms, but just as easily dissolve again under the heat of the Sun and can disappear into the Invisible, so the beginning of all of Rupa- or form-development is going on in the Saturn sphere. It is a very significantly task of the ether body

---

[411] GA 119 "Makrokosmos und Mikrokosmos" (Macrocosm and Microcosm), Vienna, Lecture of 25 March 1910

to create lasting forms and finally even such ones into which materials of the Earth will fit. This activity begins in the Saturn sphere. [412]

With the entry into the already somewhat denser Jupiter sphere, man repeats, during his prenatal descent into a new life on Earth, the developmental processes of the human ether body on the Rupa globe of the ancient Moon. There it was endowed with the ability to build fluid forms, still very mobile and changeable, but of much higher density and longer durability than the volatile, gaseous formations on the ancient Sun. The individual forms are not yet completely separated from each other. They still interpenetrate and form a common great unity. They are thus an expression of the unity of all life, which manifests in the Jupiter sphere as flowing, streaming, according to which this sphere is called the "Oceanic Region" of the spirit land. Here are also the spiritual foundations of the ancient Moon's sea existence, which was permeated by various life streams and in which even the senses of man were still alive, as the contemplation of the previous weekly verse has shown.

The ability to build solid, clearly separated forms and to sustain them for a long time was woven into the spiritual archetype of the human ether body on the Rupa globe of the Earth development for the first time. This process took place in the Mars sphere, the lowest Rupa region of the world of thought. It is therefore called the "Continental Region" in reference to the solid forms on Earth. This is by no means just an analogy, but all physical forms have their spiritual archetypes there, which sustain them. The prenatal passage of the human spirit-soul through the Continental Region of the spiritual world or the Mars sphere is the subject of the next weekly verse.

Return to the Mars Sphere – 47th Week

In the depths of the cosmos, the human spirit-soul lives usually for centuries without any sense of heaviness and form. But at some point a longing for earthly heaviness begins to stir in it. Coming from the vastness of the Jupiter sphere it contracts in order to enter the Mars sphere or lowest region of the spiritual world and to continue there its preparation for the forthcoming new life on Earth.

"Then man, returning to earth, yearns again to live in the heaviness of the Earth. But he first passes the Jupiter sphere. Jupiter also radiates a heaviness, but one that is suitable to add a certain joyfulness to the yearning for the heaviness of the earth. So not only the yearning for the heaviness of the earth will live in the soul, but this yearning will receive a joyful nuance of mood. Man passes through the Mars sphere. He yearns for the heaviness of the earth. A joyful mood is already in him. Mars also affects him with its heaviness, plants in, inculcates, as it were, into the joyfully yearning soul the activity to enter this heaviness of the earth, in order to powerfully use the next physical life between birth and death. Now the soul is already so far that in its subconscious depths it has the impulse to clearly yearn for the heaviness of the earth and to use the earthly incarnation powerfully, so that the yearning joy, the joyful yearning is expressed with intensity." [413]

The human spirit-soul, meanwhile filled with joy and vigor, one could even say, "bursting with energy", encounters in the Mars sphere the world forces building up the sensory world and underlying the sense-appearance. These forces now reveal themselves ever more strongly, almost with lust or pleasure to become. Our sensory organs, as slightly enlivened physical instruments, are components of our physical body. Hence they are closest to the lifeless world that surrounds us in life on Earth and which includes also the mineral sheaths of all living beings. It is precisely for this reason that we can perceive the physical world sensorily at all and call the totality of these perceptions a "sensory world". Nowadays we also attribute to it those areas of the physical world that we can only perceive with the help of technical equipment such as microscopes, telescopes or similar instruments. But all physical form has its foundation in the Mars sphere or the first or "Continental Region" of the spiritual world, as Rudolf Steiner writes in his "Theosophy":

"The first region contains the archetypes of the physical world, insofar as it is not gifted with life. The archetypes of minerals can be found here, as well as those of the plants; but only insofar as they are purely physical, that is, insofar as life in them is not taken into consideration. Likewise one meets here the

---

[412] GA 212 "Menschliches Seelenleben und Geistesstreben im Zusammenhang mit der Weltentwicklung" (Human soul life and spiritual aspiration in connection with world development), Dornach, Lecture of 26 May 1922

[413] GA 291 "Das Wesen der Farben" (The essence of the colours), Dornach, Lecture of 10 December 1920

physical forms of animals and humans. This should not be the end of what is in this region; it should only be illustrated by obvious examples".

In the first region of the spiritual world, the Mars sphere, the human being, approaching his next life on Earth, continues his work on the spiritual archetype of a new ether body, because later on in life on Earth it should finally be able to grasp the lifeless substances of the physical body in order to include them in life processes and thus to sustain the organ functions of the physical body for the duration of life on Earth. Although the archetypes of all lifeless, solid and purely mineral physical things are by no means everything that belongs to this region, as Rudolf Steiner expressly emphasizes – for here, man not only continues his work on physical forms, but in addition on the spirit-germ of his ether body – the region has nevertheless received its name from them.

"This region makes up the basic structure of the «spirit land». It can be compared to the solid land of our physical earth. It is the continental mass of the «spirit land». Its relationship to the physical-corporeal world can only be described comparatively. You can get an idea of it by something like this: Think of any limited space filled with physical bodies of the most varied kind. And now think these physical bodies away and in their places hollow spaces with their forms. The previously empty interstices in turn, imagine as to be filled with the most varied forms, which are in manifold relationships to the previous bodies. – This is approximately what it looks like in the lowest region of the archetype world. In it, the things and beings that are embodied in the physical world are present as «cavities». And the movable activity of the archetypes (and of the «spiritual music») takes place in the interstices. In the physical embodiment, the cavities, as it were, are filled with physical substances. Whoever looked into space with physical and mental eyes at the same time would see the physical bodies and in between the movable activity of the creating archetypes." [414]

We experience vividly this movable activity of the creative archetypes during our descent through the Mars sphere. Here, "out of the world-womb wants to rise, to quicken sense-appearance, the pleasure to become". For, the sensory world, as we will get to know it during our gradually approaching a new life on Earth, is just an "appearance". It is sustained in its existence and constantly "quickened" anew, refreshed by the spiritual archetypes of the Mars sphere, which are constantly in a pleasure to become. They are the reality behind the sense-appearance. For that we may never forget this when we will have arrived on Earth, we need "divine powers" that we bring with us from the spiritual world. They should also live "strongly" and thus Mars-like in our inner being and, as a spiritual power, prevent our thinking from falling into the error that the sense-appearance would be a reality on its own, independent of the spiritual world. Just here in the lowest region of the world of thought, just before we descend into the uppermost region of the soul world, all the power of the Holy Spirit must once again "strongly" revive within us and incorporate itself into the spirit-germ of our ether body as the bearer of our thinking.

47th Week (23 February - 1 March)	*47. Woche (23. Februar – 1. März)*
Out of the world-womb wants to rise,	Es will erstehen aus dem Weltenschoße,
To quicken sense-appearance,	Den Sinnenschein erquickend, Werdelust.
The pleasure to become.	Sie finde meines Denkens Kraft
May it now find my thinking's power	Gerüstet durch die Gotteskräfte,
Equipped enough by divine powers,	Die kräftig mir im Innern leben.
Which strongly live inside of me.	

From here, the spiritual archetype of the new earth-man works vigorously down into life on Earth, and the attraction between it and the Earth becomes more and more powerful.

"The archetype of a new life becomes more and more definite, and it causes that by the forces placed in man, he feels driven down to a physical life on earth, feels driven down in such a way that he feels attracted to the parent couple who can give him the physical sheath that corresponds most to the archetype of his coming life on earth, which was created in the spiritual world. Thus, a Threefold unites in the rebirth of man: the Masculine, the Feminine and the Spiritual. One can say: Long before man enters his new life on earth with birth, this developed power moves towards the respective parental couple; because man is

---

[414] GA 9 "Theosophie" (Theosophy), Chapter "Die drei Welten" (The three worlds), Section III "Das Geisterland" (The spirit land)

inwardly, substantially, this power, which grows out, one could say, as the power, which firstly strives towards the archetype and then towards the new life on earth." [415]

The driving force of a becoming and emerging of new sense-perceptible body forms can be experienced in the course of the year on Earth at best at that time when the very first signs of a new emergence of form in the plant world become apparent at the meteorological beginning of spring in the transition from February to March, when more and more sprouts break through the uppermost layer of the Earth, out of the "world-womb", and reveal the strong effectiveness of powers that will produce a complete, new vegetation period in the sensory world. With the entry of the Sun into the zodiac sign of Pisces in the last week of February, the Earth itself becomes a parable-like, sense-perceptible, earthly likeness of the spiritual "world-womb" and its "pleasure to become".

Return to the Sun Sphere – 48th Week

In order that the "thinking's power", which is now "equipped enough with divine powers, which strongly live inside of me", as it is said in the preceding Mars verse, will not live itself out in the new life on earth only as a formative power of the new ether body, which remains completely unconscious to the human being, but that it can also be experienced consciously in the form of thoughts and imaginations by the human soul, the human ether body must additionally be pervaded by an astral body. Only an astral body is suitable as a bearer of soul and consciousness, though only for a rather dreamlike consciousness, which surges up and down, and which by no means reaches to a completely awake-conscious and I-controlled thinking, let alone that in addition the human being could become aware of himself as an independent being.

"Furthermore, as an inner member of the human being, we have the astral body, the bearer of everything that man takes in with consciousness, what he really experiences during his day life in such a way that he can receive it mirrored from his body. Between the astral body and the physical body lies the bearer of what are imaginations that remain unnoticed for years, which are then brought up into the astral body and develop fully. In short, we speak of the fact that the ether body of man is active between the astral body, the bearer of consciousness, and the physical body." [416]

After his death, the human being gradually had put off the astral body of his previous earth life in the course of his passage through the sub-solar planetary spheres and finally completely in the Sun sphere. There his ethical review of his last life on earth ended. The old astral body had thus fulfilled its task.

"Only after taking off the astral body, after the life assessment was completed, man enters the spiritual world. In this he is in such a relationship to beings of pure spiritual kind as on Earth to the beings and processes of the nature kingdoms. In the spiritual experience, everything that was outside world in life on Earth becomes inside world then." [417]

Without an astral body, but instead clothed in a spiritual body conferred by the Hierarchies, man moved into the first region of the spiritual world, the Mars sphere, after his death. When, in preparation for his new birth on Earth, he descends in the opposite direction, coming from the Mars sphere, entering the Sun sphere, he immediately begins to clothe himself in a new astral body there. For this, however, he does not need to build up another spiritual archetype, as it is necessary for the physical body and the ether body. That is the great difference between the physical and the ether body on the one hand as the two lower members of the human being and the astral body and the I on the other hand as the two higher members of the human being, insofar as we regard him as four-membered. The archetype of the new astral body is first of all the human soul itself with all its enrichments and gifts of God that it was allowed to receive in the course of its passage through the higher regions of the spiritual world and its contact with the Budhi plane in the middle between two incarnations. According to its own being and stage of development, as much of the astral light-substantiality flows and streams to it from the Sun sphere as it can unite with itself in accordance to its inner nature. But in the highest region of the soul world, which is not yet clouded by the subjectivity of human thinking, the powers of the objective world thinking also stream to it, based on which the whole cosmos was built and rests securely. Pure astral light as well as the world-thinking's objectivity

[415]   GA 63 "Geisteswissenschaft als Lebensgut" (Spiritual science as a treasure of life), Berlin, Lecture of 19 March 1914

[416]   GA 60 "Antworten der Geisteswissenschaft auf die großen Fragen des Daseins" (Answers of the spiritual science to the great questions of existence), Berlin, Lecture of 24 November 1910

[417]   GA 26 "Anthroposophische Leitsätze" (Anthroposophical Leading Thoughts), Leading thought No. 26

and secureness stream into the human soul from all sides in the Sun sphere. This process is described in the first part of the weekly verse, which deals with man's descent into the Sun sphere.

Within the light that from world's heights	Im Lichte, das aus Weltenhöhen
Desires to stream powerfully to the soul,	Der Seele machtvoll fließen will,
May now, to solve soul's mysteries,	Erscheine, lösend Seelenrätsel,
Appear secureness of world-thinking ...	Des Weltendenkens Sicherheit ...

By means of this objective thinking, the human soul can once again receive answers to all its questions about the meaning of his own existence in the world, his origin, his development up to now as well as about the high goal at the end of his earthly and cosmic development, because here, in the highest region of the soul world, the soul is a virginly pure, still completely unclouded mirror of the spirit. There, the mentally internalized and in the purest way subjectivized world thinking can still preserve its objectivity even within the soul.

The formation of an independent human astral body started on the astral globe of the ancient Moon and was further developed on the astral globe in each next Moon-round as well as in the Earth-rounds completed to this day. As a member of being that is destined to become a bearer of the human soul and to interpenetrate with it, this could only be developed in the soul world or astral world. At his entry into the Sun sphere, the human being first enters the highest region of the soul world. From its heights the astral light streams to the human soul in its purest substantiality. Therefore, the weekly verse says, "Within the light that from *world's heights* desires to stream powerfully to the soul." The powerful radiance of even the earthly Sun is thus a very vivid sensory image of man's experience in the Sun sphere. This astral radiance of light, however, is merely the external appearance of the beings of the third Hierarchy, which are acting as the "world-thinking". Rudolf Steiner commented on this in his "Instructions for an esoteric training" in connection with the meditation formula "It thinks":

"«It» is the power-word for the world-thinking, that is, those beings in the higher world, who are endowed with creative thinking to the same degree as the human beings below them are endowed with the sensory looking." [418]

And on another occasion Rudolf Steiner notified:

"The beings of the third Hierarchy manifest in the life that unfolds in human thinking as a spirit-background. This life is hidden in the activity of human thinking. If they continued to function in their own way, man could not attain independence. Where cosmic thinking ends, human thinking begins." [419]

In order to achieve independence, it had to be possible for the human being to fall into error and lies. Quite different is the situation with regard to the beings of the third Hierarchy. As long as they remain true to their own nature, they can neither err nor lie. On this fact the "secureness of world-thinking" is based:

"I ask you to bear in mind, my dear friends, that by ascending to the higher category of beings that are no longer outwardly perceptible to humans, we are dealing with such beings who perceive by manifestation, by expressing what they themselves are. And they actually perceive their own being only as long as they want to manifest it, as long as they express it in some way to the outside world. They are, we could say, only awake by manifesting themselves. And if they do not manifest themselves, if they do not enter into a relationship with the environment, with the outer world through their will, then a different state of consciousness occurs to them, then they sleep in a certain way. However, their sleep is not an unconscious sleep as in humans, but their sleep is a kind of diminishing, a kind of loss of their sense of self. They have their sense of self as long as they manifest themselves to the outside world, and they lose their sense of self in a certain way when they no longer manifest themselves. Then they do not sleep like men but then something enters into their own being like the revelation of spiritual worlds which are higher than they themselves. They are then filled with higher spiritual worlds within themselves. ... The possibility of a lie does not exist in the beings of the third Hierarchy if they maintain their nature. For, what would happen if a being of the third Hierarchy wanted to lie? Then it would have to experience something inside itself that it would transmit to the outside world in a different way than it experiences it. But then this being of the next higher category would no longer be able to perceive this, because everything that these beings experience in their inner being is manifestation that passes into the external world immediately. These

---

[418] GA 245 "Anweisungen für eine esoterische Schulung" (Instructions for an esoteric training), Section: "Erklärungen zu den beiden vorhergehenden allgemein gegebenen Hauptübungen" (Explanations to the two preceding general exercises, given in general)

[419] GA 26 "Anthroposophische Leitsätze" (Anthroposophical Leading Thoughts), Leading thought No. 66

beings must live in a kingdom of absolute truth if they want to experience themselves at all. If we assume that these beings would lie, would have something inside of them that they would transform in their manifestations in such a way that it would not coincide with the manifestations, then they would not be able to perceive it, because they can only perceive their inner nature. They would immediately be dazed under the impression of a lie, immediately shifted into a state of consciousness, which would be a Dimming, a Tuning down of their ordinary consciousness, because it can only exist as manifestation of their inner being. So above us there is a class of beings who must live in the kingdom of absolute truth and sincerity through their own nature if they do not want to deny this nature. And any deviation from truth would numb these beings, diminish their consciousness." [420]

Man has no direct part in this divine truth initially. He must laboriously search for answers to his soul puzzles. These can best be solved in the soul world. In the course of his existence between death and new birth man stays there twice: once coming from the Earth after his death, beginning with his entry into the Moon sphere, the lowest region of the soul world, and a second time usually centuries later when he contracts himself from cosmic expanses into the soul world from above and then first into the Sun sphere as its highest region. Therefore, both in the 28th weekly verse, which deals with the entry of the newly deceased into the Moon sphere, and in the 48th weekly verse Rudolf Steiner points out the possibility of solving the mysteries of the human soul, which is given especially in the soul world. And he emphasizes already in the 28th weekly verse that this happens with the help of the world-thinking of the third Hierarchy. He describes it there as "rays of thought out of the sun-might of the soul" in which man is allowed to have a share beginning with the Moon sphere, i.e. immediately with his entry into the soul world: "I can, revitalized inside, feel now own being's vastness and forcefully give rays of thought out of the sun-might of the soul to solve the mysteries of life, and grant fulfillment many a wish, though hope already paralyzed its wings."

But man is destined to develop the qualities of independent, free will and of love in the cosmos. Solely on the basis of world-thinking, he never could attain independence. To this end, there must be planted a self-will in him that gives him independence as the basis of a human thinking activity on its own. As long as this self-will is in contradiction to the will of God, man can err and lie. If, however, man freely chooses to unite his own will to the divine will and permeates his thought-life with it, then this will make him free, will lead him to independence. Conversely, man must permeate his will-life with thinking in order to reach love. But this also leads to the goal desired by God only if man's own thinking corresponds to the pure world-thinking of the Sun sphere. This is particularly the case during man's prenatal passage through this sphere and for this reason the power of love is awakened in him precisely there.

"Just as we attain independence and free will through irradiating our thought-life with will, so we attain love by permeating our will-life with thoughts. We develop love in our actions by making thoughts radiate into the Volitional." [421]

But the will impulses of man flow through his heart with the help of the blood, or rather, the blood heat. In this way the heart can receive the impulse of love and become a true centre of love as the main organ of the human blood circulation. This is depicted in the Christian tradition as the flaming heart of Christ. The "Christ in us" livens up in the love of our heart. Therefore, the 48th weekly verse about the prenatal experience in the Sun sphere reads in its entirety:

48th Week (2 - 8 March)	*48. Woche (2. – 8. März)*
Within the light that from world's heights	Im Lichte, das aus Weltenhöhen
Desires to stream powerfully to the soul,	Der Seele machtvoll fließen will,
May now, to solve soul's mysteries,	Erscheine, lösend Seelenrätsel,
Appear secureness of world-thinking	Des Weltendenkens Sicherheit,
And, focusing the power of its rays,	Versammelnd seiner Strahlen Macht,
Awaken love in human hearts.	Im Menschenherzen Liebe weckend.

Of all the organs of the human organism, especially the heart is significantly developed in the Sun sphere. It is true that the zodiacal forces are involved, too, particularly those of Leo, but in the Sun sphere these must be substantially supplemented by the etheric forces of the Sun.

---

[420] GA 136 "Die geistigen Wesenheiten in den Himmelskörpern und Naturreichen" (Spiritual beings in the celestial bodies and in the kingdoms of nature), Helsingfors, Lecture of 5 April 1912

[421] GA 202 "Die Brücke zwischen der Weltgeistigkeit und dem Physischen des Menschen" (The bridge between universal spirituality and the physical constitution of man), Dornach, Lecture of 19 December 1920

"The forces from which the heart is prepared are at first purely moral-religious forces in the direction of Leo; initially purely moral-religious forces are planted into our heart like a mystery. To those ones who realize this, it actually seems nefarious that today's natural science regards the stars as indifferent, neutral physical masses, without seeing the Moral. And when man passes through the Sun region, these moral-religious forces are seized by the ether forces. And only when man comes closer to the Earth, the warmth, the fire region, the last steps are added to the preparation, so to speak. There those forces begin to work, which then shape the physical germ for the man, who descends as a psycho-spiritual being." [422]

The spirit-germ of the physical heart first emerges under the influence of the fiery sign of Leo or, respectively, the forces of the higher spiritual world underlying it. The spirit-germ of the etheric heart, on the other hand, is mainly formed in the Sun sphere. Therefore it is a particularly important sphere among the seven planetary spheres, from whose forces the archetype of the human ether body is woven. However, the heart is primarily a muscle organ and the muscle system of the human body is pervaded by the astral body, the bearer of the human soul, especially by the soul force of willing. Hence, in the astral light-fire of the Sun, before the descent of the human spirit-soul into a new life on Earth, in particular his will is once again strongly Christ-imbued, but always depending on the stage of development of each human being.

The preparation for the later absorption of physical substances into the archetype of the embryonic human heart, taking place only in a mother's womb on Earth, is done during the passage through the warmth- or fire-region of the Earth. Natural science correspondingly calls this region close to the Earth thermosphere and describes an ionized, plasmatic state of the atoms there under a gradual rise in temperature up to about 1,200 °C (2,190 °F) at an altitude of about 500 km (310 mi) and the influence of the ultraviolet radiation. This region forms a real coat of warmth around the Earth as protection against the extreme cold of the outer space. Thus, far above the Earth's surface, high above the water sphere of the oceans and even beyond the stratosphere's sheath of cold air, in which the temperature dips to a low frost range of approximately -90 °C (-130 °F), the thermosphere is located as the fourth sphere of the Earth and as a representative of the solar forces on Earth. In a similar way, the Sun sphere as the fourth of the planetary spheres is the representative of the zodiac sphere of fourth region of the spiritual world, which in turn is the representative of the fourth world among the seven worlds, i.e. the Budhi plane. Therefore, the development of the Budhic power of love and the human I as an expression of the zodiacal forces, as well as the development of the human heart as Budhi organ always take place in connection with one of these respective fourth spheres. They always act as mediators between three higher and three lower parts of a total of seven. This shows how complicated the process of "ex deo nascimur" for the formation of a new human being on Earth is. As a microcosmic likeness of the macrocosm, the human being is as complex as the cosmos itself.

Return to the Venus Sphere – 49th Week

In the Sun sphere, the human spirit-soul was allowed to witness the work of the spiritual Hierarchies mainly on the human soul forces of thinking and willing. Imaginatively, this activity was presented to it in the image of light and fire. In the next-lower Venus sphere, the focus of development is then on the soul power of feeling. Here, too, everything is still strongly irradiated by light and warmth, simply because the lower part of the Sun sphere and the upper part of Venus sphere interpenetrate. In general, at this point it should be pointed out once again that there are no definite boundaries between the spheres, but each one merges into the other. The fact that it is possible nevertheless to speak of clearly distinguishable spheres can be illustrated by the example of the solar spectrum. It includes seven clearly distinguishable colours. However, the boundaries between them cannot be determined exactly. Whether, for example, a colour can be just assigned to orange as a yellowish orange, or perhaps rather to the neighbouring yellow as an orange yellow, will depend in the truest sense of the word on the eye of the beholder; for we perceive the finer nuances of the colours quite differently. On the other hand, there will be no disagreement about the middle range of each of the seven colours, provided they are viewed with an organically healthy eye. The same is true of the spheres. Each one emerges gradually out of the previous one and merges into the next one. In their middle areas, however, their characteristics are undeniably different from those of the two neighbouring spheres. This again shows that in the Creation the Ahrimanic principle of distinction and

---

[422] GA 239 "Esoterische Betrachtungen karmischer Zusammenhänge" (Esoteric reflections on karmic connections – karmic relationships), Volume 5, Prague, Lecture of 30 March 1924

delimitation on the one hand and the Luciferic principle of blurring and dissolving all boundaries on the other are in balance.

In the Venus sphere, once again a vivid memory rises in the human soul longing for the Earth that it was formed out of the macrocosm in long-lasting stages of development as human self and likewise its complicated sheath nature. For the last time it looks back on its entire process of becoming since its passage through the midnight hour of existence, when its "ex deo nascimur" in dark world nights first began with a retracing and reproducing of the development processes of ancient Saturn. It was endowed with forces of the Budhi plane and the regions of the spiritual world, with cosmic forces of various kinds, which it absorbed during its existence as a world-being. All these forces, originating from the cosmic circumcircle, were internalized meanwhile and thereby turned into soul forces. This is what the human spirit-soul feels then in full clarity:

I feel the force of world-existence:	Ich fühle Kraft des Weltenseins:
So speaks the clarity of thought,	So spricht Gedankenklarheit,
Remembering own spirit's growth	Gedenkend eignen Geistes Wachsen
In world's dark nights ...	In finstern Weltennächten ...

Here, the last look back becomes possible for the human soul before the new incarnation, because it still has a share not only in the divine willpower of the Sun sphere that awakens love, but also in its wisdom-filled light, which is woven into the germ of the future ether body. Love, in turn, in the Venus sphere will in the further course of its development more and more be transformed from selfless divine love to a human feeling already saturated with self-will. From the all-encompassing love the first predilections are evolving. Thus love itself is shaded in different nuances, starting from the purely spiritual love of the Sun sphere, reaching down to the upper half of the Venus sphere, as an expression of the Budhi plane's divine love in the soul world, then as the gradually developing preference for a certain religious and spiritual community, to which the human soul feels increasingly attracted and with which it identifies itself, down to emotional, passionate and ultimately physical love, which will come more clearly into the foreground of human soul life not before the third set of seven years of the earthly life when it awakens as sexual love. In this process, the spirits of the Venus sphere play a decisive role.

"At the same time one learns to recognize which beings are preferably connected with the Venus existence, the beings from the Hierarchy of the Archai, the Primal Forces. And then you get to know an important truth, again something that, when you really get to know it, astonishes you tremendously. One looks at the beings connected with the Venus existence, which have a reflection in human life after sexual maturity. And these beings are then those that are linked as Primal Forces with the emergence of the world itself. These beings, which are linked as Primal Forces with the emergence of the cosmos itself, are again active in their reflection in the emergence of the physical human being in the sequence of the generations. The great connection between the cosmos and human life reveals itself in this way." [423]

Rudolf Steiner calls the Venus sphere as the second highest region of the soul world also the "Region of active Soul Power".[424] Beside his own newly acquired soul power, the human being experiences there, first and foremost through feeling, the activity of the Archai in the process of Creation and the further configuration of the human astral and ether body. This too is a "force of the world-existence". In contrast to life on Earth, however, man in the soul world has to illuminate, with the help of his ability to radiate his own soul light, the outside world, which appears otherwise dark to him. His ever more intense turning to the sensory world of the Earth, where the Sun will illuminate the whole world from the outside, causes that the time in the past appears to him as a life in "world's dark nights". Even in the spiritual world Lucifer always had to brightly illuminate with his light every section of that world to which man was to give attention to. But now all hope and all longing of the human soul is directed entirely towards "the world's near day" in the next earthly life. Accordingly, the 49th weekly verse reads completely:

---

[423] GA 239 "Esoterische Betrachtungen karmischer Zusammenhänge" (Esoteric reflections on karmic connections – karmic relationships), Volume 5, Paris, Lecture of 24 May 1924

[424] GA 9 "Theosophie" (Theosophy), Chapter "Die drei Welten" (The three worlds), Section I "Die Seelenwelt" (The soul world) and Section II "Die Seele in der Seelenwelt nach dem Tode" (The soul in the soul world after death)

49th Week (9 - 15 March)	*49. Woche (9. – 15. März)*
I feel the force of world-existence:	Ich fühle Kraft des Weltenseins:
So speaks the clarity of thought,	So spricht Gedankenklarheit,
Remembering own spirit's growth	Gedenkend eignen Geistes Wachsen
In world's dark nights,	In finstern Weltennächten,
And to the world's near day	Und neigt dem nahen Weltentage
It turns the inside's rays of hope.	Des Innern Hoffnungsstrahlen.

"We can then summarize this in the words: The closer we approach a new earthly life, the more man as a universe contracts, so to speak. We become more and more aware of how this first majestic universe – especially in the middle between death and a new birth it is majestic – of how man, being this majestic universe, shrinks to a certain extent, how the planets we carry within us, the weaving of the planets turns into that which then vibrates, pulsates in the human ether body; how what the fixed stars in the zodiac are turns into that which forms our sensory and nervous life. That shrinks, that takes shape, becomes first a spiritual, then an etheric body. It is received by a mother's womb and clothed in earthly matter only when it has become very small. And then the moment comes when we approach earthly life, where we feel, so to speak, that the universe that we have had before is disappearing. It shrinks, it gets smaller. And this creates in us the yearning to come down to Earth again, to connect ourselves with a physical body again, because, in a sense, this universe withdraws from the spiritual gaze. We look at how we become human." [425]

Return to the Mercury Sphere – 50th Week

In the course of his passage through the Venus sphere, the human being has dissolved from his humanity-wide feeling, which still had a decisive influence on his soul life in the Sun sphere. He already turned his attention to that special part of humanity belonging to the cultural and religious connections in which he wishes to incarnate. With the transition from the Venus sphere to the Mercury sphere, the circle of humanity is further narrowed. The human spirit-soul comes here mainly under the influence of the Archangeloi. In their quality as Folk Spirits, they prepare the next incarnation of man within a very particular people on a confined area of the surface of the Earth, which is under their rule. This brings man still closer to the earthly sensory world. The consequence of this is that his perception of the spiritual Hierarchies that lead him increasingly fades away. Like a final, very last remembering of his sublime, divine-spiritual origin and an unmistakable pointing out of his great task in the cosmos, the Hierarchies once again focus directly to man's innermost being, to his I, through which he is a member of the spiritual world, one of them. This is still possible in the Mercury sphere especially because it is pervaded by the lowest region of the spiritual world, the Mars sphere or Continental Region. [426] So, the direct influence of the spiritual world reaches as far as there. In the Moon sphere bordering the Earth, on the other hand, man will be predominantly subject to the influences of the soul world through his astral body. But before that, for the last time, the Hierarchies of the spiritual world, which are no longer directly perceptible to him, manifest themselves to him through their joyful, powerful, world-creating activity, which the human being witnesses as the world-existence's real desire to become. It is that vigorous and powerful pleasure to become to which Rudolf Steiner already drew attention in the 47th weekly verse about the Mars sphere and which can be brought to the consciousness of the human soul once again here, precisely because of the fact that the Mercury sphere is pervaded by that sphere.

And to the human I now speaks,	Es spricht zum Menschen-Ich,
In powerful manifestation	Sich machtvoll offenbarend
And loosening its being's forces,	Und seines Wesens Kräfte lösend,
The world-existence's desire to become:	Des Weltendaseins Werdelust:

---

[425] GA 214 "Das Geheimnis der Trinität" (Mystery of the Trinity), Oxford, 22 August 1922

[426] See Figure 2 in the chapter about the 7th weekly verse (Spheres of Jupiter- und Saturn).

The last spiritual awakening call of the choir of Hierarchies to the human being, however, means at the same time taking leave of each other, at least as far as human consciousness is concerned, for in the following time it will increasingly turn to the sensory world, so that finally even the only indirect perception of Hierarchies by their manifestation will be lost to him. The work of the creative Hierarchies working from the spiritual world to prepare for a new incarnation of man is coming to an end. They now release him from their sphere of power and entrust him, "loosening" their own creative-forming forces, to the care of their messengers, first of all the arch-messengers or Archangeloi, who will accompany him in the further steps towards a new incarnation.

However, so that man in earthly life may not completely succumb to the influence of the sensory world and forget his spiritual origin as well as his most important cosmic task within the overall context of all spirit-beings involved in the world's creation, his great cosmic mission is brought to his consciousness once again in all clarity. Therefore the divine-spiritual world as a whole speaks to the human I that is about to begin a new incarnation on Earth the deeply significant words:

By giving into you my life	In dich mein Leben tragend
Out of its magic spell,	Aus seinem Zauberbanne,
I gain my real goal.	Erreiche ich mein wahres Ziel.

When the spiritual world once had accomplished everything that was to be accomplished by its creative powers, in the centre of its spirit- and self-awareness the insight arose that it needed rejuvenation and a new impulse both for its own further development and that of the world-existence. Like an annual plant that needs new powers to develop its innermost being, which can only be attained through the passage through a new germinal stage in order to grow and flourish in a new form, the totality of spiritual Hierarchies as the last great act before their overall creative activity faded away and came to rest, once made the decision: "Let us create man" as a microcosmic germ for a new macrocosm. And again comparable to a plant which, after it has formed all its green leaves, is dwindling in growth and is about to infuse all its forces, all its life into one, several or even countless small germs, and to develop these to seeds so that a multitude of new plants may emerge from them next spring, the spiritual world also makes all its forces, all its life, flow into billions of human souls and "I"s as germs of a new cosmos, which is to arise one day from their multiplicity as a new unity. The creative activity of the old world finds its coronation and perfection in it. The spirit is "concealed by an enchantment" into the sensory world, the sense-appearance, and is subject to a "magic spell" there from which it can only be redeemed by humanity, provided it may achieve its God-given goal of development. This is actually the "true goal" of the spiritual world in which it is strongly involved and for this purpose has sent to mankind the Anointed, the Christ, as representative of the life underlying all Creation, the Spirit of Life or the Life Spirit, and the bearer of the threefold and triune Logos, too. Rudolf Steiner once summarized this in two short sentences:

"In man is the seed for the future. But this seed must be fertilized by the Christ Jesus." [427]

For most people the spiritual world's last prenatal unmistakable statement "By giving into you my life out of its magic spell, I gain my real goal" slumbers in deeper layers of their souls during their life on Earth. It does not penetrate into the waking consciousness. But, there are human souls who remain so strongly attached to the spiritual world even in earthly life that the above farewell words of the Hierarchies reverberate in them and enter into their awake I-consciousness. Such a person, for example, was the German philosopher Friedrich Schelling, who lived in the transition from the 18th to the 19th century and thus still before the flood of theoretical materialism around the middle of the 19th century. Rudolf Steiner commented on Schelling's world view with the words:

"To Schelling the world puzzle takes shape by the fact that he finds his soul, which has awakened to the «I», confronted with the seemingly dumb, dead nature. Out of this nature the soul awakens. This fact reveals itself human observation. And into this nature the recognizing, the feeling human spirit immerses itself and fills itself through it with an inner world, which then becomes spiritual life in him. Could this be the case if there were not an inner deep relationship between the soul and nature that was initially hidden from human recognition? But nature remains dumb when the soul does not turn into its tool of speech; it seems dead when the human spirit does not release life from its enchantment in the appearance. ...

---

[427] GA 181 "Erdensterben und Weltenleben – Anthroposophische Lebensgaben – Bewusstseinsnotwendigkeiten für Gegenwart und Zukunft" (Earth's dying and world's life - Anthroposophical gifts to life – Necessities of awareness for present and future), Berlin, Lecture of 6 August 1918

Schelling sought the Spirit in nature through an intellectual view: the Spiritual, which by the power of its creative work made nature sprout forth. Nature once was the living body of this Spiritual, just as man's body is that of the soul. Now it has been spread out, this body of the World Spirit, revealing in its features what the Spiritual once incorporated into it, showing in its becoming and weaving the gestures that represent the effects of the Spiritual. This spiritual activity in the world-body had to precede the present state of the world so that it hardened and procreated a bone system in the mineral kingdom, a nervous system in the plant kingdom and a precursor of man's soul life in the animal kingdom. Thus from its youth, the world-body was developed into its old age; the present mineral, plant and animal kingdoms are, in a sense, the hardened products of what was once spiritually-corporeally accomplished in a process of becoming that has expired at the present time. But from the womb of the world's old-age-body the creative spirituality could make arise the human being gifted with soul and spirit, in whose inside the ideas by which the creative spirituality first formed the world-body light up to his recognition. As if enchanted in the present nature, the once alive and effective spirit rests in it; in the human soul it is released from its enchantment." [428]

This is how true knowledge speaks about the connection between man and world on the one hand and man's great cosmic destiny on the other. Less intellectually and more touching the emotional life of the people, the fairy tales spoke of the same truth to the deeper layers of human souls in the centuries and millennia before:

"The fairytale world is based on the well-founded belief that everything we have around us is the enchanted spiritual reality, and that the human being attains the truth when he releases the spiritual world from its enchantment." [429]

In this sense, the deeply significant words of the 50th weekly verse may resound once again at the end of this reflection.

50th Week (16 - 22 March)	*50. Woche (16. – 22. März)*
And to the human I now speaks,	Es spricht zum Menschen-Ich,
In powerful manifestation	Sich machtvoll offenbarend
And loosening its being's forces,	Und seines Wesens Kräfte lösend,
The world-existence's desire to become:	Des Weltendaseins Werdelust:
By giving into you my life	In dich mein Leben tragend
Out of its magic spell,	Aus seinem Zauberbanne,
I gain my real goal.	Erreiche ich mein wahres Ziel.

Return to the Moon Sphere – 51st Week

How does the life of the spiritual world get into the human I, so that man may release it from its magic spell in the physical outside world, in anticipation of a new spring of world-existence, as it says in the previous weekly verse? Perception of the physical outside world is possible for the human I only with the help of its sensory organs, of which the most important representative is the human eye. Just as the Sun's light in the darkness of the night is reflected on the outer surface of the Moon, the light phenomena of the physical outside world are reflected on the dark inner surface of the eye. The next weekly verse speaks of this:

51 Spring-Anticipation	*51 Frühlings-Erwartung*
Into the inside of the human being	Ins Innre des Menschenwesens
The richness of the senses pours.	Ergießt der Sinne Reichtum sich,
World Spirit finds itself	Es findet sich der Weltengeist
As mirror image in the human eye,	Im Spiegelbild des Menschenauges,
Which has to recreate from it	Das seine Kraft aus ihm
Its force completely new.	Sich neu erschaffen muss.

---

[428] GA 20 "Vom Menschenrätsel" (About the riddle of Man), Chapter "Der Idealismus als Natur- und Geistesanschauung (Idealism as a view of nature and spirit): Friedrich Wilhelm Joseph Schelling"

[429] GA 108 "Die Beantwortung von Welt- und Lebensfragen durch die Anthroposophie" (Answering world and life questions through anthroposophy), Berlin, 26 December 1908

What man experiences through his senses, but especially through the "human eye", is the richness of the sensory impressions of the earthly outside world and the extraterrestrial cosmos, too. The World Spirit was concealed in this Maya of the sensory world by enchantment. It pours through the human eye as "the richness of the senses" into the inside of the human being, however, by no means only into the inside of the physical eye, but with the help of the ether body and the astral body into the human soul. The 51st weekly verse therefore does not begin with the words "Into the inside of the human *body* ...", but in a much wider sense with the words "Into the inside of the human *being*", i.e. first into the human soul. But man is more than just a soul being. He is also a spirit being. As such he reaches with his various bearers from the spiritual world down to the physical sensory world and can therefore lead the world spirit, which was poured out into the sensory world, up and back again into the spiritual world, now, however, enriched by all those experiences which are only possible for a human being and can be achieved only within the physical sensory world. When the sensory experiences, which are reflected in the human soul, are seized by the human I, and their spirituality, through which they were once created, is recognized by the awake-conscious human thinking, then they are filled with the power of the World Spirit and released from their magic spell. But the initially completely passive mirror image in the human eye inside the human being, in the human soul, must first recreate its force from the World Spirit by means of the human I. In this way, the Creation experiences a new spring through the human being. While the outside world is already dying and approaching its death, the life of the spiritual world-existence undergoes a gradual resurrection within humans.

The higher spiritual members of being have started to flow into the human soul, especially into the human I. First it is Manas or the spirit self and Budhi or the life spirit. But the latter can only flow into the human I when it is inwardly connected with Christ, who has the life spirit as his lowest member of being. In order to connect this to mankind, Christ himself became man, accomplished his great sacrifice of love, suffered as man and died as man in order to rise again in the passage through the human stage to a new, higher life. Christ thus acts as mediator and link between the old dying Creation on the one hand, and a new, spring-like new Creation on the other. To participate in this process is the great cosmic task of man. For this purpose he was created as a great, last and highest artwork of the gods.

To those people who have preserved the feeling of their divine-spiritual origin even in life on Earth, the knowledge of the great cosmic mission of mankind may be revealed inwardly. Rudolf Steiner, for example, tells us about Goethe:

"Out of Goethe's way of thinking, the word is spoken that can make such a deep impression: What would the countless stars, what would all the heavens be, if they did not shine into a human eye, if they were not reflected in a human soul and perceived by a human heart? He who understands Goethe's way of thinking knows that there is a nobler work of art than all cathedrals, that there is a nobler work of art than all the artworks of human beings, however much he admires them; he knows that there is the gods' artwork of Man!" [430]

That man can have an eye, is the fruit of a long evolutionary process in which the sensory light of the outside world created the human eye. Goethe recognized this too, as can be seen from his words in the didactic part of his Theory of Colours: *"The eye owes its existence to the light. From indifferent animal auxiliary organs the light produces an organ that becomes its equal; and thus the eye is formed on the light and for the light, so that the inner light comes up to the outer."* [431]

However, it is not only the outer light that builds the human eye, but a multitude of forces of the World Spirit must cooperate to produce this very special organ, together with the physical sunlight, so that the World Spirit can reflect itself in it and carry his life into the human being. As already mentioned, together with the World Spirit the spiritual forces of the higher human members stream "into the inside of the human being", and indeed through the eye, as Rudolf Steiner once explained:

"The white magician uses only the higher powers in man, all of which are contained in his head. Through the seven gates of his head he is connected to the seven reflections of the world-forces. (Right, left eye, right, left ear, right, left nostril, mouth = 7). Through an organ at the top of the head, which has not yet been opened, man is connected with Atma; through the right eye the life spirit, Budhi, streams into him; through the left eye the spirit self, Manas, streams into him. Budhi is reflected in his mind as intellectual

---

[430] GA 64 "Aus schicksaltragender Zeit" (From fateful time), Berlin, Lecture of 29 October 1914 on "Goethes Geistesart in unsern schicksalsschweren Tagen und die deutsche Kultur" (Goethe's way of thinking in our fateful days and the German culture)

[431] GA 6 "Goethes Weltanschauung" (Goethe's world view), Chapter "Die Erscheinungen der Farbenwelt" (The phenomena of the world of colours)

soul and sentient soul. With his right ear he is connected to everything that streams through the world as thoughts, through his left ear the sensations in the world stream into him. Manas is reflected in his soul as the sentient body and the ether-double-body." [432]

Not only the human being as a whole is artwork of the gods, but every single one of his sensory organs, as well as all other organs. They all are wonderful creations of cosmic world-spiritual. Whole worlds are planted in them as germs of a future cosmos.

"We already bear a part of the cosmos within us, but with ordinary recognition we do not know that. When man advances through Imagination, Inspiration, Intuition to the recognition of the spirit, his inner experience becomes at the same time ever greater and greater in the soul. Oh, what is the human eye as ordinary consciousness knows it today! But this human eye is in every detail a cosmos, great and mighty like the macrocosm. Every single organ reveals itself as a world in the physical body already. Therefore the human being, when he looks around as an initiate, sees a world, a world down here with its elements, up there with the stars, with Sun and Moon. When he looks inside himself: every organ, eye, ear, lung, liver and so on is a world of its own, and a great interplay of worlds is this human physical body: worlds that are finished, worlds that are still germ-like, worlds that are sensory, worlds that are half extrasensory, worlds that are completely extrasensory. Man truly bears more and more worlds within himself as he develops through evolutions." [433]

Coming from the cosmic vastness of the stars, man as a spirit- and soul-being has contracted more and more until he finally prepares himself under the influence of the Sun sphere, the gate to the world of the spirit, and the influence of the Moon sphere, the gate to the world of the soul, to enter a new small human germ in the body of his future mother. The way in which the human being himself experiences this prenatal process and what role the human eye plays in this context becomes clear from the following words of Rudolf Steiner:

"When man approaches earthly life, then he still has Sun and Moon within him. But gradually Sun and Moon are shrinking. You sense that then just as if you feel your two lungs shrinking in you. This is how you then feel your cosmic existence, your Sun and Moon organs, shrinking. And then something separates from the Sun, and something separates from the Moon. Then, instead of having Sun and Moon in you as before, you have something in front of you that is a kind of likeness of Sun and Moon. Shining, glittering you have two huge spheres in front of you, of which one sphere is the spiritualized Sun, the other sphere is the spiritualized Moon: one sphere in bright shining light, the other ball glowing, more warm in itself, warming fiery and more selfishly holding the light to itself. These two spheres, which detach from the cosmically transformed human being – from this still existing Adam Kadmon –, these two spheres, which detach, are approaching each other more and more. When you come down to Earth you say: Sun and Moon become one. And that is what guides you, that is what leads you – already from the great-great-great-grandmother, great-great-grandmother, great-grandmother, grandmother and so on – to the last mother who is to give birth to you. There Sun and Moon lead us, but they are getting closer and closer.

And then one sees a task ahead of oneself. Then, as if it were a single point, one sees what is still far away in the human embryo. And one sees what has emerged from the Sun and the Moon as a unity, approaching the mother. But you see a task ahead of you that I can characterize in this way: Think that this here [the glove] would now be the One moving before you as the united Sun and Moon, and you know: When your cosmic consciousness will have completely vanished, when you will pass through a darkness – that is after the conception, when man immerses into the embryo –, then you will have to evert it, so that the inside comes out. You have to evert what Sun and Moon have been, and then a small opening emerges, through which you have to enter with your I, and this, in the likeness, will then be your human body on Earth. Well, this is the pupil in the human eye. From this One are made the Two then, as if two mirror images would emerge: These are the two human eyes, first united together, but united as Sun and Moon, then everting.

This is the task that one carries out unconsciously: One has to turn the whole thing around, put the inside out and enter through the small opening. Then it expands: Two physical likenesses are formed in an

---

[432] GA 89 "Bewusstsein – Leben – Form" (Consciousness – Life – Form), private lesson "Über die Logoi" (About the Logoi), without date, presumably 1904

[433] GA 346 "Vorträge und Kurse über christlich-religiöses Wirken – Band V – Apokalypse und Priesterwirken" (Lectures and courses on Christian religious work - Volume 5 - Apocalypse and work of the priests), Dornach, Lecture of 7 September 1924

embryonic state. For, the physical embryonic eyes are two images, which were created from the Sun and the Moon." [434]

Indeed, deep secrets are connected to the human eye. Without participation of man's spirit and soul, however, it would never be able to produce experiences of consciousness. This requires the action of the extrasensory human being:

"Thus it is the Psycho-Spiritual that works on the eye and causes certain processes in the eye. When these processes have been caused, then the eye reflects back into the Psycho-Spiritual that which we call colour. So it is the deeper Psycho-Spiritual that works in the body. And this is where spiritual research will lead humanity to: to recognize that it is we ourselves who live within our imaginations, and who prepare, with our deeper beings, the bodies for ourselves beforehand, so that they become mirroring apparatuses for what the souls then experience. This is the way it is, in ordinary, external, spatial life." [435]

Spring in Life on Earth – 52nd Week

After the human spirit soul has connected itself to an astral body as a bodily bearer, it is not yet in a position to also connect itself to a physical body in order to be able to experience through its senses the physical outside world into which the world spirit was enchanted. This requires a link between the astral body as a bearer of the human spirit-soul on the one hand and the physical body on the other. This link is the human ether body.

The spiritual archetype of a new ether body was already built up by man during his prenatal descent through the planetary spheres. As soon as this archetype creating activity has found its conclusion in the lowest planetary sphere, the Moon sphere, the human spirit-being striving for incarnation, who in the course of his passage through the soul world has already enveloped himself with a soul body, can contract, according to the ether body's spiritual archetype, the matching substances from the surrounding world-ether. In this way a new human ether body comes into being. It is filled with formative forces, because the harmonies of the spheres of the entire planetary world work in it. Rudolf Steiner therefore often called it "Bildekräfteleib", which means body of formative forces. These are able to seize the lifeless, passive, physical substances and to shape them into the most diverse forms, to enliven them and to fill them with inner spiritual light. All earthly beauty has its origin in the heavenly world. From the distant space it comes down to Earth. The beauty and colourfulness of the plant world, which presents itself to us every spring in an extremely varied, really enchanting splendour of form and colour, is mainly based on the etheric formative forces. The beauty of many animal forms also requires the participation of astral soul-forces from the cosmos and the emergence of human beauty requires the intervention of the spirit from the depths of the cosmos through the human I, which reveals to us its presence on Earth in the image of a human form, for:

"This is something thoroughly spiritual. It should cause a solemn mood to perceive with physical senses in the physical world a Spiritual as a human form. For the one who can see spiritually, it is such that he sees in the human form a real Imagination that descended into the physical world." [436]

However, the prerequisite for this is that the human I as spirit-being has enveloped itself with an astral body beforehand as well as with an ether body, which is able to connect it with the embryonic substantial germ of a human physical body. Only in this way can a well-formed human body, human beauty, emerge on Earth. But, the ether body alone is an extremely magnificent structure. According to Rudolf Steiner, there are *"currents and organs of wonderful variety and splendour"* in it. [437]

Together with the cosmic forces that bring about all earthly beauty, life force streams from space and the distant heaven into the physical germ resting in an earthly mother's womb, for the etheric body is the

---

[434] GA 214 "Das Geheimnis der Trinität" (Mystery of the Trinity), Oxford, Lecture of 22 August 1922

[435] GA 153 "Inneres Wesen des Menschen und Leben zwischen Tod und neuer Geburt" (Inner nature of man and life between death and new birth), Vienna, Lecture of 8 April 1914

[436] GA 26 "Anthroposophische Leitsätze" (Anthroposophical Leading Thoughts), Chapter "Erster Teil der Betrachtung: Was offenbart sich, wenn man in die vorigen Leben zwischen Tod und neuer Geburt zurückschaut" (First part of contemplation: What is revealed when one looks back into the previous lives between death and new birth), Goetheanum, at the turn of the year 1925

[437] GA 94 "Kosmogonie" (Cosmogony), Berlin, Lecture of 19 February 1906

bearer of life. As soon as it pervades the fertilised egg cell, enormous processes of transformation start immediately within the earthly human germ, and the human spirit-being, which has passed through the depths of the soul world, connects in this way with the earth world. It turns to the physical world existence. This incarnation process as a conclusion of man's prenatal existence is the subject of the last weekly verse. Through embodiment the human being becomes the direct representative of the Spirit on Earth. Through all other earthly kingdoms, the mineral, plant and animal kingdoms, the Spirit can only work indirectly, but through man directly. For this reason, the ancient Greeks revered the human form as the highest earthly form of all and depicted their gods always in human form to honour them. If in the physical outer world, into which all Spiritual was enchanted as if by a magic spell, a being of the spiritual world wants to be present with a consciousness of himself and in full spiritual power, it must descend into the existence as a human being on Earth. Even Christ had to take on human form in order to be able to work directly on Earth as a bearer of the Logos and divine being to overcome the earthly forces of death for the benefit of mankind and the Earth. When the spirit of all life, the Life Spirit or the Budhi, coming from the depths of the soul world, turned to the physical, outer world-existence, He connected the immortal essence of the spirit with human existence. It is this sacrificial divine deed, too, of which the words of the 52nd weekly verse speak to us in a pre-Easter-atmosphere:

52nd Week (30 March)	*52. Woche (30. März)*
When from the depths of soul	Wenn aus den Seelentiefen
The spirit turns to outer world-existence	Der Geist sich wendet zu dem Weltensein
And beauty wells from distant space,	Und Schönheit quillt aus Raumesweiten,
Then streams, out of the heavens far,	Dann zieht aus Himmelsfernen
Life's vital power into human bodies	Des Lebens Kraft in Menschenleiber
And unites mightily the spirit's essence	Und einet, machtvoll wirkend,
With the existence as a human being.	Des Geistes Wesen mit dem Menschensein.

In one of his lectures Rudolf Steiner once explained in more detail how the incarnating human spirit-being contracts his ether body "out of the heavens far":

"When entering into a new embodiment, it is like this: The I descends from the spiritual world, with all previously acquired imperishable extracts of both the Etheric and the Astral. First it naturally contracts all astral qualities forming a new astral body, which correspond to its previous development, and only then in the same way the etheric qualities. All this takes place in the first days after the conception, and it is not before the eighteenth to twentieth day afterwards that the new ether body works independently on the development of the physical human germ, whereas in the days before the ether body of the mother accomplishes what has later to be done by the incoming ether body. Only on this eighteenth to twentieth day after the conception the individuality, who wants to embody there and until then has enveloped his I with a new astral body and ether body, takes possession, so to speak, of the physical body formed by the mother until then.

At a moment before this seizure takes place, the human being is composed of exactly the same members of being as at the moment of death; in the latter case man has just discarded the physical body at that moment, in the former case not yet seized the physical body. From this it will be easy for you to understand that at the moment when a human enters his new physical body, something analogous to the moment when he discards it appears. At this moment man has a kind of preview of his coming life, just as at the moment of death he had a look back at his passed life. But man forgets this preview, because the constitution of his physical body is not yet suitable for keeping this preview in memory." [438]

In the course of this preview man also looks on the experiences which were interwoven into his impending new earthly life in order to compensate his karma, for when he passed the Moon sphere he also took up the fate package of his not yet mastered karma which he had deposited there soon after his last death. Just before his new incarnation it is woven into the I, astral body, ether body and physical body.

"But now you are still in the spiritual world. The spirit-germ of the physical body has already gone down, the human being himself is in the spiritual world. Then a strong deprivation, a strong feeling of deprivation arises. One has lost the germ of his physical body. It is already down. It has arrived at the end of the line of generations you have seen. You are still up. Hence the deprivation is asserting itself enormously. And it is this deprivation that attracts the appropriate ingredients from the world-ether all over the world. After one

---

[438] GA 100 "Menschheitsentwicklung und Christuserkenntnis" (Human development and understanding of Christ), Kassel, Lecture of 23 June 1907

has already sent the spirit-germ of the physical body down to Earth, and is left behind as a soul, as an I and as an astral body, one attracts etheric substances from the world-ether and forms one's own ether body. And with this own ether body, which one has formed, one unites then approximately in the third week after the fertilization on Earth has occurred, and unites with the bodily germ, which was formed according to the spirit germ in the described way. But before one unites with one's own body-germ, one still forms one's ether body in the way I have characterized it. And into this ether body is interwoven the package of which I have spoken, which contains the moral value. You interweave this then into your I, into your astral body, but into your ether body, too. That's what you then combine with the physical body. And that is how you carry your karma to Earth. First it was left behind in the Moon area, because one would have formed a bad, a corrupted physical body if one had taken it into the Sun area. The human physical body becomes individual only by the fact that the ether body permeates it. The physical body of every person would be equal to the physical body of another one, for in the spiritual world the human beings weave actually equal spirit-germs for their physical bodies. We become individual according to our karma, according to how we have to weave our package into the ether body, which then, while we are still in the embryonic state, individually shapes, constitutes, pervades our physical body." [439]

This descent of the ether and life body into the physical human germ is in addition associated with a mystery which must not yet be revealed to mankind at its present stage of development. Therefore Rudolf Steiner made only a suggestion:

"The ether organism exhales light, and gives us this light. And by exhaling light and giving us the light, we live through its light. And it inhales light. Just as we breathe in and out air, so our ether body breathes out and in light. And breathing in light, it processes the light in itself as we physically process the air in us. Read about this in my mystery dramas, where at a certain point this very secret of the ether world is dramatically presented.[440] *The ether body inhales light, processes the light within itself into darkness, and into this darkness it can absorb as its food the sound of the world, which lives in the harmony of the spheres, and can absorb the impulses of life. Just as we eat physical food, so does the etheric being that lives within us breathe in and out light. Just as we process air in us as oxygen and transform it into carbonic acid, so the ether body processes the light and permeates it with darkness, whereby it appears in colours and the ether body appears to us, to the clairvoyant gaze, in waving colours. But while the ether body is preparing the light for the darkness and thus performing an inner breathing work for itself, it lives by absorbing the world-sound, by processing the world-sound into world-life. But what we receive as our ether body in this way comes down to us at certain times from the vastness of the cosmos.*

It is not yet possible today to point out the circumstances of how the human ether body streams down on the paths of light when these paths of light are directed through the star constellation in a certain way. In order for this to be said one day, people must rise to a still higher level of morality. For even today, this very mystery of the human ether bodies' streaming down as if on paths of light and paths of sound from the harmony of the spheres would be abused by man in the most terrible way if he knew it. For this mystery includes everything that would give the ancestors unrestricted power over the whole progeny, if people with lower desires wished to acquire it. You will therefore believe that this mystery of how the ether bodies come to the people, who embody themselves, on the paths of light and on the paths of sound from the harmony of the spheres, that this mystery will have to remain a mystery for a long time to come. ... Wisely it is wrapped in unconsciousness to mankind, and thrives quite well in unconsciousness through the will of the wisdomfilled world-guidance." [441]

Nevertheless it is of extraordinary importance that people today already acquire detailed knowledge that they descend as immortal spirit- and soul-beings from cosmic expanses to the Earth in order to live here for some time with forces which can only be acquired in extraterrestrial existences in spiritual worlds between two lives on Earth. In order that this can happen in the required way and intensity, man must prepare himself already in earthly life by his conscious turning to the spirit. He must acquire concepts and imaginations that can be attained only on Earth and only through the science of the spirit that Rudolf Steiner brought to Earth for the benefit of the further development of mankind.

---

[439] GA 226 "Menschenwesen, Menschenschicksal und Welt-Entwicklung" (Man's being, his destiny and world-evolution), Kristiania (Oslo), Lecture of 17 May 1923

[440] GA 14 "Vier Mysteriendramen" (Four mystery plays), "Die Pforte der Einweihung" (The portal of initiation), 7th scene.

[441] GA 171 "Innere Entwicklungsimpulse der Menschheit – Goethe und die Krisis des 19. Jahrhunderts" (Inner human impulses for improvement – Goethe and the crisis in the 19th century), Dornach, Lecture of 2 October 1916

"Spiritual science must become something to us with regard to the trivialities of life, too. More and more it will become clear what life forces can be acquired between death and new birth. People will be born with withered bodies because of the fact that by their refusal against spiritual science they have not prepared themselves to get forces from the cosmos. People must already gain an understanding of spiritual science for the sake of the Earth's development! To know, before this life you were in a spiritual world, will make people happy when they have opened themselves up to spiritual science. «The starry sky above me, the moral law within me», that's what makes the world great. Man says to himself: My inner life is what I absorbed in the world of the stars; what I experienced in the universe now lights up in my soul. You have bad instincts in your soul, because during your life in the stars you did not try to absorb their forces and the spirit-forces of Christ.

We must learn to become related to the macrocosm. Today man can only guess and feel what is going on between death and a new birth. He feels: In your existence on Earth you live in your soul and hold in your spirit forces of the starry sky. When man experiences this sentence meditatively in the right way as an idea, it will turn into a force that is of immense importance." [442]

The "forces of the starry sky" which we hold in our spirit must however include the "spirit-forces of Christ". In the ether region of the Earth, Christ is already preparing the next setting of human development, as he himself says: *"In my Father's house are many dwellings; if it were not so, would I have told you that I go to prepare a place for you?"* (John 14:2). People will have to develop from the sense-perceptible Physical to the extrasensory Etheric. But for this they must absorb the forces of life into themselves in order to be able to overcome those of death. This will only be possible through the intimate turning of each individual towards Christ, the Spirit of Life, on the basis of spiritual science. In this we are assisted by the fifty-two weekly verses of the Anthroposophical Soul Calendar, because through them we can experience in our souls, in harmony with the changing nature moods in the course of the year, how Christ leads us on our incarnation cycle through the many "dwellings" in the house of His and our Father and endows us with all those forces that we need on our further path of development. Solely under His guidance can we reach the goal of human evolution and transform the Earth into a cosmos of love, which is to resurrect one day as a new cosmic existence and flourish in new splendour. That will only succeed if we get closer and closer to Christ in each of our earthly lives, and inwardly unite with Him more and more closely, so that His life may live up within us, in keeping with Paul's words: *"Now, no longer do I live, but Christ lives in me."* (Gal 2:20) We should commemorate this fact throughout the year, but especially at every Easter time.

---

[442] GA 130 "Das esoterische Christentum und die geistige Führung der Menschheit" (Esoteric Christianity and the spiritual guidance of mankind), St. Gallen, Notes from the Lecture of 19 December 1912

Christ and the Course of the Year

How can man get closer to Christ? This is a question that deeply concerns all true seekers of Christ who know of the great importance of the Christ Being for the further fate of mankind and the Earth. Rudolf Steiner was often asked this question as well, as he himself states:

"Many ask again and again: So how do I get closer to that being that we address as the Christ? You can't give a simple formula: Do it this way or another! But certain more important things of the whole spiritual science today are such that they lead one into the region of Christ as he is present. Just take the fact, which we know well: As a physical man, the Christ walked the earth only at the time of the mystery of Golgotha. Thus, to experience him as a physical person in physical events was only possible at that time. If you want to get close to him today, you have to look for him as he lives in the Earth sphere. But he does not live in the rough connections, but rather lives in finer connections. So that just what I told you today, the search for finer, more distant connections, the schooling of oneself on finer, more distant connections can bring people into that region of consciousness where they really experience the Christ. Of course, in doing so you may be touched by a, I would like to say, materialistic hand. Someone may say: Well, then you tell us that one just cannot comprehend the Christ in the ordinary conception as it is applicable to natural things! – People who apply such a thought at all, who actually speak from the sensation, that only what is conceived according to the sample of natural things is justifiable, as all materialists do, they cannot be guided at all in such a way that they perceive the Spiritual.

It may be daring, but just think, a being would be of such kind that you could only perceive it if you dream it. To the eyes, to the ears it does not show itself, even to ordinary everyday thinking it does not show itself; but it shows itself to the dream. Thus, the person who wants to experience something of this being would have to engage in developing the art of dreaming. Otherwise the being cannot be there to him. Well, if someone says, dreams don't give me anything Real, it is his fault that he can't get close to this being. In this respect, people think the wrong way, actually by making demands of their own. And if something does not fulfil these demands, then it is not of value to them. But, if the thing is of such kind that it is not there with regard to this demand, then the people who make such demands must miss it. So you definitely have to be clear about the fact that you must develop a special way of thinking or inner life as a whole to which what is not in the outer nature can show itself. We have to go to these beings, not they come to us. That's the important thing!" [443]

"We have to go to these beings", says Rudolf Steiner. But how do we go to Christ? The words "to go" cannot mean any spatial walking in this case, of course, for after his Resurrection and Ascension Christ is no longer present in a physical body perceptible to earthly sensory eyes. Since then he has been present extrasensorily in the ether sphere of the Earth. There he shall be sought by us, in the Etheric, in the ether body. The ether body, however, is primarily not a spatial body, but a temporal body. When we speak of the human ether body, we speak of a temporal organism that extends over man's entire life on Earth. This extrasensory organism can only be perceived if one develops the soul power of thinking to the next higher level of consciousness, that of Imagination. The existence of the ether body can be understood with the normal thought forces of man already. But it can only be really perceived by the soul, extrasensorily seen through the development of "imaginative" thinking.

"If one has learned exactly for some time to live in «imaginative» thinking, to engage inwardly one's whole being within this «imaginative» thinking, then one will find that with this «imaginative» thinking one immerses oneself into a reality, submerges oneself into a reality that one has never known before. For then, with this «imaginative» thinking the first stage of the extrasensory world is attainable. One gradually finds that, through this «imaginative» thinking, one now experiences in oneself a second human being, a human being who is as real as otherwise only the outer physical spatial human being. And just as this outer physical spatial human being is an organism whose individual members are in an alternating relationship to each other, how the head is dependent on the hand, and again the hand is dependent on the head, how the right hand is dependent on the left, how all members of the human spatial organism are dependent on each other, so one discovers a second human being in oneself, whom I must call a time-organism. It is a temporal organism. There is nothing Spatial. But it stands like a huge tableau in front of your soul's sight. If we have progressed enough in «imaginative» knowledge, then we no longer look back at individual

[443] GA 176 "Menschliche und menschheitliche Entwicklungswahrheiten – Das Karma des Materialismus" (Developmental truths of man and humanity – The karma of materialism), Berlin, Lecture of 10 July 1917

reminiscences from memory, but then we look back at our past life on earth since the first years of our childhood, at first. We look back surveying everything at once, as in a single image, but in an image that we know is not a spatial image. If we painted it, we would paint something like lightning, like something that can only be captured in a moment. It is what I have called the body of formative forces, the ether body. But it cannot be painted just this way, because we have to be aware that we paint a cross section of a temporal organization." [444]

All spatial representations of the ether body, as given to us by Rudolf Steiner as sketches, in which the ether body surmounts the physical body all around a little, are thus merely illustrations of an instantaneous cross section of the ether body. Only in relation to this cross section we can speak of spatiality also in the ether body. But as soon as we want to look at the ether body as a whole, we have to rise from the Spatial to the Psychological, because everything Temporal we can only experience inwardly in the soul. We will look in vain for yesterday's events in the physical outside world. But they are still present in our ether body as events of the soul, experienced in the stream of time, and they remain with us even after the death of our physical body. They continue to exist independently of the spatial physical body on a level of temporal existence. To this level of the Temporal man can rise mentally.

Moreover, the ether body is the also a bearer of life. He is a vital body. As such it causes all rhythmic vital processes of the earthly human body going on in time. May we not therefore expect something similar from the ether body of that being who has taken the Earth to his body? Should not his ether body encompass all vital processes of the Earth as well? Would the temporal rhythm of the earthly course of the year not be exactly the expression of the work of this ether body? – However, an observation of the coarse, sense-perceptible changes of Earth's nature in the course of the year will only tie our consciousness to the physical sensory world. In this way we will not be able to find access to the ether region of the Earth. But if we allow ourselves to be inspired by the moods of nature lingering in our souls, in their temporal succession, we may succeed in penetrating into finer, more hidden connections behind the Maya of the physical outside world, into that region in which we can find the Christ, too. This is what Rudolf Steiner meant when he spoke the words already quoted above:

"If you want to get close to him [Christ] today, you have to look for him as he lives in the Earth sphere. But he does not live in the rough connections, but rather lives in finer connections. So that just what I told you today, the search for finer, more distant connections, the learning on finer, more distant connections can bring people into that region of consciousness where they really experience the Christ."

The first earth-man who was allowed to consciously experience the presence of Christ in the ether sphere of the Earth was Paul in his experience of revival before Damascus. It will be experiences of a similar kind that will be accessible to more and more people in the future. So let us recall Rudolf Steiner's answer to a related question by Friedrich Rittelmeyer, which the questioner left us with his own written records:

"To my question, what could be done to prepare for Damascus-like Christ-events, he [Rudolf Steiner] replied: This is only possible when one experiences Christ in the course of the year. Also for that, one may compare our meditations." [445]

In the course of the year, in the Temporal only, we can get closer to Christ, in experiencing the rhythms of time and life, but in such a way that these become an expression of finer, more distant connections. Such more distant connections are already contained in the human ether body considered separately, for by dividing the human lives on Earth into groups of seven years the human ether body reveals, as a temporal body, its inner connection with the seven planetary spheres between the Zodiac on the one hand and the Earth on the other. At the moment of the union of the ether body with the physical germ in the motherly womb, this becomes visible "imaginatively". Rudolf Steiner illustrated this in his sketch, shown as Figure 23 in the chapter on the 46th weekly verse.

But behind this development history of the ether body during man's prenatal existence in the planetary spheres are even finer, even more distant connections, for the ether body as such emerged only in the course of a long evolutionary process. This too is mysteriously inscribed in it. Through his close connection with the physical body, which persists throughout a human life on Earth – in contrast to the astral body and the I, which separate each night from the physical body and ether body – become visible in the ether body under certain conditions, as even finer, even more distant connections, images of those spiritual beings who formed it in the course of great creation periods, beginning with the ancient Saturn and the ancient

[444] GA 211 "Das Sonnenmysterium und das Mysterium von Tod und Auferstehung" (The mystery of the Sun and the mystery of death and resurrection), London, Lecture of 14 April 1922

[445] See notes 142 and 143 (pages 77 and 78).

Sun, and who even today still sustain it every night, precisely when it is temporarily left by our astral body and our I. An initiate can see this as in the form of astral images, Imaginations, after they have made their impressions on his ether body. For this, at least that part of the ether body which animates the upper part of the human body must be loosened for some time from its close connection with the physical body by a special process. According to Rudolf Steiner, the initiate then sees a picture of that kind which John the Evangelist described as the second seal of his revelation.

**Figure 24: Second seal of the Revelation of John (Rev 4:6 ff.),
painted by Clara Rettich according to Rudolf Steiner's instructions (GA 104)**

"Thus the initiate first looks back into this image of prehistory. But now we must ask ourselves: Why does the initiate see this picture? – Because in this picture are represented symbolically and astrally the forces which have formed the human ether body in its present form and then the physical one. You can easily imagine why this is so. Imagine, a man lies in bed, leaves with his astral body and I his physical body and ether body. But to the physical body and ether body as they exist today, to the present physical human body and ether body belong the astral body and the I. This physical body and this ether body cannot exist on their own. They have become what they are because the astral body and the I are integrated into them. Only a physical body in which there is no blood flowing and no nervous system can exist without an astral body and I. Therefore a plant can exist without astral body and I, because it has no blood and no nervous system. For, the nervous system is connected to the astral body and the blood to the I. There is no being having a nervous system in the physical body that is not pervaded by an astral body, and there is no being having a blood system in the physical body into which the I has not entered. Think about what you do every night. You disdainfully desert your physical and ether body and leave them with the blood and nervous systems to themselves. If it were only up to you, your physical body would perish every night as you leave your nervous and blood systems. It would die right at the moment that the astral body and the I leave the physical and the ether body. But the clairvoyant vision sees that other beings, higher spiritual beings fill it then. He sees that they enter it and do what man does not do at night. They supply the blood and nervous systems. But these are the same beings that created man, as far as he is composed of a physical body and ether body, not only today, but from incarnation to incarnation. They are the same beings who created the very first preliminary stage of the physical body on ancient Saturn and who formed the etheric body on the Sun. These beings, who have ruled in the physical and ether bodies from the very beginning of the Saturn- and Sun-existences, they rule therein every night, while man sleeps and leaves his physical and ether

bodies disdainfully, so to speak abandons them to death. These beings penetrate and supply his nervous and blood systems.

Therefore, it is understandable that at the moment the astral body touches the ether body in order to imprint itself in it, man is pervaded by these forces that have formed him, that then he sees the image of these forces, which are symbolized in the second seal. What sustains and connects him to the whole cosmic outer space flashes up in this moment of initiation." [446]

The reason why such forces or beings appear as animals is given in the fact that the spiritual archetype of the ether body is formed mainly in the lower spiritual world and in the higher soul world pervaded by it, the planetary plane of the cosmos, as shown in Figure 17, for example, in the chapter on the 20th weekly verse. Man only gains access to this level through the higher consciousness state of Inspiration. On this level, spiritual beings and powers show themselves in animal form. Even beings of the higher spiritual world, which is basically only accessible to Intuition, present themselves to "inspirative" consciousness in animal form. Therefore even the Holy Spirit, who is at home in the higher spiritual world, appears to the person who watches "inspiratively" in the form of a dove.

"During the period of atavistic clairvoyance, as it still existed in the first four Christian centuries, at least still during the time of the mystery of Golgotha, it was not merely a superficial, vain symbolism, but a true inner knowledge that portrayed higher spiritual beings, which can be found through Inspiration, in forms of animals. And it is entirely in accordance with this that the Holy Spirit was indicated in the form of a dove by those who drew attention to Inspiration. How should we conceive it today when we hear spoken of the Holy Spirit as in the form of a dove? We have to conceive it in that way, saying, those who spoke like that were inspired people in the ancient atavistic sense. In the region, where the Holy Spirit showed himself to them purely spiritually, they saw him in this form as an Inspiration." [447]

The fourth figure in the second seal image, which already bears a human-like face, began to unfold its effectiveness in the human ether body in the course of the development of the Earth at first, when this body was prepared to be pervaded by an I as the fourth member of the human being, which is destined to become a bearer of forces of the higher spiritual world and even more sublime world planes. On the ancient Moon, the human ether body only contained three images. They were reflections of the activity of three spiritual beings working from the Sun after it had set the ancient Moon out of itself. As a result, the human bodies, which developed on the ancient Moon, could be raised to the stage of animals:

"On the Moon, humans evolved to the rank of animals, so to speak, although they were not animals. With a certain degree of justification, with regard to the animal kingdom one always distinguished animals of different stages. The animal-humans on the Moon appeared quite significantly different in three stages, which are called in spiritual science the stage of the «Ox», the «Lion» and the «Eagle» These are typical forms, as it were, of animalhood. So there were three different groups on the ancient Moon: Ox Humans, Lion Humans and Eagle Humans. ... On the Sun, however, there were the spiritual counter-images of them. There were three groups, too. While the development of the Astral on the Moon formed these three different animal-humans, the corresponding spiritual humans emerged on the Sun, namely as angel-like beings, spiritual entities, which are also called – but as the spiritual counter-images – Lion, Eagle and Ox. So when you look at the Sun, you find spiritual beings of whom you say to yourself: they present to me the beautiful, wisdom-designed archetypes! And on the ancient Moon you have something like hardened likenesses of what is up there on the Sun." [448]

The three groups of spirit beings influenced as group souls their hardened likenesses on the ancient Moon, for *"there is a spiritual connection between archetype and likeness. Because the group soul is the archetype and works as archetype on the likenesses. The forces emanate from the group soul and direct the likenesses below: the Lion Spirit directs the beings that are his likenesses as Lion Humans, the Eagle Spirit the Eagle Humans and so on. If these spirits, who are up there, had remained united with the Earth [under the conditions of the ancient Moon], if they had remained bound to their likenesses, if they had to dwell in their likenesses, they would not have been able to take action, they would not have been able to exercise the powers they had to exert for the salvation and development of the likenesses."*

The evolution of the ancient Moon finally ends with the transition into a Pralaya state or a world night. *"After this world night, out of the darkness of the world-womb, our Earth state emerges, which is called to bring man so far that he can add the I or the I-bearer to the physical, etheric and astral body."* For this,

---

[446] GA 104 "Die Apokalypse des Johannes" (The Apocalypse of John), Nuremberg, Lecture of 19 June 1908

[447] GA 214 "Das Geheimnis der Trinität" (Mystery of the Trinity), Dornach, Lecture of 28 July 1922

[448] GA 112 "Das Johannes-Evangelium im Verhältnis zu den drei anderen Evangelien" (The Gospel of John in relationship to the three other Gospels), Kassel, Lecture of 26 June 1909

again spiritual beings had to work from the Sun as spiritual archetypes on the humans, who were now evolving on Earth.

"What kind of beings were these? They were the descendants of those beings who during the ancient Moon state had already developed on the Sun as Ox Spirit, Lion Spirit and Eagle Spirit. And the highest, the most advanced of them, were those who had united the natures of Eagle, Lion and Ox into a harmonious unity. The most advanced spiritual beings that now took their dwelling place on the Sun were the beings that can be described as «Human archetypes», as «Spirit-Humans» in the true sense. So imagine that among those spiritual beings that were found on the Sun during the ancient Moon time as the Ox Spirit, Eagle Spirit, Lion Spirit, there were those that had attained a higher level of development. They are the actual Spirit-Humans, who now preferably take their place on the Sun. They are, so to speak, spiritual counter-images of what is developing down there on the separated Earth plus Moon. ...

If the Earth had remained with the Sun, man could never have come to his present development; he could not have kept pace with a development that the beings on the Sun needed. What developed up there was not man as he lives on Earth; there, a spiritual archetype of man developed, of which today's man, as we meet him in his physical form, is basically only a likeness."

All four kinds of spirit beings are still active in the human ether body night after night and present themselves pictorially to initiates as the four living creatures of the second seal of the revelation of John. In their midst, however, a fifth figure appears.

"In ancient initiation, the figure in the middle of the second seal image was only indicated as the fifth of the group souls. It is that which existed in humanity of ancient days only in a germ-like state and only came out in Christian initiation as that which is also called the Son of Man who rules the seven stars when he appears before man completely in his true form." [449]

But in the state of Inspiration, even the fifth living creature could be seen as an image impressed on the ether body only in animal form, as the Lamb with the Book of Life, as shown in Figure 24.

"And in what way would these atavistically inspired contemporaries of the mystery of Golgotha have characterized the Christ? They may have seen him on the outside, they saw him as a human being. To see him as a human being in the spiritual world, they should have had Intuitions. But such people who could see him as an I in the «intuitive» world were not there even in the time of the mystery of Golgotha; they could not do that. But they could still see him in atavistic Inspiration. Then they also needed animal forms to express the Christ on their own. «Behold, this is the Lamb of God» is for that time a proper way of speaking, a speaking in which we must immerse ourselves when we wish to comprehend what Inspiration is, or how one sees by Inspiration that which can appear in the spiritual world: «Behold, the Lamb of God!». It is important that we learn to recognize again what is «imaginative», what is «inspired», what is «intuitive», and that by doing so we learn to understand the way of speaking that sounds up to us from ancient times." [450]

The spiritual principle of the seven-number, which underlies the formation of the ether body, has its effects into the physical body. This connection of the ether body with the physical body presents itself to the clairvoyant as a kind of rainbow enclosing the five living creatures.

"This is how the clairvoyant image appears. So man comes out of the darkness of the spirit land. And the force that has formed it appears as a kind of rainbow formation. The more physical forces surround the whole formation of man like a rainbow." [451]

But just as the seven planetary spheres are surrounded by the zodiac, which is structured according to the twelve-number, so in the vision of John the Rainbow was surrounded by higher forces, structured according to the principle of the zodiac, the twelve-number.

"This is surrounded by something that is quite different in essence and nature from that which emerges from the indeterminate Spiritual. And what it is surrounded by was symbolized in ancient times in the zodiac, in the twelve signs of the zodiac."

The twelveness of the zodiac represents in spiritual vision that the ether body is closely connected with the physical body in which it causes the vital processes which are running rhythmically, that is in terms of time. Physical body and ether body were both created on the ancient Saturn and the ancient Sun. Already during the second half of the ancient Saturn state, changes were made to the physical body in order to prepare it for being pervaded by an ether body in the following Sun state. The entire creative activity for the

---

[449] GA 104 "Die Apokalypse des Johannes" (The Apocalypse of John), Nuremberg, Lecture of 19 June 1908

[450] GA 214 "Das Geheimnis der Trinität" (Mystery of the Trinity), Dornach, Lecture of 28 July 1922

[451] GA 104 "Die Apokalypse des Johannes" (The Apocalypse of John), Nuremberg, Lecture of 19 June 1908

physical body and the ether body therefore extended over seven Saturn rounds and five subsequent states of Pralaya as well as seven Sun rounds and five subsequent states of Pralaya. This results in a total of twice twelve or twenty-four cycles. Rudolf Steiner explained:

"If you want to have it quite according to our reckoning of time, then you sum up two planetary states, Saturn and Sun [on the one hand], Moon and Earth [on the other]. Then you get twenty-four rounds each. These twenty-four rounds are important epochs in the representation of the world, and these twenty-four epochs are thought to be regulated by beings in the cosmos, which in the apocalypse are hinted at as the twenty-four elders, the twenty-four regulators of cosmic revolutions, of cosmic periods. On the seal picture [Figure 24] they are indicated as the world clock. The individual numbers of the clock are only interrupted here by the double crowns of the elders to indicate that these are the kings of time, because they regulate the revolutions of the cosmic bodies." [452]

This is what can be seen when the spiritual view of a man's ether body and physical body opens up to him. The four group souls of mankind and the twenty-four regulators of the rounds or world periods continued to be active in the ether body and physical body, however, even after the ancient state of the Sun, and indeed they are still active today. In order for the two lowest members of the human being to be pervaded by an astral body and finally by an I, further rounds had to be gone through during the ancient Moon's and our Earth's development. From the beginning of the ancient Moon to the end of the Earth's evolution, when the I will be fully developed in a part of humanity, another total of twenty-four rounds or states will be performed. If we sum up all forces and periods which have been effective in the ether bodies of mankind and of the Earth, we finally get twice twenty-four periods subject to the regulators, i.e. forty-eight periods. Supplemented by the four group souls of humanity, which work on the human members of being too, this ultimately results in fifty-two beings working on the ether body and the physical body.

The human ether body shows the peculiarity that it is always equipped with the forces of the entire period for which it is intended to serve as a time-organism, even if for karmic reasons death should occur much earlier, sometimes in childhood already.[453] Correspondingly within the Earth's own ether body as well, today all forces are already contained up to end of the entire earth evolution. If they all wanted to express themselves one after the other in succession, they would have to form a temporal rhythm of forty-eight plus four, that are fifty-two units of force. But this is exactly the division of time manifesting in the Earth's course of the year. Fifty-two weeks with seven days each – since the ether body is based on the principle of the seven-number – result in 364 days. In the end there is only one day left to complete the 365 or 365 ¼ days of a solar year. In the number of days of a year, this one day represents the superior unity, from which all subdivision emerges, the unity of the Budhi, the Lamb or the Christ. As the highest Sun Spirit, as a Unity Being and Spirit of Life, it regulates all partial forces of the ether body of the Earth in their chronological sequence and thus all life processes in the course of the earthly year. Of course, this single additional day does not change the number of weeks. It remains at fifty-two weeks.

In the ether body of the Earth are thus effective the forces of the four group souls of mankind, which are grouped around the Lamb, as well as the twenty-four rulers over the time periods, who are active twice. Hence the course of the year turns out to us as a temporally experienceable likeness of the Earth's ether body and the spirit beings effective in it, above which Christ as the Earth Spirit is at the highest and central place. Figure 25 illustrates these relationships. And indeed, the order in which the four human group souls are expressed as etheric qualities of force throughout the year corresponds exactly to the order in which John in his revelation lists the four living creatures around God's throne and the Lamb, but in retrograde, since it is an astral experience. In the ether body of the Earth the order runs from Leo or the Lion group spirit in summer, to Taurus or the Ox group spirit in spring, then to Aquarius or the Angelic-Human group spirit in winter until Scorpio as representative of the forces of the Eagle group spirit in autumn:

"the first living creature like a lion, the second living creature like an ox, the third living creature with the face of a man, and the fourth living creature like a flying eagle." (Rev. 4:7)

Figure 25 shows the series of the 52 weekly verses in Arabic numerals, and in addition inwardly in Roman numerals the epochs of the 24 elders, which are expressed twice in the course of the year, beginning with the Roman number one in the sign Pisces and later once more in the opposite sign Virgo. In the two rows of the 24 elders, the four group spirits, who rule the four seasons, additionally fit in as direct

---

[452] Ibidem

[453] See Rudolf Steiner's statements on the continuing effect of the forces of the ether body of Theo Faiß, who as a little boy died through an accident on the Goetheanum site, and on the continuing effect of the forces of the ether bodies of all the many "war dead" of youthful years in World War I in GA 174b "Die geistigen Hintergründe des 1. Weltkrieges" (The spiritual backgrounds of World War I), Stuttgart, Lecture of 14 February 1915

rulers of a week of their own, always at the end of that month of the zodiac belonging to them, that is in the transition to the following sign, because then the effect of their respective power has reached its climax in the course of an earthly year. But it is not only from this point of view that they are correctly positioned there. Even from the point of view of the great planetary states of development, they fit into the course of the year in a meaningful way just there. So, on ancient Saturn, for example, an outer materiality of the physical body, which was increasingly seized and pervaded with life by the Ox group spirit, can only be spoken of from the middle of ancient Saturn. In the figure, this point of time corresponds exactly to the middle of the sign Aries, when Rudolf Steiner also lets begin the first weekly verse. In the period before, there was only inner, spiritual warmth on ancient Saturn. Here the transition from the inside to the outside took place. Likewise, only from the middle of the ancient Sun the ether body had progressed so far in its development that the preparatory activity of the Lion group spirit for the later interpenetration of the ether body with an astral body could take place over the entire second half of the Sun development. And it is only from the middle of the ancient Moon that we can speak of a soul-inwardness and preparation for the subsequent development of the Earth. Even the I, with which the transformation of the bodily members of being into spiritual members of being begins, was only given to man in the fourth, thus middle round of earth development. The peak of the spiritual activity of a group spirit always is reached in the midst between two planetary states of development. Thus the four special weeks of the four group spirits coincide exactly with the 7th, 20th, 33rd and 46th weeks, for which Rudolf Steiner has inserted the four conspicuously different threshold weekly verses as special features between the forty-eight remaining weekly verses.

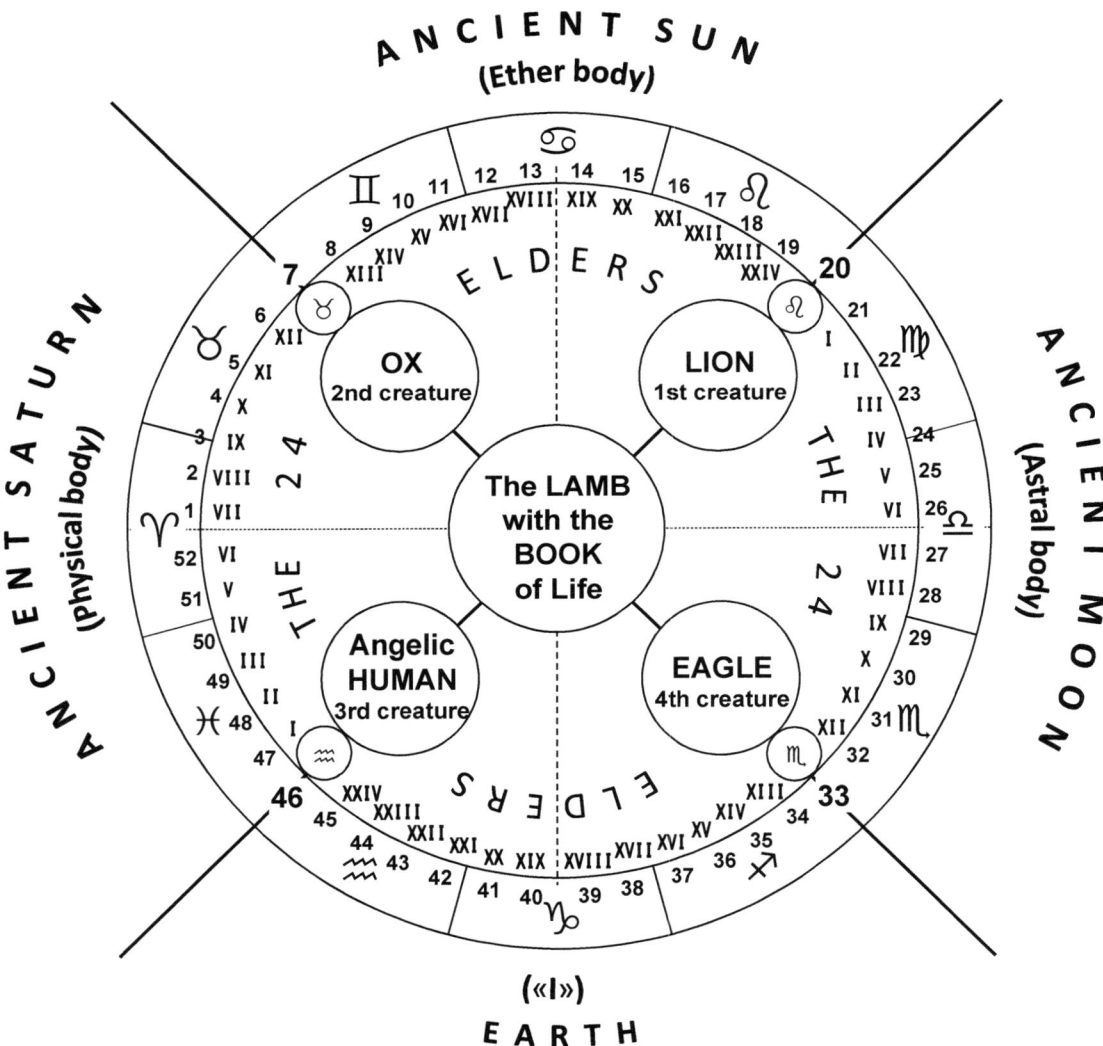

Figure 25: The activity of the twenty-four Elders, the four Group Spirits and the Christ Being as the Sun and Life Spirit in the course of the year

The second half of the Earth's development is that period in which mankind is to connect itself with Christ and develop into the very first preliminary stages of an Angelic existence on the future Jupiter. Thus it becomes clear why Christianity quite rightly commemorates the physical presence of Christ on Earth and the earthly lifetime of Christ just during that time of the year when the Sun passes through the winter quarter from 15° Capricorn at Epiphany, the day of remembrance of the Baptism in Jordan, to 15° Aries at Easter, the day of remembrance of Christ's resurrection. In this way, the three monthly steps starting at 15° Capricorn to 15° Aquarius and 15° Pisces until 15° Aries reflect the three years of Christ's stay in a human body on Earth. With reference to the human incarnation cycle, this quarter reflects as well the creation of the bodily members of the human being, which ultimately culminates in the human form as a physically visible image of the human I and the "I am", which is the unity of Father and Son in man according to the words of Christ: *"He who sees me sees the Father"*. (John 14:9) Obviously, the occult borders of the seasons do not coincide with the astronomical borders. The latter are just one of several ways of subdividing the course of the year. From a meteorological point of view, science itself sets other borders. Thus, the meteorological beginning of spring on the northern hemisphere of the Earth is March 1st and the meteorological beginning of the other seasons is also always a good three weeks before the astronomical.

Not only in the ether body of the Earth, but also in the human ether body, the four group spirits have their very own territories each. The forces of the Ox group spirit work mainly in the lower part of the human body, where they mainly control the metabolic processes. There the material is seized and integrated into vital processes. The Lion spirit, as the Sun-sign Leo, represents the incoming life forces of the Sun on the one hand. On the other, astral forces too are already flowing through it from the cosmos in order to build up an astral body as an external bearer for the human soul and to raise the bodily life to soul life. Hence, the heart, the organ of Leo, is considered to be the seat of the soul. The Eagle spirit rules above all the human head with the brain as an organ of consciousness. It enables man to bring his inner emotional and spiritual experiences up to I-consciousness. By means of the I-consciousness, the human being then has the possibility of consciously controlling the instinctual life in his astral body. He learns to tame the dragon in himself through the power of Michael and gradually transform the astral body into Manas or spirit self.

But in order for man to become a bearer of the "I am", a bearer of the Budhi, the Lamb or the Christ, the forces of the Ox, Lion and Eagle group spirits must be brought into harmony. This task is accomplished by the group spirit with the human-like face. Through him a power works that emanates from the divine "I am" of the Budhi plane. So the task of the first three group spirits is mainly to develop man up to the human level, whereas the group spirit with the human-like face, which is connected to the zodiacal image of Aquarius, has the task of preparing man for future stages of development and for that purpose endow him with superhuman abilities already. For, in order to prepare Manas in man for the reception of Budhi, Angelic powers are needed. The Angeloi are those who work on the formation of Manas in the human astral body. Accordingly, Christ had to be preceded by an Angel, whose noble task was to assist at the Baptism at the Jordan in the unification of Jesus of Nazareth with Manas and Budhi brought along by Christ. Bearer of this Angel was John the Baptist. He was prepared for this task by the special stage of the "Aquarius Initiation". From then on, an angelic being worked through him.[454] That is why Christ himself said of John the Baptist: *"It is he of whom it is written* [in Malachi 3,1]: *"Behold, I send my Angelos before thee; he shall prepare thy way before thee."* (Lk 7:27 and Mark 1:2)

Figure 26 presents the interrelationships from a slightly different perspective than the preceding Figure 25: Christ is the great leader of the evolution of mankind extending in cosmic rounds over three worlds or four world levels. According to the hermetic law "as in the large scale so in the small", the incarnation cycles of the individual people are designed according to these great, cosmic cycles. They extend over the same three worlds or four world levels. This is why we can approach the activity of Christ precisely by turning our attention towards the human incarnation cycle. If we consider, that both the cosmic cycles and the incarnation cycle of man can be experienced in harmony with the changing moods of nature in the earthly cycle of the year, it becomes understandable why Rudolf Steiner suggests this approach to Christ in the Ether sphere. After all, it is precisely the ether body of the Christ, who has become the Spirit of the Earth, which underlies the annual rhythm of all earthly life as a temporal organism.

With regard to the human incarnation cycle, however, it should be noted that in the higher worlds man has both outer and inner experiences as well as in life on Earth. In the course of the year, the life of the human soul proceeds in such a way that in the summer half-year we are primarily turned towards the outside world and in the winter half-year more towards our inside world. According to divine wisdom, the

---

[454] GA 124 "Exkurse in das Gebiet des Markus-Evangeliums" (Excursions into the field oft he Gospel of Mark), Berlin, Lecture of 6 December 1910, and Munich, Lecture of 12 December 1910

natural moods of the summer half-year are therefore mainly related to man's outer experiences in the higher worlds between death and new birth, whereas the natural moods of the winter half-year are complementary to his inner experiences. Only the two together give an overall picture.

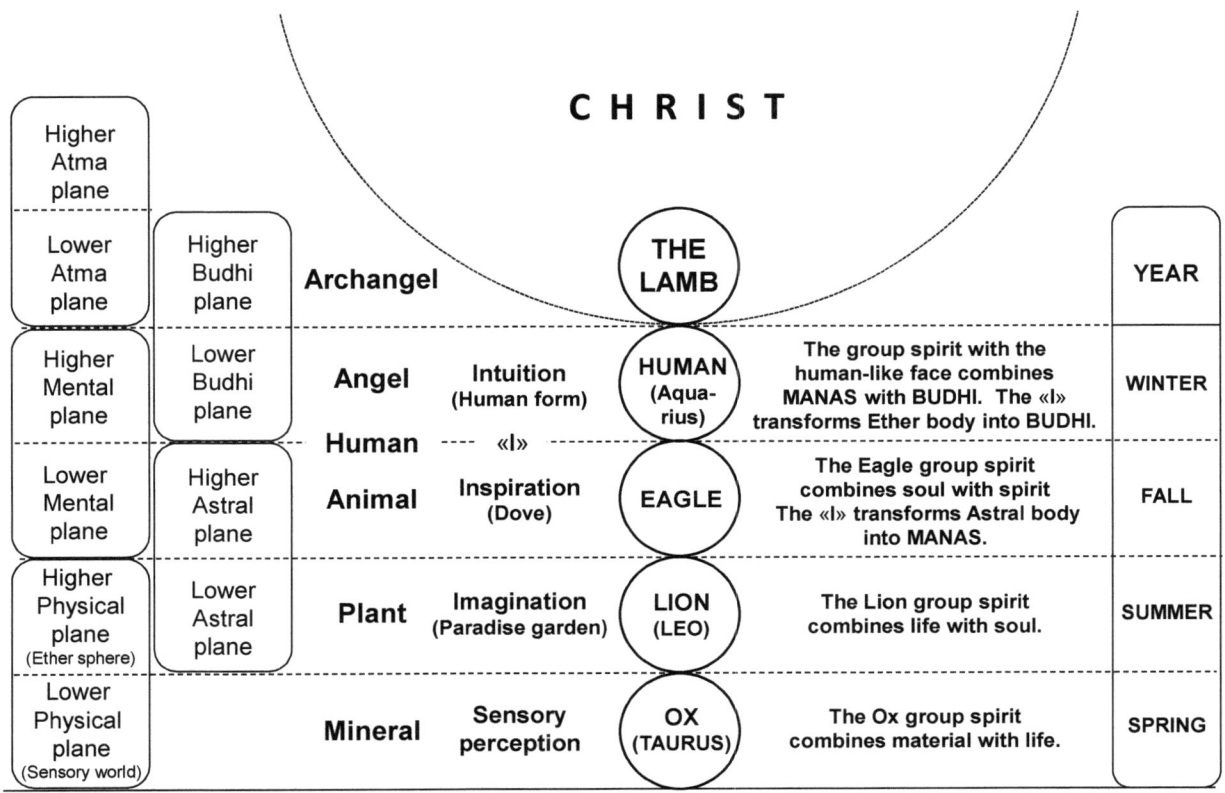

Figure 26: The four human Group Souls and the Lamb

Christ of the West and the East

Christ as the ruler over the course of the year and the time-rhythm of all life on Earth is assisted by several Archangels serving him. The actual Time Spirits are of the rank of the Archai. However, these rule over whole ages. Shorter time periods are ruled by Archangels who are already developing into the rank of a Time Spirit. Five of them perform special tasks in the course of the year. Four of these each rule over a quarter of a year. Their main time of activity is in each case at the transition between two seasons. Thus Raphael reaches his culmination right at the beginning of spring as healer of the body. He works in harmony with Christ as the Saviour who, through the mystery of Golgotha, which we just commemorate at Easter, saved for mankind the form-shape or phantom of the physical body, as Rudolf Steiner occasionally called it: *"This phantom is the form-shape of man, which as a spiritual texture processes the physical substances and forces, so that they get into the form which we encounter as man on the physical plane."* [455]

At the summer solstice, when people are completely devoted to the etheric expanses, Uriel most strongly works down from the heights of heaven as a servant of Christ in His capacity as Lord of karma. The ether body of the Earth is the Book of Life in which the karmic guilts of all human beings are recorded just as it happens for each individual in his own ether body. In this regard, Rudolf Steiner points out a passage in the Gospel of John: *"There is a strange passage in the eighth chapter: When the Pharisees asked Jesus for his opinion about the adulteress, he bent down (verses 6 and 8) without saying a word and*

---

[455] GA 131 "Von Jesus zu Christus" (From Jesus to Christ), Karlsruhe, Lecture of 10 October 1911

wrote with his finger on the Earth. But the Earth, as we have seen, is his own body. He does not condemn the adulteress, but he inscribes her deed in his own organism." [456] Christ as the Lamb has connected himself with the karma of mankind by taking over the ether body of the Earth. He carries the sins of mankind and helps each individual to work through and compensate his individual karmic guilt. For this he is also helpful at our sides during our incarnation cycles between our earthly lives. Uriel, as his servant in ordering the human karma, annually examines the guilts accumulated in the ether body of the Earth and in the human ether bodies, strengthens conscience as an ethical cognitive force and calls upon people to overcome their remaining vices. On the other hand, he also appreciates all the virtues of humans already attained: *"And I have spoken to you of how Uriel's gesture is an admonishing gesture, in a sense a debit addressed to men, which challenges them when they understand it, to transform their mistakes into virtues. For above in the clouds appear the images of beauteousness, the images of beauty woven from the Sun-gold, of all that which humans accomplish in virtues."* [457]

At the beginning of autumn it is Michael who reaches the climax of his powerful activity. Through him Christ's power to overcome is expressed, through which He defeated the adversary powers active within mankind and in the Earth and put them in their places. Michael gives people the courage and the iron willpower they need to overcome the imperfections recognized under Uriel's examining gaze, to tame the dragon in their astral bodies and to submit human action to the dominion of the I-consciousness. Through Michael is to grow *"all that, which should develop against comfort, against anxiety, but towards inner initiative, towards the free, strong, brave will in man."* [458]

But everything that the Archangels of the beginning of spring, the summer solstice and the beginning of autumn give to mankind is based on the fact that the Archangel Gabriel, who has his main time of activity at the winter solstice, has brought to Earth that pure, primeval human being, untouched from the Fall, the Krishna soul of the Nathan Jesus boy. This is a being that emanated directly from the Budhi plane, filled with the purest, divine love. Only such a love-being could mature on Earth as a human being in order to become the bearer of Budhi itself, the Christ. From Christmas time onwards, with the participation of Gabriel, Christ makes the Budhi, the love, flow into the people, and with it the "I am" that underlies the human form as an Imagination and finds its highest expression in the human face.

Likewise the year as a whole is under the rule of a special Archangel being. Through this, Christ, the Lord of life or the Life Spirit, reveals Himself as a unitiy-being and as the Lord of the Year. This close connection of Christ with an Archangel may surprise at first. However, it becomes immediately understandable when we consider that Christ himself belongs to the Hierarchy of the Archangels, those beings who work especially on the ether bodies of men. At the time of the ancient Sun, when the Archangels passed through their stage of humanity, Christ had already advanced to their highest initiate and had connected himself with the Logos, as it was explained in detail in the chapter "The Christ Being". He became the ruler over the spiritual counterpart of the ether or life body: the life spirit.

"For Christ Jesus reveals himself through the life spirit. He reveals himself through a being of the kingdom of Archangeloi. Of course, he is an infinitely higher being, however, it does not matter now, but that he reveals himself through a being of the kingdom of Archangeloi. So that through this encounter we are especially close to Christ Jesus with regard to today's development, to the development since the mystery of Golgotha, and that we also can call the encounter with the life spirit, in a certain way, the encounter with Christ Jesus that takes place in the deep undergrounds of the soul. If now a person – be it through the development of the spirit-consciousness in the area of religious deepening and religious exercise, or be it, supplementing this religious exercise and religious feeling, also by acceptance of conceptions of the spiritual science –, if a person deepens his emotional life, spiritualizes it in the way described, he will experience the after-effect of the encounter with the life spirit, respectively with the Christ, just as he can experience the after-effect of the encounter with the genius [his Angel] in his awake life. And it is indeed the case that in the time that now follows the indicated Christmas time until Easter time, the conditions are particularly favourable in order to bring to consciousness the encounter of the human being with the Christ Jesus.

In a profound way – and one should not blur this today by an abstract materialistic culture – the Christmas time is bound to processes of the Earth, because man together with the Earth undergoes the

---

[456] GA 100 "Menschheitsentwicklung und Christuserkenntnis" (Human development and understanding of Christ), Basel, Lecture of 25 November 1907

[457] GA 229 "Das Miterleben des Jahreslaufes in 4 kosmischen Imaginationen" (The experience of the course of the year in 4 cosmic Imaginations), Dornach, Lecture of 13 October 1923

[458] Ibidem, Dornach, Lecture of 5 October 1923

Christmas change of the Earth. The Easter period is determined by events in the sky. Easter Sunday is to be set on the first Sunday, which follows the first full moon after the Spring Equinox time. Thus, the Easter season is determined from above, whereas the Christmas season is determined by the conditions of the Earth. For just as true as we are connected with the conditions of the Earth through all that we have described, just as true are we connected with that which I now have to describe, with the conditions of the sky, with the great cosmic-spiritual conditions. For Easter season is that time in the concrete course of the year when everything that was caused in us by the encounter with Christ in the Christmas season, in turn connects itself so properly with our physical earth-man. And the great mystery, the Good Friday mystery, which brings to the human mind the mystery of Golgotha during the Easter season, has, besides everything else, even this meaning, that the Christ, who walks, as it were, alongside us in the time I have described, now approaches us the most, as it were, roughly speaking, disappears into ourselves, pervades us, so that He can stay with us for the time after the mystery of Golgotha, in the time that now comes as summer time, when in ancient mysteries at St.John's Day people wanted to connect themselves to the macrocosm in a different way than it must be done after the mystery of Golgotha." [459]

At this point the question may arise: Does only the Christian part of humanity know of these extraordinarily significant connections, of the earthly presence of Christ as the highest Sun Spirit, who has taken the body of the Earth as his new macrocosmic body and directs the development of life on Earth through the ether body of the Earth as its time-organism? It seems that the omnipresent Christ gradually leads the other religions to an understanding of these interrelationships too, in order ultimately to lead them to a realization of the mystery of Golgotha. For example, in Tibetan Buddhism, founded in the transition from the 8th to the 9th century AD by the sage Padmasambhava, we also find the teaching of four archangel-like beings, so-called Dhyani Buddhas.[460] They rule over the four cardinal points: Akshobhya in the East, the direction of sunrise, corresponding to the beginning of spring in the course of the year. He gives the power of mirror-like wisdom or mirror knowledge. It enables us to look at things passionlessly, to reflect them objectively in us, just as the physical senses, above all the eyes, reflect the outside world. Ratna-sambhava reigns in the South, where the Sun reaches its highest point every day, especially at the summer solstice. His wisdom is that of the equivalence of all living beings. When we violate it, we create karmic guilt. Amitābha works from the West, where the Sun sets and the transition from light to darkness occurs, which in the course of the year corresponds to the beginning of autumn as a natural image of the transition from the outside world to the inside world. Amitābha therefore gives the power of introspection, of meditation, of self-examinination, of discriminating wisdom, for example with regard to the question whether a supposedly selfless action might perhaps arise rather from an egoistic drive of the astral body. Amoghasiddhi works from the North, where the Sun reaches its lowest position every night, above all at the winter solstice. He is the representative of the all-acting, all-perfecting wisdom, the wisdom of transforming the most inner and supreme spiritual impulses into an outer existence. His wisdom is therefore creative, even world-creating.

But in the midst of these four sublime entities there is a fifth being of higher rank enthroned. It is Vairocana. His name appeared in the spiritual writings of the east already in the 5th century AD. It means something like "the Sun-like" or "the Radiant". On some presentations Vairocana is depicted with four faces looking in the four directions of the sky. He is regarded as the creator of all appearances, as cause of all causes and as the unifier of all opposites. It is also taught that he has the wisdom of all Buddhas. He represents the universal wisdom of the cosmic law, the all-encompassing wisdom, and is revered as the head, indeed the archetype, of all Buddhas. There is only one being, even more hidden, that is higher than him: the Adibuddha Samantabhadra, the "All-Good". Who does here not immediately feel reminded of the words of Christ Jesus, which he spoke to his disciple Philip: *"Why do you call me good? Nobody is good but God alone."* (Luk. 18:19 and Mark 10:18)

It seems that as a result of the Christ impulse working within humanity on Earth, the Eastern world has also been worshipping Christ for centuries, albeit under a different name and without knowing the more precise connection with the mystery of Golgotha. But even this is already hinted at in the Eastern teachings, because Vairocana, the central being, is usually depicted with a body of white colour in front of a blue background, like the white sunlight in front of the blue sky. Akshobhya, the Dhyani Buddha of the East and the beginning of spring at which Christians celebrate Easter, is depicted just the other way round, with

---

[459] GA 175 "Bausteine zu einer Erkenntnis des Mysteriums von Golgotha" (Building stones for an understanding of the mystery of Golgotha), Berlin, Lecture of 20 February 1917

[460] See, for example, "The Tibetan Book of the Dead", W. Y. Evans-Wentz, London, Oxford University Press, H. Milford, 1927, and "Creative Meditation and Multi-Dimensional Consciousness", Lama Anagarika Govinda, London 1976, Allen and Unwin.

a body of blue colour in front of a white background. So he is mirrored in the colour sense. Akshobhya is, so to speak, the earthly reflection of Vairocana. At his side is the Bodhisattva Maitreya, who is supposed to ascend next to the dignity of a Buddha.

However, not only the Buddhists worship Christ-Vairocana, but the Hindus too, although again under a different name. To them, the second person of the divine Trinity is revealed through Vishnu, the Sustainer of Creation. "*In Brahmanism the time from Christmas to Easter was dedicated to Vishnu*", as Rudolf Steiner pointed out.[461] His epithet in his capacity as all-creator, world-builder, architect and artist of the gods was Vishva Karman.[462] Vishnu is worshipped as the deity of spiritual sunlight and cosmic warmth, in the sense of the divine heart warmth of the Budhi plane. Being at home beyond the zodiac, in the pictorial representations he rests on the world serpent. This is reminiscent of the seal that Rudolf Steiner prefaced to his fourth mystery play and which contains the Mystery of the I (see Figure 3 in the chapter on the 8th weekly verse). It means that Vishnu's spiritual home is beyond the zodiac. Even the higher spiritual world is still below the Budhi plane. Therefore the eagle-like bird Garuda is attributed to Vishnu as a mount. It corresponds to the Eagle group spirit of the Western spiritual teachings. Above the world snake and above the eagle ascending to heavenly heights the actual region of Vishnu is located. And since he is the Lord of four worlds, he is represented with four arms. In each of his four hands he holds a symbol of his power over one of these four worlds. In one of his two lower hands he holds a mace as an expression of his power over the physical world and in the second he holds a lotus blossom, the most beautiful aquatic plant, as an expression of his power over the soul world or astral world, which is always associated with the flowing element of water (see Figure 4 in the chapter on the 8th weekly verse). In his two upper hands he holds the symbols of his power over the spiritual world and the Budhi world, which correspond to the elements air and fire. Vishnu's power over the spiritual world is represented by a conch or snail horn through which he blows. It symbolizes the sound of the creative world word. His power over the flaming Budhi plane, which underlies all development, is represented in a wheel of fire, which is often depicted as a light-chakra or shining disc as well and is considered his most powerful tool.

The Eastern teachings are full of wisdoms about Vishnu's activity in connection with the creation and becoming of the world, but primarily about the past of the world's evolution, essentially up to its middle. With regard to the future, the East was only granted a glimpse of the end of the Earth's development. Thus it is said that the god Vishnu, who once emanated Krishna as the earthly representative of his Budhic love and as the primeval soul of mankind, will return at the end of time in his emanation as Kalki. He will appear as a rider on a white horse. Some Hindu denominations recognize in it a connection with Christ as he is described towards the end of the Apocalypse: "*And I saw the sky opened; and behold, a white horse. And he who sat on it was called Faithful and True, and he judges and fights in righteousness. His eyes are like a flame of fire, and on his head many crowns; and he had written a name which no one knew but himself. And he was clothed with a garment sprinkled with blood; and his name is called: «The Logos – the Word – of God».*" (Rev 19:11-13)

However, little does the East know about all that is connected with the events concerning the mystery of Golgotha. The way, in which Christ-Vairocana-Vishnu together with the Krishna soul of the Nathan Jesus has worked and will continue to work for the future of the Earth and mankind is included in the wisdom teachings of the West. They begin with the Genesis of the Old Testament as a short summary of the high and sublime wisdom of the East about the origin of the world and with the descent of mankind into the world of Maya through the Fall of Man, and then outline the world-historical mission of the Jewish people to prepare a physical bearer for the long-awaited incarnation of the Redeemer of mankind from the Fall of Man, are continued immediately in the New Testament, which preserves the knowledge of the Incarnation of Christ and the mystery of Golgotha as the most important events in the entire history of Earth and mankind at all, and reach far into the future, through the Apocalypse of John, until the end of the evolution of mankind within the physical world and its transition to the astral globe. Thus, only both sides, the time-honored teachings of the East and the younger teachings of the West, give a complete picture of the development of the Earth and mankind. They complement each other in full harmony. Only we must not cling to the name "Christ", but we must strive for a more comprehensive view.

Using another name, it was precisely the northern and central European peoples who were particularly prepared for an understanding of the etheric reappearance of Christ, which, according to Rudolf Steiner, has already been perceptible to a few human beings since the early 20th century. The ancient Germanic

---

[461] GA 266a "Aus den Inhalten der esoterischen Stunden" - Volume 1 (From the contents of the esoteric lessons), Appendix, internal lecture, presumably Berlin, 1904

[462] See for example GA 114 "Das Lukas-Evangelium" (The Gospel of Luke), Basel, Lecture of 21 September 1909

peoples knew both of the Twilight of the Gods, the fading away of an ancient time of innate clairvoyance and wisdom, as well as of the fact that one day from among their gods, who were predominantly Angelic and Archangelic beings, a special Archangel would come to the fore, who had remained more in the background so far, and would introduce a new era. It was prophesied to them that the Archangel Widar would in the future overcome the forces of the ancient, atavistic clairvoyance, the Fenris wolf, and lead mankind to a new, fully conscious spiritual vision by which they would be able to see Him in an etheric form.

"But this different thing is known to Germanic-Nordic mythology. Of this it knows, that it exists. It knows, that there exists the etheric form in which is to incarnate that which we shall once again see as the etheric form of Christ. And this alone will succeed in driving out the confused clairvoyant power which would bewilder mankind, if Odin did not overcome the Fenris Wolf, which represents nothing but the backward clairvoyance. Vidar, who has been silent all the time, will overcome the Fenris Wolf. This is what the Twilight of the Gods tells us, too.

Whoever recognizes Vidar in his significance and feels him in his soul will find that in the twentieth century people can again be given the ability to see the Christ. Vidar will stand before him again, who is common to all of us in Northern and Central Europe. He was kept secret in the mysteries and secret schools as a God who will receive his mission only in the future. Even his image is only spoken of indefinitely." [463]

In vain, however, men will look with their physical eyes for Christ in the form of Vidar, for physical eyes can only see physical forms, but not an etheric form that reveals itself to us from the astral world. At the time of the fourth post-Atlantean culture, in the Greek-Roman age, when the Twilight of the Gods had become reality and the direct spirit-vision had already been lost to the most advanced peoples, men could perceive God only as an external sensory image in a physical human body. In the meantime, however, humanity has developed further. Today we live in the fifth post-Atlantean culture, the age of intellect and imaginations, both of which have the human ether body as their bearer. We are already on the way to a new, higher way of perception.

"In our time one finds as characteristic that of the enumerated impulses [perceptions, imaginations, emotions and moral will-impulses] the greatest value is placed on imaginations. We live in a culture of imagination. The intellect is developed. In the Greek and Roman culture people did not think so much, but they perceived more than today's people do. ... Therefore we can distinguish two epochs: an epoch of perceptions and one of imaginations. Then a third will follow, through which the emotions will be developed, which today go only along the side. ... So if an impulse should come to man in Greek and Roman times, man was trained then to especially perceive what approaches outwardly. Therefore the impulse of the Christ event enters the world as an external perception. Today we live in the culture of imagination. Therefore, our cultural epoch will reach its goal by knowing Christ as something that is perceived from the astral world as an inner imagination. As an ether figure he will present himself out of the astral world. ... So also the perception of Christ will develop further. In his imaginations, in his Imaginations man will perceive Christ in a natural way now." [464]

But, perceiving is not automatically understanding of what one perceives. In order to really recognize the ether form of the Vidar as such and, beyond that, to understand it as the reappearance of the Christ, we need sufficient preparation through acquiring a deeper understanding of the Christ Being. Here it is precisely the weekly verses of the Anthroposophical Soul Calendar that can be of extraordinary help to us. The contemplation of the more hidden and distant connections which underlie the course of the year with its rhythmically changing moods of nature as an expression of the Earth's temporal or ether body can lead us to a deeper understanding of both the Christ Being and the human being. After all, the ether body of the Earth is the macrocosmic ether body of both the Christ and the Krishna Being, the primeval Adam of mankind. Through cognitive learning and emotional fathoming out anthroposophy, we can expand our world of imaginations in such a way that, in addition to the inner images of the outer sensory world, other completely new images will soon be added which are not illusions, but expressions of higher realities, albeit initially only of a pictorial nature, as Imagination. All higher seeing, however, must always first be prepared by the acquisition of an understanding that leads up.

---

[463] GA 121 "Die Mission einzelner Volksseelen" (The mission of folk-souls), Kristiania (Oslo), Lecture of 17 June 1910

[464] GA 143 "Erfahrungen des Übersinnlichen – Die drei Wege der Seele zu Christus" (Experiences of the extrasensory – The three paths of the soul to Christ), Winterthur, Lecture of 14 January 1912

"If a number of people will have developed a feeling of it through spiritual-scientific understanding, then it will happen that these people will just as well be able to convince themselves of the truth of the Christ event, as Paul was able to convince himself of it at the event of Damascus. Between 1930 and 1940 there will be a small number of people who will develop this ability, and then over 2500 years more and more people will see the Christ in the ether body. If they evolve up to etheric vision, people will see the Christ in the ether body. But they can only achieve that through spiritual understanding and feeling. This is the new descent of Christ to the earth-men. In truth, it is rather an ascent, for it will no longer be that the Christ will embody himself in the flesh. But the people who develop themselves up to him will be able to perceive him in the ether body. They will know from their immediate experience that Christ is alive. For those who want to recognize Christ, he will reappear in his ether body. They will know of the Christ through seeing." [465]

The Year 1912 and the Date of the Mystery of Golgotha

Finally, let us turn to the issue as to whether there were reasons why Rudolf Steiner published the Anthroposophical Soul Calendar just in 1912. After all, it is hardly conceivable that he would hand over such a precious spiritual treasure to his pupils and listeners at any time. On closer inspection, the year 1912 actually has some special features.

At first, it may be surprising that Rudolf Steiner lets the first weekly verse begin with Easter Sunday of 1912 on April 7, because this is not the date of the historical Easter Sunday on which the Resurrection took place. Rudolf Steiner nevertheless used this date expressly for the beginning of the Soul Calendar, in that he overwrote the first weekly verse with the words: "Easter-Atmosphere (7 – 13 April)". The historical Easter Sunday, however, was not on April 7 but on the April 5 of the year 33 A.D. as we know from Rudolf Steiner, since he explicitly indicated April 3 as the date for the historical Good Friday, two days before the historical Easter Sunday.

"On a Friday, April 3 of the year 33, three o'clock in the afternoon, the mystery of Golgotha took place. And there also took place the birth of the I in the sense that we have often characterized it." [466]

Would not it have been better if Rudolf Steiner had waited with the publication of the Soul Calendar until Good Friday had fallen again to April 3 and Easter Sunday to April 5? At first glance this may seem reasonable. However, the consequence would have been that the Soul Calendar could not have been published before 1931, because this was the first year of the 20th century in which Good Friday fell to April 3. Otherwise, only the years 1942 and 1953 would have come into question for this purpose in the same century. By the way, in the first half of our 21st century Good Friday was or will be on April 3 in the years 2015, 2026, 2037 and 2048.

Regardless of the fact that Rudolf Steiner would have to wait until 1931, we must consider that the historical Good Friday of the year 33 A.D. was on April 3 only according to the rules of the Julian calendar, which was prevailing in the Roman Empire at that time. According to the Gregorian calendar, which is valid today and more accurate, the Crucifixion took place on April 1 of the year 33 AD. This does not mean at all, that Rudolf Steiner's statement of April 3 was wrong, because for that time this statement is quite correct. For us today, however, the times given on the basis of the Gregorian calendar apply. But ultimately only the positions of the Sun and Moon in the zodiac at that time are decisive. When the Sun set on the historical Good Friday in the West in 11.5° Aries the full Moon rose in the East in 11.5° Libra simultaneously. Whether this day is called April 3 according to the one rule of calculation or April 1 according to the other is of secondary importance at first, although it is certainly not by chance on the other hand that according to the rule of calculation at that time it was just April 3, and thus in the historical date of April 3 of the year 33 A.D. the principle of the divine Trinity is expressed, which acted through Jesus Christ in human form directly on Earth.

In the year 1912 the peculiarity arose that the first full moon after the beginning of spring took place on the same day as at the Crucifixion, which we call April 1 according to today's calculation. Although in 1912 this was a Monday, nevertheless just that constellation between Moon and Sun, which was seen in the sky

[465] GA 118 "Das Ereignis der Christuserscheinung in der ätherischen Welt" (The event of the appearance of Christ in the etheric world), Düsseldorf, Lecture of 20 February 1910

[466] GA 143 "Erfahrungen des Übersinnlichen – Die drei Wege der Seele zu Christus" (Experiences of the extrasensory – The three paths of the soul to Christ), Cologne, Lecture of 7 May 1912

on the historical Good Friday, happened once more on the correct date, albeit the Moon became full only some hours later in the night of April 1 to April 2.[467] If Rudolf Steiner had wanted to wait for a year in which April 1 coincided with Good Friday, he would have had to live for far more than a hundred years, because that was only the case again in 1983, 1988 and 1994, but even then without a simultaneous full moon. In our 21st century, Good Friday will not fall to April 1 again until 2067 at the earliest. But the full moon will then fall on the day before, on Holy Thursday.[468] So it is not easy at all to find a reasonably suitable year in which the date of Good Friday fulfils the demands of both the historical and occult laws.

A second special feature of the year 1912 is the following: Good Friday of that year fell on April 5, two days before Easter Sunday on April 7, which Rudolf Steiner chose for the beginning of the first weekly verse. On that Good Friday the Sun exactly reached 15° Aries and thus that position in the zodiac which, according to the etheric or temporal body of the Earth, represents the occult point of time of the transition from the winter half-year to the summer half-year (see Figure 25). With his death on the cross and the subsequent entombment, Christ was born out of the microcosmic body of the human Jesus into the earthly outer world. He took up the physical and ether body of the Earth as his new macrocosmic body. With this he completed the transition from inwardness to outwardness. Thus, Rudolf Steiner came very close to this day by choosing the year 1912 for the publication of the Soul Calendar. Although the difference was two days, for Good Friday was on April 5 instead of April 3 in 1912, the full moon after the beginning of spring was on the correct date for today, April 1.

The actual circumstances concerning the historical date of the mystery of Golgotha are even more complex. According to another statement by Rudolf Steiner, the great change in human history should have taken place originally only in 333 AD, exactly in the middle of the Age of Aries. At this time, the cultivated mankind of the occident reached the middle of the period that was intended for the development of the intellectual and emotional soul, that is, the Greek-Latin culture. The last remnants of ancient clairvoyance faded more and more. There was a turning of the people from their inner world to the outer world. However, certain adversary powers wanted to bring about the climax of the development of the consciousness soul in a completely premature way and to the detriment of mankind already shortly after the middle of the age of the intellectual and emotional soul.

"What should have happened only in the middle of our period, what is to happen 1,080 years after the year 1413, what is to happened only in the year 2493 – then only man is to develop so far with reference to the conscious grasping of his own personality – should have been inoculated into man already in 666 by Ahriman-Luciferian powers." [469]

In order to avert this extremely harmful influence on humanity, the mystery of Golgotha and thus, of course, the birth of Jesus of Nazareth preceding it, had to be brought forward by exactly the same period, as Rudolf Steiner communicates in the same lecture.

"333 is therefore a very important time in the development of mankind, the middle of the Greek-Latin cultural period. 333 years before this middle the birth of Christ Jesus took place, that is, what led to the mystery of Golgotha. ...

Just as many years as the mystery of Golgotha preceded the middle of this period, 333 years, just as many years after this period was intended by certain spiritual powers to lead the evolution of the Earth in completely different ways than it then was led, because the mystery of Golgotha was there. 333 years after the year 333 is 666; this is the year of which the scribe of the Apocalypse speaks with a great temperament. Read the relevant passages where the scribe of the Apocalypse speaks of what refers to 666! Something should have happened to humanity according to the intentions of certain spiritual powers, and it would have happened if the mystery of Golgotha had not occurred."

So, the Mystery of Golgotha did not take place in 333 AD, which corresponds to the middle of the Aries Age, and thus to its 15th degree.[470] Even on Good Friday of 33 AD, the Sun was not in 15° Aries, because

---

[467] See "The Rosicrucian Ephemeris 1900 – 2000", as well as the "Swiss Ephemeris for the year 1912" or use the "Osterrechner" (Easter calculator), http://www.nabkal.de/ostrech2.html

[468] See for example the list of Easter dates of the University of Bamberg, Section of Liturgical Science (http://www.maa.clell.de/StarDate/feiertage.html)

[469] GA 182 "Der Tod als Lebenswandlung" (Death as a metamorphosis of life), Zurich, Lecture of 16 October 1918

[470] Relative to the starry sky, the vernal equinox already arrived at 0° Aries at that time, and thus at the point of transition to the constellation Pisces. Rudolf Steiner always calculated the ages offset by 15° in relation to the constellations of the zodiac. Hence, when the Pisces Age began in 1413, the vernal equinox had already traveled backwards through the zodiac to the 15th degree of the constellation Pisces.

the full moon occurred in advance, namely by three and a half degrees. At the time of death on the cross the Sun was therefore in 11° 30' Aries. Simultaneously with the sunset in the West, the full moon rose in the East.

The Sun as a physical-sensory likeness of Christ as the highest Sun Spirit is indeed ruler over the day and the outside world. But Christ is also ruler over the inner world of man, which in the sky has its representative in the Moon, the ruler of the night. It reflects the outer sunlight in a similar attenuated way as the bright outer sensory world is reflected in the darkness of the human eye and subsequently in the human soul. Thus, if Christ, as ruler of the Sun and the Moon, of the light of day and night, wanted to accomplish his transition from the inner world of a human being – the Jesus of Nazareth – to the outer world of the Earth, then not only the laws of the Sun's path but those of the Moon's too, had to be observed. By the latter, in particular the ancient Jews were guided. Long before the mystery of Golgotha, Yahweh had set the month of Nisan as the spring month and the first month of the year, through Moses. On the 14th day of this month they were to slaughter a young ram and celebrate the Passover. Since every lunar month begins with a new moon, the 14th day was always that of the full moon.

"The Lord said to Moses and Aaron in the land of Egypt: «This month shall mark for you the beginning of months; it shall be the first month of the year to you. Tell the whole congregation of Israel that on the tenth of this month they are to take a lamb for each family, a lamb for each household. If a household is too small for a whole lamb, it shall join its closest neighbour in obtaining one; the lamb shall be divided in proportion to the number of people who eat of it. Your lamb shall be without blemish, a year-old male; you may take it from the sheep or from the goats. You shall keep it until the fourteenth day of this month; then the whole assembled congregation of Israel shall slaughter it at twilight. They shall take some of the blood and put it on the two doorposts and the lintel of the houses in which they eat it.»" (Exodus 12:1-7)

About one and a half thousand years later, Christ Jesus Himself celebrated the Passover with his closer circle of disciples according to the traditional rules as the so-called Last Supper. However, this also was done early, on Nisan 13 already, instead of Nisan 14, as stated in the Gospel of John: *"Before the Passover, since Jesus knew that his hour had come ..."* (John 13:1). The reason for this was that on the next day, Nisan 14, when the Moon became full and the Jewish people celebrated the Passover, Christ Jesus Himself was to be killed and his blood shed from the cross as the true Passover Lamb.

But, the day of the death, which was the day of the birth of Christ Jesus into the earthly outer world as well, could not be arbitrarily far away from that day on which the Sun reached 15° Aries and thus the midpoint of the zodiac sign of the Lamb. This time was given by the solar year in accordance with the laws of the ether body of the Earth. The Sun is elevated in Aries or the Lamb. There it has its greatest power. But, each sign of the zodiac is threefold in its nature, and each Age as well. The three sections are called decans. The Sun shows its most sublime power in the middle third or decan of Aries and so it is with respect to the Age of Aries. The middle third extends over the range from 10° to 20° in each case. According to Rudolf Steiner's statements in a lecture on the five post-Atlantean ages and the planetary rulers of the individual decans of these ages, *"the decans of the Aries period are: Mars, Sun, Venus."* [471] Rudolf Steiner drew a sketch on the blackboard, according to which Venus reigns over the first decan of Aries, the Sun over the middle decan and Mars the third decan (see Figure 27).

The first third of the fourth post-Atlantean cultural epoch, which began in 747 B.C., was therefore under the rule of the planet Mars in the third decan of Aries. Since the position of the vernal equinox passes through one degree of the zodiac in 72 years, it took 10 × 72 years, i.e. 720 years, for the 10 degrees of this decan. In the year 27 B.C., the spring equinox, moving retrogressively through the zodiac (in the illustration from lower left to upper right), had passed through the 3rd decan of the Aries Age and crossed the border to its second or middle decan. All events of Christ-Jesus' life on Earth therefore took place in connection with the entry of the vernal equinox into the middle decan of the Age of Aries and under the influence of the Sun reigning from then on with its most sublime power, beginning with the 20th degree. The next degree of the middle decan, the 19th degree of the Age of Aries, was reached by the backward wandering vernal equinox not before 45 A.D., twelve years after the mystery of Golgotha.

The entry of the vernal equinox into the middle decan of the Aries Age apparently had a reflection in a smaller scale, for in the night from Wednesday, April 1, to the historic Holy Thursday on April 2 in the year 33 A.D., according to the Julian calendar, which was in use at that time, the Sun reached the middle decan of Aries. But because the Sun moves forward in the zodiac – in contrast to the retrograde movement of the vernal equinox – it entered the middle decan of Aries from the other side, of course, not at 20°, but at 10°. According to the Gospel of John, this day coincided with Nisan 13 of the Jewish lunar calendar, on which

---

[471] GA 180 "Mysterienwahrheiten und Weihnachtsimpulse – Alte Mythen und ihre Bedeutung" (Mystery truths and Christmas impulses - Ancient myths and their meaning), Dornach, Lecture of 8 January 1918

Christ Jesus celebrated the Passover – which he brought forward one day for the above-mentioned reasons – with his closer circle of disciples, and washed the feet of the twelve apostles. It was that same night when Judas committed his betrayal and Christ Jesus was captured. On the following day, Nisan 14 of the Jews and April 3 according to the Julian calendar, the Crucifixion, the Death on the Cross and the Entombment took place. On this day, when the Moon became full, the Sun passed from 11° to 12° Aries.

Figure 27: Decans of the Zodiac Signs of the five post-Atlantean Ages (GA 182)

On the historic Holy Saturday, the day of the rest in the grave, the Sun moved from 12° to 13° Aries. On Easter Sunday, before sunrise, with the first beginning of dawn at about 4 o'clock, the Sun completed its course through the first three degrees of the middle Aries decan by crossing 13° Aries. Thus all events concerning the Mystery of Golgotha took place in the first three degrees of the Middle or Sun decan of the Sign of the Lamb.

One of the peculiarities of the year 1912, whose weekly division Rudolf Steiner took as a basis with exact dates for the Soul Calendar, is the fact that also in that year the Moon became full as in 33 A.D. on the day, when the Sun passed from 11° to 12° Aries. The only thing is that in 1912 it did not happen on a Friday, but on a Monday, as already mentioned above.

Due to all these circumstances, the bringing forward of the birth of Jesus of Nazareth by 333 years, the obeying of the laws of the Sun's and the Moon's path, the retrograde movement of the vernal equinox and the periods of the Sun's reigns in the signs of the zodiac and their decans – possibly for other reasons, too – the mystery of Golgotha and with it the birth of Christ Jesus into the body of the Earth took place two days earlier than the path of the Sun alone would require, that is, not at the time when the Sun passed through 15° Aries, but two days earlier, when it passed through 13° Aries.

The fact that Rudolf Steiner based his Soul Calendar just on the year 1912 may therefore be due in particular to the following three peculiarities. Firstly, on Good Friday 1912 the Sun was in 15° Aries, completely in harmony with the occult division of the seasons shown in Figure 25 and as an expression of the transition from the inner world to the outer world. As a second special feature, the full moon in 1912 occurred exactly on the date of the historical day of the Crucifixion, April 1, according to the Gregorian calendar valid today (corresponding to April 3 of the ancient Julian calendar). The third special feature of the year 1912, which is important for the practical handling of the Soul Calendar, was that Easter Sunday in that year fell almost exactly in the middle of the period between the limits of which it is allowed to sway according to the calculation rules of Western Christianity. As a result, in that year there were no shifts of the weeks immediately preceding and following Easter. The verses of the first half of the year could be distributed evenly between the immovable feasts of Christmas and St. John's Day at weekly intervals, and thus all verses of the entire year could be provided with the dates given to us. In this way Rudolf Steiner was able to hand over an extraordinary precious treasure of spirit and soul to his pupils and listeners, closely following the underlying historical and occult laws.

Overview of the

Weekly Verses

Rudolf Steiner added capital letters in alphabetical order to the individual weekly verses, omitting the letter J and not assigning a letter to one verse in both the summer and winter half-years.

World of the Life-Spirit
(Budhi Plane)

2nd Sphere

1st Sphere

7th Sphere

Higher
Spiritual World
(Arupa-Region)

6th Sphere

5th Sphere

Zodiacal
Region

4th Sphere

Lower
Spiritual World
(Rupa-Region)

2nd and 3rd Spheres
(Jupiter- and Saturn-Spheres –
Oceanic and Atmospheric Regions)

14th Week (7 – 13 July)   N
Surrendered to the senses' revelation,
I lost own being's drive,
A thought-dream seemed, benumbing,
To rob me of my self,
World-thinking yet draws near
In sense-appearance to wake me up.

15th Week (14 – 20 July)   O
I feel the spirit's weaving in the world-appearance
As if concealed by an enchantment:
It has enwrapped my separate being
In senses' dullness
To give the force to me:
Which, powerless to give it to itself,
My I cannot give, in its limits.

16th Week (21 – 27 July)   P
To save the spirit-gift within,
Is my presentiment's strict order
That divine bounties, ripening
And fruiting in soul's grounds,
May bring the selfhood's fruits.

17th Week (28 July – 3 August)   Q
The World Word speaks,
Which through the senses' doors
I was allowed to lead into soul's grounds:
Imbue your spirit-depths
With my worlds' vastness
To find me within you one time.

18th Week (4 – 10 August)   R
Can I expand the soul
That it unites itself
With the received World-Germ-Word?
I sense that I must find the strength
To shape the soul worthy of it,
To mould it to the spirit's dress.

19th Week (11 – 17 August)   S
To encompass the newly-got
With memory mysteriously
Shall be my aspiration's further point:
This shall awaken, getting stronger,
Own powers in my inner being
And, growing, give me to myself.

20th Week (18 – 24 August)   T
In this way only, I feel my existence,
Which far from world-existence
Would in itself obliterate itself
And, building merely on its own foundation
Inside, would deaden finally itself.

1st Sphere

2nd Sphere

World of the Life-Spirit
(Budhi Plane)

7th Sphere

Higher
Spiritual World
(Arupa-Region)

6th Sphere

5th Sphere

Zodiacal
Region

4th Sphere

Lower
Spiritual World
(Rupa-Region)

13th Week (30 June – 6 July)   M
And am I in the senses' heights,
Then flames in my soul's depths
Out of the spirit's fire-worlds
The Truth Word of the Gods:
In spirit's backgrounds seek, by sensing,
To find yourself akin to spirit now.

12 John-Atmosphere (24 June)
The sheen of the worlds' beauteousness
Compels me from the depths of soul
To set my own life's divine powers
Free for the world-high flight;
To leave myself
And confidently seek myself
In world-light and world-warmth.

11th Week (16 – 23 June)   L
In this hour of the sun
It's up to you, to recognize wise news:
Surrendered to worlds' beauteousness,
Pervading feelingly your self in you by living through:
The human I can lose itself
And in world's I retrieve itself.

10th Week (9 – 15 June)   K
Up to the summer's heights,
The sun's bright being rises;
It takes along my human feeling
Into its spatial vastness.
Sensation stirs inside,
Like a presentiment announcing dimly,
Once you will recognize:
A divine being has felt you now.

9th Week (2 – 8 June)   I
Forgetting my will's peculiarity,
World's warmth, announcing summer,
Fills up my spirit and the essence of my soul;
To lose myself into the light
I am commanded by the spirit-vision,
And strongly tells presentiment:
Now lose yourself to find yourself.

8th Week (26 May – 1 June)   H
The senses' might is growing
In league with the creative work of gods.
It presses down the force of thinking
To dullness of a dream.
When divine being
Wants closer union with my soul,
Then human thinking must
Be content with a state of dream.

7th Week (19 – 25 May)   G
My self is threatening to flee away,
By world's light mightily attracted.
Now exercise, intuitive assumption,
Your rights with strength.
Replace the might of thinking,
Which in the sense-appearance
Is just about to lose itself.

**1st Sphere
(Mars Sphere –
Continental Region)**

21st Week (25 – 31 August)   U
I feel strange power fruiting,
Increasing, giving now myself to me.
I sense the seed maturing, and
Presentiment weaving with its light
Within me on the selfhood's power.

**7th Sphere
(Sun Sphere)**

22nd Week (1 – 7 September)   V
The light out of the vastness of the world,
It lives on forcefully inside:
It turns into a soul-light
And shines into the spirit-depths,
To loosen fruits
That make mature the human self
Out of the World Self in the course of times.

**6th Sphere
(Venus Sphere)**

23rd Week (8 – 14 September)   W
Autumnally is dimming now
The senses' quest for stimuli;
Into light-revelation
The mists' dull veils are blending.
I see, out in the distant space,
The autumn's winter sleep.
The summer has given utterly
Itself to me.

**Soul-
World**

**5th Sphere
(Mercury Sphere)**

24th Week (15 – 21 September)   X
By constant self-creation
The soul-existence perceives itself;
The cosmic spirit keeps on striving,
Revitalized in self-cognition,
And forms out of soul-darkness
The will-fruit of the sense of self.

**1st to 4th Sphere
(Moon Sphere)**

25th Week (22 – 28 September)   Y
I may belong now to myself
And brightly spread the inner light
Into the dark of space and time.
While nature's being strives for sleep
The depths of soul must be awake
And waking carry sunny glowing
Into the winter's chilly floods.

Earth Sphere

26 Michaelmas-Atmosphere   Z
Nature, your motherly existence,
I bear it in the will part of my being;
And my will's fiery might,
It steels my spirit's drives,
That they give birth to sense of self,
To hold me in myself.

**Lower
Spiritual World
(Rupa-Region)**

**1st Sphere
(Mars Sphere –
Continental Region)**

6th Week (12 – 18 May)   F
Arisen out of separate being
Is now my self and finds itself
As revelation of the world
In temporal and spatial forces;
The world presents to me all over,
As divine archetype,
The truth of my own likeness.

**7th Sphere
(Sun Sphere)**

5th Week (5 – 11 May)   E
Within the light that out of spirit-depths
Reveals the gods' creative work
By weaving fertilely in space:
In it, the essence of the soul appears
Expanded to the world-existence
And resurrected
From narrow selfhood's inner power.

**6th Sphere
(Venus Sphere)**

4th Week (28 April – 4 May)   D
I feel now essence like my essence:
So speaks sensation,
Which in the sunlit world
Unites with floods of light;
It wants to give to thinking
Warmth for the clarity
And firmly bind together
Man and the world in unity.

**Soul-
World**

**5th Sphere
(Mercury Sphere)**

3rd Week (21 – 27 April)   C
And to the universe now speaks,
Forgetting gradually itself,
Recalling yet its origin,
The growing I of man:
In you, I free myself
Out of the fetters of my personal traits
And fathom out my real essence.

**1st to 4th Sphere
(Moon Sphere)**

2nd Week (14 - 20 April)   B
Into the sensory universe's outer region
Thought power loses own existence.
Spiritual worlds now find
The human shoot again,
Which has to find its germ in them,
Its own soul's fruit yet in itself.

Earth Sphere

1. Easter-Atmosphere (7 – 13 April)   A
When from the vastness of the world
The sun speaks to the human sense
And pleasure from the depths of soul
Unites with light, in looking,
Then soar, out of the selfhood's sheath,
Thoughts to the distant space
And dully bind man's essence
To the existence of the spirit.

27th Week (6 – 12 October) A
Ingress into my being's depths:
This is encouraged by a prescient longing,
So that I find myself in self-reflection,
The summer's sunny gift, which warming lives
As gem in autumn-mood,
As drive of forces in my soul.

28th Week (13 – 19 October) B
I can, revitalized inside,
Feel now own being's vastness
And forcefully give rays of thought
Out of the sun-might of the soul
To solve the mysteries of life,
And grant fulfillment many a wish,
Though hope already paralyzed its wings.

29th Week (20 – 26 October) C
To kindle thinking's luminousness
Vigorously inside oneself,
Construing the experiences' deeper meaning The
From cosmic spirit's source of forces,
Is now the summer's heritage to me,
Is autumn's rest and winter's hope as well.

30th Week (27 October – 2 November) D
In soul-sunlight sprout for me
The thinking's ripened fruits,
Into safeness of self-confidence
All feeling is transforming.
With pleasure I can sense
Autumn's awakening of the spirit:
The winter will arouse in me
The summer of the soul.

31st Week (3 – 9 November) E
The light from spirit-depths
Strives to the outside like a sun:
It turns into a life-will-power
And shines into the senses' dullness
In order to set forces free
That make creative powers out of soul-drives
Ripen in the work of man.

32nd Week (10 – 16 November) F
I feel my own force fruiting,
Increasing, giving myself to the world;
And my own being I feel forceful
Turning to clearness
In weaving of life's destiny.

**Lower
Spiritual World
(Rupa-Region)**

Earth Sphere

1st to 4th Sphere
(Moon Sphere)

5th Sphere
(Mercury Sphere)

**Soul-
World**

6th Sphere
(Venus Sphere)

7th Sphere
(Sun Sphere)

1st Sphere
(Mars Sphere –
Continental Region)

**Soul-
World**

52nd Week (30 March) Z
When from the depths of soul
The spirit turns to outer world-existence,
And beauty wells from distant space,
Then streams, out of the heavens far,
Life's vital power into human bodies
And unites mightily the spirit's essence
With the existence as a human being.

51 Spring-Anticipation
Into the inside of the human being
The richness of the senses pours.
World Spirit finds itself
As mirror image in the human eye,
Which has to recreate from it
Its force completely new.

50th Week (16 – 22 March) Y
And to the human I now speaks,
In powerful manifestation
And loosening its being's forces,
world-existence's desire to become:
By giving into you my life
Out of its magic spell,
I gain my real goal.

49th Week (9 – 15. 3.) X
I feel the force of world-existence:
So speaks the clarity of thought,
Remembering own spirit's growth
In world's dark nights,
And to the world's near day
It turns the inside's rays of hope.

48th Week (2 – 8 March) W
Within the light that from world's heights
Desires to stream powerfully to the soul,
May now, to solve soul's mysteries,
Appear secureness of world-thinking,
And, focusing the power of its rays,
Awaken love in human hearts.

47th Week (23 February – 1 March) V
Out of the world-womb wants to rise,
To quicken sense-appearance,
The pleasure to become.
May it now find my thinking's power
Equipped enough with divine powers,
Which strongly live inside of me.

**Lower
Spiritual World
(Rupa-Region)**

Lower Spiritual (Rupa-Region)

Zodiacal Region

2nd and 3rd Spheres (Jupiter- and Saturn-Spheres – Oceanic and Atmospheric Regions)

Higher Spiritual World (Arupa-Region)

World of the Life-Spirit (Budhi Plane)

4th Sphere

5th Sphere

6th Sphere

7th Sphere

1st Sphere

2nd Sphere

33rd Week (17 – 23 November) G
In this way only, do I feel the world,
Which, without my soul's experience,
Would merely be a frosty, empty life
That, manifesting without might
To recreate itself in souls,
Would in itself find only death.

34th Week (24 – 30 November) H
To feel the old-preserved
With newly risen self-existence
Coming to life inside mysteriously:
This shall pour forth, awakening,
World forces into my life's exterior work
And, growing, imprint me into the existence.

35th Week (1 – 7 December) I
Can I distinguish the existence
So that it reappears
In soul's urge for creation?
I feel, I've been endowed with might
To humbly live into the World Self
My own self as a member.

36th Week (8 – 14 December) K
Within my being's depths now speaks,
Urging for revelation,
The World Word so mysteriously:
Imbue your labour's aims
With my spiritual light,
To sacrifice yourself through me.

37th Week 15 – 21 December) L
To carry spirit-light into world-winter-night,
Is what my heart's drive longs for blissfully,
That soul-germs take their roots
In cosmic grounds luminously
And in the senses' darkness sounds, transfiguring,
The Word of God through all existence.

38 Consecration-Night Atmosphere M
I feel the spirit-child in my soul's womb
As if released of an enchantment;
In brightness of the heart,
The holy World Word has begotten
Hope's fruit from heaven,
Which jubilantly grows in cosmic distances
Out of my being's divine ground.

39th Week (29 December – 4 January) N
Surrendering to spirit-revelation,
I gain World Being's light.
Thought force grows and clears
To give myself to me,
And from thinking's might emerges
The sense of self to wake me up.

40th Week (5 – 11 January) O
And am I in the spirit-depths,
Then, in my soul's deep grounds,
Out of the love-worlds of the heart
All separate being's void delusion
Fills with the World Word's firepower.

41st Week (12 – 18 January) P
The soul's creative power
Strives from the heart's deep ground
In order to inflame the forces of the Gods
To right activity in human life,
To shape itself
In human love and human work.

42nd Week (19 – 25 January) Q
In this winter-dark,
To manifest own power
Is now the soul's strong drive,
To guide it into darkness
And feel, like a presentiment,
Through warmth of heart the senses' revelation.

43rd Week (26 January – 1 February) R
In wintry depths
The spirit's true existence warms.
It gives to world-appearance,
By powers of the heart, mights of existence.
The inner fire of the human soul defies,
With growing strength, the coldness of the world.

44th Week (2 – 8 February) S
In grasping of new sensory stimuli,
Soul-clarity, in retrospect of spirit-birth,
Fills the confusing, sprouting
Becoming of the world
With the creative will of my own thinking.

45th Week (9 – 15 February) T
The might of thought consolidates
In league with spirit-birth.
It brightens up the senses' gloomy stimuli
To total clarity.
If soul-abundance
Wants to unite with world-becoming,
Then senses' revelation must
Receive the light of thinking.

46th Week (16 – 22 February) U
The world is threatening to daze
The inborn power of the soul.
Come forth, you, memory,
Refulgent from the spirit-depths
And reinforce my looking,
Which only by volitions
Is able to sustain itself.

LIST OF FIGURES